Who Invented the Stepover?

AND OTHER FOOTBALL CONUNDRUMS

First published in Great Britain in 2013 by

PROFILE BOOKS LTD

3A Exmouth House
Pine Street
London EC1R 0JH
www.profilebooks.com

1 3 5 7 9 10 8 6 4 2

Printed and bound in the UK by
CPI Group (UK) Ltd, Croydon, CR0 4YY

A CIP catalogue record for this book is available from the British Library.

ISBN 978 178125 0068
eISBN 978 184765 8425

The paper this book is printed on is certified by the © 1996 Forest Stewardship
Council A.C. (FSC). It is ancient-forest friendly. The printer holds FSC chain of
custody SGS-COC-2061

Who Invented the Stepover?

AND OTHER FOOTBALL CONUNDRUMS

Paul Simpson & Uli Hesse

PROFILE BOOKS

Contents

Stars

Gaffers

Records

Culture

For Yannick and Jack, who'll never walk alone

Introduction

Who invented the stepover? The thought must have occurred to many of us while watching Cristiano Ronaldo taunt an opponent with this trick. Maradona, perhaps? Pelé? Surely some South American. I was editing *Champions* magazine, so did some initial research and traced the trick back to a Dutch footballer called Abe Lenstra in the 1950s. But there the trail went cold. Picking up the investigation for this book, the answer became much more complex and entertaining, touching on the careers of Bob Marley, a player celebrated as 'Adam the Scissors Man' and a Boca Juniors legend who played in espadrilles instead of football boots.

That question, inevitably, led to other conundrums – who invented the bicycle kick and the long throw, who had the hardest ever shot, what was the greatest of all great escapes, what is the point of corner flags and dugouts, and just where did all those football pop singles come from? I'd always found the *New Scientist* question and answer books, such as *Why Can't Elephants Jump?*, curiously addictive and began to wonder if a similar approach would shed new light on the game of football – its origins, development and culture. When my co-author Uli Hesse suggested that one of the questions we could answer was 'Can elephants take penalties?', it seemed excitingly obvious that it could.

The selection of questions posed and, in general, answered here has led us into various corridors of uncertainty, sharpened our reading of the game and left us still pondering the connection between parrots, football and misery. They have also introduced us to a fascinating gallery of characters – the German coach who was shot in the jaw while sharing a bed with a suspected CIA agent, the striker who used to smoke dollar bills at half-time, and a doomed Dutch prodigy who learned how to beat defenders by watching people speed skate over frozen canals – who barely feature in the orthodox version of football's rise to become the most popular sport in the world.

Along the way we also consider the synergy between tobacco and football, the mysterious origins of 4-4-2 and whether Argentina would have won the 1986 World Cup without Maradona. (Not the toughest question we had to answer.) The end result is a book that shreds shibboleths, challenges assumptions and could inspire a truly epic pub quiz – or possibly incite a riot at one.

Paul Simpson, October 2013

Inventions

🌐 Who invented the **bicycle kick**?

If you believe Uruguayan writer Eduardo Galeano's *Football In Sun and Shadow*, this question has a straightforward answer. To quote Galeano: 'Ramón Unzaga invented the move on the field of the Chilean port Talcahuano: body in the air, back to the ground, he shot the ball backwards with a sudden snap of his legs, like the blades of scissors.'

Galeano does not date this historic moment but popular tradition has it that Unzaga invented this move in 1914 in Talcahuano. A naturalised Chilean – he had emigrated from Bilbao with his parents in 1906 – Unzaga loved launching bicycle kicks both in attack and defence. After he showed off his trademark move in two Copa Americas (1916 and 1920), the Argentinian press dubbed the bicycle kick *la chilena*.

As comprehensive as that narrative might sound it finds no favour in Callao (Peru's largest port), nor with Argentine journalist Jorge Barraza, whose investigations suggest the move was invented by a *chalaco* (as Callao locals are known) of African descent who tried out the acrobatic manoeuvre in a game with British sailors. Peruvian historian Jorge Bazadre suggests this could have happened as early as 1892. The Chileans could, Barraza speculated, have copied the bicycle kick from regular matches between teams from Callao and the Chilean port of Valparaíso. If you believe this theory, the bicycle kick is truly *la chalaca* (Chalacan strike).

In his 1963 novel *The Time Of The Hero*, Mario Vargas Llosa suggests that people in Callao must have invented the bicycle kick because they use their feet as efficiently as their hands. However, neither Chile nor Peru will ever relinquish their claim to have invented this spectacular move. Which, when you think about it, is strange, because a bicycle kick presupposes that somebody else has not done their job properly. German scientist Hermann Schwameder, an expert on motion technique, says what you need is 'instinct, a lot of

The much-decorated Chilean Ramón Unzaga, putative inventor of the bicycle kick. The equipment, right, is not recommended for home use.

courage – and a bad cross'. Klaus Fischer, who scored with the most famous bicycle kick in World Cup history (it tied the 1982 semi-final between France and West Germany at 3-3 in extra time) agrees: 'By and large, you have to say that every cross that leads to a bicycle kick goal is not a good cross.'

Yet, on one famous occasion, a not very good penalty led to a bicycle kick goal. In May 2010, in the Hungarian top flight, Honved were 1-0 up against their great rivals Ferencvaros, when they won a penalty. Italian striker Angelo Vaccaro stepped up to seal the victory. He struck the ball at a perfect height for the keeper who punched it into the air. Vaccaro waited for the ball to come down and, with half an eye on the on-rushing defenders, flicked it over his head (and the keeper) and into the net.

Even if you don't miss a penalty first, a good bicycle kick is a shortcut to glory – though sometimes that glory is short-lived. Zlatan Ibrahimović's overhead wonder goal against England in November 2012 was feted as one of the greatest ever. That same month, trying to replicate his effort in a French Cup tie for PSG against Saint-Étienne, he missed the ball completely.

Wayne Rooney's spectacular overhead kick in the Manchester derby in February 2011 was voted the best goal in the history of the Premier League. The player didn't romanticise his achievement, saying: 'I saw it come into the box and thought, why not?' Therein, perhaps, lies the secret of the move's enduring appeal: it is rare in life that we see human error (a bad cross) so swiftly redeemed by human genius.

Even a missed bicycle kick can have unforeseen consequences. At USA 94, with the hosts minutes away from a 2-1 victory against Colombia, Marcelo Balboa startled the Rose Bowl crowd with an inspired bicycle kick that flashed just over the left-hand corner. If it had gone in, it would have become one of football's most famous YouTube clips. It didn't

Rooney pulls it off. His great bicycle kick against City was improvised from a mis-hit cross from Nani. The move is said to have been introduced to England in the 1960s by United's Denis Law, who had picked it up at Torino.

but it still inspired Denver billionaire Philip Anschutz who vowed: 'That's the guy I want to play for my team.' Balboa was signed by Anschutz's Colorado Rapids and the billionaire became such an enthusiast he invested in the Chicago Fire, New York/New Jersey Metro Stars, the LA Galaxy, DC United and the San José Earthquakes – six out of ten Major League Soccer franchises. So you could say Balboa's bicycle kick launched the MLS.

There are other, less convincing, claimants for the honour of inventing the bicycle kick. Legendary Brazilian striker Leônidas, whose elasticity earned him the nickname Rubber Man, claimed the move was his creation. But he first used it, records suggest, for his club Bonsucesso in 1932 – more than a decade after Unzaga. Chronology counts even more decisively against Carlo Parola, the Juventus centre-back who used the trick so often he was known in Italy as Signor Rovesciata (Mr Reverse Kick) and Doug Ellis, the 'deadly' Aston Villa chairman who claimed to have invented this move while playing for Southport during World War II.

By then, though, the bicycle kick had achieved international notoriety. In 1927, Chilean club Colo Colo toured Europe and their 24-year-old striker, captain and founder David Arellano performed the trick so often he was the toast of Spain – until he was killed, struck down by peritonitis after colliding with another player during a match in Valladolid. The black line above Colo Colo's club emblem is a memorial to a flamboyant striker whose memorably premature death is a grim warning about the perils of showboating.

⚽ Who recorded the first celebratory football song?

Regal Records in 1932: the first FA Cup final souvenir disc was a 78rpm record commemorating the clash between Arsenal and Newcastle. This first entry in a genre we might call FA Cup vinyl was very different to its successors. For a start, the record was released before the final. And instead of the catchy, platitudinous pop songs that became obligatory, this record consisted of interviews with the players. Each finalist had a side of the record to themselves.

Controversial it isn't. The announcer, who sounds as if he's killing time before narrating his next Pathé newsreel, introduces the Gunners 'popular captain Tom Parker … the right full-back, a wholehearted player, who is respected by his colleagues and opponents throughout the football world,

and is equally as a good a fel-low.' Parker then describes the recording as a greater ordeal than anything that Wembley has to offer before promising that his team will play the game and play it well. (In the event, they lost 2-1, with Newcastle equalising controversially from a move during which the ball had gone out of play.)

There was then a strange lull before the vinyl baton was picked up in France, Germany and the Netherlands. Before the Bundesliga was founded in 1963, the national champion-ship was decided by a cup final. In 1959, a composer called Horst Heinz Henning decided to celebrate the fact that local rivals Eintracht Frankfurt and Kickers Offenbach had reached the final by releasing a record which had an Eintracht song on one side and a Kickers tune on the other. A one-man hit factory with more pen names than Jonathan King, Henning never showed a trace of humour in his songs but, in 1977, surprised everyone by releasing a record called 'The House At The Arse End Of Nowhere'.

Neither team were involved in this commemoration of a 'dream final', but a point had been proved. In 1965, Borus-sia Dortmund won the Cup Winners' Cup, the first time a German club had won a European competition, and the team were inspired to record two songs. One was the Dortmund club song 'Wir Halten Fest Und Treu Zusammen' (which translates as 'We stick together firmly and faithfully') while the other was a popular carnival song from the early 1950s.

Two years later, French singer Antoine was so inspired by Ajaccio's surprising promotion to Ligue 1 he wrote and released 'Le Match De Football'. After a downbeat opening in which the football-supporting farmer wishes his cows would give him wine instead of milk, the song mysteriously notes that life is sweet, going badly, yet will be redeemed by the football on Sunday which he will watch on TV, dreaming of the fantastic day when the Corsicans win the Olympics. The song was the main attraction on an EP with a lovely old-school cover featuring a classic team photo.

In 1970, as the tuxedoed members of the England World Cup squad were singing 'They'll be thinking about us back home', Feyenoord celebrated winning the European Cup with their own single. The golden – if that's the appropriate metal to be invoking – age of the celebratory record had just started. Arsenal, Brighton, Bristol City, Cardiff City, Chelsea, Coventry City, Crystal Palace, Everton, Leeds United, Lincoln City, Manchester United, Middlesbrough, Nottingham Forest, Scotland, Spurs and Yeovil have all graced – or disgraced – the charts with their ditties. So popular were these singles that Chelsea recorded 'Blue Is The Colour' in 1972 just to celebrate the fact that they had reached the League Cup final (which they lost to Stoke City). 'Blue Is The Colour' has since been adapted (although the colour has often changed) by the Vancouver Whitecaps, Norwegian champions Molde and Finnish giants HJK.

Apart from the classic 'Anfield Rap' and the almost-credible 'World In Motion' (New Order with John Barnes), most of these cash-in singles were cheesily predictable. It took the Belgians to show Britain how these things should be done. In 1985 Belgian singer Grand Jojo, best known for his drinking songs, cut 'Anderlecht Champions' with the Mauves squad that had just won the Belgian title. The first verse features the usual platitudes about growing up as a fan but in the second verse, the song takes a bizarre, entertaining diversion in which the singer complains that he went to see another team, but there wasn't even a cat nearby and the car park was deserted. The baffled fan sings: 'But in front of me there were three turnstiles open. At one of the turnstiles I said: "Has the match been put off until Easter or Christmas?" The bloke in front of me said, "Don't worry mate! As you've come on your own, we'll start whenever you want!"'

It's an old gag but it is surely better than, for example, 'And we'll play all the way for Leeds United'.

⚽ Who invented **4-4-2**?

The orthodox view is that the classic 4-4-2 formation was invented by Victor Maslov. Jonathan Wilson's *Inverting The Pyramid* makes this case eloquently, noting: '[Sir Alf] Ramsey is regularly given the credit (or the blame) for abolishing the winger and, given the lack of communication between the USSR and the West in those days, there is no suggestion he did not come up with the idea independently, but the 4-4-2 was first invented by Maslov.'

This invention was perfected at Dynamo Kiev, coached by Maslov from 1964 to 1970. Looking at the 4-3-3 with which Brazil had won the 1962 World Cup with forward Mário Zagallo falling back on the left, Maslov decided to go one better and pulled back his right-winger too. The idea was to give his players, especially his playmaker Andriy Biba, the freedom to create. But just as Ramsey dispensed with tricky wingers (because they held on to the ball too long), so Maslov parted with his gifted winger Valeriy Lobanovskiy. The 4-4-2 Maslov created was, in part, a formal shape that made it possible for his players to interchange because they knew which shape they had to keep. A defender pressing forward in this system knew a team-mate would cover the space he had left. Without that structure, the team could not be creative and remain competitive.

Coaches whose experiments succeed are regarded as deep thinkers, those whose ploys don't pay off are derided as 'tink-erers'. Yet as Maslov's reign in Kiev shows, great coaches are usually both. By October 1967, when his team knocked out European champions Celtic in the first round of the European Cup, Maslov had his side playing 4-1-3-2 with Vasili Turian-chik as a holding midfielder sitting in front of the back four.

Oddly enough, as Wilson points out in his book, this is probably the most accurate description of the formation with which Ramsey's England won the 1966 World Cup final. In front of the back four was Nobby Stiles, playing behind a midfield trio of Alan Ball, Bobby Charlton and Martin Peters, with Geoff Hurst and Roger Hunt as the attacking two.

Yet tactically the most significant matches in that tournament might well have been in Group 1. The scoreline in England's routine 2-0 win over Mexico was a tactical triumph for coach Ignacio Trelles. In May 1961, Mexico had lost 8-0 on their first visit to Wembley. Desperate to avoid such humiliation, the players agreed to emulate Uruguay (who had held the hosts to 0-0 in the opening game) and play for a draw. 'We played them using a 4-4-2 which we weren't used to and was considered super defensive,' said Trelles. 'We gave the English a lot of work to do. Only a great goal by Bobby Charlton opened us up.' Defender Jesús del Muro, who shrugged off injury to play that game, recalled later: 'That was the day they said Nacho Trelles put out the "formation of fear", because he played 4-4-2. Imagine – in 1986, they were all playing it.'

Uruguay, under coach Ondino Viera (the man who famously observed 'other countries have their history, Uruguay has football'), also set out to play 4-4-2 against France, although this changed when they went a goal down after 15 minutes. So what we have is the spectacle, in one round of games halfway through Group 1, of two sides, Mexico and Uruguay, playing 4-4-2 for some or all of their World Cup match in 1966 – just two years after Maslov had begun experimenting with this formation in Kiev.

It is extremely unlikely – given the lack of communication between East and West that Wilson acknowledged – that either Viera or Trelles had consulted with Maslov, let alone Ramsey. The timeline may still favour the Russian coach, yet Trelles was a great tactical innovator (and was often criticised for it by the Mexican media) so it is hard to settle this argument definitively. In his book *Where Good Ideas Come From*, author Steven Johnson points out that four different scientists in four different countries all 'discovered' sunspots in the same year, 1611. His theory of innovation is that they are created not by lone geniuses but by a process he calls the 'adjacent possible'. This is his way of saying that only certain kinds of next steps are possible – you can't invent the printing press without moveable type, ink and paper.

So applying this theory, 4-4-2 became an adjacent possibility as soon as a team proved you could succeed playing 4-3-3. At its simplest, the distinction between the two is merely the positioning of one winger. Which means that almost any reasonably intelligent, open-minded coach could have studied what Brazil did in 1962 and drawn the same conclusions as Maslov, Ramsey and Trelles.

⚽ Who was the first **attacking full-back?**

On 15 May 1949, Arsenal beat the Brazilian side Fluminense 5-1 in the Vasco da Gama stadium in front of 60,000 excited fans. As comfortable as that margin of victory sounds, the Arsenal defenders endured much discomfort. As full-back Laurie Scott recalled in Aidan Hamilton's *An Entirely Different Game*: 'Suddenly, a bloke comes dashing through and he's had a shot at goal and the ball went wide. And we started looking around to see who we'd got to blame for this. We found out it was their full-back. See, they didn't care. I never went up there like that. I used to go down the sideline, yes, but never like that.'

As the great Dutch coach Rinus Michels famously said, the problem is not persuading full-backs to go forward, they all want to do that, the problem is to persuade them to track back. This is especially true in Brazil. So the honest answer to this question is that it could have been any Brazilian full-back at any time from the 1930s onwards.

Then again it could have been an Englishman. In the 1930s, left-back Samuel Barkas won five England caps while on Manchester City's books. In Douglas Lamming's stuffy but compelling *An English Football Internationalists' Who's Who*, he quotes a contemporary appraisal of Barkas which sums him up as 'clever and stylish with a liking for an occasional foray upfield'. It's worth noting that Barkas could have indulged this liking as a left-half and inside-right – he was good enough to play in most positions – but there is at least a possibility that he was given licence to enjoy this role.

The first gifted pioneers to make an impact on a World Cup as attacking (or overlapping, as they were called back in the 1950s) full-backs were the Hungarian right-back Jeno Buzanszky and left-back Mihály Lantos. The Hungarian duo were such paragons of virtue that even Michels would have approved. Steady, reliable and strong in the tackle, they were primed to launch counter-attacks. Buzanszky loved to dribble up the wing and cross into the centre, while Lantos had a powerful driving shot.

Hungary should have won the 1954 World Cup with their attacking full-backs. Four years later, Brazil did just that with the unrelated Djalma and Nilton Santos on the right and left of their back four. The latter had made his mark as a prolific striker, been bought by Botafogo as a reserve centre-half and then made his debut at left-back. He never really regarded his new role as purely defensive and, sweeping up the flanks like a frustrated striker, he perfected the attacking full-back role. He overlapped brilliantly with Djalma who was slightly less enterprising but still provided the cross for Brazil's third goal in the 1962 World Cup final.

By proving that goals could be made or scored from almost any position, the Santoses liberated the game tactically. Paradoxically, the most compelling proof of their enduring

Brazil's World Cup winners, 1954. Standing, from left: Djalma Santos, Zito, Gilmar, Zozimo, Nilton Santos, Mauro. Squatting: America, Garrincha, Didi, Vava, Amarildo and Zagalo.

influence was offered by Helenio Herrera's Inter Milan, who dominated European football with their counter-attacking *catenaccio* in the 1960s. When Herrera was criticised for his team's sterile tactics, he would point to the *Nerazzurri*'s elegant attacking left-back, Giacinto Facchetti.

Facchetti was a full-back who wanted to be a centre-forward but put his frustration to good use, becoming, in 1971–72, the highest-scoring full-back in the history of Italian football. 'It was a trait I brought with me from my days playing at the church youth centre,' Facchetti said once. 'I didn't like to sit back, I preferred to follow the action and finish it.' Among his legion of admirers was a young centre-back called Franz Beckenbauer. 'He inspired me to play in my own style,' said the Kaiser. 'He was one of the few who turned a defensive role into an attacking one. As a left-back, he went up and down the entire wing, which made him unpredictable. He even scored goals. His options were limited – in his position he could move only straight ahead or to his right – whereas for me, in the centre, everything was possible.'

Today, football seems to be teeming with full-backs who look better going forward than running back. Some fans still pine for the old-school full-back who tackled like a beast and believed the only appropriate use of the ball was to belt it into Row Z. For the diehards, the man who must shoulder the blame is Djalma Santos. Not only was he supremely effective in attack, he was one of the first, great full-backs to prove that scything tackles were overrated, showing that you were usually better off shepherding the attacker into such a useless part of their pitch that, in their demoralised state, they could be dispossessed with ease.

⚽ Which goalie first wore **gloves?**

One of the great old-time goalies, Heiner Stuhlfauth, who played for Nuremberg and Germany in the 1920s, recalled: 'When it was raining, I would wear gloves made of rough wool. A wet ball will stick to such gloves. It was something I learned from life – I knew you cannot hold an eel with your bare hands, that you have to grip him using a rough piece of cloth.'

His contemporary, the Spanish keeper Ricardo Zamora, rarely stepped onto the pitch without gloves, though they may have primarily been a fashion statement. The man they called El Divino was very fastidious about his appearance. His trademark accessories were his legendary white V-neck sweater and a black turtleneck. Zamora smoked 65 cigarettes a day in the latter stages of his career and liked to calm his nerves at half-time with a quick ciggie. He never went anywhere without his good luck charm – a crude doll in a dark frock. So perhaps the well-dressed superstar simply considered gloves part of a gentleman's proper attire. However, Zamora's gloves weren't of much use on his blackest day, when Spain lost 7-1 to England in December 1931. So many balls slipped out of the divine one's grasp on a muddy Highbury pitch that one newspaper complained that Spain might as well have put Zamora's lucky charm between the sticks.

Stuhlfauth and Zamora pre-date two famous keepers who are often credited with pioneering the use of gloves in the 1940s: Charlton's Sam Bartram, and Argentinian keeper Amadeo Carrizo, both of whom are pictured with and without gloves. One famous contemporary of Carrizo's always wore gloves, the great Lev Yashin. Dubbed the Black Panther because of the colour of his kit, he looked fashionably monochrome with black gloves. Yashin wore tight leather gloves, not ones made of wool, so he wasn't wearing them to warm his hands. Indeed, after the 1956 Olympic final, Yashin approached the Yugoslav keeper, Petar Radenković, urged him to switch to wearing gloves and gave him a pair to use.

Yet none of these gloves were the special custom-made products that spread like wildfire in the 1970s. Germany's Sepp Maier is widely considered the first to wear oversized gloves with padding and rubber inlays. The move towards modern gloves began when Maier took up wearing gloves made of terry cloth instead of wool or leather. 'One day I was drying the ball with a towel and noticed it stuck to the ball,' he recalls. 'So then I had gloves made from this material.' Ultimately, Maier's experiment led to the huge gloves that

Cap, check. Gloves, check. Lev Yashin lines up, fully prepared, for the USSR, 1958.

became his trademark. Bob Wilson once said: 'I remember making fun of the big gloves Maier wore at the 1974 World Cup. Within a year, everyone was wearing them.'

John Burridge, easily as eccentric as the renowned practical joker Maier, says: 'I was the first keeper in England to wear gloves. I'd seen Sepp Maier wearing them. I had to get them from Germany; you couldn't get them in England. Pat Jennings and Peter Shilton rang me for pairs.'

Maier collaborated with Gebhard Reusch, whose father had founded a company that was producing winter sports equipment, including skiing gloves. In 1973, Reusch introduced a range of goalkeeping gloves bearing Maier's name. At roughly the same time, Wolfgang Fahrian, West Germany's goalkeeper at the 1962 World Cup, had been experimenting with cutting up the rubber sheets used on table-tennis racquets and glueing them onto gloves for a better grip. Fahrian teamed up with sportswear entrepreneur Kurt Kränzle and put out his own range. Fahrian had the same nickname as Yashin – the Black Panther – and fought Radenković for a place in 1860 Munich's goal.

⚽ Who invented the **league**?

No one's going to like the answer to this, so let's delay the inevitable for a while and start with some linguistics. The term 'league' comes from the Latin word 'ligare', meaning to bind, and refers to a group of people, nations or institutions bound together for and by a purpose. What we now call league football began, in 1888, when William McGregor of Aston Villa invited several professional clubs to a meeting to create an association that would organise regular, scheduled games. This organisation could have been called the Football Association, but since that name was already taken, McGregor and his associates settled on the Football League. In its inaugural year, the league was contested by twelve clubs from the north and Midlands: Accrington, Aston Villa, Blackburn Rovers, Bolton Wanderers, Burnley, Derby County, Everton, Notts County, Preston North End, Stoke F.C., West Bromwich Albion and Wolverhampton Wanderers. The winners were Preston, who were unbeaten, and also won the FA Cup.

The first-ever football league winners – Preston North End, 1889.

This derivation explains why there are football leagues that don't really play league football. Consider, for instance, the ACDV League. ACDV stands for Attività Calcistica dei Dipendenti Vaticani and refers to the Vatican City State FA. There are normally 16 teams in this league (one is called, and we're not making this up, North American Martyrs). The precise championship format varies, but usually the teams are divided into groups, from which the best teams qualify for a knock out cup tournament, the Clericus Cup, fittingly played after Easter.

But forming a league is only the first step. The next one for McGregor and his allies was designing some kind of system for a competition. We all know how it eventually turned out – each team played the other once at home and once away;

two points were awarded for a win and one for a draw – but these are just details, as the number of games, where they are played or how many points are distributed is ultimately of no relevance to what we consider a league system.

The best and shortest description of what we are looking for is this: 'A league uses a prearranged schedule of games to decide on a championship from among its members.' This definition comes from *The Dickson Baseball Dictionary*, a book that should know what it's talking about, because the league system was invented in the United States and first introduced in baseball. In America, the National League was already into its twelfth season when McGregor and the others formally created the Football League at the Royal Hotel in Manchester.

The National League, the oldest existing professional team sports league in the world, was founded on 2 February 1876, but the first professional sports league, the National Association of Professional Base Ball Players, was formed five years earlier. This association originally comprised ten clubs, nine of which fielded a team for the inaugural season. The clubs played between 27 and 35 games against each other (scheduling was still a problem). Philadelphia Athletics won the most games (22) and were declared champions. This was a league, as we understand this today, in all but name, and it was born in the same year as Marcel Proust and Orville Wright.

Of course, a league is not always a straightforward thing. In Argentina, a truly arcane system determines the clubs to be relegated, based on their average points per match over a three-year period. (Relegation, introduced by way of play-offs in 1894, was the great English innovation, as it remains unknown to baseball.) And between 1991 and 2012, Argentina had a somewhat unusual method of deciding the title, with the country producing two champions per calendar year, the winners of the so-called Apertura and Clausura seasons, respectively. Though the homeland of Maradona and Messi has since switched to a league with one champion a season, this system remains popular in Latin America and some countries, such as Venezuela, then crown an overall champion through a two-legged final between the winners of these tournaments. A bit like baseball's World Series.

Sometimes, the oddities are subtler. This final table in Morocco in 1965–66 is famous as one of the most competitive leagues ever, with only eight points separating the champions from the two relegated clubs.

	P	W	D	L	F	A	Pts
1. Wydad Athletic Club (Casablanca)	26	11	9	6	26	18	57
2. Raja Club Athletic (Casablanca)	26	9	12	5	27	20	56
3. Renaissance Sportive de Settat	26	10	8	8	28	15	54
4. Sporting Club Chabab de Mohammédia	26	8	12	6	19	17	54
5. Kawkab Athletic Club de Marrakech	26	9	9	8	21	21	53
6. TAS (Casablanca)	26	8	10	8	21	20	52
7. Hassania Union Sport Agadir	26	6	14	6	32	33	52
8. Stade Marocain (Rabat)	26	8	9	9	27	27	51
9. Mouloudia Club Oujda	26	5	15	6	27	28	51
10. Racing Athletic Club (Casablanca)	26	7	10	9	17	21	50
11. Maghreb Association Sportive (Fès)	26	6	12	8	13	16	50
12. Fath Union Sport (Rabat)	26	7	10	9	25	31	50
13. Club Omnisport de Meknès	26	7	9	10	16	23	49
14. Maghreb Athletic Tetouan	26	7	9	10	21	30	49

Yet it's also notable because of the points system. Morocco awarded three points for a win (15 years before that was adopted in England and 28 years before it was first used in a World Cup), two for a draw and – oddest of all – one point for a defeat. The innovative idea of rewarding losers has never caught on and Morocco now awards three points for win, one for a draw and nothing for a defeat.

Who invented the long throw?

Not Rory Delap certainly. The devastating monotony with which the Stoke City legend hurtled the ball to the far post so infuriated Arsène Wenger that he proposed FIFA should replace throw-ins with kick-ins or abolish the rule that players can't be offside from a throw-in. If either of Wenger's proposals were adopted, Delap and his fellow practitioners would have to find a new trick and the beautiful game, for which the French coach has appointed himself moral guardian, would be a little less ugly. But Wenger is blaming the wrong man.

If you assess the quality of a long throw purely on distance, the king of the flingers is Dave Challinor who, while on Tranmere's books, threw a record 46.34 metres. But Chelsea fans insist that, in terms of sheer effectiveness, it is hard to beat the great Ian Hutchinson. Hutch's most famous throw, launched into the penalty area at Old Trafford in the 1970 FA Cup final replay, caused such havoc in the Leeds United defence that Dave Webb rose home to head the winner.

Hutch's prowess was exceptional but he was hardly unique. Hennes Weisweiler, who coached the great Borussia Mönchengladbach side of the 1970s, complained in 1978 that: 'Every English team has one player who is expert at the long throw.' Fulham and Spurs certainly did. In the late 1950s and early 1960s, Fulham left-back Jim Langley's ability to wind himself up for throws and launch the ball on to the head of striker Maurice Cook created many goals for the Cottagers. At White Hart Lane, as one Spurs fan noted, 'long throw by Chivers to Alan Gilzean who would flick the ball on with his strangely pyramid-shaped head for Martin Peters to ghost in at the far post to volley home. Worked every time!'

Where some see art, others look for science. In 2006, researchers of Brunei University found that the optimal angle to release the ball for a long throw was 30 degrees. That maximises height while minimising air resistance. In the summer of 1933, a promising young right-half called Bill Shankly was doing his own experiments. Having just broken into the Carlisle United first team, he returned to his home village Glenbuck for the summer and spent days trying to perfect this tactic, throwing the ball over a row of houses and persuading local boys to fetch them back for him.

Shankly may have been inspired by Samuel Weaver, a left-half whose throw-ins were said to reach distances of 32m when he was at Hull City in 1928–29. In August 1936, Weaver joined Chelsea and there is a famous photo of him showing off his technique to his new team-mates. They don't

Chelsea's long-throw specialist Sam Weaver could also throw himself over his team-mates. It was unclear what match-winning ploy he had in mind.

look like they're taking the demonstration that seriously. They certainly wouldn't have dreamed that, 34 years later, the club would win the FA Cup with that very technique.

☻ Why do football matches last ninety minutes?

Nobody really knows. The laws of the game did not evolve with Darwinian efficiency. Although Ebenezer Cobb Morley, the first secretary of the FA, published an approved list of the laws of the game on 5 December 1863, those laws did not mention the duration of a game or even specify how many players constituted a team.

In the 1850s and 1860s, Sheffield was the most influential football city in the world. Sheffield FC – the world's oldest club – was formed on 24 October 1857 and a year later, the first laws of the game, known as the Sheffield Rules, were published. These didn't specify how long a game would last or how many players should be on each side either. Adrian Harvey's painstaking history *Football: The First Hundred Years* suggests that Sheffield played with 20 a side and for two hours in the late 1850s. As late as 1862, Harvey says: 'The rules provided no guidance as to the length of time of matches and these could range from anything between one and three hours.'

At this point, the steel city was home to fifteen football clubs and the Sheffield Rules were much more widely used than the Morley/FA rules. The first game we know to have been played over 90 minutes was an inter-city match between Sheffield FC and a team drawn from the London clubs at Battersea Park on 31 March 1866. At the time, the duration of the game seemed less interesting than the Sheffield team's display of aerial prowess which, according to the Sheffield FC website, 'reduced the London players and fans to fits of laughter.' It is certainly possible that the length of that match was dictated by something as prosaic as the duration of the train journey from Sheffield to London. The precedent soon caught on. In 1871, the first rules for the FA Cup stipulated that 'the duration of each match shall be one hour and a half'.

For those who prefer to think the selection of 90 minutes wasn't as arbitrary, Peter Seddon suggests in *Football Talk* that the duration springs from a historic obsession with the number 60 which he dates back to the Middle Ages and the 'division of a clockface into 60 minutes'. Six hundred years ago, Seddon says, 60 represented entirety just as 100 does today. He even suggests that this accounts for the rather arcane scoring system in tennis (15, 30, 40 and game – i.e. 60) if you accept that 40 started as 45 and was shortened on the 'grounds of laziness'. So if, like Seddon, you accept that 'fifteen minute divisions, or multiples thereof, are historically 'tidy", there might be some logic in the choice of 90 minutes. Certainly, as Seddon points out, coaches often urge their players to keep it tight for the first 15 minutes, the traditional half-time break used to last for 15 minutes and commentators love to crank up the tension by declaring that a game has entered the final 15 minutes.

Indeed Arsène Wenger has even suggested that, 'from a coaching perspective, the key element of the UEFA Champions League is the last ten to fifteen minutes.' The history of European Cup finals bears him out. Eight have been won by decisive goals after the 75th minute and in two others late goals have helped swing the result by setting up extra time.

So football isn't a game of two halves. If Wenger's right, it's a game of six sixths.

⚽ Who first **parked the bus?**

José Mourinho is credited with first using this term after his Chelsea side had been held to a 0-0 draw by (of all teams) Tottenham at Stamford Bridge in September 2004. The Portuguese coach fumed: 'As they say in Portugal, they brought the bus and they left the bus in front of the goal.' Almost six years later, Mourinho's Inter parked the bus to triumph against Barcelona at the Camp Nou in the semi-final second leg on their way to winning the UEFA Champions League. Two years later, that template came in very handy as Roberto Di Matteo's Chelsea upset the same opponents at the same stage of the competition at the same ground.

Yet Spanish coach Javier Clemente is also famous for using the phrase, promising that his Murcia side would 'park the bus' in front of goal away to Real Madrid in April 2008. Leaving out two strikers, Clemente's Murcia maintained their 7-2-1 formation even after the 19th-minute red card for Real defender Miguel Torres Gómez ... but his side lost 1-0.

Mourinho and Clemente may have coined the term but the tactic is almost as old as the game itself. Helenio Herrera had perfected the defensive art of *catenaccio* in the 1960s, drawing inspiration from – among others – Austrian coach Karl Rappan. In the 1930s, Rappan devised a system to help his semi-professional squad at Servette compete with professionals by minimising the risk of being

The fiendish Helenio Herrera.

caught out in one-on-one encounters. His system, known as *verrou* (the bolt), essentially conceded midfield, encouraging opponents to attack while funnelling their play into the centre of the pitch where they ran into a defensive block moving as a unit. Often criticised as defensive, this system could lead to swift counter-attacks in which six or seven players took part.

In a rare interview, Rappan justified this formation saying: 'The Swiss is not a natural footballer, but he is usually sober in his approach to things. He can be persuaded to think ahead and calculate ahead.' Many coaches, fearing that their players are not naturals, have felt obliged to follow Rappan's example. A few have taken it to extremes. In the 1956 Olympic football tournament, Indonesia held the Soviet Union to a 0-0 draw after their Croatian coach Antun Pogacnik ordered them to keep ten players in their own area whenever they lost possession. They lost the replay 4-0.

⚽ Who was the first playmaker?

You could argue that there is no real godfather to all the classic playmakers that come to mind – from Johan Cruyff or Günter Netzer to Michel Platini, Diego Maradona and Roberto Baggio all the way up to Zinedine Zidane – because the role is almost as old as the game itself. Indeed it was so vital to football that from the 1880s into the 1920s every team contained a playmaker. That's because the pyramid formation so popular in so many countries, the 2-3-5, stood and fell with the man in the middle of what we would now call a three-man midfield: the centre-half.

And yet we would probably not recognise any of the great old centre-halves as a playmaker if we actually saw them play. The reason is as simple as it is surprising – the laws were different. To be precise, the offside laws. Back in the heyday

Arsenal, back in their south London heyday, when the dancing centre-half ruled supreme.

of the original centre-halves – until 1925 – three opposing players (rather than the modern two) were required between the attacker and the goal line when the ball was last played for the striker to be onside. It's hard to visualise the consequences of this rule for a modern fan, so just think about how often a player is offside today following a through ball or a long vertical pass. Now don't multiply this number but square it, and you will quickly understand why back then it was nearly impossible to split a defence or get behind the backline. The pre-1925 game asked for pace and muscle and dribbling skills, not the vision of a playmaker.

Only after that all-important rule change did the modern playmaker begin to emerge, in the 2-3-5 and the new W-M system, usually credited to Arsenal under Herbert Chapman. In this formation, the centre-half became a third back, which meant that the hitherto most creative position became primarily a destructive one. At the same time, the two inside-forwards, previously part of the five-man forward line, were pulled back into a deep-lying position. One of those two would evolve into the team's playmaker, replacing the old attacking centre-half as the main man. It's why Arsenal's Alex James, a star of the 1930s, has often been called the first modern playmaker. Just listen to Brian Glanville, who enthused that 'his beautifully judged and powerfully struck passes from midfield, some through the middle to a charging, challenging centre-forward, some inside the full-back to Bastin, on the left wing, some across field to the racing Joe Hulme, were of priceless effect'.

There were other notable string-pullers like James during this decade. Sunderland's Raich Carter, for instance (whom Sir Stanley Matthews called 'bewilderingly clever, constructive, lethal in front of goal, yet unselfish'). Or the brilliant Argentine Antonio Sastre, who orchestrated Independiente's play in the 1930s.

All of these great players, and others, have been hailed as the inventor of the playmaking role but to find the true originator you must go back further still. The offside rule changed in 1925 but James only emerged as Arsenal's key man in 1929. Two players filled the role of the scheming, withdrawn inside-forward in Chapman's system before James. His immediate predecessor was Charlie Buchan. He had suggested the W-M in the first place, had always wanted to be the deep-lying link man and filled that role until he retired in 1928. But when Chapman introduced the new system, he didn't use Buchan as link man, turning instead to the veteran Andrew Neil, about whom he noted, 'he is slow as a funeral but has ball control'.

Yet it's not simply the position that maketh the playmaker. As good as Neil and Buchan may have been, they weren't compared to an orchestra's conductor, nor did the country's intelligentsia write poems about them. Unlike the legendary Austrian Matthias Sindelar. In the 1920s, the Danubian school stuck to the 2-3-5, so you'd expect Sindelar to have filled the old centre-half role, the more so since he was lightweight, pencil-thin and disliked any form of bodily contact (all of which explains why they called him the Paper Man). But he was the centre-forward. With a twist.

Matthias Sindelar, the Paper Man, became a legend in Austria after refusing to give the Nazi salute to Hitler after the *Anschluss*.

Like the Hungarian Nándor Hidegkuti in the 1950s or Johan Cruyff in the 1970s, Sindelar was a centre-forward who loved to drop back, exchange passes with a midfielder (in the national team, this was centre-half Josef 'Pepi' Smistik) and then distribute the ball or make runs himself. He had technique, vision and style. Maybe too much style. He made his Austria debut in 1926, at 23, but fell foul of national coach Hugo Meisl two years later after his playfulness lost the team a game played on a slippery, snowy surface. Stubborn, like all great playmakers, Sindelar refused to cut down on his elegant dribbles or beloved short passes and gave away the ball so often on that cold afternoon that Meisl lost patience.

Yet fans and writers demanded Sindelar's return and Meisl finally relented in time for a game against Scotland in May 1931. Austria sensationally won 5-0. It was the birth of a side known as the Wunderteam – and Sindelar was its brains. The drama critic and essayist Alfred Polgar put it this way: 'He would play football as a grandmaster plays chess: with a broad mental conception, calculating moves and countermoves in advance, always choosing the most promising of all possibilities.' And the writer Friedrich Torberg composed a poem which said that 'he played nonchalantly, delicately, cheerfully – he always played, he never fought'. Which is as good a description of the classic playmaker as you're likely to read.

But Sindelar was not just a footballer. In 1938, after Nazi Germany annexed Austria, Sindelar led Austria to victory in a celebratory game between the two nations, pointedly refusing (along with fellow scorer Karl Sesta) to make a Nazi salute to Hitler beforehand. He then refused to play for a united German team. In 1939, he was found dead, probably due to carbon monoxide poisioning, though Gestapo involvement was strongly suspected. His club, Austria Vienna, received 15,000 telegrams of condolence.

⚽ Who was the first **sweeper-keeper?**

'**Go out and make mistakes.**' That's what Ajax coach Johan Cruyff told his young keeper Stanley Menzo in 1985–86. A brilliant shot-stopper, Menzo was usually adept at clearing up behind the defence but sometimes took his coach's advice too literally. Two blunders by Menzo against Auxerre in 1993 – under Cruyff's successor Louis van Gaal – smoothed the way for Edwin van der Sar to perfect the sweeper-keeper role.

This style of goalkeeping had been influential in Dutch football ever since the 1970s. Selecting his 1974 World Cup squad, Netherlands coach Rinus Michels decided that Jan Jongbloed's ability to operate as an extra defender, playing 20 yards from his goal with his feet, was more useful than the agile, shot-stopping of Jan van Beveren. Jongbloed's brief wasn't that sophisticated: he usually had to get the ball first and kick it into touch but Van der Sar became the pivot of Ajax's rapid 'circulation football', a style Van Gaal exported to Barcelona, laying the foundations for tiki-taka. As Chris Keulemans, an amateur goalkeeper and Dutch novelist, told David Winner, 'some goalkeepers regard the ball as their enemy because it is trying to penetrate their sacred area, but Van der Sar regards it as his friend.'

In the 1990s, Van der Sar, Peter Schmeichel and the gifted, but erratic, Fabien Barthez emerged as gifted sweeper-keepers. Today, the best exponent of that role is probably Barcelona's Víctor Valdés. But they weren't the first players in that position to regard the ball as a friend. Before the 1990 World Cup, Colombia coach Francisco Maturana put his faith in René Higuita who, he wrote, 'gives us something no one else has. With René as sweeper, we have eleven outfield players'.

In hindsight, Higuita's career has been telescoped into one scorpion kick and one famous failure to sweep up that let Roger Milla score for Cameroon at Italia 90. At the very moment Higuita lost the ball near his own halfway line, the Colombian TV commentator was describing him as 'an exceptional sweeper'.

From such highlights, the legend of Higuita as El Loco was born. In fairness, Higuita's self-confidence had often provided the inspiration for an exceptional Colombian side. In 1988, in a friendly against England at Wembley, the keeper dribbled around Gary Lineker as if, in Maturana's words, 'it was a game in the park back home'.

Maturana had looked back to Jongbloed for inspiration. But Michels, who had selected Jongbloed, was looking back even further – to the great Hungarian side of 1953 and their keeper Gyula Grosics. Under their innovative coach Gusztáv Sebes, Hungary's shift in tactics to a 4-2-4 with a withdrawn striker created, as Grosics recalled, 'an attacking game-plan that provided more opportunities for the opposition to counter-attack when they got possession. There was space behind our defence to be exploited and I had to act as a kind of extra sweeper, outside my area, trying to reach the through ball before the opponent did.' With a looser back four, Grosics learned to roll the ball out because it was more accurate, and quicker, than just kicking it up the pitch. This tactic was so successful that Ferenc Puskás and Nándor Hidegkuti would drop back to pick up a throw. The success of this approach impressed Michels, then a no-thrills centre-forward for Ajax, who would use the same ploy when he became the Amsterdammers' coach.

Of course, there is also an entirely different way for a goal-keeper to 'exploit space' – he could, like Franz Beckenbauer would one day, run into it with the ball at his feet. In fact, there was a keeper known for precisely such suicidal forays deep, deep into the opponents' half long before the Kaiser

Put your hands in the air for the original sweeper-keeper, the man in black, 1860 Munich's Petar Radenković.

invented the attacking sweeper. And since this goalkeeper was playing in Munich, it is tempting to rewrite history and say it wasn't Giacinto Facchetti's runs down the wing that inspired Beckenbauer but a batty Yugoslav we have met before – 1860 Munich's Petar Radenković.

Radenković, who'd won three caps in the 1950s, became the Bundesliga's first foreign superstar during the league's inaugural season, 1963–64, in part because the nation finally saw what 1860's fans had already become used to: Radenković's spectacular solo runs. Like Grosics, the Yugoslav would roll the ball out, or rather: pretend to. Because if there was no opponent in the vicinity, Radenković would roll the ball into his own path – and run. His solos could literally take him as far as the other team's penalty area and he was so fearless – or reckless – that he would make them even on snowy, slippery surfaces.

This combination of eccentricity and showmanship ran in the family (see 'What was the top pop hit by a footballer', p.260). However, Radenković maintains: 'My runs had nothing to do with putting on a show. I was just creating modern goalkeeping. I had been an outfield player during my youth, and I learned that you don't just hoof the ball away.'

⚽ Who invented the **stepover**?

The global popularity of a trick that Cristiano Ronaldo turned into his signature move is reflected in the variety of terms used to describe it. In German-speaking countries, the stepover is sometimes called the *Scherentrick*, literally scissor trick, but more commonly known as an *übersteiger*, a climb over. In France, they call it, rather poetically, *un passement des jambes* (a passing of the legs), while the Italians, as if the trick was performed on the dance floor, call it *un doppio passo* (a double step) and the Spanish, confusingly, refer to it as *la bicicleta* (which they also use to describe a bicycle kick).

This profusion of terms reflects the complex roots of this showboaters' trademark. Apart from CR7, most of the famous recent exponents have been Brazilian. The Brazilian Ronaldo famously used his shuffle to win the 1998 UEFA Cup for Inter, prompting an awestruck Kevin Keegan to say: 'We've all seen those skills before – but not at 100mph.' Denilson's exuberant use of the trick prompted British rapper JME (or grime artist if we're being absolutely accurate) to cut a track in 2009 called 'Over Me' which includes the line 'I'm quick, like Denilson stepover'. And in Chile, Club de Deportes La Serena star Eduardo Rubio, is nicknamed *El Bicicleta*, the Stepover. He has also been dubbed the triathlete, because he '*corre, bicicleta y nada*' –

runs, bicycles, and *nada* – which means both 'swims' and 'nothing' in Spanish.

So the obvious place to look to trace the evolution of the stepover might seem to be South America. But to do that would be to ignore the contributions made by two of Gazza's best mates, a German midfielder nicknamed after asparagus, and a tragic Dutch speed skating aficionado.

Let's start in the not too distant past with Gazza's former mentor, Glenn Roeder. In the 1980s, Newcastle United's languid central defender used the stepover to get out of trouble. He did this so often – sometimes twice on the same opponent – that it was called the Glenn Roeder shuffle. When asked to explain the origins of this move, Roeder said his dad taught him it 'many moons ago'.

'Go across the ball with the outside of the right or left foot, feint with the upper part of the body and cut inside.' Cristiano Ronaldo prepares to roll.

Roeder was hardly the only player to realise the fun that could be had by stepping over the ball. The same thought had occurred, to mention just a few names, to Francesco Totti, Luís Figo, Robinho, Zinedine Zidane and Chris Waddle. In his prime at Marseille, Waddle, Gazza's long-suffering former room-mate, liked to deceive defenders by doing the stepover at jogging pace or at a standstill, lazily jabbing his foot over the ball before he dropped his shoulder and accelerated away.

For fans in Germany and the Netherlands, such artistry was impressive but hardly new. In the 1970s, this sleight of foot was the making of Hans 'Hannes' Bongartz, the great Schalke midfielder nicknamed Asparagus Tarzan (the plant is often used to describe long-legged German footballers). It led to him being lauded, in one club history, as the inventor of the stepover. Was he? Alas, no – not even in Germany. Earlier in the decade, coach Karl-Heinz Heddergott had published a book called *Neue Fussball Lehre* (New Football Teaching) in which the move – referred to as the *Scherentrick* (scissor trick) is described in detail. The book instructs players: 'Go across the ball with the outside of the right or left foot, feint with the upper part of the body and cut inside.'

Ajax's reclusive legend Piet Keizer had no need of such instructions. Dutch coach Bert van Marwijk recalled watching Keizer and copying his moves, saying, 'Piet was more Mr Stepover like Ronaldo.' But where did Keizer get the idea? Possibly from watching Abe Lenstra, the tricky left-sided player who won 47 Dutch caps between 1940 and 1959 and would have won many more if he hadn't insisted the selectors play him in his preferred inside-forward position. There is a YouTube clip of Lenstra rehearsing his stepover on the training ground.

Lenstra may have been perfecting the manoeuvre at around the same period as Chilean left-half Augusto 'The Kid' Arenas was insisting he had invented it. The left-half, who won the Chilean title with Everton de Viña del Mar in 1952, was determined that no one else would get the credit, saying: 'The stepover is mine, all who saw me know that.' Yet other remarks made by Arenas suggest we shouldn't take his assertion at face value. The left-half told the newspaper *La Cuarta*: 'This is nothing – several times I dived from the top of the cranes on the Vergara pier, I was featherweight champion, played basketball – and gave mambo dancing classes.'

Arenas' bombast would be disputed by fans of forward Jair da Rosa Pinto, who was credited, in his native Brazil, with inventing the move. Yet by a tragic quirk of football history, the claims of Master Jaja – as he was known – have largely been overlooked. His career – indeed his life – never recovered from his participation in the de facto final of the 1950 World Cup which Brazil, as hosts and favourites, catastrophically lost 2-1 to Uruguay.

Yet as far back as the 1930s, Italy's World Cup-winning midfielder Amedeo Biavati was thrilling crowds, and *Azzurri* coach Vittorio Pozzo, with this same technique. At the time Pozzo said: 'Biavati perfected the stepover. The public expected it every time he took off down the touchline. And the opponent expected it too. But there was nothing he could do. At full speed Amedeo executed a kind of little jump in the air, it seemed as if he was going to do a back heel. The defender slowed down for an instant, Biavati surged past him,

touching the ball with his second foot and was off.' Such feints inspired a young Bologna supporter called Pier Paolo Pasolini who said later: 'When I played, I said "I am Biavati".'

The film director's idol was one of the first players to make the stepover famous. But he was not the first. A fragile genius from the Dutch East Indies (as Indonesia was then known) called Law Adam had already perfected this trick. In October 1932, the Dutch newspaper *Het Vaderland* covered a friendly between the Netherlands and Belgium in Brussels. With 15 minutes to go, and the score at 2-2, Adam slipped past one opponent and then beat Belgian skipper Nicolas Hooydonckx with a trick the paper refers to as his *bekende schaarbeweging* (well-known scissor move). The paper's description suggests the stepover may have been Adam's signature move, and contemporary accounts suggest he got the idea from watching speed skaters. Speed skating over frozen canals, often over long distances, was then a popular Dutch pastime. Speed skaters make these stepover movements and do so in such a way that it's easy to see why this trick might be dubbed the scissor move.

Adam might be more famous had he not suffered from a heart condition which forced him to retire at the age of 25, in 1933, and killed him on 15 May 1941. His final hours read like a scene in a Victorian adventure novel. Back in Asia, he was playing a friendly in Surbaya, his home town. After two goals and three assists, he left the pitch in the 53rd minute with his hand on his heart. He assured the referee it wasn't serious, that he was leaving because victory was assured, but within an hour he was pronounced dead. Still, the legend of Adam's scissor move still resonates in Dutch popular culture. In 1974, the Dutch author Jan Wolkers published a novel called *De Walgvogel*. In the first chapter – entitled 'Adam de Schaarman' (Adam The Scissors Man) – the first-person narrator describes his uncle's attempt to perfect the move.

Spoiler alert. This is Pedro Calomino – the man who invented the stepover.

Adam may have introduced the stepover to Europe but even he didn't invent it. The balance of evidence suggests that the man who first perfected this move was Argentinian footballer Pedro Calomino. Authoritative claims that the Boca Juniors legend invented the stepover can be traced back as far as 1910. In *Soccer vs. The State: Tackling Football And Radical Politics*, Gabriel Kuhn says Calomino was one of the stars of Boca's first golden age: 'Spectators no longer came just to watch their teams – they came to watch their idols. One of them was Pedro Calomino, cheered on by the Boca fans in Genovese Spanish: "*Idaguele Calumín, dáguele!*" ("Do it, Calumín, do it!"). Calomino was always oblivious to the stands. He stood on the field, waited for the ball and made defenders dizzy with his incredible dribbles. He was the inventor of the *bicicleta*, the stepover.'

One reason Calomino was so popular was that he seemed to embody the club. The influence of Genovese immigrants in Boca's early history was so profound that even today the club is still nicknamed Xeneize (Genovese). Calomino's family were Genovese and he painted boats to support his family before becoming a footballer. He was an old-fashioned winger, so old-fashioned he didn't like to wear boots. Boca got permission for him to play wearing espadrilles. None of this prevented him from destroying opponents with his stepover. Fairly reliable sources tell of a game between Argentina and a Basque XI in which defender Arrate, tiring of the Boca star's tricks, told him: 'You can go forwards, you can play backwards, but just play with good faith.'

Calomino won four league titles at Boca, scored 82 goals in 182 games there (he was top scorer for six seasons) and starred in the Argentine side that won the 1921 Copa America. He retired in 1924, aged 32, because he had trouble with his right eye. But he remains a legend at Boca where he invented the stepover at their stadium.

That trick continues to delight fans and footballers – even amateurs. Reggae legend Bob Marley was so passionate about football he insisted on having access to a pitch on his world tours. A skilful midfield general – with a hard man called Skully acting as a kind of security guard on the pitch – Bob can be seen doing a stepover in the 2012 documentary film, *Marley*.

⚽ Who invented Total Football?

The usual answer – Rinus Michels' Ajax – is not necessarily right. In the early 1970s, Michels' Ajax, led by the paradigm shifting genius of Johan Cruyff, thrilled and conquered Europe with a stylish brand of football in which every outfield player could play in any position. But they didn't entirely invent it.

Tactical guru Jonathan Wilson argues that the innovative Russian coach Viktor Maslov (see 'Who invented 4-4-2?', p.8) had laid the basis for such fluidity, introducing the pressing game at Dynamo Kiev in the 1960s. You could only pressure the ball if you were absolutely confident a team-mate would

Rinus Michels – a man synonymous with Total Football – explains how he wants everyone to play. But did he learn it all from Leicester City?

cover for you and that could only happen if every player could see beyond their own specialist role and read the game.

Affectionately known to his players as Grandad, Maslov started coaching Kiev in 1964. Dynamo midfielder Yozhef Szabo says in Jonathan Wilson's book *Inverting The Pyramid*: 'In the course of the game there was complete interchangeability. This team developed the prototype of Total Football. People think it was invented in Holland but that is just because, in western Europe, they didn't see Maslov's Dynamo.' Or as Valeriy Lobanovskiy, another great Dynamo coach, who played under Maslov, put it: 'There is no such thing as a striker, a midfielder, a defender. There are only footballers and they should be able to do everything on the pitch.' To make his point, Lobanovskiy would make his players wear blindfolds in five-a-side games.

Yet – somewhat bizarrely – one year before Maslov even took charge at Kiev – and eight years before Ajax won their first European Cup at Wembley – a variant of Total Football was already being played by Matt Gillies' Leicester City, who reached the 1963 FA Cup final, losing 3-1 to Matt Busby's Manchester United. Football historians who have an instinctive preference for setting every tactical innovation in a wider, socio-political context might baulk at this suggestion. There is a kind of cultural snobbery at work which makes it easier to imagine revolutionary new tactics being honed in the glamorous fervent of 1960s Amsterdam or in the pseudo-scientific, quasi-academic world of Soviet sport than on a training pitch in the East Midlands.

Or at a very unfashionable club in the heart of West Germany's decidedly unglamorous Ruhr region. Because at the same time that Leicester stunned England, a Meidericher SV (now MSV Duisburg) team assembled on a shoestring budget shocked the Bundesliga by finishing as runners-up in 1963–64. The secret of their success was a tactical system their coach had improvised to suit his players. The coach was Rudi Gutendorf (see 'Who has coached the most national teams?') and his strategy became known as *der Riegel*, the bolt. This name, and the fact that Meidericher SV were hardly a superpower, led many to presume that Gutendorf's game was ultra-defensive. In a way, it was – because everybody defended. But at the same time, and this has been forgotten, almost everybody attacked.

Gutendorf's system was dubbed *der Riegel* because the whole team would move forward and backwards, like a bolt. While most teams were playing the W-M system, Meiderich used only two men up front, being cautious but also giving those attackers more room in which to operate. Their job was to pull defenders out of position and open up space for attacking full-backs. In November 1964, the noted magazine *Der Spiegel* said: 'Meiderich defended with attackers and attacked with defenders.' (It also quoted national coach Sepp Herberger as saying: 'This is modern football.' He might as well have said: 'This is Total Football.')

The new system didn't catch on because it demanded too much of players steeped in a simpler game. Even though Meiderich finished second, captain Werner Krämer approached Gutendorf in pre-season training and told him the team was unhappy because all the running up and down the pitch was wearing them out.

Leicester's players were more obedient. In the 1963 FA Cup Final programme *Sunday Mirror* journalist Sam Leitch has this to say of City's style: 'Millions of words have sought to explain the successful formula of the Leicester play. Tactics, that mysterious seven-letter word that is so easy to write but more difficult to explain, has been behind it all. Gillies is the first to admit football is a simple game but it can be changed around. Why should the number of players' shirts shackle them to a fixed role? If eight men can attack, why cannot eight defend?'

The Leicester manager was a tactical pioneer in a period of British football when, he said, 'players hadn't gone beyond thinking about numbers'. A ploy as simple as swapping right-half Frank McLintock and inside-right Graham Cross was enough to confound many opponents.

Inspired by the great Austria and Hungary teams of the 1950s, Gillies had Leicester playing a patient, possession-based game relying on short, probing passes and the flexible, position-swapping play of wing-halves, inside-forwards and wingers. While Cross and McLintock interchanged on the right, tireless winger Mike Stringfellow and playmaking inside-forward Davie Gibson swapped on the left. Defenders never knew if Gibson was going to feed Stringfellow or drift out wide and play a sharp, angled pass into the box for con-verted centre-forward Ken Keyworth to exploit.

Such tactics were startling – and successful – enough to take Leicester to two FA Cup finals in three years (they also lost in 1961 to Bill Nicholson's double-winning Spurs) and fourth place in the old First Division in 1962–63. They also inspired Bill Shankly who soon ordered Liverpool's Gordon Milne and Tommy Smith to swap places, like Cross and McLintock.

Gillies was a trailblazer, not the inventor. Like Michels, he had been inspired by the free-flowing style of Gusztav Sebes' great Hungarian side illuminated by the talents of Ferenc Puskás, Nandor Hidegkuti, Zoltan Czibor and Jozsef Bozsik. But even Sebes didn't invent Total Football. In the 1930s, the Austrian Wunderteam, under Hugo Meisl, played with such improvisational genius that opponents were stupefied. In 1955, Hugo's younger brother Willy wrote a classic book called *Soccer Revolution* in which he dubbed this system 'The Whirl'. In the book, he demanded: 'We must free our soccer

Hugo Meisl's Austrian Wunderteam take to the field in the 1930s – the painting is by Paul Meissner. Sindelar is fourth from right. Meisl has the hat and cane.

youth from playing to order, along rails, as it were.' He also suggested, a decade before Michels started coaching at Ajax: 'Every man-jack must be able to tackle anybody else's job temporarily without any ado.'

Meisl's Wunderteam wouldn't have been as dazzling without the great, unpredictable genius of Matthias Sindelar (see 'Who was the first playmaker?'). Austrian football writer Friedrich Torberg said of Sindelar: 'He had no system nor set pattern. He just had … genius.'

And therein lies some of the difficulty in tracing the tortuous history of Total Football. Traditionally, this philosophy's development is described almost exclusively in terms of coaches, tactics and systems, yet the quality of the players was crucial. Instead of a Sindelar or a Cruyff, Leicester manager Gillies had Gibson and McLintock – gifted players but hardly the icons to inspire a revolution. As innovative as Gillies' tactics were, the Foxes won more plaudits than silverware – even with Gordon Banks in goal. The Scot won the League Cup in 1964, suffered tuberculosis and left Filbert Street in November 1968. Six months later, City lost their third FA Cup final in nine years and were relegated.

As visionary as Michels was, he inherited – rather than invented – the genius of Cruyff. And it was free-thinkers like Cruyff, Franz Beckenbauer has suggested, who were at the heart of that football revolution. 'It owed more to the element of surprise than any magic formula,' said the Kaiser. 'The Dutch got away with it so long because the opposition could never work out what tactics they were facing. There were no tactics at all. Just brilliant players with a ball.'

Oddities

⚽ **Do you always have to wear boots to play football?**

You do now – since FIFA changed the laws. The team that most famously fell foul of the custom of wearing boots was India's 1950 World Cup side that missed the tournament because they wanted to play barefoot. Except, as you will discover, the story is a bit more complicated than that.

First, whenever this anecdote is retold, people assume that India was a backward football nation at the time. That was not quite the case. Delhi's annual Durand Cup is the third oldest football competition – after England's FA Cup and the Scottish Cup. But it is true that the Indian FA joined FIFA in 1948 partly so the national team could compete in that year's

London Olympics and it is true that field hockey, not football, was – and is – India's national sport.

Some of the best Indian footballers started out playing hockey or represented their country at both games. In India, hockey was often played barefoot. Not because the players couldn't afford shoes, but because they found it easier and more comfortable to play that way. In the final of the 1936 Olympic hockey tournament, India played in shoes and were losing at half-time (to hosts Germany). After star player Dhyan Chand took off his shoes, India won 8-1.

When India sent a football team to the 1948 Olympics, contrary to popular myth, the players were neither bad (they only lost 2-1 to France after missing two penalties) and didn't all play barefoot. Many did, because they were used to it from hockey – and at the time, this wasn't officially forbidden – though 'barefoot' is perhaps a misleading term. Those players who didn't have boots protected their feet with bandages.

Two years later, India qualified for the 1950 World Cup without playing a game, as their three qualifying opponents – Burma, Indonesia and the Philippines – all withdrew at the eleventh hour. Many countries, in fact, didn't bother with the 1950 World Cup in Brazil. Austria, Belgium, Finland and France all declined to take part due to the expensive, arduous travel involved. Which is why FIFA were so keen for India to play they even offered to pay for the flights to Brazil. But the Indian FA kept making new demands – until finally they asked for an exemption from a new rule, the one that said players had to wear boots. FIFA refused, India stayed home.

The truly strange thing about this saga is that the Indian FA didn't consult their players. Most of them would have happily played in boots in Brazil. Indeed, the whole team wore boots at the 1956 Melbourne Olympics. For that tournament,

The Indian team training barefoot for the 1948 Olympics.

they asked the organisers if players could take them off if the boots' weight caused cramps but – boots or no boots – India's team came fourth, winning a quarter-final 4-2 against hosts Australia. Coach Syed Abdul Rahim, a student of Hungary's free-flowing Magical Magyars, played Samar Banerjee as a withdrawn centre-forward, a revolutionary tactic that flummoxed opponents. The affronted Australians demanded a rematch after the Olympics (which they lost 7-1).

The most likely, though no less mysterious, explanation for India's failure to compete in the 1950 World Cup is that the Indian FA had absolutely no interest in sending a team to this or any other tournament. Because four years later, ahead of the 1954 finals, they sent in their registration only after the deadline for doing so had expired. After that, FIFA would not hear anything from Delhi for three decades. Which is why India played its first-ever World Cup qualifier on 21 March 1985, losing 2-1 to Indonesia. Krishanu Dey, an attacking midfielder revered as the Indian Maradona, scored his country's first goal in the history of the competition.

⚽ Who was the first player to wear coloured boots?

In October 1973, Bayern Munich needed a shoot-out to edge past Swedish champions Åtvidaberg in the first round of the European Cup. Conny Torstensson had stood out for the Swedes – because he scored twice in the second leg and because of his footwear. Wilhelm Neudecker, who was Bayern's president, said: 'I want the striker with the red boots' and the club soon signed him.

Torstensson's red boots were distinctive but not historic. Four years before, Alan Ball had worn white boots for Everton in the Charity Shield. Yet these boots weren't quite what they seemed. As Brian Hewitt, who was marketing director for Hummel Football Boots recalled, 'When the boots were first introduced to the UK, I made them white to make them stand out from adidas and Puma. But while Hummel did make boots, Alan couldn't initially wear them so we actually had his adidas boots painted white and delivered them to him ten minutes before the start of the game.'

Before Ball's flamboyant gesture, boots had traditionally been black or brown. Yet sixty or so years before Hummel got the paint brushes out, a tubby striker called Herbert Chapman had decided that bright yellow boots would make it easier for his team-mates to spot him. The stats suggest they also made it simpler for defenders to mark him. In one prolific spell at Northampton Town, Chapman scored 14 goals in 22 games but his strike rate at Spurs – 16 goals in 42 games between 1905 and 1907 – was more representative of his career as a whole.

Chapman's flamboyance was a harbinger of an age where, despite the grumbling of such old school coaches as Martin O'Neill, black boots have become the exception rather than the norm. Football boots is one branch of the fashion business where the hot trendy thing – the new black if you will – will never be black.

Alan Ball white boots: every English schoolboy's dream, c.1967, along with George Best's purple-and-black Stylo Matchmakers.

⚽ What was the **most brutal game of football ever?**

Traditionally, the South Americans are the specialists – and indeed they were involved in all three World Cup matches that are quasi-officially designated battles: the Battle of Bordeaux (1938), the Battle of Berne (1954) and the Battle of Santiago (1962). But Italians and Glaswegians have played significant supporting roles.

Bordeaux actually seems more of a skirmish compared to the mayhem of the following two. A 1-1 draw between Brazil and Czechoslovakia was marred by three sending offs (Manchado and Zezé Procópio for Brazil; Jan Riha for the Czechoslovaks), while Oldrich Nejedly suffered a broken leg, captain Frantisek Planicka's right arm was broken and Josef Kostalek was injured in the stomach. The carnage was completed by injuries to the tournament's top goalscorer Leonidas and Brazilian striker José Perácio.

Sixteen years later, Brazil were embroiled in an even more violent tussle with Hungary. The tone was set in the third minute when Hidegkuti gave Hungary the lead only to have his shorts ripped off as he scored. Both sides conceded penalties with rash defending but referee Arthur Ellis, later renowned for his benign officiating on *It's A Knockout*, had to send off Bozsik and Nilton Santos for fighting, and then young Brazilian left-back Humberto Tozzi for kicking Gyula Lóránt. Scoring the winner to make it 3-2 must have been especially thrilling for Zoltán Czibor given that, as Brian Glanville notes in his *The Story Of The World Cup*, 'he had been chased around the field by an incensed and threatening Djalma Santos'.

The violence escalated as the match ended. Someone – some witnesses say it was Puskás, though he denied it – threw a bottle at the Brazilian centre-half. Enraged, the Brazilians invaded the Hungarian dressing room, leaving coach Sebes needing four stitches after the confrontation. Brazilian fans spat on Ellis's car as he left the stadium. The official's verdict on the match? 'Whether it was politics or religion I don't know but they behaved like animals.'

Another Englishman, commentator David Coleman, would be even more eloquent about the Battle of Santiago in 1962. He introduced the BBC's coverage of the match between hosts Chile and Italy with these unforgettable remarks: 'Good evening. The game you are about to see is the most stupid, appalling, disgusting and disgraceful exhibition of football possibly in the history of the game.'

English referee Ken Aston sends off Italian player Mario David, as an injured Chilean lies on the ground, during the World Cup clash at Santiago, 1962.

Coleman wasn't exaggerating. The game started with the Chilean players spitting at their opponents and the eighth-minute sending off of *Azzurri* midfielder Giorgio Ferrini. It took eight minutes – and police intervention – for Ferrini to leave the pitch. Chilean midfielder Leonel Sánchez responded to a series of kicks from Italian defender Mario David by flattening him. When British referee Ken Aston gave no foul, David took matters into his own hands, or feet, and was sent off for kicking the midfielder in the neck. Sánchez celebrated by breaking Italian forward Humberto Maschio's nose with a left-hook his dad, a professional boxer, would have been proud of. The linesman ignored the punch so Sánchez stayed on.

Aston later complained that he wasn't 'reffing a football match, I was acting as an umpire in military manoeuvres'. The Italians insisted the English referee had been bought. In reality, he had just reacted incompetently as the game descended into violence, though he did give every significant decision to the home side as Chile won 2-0.

As grim as all that sounds, it's nothing compared to the violent mayhem that made the play-off to decide the 1967 Intercontinental Cup memorable for all the wrong reasons. Before the second leg in Buenos Aires, Celtic keeper Ronnie Simpson had been knocked out cold by a stone hurled from the stand and with Jimmy Johnstone kicked around the pitch with impunity, Racing Club won 2-1 to tie the series and necessitate a play-off in Montevideo. The game was so dramatic that trying to reconstruct who did what to whom and why they were sent off is extremely difficult. After 25 minutes, Paraguayan referee Rodolfo Perez Oserio was so alarmed by the way the game was being played, he called the captains together and warned them. It had little effect.

When Johnstone was chopped down for the umpteenth time, he retaliated. Racing defender Alfio Basile (who later coached Argentina) spat at Celtic winger Bobby Lennox and, after the predictable mass pugilism, both players were sent off (although Basile had actually been fighting with John Clark and Lennox was far away when the offence was committed). Racing keeper Agustín Cejas admitted later that Basile's foul on Johnstone was 'one of the most violent I've ever seen', but that didn't stop him walking up to his injured opponent and 'kicking him as hard as I could for getting my team-mate sent off'.

At half-time, Johnstone had to wash opponents' spit out of his hair. Three minutes into the second half, 'Jinky' was dismissed for the crime of being rugby tackled by Racing defender Oscar Martin. French journalist Francis Thébaud, covering the match for *Miroir du Football*, looked on incredulously: 'He who had been the constant target of the aggression since the beginning of the match became the victim of the man who was supposed to protect the footballer against the fakers and foulers. It was a staggering decision.'

Among all the carnage, Racing striker José Cardenas found time to score the only goal and Tommy Gemmell seized the opportunity to kick an opponent up the backside. All that remained was for Celtic forward John Hughes to be sent off after a foul on Racing keeper Cejas and for Rulli to be dismissed too, for a relatively mild offence. Two minutes later, after another free-for-all, Oserio seemed to send off Bertie Auld but the headstrong Celtic midfielder refused to leave the pitch.

After six sendings off (even though Auld didn't leave) and 51 fouls, the finale to the play-off was grimly appropriate. Racing's attempted lap of honour was curtailed as they were pelted with whatever the Uruguayans in the crowd could find to throw at them. The Argentinian paper *La Racon* crowed: 'Racing have recovered the glory days.' The *Miroir du Football* had a different take in its headline: 'Racing: Champions of the world of violence, treachery and theatrics.' Celtic directors were so appalled they fined their players £250 each. If you've ever wondered why Jock Stein never got his knighthood, this might be the reason.

Needless to say, there is some terrific footage of all these battles on YouTube.

⚽ Who were the most **careless owners** of a trophy?

Sometimes you wonder why athletes invest so much time and effort trying to win a trophy, when they often seem to lose all respect for the object of desire once it's theirs. The tragi-comic history of carelessness starts with the very first football trophy – the original FA Cup was stolen in 1895 from a Birmingham shop window, where winners Aston Villa had put it on display, and was never recovered.

Yet the English obviously didn't learn from the experience, as 71 years later, while staging the World Cup, they allowed the Jules Rimet Trophy to be nicked while on display at Westminster Central Hall. Luckily, the cup was found a week later by Pickles, a black and white collie dog. (Fearful of a repeat, the FA secretly commissioned a replica of the trophy. It's this replica that Bobby Moore holds aloft in English football's most iconic image.)

Alas, dog and trophy suffered sad fates. Pickles became famous enough to have the same agent as Spike Milligan but, after a brief appearance in the British comedy *The Spy With A Cold Nose*, strangled himself on his lead while chasing a cat in 1967. And in December 1983, the real Jules Rimet Trophy was stolen again, from the headquarters of the Brazilian FA in Rio. No dog came to the rescue so the Jules Rimet is not still gleaming – as the David Baddiel and Frank Skinner lyrics

Pickles the collie being interviewed at the crime scene where he discovered the World Cup trophy, discarded in a ditch.

to 'Three Lions (Football's Coming Home)' might suggest – having almost certainly been melted down by the thieves.

Club sides don't treat their trophies much better. The Germans are almost as careless as the English. In 1978, Magdeburg won the East German FA Cup for the fifth time and were allowed to keep it. In 1990, it disappeared. Just like that. Maybe it was stolen, maybe not – it's just not there anymore. In 2002, in a reunified Germany, Schalke paraded the cup in triumph through their home town Gelsenkirchen only for the trophy to slip from the grasp of business manager Rudi Assauer and loop on to the asphalt. The club brought the badly damaged cup to Wilhelm Nagel, the Cologne goldsmith who had created the modern trophy in 1964. 'The first time I saw it, tears welled up in my eyes,' Nagel said. The then 75-year-old worked for five months until he had restored the cup to its former glory. (Assauer paid the £21,000 bill for repairs.)

Careless hands struck again in April 2011, when Real Madrid paraded the Copa del Rey, which they hadn't won in 18 years. Dropped by defender Sergio Ramos, the trophy was crushed under the bus's front right wheel. Only a few weeks later, Dutch side Ajax rode through Amsterdam to present the Eredivisie trophy to their fans. Goalkeeper Maarten Stekelenburg, of all people, dropped the silver plate and watched it bounce along the road. A year later, Ajax dropped the trophy again. This time defender Jan Vertonghen let it fall on to his left foot after Ajax had clinched the title. The trophy was undamaged but Vertonghen's sock was left soaked with blood.

That same month the *Daily Mail* reported that 'three members of Chelsea's staff have been suspended after the Champions League trophy was damaged'. The newspaper explained: 'One of the handles was left hanging off after the three security personnel posed for pictures with the trophy to show off to friends.'

Posing for pictures, as Aston Villa can testify, is often where the trouble starts. In May 1982, when the Villains won the European Cup, left-back Colin Gibson and midfielder Gordon Cowans were tasked with bringing it back from Rotterdam. In celebratory mood, they took the gigantic silverware to the Fox Inn near Tamworth. After a few photos, and a few drinks, the players began a darts match until, at some point, Gibson recalls, 'someone turned around and said the cup's been stolen'. Luckily, it turned up – 100 miles away at West Bar police station in the centre of Sheffield. Before their colleagues from the West Midlands arrived to retrieve the trophy, the younger police on duty at West Bar played in full uniform for the honour of 'winning' the European Cup. What the police in Sheffield and the West Midlands still don't know, more than 30 years later, is who stole the trophy, why and how it came to end up in Sheffield.

What is the **strangest criteria** to decide which clubs enter a cup?

The Inter-Cities Fairs Cup, which UEFA like to call 'the father of European football tournaments', was initially open to teams from the 60 or so cities across Europe which hosted major industrial trade fairs. Ernst Thommen, a Swiss pools magnate on FIFA's executive committee, had, as UEFA's official history puts it, 'the idea of juxtaposing commerce and football' and thought this tournament 'could constitute the ideal meeting point for sport and business'.

This strange beast kicked off on 4 June 1955, three months before the European Cup, so the honour of scoring the first goal in a UEFA competition goes to Eddie Firmani, who found the net in the 35th minute as a London XI beat a Basel XI 5-0 in Switzerland. These teams were true XIs, drawn from various clubs within the city that hosted the trade fair. Some cities didn't like this idea, though, so Birmingham City FC were the sole representatives from the Venice of the Midlands.

The idea of playing fixtures to coincide with trade fairs meant that the first competition staggered to a conclusion three years after the first match with Barcelona trouncing a London XI 8-2 on aggregate. After the second tournament, city teams became the exception rather than the norm. In 1960–61, the criteria changed, with UEFA taking a hand in the organisation, and the Fairs Cup was opened to top clubs who weren't involved in either the European Cup or the Cup Winners' Cup and was completed within a season.

The new, improved competition was used to test new rules: away goals gave Dynamo Zagreb the edge in their 1966–67 tie with Dundee United and Spartak Trnava edged past Olympique de Marseille after a penalty shoot-out in 1970. It was renamed the UEFA Cup in 1971, metamorphosing into the UEFA Europa League in 2009. But before it ceased to be the Fairs Cup, the competition spawned a mutant knockout tournament called the Anglo-Italian Cup.

In 1969, Swindon Town were the shock winners of the League Cup but, as a Third Division side, were not allowed entry into the Fairs Cup; the same fate had befallen QPR, League Cup winners in 1967. Concerned that this rule unduly punished such plucky giant killers, the Football League created the Anglo-Italian League Cup, in which the League Cup winners took on the Coppa Italia holders. This was something of a departure for the Football League which was then

run by Alan Hardaker, a man who famously said he didn't like European football because there were 'too many wops and dagoes'. Yet Swindon enjoyed their European campaign, losing 2-1 to AS Roma in the Stadio Olimpico and winning 4-0 at the County Ground, against a side that included Fabio Capello.

The Anglo-Italian League Cup inspired – and was succeeded by – the Anglo-Italian Cup. Rapidly becoming *calcio*'s nemesis, Swindon won this competition, too, in

1970, awarded victory in Naples when the game was abandoned due to crowd trouble when they were 3-0 up against Napoli. The Anglo-Italian kept going in various forms, including a semi-professional phase from 1976 to 1986, and then a brief second-tier professional revival in the 1990s.

These tournaments soon spawned a host of pre-season competitions. The Watneys Cup, contested by the top scoring side in the four divisions of the Football League, is chiefly notable because, in the 1970 semi-final between Manchester United and Hull City, Denis Law made history as the first man to miss from the spot in a penalty shoot-out. This competition – and its rival Texaco Cup – are still remembered with a rosy, nostalgic glow. The same could not be said for the Full Members Cup (1985–92), created to fill the gap left in the fixture schedules by UEFA's ban on English clubs after the Heysel tragedy.

One glance at the list of miscellaneous cup competitions between national sides on rsssf.com proves that countries will find any excuse to start a football tournament. The more obscure knockout competitions include the Eco Tournament (contested in 1993 by seven countries in a regional trade pact: Azerbaijan, Iran, Kazakhstan, Kyrgyzstan, Pakistan, Tajikistan and Turkmenistan), the Games of the New Emerging Forces (mainly contested by Communist states in Asia and Africa between 1963 and 1965, but also briefly featuring university teams from Argentina and Uruguay) and the Arab Police Championship (no explanation necessary).

As odd as these all sound, they are not quite as weird as the laudable but transient Glasgow Dental Cup. This was staged once, in 1928, to raise funds to build, as the name suggests, a new dental hospital in Scotland's biggest city. Contested by five clubs – Celtic, Clyde, Partick Thistle, Queen's Park, Third Lanark and Rangers (who mysteriously entered at the semi-final stage) – it raised £819 (£40,000 in today's money). In the final, on 11 December 1928 in front of 5,000 spectators, Partick beat Rangers 2-0 with a goal from Davie Ness and a penalty by John Torbet, who banged in 116 goals for the Jags.

What was the **earliest kick-off** time for a professional game?

Fans like to bemoan the fact that, these days, there are almost as many kick-off times as there are games. And it's not just a British disease. On the weekend of 17/18 November 2012, all 10 Spanish Liga fixtures kicked off at different times. Pay-per-view television doesn't like too many simultaneous matches. What especially annoys supporters, if they come from countries with a tradition of away support, is that matches seem to start earlier and earlier. Many leagues, like Spain's, now pander to lucrative faraway markets with a considerable time difference. In Scotland, potentially troublesome games often kick off as early as noon to restrict pre-match drinking.

Mind you, it's not easy to clarify what is a traditional kick-off time. In Britain, 3pm on a Saturday is regarded as the hallowed, classic kick-off time. Queen's Park claim they were the first to adopt this as their customary kick-off time, though that's hard to establish. It is recorded, however, that on the day league football began – Saturday, 8 September 1888 – only one game started at that time: Aston Villa v Wolverhampton Wanderers. If you look at the results of that day, you'd presume that Fred Dewhurst has the honour of having scored the first-ever goal in league football, because he found the target for Preston North End against Burnley after all of three minutes. But that game kicked off at 3.50pm, which means it was seven minutes to four when Dewhurst scored. At that

If only they had fixed a regular 3pm kick-off time, Gershom Cox would have avoided infamy – as the first league (own) goalscorer.

time, Villa and Wolves were already enjoying their half-time tea with the score at 1-1. The visitors had taken the lead on the half-hour, at 3.30pm, when Villa defender Gershom Cox fumbled the ball across his goal line, scoring an own goal that entered the record books.

Kick-off times have always been more diverse than the conventional wisdom suggests. Italy's Serie A traditionally plays on Sunday afternoons, while games in Spain used to kick off late on Sunday evenings. In Germany, fans will tell you that the classic kick-off time is almost the same as in England, namely 3.30pm on a Saturday. But that's not quite true. On the Bundesliga's very first matchday – Saturday, 24 August 1963 – every game kicked off at 5pm, a common time during this inaugural season. In the decades before the Bundesliga, games in Germany were normally played on Sundays because many of the players, who were semi-pros or amateurs, worked on Saturdays.

One wonders how they would have reacted if they had been told their next league game would kick off five minutes after midnight on a Wednesday. That's when Barcelona's home game against Sevilla began on 3 September 2003.

The story behind this unusual time was a dispute between Sevilla and Barcelona's new president Joan Laporta. When Laporta realised that nine of the internationals in Barça's squad would have to play for their respective countries on the Saturday after this game, scheduled for Wednesday, he asked Sevilla to move the match to Tuesday. But Sevilla president Jos del Nido refused on the grounds that his team faced Atlético Madrid the Sunday before. Whereupon an angry Laporta threatened that if Sevilla insisted on Wednesday, Barcelona would choose a kick-off time as close to Tuesday as possible, namely shortly after midnight. Sevilla called his bluff – and Laporta was true to his word.

'This is a throwback to the Spain of guitars and tambourines, when every ruse was legit,' Sevilla's skipper Pablo Alfaro complained. And Javier Irureta, then coaching Deportivo La Coruña, said: 'What do you think your wife's going to say when you tell her you're going to a football game at midnight? She thinks you're cheating on her!' But when Laporta noted how much publicity he was getting and that there was nothing in the Spanish FA's statutes that prevented him from doing it, he went ahead with his plan. The game started at 0.05am, watched by 80,200 fans at the Camp Nou. It finished 1-1. Barcelona's new signing Ronaldinho equalised with a wonder goal on his home debut, capping off a solo run across half the length of the pitch. At 1.24am.

⚽ Can elephants take penalties?

They have been known to do so occasionally, albeit not in a competitive match on a conventional football pitch. One of them was so good at it that he beat a group of professional footballers in a penalty shoot-out. The pachyderm in question was a performer in 'Lord' George Sanger's travelling circus. The title was self-awarded, but it suited the eccentric millionaire's image and looked good on posters. His wife used to dance in the lions' cages but Sanger, though he loved working with any animals, was particularly fond of elephants.

According to Andrew Ward's *Football's Strangest Matches*, this particular elephant was so good that when the circus hit Leicester in the late 1890s, Sanger issued a challenge to the city's professional footballers. Four Leicester Fosse players duly accepted and took on the elephant.' Each contestant had to take four penalties and then go between the sticks and try to keep out his opponent's four shots.

LORD JOHN SANGER AND
(LIMITED).
REAT BRITAIN'S LARGEST AND GRANDEST AMUSEMENT
THE LARGEST AND GRANDEST SHOW IN THE W
unded in 1837 by John Sanger (the Eldest and Original Sanger). The only Travelli
has been commanded by Her Majesty the Queen to appear at Windsor C
THE FIRST VISIT OF LORD JOHN SANGER AND SONS', LTD.,
ENGLISH SHOW.

THE GREATEST NOVELTY IN THE WORLD! THE ELEPHANTS
FOOTBALL MATCH.
FOOTBALL MATCH, ELEPHANT V. MAN,
e a very MASSIVE GOBLET, which will be on view at Mr. W. H. RUSSELL
. W. KEECH, Centre Forward, Loughborough Football Club, has arranged to compe
CENTRE FORWARD ELEPHANT, which can kick the most goals out of
Mr. W. KEECH and the ELEPHANT to keep goal in turn

To this day, Leicester fans stubbornly point out that the elephant's size gave him a bit of an edge when he went in goal. (Chelsea's man mountain of a keeper, William 'Fattie' Foulke, used the same tactic at about the same time.) The ball also happened to be six times larger than normal. Which is why FIFA's official home page says: 'Back in the 1890s, long before there were any FIFA standards governing the circumference of the ball, an elephant caused red faces among the professional players at English club Leicester Fosse when Sanger's Circus bet that no one could score past its elephant in a penalty shoot-out using an oversize ball.' This is, in fact, nonsense. There were no FIFA standards regarding the ball at the time, because FIFA didn't actually exist. The FA, however, had strict regulations governing the size of the ball.

On this particular occasion, the shoot-out was not held under FA rules, thus the famous, but sadly anonymous, elephant could take on the Leicester players, three of whom were soundly beaten and shall thus remain equally nameless. The fourth was William Keech who, says Ward, 'used a crafty penalty-taking technique. Keech feinted to take the ball one side of the elephant, then, as the elephant raised his foot in anticipation, Keech slotted the ball into the other corner.' Steve Russell, of the website Independent Rs, adds: 'He went on to repeat this trick successfully but when Keech took his turn in goal, the elephant copied the same trick and scored twice in the same fashion. This resulted in a replay and Keech once again deceived the elephant with the same tactic and won the competition by three goals to two.'

Keech was almost as well-travelled as the elephant he defeated. He was born in Irthlingborough in 1872 and while he is best known as a Liverpool, Leicester and Queen's Park Rangers player, he also played for Wellingborough, Finedon, Kettering Hawks, Irthlingborough Wanderers, Barnsley St

Peter's, Blackpool, Loughborough Town, Brentford and Kensal Rise United. According to Tony Williamson's book about the history of QPR, Keech later became 'a billiards marker' (a man who keeps scores made by players and indicates them on a scoring board). One of the pubs he regularly worked in was on 464 Harrow Road in North Kensington, London; it was, of course, called The Elephant and Castle.

⚽ Do footballers have **small feet**?

In Eva Menasse's novel *Vienna*, the heroine's footballing father declares: 'The best footballers have small feet.' This is certainly a popular theory – the great Bulgarian Hristo Stoitchkov once attributed his success to his size 5 feet – but is it true?

There is no shortage of famous players with dainty feet. The smallest foot size we have come across in professional football is size 2 (though other reports say 3 and 4), worn by Johnny Hancocks (pictured), the England inside-right whose blistering shot helped him score 158 goals for Wolves, with whom he won the league in 1954. And when we say blistering we mean it quite literally: his tough manager Stan Cullis once made the mistake of saving a Hancocks penalty in training and needed physio on his injured hand for a fortnight.

Brazilian striker Adhemar had size 3.5 feet. Lothar Matthäus and Romania's most naturally gifted footballer Gheorghe Hagi wore size 5 boots, while David Villa, like Roberto Carlos, wears size 6. Gerd Müller preferred size 7 and 6.5. In his 1973 autobiography, Der Bomber recalled: 'I have healthy feet but they do not have the same size. Football boots need to feel like a second skin and so adidas manufactures them specially for me – the left larger than the right.' This disproves the legend that Müller wore boots too big for him because they helped him turn more quickly.

Jackie Milburn, the Newcastle and England centre-forward, was so keen to make his boots feel like a second skin that he says in his memoirs: 'I always wore a size 6 boot even though

Jackie Milburn's boots.

my feet were size 8, so I used to break them in by wearing them without socks and soaking them in cold water until they moulded to my feet.' To ensure his boots were broken in beyond reasonable doubt, Milburn wore them down the pit when he worked as a miner.

The Toon legend's concept is not unusual. The great Austrian midfielder Johann 'Buffy' Ettmayer, who played for Eintracht Frankfurt in the 1970s, always chose a smaller size because, as he famously put it, 'football boots have to be like condoms for your feet'. Lionel Messi (popularly supposed to wear size 10 boots) likes 'boots to be really tight so they adjust to your feet and seem more like slippers than shoes'.

The experience of Argentinian midfielder Mafias Alameda, who signed for Sevilla in 1996, shows how perilous big boots can be. More than 10,000 supporters gathered at the club's Ramón Sánchez Pizjuán stadium to welcome him but the introduction soon went horribly awry. 'I realised they were mistaken about me, I was a midfield destroyer, not a striker,' Alameda recalled. 'And I'd forgotten my boots. Someone gave me a pair, but they were size 10.5 or 11, and I'm a 9.5. The crowd started chanting for tricks, but I couldn't control the ball, it ended up in the stands.'

With vicious irony, when rebellious midfielder Matthias Sammer was deemed to be getting too big for his boots by officials at Dynamo Dresden in the 1980s, they ensured that, when the whole squad received new footwear, Sammer's were three sizes too large. 'It was pure harassment, individualism wasn't tolerated,' he said.

Giacinto Facchetti had the opposite problem. When he started at Inter in the 1960s, the conventional wisdom in Serie A was that any player whose feet were bigger than size 7.5 couldn't be a good player. His Inter team-mate Sandro Mazzola recalled, 'Giacinto bandaged his toes with sticking plaster before games to squeeze his feet into a smaller boot size. Jair saw him and ribbed him, "Giacinto, you can't put Milan inside Treviglio" [a small town near Milan].'

The average shoe size in the UK is 9 – Wayne Rooney's boot size – and players typically wear size 8.5 to 9.5 boots. Famous footballing Bigfoots include Peter Crouch, whose robot dance celebration might have looked less tacky if he didn't have size 11 feet; Günter Netzer, who wreaked havoc in midfield in the 1970s with size 12 feet; and Nigerian striker Kanu who bamboozled opponents with his tricky size 15 feet.

Garrincha, the tragic Brazilian genius who won two World Cups, probably had the most enigmatic feet in football.

Stricken by polio as a child, the Little Bird's right leg turned inwards while his left leg turned outwards. Before kick-offs, he often stood with his feet splayed apart like a scarecrow. Because of his unusual shape and sorcery on the ball – in the first 34 seconds of a 1958 World Cup match against the Soviet Union he beat seven opponents with his dribbling skills – he was likened to a *curupira*, a demon in Brazilian rural folklore whose feet were believed to be back to front. Yet before the 1958 World Cup, doctors were astonished by results of the Brazilian squad's medical tests which showed, as biographer Ruy Castro noted, that 'in spite of being grotesquely off centre, Garrincha had the poise of an angel. They took plaster casts of all the players' feet, but no one's toes, arch and instep were as neatly aligned as Garrincha's.'

Garrincha – the Little Bird – on the ball at the World Cup 1962. The hapless defender is England's Ray Wilson.

⚽ Why did **Independiente** hold a minute's silence for **Neil Armstrong?**

The first man to walk on the moon left a very special souvenir up there: a pennant from Independiente de Avellenada. As soon as the crew for Apollo 11 was named, the club's press officer Hector Rodriguez proposed making Armstrong, Buzz Aldrin and Michael Collins members of Independiente. The membership cards – Armstrong was member No. 80,400 – and some memorabilia, including pennants, were sent to the astronauts. Armstrong wrote back thanking the club in May 1969, two months before his historic journey to the moon.

After Armstrong took his giant step on 20 July 1969, the Argentinian club's officials suggested he had left a pennant on the moon. Nobody took them too seriously until Armstrong visited Buenos Aires in November 1969 on the Apollo 11 crew's exhausting world tour. At an embassy reception, Armstrong assured Rodriguez he had taken the pennant to the moon, that it had brought him good luck and he had left it there. So when he died on 25 August 2012, the club held a minute's silence before their next home game, against Arsenal de Sarandi. As *FourFourTwo* magazine noted: 'Afterwards everyone in the stadium applauded as if Armstrong was a club legend. And in a unique way, he was.'

⚽ What was the oddest method to separate teams **level on points?**

Every league system has one obvious drawback – what happens if teams end up with the same amount of points? Today, we take it for granted that goal difference – when goals conceded are subtracted from goals scored – takes care of that. However, for a very long time, the more mathematically challening goal average was in use (the number of goals scored divided by the number of goals conceded).

The goal average system seems absurd in retrospect, because it didn't reward going for goals (scoring 3 goals and conceding 1 for a goal average of 3.0 is better than scoring 10 and conceding 4 for a goal average of 2.5) as well as needing a calculator. But the French Ligue 1 used it until 1964, the German Bundesliga until 1969, and the Football League stuck with it until 1976.

One league briefly broke the mould. The Soviet Union had switched from goal average to goal difference as early as 1961 but felt this was not a great way of deciding titles or relegations. So there were regular play-off games from 1961 to 1977 to decide who won the league and who went down. For the rest of the table, goal difference remained the first tie-breaker ... with one exception.

In 1970, the powers that be hit upon a fantastic new idea. For this one season, the new tie-breaker was the number of footballers in a squad that played for the national team. After taking such a revolutionary step – quite a bold one given the stagnation that typified the USSR under Brezhnev – the authorities scrapped this system the next year. The difficulty may have been that not many clubs had internationals in their squads. The USSR's 1970 World Cup squad, for example, contained players from seven clubs – and two of those, CSKA Moscow and Dynamo Moscow, were involved in the play-off for the title. So in a league containing 17 clubs, this rule could easily end up making absolutely no difference whatsoever. So it was back to boring old goal difference in 1971.

⚽ What formation did **North Korea** play in 1966?

When North Korea qualified for the World Cup in 1966, they didn't have diplomatic relations with the hosts, England. After some sporting diplomacy, the team were allowed to participate as long as their national anthem wasn't played before games. Inspired – or terrified – by their great leader Kim Il-Sung (who urged them, 'As the representatives of the Africa and Asia region, as coloured people, I urge you to win one or two matches'), they surprised everyone by knocking out Italy, and then reaching the quarter-finals, where they raced into a 3-0 lead against Eusébio's Portugal before losing 5-3. Their heroic overachievement was one of the highlights of the tournament but opinion still differs over their formation.

To Western eyes, their game was distinctly unusual. Dennis Barry, a Middlesbrough fan who watched their group games at Ayresome Park, told the BBC: 'They played good football. They were small and that was a novelty in itself. It was like watching a team of jockeys playing. They moved the ball around really well and they played attacking football. There was nothing defensive about their game.' Their manager, Myung Rye Hyun (the name means 'Sternly Rising Sun'), attributed their success to a fast, position-swapping style of play he called *Chollima Lightning Football* (Chollima was a horse that, according to Far Eastern mythology, could run at 1,000 miles an hour.) Dan Gordon, who produced a BBC documentary on the team, hailed them as pioneers. 'Football was incredibly slow in 1966. Nowadays teams play fast, like the Koreans in 1966.'

Forget Total Football. The Koreans modelled themselves on a horse that could run at 1,000 miles per hour.

Perhaps because the country's football developed in such extreme isolation, there has been talk that the North Koreans played in a formation the game had never seen before. Wilhelm Fischer, in his book *Fussball Weltmeisterschaft*, published in Germany a week after the final, suggested they played 'an unusual 9-1-1 formation' against Chile before incongruously adding that they 'either defended with eleven men or attacked with nine'.

Yet the FIFA technical report on the finals doesn't mention any such system which, given that it comments on Uruguay's 1-4-3-2, it surely would have if Korea's formation had been so revolutionary. Is it possible that, given the speed of their play, their tireless efforts, and their attacking style, such an unusual formation could have gone unnoticed by a panel of experts which included one former England manager (Walter Winterbottom) and one future Three Lions boss (Ron Greenwood)?

The best books about those finals don't clarify anything. Most don't even mention Korea's tactics, a few have them playing 4-2-4 while another says that, at times, they played three up front. Brian Glanville, in his definitive *The Story of the World Cup*, describes them as a 'team of little men who moved sweetly and finished splendidly'. It is just possible that their movement, attacking play and pace, and what Glanville refers to as 'the charisma of the unknown', convinced less informed observers that their formation was radically different.

⚽ What is an **Olympic goal**?

An Olympic goal is what South Americans call a goal scored direct from a corner. On 2 October 1924, Uruguay returned from winning gold at the Olympic football tournament in Amsterdam, and Argentina beat them 2-1 in a friendly with a goal scored in just such fashion.

The scorer was left-winger Cesáreo Onzari. The goal made this stalwart of Atlético Huracán famous across Argentina. In *Football In Sun And Shadow*, Eduardo Galeano notes: 'It was the first time in the history of football a goal was scored that way. The Uruguayans were speechless. When they found their tongues, they protested. They claimed their goalkeeper was pushed when the ball was in the air. Then they howled that

Onzari's 'Olympic Goal' for Argentina against Uruguay. Did the wind get an assist? It depends on your nationality.

Onzari hadn't intended to shoot at the net and that the goal had been scored by the wind.'

As you might expect, the goalscorer insisted then – and for the next 40 years of his life – that the ball had done just what he intended. 'Maybe the keeper got out on the wrong side of the bed that day,' he reflected later. 'Or players may have blocked his path. But I never scored a goal like that again. To be honest, when I saw the ball go in, I couldn't believe it.' Such a strike was so rare it became known, either – as Galeano says – 'in homage or in irony' as the 'Olympic goal'.

Onzari's timing was certainly remarkable. Scoring straight from a corner had only become legal since the beginning of August 1924, after the International Football Association

Board decided to change the rules. However, FIFA disagrees with Galeano about Onzari's being the first goal to be scored in such a fashion. The game's blazers-in-chief say that a little known Scottish striker called Billy Alston scored straight from a corner in the Scottish Second Division in late August.

Inspired by the legend of Onzari's goal, other Argentinian footballers sought to emulate him. One of the most effective was Juan Ernesto Cochoco Alvarez. In six seasons at Colombian side Deportivo Cali, he only scored 35 goals – but eight of them were direct from corners. He once scored twice from a corner in the same game. The secret, he said, was a training ground competition with Colombian teammate Angel Maria Torres to see who could score the most from corners.

Anibal Francisco Cibeyra wasn't quite as prolific. But playing for Ecuador's Emelec in the 1970s, he once scored three Olympic goals in successive derbies against Barcelona de Guayaquil, a feat that earned him the nickname *El Loco De Los Goles Olimpicos* (The Olympic Goal Fanatic).

Such fanaticism looks less extreme when you consider: Eintracht Frankfurt star Bernd Nickel who has scored an Olympic goal from all four corners of the club's ground; Morten Gamst Pedersen who as a junior player in Norway scored six from corners in the same match; and Northern Ireland international Charles Tully who, in 1953, scored directly for a corner for Celtic against Falkirk and, when the goal was disallowed because the ball wasn't in the arc, retook the corner and scored again.

Most prolific of all is the great Turkish striker Sükrü Gülesin who, between 1940 and 1954, scored 32 Olympic goals. As Özgür Canbas, a presenter on Turkey's Radio Spor, noted: 'His major characteristic was that he could score from the left and the right sides even though he was left-footed.'

⚽ Why can't you score an **own goal from a direct free-kick?**

The rules on this are clear, even though few people are aware of them. Law 13 states: 'If a direct free-kick is kicked directly into the team's own goal, a corner kick is awarded to the opposing team.' When you think about it for a second, Law 13 is a bit odd. If you're awarded a direct free-kick and decide to hit the ball in the general direction of your own goal, possibly because you want to involve your goalkeeper, the free-kick should be considered taken the moment the ball leaves your foot – and after that, officials should let events take their course.

But the custodians of the game felt it would be profoundly unfair if you could score an own goal from such a set-piece. You can't concede an own goal from an indirect free-kick because someone else has to touch the ball. So if you could score an own goal straight from a direct free-kick, your opponents would, in a circuitous way, be rewarded for the severity of their infringement.

You might think that the question was entirely academic, but Wally Downes proved otherwise. It's been 30 years since he made his mark by scoring an own goal from a free-kick.

The telling and retelling of the tale may have added the odd flourish here and there. What we know is this: on 27 December 1983, Wimbledon played Millwall at Plough Lane in the old Third Division. Going into stoppage time, the Dons led 4-2 and had just been awarded a free-kick, which was taken by midfielder Downes. He turned around, hit the ball towards his own goal and somehow it went in, past mystified keeper Dave Beasant. The referee pointed towards the centre circle to make the score 4-3. Luckily for Downes, the Dons held on for another five minutes to win the match.

Now, it's entirely possible that Downes wanted to play a back pass, missed the goalkeeper and was unlucky that referee John E. Martin, oblivious to the arcane Law 13, didn't seem to know the appropriate rule and failed to award Millwall a corner. But it could have been a prank. An inveterate practical joker, Downes is the player who some credit as starting the myth of Wimbledon's Crazy Gang. He once called a TV show Dave Beasant was on, claiming to be a Liverpool official and offering him the chance to leave the hopeless Dons. In any case, as Downes left the pitch, he told a reporter that the referee didn't know the laws of the game and the goal shouldn't have been allowed to stand. He, for one, was well-versed in Law 13.

⚽ Who is the greatest **penalty saver** in football history?

After saving three Valencia spot-kicks to win Bayern Munich the UEFA Champions League in 2001, Oliver Kahn said of the shoot-out, 'I reached a level of concentration I had never been before. I felt like I was on an undetected planet.'

Kahn hadn't, hitherto, stopped that many penalties but that didn't matter much in Germany where the prevailing view is that great keepers, like Kahn and Sepp Maier, don't necessarily stop spot-kicks. There are certain exceptions to this rule, notably Gianluigi Buffon and Edwin van der Sar, but even Liverpool fans might agree that their shoot-out heroes Bruce Grobbelaar and Jerzy Dudek weren't world-class.

Indeed, one of the most effective penalty stoppers in English football – Paul Cooper, who saved eight out of ten for Ipswich Town in 1979–80 – never won a cap at any level for England. And Steaua Bucharest icon Helmuth Duckadam,

Gotcha! Helmut Duckadam saves Barcelona's fourth and final penalty to win the 1986 European Cup for Steaua Bucharest.

who saved all four penalties to clinch the 1986 European Cup final, won just two caps for Romania and was fourth choice behind Silviu Lung, Dumitru Moraru and Vasile Iordache.

Duckadam's saves in Seville show why Germans don't take penalty-stopping too seriously. The first three penalties – taken by Barcelona's José Ramón Alexanko, Angel Pedraza and Pichi Alonso (Xabi's dad) – were shot at the same spot: low and to the keeper's right. If Duckadam guessed correctly he was bound to make contact with the ball. The fourth taker, Marcos, aimed at the other side, but low enough for the Steaua keeper to block easily if he went the right way. Nonetheless, saving four penalties in a row is a feat no other keeper has matched in a game of that magnitude.

⚽ Which teams won the league and were **relegated next season?**

It is richly symbolic of Manchester City's proud record of false dawns and flashy underachievement that they should hold this dubious distinction in England. What's more, when they slipped out of the old First Division in 1937–38, they did it the hard way, contriving to finish 21st out of 22, despite scoring 80 goals, more than any other team, and registering the season's biggest away win, trouncing Derby County 7-1 at the Baseball Ground.

No team in England has duplicated this dubious achievement. The only other major European league in which anything like this has ever happened is the German Bundesliga, where Nuremberg won the title in 1968 and were relegated a year later, fair and square, on the field of play, without any deductions of points or other penalties.

If it's any consolation for City, the relegation of reigning champions is a common phenomenon in Scandinavia. Thanks to some truly exhaustive research by Karel Stokkermans, one of the founders of the Rec.Sport.Soccer Statistics Foundation, we know it has happened four times in Sweden (the most recent victims being IFK Gothenburg in 1970) and Norway, and three times in Denmark and Finland. Stokkermans concludes that Finland is 'the only country which had reigning champions relegated in consecutive years'. Tampereen Pallo-Veikot won the Veikkausliiga in 1994, then went down in 1995 just as Haka Valkeakoski lifted the championship only to be relegated themselves in 1996.

In an answer that testifies to the predictably unpredictable nature of football, it would be remiss not to mention Algerian club EP Sétif. Champions in 1987, they were relegated in 1988 – and won the African Cup of Champion Clubs, the only team from outside the top flight to do so.

⚽ What is the strangest **sending off**?

One of the odder stories of English football in 2013 was when the Chelsea player Eden Hazard, showing all the class that his club had displayed throughout the season, was sent off for kicking one of Swansea City's ball boys, who was doing a spot of actorish time-wasting in a League Cup semi-final. It was put forward, with some justice, as one of the strangest sendings off of all time. But, of course, given football's rich history, there are plenty of rival claims.

Swinging on the crossbar – and breaking it twice – earned Athlone Town goalkeeper Mick O'Brien a red card in an Irish Cup semi-final against Finn Harps at Oriel Park on 31 March 1974. Before you rush to the judgement that the referee was an officious killjoy, it's worth pointing out that the first breakage had taken fifteen minutes to fix while the second forced the PA announcer to ask, 'Is there a carpenter in the ground?'

At St Mel's Park, Athlone's home ground, the crossbars were made of metal. Trusting in their resilience, O'Brien had got used to swinging on the bar to entertain fans, stave off boredom or, he said, to 'make sure the ball went over'. Oriel Park's wooden crossbars were not made for swinging. When play resumed after the first breakage, Finn Harps scored two quick goals to make it 4-0 and O'Brien was seen to climb the netting and throw himself bodily onto the bar, bringing the whole goal crashing down. That earned him a straight red card, the derision of the Irish media and a half-hearted defence from manager Amby Fogarty who declared, 'he is very dedicated and a bit headstrong'.

Some Athlone fans suggested his antics were prompted by shame at the team's abject performance but O'Brien had his own explanation for his behaviour. 'I was trying to fix it when it came crashing down on me. The corner of the post seemed a bit loose so I jumped up to mend it. When I touched it the post came away in my hand.' He then explained why somersaults and swinging on crossbars had become such an essential part of his game: 'I think I might be over-fit'.

Lest you assume O'Brien was merely trying too hard to prove the cliché that goalkeepers are crazy, it is only fair to add that, on 22 October 1975, he kept a clean sheet when Athlone held AC Milan to a 0-0 draw in the UEFA Cup.

⚽ What are the oddest reasons for stopping play?

Failing floodlights, holes suddenly appearing on the pitch during play (famously caused by subsidence at Watford's Vicarage Road ground in a match against Grimsby in December 1961) all sound pretty humdrum alongside the remarkable story of the ten-minute stoppage during a reserve match in Florence in 1954.

On 27 October 1954, in Tuscany's most famous city, Fiorentina played US Pistoiese in the now forgotten Campionato Riserve, Italy's reserve team league. The reports agree that some 10,000 people were on hand at the Stadio Comunale. That seems an astonishing crowd for a reserve game against what was then a fourth-division club. But that Wednesday afternoon Fiorentina gave their entire first team a brief run-out during the first half. Eight of these men – including the great Swedish forward Gunnar Gren – would win Serie A the following season, so maybe word had spread.

And supporters who came out to see their stars also saw something entirely unexpected.

In the second half, Fiorentina played their normal reserve team. But a few minutes after the restart, at roughly 2.30pm, the referee noticed a noise from the stands out of all proportion to what was happening on the pitch. He could see spectators pointing at the sky and when the players began looking up he finally halted play. 'I saw something like small rings in the distance,' Pistoiese's captain Romolo Tuci later said. 'What they actually were I really don't know.'

Many others, however, saw much more clearly. Reports speak of at least 20 unidentified flying objects in various shapes and sizes in what remains one of the best-documented UFO sightings in history. The objects had previously hovered

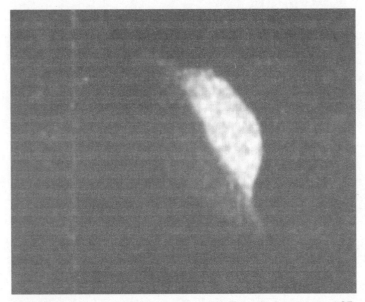

One of the alien spacecraft that came to watch Fiorentina's reserves on 27 October 1954.

over Florence's Duomo for so long that eye-witnesses had jammed newspaper phone lines and journalists were despatched to catch the second sighting of that day, over the Stadio Comunale. When the objects eventually whizzed out of sight, they dropped so much of the substance that ufologists call 'angel hair' that it looked as if snow was falling over Florence. After a break in play of ten minutes, Fiorentina and Pistoiese resumed their game. (On the same day, these objects were also sighted over Venice.)

With Italian football having such a defensive reputation at the time, it is tempting to assume that the crews in these UFOs might have been bored rigid by the dourness of the sporting spectacle below. Yet the visitors from outer space struck lucky: there was almost certainly no *catenaccio* on display in Florence on that day. Fiorentina were coached by the legendary Fulvio Bernardini, who preferred a version of the W–M system that prefigured Brazil's 4-2-4. Unusually for an Italian coach, Bernardini once declared: 'Tactics are not important. A team is only as strong as the feet of its players.' So if they do play football in space, it's probably fun to watch.

⚽ What is football's strangest transfer deal?

There is an apocryphal tradition that Aston Villa acquired a player from Gillingham in 1937 for three used turnstiles, two goalkeeper tops, three cans of weed killer and a typewriter, but it's hard to find any proof that this deal ever happened.

To stick with transfers we know definitely did happen, Roger Fallas's move from Costan Rican second division club Puma to Universidad de Costa Rica in July 2013 was for 50 footballs. The 26-year-old defender's contract was running out so, instead of a fee, Puma's technical director Rigoberto Chinchilla requested footballs. Universidad were happy to oblige.

Being sold for a bag of balls might sound a tad undignified but other members of the footballing profession have been traded for much more embarrassing commodities. In the English game, tracksuits and training kits were used to facilitate the moves of John Barnes (from Sudbury Court to Watford), Tony Cascarino (from Crockenhill to Gillingham) and Gary Pallister (from Billingham Town to Middlesbrough). Although Manchester United's club record fee is £30.7m for Dimitar Berbatov, in 1927 they snapped up half-back Hugh McLanahan after donating a freezer full of ice cream to Stockport County.

Players' frequent lament that clubs buy and sell them like meat took on a horribly literal meaning in February 2006 when Romanian club UT Arad sold defender Marius Cioara to fourth division side Regal Horia for 15kg of meat. The buying club was understandably upset when, days later, Cioara decided to give up football to find a job in Spain in agriculture or construction. A Regal Horia official complained, 'we lost twice – we lost a good player and our team's meat for a week.'

In Norway, a country which consumes around 105,000 tonnes of seafood a year, shrimp were used to facilitate the move of Kenneth Kristensen from third division club Vindbjart to local rivals Floey. The 23-year-old desperately wanted to play for Floey so Vindbjart president Vidar Ulstein proposed that he be sold for his own weight in shrimp. Kristensen was duly weighed before the next game between the clubs and the fee was agreed: 75kg in shrimp.

The oddest free transfer in the game's history must surely be the arrival of Al-Saadi Gaddafi, third son of the Libyan dictator, at Perugia in 2003. Gaddafi, an inside-forward

Al Saadi Gaddafi, son of Libyan leader Colonel Muammar Gaddafi, with Perugia president Luciano Gaucci.

who ran the Libyan FA, and fancied himself as the Libyan Maradona, was a 30-year-old billionaire when he came to Italy. The move was inspired by the player's performance for 30 minutes in a friendly in Perugia and a conversation with the club's eccentric president Luciano Gaucci that started out as a joke. Yet the player was keen and the president was curious, especially when, he insists, Silvio Berlusconi (then prime minister of Italy) told him the transfer would be politically advantageous.

The only man who didn't find any of this amusing was Perugia's coach Serse Cosmi who refused to play Gaddafi because he wasn't good enough. Given that the president boasted of sacking a youth team coach who wouldn't give Gaucci Jr a game, this was a brave stand.

The player, meanwhile, was so determined to improve and get in shape he employed Diego Maradona as his technical consultant and Canadian sprinter Ben Johnson (who won the 100m at the 1988 Olympics and was banned for taking steroids), as his personal trainer. Before Gaddafi could make his Serie A debut, he was banned when a drugs test revealed that he had too much nandrolone, the performance-enhancing steroid, in his system. Gaucci, however, managed to get the automatic two-year ban reduced to three months.

In May 2004, with Perugia leading 1-0 against Juventus in a game they needed to win to avoid relegation, Cosmi finally gave in. Signalling to his bench, he brought on Gaddafi in the 75th minute. The move had little impact: Gaddafi didn't touch the ball and Perugia held on to win. The Italian newspaper *La Repubblica* was especially scathing about the player's performance: 'Even at twice his current speed he would still be twice as slow as slow itself.'

Afterwards, Cosmi insisted that 'Gaddafi came on because he is a player and not because any of us wanted to go down in history as the one who first played the son of a head of state in the Italian championship.' Neither the change of heart – nor averting relegation – could save Cosmi, who was sacked.

His only consolation was that a year later, the club went bankrupt and Gaucci had to flee to the Dominican Republic to avoid being arrested for fraud. He has since returned to Italy. Gaucci's former protégé, Al-Saadi Gaddafi, played another ten minutes in Serie A – as a sub for Udinese the next season – before returning to Libya. During the civil war in which his father was killed, Al-Saadi fled to Niger where he has been granted political asylum by the president.

⚽ Which is the most unlikely club to break a transfer record?

Falkirk paid a world record fee of £5,000 to acquire Sydney Puddefoot in February 1922. The sale of West Ham's prolific striker almost caused a riot in east London but the club insisted the move was entirely the player's doing, saying in a statement: 'Everyone has one chance in life to improve themselves and Syd Puddefoot is doing the right thing for himself in studying his future. We understand that he will be branching out in commercial circles in Falkirk and when his football days are over he will be assured of a nice little competency.'

The truth is that Puddefoot didn't want to go. Not even when West Ham said his brother Len could move with him and he

Syd Puddefoot (right, with William Rankin) in happier times at Blackburn Rovers, where he won the FA Cup.

realised he would be paid a one-off fee of £390 (at a time when the footballer's maximum wage was £8 a week). It's possible, too, that West Ham manager Syd King didn't want to sell him. One explanation for the sale – which was oddly timed given that the Hammers were pushing for promotion – is that King named a price he thought the club would never pay. When Falkirk matched the valuation, and with West Ham in some financial difficulty, King was left with no option but to sell.

So how did Falkirk come to have the money? Their supporters raised it – indeed so generous were they that Falkirk could have paid as much as £6,000. The fans were desperate for the Bairns to regain the impetus that had led them to victory in the Scottish Cup in 1913. Scottish football was booming after the end of the First World War and with Falkirk in the top flight, the transfer might have transformed the club's prospects. It almost worked: the Bairns came fourth in 1923–24 but slid down the table when Puddefoot moved on.

Puddefoot scored 45 goals in three years at Falkirk but never really settled – he later complained that the players wouldn't pass to him – and moved on to Blackburn Rovers for £4,000. No Scottish club has ever set a world transfer record since.

⚽ Has a league-winning team ever been unable to defend their title?

The wrong answer is Juventus. The *Bianconeri* won Italy's Serie A in 2006 but, after their involvement in the Calciopoli bribe scandal was exposed, they were consigned to Serie B. But if you follow the letter of the law, Juventus were stripped of the 2006 and 2005 championships, so technically the title wasn't theirs to defend in 2006–07.

There is one very strange case of a famous, proud and strong team that couldn't defend the title they had won. This team was CSKA Moscow, the club closely associated with the Soviet army. In 1951, CSKA (then called CDSA) won the USSR's top flight by seven points and lifted the Soviet cup. But the next season, says Robert Edelmann in *A History of the People's Team in the Workers' State*, his book about Spartak Moscow, 'proved to be one of the strangest in Soviet soccer history'. The 1952 Olympics in Helsinki were to blame. For the first time, the USSR had decided to send athletes to the Games, expecting to prove the triumph of the Soviet system in the Olympian fields. 'Great attention was paid to the football competition,' says Edelmann. The 1952 season, which would have been interrupted by the Games, was cut to 13 rounds of matches, played after the Olympics, allowing the USSR team a very long time to prepare.

Boris Arkadiev, CSKA's coach, was chosen to assemble and manage the team. Roughly half the squad came from CSKA. The team beat Bulgaria in the first round, then played a legendary game against Yugoslavia, in which the Russians came back from four goals down after an hour to draw 5-5. Vsevolod Bobrov (who was also a member of the famous Russian national ice hockey team) scored a hat-trick and was on target again after six minutes of the replay. But this time the Yugoslavians came back, scoring three goals to defeat Arkadiev's men 3-1.

Edelmann writes: 'A political defeat at the hands of the representatives of the defiant Marshall Tito was intolerable.' When the sports committee concluded that CSKA Moscow were at fault for this intolerable defeat, the club's fate was sealed. The team played the first three games of the 1952 season (and won them all), but on 18 August 1952, the committee decreed that the club was to be disbanded. Thus the reigning league champions and cup winners could not defend their titles. It took the thaw that followed Josef Stalin's death in 1953 for the apparatchiks to allow CSKA to reform.

The only comparable case we know of occurred in Macau. Clube Desportivo Monte Carlo, founded in 1984, won the 2008 league title but then quarrelled with the Macau FA about a change in the regulations – whereupon the authorities swiftly banned the club for the 2009 season for 'subversiveness'.

⚽ Why did **Venezia fans start booing white players?**

Venezia's Ultras took a leading role in the campaign against the racist chanting that was afflicting many Italian grounds in the 1990s. As John Foot says in *Calcio: A History of Italian Football*: 'This opposition took the form of banners, leaflets and sarcasm. In one game against Verona – notorious for its hard-core support – Venezia's fans turned the racist *bu-bu* chants against Verona's white players, thereby rendering the whole concept of the chant absurd.' It wasn't exactly a long-term solution to the problem but it's hard to think of a more disconcerting riposte to racist chanting inside stadiums.

Stars

⚽ Who was **Britain's first black footballer?**

In 1880–81, the Scottish Football Association annual included this entry: 'Watson. Andrew: One of the very best backs we have; since joining Queen's Park has made rapid strides to the front as a player; has great speed and tackles splendidly; powerful and sure kick, well worthy of a place in any representative team.'

That entry is remarkable for what it does not say about this fine young footballer. It does not say, for example, that Watson is black – and is probably the first black footballer to play for a British club. Playing as an amateur a decade before Arthur Wharton became the first black professional footballer in Britain (keeping goal for Rotherham and Sheffield United), Watson was the first black player to win the Scottish Cup, the first black player to appear for (and captain) an international team and the first black footballer to appear in the FA Cup. Astonishingly, Watson's importance only came to light by accident in 2003 when Ged O'Brien, then a director of the Scottish Football Association's museum, spotted him in a photo of a Queen's Park line-up and realised that here was a story that could rewrite football history.

Born in 1857 in Georgetown, British Guyana, the son of a Scottish planter and a Guyanan woman, Watson came to study at King's College in London where he soon revealed a talent for football. He started playing for Queen's Park while studying natural philosophy, maths, civil engineering and mechanics. He later became club secretary, making him the first black football administrator in Britain, and won two Scottish Cups and three caps for Scotland, being appointed captain in 1881. His record was impressive: he was captain and right-back when Scotland beat England 6-1 on his debut on 12 March 1881. In his next two games, the Scots beat Wales and England 5-1.

Like many players of his era, Watson would travel any-where to get a game, and when he moved south of the border – appearing in an FA Cup tie in 1884 for London Swifts – he effectively ended his international career, as the Scottish FA would not select footballers playing outside Scotland.

While we still don't have a full, rounded picture of Watson's career, his success is remarkable. Football was almost exclusively a white man's sport and in Glasgow, where he made his name as a footballer, Afro-Caribbeans were almost invisible in the 1870s and 1880s. The extant contemporary records do not suggest that he suffered racial abuse, one newspaper account suggesting that spectators were intrigued

Andrew Watson with members of his Scotland team that beat England at the original Hampden Park on 11 March 1882.

by the colour of his boots (brown rather than black, as was customary at the time) but not by the colour of his skin.

So Watson may have been luckier than forward Walter Tull who, while playing for Northampton Town in 1909, was abused by Bristol City fans in a manner the Northampton Echo found 'cowardly'. The nature of the abuse is clear when the correspondent tells the Bristol hooligans that 'Tull is so clean in mind and method as to be a model for all white men who play football'.

The same could be said of Watson. In 1926, the sportswriter J.A.H Catton, editor of *Athletic News*, named Watson in his all-time Scotland team. Yet long before then

Watson had drifted into the kind of obscurity typical of many footballers. After leaving Queen's Park, he had played for Bootle, Glasgow's Crusaders, and the Corinthians. After he hung up his brown boots, the consensus is that he emigrated to Australia, probably with his wife, son and daughter, where he died in around 1902, when he would have been about forty-five.

In May 2004, one hundred and two years after Watson's death, Nigel Quashie took to the field against Estonia to become the second black player to represent Scotland.

⚽ Who was the **greatest diver** of all time?

As with most rankings, this depends on your criteria. What do you value most – artistic expression, technical merit or originality? If it's the first, then the trophy probably has to go to German midfield genius Andreas Möller, who once went down so spectacularly that he was suspended, making him the first – and so far only – Bundesliga player to be punished for a dive after the fact, with the use of video technology.

Then again, nobody really needed technology to expose the trickery. When Möller went down on 13 April 1995, with 15 minutes to go in a match between his team Borussia Dortmund and visiting Karlsruhe, everyone on the pitch and in the stands knew the midfielder had dived. Karlsruhe's Dirk Schuster didn't just fail to make contact with Möller, he didn't get anywhere near him. When Schuster said 'a small car would have fitted between me and him', he was not greatly exaggerating. The only person who was fooled was referee Günther Habermann. He awarded Dortmund a penalty from which the home side equalised before going on to win. The

Andreas Möller in his pomp at Dortmund, secure in the knowledge that his diving is unrivalled in Europe.

dive was so blatant that the German FA suspended Möller for two games and fined him 5,000 Deutschmarks. Yet the result stood. Two months later, Dortmund were crowned league champions, one point ahead of Werder Bremen.

If you admire technical difficulty more than athleticism, it's hard not to give first prize to someone who smuggled a razor blade on to the pitch to inflict bleeding wounds upon himself. Then again, the Chilean Roberto Antonio Rojas, known to his admirers as the Condor, had an occupational advantage – as a goalkeeper he could conceal the instruments of deception in his gloves.

On 3 September 1989, Rojas kept goal for his country in a World Cup qualifier against Brazil in Rio, in front of 160,000 Brazilian fans. The first tie, also a tumultuous affair, had ended 1-1, so it all came down to this game. Brazil needed only a draw to qualify and took a 1-0 lead. Chile's hopes were ebbing away until, twenty minutes from time, Rosenery Mello do Nascimento Barcelos da Silva – a good-looking 24-year-old Brazilian girl – hurled a flare on to the pitch. It landed only a few steps away from Rojas, who went down, writhing on the ground and covering his face with his hands. By the time the physios got to him, he was bleeding profusely from facial wounds. Since no stretcher was forthcoming, his team-mates carried Rojas off the field and into the dressing room, where they stayed, refusing to finish the match.

Brazil were lucky that photographer Ricardo Alfieri Junior had taken a picture of the moment the firework hit the ground. The photo showed that the flare clearly didn't touch Rojas. FIFA then discovered he had cut himself with the blade hidden in his glove. The Chilean keeper was banned from football for life. Mello milked her notoriety. She was subsequently paid $20,000 to appear in Brazilian *Playboy*, became a model and acquired the nickname *La Fogueteira* (the pyrotechnician).

Neither Möller nor Rojas, however, can match the great Dane, Allan Simonsen, who faked his own death. In a crucial World Cup qualifier, Simonsen pretended he had been shot in the back. In 1977, director Tom Hedegaard was filming *Skytten* (*The Marksman*). The title character was a militant activist who wanted to alert Denmark to the dangers of nuclear power by killing people. His most prominent victim was to be Simonsen. Hedegaard couldn't afford to re-enact an entire international, so the player agreed to fake his death in a real match. The shoot was on 1 May 1977, when Denmark met Poland in a World Cup qualifier in Copenhagen. When the hosts won a corner, Simonsen decided to get it all over with. As the cross came in, he started for the ball – and threw himself to the ground as if he'd been shot in the back.

It all looked halfway believable in the movie (you can see it on YouTube: search for 'Allan Simonsen vs Jens Okking'). But there was one problem. When Simonsen made his dash into the box, he lost his marker who was too slow in reacting.

Allan Simonsen about to fake his own death, live, in front of a capacity crowd for a World Cup qualifier. You couldn't make it up.

As the cross sailed in, the striker would have been in a good position to make contact with the ball ... if he hadn't dived. So there were losers all around: *Skytten* flopped, Simonsen didn't get an Academy Award and Denmark lost the game 2-1, failing to qualify for the World Cup in Argentina.

⚽ How two-footed are two-footed players?

Not very two-footed. Intrigued some years ago by an injury to Graeme Le Saux, and the ensuing media panic about England's dearth of left-footed players, Bangor University's Dr David Carey began researching footedness in football. He found that four out of five players were right-footed and, after studying nine games at the 1998 World Cup, plotting every touch, found that every player had a strong preference for one foot. Although the media is full of praise for certain two-footed players, Carey's research suggested that the genuinely two-footed player, who used their feet interchangeably on a 50/50 basis, did not exist.

The closest he came to finding such a paragon player was Slovakian international Lubomir Moravcik, who used his right foot only 64 percent of the time. 'That's about as two-footed as it gets,' Carey told *Champions* magazine in 2011. Moravcik took penalties with his right foot but used his weaker left foot for other set-pieces.

German defender Andreas Brehme was another exception to the rule. 'When I was young my father would throw the ball at me alternately from the right and left,' he recalled. 'That's why my so-called weaker left foot is as strong as the right. My left foot shots are more powerful, the ones with the right are better placed, like all penalties.' He scored the winner in the

1990 World Cup final from the penalty spot – with his right foot. 'It's like choosing a weapon,' said Brehme.

Further research by English Premier League Index blogger S. McCarthy, crunching Opta stats for the English Premier League from 2008–09 to 2011–12, qualifies Carey's conclusions but doesn't seriously contradict them. He noted that Peter Odemwingie had taken 81 shots with his right foot and 85 with his left. Obviously counting shots isn't the same as monitoring touches but this does suggest that the Nigerian international is closer to the 50/50 ideal than Moravcik. Yet in many ways McCarthy's results reinforce Carey's point, with only seven players taking shots with their weaker foot more than 40 percent of the time.

Carey's studies don't suggest that bilateralism is that common in any football culture. But developing more two-footed players has long been a focus in the English game. An FA players' development adviser once told *When Saturday Comes*: 'In places like Brazil, Holland and Africa, there's an emphasis on players making decisions for themselves during games. If coaching is too regimented then, under pressure, players will revert to type and won't risk their weaker foot.'

A player's starting position is vital. If youngsters get used to taking their first step with their left, they are more likely to kick with their right. So changing that – and teaching children to kick with both feet – is one long-term answer. Yet given that a 2010 study, by Alex Bryson of the National Institute of Economic and Social Research, found that teams with more two-footed players do not amass 'significantly' more points over a season, some clubs may wonder if there is any point. Maybe the last word should go to that left-footed genius Puskás: 'In football, you have to swing with one leg and stand on the other, so I chose to stand on my right.'

🌑 Who was the first **foreign footballer in the English game?**

Raymond Braine could have been British football's first foreign superstar. A gifted striker, he scored over 360 goals in a 17-year-career for club and country. Belgian football was still an amateur sport in the 1920s and Braine, like many of his peers, made ends meet by running a café. When the authorities decreed that such a sideline was only permitted for reserve team players, the 23-year-old striker decided to play abroad. Clapton Orient were keen to sign him but Braine couldn't get a work permit and joined Sparta Prague instead. Burnley chairman Charles Sutcliffe, the most powerful figure in the Football League in the 1920s, had publicly declared that the 'idea of bringing in foreigners to play in league football is repulsive to the clubs, offensive to the players and a terrible confession of weakness in the management of a club.'

The target of Sutcliffe's xenophobic fury was Herbert Chapman, the Arsenal coach who had tried to sign Austrian goalkeeper Rudolf 'Rudi' Hiden and, after the player was denied a work permit, managed to recruit Dutch goalie Gerrit Keizer by insisting he was an amateur. Fearing that Braine, Hiden and Keizer would prove the first of many, the FA insisted that foreigners could only play after living in the UK for two years. This de facto ban endured until 1978.

If maverick Egyptian striker Hassan Hegazi had shown less loyalty, the FA might have felt obliged to act earlier. In 1911, this spoilt son of an Egyptian aristocrat came to London to study engineering. He had loved football ever since he had played against British soldiers as a boy, so he joined local non-league side Dulwich Hamlet. Lively, agile, with superb ball control, an eye for a pass and a taste for over-elaborate play,

Born in Accra, Arthur Wharton kept goal for Preston North End's 'Invincibles' of the 1880s before turning professional with Rotherham, Sheffield United, Stalybridge Rovers and Stockport County.

Hegazi was dubbed 'Nebuchadnezzar' by the fans. Fulham tried to buy him and he played once for the Cottagers, scoring in a 3-1 win over Leeds, but he decided, loyally, to stay with Dulwich. In 1914, he returned to Egypt, where he represented his country in two Olympic tournaments and had a street named after him in Cairo's Garden City area.

Before Hegazi, long before German striker Max Seeburg had played in the Football League for Spurs in 1908–09, and even before Ghanaian-born sportsman Arthur Wharton had become the first black footballer in the Football League in 1893–94, a Canadian full-back, Walter Wells Bowman, had scored on his debut for Accrington on 23 January 1892 in a 4-2 victory over West Bromwich Albion.

Bowman had first come to England four years earlier, on tour with the Canadian national team. The touring party certainly aroused curiosity, with one paper saying: 'Some queer ideas have been dispelled as to the colour, language and manners of the inhabitants of Canada as shown by its representatives on the football team. The idea that foreigners can produce something in the way of football worth going to see is growing gradually on the mind.' A second tour, in 1891, aimed to showcase the players in the hope that British clubs would buy them.

Born in 1870, Bowman made his name at Berlin Rangers in Ontario, the Canadian province where football was most popular. On the 1891 tour, he impressed Accrington, one

Man City's first foreign signing, Walter Wells Bowman.

of the Football League's founder members. He played five games for Stanley before joining Division Two side Ardwick and, when that club went bust, staying on to play for its successor Manchester City. Making 47 appearances between 1892 and 1900 for Ardwick and City, Bowman never really hit the headlines, though he once turned out as an emergency goalkeeper in a derby game against Newton Heath (later Manchester United). Even the indefatigable Nick Harris, author of *England, Their England: The Definitive Story Of Foreign Footballers In The English Game since 1888*, concludes: 'What happened next remains something of a mystery.' Bowman was, Harris's researches suggest, 'last heard of in Butte, a copper mining city in Montana'.

In 2011–12, 68 nationalities were represented in the Premier League and 67 in the Championship. Canada supplied just two Premier League players – Junior Hoilett (then at Blackburn Rovers, now at QPR) and Simeon Jackson (Norwich City). In what may be a sign of how complex football nationality has become in the 120-something years since Bowman made his debut, Jackson was born in Jamaica and Hoilett, who could represent Canada or Jamaica, has hinted that he would prefer to play for England.

🌑 Who was football's first global superstar?

It has to be José Andrade – carnival musician, sometime shoe-shiner and right-half in the Uruguayan national side that won the 1924 and 1928 Olympics and the 1930 World Cup. Known as the Black Marvel or Pearl – decades before such sobriquets would be awarded to Pelé or Eusébio – Andrade once famously thrilled spectators by travelling half the pitch with the ball on his head. In his appreciation of the Uruguayan star, Eduardo Galeano says: 'The first international football icon was black, South American and poor.'

In the 1920s, Uruguay weren't just successful, they were revolutionary, playing a creative, intricate, short-passing game that Europe had never seen before, a kind of chess with a football, only possible because they shared a level of technique none of their Olympic rivals could match. Their first opponents, Yugoslavia, spied on them. Forewarned, the Uruguayans trained like clowns – and proceeded to win the match 7-0, even though their flag was raised upside down and the Brazilian anthem was played by mistake before kick-off. Uruguay's 1924 Olympics campaign was almost a ceremonial progression. Their record was: Played 5, Won 5, For 20, Against 2. They beat hosts France 5-1 in the quarter-finals before defeating Switzerland 3-0 in the final. After winning gold, they did a lap of honour, believed to be the first in the history of the event, a ritual that is still known in Spanish as 'vuelta olimpica'.

Good enough to play as full-back, down the wings or in central midfield, with enough tricks to dribble past an opponent if he couldn't pass around them, Andrade masterminded Uruguay's attacks. Asked by the media to explain the team's revolutionary style, he swore that the players trained by chasing chickens that fled, making S-shapes on the ground. The media were so credulous – and fascinated by Andrade – they published this as the truth. French football writer Gabriel Hanot, one of the inventors of the European Cup, was not fooled, writing: 'The principal quality of the victors was a marvellous virtuosity in receiving the ball, controlling it and using it. They created a beautiful football, elegant but varied, rapid, powerful, effective.' He concluded that 'these fine athletes are to the English professionals like Arab thoroughbreds next to farm horses'.

The only black player among these thoroughbreds was Andrade. The charismatic star stayed on in Paris for a while, basking in France's adoration, living as, in Galeano's words, 'a wandering Bohemian and king of the cabaret'. But he returned to South America as Uruguay faced their rivals Argentina in a hastily arranged friendly. After a 1-1 draw in Montevideo, the rematch in Buenos Aires was marred by crowd trouble. In

The Pearl – José Leandro Andrade – gets poured a half-time cup of tea at the 1928 Olympics.

the closing minutes, the home fans started throwing stones at Andrade who flung them straight back, sparking a near riot in which the Uruguayan team walked off the pitch.

Andrade – and Uruguay – would have their revenge in 1928, beating Argentina 2-1 to win their second successive Olympic gold. The organisers of the Amsterdam Games had 250,000 requests for tickets from across Europe to watch that final. Such demand led to the agreement, at the 1928 Olympics, to launch the World Cup. Andrade would be one of the best players in that first mundial even though he was already suffering from syphilis and an eye injury sustained after he crashed into a post in the 1928 semi-final.

Richard Hofmann, the German centre-forward who scored 24 goals in 25 games for the national team, said: 'Uruguay then were the best team in the world. Their star was Andrade. He was a football artist who could do simply anything with the ball and was always ahead with his thoughts by several moves.' Like so many football superstars to come, Andrade was better at reading the game than he was at reading life. He spent his last days, alcoholic, blind in one eye, in a dilapidated flat in Montevideo, with a beautiful wife, and his medals in a shoebox. He died of tuberculosis on 4 October 1957, at the age of 56. Yet for much of the 1920s, José Leandro Andrade had been the most famous footballer in the world, the player with the golden feet.

⚽ Who has scored **most goals** in the history of the game?

The official answer is Pelé. FIFA states unequivocally that the Brazilian legend's 1,281 goals is a world record. However, the International Federation of Football Historians and Statisticians gave their Golden Ball as the greatest goalscorer of the last century to Austrian goal machine Josef Bican, as he had been top scorer in a domestic league for 12 seasons (one more than Pelé).

Bican, the fearsome striker at the heart of Austria's Wunderteam in the 1930s, is officially credited with 649 goals by the IFFHS, although on rsssf.com his tally is enigmatically stated as '805+'. Supplementary information suggests that Bican scored another 663 in friendlies, which would give him a tally of 1,468 – 187 more than Brazil's greatest No 10. The difficulty

Artur Friedenreich (centre) with Pelé and the Brazilian football writer, Silvio de Oliveira.

here is ascertaining which friendlies and unofficial matches FIFA chooses to recognise and why. The Federation is unlikely to shift from its official position but given that the Brazilian and the Austrian scored hundreds of goals in non-competitive matches, it is hard to come to a definitive reckoning.

To confuse matters still further, another Brazilian striker has a claim to the title – the great, but largely forgotten Artur Friedenreich. Once described as a better all-rounder than Pelé and more elegant than Alfredo di Stéfano, Friedenreich made his name in the 1910s and 1920s, scoring the goal that won Copa America for the *Seleção*. A mulatto who played in an era in Brazilian football when the game was dominated by the country's white elite, Friedenreich only managed to play by pretending, as the magazine *Placar* put it, 'to be a white man with an all-year tan'. He invented, as Eduardo Galeano wrote it in *Football in Sun and Shadow*, 'a style open to fantasy, one which prefers pleasure to results'. You could argue that he defined what we now think of the Brazilian style decades before Pelé, Didi and Garrincha. And he scored 1,329 goals – 48 more than Brazil's most famous footballer.

Unfortunately for Friedenreich, the statistical records which his father Oscar and, later, Arthur's Paulistano teammate Mário de Andrade, lovingly compiled, which could have proved his goal tally, vanished after Andrade's death in the mid-1960s. The bereaved family are believed to have junked the records and, by the time a Brazilian football journalist tried to find them, they had disappeared into a Sao Paulo rubbish skip. In an attempt to solve the mystery, Friedenreich was tracked down to his house in Sao Paulo. As soon as the unofficial delegation of journalists and statisticians found him, they realised their quest was hopeless. He answered all their questions vaguely, while staring at an indefinite point in the distance. By the time Friedenreich died at the age of 76, on 6 February 1969, he had forgotten his name. Since his death, football has largely forgotten his claim to be the game's greatest goalscorer.

⚽ Has any footballer ever succeeded in gridiron?

It is fashionable to describe a certain style of passing midfielder – think Andrea Pirlo or David Beckham – as a quarter-back. But has any footballer ever succeeded in gridiron?

The most conspicuous success is Toni Fritsch – or Wembley-Toni as he is still known to Austrian football fans of a certain age. In 1965, the speedy, diminutive winger escaped the shackles of Nobby Stiles to score twice as Austria came back from 2-1 down to win 3-2 against an England team that would win the World Cup nine months later. One of those goals, a long-range screamer with Fritsch's famous right foot, hinted at a career change to come. Six years later, when the Dallas Cowboys visited Vienna on a European tour, they were looking for a specialist place kicker. Austria coach Leopold Stastny suggested Rapid Vienna star Fritsch who had lost much of his pace but still knew how to kick a ball.

Fritsch could speak no English and had never seen an American football before. Taken to the 19th district, where some gridiron goals erected by GIs in the 1950s still stood, he booted the ball over the bar and signed a contract there and then. Delighted but bemused that he was offered money to

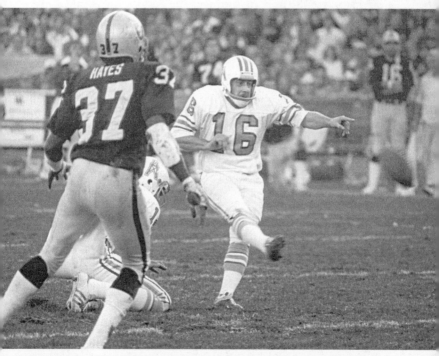

Wembley-Toni (No. 16) kicking for Houston Oilers against Oakland Raiders, towards the end of his gridiron career in the 1980s.

'play this strange sport', Fritsch quickly made an impact in Dallas. In the Cowboys first game of the 1971 season, with the scores tied against the St Louis Cardinals, Fritsch was brought on to kick a field goal. One of his opponents shouted 'Choke Fritsch choke!', but the Austrian, knowing no English, kicked the field goal and won the game. In 1972, he became the first – and, to date only – Austrian to win the Super Bowl and when he stopped kicking in 1985 he had scored 157 field goals, including 13 in consecutive play-off games. Gil Brandt, then the Cowboys personnel director, said: 'He was one of the guys from the day he got there. He knew nothing about American football, he just knew how to kick the ball.'

Fritsch is the only man to win the Super Bowl – and score twice against England at Wembley. As successful as he was in America, he never forgot the game that made him famous. When he died in 2005, of a heart attack at the age of 60, he had just collected his tickets to watch Rapid Vienna's return to the UEFA Champions League, after a nine-year absence, to face Bayern Munich.

Another Austrian Toni came close to matching Fritsch's success: Anton 'Toni' Linhart. Linhart won six caps for Austria in the 1960s and later played for the Baltimore Colts in the NFL. In 1975 and 1976, the Colts made the play-offs but didn't reach the Super Bowl, though Linhart was voted onto the Pro Bowl (the All-Star game) team in both years. In Britain, Linhart is remembered neither for his footballing skills nor for his gridiron heroics – but for playing an important part in one of the most infamous games on British soil.

On 8 May 1963, Scotland met Austria in front of 94,596 at Hampden. It was a friendly, although Scotland's Dave Mackay begs to differ. He remembers the game as inexplicably vicious, saying: 'It all started with them spitting at us. They were off their heads.' With eleven minutes left on the clock, and Scotland leading 4-1, Austria were down to eight men, because one player had been carried off injured while two others had been dismissed (Horst Nemec for dissent, Erich Hof for what the press referred to as a 'diabolical tackle at waist-height'). Mackay says the Scots weren't protecting their lead – but their leader: 'We were trying to protect Denis Law, who they were chasing like a rabbit,' he says. The one who finally got him was Austria's lone goalscorer, future NFL hero Linhart. On 79 minutes, he sent Law to the floor and when the United star didn't get up again, the disgusted referee Jim Finney had had enough. He ended the game there and then. 'I felt that I had to abandon the match or somebody would have been seriously hurt', Finney explained.

⚽ Who scored the **most headers** in a match?

The unlikely candidate for this honour is probably a tall, strong Brazilian striker by the name of João Ramos do Nascimento, aka Dondinho. He played for several clubs in the 1930 and 1940s, notably Atlético Mineiro and Fluminense. Why 'unlikely'? Well, as his son later wrote: 'Usually this sort of player would be English, but at that time Brazil had a footballer who scored some amazing headers called Baltazar. Everyone said that my dad was the "up-country Baltazar".'

Dondinho would probably be forgotten today if the son who wrote those words hadn't been Edson Arantes do Nascimento, better known as Pelé. In his autobiography, he added: 'It was said that Dondinho once headed five goals in the same match. Later in my career, when I reached a thousand goals, some journalists started to research this claim to see if it was true or not. And it was – they reported that the

Dinner with the Nascimentos. Dondinho is on the left, next to the teenage Pelé, who is being served up a good portion by his mum, Dona Celeste.

only goal-scoring record that didn't belong to Pelé belonged to his father!'

The matter isn't quite that clear-cut. There is some controversy about the match in which Dondinho set his record. Victor Cunha, a former president of the Atlético Três Corações, says it was a game between Atlético TC and Rio Vermelho, which the hosts won 6-1. But most sources, including old newspapers and the official home page of Pelé's former club Santos FC, point towards a match between Yura-cán AC and Smart Club, two sides from the city of Itajubá, on 5 August 1939. Playing for Yuracán, Dondinho scored five headers in his team's 6-3 win. Among those witnessing this feat was Dondinho's team-mate General Eloy Menezes, later a famous equestrian who participated in three Olympic Games and became president of Brazil's National Sports Council.

⚽ Who had the **hardest shot** in football?

Before we try to answer that, let's see how hard a really hard shot really is by considering the game usually called the world's fastest team sport, ice hockey. That's because when we call a shot 'hard', what we really mean is that it travels through the air very 'fast'.

The Russian defender Alex Riazantsev is usually credited with having hit the hardest shot in ice hockey, a 114.15 mph (183.7 km/h) rocket during a skills competition in 2012. Yet, amazingly, these small, compact, hard disks – which strong men fire into the air with the help of a wooden stick that acts as a catapult – travel slower than a much larger, relatively lightweight football struck well by a human leg. Because no matter where the football record stands, you have to have a shot faster than 125 mph (202 km/h) to get anywhere close.

In February 2007, *The Guardian* published a list of hard hitters headed by Sheffield Wednesday striker David Hirst, who'd had a shot clocked at 114 mph (183.47 km/h) in 1996. Other sources pointed to a famous 125 mph (202 km/h) strike by Roberto Carlos, delivered in early 2000. Then a week later, a *Guardian* reader found a video of a goal by Brazilian hotshot Ronny Heberson Furtado de Araújo for

David Hirst, of then top-division Sheffield Wednesday, prepares to unleash his 114 mph shot.

Sporting Lisbon against Naval in November 2006. The editors calculated that Ronny's shot travelled at 131.82 mph (210.9 km/h).

We'll never know for sure who had the hardest shot, if only because conditions are never the same. The playing materials, for instance, keep changing. There are claims that Luigi Riva would have had a shot clocked at around 124 mph if he had been using a modern ball. (Riva was renowned for the power of his shots – in October 1970, one of his strikes broke the arm of a boy watching a Cagliari practice match.) Many other heroes of the past never had their shots measured. In the 1960s, the Eintracht Frankfurt player Bernd Nickel earned the nickname Dr Hammer for his ferocious shots. Nickel spent much of his childhood shooting a ball against a huge barn door. 'It's no longer there,' he says. 'Guess I've worn it out.' But his strikes were never properly timed. The same goes for Puskás. Anyone who saw him play swears that no living soul ever shot harder. Which is why he was known in Spain as *Canoncito Pum* (Booming Cannon).

Finally, sometimes a shot is too hard to be clocked. In November 2004, Anderlecht's Walter Baseggio volleyed home from the edge of the penalty area against La Louviere in the Belgian league. Baseggio hit the ball so hard that it exploded upon impact and crossed the line with the bladder hanging out. The referee allowed the goal and Anderlecht won 2-1.

🌐 Why didn't **hat-trick Hurst** get the 1966 World Cup final matchball?

When the final whistle rang at Wembley in 1966, West German striker Helmut Haller, who had scored the opening goal in that final, grabbed the ball and walked to the dressing room. Normally, it is the referee's duty to collect the ball but Gottfried Dienst didn't do so. Haller later explained his actions saying, 'It is an old German tradition – if the winners get the cup, the losers get the ball.'

Contrary to popular opinion in Britain, there was nothing clandestine about the way Haller made off with the ball. The unwritten rule that a player who scores a hat-trick gets to keep the match ball was then unknown in Germany. Indeed, according to the German definition, Hurst's three goals weren't even a hat-trick. To score a proper hat-trick in German football, a player had to score three goals consecutively and in the same half. Hurst later admitted that 'amid the euphoria of the World Cup win' he didn't try too hard to retrieve the ball. He certainly had the opportunity as Haller later asked all the England players and a few other stars of the tournament, such as Eusébio and Pelé, to autograph it before he took it home.

In the build-up to Euro 96, the British tabloids suddenly decided the matchball should return to England and launched an investigation into its whereabouts. This was a tad unnecessary, as Hurst had known for years that Haller had the ball.

Eventually, the Mirror Group, with support from Virgin and Eurostar UK, paid the German international (who died in 2012, at the age of 73) £80,000 for the famous pig's bladder and proudly displayed the ball at Waterloo Station.

Unfortunately, the new owners of the most famous matchball in the history of the game neglected it. 'It was left in direct sunlight and all the signatures faded,' said Mark Bushell, the marketing director of the National Football Museum, which now has the ball. 'It's unbelievable.'

⚽ Is there any real advantage in having a **low centre of gravity**?

In February 2011, Partizan Belgrade signed Ghanaian striker Dominic Adiyiah on loan from AC Milan. It was his header that Luis Suarez punched away in the quarter-finals of the 2010 World Cup. Milovan Rajevac, the Serbian coach of that Ghana side, said Partizan's new arrival was 'a very dangerous player, with a very low centre of gravity, explosive and quick.' When a journalist replied, 'Sounds like you are describing a player like Romário,' Rajevac said, 'Let's say they have certain similarities.' That was enough for Adiyiah, who is now playing for Arsenal Kiev, to be hailed in headlines as the 'African Romário'.

The idea that certain footballers have a low centre of gravity – and that this is an asset – has not pervaded every football culture. In Germany, pundits rarely use the phrase and, if they do, they invariably use the English words because there is no German equivalent. Elsewhere the term is used and translated almost word for word – *un centre de gravité bas* (in French) and *baricentro basso* (literally 'gravity low' in Italy. In the Spanish and South American game, where such diminutive geniuses as Maradona have shone, having a low centre of gravity is regarded as essential for a *fantastista*, the playmakers who change games with their creativity.

Although Maradona's low centre of gravity has been retrospectively lauded, it was Romário's success that made people take note of the term. The 5ft 6in forward, the greatest player in Brazil's 1994 World Cup winning side, was hailed for his stature and balance in Jimmy Burns' book on Barcelona, *A People's Passion*. As a young player, he was known as *O Baixinho*

One for the physicists to calculate as Romário sweeps past Italy's Dion Baggio in the 1994 World Cup Final. Brazil won on penalties.

(Shorty), but with the innate self-confidence that would later inspire him to paint unflattering caricatures of his enemies on the walls of his nightclub, he just ignored the nickname and focused on goals – indeed he claims to have scored over 1,000 of them. (FIFA don't agree.) Ever since he dazzled the world with his speed, power and eye for the net, many up and coming forwards have been likened to him – not just Adiyiah, but Lionel Messi, Sergio Agüero, Luis Suárez and Islam Feruz, the 18-year-old 5ft 4in striker who joined Chelsea in 2011 and is being hailed as the future of the Scotland team.

The proof that having a low centre of gravity makes for better control of the ball is convincing, if not conclusive. American youth coach Alex Kos has long argued that size does matter – the excuse clubs use when turning away prospects like Kevin Keegan because they are deemed too short – but not in the way many scouts think. A low centre of gravity, he suggests, makes it much easier for players to 'dribble, make fakes and feints, and change direction'. He also believes that coaches should 'never underestimate the toughness of a short player. They are usually tougher and more physical than taller players.' He cites Pelé (5ft 8in), Maradona (5ft 5in) and Messi (5ft 7in) in support of his case.

However, a roll call of the shortest players in the major European leagues suggests that around 5ft 3in is the threshold for players competing at this level. In other words, centres of gravity can be too low. (The shortest England internationals – Fanny Walden and Jack Crawford – played between the 1910s and 1930s and were just over 5ft 2in.)

Sometimes, having too many players built like Romário can be too much of a good thing. In Argentina, which has produced these players in industrial quantities – apart from those already mentioned, think of Pablo Aimar, Javier Saviola and Carlos Tevez – they are called *bajitos*, short ones. The

Can you win a World Cup with *bajitos*? We may soon find out. Messi, Sergio Agüero and Carlos Tevez celebrate with Maxi Rodríguez.

term is intended as a compliment so fans might say 'the coach won the game because of *los bajitos*'. Yet if they're not performing, these players can be derided *enanos* (dwarves), with their lack of stature being blamed for their failure to undo a physically imposing defence.

In recent years, Argentinian fans have demanded that Agüero, Aimar, Messi, Saviola and Tevez play in the same national side. Julio Grondona, the plain-speaking president of the Argentinian FA, dismissed the very notion saying, 'If someone wants that, better rent *Snow White And The Seven Dwarves*. You cannot use that formula to win a World Cup.' He pointed out that this kind of player might not be as useful in defence where, in his opinion, World Cups are really won. Grondona has a point: how many centre-backs get praised for their low centre of gravity?

⚽ Which player has represented the most national teams?

If we ignore the legion of players who have represented a second country – or even a third – after the first has disintegrated, two players stand out. Both of them were banned by FIFA, neither played in a World Cup finals yet they ended up playing in the same national side.

The great Alfredo di Stéfano first tasted international football with Argentina, scoring six goals in six games in the 1947 Copa America and, between 1957 and 1961, found the net an impressive 23 times in 31 appearances for Spain. While he was at Millonarios in Bogotá, he made four appearances for Colombia but those caps aren't recognised by FIFA because it had blacklisted the league (in 1948) and the national team (between 1951 and 1954) after Argentinian complaints that Colombian clubs were pirating their players (see 'What was the most entertaining league season ever?'). So, officially, if not in reality, Di Stéfano only played for two countries. He may also be the greatest footballer never to play in a World Cup finals. Argentina didn't enter in 1950 out of pique, FIFA wouldn't let him represent Spain in 1954 – and La Roja missed out on qualification anyway – and, after he had acquired Spanish citizenship, he was injured for the 1962 finals.

Millonarios (and Real Madrid) legend, Alfredo di Stéfano.

Di Stéfano may be indelibly associated with Real Madrid but he could easily have stayed at FC Barcelona had Franco not helped force through the move for the political and sporting glory of the capital and Spain over the troublesome Catalans. If Di Stéfano had stayed at Barcelona, there would have been the intriguing propsect of him sharing the limelight with the Hungarian star Ladislao Kubala, who, to quote Brian Glanville, was 'a superb player and a remarkable, somewhat Rabelaisian personality'.

The variety of countries Kubala played for offers a snapshot of his life and the tragic fashion in which wars and revolutions rewrote the history of European football in the twentieth century. Born in Budapest, to Slovak parents,

Kubala started out at Ferencvaros but was impressing up front for Slovan Bratislava when he made his debut for Czechoslovakia in October 1946. He won his sixth – and last – cap for that country in December 1947. Five months later, after returning to Budapest to avoid Czech military service, he made his debut for Hungary in a 0-0 draw away to Albania in the Balkan Cup. He was to make just two more appearances for his homeland before he jumped into the back of a truck, disguised as a Soviet soldier, and fled to Italy in January 1949. Banned by FIFA after Hungarian protests, Kubala was invited to join the all-conquering Grande Torino side flying to Lisbon for a friendly against Benfica in May 1949. However, his son was ill so he stayed at home and thus wasn't killed in the Superga air disaster.

In Italy, desperate to play football, Kubala formed a team of Hungarian exiles and, on a tour of Spain, impressed Real Madrid president Santiago Bernabéu. Kubala said he would sign for the *Blancos* if his father-in-law Ferdinand Daucik became coach. In the event, Daucik ended up coaching Barcelona and Kubala followed him to Catalonia. Acquiring Spanish citizenship, Kubala made his debut for his third footballing nation in July 1953. He scored 11 goals in 19 games for Spain, but played his last international in April 1961, missing out on the World Cup in Chile.

So Kubala is the only player officially recognised to have played for three countries. And unofficially, the tally is four. Kubala also played four games for Catalonia, a footballing identity FIFA does not recognise. But whether three or four, this is a record nobody can take away from the man whom supporters, in a 1999 poll, chose as the greatest player to wear the Barcelona shirt. He is commemorated by a statue outside the Camp Nou.

⚽ Which player has been capped in the **most positions?**

'**Mr Versatility**, a centre-half by trade, he always gave everything, wherever he was played, centre-half or right-half, right or left full-back, he often played in goal as well and not just for the craic.' When Peter Goulding, of Football Poets, paid tribute to Irish footballer Cornelius (Con) Joseph Martin he wasn't taking any licence.

Consider the facts: Martin scored four goals in three internationals playing as a centre-forward, was bought by Aston Villa as a centre-half, played at inside-forward for Leeds United and rejected a bid from Manchester United because they wanted him in goal. There seemed no end to Martin's versatility: he played for Ireland and Northern Ireland and also won honours in Gaelic football.

He made his debut for Ireland in goal on a tour of Iberia in 1946 and scored six goals – four from the penalty spot – in 30 internationals. Though his preferred position was centre-half, Martin led the attack, and helped out at full-back and in goal when called upon. One of his penalties was scored against England at Goodison Park on 21 September 1949 when Ireland won 2-0, inflicting England's first defeat on home soil by a foreign team. Con was playing for Villa at the time and, after this historic result, got a lift back on the England team bus to Birmingham.

Belgium's bespectacled midfielder Armand Joseph 'Jef' Jurion was even more versatile, playing in seven different positions for Belgium in the 1950s. Yet neither he nor Martin covered as many positions as the legendary Austrian Gerhard Hanappi who represented his country in every position except goalkeeper.

Mr Utility, Gerhard Hanappi, at the Rapid Vienna stadium, 1961.

Hanappi made his international debut in 1948 when he was 19 as a right-half (and would not miss any of the next 55 internationals, an Austrian record) but was signed by Rapid Vienna to link defence and attack, which is why he was usually described as a centre-half. 'Signed' is probably not the right word. Hanappi desperately wanted to join Rapid, Austria's most famous working-class club, in 1950 but his club, Wacker Vienna, didn't want to sell him. So Hanappi disappeared. He claimed to have been kidnapped by Rapid's director of football Franz Binder and didn't show up for six months until Wacker relented. Yet during those 'lost' months, national coach Walter Nausch kept calling him up for international duty – and fielding him in all kinds of positions.

'He can play everywhere,' Nausch liked to say about Hanappi. This was no exaggeration. Hanappi scored 21 goals for Rapid in the 1952–53 season, a haul that made him the club's second-best forward; but he played at left-back for the Europe XI which faced England at Wembley in October 1953, marginalising the great Sir Stanley Matthews.

Hanappi's versatility didn't just extend to the pitch. A poor working-class boy who grew up with his aunt after his mother had died young, Hanappi studied architecture and designed Rapid's new stadium in the early 1970s. After he succumbed to cancer in 1980, the ground he had built was renamed Gerhard Hanappi Stadium. A footballer who could cover any outfield position and design his own stadium – that's what you call a utility player.

⚽ Have outfield players worn No. 1?

Dutch striker Ruud Geels enjoyed a long career, winning 20 caps for his country, but Netherlands coach Rinus Michels denied him his chance to make history. For the 1974 World Cup, the Dutch did not assign shirt numbers the normal way – 1 for goalkeeper, 2 for left-back and so on – but instead alphabetically. (The exception was Johan Cruyff, who demanded his customary 14.) Under this system, Geels was given the No. 1 shirt – but Michels refused to play him. There was no place in the world of Total Football for a goal machine whose greatest gift was his ability to head the ball. By the time Geels got his chance, at the 1976 European Championships, the Dutch had reverted to the normal system and he wore No. 13.

Such eccentricity wasn't unique to the Dutch. At the 1974 World Cup, Argentina allocated shirt numbers alphabetically, but made an exception by reserving numbers 1, 12 and 21 for the goalkeepers. Then four years later, as World Cup hosts, Argentina went all the way. River Plate midfielder Norberto 'Beto' Alonso wore 1, Osvaldo Ardiles 2, substitute goalkeeper Hector Baley 3 and so on. Argentina's coach Cesar Luis Menotti didn't really rate Alonso (and may have called him into the squad partly due to pressure from the junta), but he brought him on in the first group game, against Hungary, with fifteen minutes left, treating the world to the spectacle of an offensive midfielder wearing the No. 1. (At his club Alonso wore the iconic No. 10 with pride.)

There is nothing in the rules to stop an outfield player wearing No. 1, so Argentina used their system again for the 1982 and 1986 World Cups. They made exceptions for such stars as Diego Maradona, Daniel Passarella and Jorge Valdano but Ardiles didn't mind being No. 1 in 1982.

Though numbers no longer rigidly define the wearer's roles, it is rare to see an outfield player donning the No. 1 shirt. Yet in 2000, Aberdeen's Moroccan striker Hicham Zerouaki wore No. 0 after being nicknamed 'Zero' by Dons fans. The Scottish FA outlawed the number after the season was over. That was not the end of the zero shirt, however: in 2006, LA Galaxy keeper Steve Cronin adopted zero.

The Scottish FA were not the first members of the football bureaucracy to limit a player's freedom of choice. In the 1990s, Finnish midfielder Mika Lehkosuo wore 96.2 – the FM frequency of a local radio station. When HJK Helsinki qualified for the UEFA Champions League, Lehkosuo was told that UEFA only allowed players to choose from 1 to 99. He chose 96.

The Asian Football Confederation is more dogmatic, stipulating that players keep the shirt number they are given at the start of an Asian Cup qualifying campaign. This meant that winger Tommy Oar, who was obviously a long way from being the first name on Australia coach Pim Verbeek's team-sheet for the qualifiers for the 2011 Asian Cup, made his debut in a 1-0 victory against Indonesia in March 2010 with No. 121 on his back.

⚽ Which player has had the most elaborate pre-match ritual?

Putting your shirt on last (Paul Ince), placing your boots under a bust of your dad on matchday (Cristiano Ronaldo) and filling up with petrol at the same station even when you know you have enough fuel to drive home from the match (Pepe Reina), all look pretty humdrum when you consider the elaborate series of rituals with which Newcastle United striker John Tudor protected himself against ill fortune on a matchday in the 1970s.

Here is a snapshot of his typical matchday from the *Rough Guide Newcastle United 11* book: 'The striker always had lunch at noon. Always the same lunch – beans on toast and a drop of rice pudding. On the coach, he had to have a piece of spearmint gum unwrapped and given to him personally by the physio Alec Mutch. This gum was chewed throughout the game and only removed after the final whistle. Nearing the dressing room he had to have a slug of whisky – again handed to him by Mutch. Then, with striker Malcolm Macdonald, he would open a large tin of elastoplast, and use all the plaster to strap his ankles tightly. Supermac would take the empty tin, fill it with water, take out his four front false teeth, put them in the tin, close the lid and then put the tin away.' Only after this rigmarole had been completed did Tudor consider himself ready for kick-off.

⚽ Who was the first **Scotsman to score** in a World Cup finals?

Not Jimmy Murray, though the Hearts striker did score Scotland's first goal in the finals – to earn a 1-1 draw with Yugoslavia in 1958 in Sweden. The honour instead belongs to another Edinburghian forward, Bart McGhee, who scored the USA's first goal in a 4-0 victory over Belgium in Montevideo on 13 July 1930.

Born on 30 April 1899, McGhee was the son of James McGhee, a prolific inside-forward for Hibernian who won one cap for Scotland and managed Hearts. He suspended

Legendary Scottish winger Bart McGhee (left) playing for the USA against Argentina in the 1930 World Cup.

the club's star player Bobby Walker for missing a game and when the board sided with the Hearts star, quit and emigrated to the USA where, in 1912, his sons Bart and Jimmy joined him.

Bart shone on the wing for such picturesquely named clubs as New York Shipbuilding, Fleisher Yarn and Indiana Flooring and was playing for the New York Nationals when he was called up into the US squad for the first World Cup. An ever present as the Americans topped their group and reached the semi-finals (where they were thrashed 6-1 by Argentina) McGhee, who was 31 when the finals finished, never won another cap after the tournament was over.

The end of this pioneering Scot's career is shrouded in the fog of the Great Depression – when the game's statistics suddenly became sketchy – and a dispute between the American Soccer League and the US FA about fixtures which ultimately finished off the League. McGhee is officially credited with 137 goals in nine seasons with US clubs. Although McGhee didn't die until 1979, it isn't clear where or when he played his last competitive football. We do know it wasn't Hull City. Despite persistent reports linking him with the Tigers, his son Ed insisted that Bart had only left the US once – to represent his adopted country in Uruguay.

⚽ Who is the **most travelled player?**

Long after memories of John 'Budgie' Burridge turning out for Wolves with a Superman outfit under his kit have faded, this eccentric, nomadic, goalkeeper's legend will endure in the record books because he has played for more English league clubs – fifteen, count 'em! – than any other footballer.

Those fifteen were: Workington Town (1969–71), Blackpool (1971–75), Aston Villa (1975–78), Southend United

(1977–78), Crystal Palace (1978–80), Queen's Park Rangers (1980–82), Wolves (1982–84), Derby County (1984), Sheffield United (1984–87), Southampton (1987–89), Newcastle United (1989–91), Scarborough (1993), Lincoln City (1993–94), Manchester City (1994–95) and Darlington (1995–96). Burridge's wanderlust was so great that he also played for five Scottish teams: Aberdeen, Dumbarton, Falkirk, Hibernian and Queen of the South. Since hanging up his gloves, he has become a pundit-cum-goalkeeping coach in the Middle East where he mentored Omani goalkeeper Ali Al-Habsi, who made his name at Wigan Athletic and once declared 'after God, John Burridge is the main person.'

Yet Burridge looks distinctly unadventurous when you consider goalkeeping's Phileas Fogg, Lutz Pfannenstiel. The German keeper may look like he would rather have been a wrestler, rock musician or porn star than a footballer but he has the unique distinction of being the only man to have played professionally in all six FIFA football continents: Africa, Asia, Europe, Oceania, North America and South America.

A German Under-17 international, Pfannenstiel's career started unremarkably enough at local Bavarian side Bad Kötzting in 1990. But three years later, aged 20, he signed for the Malaysian League's Penang state side, a surprising sideways move that set the nomadic precedent for the decades ahead. In 20 years between the sticks, Pfannenstiel has been on the books of (or played for) at least 27 clubs in 14 countries, completing his set of FIFA continents with spells at the Orlando Pirates (Africa), Dunedin Technical (Oceania), Calgary Mustangs (North America) and Atlético Ibirama (South America).

With the kind of plucky resolve hitherto associated with unflappable nineteenth-century explorers, Pfannenstiel has kept goal in Albania, Armenia and Namibia and been jailed on suspicion of match fixing in Singapore – even though he

Lutz Pfannenstiel finds his true home, Global United, set up to raise aware-ness of climate change. 'We love football, we love the planet' is their slogan.

won the games in question. (He was charged, bizarrely, with keeping goal 'suspiciously well'. Strangely, but in the circumstances understandably, Pfannenstiel denied this and the case never came to court.) He has also had run-ins with Ukrainian gangsters, which is why he prefers not to reveal which clubs he played for in that country.

Pfannenstiel – the name translates as 'panhandle' – never really made it in any of Europe's biggest leagues. A reserve keeper at Nottingham Forest from 1995 to 1997 (his nickname, predictably, was 'The German') Pfannenstiel was invariably loaned out. He is best remembered in England for having to be given the kiss of life after he stopped breathing three times while playing for Bradford Park Avenue in 2002.

Two years later, at the age of 31, he impressed AC Milan but was promptly loaned to the Calgary Mustangs. Pfannenstiel felt most at home in Norway – 'to relax and fish in a mild Norwegian summer is a dream' – where he had four spells at three clubs and came to regard Second Division side Baerum as a second home.

After hanging up his boots, Pfannenstiel formed a club, called Global United FC, which plays charity games in order to, as the team's badge says, 'fight global warming'. In March 2012, Pfannenstiel lived in an igloo for five days to raise awareness. One of the few people alive who can authorita-tively make such a comparison, he insists that living in an igloo is preferable to a prison cell in Singapore. Now a scout for Hoffenheim, Pfannenstiel says: 'I don't think anyone will break this record because there aren't many people as crazy as me.'

⚽ Has any footballer ever played **two matches on the same day?**

On 27 January 1957, midfielder Can Bartu made a strange kind of history, scoring twice as Fenerbahçe beat Beyoğlus-por 4-0 before scoring ten points in a 44-43 victory for the sports club's basketball team. Bartu had initially made his name on the basketball court but when he decided, at the age of 21, to focus all his energies on football, he was good enough to win 28 caps for Turkey and spent six profitable seasons in Serie A in the 1960s, probably the best league in the world at that time.

If you're looking for players who've starred in two football matches on the same day, three names stand out – and two of them, by a bizarre coincidence, played for Bayern Munich.

On 13 November 1985, Søren Lerby played 58 minutes as Denmark beat the Republic of Ireland 4-1 in a World Cup qualifier in Dublin. After leaving the pitch, he took a private jet back to Munich to play, as a substitute, in a German Cup match which Bayern drew 1-1 with Bochum. Almost two years to the day, Bayern organised another private jet so that Mark Hughes could play for Wales, who lost 2-0 to Czechoslovakia in Prague, and still be back in time to help Bayern beat Borussia Mönchengladbach 3-2 in a cup replay.

Mexican keeper Jorge Campos represented LA Galaxy and Mexico on the same day on 16 June 1996. The flamboyant goalie, famous for designing his own colourful kits, didn't have to leave California to double up. It was probably worth the effort because Mexico's 2-2 draw with the USA was enough to win them the US Cup for the first time.

Yet Chris Balderstone probably surpasses Bartu, Campos, Hughes and Lerby. One of England's great cricketing footballers, Balderstone made 51 not out for Leicestershire against Derbyshire in Chesterfield on 15 September 1975 before jumping into a taxi to head to Doncaster Rovers' Belle Vue ground for an evening kick-off against Brentford. After a 1-1 draw with the Bees, he was back at the crease the next day. Not content with his innings of 116 runs, the versatile 35-year-old took three wickets for 28 runs as Leicestershire wrapped up their first-ever County Championship.

Balderstone was not the first man to achieve this double and become a champion. On 30 August 1920, fast bowler Jack Durston represented Middlesex against Surrey at Lords. But he was excused fielding duties so he could keep a clean sheet for Brentford in a 1-0 victory over Millwall, in the second Football League match in the Bees' history. The next day, he took the wicket of Surrey captain Percy Fender as Middlesex won the match and the County Championship.

⚽ Did any one player **win the World Cup single handedly?**

'Football is a game of individuals,' one French international told football writer Philippe Auclair. A zillion motivation experts may have assured us that there is no 'I' in team (although there is a 'me'), but World Cups are often decided by the intervention of a genius. Just think about the contributions made by Garrincha (in 1962), Pelé (1970), Zizou (1998) or even Paolo Rossi (1982). And then consider the decisive intervention of Diego Maradona in 1986.

The abiding memories of that World Cup are two goals by Maradona: the brilliant, criminal improvisation of the Hand of God against England and the divine feet with which, four minutes later, he runs from his own half, leaving Peter Reid panting behind him, cuts inside Terry Butcher, touches the ball past Terry Fenwick in such a way that, as Rob Smyth noted, 'it takes Fenwick out of the game before he even knows he's in it', and slides the ball past Peter Shilton into the net.

For Maradona's team-mate Jorge Valdano, the goal symbolised El Diego's 'personal journey'. It looked like a once-in-a-lifetime goal but four days later, albeit from a more central position further up the field, he scored with a carbon copy run against Belgium in the semi-final. That slalom may have been inspired by the memory of Belgian keeper Jean-Marie Pfaff's pre-tournament verdict on the little No. 10. 'Maradona,' Pfaff had insisted, 'is nothing special.'

Apart from those three goals what did he do? Well, he scored five and was credited with five assists – one of them being the winner in the final. So he played a part in ten of the 14 goals Argentina scored in the finals. His other stats aren't bad either: he embarked on 90 dribbles (three times as

Diego Maradona skips past Terry Butcher and Peter Shilton points the way to eternal glory.

many as any of his team-mates), won 53 free-kicks (more than twice as many as any team-mate) and attempted or set up over half his side's shots. No wonder he won the Golden Ball with 1,281 votes, with Harald Schumacher, who had made such an indelible impression on Patrick Battiston in 1982, a distant second on 344. (A bizarre postscript to this vote: the trophy presented to Maradona was later stolen while on tour and melted down into gold bars on the orders of a mafia don.)

Argentina, mind you, were not a one-man team. Striker Valdano, midfielders Sergio Batista and Jorge Burruchaga, and defenders Daniel Passarella and Oscar Ruggeri were all considerable talents. Indeed, coach Oscar Bilardo's side were so efficient at the back that they only conceded five goals, keeping three clean sheets in seven games. Yet Bilardo, who changed his tactics to give Maradona a free-floating role as the second striker from the quarter-finals onwards, certainly did his utmost to build the team around a footballer who was easily the greatest player in the world at that time.

You can imagine Brazil still winning without Pelé in 1970 (as they had in 1962). It's harder to envisage France still triumphing in 1998 without Zizou. But it is impossible to conceive of Argentina winning in 1986 without the transcendental, game-changing genius that was Diego Armando Maradona in his prime. As an enraptured Clive Gammon wrote in *Sports Illustrated*: 'How many games can a single genius win on his own? As many as he needs to.'

Gaffers

🌑 **Who was the first coach to discover the importance of diet?**

In October 1996, Arsenal players staged the great Mars bar revolt. Travelling away to Blackburn for their first match under new coach Arsène Wenger, the players at the back of the bus began chanting: 'We want our Mars bars!' The aforementioned items of confectionery, hitherto a staple of the team's matchday diet, had been banned by their French coach on the grounds that: 'I find it stupid that a player can practice all week and spoil his game because he eats something silly 24 hours before.' Wenger didn't back down, telling his players: 'Food is like kerosene. If you put the wrong one in your car, it's not as quick as it should be.'

At the time, Wenger's views on diet – along with his insistence on improving the dressing rooms' feng shui and pre-match muscle-honing stretches – led a credulous British media to position him as the latest in a grand Gallic tradition of scientific pioneers that stretched back to Marie Curie and Louis Pasteur. Yet he was far from the first coach to realise that there was a connection between a footballer's diet and their performance.

The same thought had occurred to the Chilean World Cup squad in 1962. Food and drink formed a central part of their pre-match preparation, albeit not in a way Wenger would have understood. The hosts of the 1962 mundial ate cheese before their opening game against Switzerland (which they won 3-1), tucked into spaghetti on the eve of their clash with Italy (which they won, controversially, 2-0) and downed vodka before they overcame USSR 2-1 in the quarter-finals. Chile then succumbed to Brazil in the semi-finals possibly because their pre-match sampling of their opponents' cuisine was restricted to a few cups of coffee.

One of the USSR stars to miss out on a place in the 1962 World Cup was winger Valeriy Lobanovskiy. A supreme individualist as a player, Lobanovskiy became, as Dynamo Kiev coach, an influential advocate of a scientific, systematic approach to the game that regarded players as components, not people. As components, they had to be in perfect condition so he insisted his players follow a strict dietary regime.

Lobanovskiy's dietary regime was following in the footsteps of one of European football's greatest autocrats, Helenio Herrera. In the 1960s, the Argentine mastermind of the all-conquering *Nerazzurri* side known as Grande Inter had given players their own diet sheets and forbidden them from smoking or drinking 'super-alcolici' (a blend of whisky and grappa). To make it easier to enforce these rules, Herrera

No Mars bars for the boys. Britain's favourite nutty professor, Arsène Wenger, chews the cud with the then England manager, Sven Goran Eriksson.

insisted his players prepared for a game by getting together for a *ritiro* (retreat).

Yet decades before Herrera laid down the law, a revolutionary, detailed approach to diet and training helped Tom Watson win the English league at Sunderland (1892, 1893 and 1895) and Liverpool (1901). The players' day started at 7.30am with a stroll, breakfast at 8.30am ideally consisted of weak tea, chops, eggs, dry toast or stale bread. Training started at 9.45am and again at 3.30pm. A glass of beer or claret was recommended at dinner, during which tobacco could be 'sparingly used'. The players then rounded off the day at 7.30pm with an hour's stroll.

As unscientific as all this may sound, it certainly marks a step forward from the dietary regime Blackburn Olympic laid down for their players before the 1883 FA Cup final. As Hunter Davies recalls in *Boots, Balls And Haircuts*, 'Their diet consisted of a glass of port wine at six in the morning, followed by two raw eggs and walk along the sands. For breakfast they had porridge and haddock. Lunch was a leg of mutton. Tea was more porridge and a pint of milk. Supper was a dozen oysters each. It seemed to work. They beat the Old Etonians 2-1.'

In such a context, Watson's views were nothing less than revolutionary. Ninety years before Wenger famously complained that the British diet contained too much sugar and not enough vegetables, sugar was one of the ingredients – along with butter, milk and potatoes – that Watson urged his players to avoid.

⚽ Who was the **best-dressed coach?**

Clothes maketh the manager. They were certainly central to the aura that surrounded Mourinho when he arrived at Stamford Bridge in 2004, with his couture suits and shirts, top button undone and tie slightly askew. The Portuguese coach's Armani overcoat came to symbolise his distinctive style, inspiring a cult T-shirt (with the words 'Mourinho's coat' emblazoned across the top) and famously fetching around £22,000 at a charity auction.

On his return to the Premier League, Mourinho has dressed more soberly, almost as if he's signalling his desire to focus on the serious business at hand. His toughest competition in the best dressed stakes is probably his old protégé, André Villas-Boas, although the Spurs manager lost points on style when he was spotted wearing a thermal vest under his tasteful dark suit. Both fare better than Arsenal boss Arsène Wenger whose elongated parka has been likened to a Michelin Man and has inspired a Facebook page 'Buy Arsène Wenger a New Coat'.

Style had not previously been the buzzword among coaches in England's Premier League, who had, according to Sarah Lyall in the *New York Times*, traditionally gravitated towards three looks: Italian playboy, 1970s East German apparatchik, and slob in tracksuit. But it had not always been thus. In 1970, Vic Buckingham, the debonair, eccentric, much-travelled English coach, who had managed West Brom to victory in the 1954 FA Cup and given a promising 19-year-old called Johan Cruyff his Ajax debut, took over at Barcelona. As Jimmy Burns recounts in his book, *La Roja*: 'He liked to dress in tweed jackets and silk ties and, in the winter months, a beige button-down jersey.' His demeanour and his liking for cocktails, golf and horseracing led some Catalans to see him as a cross between a retired Army officer and Henry Higgins.

The Higgins look was Buckingham's more flamboyant, upwardly mobile take on a style that Barney Ronay identified in his book *The Absurd Ascent Of The Most Important Man In Football*, as 'the uniform of the universal dad', as exemplified by the Crombie overcoat, trilby and pipe worn by Sir Matt Busby, presenting United's legendary boss as, in Ronay's words 'a prosperous small-town sawmill and wood chippings magnate.' This approach began to look outmoded in the 1960s when Alf Ramsey won the World Cup wearing a tracksuit, although in the public eye he was synonymous with the brown raincoat he so often wore. After the social revolution that swept through Britain in the 1960s, many managers wore tracksuits because it gave the impression that they were hands-on types who were closer to their players. The change in fashion even swayed Busby who mused, when he retired in 1969, that it might be 'time for a younger tracksuited man to take over'. Yet other coaches stood out from the crowd: Malcolm Allison was flamboyant in a fedora, John Bond looked like a TV cop (albeit not a very exciting one) in his trench coat and, by the end of the 1970s, Ron Atkinson was styling himself as the Thatcherite king of bling.

In many countries, tracksuited coaches had already made their mark. When West Germany won the 1954 World Cup, their manager Sepp Herberger was wearing a trench coat to protect him from the rain but he wore a tracksuit under that and rounded off the ensemble with adidas sports shoes. This look would inspire generations of German coaches, most notably Otto Rehhagel who won Euro 2004 with Greece. Herberger felt so at ease in his tracksuit that, according to a 1996 biography of the great man, he was buried in it.

Yet today, the tracksuit has fallen out of fashion, possibly because its mystique was destroyed by the Graham Taylor documentary *Do I Not Like That*. When Owen Coyle wears one he looks like he's trying to kid his team, the fans and himself that if all else fails he can run on to the pitch and sort it out. Most managers in Europe prefer the gravitas of suits, especially if they don't have any gravitas of their own. Italian coaches like Luciano Spalletti have shown that a really good coat is almost as important as a coaching badge.

Yet enterprising coaches can still make a statement on the touchline. Hervé Renard, the Frenchman who won the 2012 African Cup of Nations with Zambia, usually patrols the touchline in straight-leg jeans and an untucked white shirt. Although he resembled a member of a 1990s boy band, his look was certainly more successful than the flowery shirts Dunga wore as Brazil coach, or Tony Pulis's disconcerting combo of tracksuit and baseball cap.

Joachim Löw and Hans-Dieter Flick in their matching cobalt blue cashmere jumpers at the 2010 World Cup. Probably not a look suited to Roy Hodgson.

The cobalt cashmere V-neck sweaters worn by Germany coach Joachim Löw and his assistant Hans-Dieter Flick during the 2010 World Cup struck such a chord back home that upscale clothier Strenesse sold out of them. Some desperate fans even drove to the Netherlands to snap up a Jogi sweater. These V-necks may be the most distinctive good luck charms worn in the dugout since Allison's fedora. Yet by Euro 2012, perhaps disappointed that the allegedly lucky blue V-necks had taken Germany only to third place in South Africa, Löw and Flick had settled for white shirts and grey suits.

🌑 Who led the most dysfunctional World Cup campaign ever?

There's major competition here but three ill-fated World Cup campaigns spring immediately to mind: Germany's in 1938, Scotland's in 1978 and France's in 2010. And, naturally, the blame for each would rest with their managers.

Austria and Germany had both qualified for the 1938 World Cup in France. Yet after the *Anschluss*, in which Nazi Germany annexed Adolf Hitler's homeland, it was decided that only one team would enter the finals. (Sweden benefitted from this decision with a late call-up.) Felix Linnemann, head of the German FA, explained the rationale to coach Sepp Herberger: 'In our sphere as well as in the others, a visible expression of our solidarity with the Austrians who have come back to the Reich has to be presented.' The Führer demanded a 6:5 or 5:6 ratio between German and Austrian players in the team.

This was easy to say, harder to do. For a start, how do you unite a squad of 22 players around a common cause, when nine of the players are from a country that has just been annexed/invaded by the country the other 13 are from? Especially when three of the nine Austrians in Germany's 1938 World Cup squad played for Austria Vienna, whose captain Karl Musch would have to emigrate because his wife was Jewish.

The players didn't just belong to different countries, they had graduated from different football schools. Still in thrall to the legend of their sublime, free-flowing Wunderteam, the Austrians were steeped in a Vienna coffee-house view of football which saw the game as a cerebral contest, in which players must out-think, out-pass, out-play the opposition. The Germans had their own great side to revere, known as the Breslau-Elf, an exhilarating amalgam of direct English play, Scottish passing

Swiss football's finest hour, as Hitler's Germany-Austria head home from the World Cup in 1938.

game and the Danubian style. Named after the city in which they beat Denmark 8-0 in May 1937, Herberger's scintillating side won ten out of eleven games in 1937.

Herberger knew that reconciling all these factors was going to be like squaring the circle, but he tried. He arranged a practice match to, as he noted, 'get the Austrians down from their heaven of supposed superiority'. The session degenerated into a keepy-uppy contest between Viennese star Josef Stroh and Schalke's Fritz Szepan that ended with the German midfielder volleying the ball against the wall just over the Austrian players' heads and whispering, 'You arseholes.'

Despite Herberger's entreaties, Austria's best player, Matthias Sindelar, opted out of the tournament, insisting he was unfit. So with 13 Germans, nine Austrians, and two keepy-uppy kings, Herberger set off for France. The campaign kicked off against Switzerland, a country which had come to fiercely dislike its growing Fascist neighbour. Though Germany took the lead through Josef Gauchel, Switzerland equalised and it became clear that, as journalist Christian Eichler put it, 'Germans and Austrians prefer to play against each other even when they're in the same team'. In the replay five days Germany went 2-0 up and were on track for victory until the Swiss grabbed three goals in the last 26 minutes to win 4-2. For the one and only time in the history of the World Cup, Germany were out in the first round.

Fast forward 40 years to 1978 and a Scotland team facing pressures created largely by their coach Ally MacLeod, who declared: 'You can mark down 25 June 1978 as the day Scottish football conquered the world. For on that Sunday, I'm convinced the finest team this country has ever produced can play in the final of the World Cup in Buenos Aires and win.' Asked what he planned to do after winning the World Cup, MacLeod said: 'Retain it.' Even for a coach who had begun his first press conference as Scotland coach with the words 'My name is Ally MacLeod and I am a winner', this was a bit much. However, 30,000 supporters paid to cheer off their departing heroes at Hampden Park, prompting Lou Macari to remark later: 'You don't normally have a victory parade before a ball is even kicked.'

The flames were soon dampened by Scotland's performances on the pitch. Footballers are a superstitious bunch, always looking out for omens, and the sight of two dead horses on the road to the team's training ground in Cordoba must have seemed inauspicious. They also realised, as soon as the aircraft doors opened in Buenos Aires, that Argentina was hot.

Still, against Peru they played well only to lose 3-1, undone primarily by the brilliance of Teófilo Cubillas. This might have seemed a useful reality check but worse was to follow. Winger Willie Johnston failed a drug test after taking Reactivan, a mild stimulant to combat hay fever, and was sent home. As social historian Dominic Sandbrook put it: 'Scotland's march of destiny was beginning to look more like a night at the circus.'

Against Iran, Scotland played like clowns, scraping a 1-1 draw after Iranian left-back Andranik Eskandarian sliced the ball into his own net. The Scotland team had to run a gauntlet of V-sign flicking, tam-o'shanter-wearing supporters as they left the pitch. In Dundee, a record shop cut the price of 'Ally's Tartan Army' singles to 1p, inviting customers to buy as many as they wanted and smash them to pieces with a hammer on the counter. Even the magnificent 3-2 win over the Netherlands – and a sublime slalom by Archie Gemmill to score the greatest goal of his career – couldn't redeem this campaign. In the *Observer*, Hugh McIlvanney, a proud but humiliated Scot, said that in the run-up to the finals MacLeod 'behaved with no more caution, subtlety or concern for planning than a man ready to lead a bayonet charge'.

When the players returned to Glasgow Airport, they were jeered by baggage handlers. Some say the sudden, stunning revelation of the nation's footballing inadequacy accounted for Scotland's failure to endorse devolution in the 1979 referendum. Be that as it may, the Scottish Football Blog probably summed it up best: 'Football was creating a global village. Scotland would provide the idiot.'

Yet the travails of Germany and Scotland pale into insignificance compared to the agonies of France's 2010 World Cup campaign during which – and these are just the edited highlights – Nicolas Anelka was sent home for using the half-time interval to tell beleaguered coach Raymond

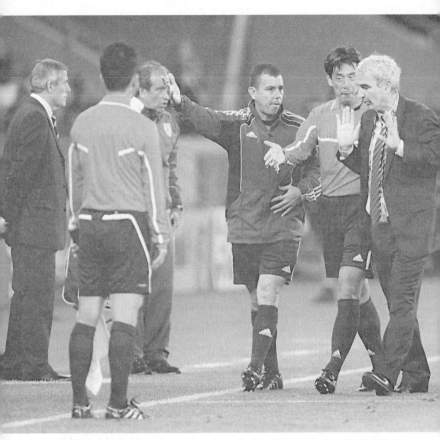

Raymond Domenech is escorted from the pitch by the fouth official and referee during the 2010 FIFA World Cup match with Uruguay.

Domenech to 'go and get yourself fucked up your arse, you and your tactics', the players went on strike for a training session in protest at his punishment, and Franck Ribéry had to appear on national television to deny, not terribly convincingly, that he had plotted against French playmaker Yoann Gourcuff.

The first World Cup strike was, as Philippe Auclair points out in his biography of Thierry Henry, 'nothing more than a symbolic downing of tools in a Sunday morning training session'. Still, as Auclair noted, there was a certain irony in the fact that the pitch in Knysna the players weren't training on – in front of a few hundred local children – was called the Field Of Dreams. On this evocatively named piece of turf, skipper Patrice Evra and fitness coach Robert Duverne almost came to blows. Duverne and goalkeeping coach Bruno Martin were, Auclair reports, 'later seen in tears, hidden behind a lorry, a few paces away from the bus where the mutineers had barricaded themselves (and on whose sides this slogan could be read: 'All together towards a new blue dream')'.

The results were almost as unedifying: les Bleus suffered their first-ever defeats to Mexico and South Africa (after the latter game, in which Gourcuff was sent off, Domenech mysteriously refused to shake hands with South Africa coach Carlos Alberto Parreira), won just one point, and scored only one goal as they finished bottom of Group A.

The only appropriate way to end such a campaign – which started with the symbolically prophetic image of William Gallas crashing his dune-buggy in pre-tournament training and ended with sports minister Roselyne Bachelot calling the team a 'moral disaster' – was for president Nicolas Sarkozy to hold an inquest at the Champs Élysées palace with Thierry Henry. By the time the dust had settled, Domenech had been replaced by Laurent Blanc, four players (Anelka, Ribéry, Evra and Jeremy Toulalan) were banned for varying numbers of matches, Henry had retired from international football and Jean-Pierre Escalettes had quit as president of the French FA.

Le Parisien caught France's national mood rather well by noting, 'To have the worst team at the World Cup was unbearable. To also have the most stupid is intolerable.'

⚽ Who was **England's first manager?**

Walter Winterbottom was the first man to be permanently given the title of England manager but he was also director of coaching at the FA and didn't usually do the one thing every modern manager insists on: picking the team. That job was given to a select committee of FA blazers and, as Barney Ronay notes in *The Manager*, in 139 matches in charge, the donnish Winterbottom had sole responsibility for picking the team just once: in October 1959, for a friendly against Sweden at Wembley. Given the historic nature of this selection, it's perhaps worth listing that XI: Eddie Hopkinson, Don Howe, Tony Allen, Ronnie Clayton (captain), Trevor Smith, Ron Flowers, John Connelly, Brian Clough (winning his second, and last, cap for England), Jimmy Greaves, Bobby Charlton and Edwin Holliday. Sweden won 3-2. True, the Swedes had reached the World Cup final in 1958, but giving Winterbottom sole charge had hardly proved an unqualified success.

The first full-time England boss to pick his own team was Sir Alf Ramsey. Yet he only secured that right after the committee's disastrous selection for his first match, against France in a freezing Paris in February 1963, led to a 5-2 defeat. Afterwards, Ramsey asked England captain Jimmy Armfield: 'Do we always play like that?' 'No,' said Armfield. 'That's the first good news I've had all evening,' replied Ramsey. By the time the 1966 World Cup started, Sir Alf was the undisputed master of team selection.

Yet neither Ramsey nor Winterbottom were the first managers of England. Ronay says the great Herbert Chapman became 'the first de facto England manager' in 1933. The Arsenal coach gave the pre-match tactical team talk, helped organise the side that drew 1-1 with Italy in Rome and lost the keys to the dressing room at half-time.

Herbert Chapman on a scouting trip to Vienna in 1932, in preparation for England international duties.

Vittorio Pozzo, Chapman's friend and rival, was surprised to see the Arsenal boss emerging from England's dressing room. When asked what he was doing in Rome, Chapman told Pozzo: 'I'm doing for my team what you are doing for yours'.' That wasn't quite true. Chapman was acting unofficially and didn't pick the team, although two Arsenal stars, Eddie Hapgood and Cliff Bastin, scorer of England's equaliser, did play. The match, the first between the *Azzurri* and the Three Lions, was played in front of 50,000 cheering fans. In the crowd was Benito Mussolini, who Hapgood hit in the midriff with a stray clearance. Il Duce dropped in to the England dressing room afterwards, Bastin recalling that the Italian dictator was so charismatic that he made Chapman seem like an 'utter nonentity'.

Writing in *The Sports Historian* in May 1996, Tony Say says that 'despite objections from selectors', Chapman 'acted as the unofficial manager to the England team' in Italy and against Switzerland in Berne when the manager's inspirational words 'helped effect a 4-0 victory over a strong Swiss team'.

Some historians have also credited Tom Whittaker, who trained the Arsenal first team under Chapman and later managed the club, as manager for six England matches, most notably in a 5-2 victory over Scotland in 1930. But the evidence that his influence extended beyond training is not compelling. So it seems most likely that Chapman was, as Ronay suggests, England's first gaffer.

⚽ Who has coached the most national teams?

Carlos Alberto Parreira and Bora Milutinović may jointly hold the record for coaching five teams in World Cup finals, but that isn't that impressive when you consider the career of a man who made the Guinness Book of World Records well over a decade ago, has published three autobiographies to date, and is known as the 'Hemingway of Football' for his countless tales of woe and wonder. Oh, and Rudi Gutendorf has coached 55 teams in 30 countries on five continents, among them 18 national teams. (That figure rises to 20 if you add the Olympic teams of Iran and China, which Gutendorf managed for the 1988 and 1992 Games, respectively.)

If he's so ubiquitous, how come you have never heard of him? Probably because he hasn't won very much. Gutendorf coached Duisburg to a sensational runners-up spot in the Bundesliga in 1964 (see 'Who invented Total Football?') and Schalke to the Cup Winners' Cup semi-finals in 1970.

But these are his only achievements in a major competition. He only actually won something in Switzerland (as player-manager of Lucerne in 1960) and Japan, where he coached Yomiuri Tokyo to the 1985 championship.

Gutendorf seldom plied his trade in the obvious places. He coached clubs in Tunisia, Tanzania, Peru and Mauritius. And if he took over a national team, it was usually a side like Fiji, Tonga, or Antigua. He came close to hitting the limelight in 1973, when his Chile side beat Peru and drew away to the USSR, qualifying for the World Cup because the Russians refused to play the second leg. But the coup d'etat that ultimately killed his friend Salvador Allende forced Gutendorf to leave Chile before the 1974 finals.

Rudi Gutendorf has another crack at glory, this time round with the Rwanda national team in 1999.

This stay in Chile is full of the kind of stories that punctuate Gutendorf's career. In his few months in the country, the then 46-year-old enjoyed an affair with a teenage Miss Chile and was shot at with a machine gun while steering his jeep through the countryside. Then he got into another affair, with a girl more than 20 years his junior. It is suspected that she was secretly working for the CIA. One night, Gutendorf and his lover were lying in bed, when a man opened the door and aimed a gun at the woman. The shot shattered Gutendorf's jawbone before hitting the woman's head, killing her instantly. He still has the scar to remind him.

Stories likes these abound in Gutendorf's autobiographies which read, at times, like magical realist novels. Yet don't be fooled: Gutendorf is no hopeless romantic – he's a fanatically determined coach. When he managed the Socceroos between 1979 and 1981, an Australian official instructed him, 'We want a coach, not a Führer.' The jibe didn't change Gutendorf's approach. As he told the *Sydney Morning Herald*, 'I can be a bastard on the field. I get too excited. I like to knife everyone when they do something I don't like. There is a saying in Germany: without sweat there is no reward.'

Who was the **scariest manager**?

'I ... Will ... Not ... Have ... A ... Coward ... In ... My ... Team.' That terrible chant was how Eddie Cramp remembered Stan Cullis, the former sergeant major who managed Wolves from 1948 to 1964, winning three league titles and two FA Cups. Some coaches are tactically innovative, others coax their teams into playing attractive football and a few enjoy record-breaking success. What set Cullis apart was that he, as Barney Ronay puts it in his book on managers, 'saw football as an absolute test of human endurance. Once one of his players,

THERE IS NO SUBSTITUTE FOR HARD WORK

Wolverhampton Wanderers manager Stan Cullis gives a team-talk in the dressing room. Not so much hard but fair as ... hard.

Ted Farmer, was brutally elbowed in the stomach. At half-time Farmer found he was passing blood. Cullis told the club doctor: 'Wait till it comes through his backside before you take him off.' Farmer was later diagnosed with a pierced bladder.'

To be fair to Cullis, he himself wouldn't have left the pitch with such an injury when he was a half-back. Badly concussed during the 1938–39 season, he played on, knowing that the next concussion might prove fatal, until 1947, retiring only when the doctors said just heading the ball would kill him. Installed as Wolves manager, he made his mark by introducing training sessions in which players endured commando-style assault courses and had to meet specific targets for running 100 yards, 220 yards, 440 yards, 880 yards, one mile, three miles and jump at least 4ft 9in into the air. War had taught him that, he said, 'proper training can cause the abnormal achievement to be the normal one'.

This military-style regimen was surprisingly popular in British football, reaching an absurd, but glorious, apotheosis in the 1970s when former Royal Marine Tony Toms organised training sessions when Jack Charlton was managing Sheffield Wednesday. In pre-season one summer, Toms took them to a commando base on the south coast where the players, in full military dress, were pushed into an S-bend pipe full of water before being hauled out at the other end by a team-mate. One player was heard calling for his mother. Wednesday's Yugoslav midfielder Ante Miročević looked at the pipe, asked 'Where's the ball?' and then ran off.

Yet even if you set Cullis in context, the Iron Manager still looks tougher than the rest. Other managers – notably Brian Clough's mentor Alan Brown – cheerfully perpetuated their tough guy image. ('You may have heard people say I'm a bastard,' Brown told Clough when they first met. 'Well, they're right.') Cullis instilled such terror that he had no need of such flourishes. When attacker Dennis Wilshaw was asked to explain why Wolves' team spirit remained so high, he replied: 'Because we all hated his [Cullis's] guts.'

Felix Magath must wish he had coached in Cullis's day. Nicknamed 'Quälix' (a play on his first name and *qual* or 'torture'), his remorseless efforts to instil the right kind of discipline at eight Bundesliga clubs have made him notorious. When he left Wolfsburg in October 2012, the first thing the gleeful players did was have a whipround to buy a CD player so they could play music in the dressing room again.

Magath's distinctive contribution to the coaching profession was probably his elaborate system of fines. Penalising players for being late for training is hardly unheard of but Magath's fines included €500 for letting the ball bounce in front of you and €1,000 for an unnecessary back pass. He famously fined Wolfsburg striker Patrick Helmes €10,000 for not working hard enough when the other side had possession. This unusual approach may explain why Jefferson Farfan, who played under Quälix at Schalke, said once: 'I would rather go back to Peru and break stones than play for him again.'

Yet Magath's method of instilling fear in his players often brought short-term results, which is why he was known as an unusually successful fireman, a coach brought in to ward off relegation.

Felix Magath looks set to dish out another fine at Wolfsburg.

Scots, of course, have a special place in management, most famously with Alex Ferguson's 'hairdryer' and the odd flying boot. One of his countrymen, Jimmy Sirrel, deserves a mention in dispatches, too. Between 1967 and 1982, the Scot managed Brentford, Notts County, Sheffield United and Notts County. At County, he developed the knack of identifying players' footsteps so he could tell which ones were sneaking into training late. He threatened to fine defender David McVay for growing a beard and once took on thousands of rampaging Manchester United supporters at Meadow Lane armed only with self-belief and a scalpel. Sirrel had his own way of solving such mysterious issues as loss of form. When County striker Trevor Christie stopped scoring, Sirrel walked up to Christie in the dressing room, punched him twice in the stomach and said, 'Big man, you're a fucking coward.' The striker scored twice that afternoon.

Such crude methods would have appalled Major Frank Buckley, the famous Wolves manager. When his striker Gordon Clayton hit a barren streak, Buckley sent him – at his wife's suggestion – to a psychologist. It worked: Clayton scored 14 goals in the next 15 matches.

Forever known as Major because he had commanded the Footballers' Battalion in World War I – he nearly died when shrapnel punctured his lungs – Buckley managed seven clubs between 1919 and 1955 but is best known for his 17-year stint at Wolves, where he revolutionised training and tactics, and enriched the club with his pioneering approach to the discovery, purchase and sale of football talent.

Buckley was a complex, often contradictory character who was willing to experiment with new tactics and even new drugs but treated his players as if they were soldiers in his private battalion. He didn't like them to marry as he feared it made them less focused. At Blackpool, he gave each player a little book outlining the behaviour he expected of them. After Wolves lost to Mansfield in the FA Cup, he humiliated his players by forcing them to walk through the city centre in their kit. His captain was, of course, Stan Cullis.

With a style of management that veered from benign dictatorship to malevolent dictatorship, Buckley was an obsessive, perfectionist, pseudo-scientific, micro-managing trailblazer, a precedent-setting genius whose distorted reflection can be seen in the careers of Sir Alex Ferguson, Arrigo Sacchi and José Mourinho.

In 1990 Sacchi's Milan became the last side to retain the European Cup. Though his training regime was as punishing as any devised by Buckley or Cullis, that wasn't why the *Rossoneri* were so frightened of him. As Carlo Ancelotti reveals in his memoirs, what really spooked them was the sight of Sacchi screaming and shouting in his sleep: 'He emitted terrifying sounds as if someone was cutting his throat. Every so often there would be a technical comment as well, even in his sleep. "Run diagonal!" or "Go back!" The man never stopped.'

⚽ Who had the **shortest managerial career?**

Leroy Rosenior is so undisputedly the record holder in this category that we have plenty of time for some honorary mentions first. No, not people like Brian Clough, whose 44 days at Leeds United was positively long-term compared to some other men who found out the hard way why they call football management the sack race.

Consider poor Alberto Malesani, who was fired by Genoa in April 2012 following a 4-1 defeat by Siena that so enraged the *tifosi* that they plastered the pitch with flares and bengal lights. When he was sacked, Malesani had been coaching the team for only 20 days. This isn't anywhere near the record but Malesani's case is worth a mention because he had already coached Genoa between June and December 2011, which means he was sacked twice in one season by the same club.

For truly short managerial reigns, you have to focus on those that didn't last even a day. Even the most ludicrously incompetent managers can't cobble together a string of poor results in just a few hours so there were all kinds of reasons for these dismissals or resignations. Pills were the undoing of Heinz Höher, a veteran German coach who had been out of a job for eight years when second-division Lübeck called him in October 1996, having fired their manager earlier that morning. Höher was so eager to revive his career, he drove to Lübeck, overseeing his first training session that very afternoon – until he suddenly lost consciousness. Officials presumed Höher had fainted but he later revealed that he had been taking medication against alcoholism and had swallowed too many pills before jumping into the car. With Höher in hospital, Lübeck began their search for a third manager that day.

In September 1998, Paul Breitner's son answered the phone, listened for a few moments and yelled: 'Dad, there's someone named Braun who wants to talk to you!' The caller was Egidius Braun, president of the German FA and he wanted to offer Breitner the post of national coach. Berti Vogts had just resigned and the mood surrounding the team was so bad that Braun felt he needed someone who would truly shake things up. Breitner's coaching experience began and ended with a local Under-10 side, but the 1974 World Cup winner had a reputation as a maverick genius. He considered the offer briefly, then said yes. A few hours later, Braun called again. 'Herr Breitner, I just want to make sure that you're not going to cop out,' he said. Breitner assured him he would stand by his word and went to bed as the new German national coach. The next morning, Braun called for the third time in 15 hours to inform Breitner that there was too much opposition within the German FA. 'I'm sorry, just forget it,' he concluded.

It took just five hours for Zbigniew Boniek to realise he was at the wrong place at the wrong time. Early in the 1991–92 season, he was asked by Pisa's long-serving president Romeo Anconetani to coach the Serie A club. On 18 September, a Wednesday, Boniek agreed to a contract and went for a celebratory dinner with Anconetani. It may have been the food, location or, as the Associated Press later reported, a disagreement over the make-up of Pisa's technical staff, but Boniek quit before the meal had finished.

However, even five hours seems like an eternity when you consider Leroy Rosenior's ten-minute tenure at Torquay. He was presented as the Gulls' new gaffer on 17 May 2007, during a press conference. While Rosenior was talking to the media, main shareholder Mike Bateson agreed to sell his stake in the club to a new consortium – and the new owners wanted a different manager. 'I did all the interviews,' Rosenior later explained. 'And within 10 minutes, Mike called me to let me know he had actually sold the club.'

This bizarre incident was widely reported, because it made Rosenior the new world-record holder. By then, he had become wearily accustomed to short periods at the helm. He had resigned as Shrewsbury Town's assistant manager after three months in 2006 and taken over at Brentford where he lasted only five months. On 7 May 2007, less than two weeks before his truncated reign at Torquay, he coached the Sierra Leone team (he had won one cap for the Leone Stars in 1994) against Leyton Orient in London, which means he was their national coach for one day.

⚽ Who was the **youngest manager** to win a league championship?

Trusting really young managers, with little or no previous experience in the dugout, is often imagined to be a modern phenomenon. In 2009, Josep Guardiola became, at 38, the youngest manager to win the UEFA Champions League and two years later, in 2011, the 33-year-old André Villas-Boas won the Portuguese league and then the UEFA Europa League with Porto, setting a record for both competitions. The bad news for AVB is that as much of a whippersnapper as he might seem, he is already too old to become the youngest manager to win the English title.

Tom Watson was only 33 when he won the old Division One with Sunderland in 1892. One of his secrets, contemporary accounts suggest, was his insistence that on really cold days his players should have whisky massaged into their chests and backs at half-time. By the time he turned 42, he had won the title twice more with Sunderland and once with Liverpool, establishing himself as the first great manager in the English game (an honour usually given to Herbert Chapman), before dying of pleurisy and pneumonia in 1915, at the age of 56.

Watson's success proves that club owners, presidents and directors have long been willing to hire coaches on the principle that 'if you're good enough you're old enough'. In 1956, the first European Cup was won by a legendary Real Madrid side coached by 36-year-old José Villalonga. The year before, at 35, Villalonga had won la Liga, a record that stood until 1983, when Athletic Bilbao won the Spanish title under Javier Clemente. Since the season ended on 1 May, eleven days before Clemente's birthday, he was still only 32 when he won the title. Youth in the dugout does not automatically translate to flamboyance on

José Villalonga enters Real Madrid legend, after his team came back from 2–0 down against Stade de Reims to win 3–2 and claim the European Cup in 1956.

the pitch, though. If you were a supporter, Bilbao's tackling was tenacious. Opponents, most notably Barcelona's coach Cesar Luis Menotti, found it crude. Clemente memorably dismissed Menotti as 'an ageing hippie'.

Thirty-two is very young for a championship-winning coach. In Germany, the record is held by Matthias Sammer, 34 when he won the Bundesliga with Dortmund in 2002. In Italy, Arpad Weisz was 34 when he won Serie A with Inter in 1930. In France, Albert Batteux lifted the 1953 championship with Stade de Reims, in a season that ended 39 days before Batteux turned 34.

It will take a real wunderkind to coach a championship-winning side at a younger age than Bob Houghton. He was born on 30 October 1947 – the importance of the date will become clear later – and started his playing career up front for Fulham. At only 23, he became player-manager of Hastings United, later taking the same role at Maidstone United and assisting Bobby Robson at Ipswich. In early 1974, he took over at Malmö and – as *The Guardian* said in 2006 – 'brought 4-4-2, pressing and revolutionary training techniques to the country'. The season, which follows the calendar year in Sweden, started on 13 April and ended on 27 October, three days before Houghton's birthday. Malmö finished the season top of the table, nine points ahead of AIK Solna, meaning Houghton was just 26 when he won his first league title as coach.

He won two more league titles with Malmö while he was still in his twenties. In 1979, at the age of 31, he stunned Europe by leading the Swedish side to the European Cup final. They lost 1-0 to Nottingham Forest, managed by 44-year-old Brian Clough. Houghton's coaching career has since taken him across the globe but whether he plied his trade in Bristol, India, Toronto or Uzbekistan, he has never won another league title.

Records

🌑 **Which side holds the record for away wins in a single season?**

In 2004–05, José Mourinho's Chelsea won 15 out of 19 games away from home, a Premier League record. Seven seasons later, Mourinho's Real Madrid won 16 out of 19 on the road to set a new La Liga record. Yet this record is held not by a team of galactical, multi-millionaires but by a young side scrambled together as the chaos of World War Two settled. In 1946–47, Doncaster Rovers' away record in Division Three (North) was Played 21, Won 18, Drew 1, Lost 2, Goals for/against 56/24.

That season, Rovers swept almost all before them. Home and away became almost an irrelevance – in those days of two points for a win they dropped only five on the road, compared to seven at their Belle Vue stadium. Donny scored 112 goals (a club record) and won 33 games (a club and Football League record). Clarrie Jordan, a 24-year-old striker who had shown promise up front for Upton Colliery during World War II, banged in 42 goals in one season (also a club record), registered three hat-tricks and scored for ten games in a row. That was as good as it got for Jordan who retired in 1954, after a career blighted by the wrong move (to Sheffield Wednesday) injuries and loss of form; he later ran a pub in Doncaster.

What was the greatest comeback?

'Greatest comeback' depends to a large degree on the definition of 'great'. Is it the occasion, the deficit, the circumstances, the time left on the clock, or a combination of all these and more? On several of these counts, it will remain hard to outdo Liverpool, who won the 2005 UEFA Champions League after trailing Milan 3-0 at half-time. At stake, after all, was the biggest trophy in club football and the opponents were Italians, not known for throwing away leads. Then again, does a comeback have to mean a big deficit? What of Manchester United's return from the dead in the 1999 final against Bayern Munich, turning 1-0 at 90 minutes into 2-1 at full time? Or, on a domestic stage, how about Manchester City's two injury-time goals against QPR, on the last day of the season in 2012, to snatch their first Premiership title in half a century?

Certainly, it's not all about numbers, and turning round a three-goal deficit is not exceptional. In recent years Sweden (against Germany) and Newcastle United (against Arsenal) have come back from 4-0 to snatch a point. On 18 September 1976 Bayern Munich proved you can not only come back from four goals down with 35 minutes to play, you can go

Liverpool players charge towards Jerzy Dudek, who has just saved Andriy Shevchenko's penalty, completing one of football's great comebacks.

on to win. Losing 4-0 at Bochum, Bayern contrived to win 6-5, with Uli Hoeness scoring his side's sixth. On 22 August 1998, Olympique de Marseille left it even later. At home to Montpellier, they went 4-0 down in 34 minutes. That scoreline stood until 61 minutes. Then Marseille scored five, including a last-minute penalty converted by Laurent Blanc, to win 5-4.

Naturally, you have to rate comebacks higher if they are pulled off against superior – or strong – opposition, or if the circumstances are against you. One of the most famous league games in Dutch history is the clash between Heerenveen and Ajax on 7 May 1950. In the 61st minute, a certain

Rinus Michels converted a penalty for Ajax to make it 5-1 for the visitors. Then Abe Lenstra, a Heerenveen legend, scored the home side's second goal and somehow the roof fell in on Ajax. Heerenveen won 6-5. Heerenveen and Lenstra specialised in that kind of comeback. In June 1947, they were 4-0 down against Masstricht's MVV after half an hour, but three minutes from time Lenstra scored the 7-6 winner – during the play-offs for the national title, no less.

In England, Charlton Athletic's comeback against Huddersfield Town on December 21 1957, in the old Second Division, is often regarded as the mother of all comebacks. In the days before substitutions, the Addicks lost their captain Derek Ufton after he dislocated his shoulder after 15 minutes and trailed 5-1 after 62 minutes. Then Johnny Summers made history by leading ten men to a stunning win. Adopting the simple credo 'We've got nothing to lose so every time I get a chance I'll have a crack,' Summers scored five that day (including a six-minute hat-trick) and set up two more for an amazing 7-6 win. His wife Betty said: 'What a weekend this has been and right on top of Christmas too.'

The Germans, too, do fine comebacks. In the 1985–86 Cup Winners' Cup quarter-finals, West Germany's Bayer Uerdingen needed to score five goals in a hurry to complete a miraculous comeback against a Dynamo Dresden side featuring Matthias Sammer, Ulf Kirsten and Torsten Gütschow. The East German side had won the first leg 2-0 and with 58 minutes of the return leg gone, led 3-1 on the night and 5-1 on aggregate. Under the away-goals rule, Uerdingen had to score five goals in 32 minutes. Inexplicably, they scored six. After the game, either out of fear or hope of a better life, Dresden winger Frank Lippmann snuck out of the team's hotel, defecting to the West.

Yet the heroics of Bayer and Charlton don't quite compare with the most amazing comeback, all things and even lower leagues considered, we have heard of. This veritable miracle took place on 10 November 2002 in Germany's multi-tiered sixth division, in Marienheide, thirty miles east of Cologne, where the local team took on Meckenheim. Marienheide scored twice in the first half and when Meckenheim's sweeper was sent off, the hosts increased their lead until it was 5-0 with only seven – yes, seven! – minutes left. (And, remember, against ten men.) But in the 83rd minute, Meckenheim scored a consolation goal. And another in the 86th minute. And another in the 88th. 'I have never seen anything like it,' Marienheide's director of football, Wolfgang Brunzel, who watched the drama with growing horror, said later. 'This was a harmless opponent! But our players must have paid more attention to the results coming in from the other grounds than to their own match.' With 60 seconds left, Meckenheim made it 5-4. And three minutes into stoppage time, they levelled the most unlikely of games at 5-5.

⚽ Who made the most **consecutive league appearances?**

Common sense says it has to be a goalie. Goalkeepers are not necessarily less injury-prone than outfield players, but since they don't have to be constantly in motion or don't need explosive acceleration over the first few yards, they can play even if they are carrying the kind of minor injuries that sideline team-mates. On top of that, goalkeepers are less likely to be benched and/or be suspended for accumulating bookings. And, before the rule about denying a player an obvious goalscoring opportunity was enforced, they had to work terribly hard to be sent off.

In France, the marathon man is keeper Fabien Cool, who made 306 consecutive appearances for Auxerre between 1998 and 2007. In Italy, it's the inevitable Dino Zoff, whose record tally stands at 332: 330 for Juventus between 1972 and 1983 and two at Napoli, for whom he played the final two games of 1971–72. In Argentina, Pedro Catalano stood between the sticks day in, day out, for Deportivo Español de Buenos Aires between June 1986 and November 1994 and beats Zoff by one game: 333.

Football writers and commentators use the adjective 'unbelievable' far too often, but it's appropriate here. Because unbelievably, the British record is held by the Tranmere Rovers centre-half Harold Bell, who played 401 league games in succession between 1946 and 1955. His record run was broken when he was dropped as an emergency centre-forward on 30 August 1955. Disappointed, because his run hadn't been ended by injury, the Bootle-born defender sat with his wife in the stands and watched Tranmere draw 1-1 with Gateshead.

Yet Cool, Zoff, Catalano and even Bell are all left in the shade by Bayern and West Germany keeper Sepp Maier. He was in Bayern's goal on 20 August 1966, the first match of the 1966–67 season, and he was still in goal on the final day of the season 13 years later, 9 June 1979. He thus made 442 consecutive Bundesliga appearances. That run wasn't interrupted for any of the usual reasons – injury, loss in form, suspension, a coach who didn't like him – but by a dreadful car accident that ended Maier's career. In July 1979, the keeper crashed into a stationary car in the fast lane, sustained internal injuries and hung up his gloves.

Maier had already been involved in a car crash in 1975, when he wrote off his Ferrari. But he was back in Bayern's goal for the next game. Of course he needed luck. During those 13 years, he couldn't go the distance in four matches and had to be substituted. In one of those instances, pitch invaders in Duisburg knocked him down. Yet in all four cases he was back in goal when Bayern played their next league match.

A very young Sepp Maier at the 1966 World Cup, with Franz Beckenbauer (flanked by Bernd Patzke and Friedl Lutz).

Asked to explain his extraordinary resilience, Maier said: 'I didn't miss a league game for ten years. Of course, I was lucky I didn't sustain any serious injuries, but it's also true that we weren't squeamish. What used to be a bruise is now a terrible haematoma. Back then, they gave you some cortisone and the pain was gone. In 1975, I drove my car into a ditch but I didn't see a doctor, I went to the club's Christmas party and played the next game.'

Which side were the **most convincing league champions?**

The best indicator of a team's superiority is not necessarily their points total or their win percentage. In some leagues, two teams are so much better than the rest that they rack up record numbers in these departments but still have a fairly close rival (Celtic and Rangers in the Scottish Premier League, Real Madrid and Barcelona in la Liga come to mind). Rather, the best way to gauge dominance is the lead a team held over second place at the end of a season. The English record stands at 18 points, set by Manchester United in 2000. Seven years later, Lyon established the French record, winning Ligue 1 by 17 points over Marseille. In Germany, Bayern won by a whopping 25-point margin in 2013 that didn't just better but pulverise the old record (which had stood at 16).

The fact that these records are all relatively recent suggests that the gap between the haves and have-nots is widening. Yet some national records come from previous eras. The Spanish record stands at 21 points and dates from 1963, when Real Madrid won the title by 12 points under the old two-points-for-a-win rule. However, using the modern three-point

Manchester United celebrate their runaway Premier League title in May 2000, having lost just three games and won twenty-eight.

system, Real's lead balloons to 21 points, because second-placed Atlético had three times as many draws.

The Italian contender also seems relatively recent. In 2007, Inter won Serie A with 97 points and led the second-placed team, Roma, by no less than 22 points. Yet it's not really a domestic record. Il Grande Torino, the magnificent Torino side that tragically perished in the Superga air disaster in 1949 were 16 points ahead of Milan when they won Serie A in 1947–48. Under today's rules, they would have won by 24 points. They also scored 125 goals, won 19 out of 20 home games and had a goal difference of +92.

Even in smaller leagues dominated by one team, it is hard to better a 24-point (Torino) or 25-point (Bayern) lead. When Rosenborg monopolised the Norwegian title in the 1990s, they never won by more than 15 points. FBK Kaunas, who all but owned the Lithuanian title for a while, only won by 21 points in 2006. In Croatia, Dinamo Zagreb won by 21 points in 2011–12, some feat given that they played only 30 games, six less than Kaunas and ten less than Il Grande Torino.

In 2011, HJK Helsinki equalled Torino's lead, winning the Veikkausliiga, Finland's top flight, 24 points ahead of Inter Turku. HJK contrived to lose four games, in a 33-match season, yet still amassed this huge lead. This puts HJK on a par, statistically speaking, with Il Grande Torino and only one point behind Bayern's all-conquering 2013 team. However, one of the world's most famous clubs can do better than all of the sides mentioned above. And easily so.

In 1972–73, Benfica won the Portuguese league 18 points ahead of Belenenses, but under the three-points-for-a-win rule, that margin would stretch to 32 points. Not bad for a season that only lasted 30 matches. Benfica won every home match, 13 away games – and drew the other two. The Eagles won their first 23 matches of the season and didn't drop a point until All Fools' Day 1973, when they were held 2-2 away at Porto, after leading 2-1 with four minutes to go. During this beautiful season, Benfica averaged 3.67 goals a game and, at the age of 31, the great Eusébio scored 40 goals to win the Golden Boot.

Yet such worthy champions were dethroned the very next season. Sporting Lisbon won the 1973–74 title, two points ahead of Benfica. The sudden fall from grace may have been sparked by a silly controversy. Jimmy Hagan, a former Sheffield United forward, coached Benfica. He was, Eusébio said, 'a strong disciplinarian … some players were physically sick after his first training session.' A few weeks into the new season, Hagan quit after a row about the selection of players for Eusébio's testimonial between Benfica and a World XI.

If Benfica in 1972–73 were the most convincing champions, AIK must surely be the least convincing. In 1998, they won the Swedish league despite scoring just 25 goals in 26 games. Even Östers, who came last, 14th, and were relegated, managed 26. The title came down to the last day of the season. Leaders Helsingborg only had to beat relegation candidates Häcken but lost, whereas AIK won 1-0 with a goal by right-back Alexander Östlund to secure their first title in 15 years. Of the club's 26 matches, ten ended 1-1, six were 1-0 victories and three were 0-0 draws. Only twice did AIK get carried away and win 2-0.

⚽ Which is the best **defensive performance** in a major league?

José Mourinho's uber-efficient Chelsea shipped just 15 goals in 38 matches as they won the Premier League in 2004–05. That works out at 0.395 goals a game. Which is pretty damn good – but it's not even the best in England. In 1978–79, Liverpool won the league with a rock solid defence that shipped 16 goals in 42 games, an average of 0.381. On this occasion, the Reds come second best. If you consider only the five biggest leagues in Europe (England, France, Germany, Italy and Spain) since 1945, Cagliari were even tighter at the back when they won Serie A in 1969–70, conceding a frankly astonishing 11 goals in 30 games, 0.367 a match. They kept 20 clean sheets and only one side, Juventus, managed to score two goals against them – though the Sardinians held on for a 2-2 draw.

Enrico Albertosi – the big man at the back for Cagliari, in a later incarnation at Inter Milan.

The irony is that, even in Sardinia, this Cagliari side is best remembered for the goalscoring prowess of Luigi Riva who was Serie A's most prolific striker that season with 21 goals in 28 appearances. In the celebrations that followed the *scudetto*, several non-Cagliari fans had been forced, at gunpoint, to wear Riva shirts. Yet the title would not have been won without the agility of goalkeeper Enrico Albertosi, who kept goal for Italy in the 1966 and 1970 World Cups. 'When I first heard of Cagliari's interest, I didn't want to go because in Florence we'd always joked that Sardinia was a penal colony,' the keeper said once. And more philsophically: 'God forbid that a goalkeeper gets devoured by doubt. A goalkeeper is never wrong, the blame is always of others.'

Oddly enough, if you widen the search a bit, you discover that, in that very season, Fenerbahçe were even more efficient than Cagliari, conceding just six goals in 30 games, 0.20 a match. That came in very handy because it meant the Istanbul side could still win their sixth league title by a seven-point margin even though their attack had scored a distinctly meagre 31 goals, a club record low.

⚽ What was the most entertaining league season ever?

There are many subjective ways of deciding how thrilling a particular season is but there are quantifiable grounds for selecting 1950 in Colombia. As David Goldblatt notes in his extraordinary book, *The Ball Is Round*, 'The League was so open and attacking that there were only six goalless draws in a whole year.' Those six came in 240 games, which included a 6-6 draw between Huracán and America de Cali, while the erstwhile Once Deportivo twice drew 5-5 (against Universidas and away at Pereira). The goals-per-game figure that season was a phenomenal 4.19.

That might have been higher if the runners-up, Millonarios, had been more ruthless. Their great player Alfredo di Stéfano, who scored 90 goals in 101 games for the club, said: 'We only scored five goals per game so as not to demoralise our opponents.' When the result was no longer in doubt, the team would switch to a passing game that became known as *Ballet Azul* (the ballet in blue – the colour of Millonarios's strip). So a team graced by the talents of Di Stéfano and his idol Adolfo Pedernera scored only 68 goals in 30 games, while Deportes Caldas, the champions, scored 91.

Credit where credit's due, this extraordinary season would never have happened without FIFA. The stampede to professionalise the Colombian game (fuelled by booming revenues from the country's staple export, coffee) meant that not all the niceties had been observed. When the amateur FA, Adefutbol, complained to FIFA, the rulers of the game decided to ban Colombian clubs and the Colombian national team. In so doing, FIFA effectively freed them from having to comply with their transfer regulations. With many Argentinian players incensed by the strikes that were paralysing football in their country, clubs like Millonarios stepped in, offering lavish salaries because there was no transfer fee to pay. When Pedernera, the heart of the legendary River Plate attack known as *La Máquina* (Machine), joined Millonarios, the revenue earned by selling tickets to his unveiling, attended by 5,000 people, was five times the typical gate receipts for a match.

Millonarios's rivals soon followed suit. By the time the 1950 season kicked off, there were 109 foreign players in Colombia (57 of them Argentinian). Among other notables were Charlie Mitten (signed from Matt Busby's Manchester United), Héctor Rial (later to win the European Cup at Real Madrid, alongside Di Stéfano), Julio Cozzi (known in Argentina as 'Goalkeeper of the Century') and Neil Franklin (the brilliant English centre-half who missed the World Cup to play for Independiente Santa Fe). This colourful cast was rounded out by such stars as Heleno de Freitas, considered Brazilian football's first '*craque problem*' (troubled genius), a gifted striker, ether addict and an inveterate womaniser whose conquests off the pitch were said to include Eva Perón.

The game was so wealthy that Deportivo Cali's Peruvian centre-forward Valeriano López used to roll up dollar bills to make his cigarettes. Legend has it that López, who scored 43 goals in 39 games for Cali, was the player Real Madrid owner

Football's first bad boy galactico, Heleno de Freitas.

Santiago Bernabéu originally travelled to Colombia to sign. When López refused, saying he didn't want to play so far away from his family, Bernabéu cast his eye over Di Stéfano.

As if the 1950 season hadn't been wild enough, the teams set a record on the very first weekend of the following campaign: on 28 and 29 July 1951, they scored 61 goals in nine games. No wonder that this era in Colombian football, which ended in 1955 when the league returned into FIFA's fold, was nicknamed El Dorado.

The only season that comes close to such thrills is 1938 in Argentina, the first professional league season in which the goals per game ratio was an astonishing 4.9. The edited highlights of this season include Racing becoming probably the only club to score 24 goals over three consecutive matches (beating Platense and Estudiantes 8-2 and Lanús 8-1), Independiente clinching the title with an 8-2 victory on the last day against Lanús, three 5-5 draws (compared to only four 0-0 draws), and Arsenio Erico, an Independiente striker idolised by a young River Plate fan called Alfredo di Stéfano, scoring 43 goals, at a rate of 1.34 a game. He could have scored more but with two games to go, he tried to set up his team-mates Antonio Sastre and Vicente de la Mata so they could score 43 goals and win a 2,000 peso reward from the cigarette company 43/70.

Erico had a wealth of nicknames – *Mister Gol*, *El Malabrista* (The Juggler), *El Hombre de Goma* (Man of Rubber), *El Diablo Sakltarín* (Jumping Devil) and *El Hombre de Mimbre* (the Wicker Man, because he scared defences and wore red) – and would be much better known if he had played for a national side. He was too loyal to his Paraguayan homeland to accept a lucrative offer to acquire Argentinian citizenship. Di Stéfano said once that Erico was better than Pelé.

⚽ Which was the first team to win an FA Cup without English players?

Cardiff City may be the only team from outside England to win the FA Cup but their giant-killing 1-0 victory over Arsenal in 1927 was achieved with the help of gifted, English left-half Billy Hardy who was born in Bedlington, in Tyne and Wear. Known as the idol of South Wales – one report says that his mere appearance on newsreel provoked ten minutes of applause in one Cardiff cinema – Hardy was ignored by the England selectors because he played for a Welsh club.

There were three Welshmen in that Bluebirds side: skipper Fred Keenor, outside-left Ernie Curtis and forward Len Davies. In 1986, there was only one Welsh player – Ian Rush – in the Liverpool side that won what is known as the Merseyside final. Alongside Rush were four Scots (Steve Nicol, Alan Hansen, Kenny Dalglish and Kevin MacDonald), three Irishmen (Mark Lawrenson, Jim Beglin and Ronnie Whelan), one Aussie (Craig Johnston), a Dane (Jan Mølby) and a Zimbabwean (Bruce Grobbelaar). The only English player to have a small role in Liverpool's triumph was Steve McMahon who watched from the bench.

To round off this answer, it seems only appropriate to list the last all-English team to win the FA Cup: Mervyn Day, John McDowell, Frank Lampard Snr, Billy Bonds, Tommy Taylor, Kevin Lock, Billy Jennings, Graham Paddon, Alan Taylor, Trevor Brooking and Pat Holland. Under West Ham United manager John Lyall, this eleven won the 'Cockney Cup Final' of 1975, beating Fulham 2-0. The Cottagers played with ten Englishmen, including Hammers legend Bobby Moore. The only non-Englishman on the pitch that day was Fulham's Irish midfielder Jimmy Conway.

⚽ Who scored the **fastest ever goal?**

Brian Clough was being a bit over-optimistic when he said, 'It only takes a second to score a goal'. But in October 2011, 35-year-old Russian midfielder Mikhail Osinov found the net for MITOS Novocherkassk after just 2.68 seconds in a Russian Second Division South match. After his team-mates had kicked off and rolled the ball back, Osinov stepped forward, chipped the Olimpia Gelendzhik keeper from 51 yards and scored what could be the world's fastest ever goal.

Nawaf Al-Abed would dispute that. In November 2009, the Saudi striker scored after just two seconds – with an improbable shot from the halfway line that caught the keeper out of position – for Al Hilal against Al Shoalah in a Prince Faisal bin Fahad Cup match. Unfortunately for Al-Abed, this was an Under-23 tournament and the game was ruled invalid after some killjoy spotted that Al Hilal used six over-age players in the second half.

So Osinov is still, for now, the fastest scorer in the professional game. But fans of the Isle of Wight's Cowes Sports FC will tell you that their striker Marc Burrows was even quicker off the mark. In 2004, assisted by a strong wind, Burrows scored for Cowes Reserves after 2.5 seconds against Eastleigh Reserves. He was modest enough to admit: 'I've tried something similar once or twice but the ball normally goes out for a throw in making me feel a right prat.' The FA declared: 'This is the fastest goal we are aware of' which seemed to implicitly acknowledge that at this level of the game, it's possible that many such goals are scored and simply not timed.

One of the difficulties in making a definitive call is that, as Ray Spiller of the Association of Football Statisticians has pointed out, there is no system for officially recognising the timing of goals. So, for example, when Jim Fryatt scored for Bradford Park Avenue against Tranmere in 1964, referee Bob Simons still had his stopwatch in hand after blowing the whistle and timed the strike at four seconds. There is no film evidence to contradict him. The fastest goal in a national competition is probably Colin Cowperthwaite's strike after 3.56 seconds for Barrow against Kettering Town in the Alliance Premier League on 8 December 1979.

Torquay United defender Pat Kruse has the unfortunate distinction of scoring the fastest own goal in British history, heading past his own keeper after six seconds against Cambridge United in January 1977. The good news for Kruse is that his world record was broken in September 2009 when Estonian defender Jaanis Kriska took just five seconds to head into his own net in a game his side, Kuressaare, lost 8-0 to Levadia Tallinn.

The record for the fastest hat-trick belongs to Ross County striker Tommy Ross who scored three in 90 seconds against Nairn County on 28 November 1964. Because there were no timekeepers at the match, his feat was not recognised by the *Guinness Book Of Records* until 2004, after the referee had confirmed the feat. Asked how he scored so many goals in such rapid succession, Ross said: 'In those days there was no kissing and cuddling when you scored a goal. You just ran back to the halfway line and got on with the game. If you were lucky, you got a pat on the head from the captain.'

⚽ When did teams first agree to fix a match?

West Germany's 1-0 victory over Austria in Spain in the 1982 World Cup is the most infamous example of this nefarious practice. With the other teams in Group 2, Algeria and Chile, playing their last match the day before, Germany and

Austria knew this result would take them both through to the second round. Algeria, who had four points, were denied the chance to make history as the first African nation to quality for the second stage of a World Cup.

There is no credible evidence of a pre-match conspiracy to fix the result so this was, if you will, a spontaneous fix. After ten minutes, Horst Hrubesch scored for West Germany. Three minutes later, Wolfgang Dremmler went clear through and was one-on-one with the keeper. If he had made it 2-0, Austria would have been forced to attack. After that, both sides saw little point in taking the risk of going forward, so there were no crosses or shots on goal. Algerian supporters in the crowd started waving banknotes at the players in outrage. As play wore on – and the denouement became painfully obvious – German commentator Eberhard Stanjek was almost sobbing as he complained: 'What is happening here is disgraceful and has nothing to do with football.' FIFA let the result stand – but changed the rules so that the last round of games in a group would always be played at the same time.

The German and Austrian teams and associations initially seemed baffled by the outrage. Hans Tschak, the head of the Austrian delegation, said: 'Naturally today's game was played tactically. But if 10,000 "Sons of the Desert" here in the stadium want to trigger a scandal because of this it just goes to show that they have too few schools. Some sheikh comes out of an oasis, is allowed to get a sniff of World Cup air after 300 years and thinks he's entitled to open his gob.'

The outrage, from everyone else, was so universal, it is easy to assume that such an arrangement was unprecedented. Yet, as Joe McGinniss has suggested in his delightful book *The Miracle Of Castel Di Sangro*, such arrangements were not uncommon in Italian football. In 1979, in the last round of Serie A matches, relegation-threatened Avellino were losing 3-0 away to third-

Softly, softly. The West Germans match the Austrians in the World Cup's disgraceful 1982 'phoney war'.

placed Juventus. Then the *Bianconeri*'s talismanic keeper Dino Zoff was replaced, with 20 minutes to go, by an unknown youngster called Giancarlo Andresselli. Avellino scored three goals to make it 3-3 and earn the draw that left them in 10th place with 26 points, two points above the relegation zone.

Six years earlier, in 1973, concern about an outbreak of dubious draws in the USSR's First Division prompted the Soviets to introduce a novelty we associate with the capitalist North American leagues: penalty shoot-outs to decide drawn games. (The team that won the shoot-out were given the point for the draw, the loser got nothing: Kairat Alma-Ata set some kind of record by drawing 11 games and winning ten of those shoot-outs.)

Non-aggression pacts, of the Germany–Austria variety, are probably as old as the game itself. When the English Football

League started, relegation and promotion was initially decided by an end of season mini-league between the two bottom teams in the First Division and the two top teams in the Second Division. In April 1898, the four teams involved in what were then called test matches were Blackburn Rovers, Burnley, Newcastle United and Stoke City. Before Burnley and Stoke kicked off their final game they knew – just as precisely as the teams in Gijón – which scoreline would suit them both. A draw would ensure Burnley and Stoke were in the top division. Neither team took any chances – or made any – in a draw that went down in history as the match without a shot. The 4,000 supporters at Stoke's Victoria Ground were so disgusted they tried to stop the game by keeping the ball whenever it strayed into the stands and even kicked one ball into the river Trent. The appalled Football League extended the First Division to 18 teams to include Newcastle and Blackburn.

In goal for Burnley, with nothing to do in that farcical fixture, was the controversial figure of 'Happy Jack' Hillman, one of the most likely instigators of the non-aggression pact with Stoke. Good enough to win a cap for England, Hillman had returned to the Clarets after being fined by Dundee for 'not trying' during matches. Ten months after the deadlock at Stoke, justice was done. Burnley were relegated after losing their last game 4-0 to Nottingham Forest, whose skipper Archie Macpherson claimed Hillman had offered his players £2 a head (£150 in today's money) to 'take it easy'. The 27-year-old keeper insisted he was only joking but the FA banned him for 12 months. The English game's first match-fixer, Hillman never played for his country again.

⚽ Which team has won the most games on the trot?

In 2010–11, Pep Guardiola's all-conquering Barcelona won 16 games in a row in la Liga, a record in Spain but not in Europe, as Benfica supporters were quick to point out: the Eagles had racked up 29 successive victories between 1971 and 1973. But Al-Faisaly, serial winners from Amman, can top that. Jordan's greatest club side won 32 matches on the trot between August 2001 and March 2003 as they monopolised the Jordanian title.

As a point of comparison, the longest winning streak in English league football is 14, a record shared by Arsenal (spanning the end of 2001–02 and the start of 2002–03 in the Premier League), Bristol City (Division Two, 1905–06), Manchester United (Division Two, 1904–05), and Preston North End (Division Two, 1950–51). Martin O'Neill's Celtic, who won 25 in a row in 2003–04, hold the British club record.

The impressive runs by Al-Faisaly, Arsenal, Barcelona, Benfica and Celtic are not record-breaking. Not by a long way. Between 1919 and 1924, Sparta Prague won an astonishing 54 games in a row in the Czechoslovakian League (including three wins in an end of season mini-tournament in 1919 and one victory in a national play-off in 1922). In 1923, the most lustrous season in this golden era, Sparta scored 94 goals as they won all 15 matches to clinch their fifth title in a row.

No one has yet been proven to have beaten Sparta's record. Their tally may be even greater than 54: it is not clear, given the sketchy state of Czech football statistics from this era, at exactly what point during the 1924 season Iron Sparta astounded themselves, their supporters and their rivals by drawing or losing a game.

The Iron Sparta team of 1922, with Scottish coach John Dick in his tweed suit. Alas, the keeper here is not the comedian Vlasta Burian.

This invincible outfit were inevitably known as Iron Sparta. The photograph of the 1922 team on the club website describes the team as 'almost unbeatable' and shows the team's Scottish manager, a former Arsenal centre-half called John Dick, in suit, hat and tie giving the photographer his best 'can we get this over with?' stare. Iron Sparta's relentless efficiency was especially impressive given that their goalkeeper Vlasta Burian was hardly the embodiment of single-minded professional focus. A cabaret artist, comedian and manic depressive, Burian starred in his first movie in 1923, becoming so successful he was dubbed the king of Czech comedy, had a rose named after him and considered running for president.

Which team has endured the worst goalscoring drought?

'**I would wait 500 minutes** and I would wait 500 more, just to be the man who waits a thousand minutes to see our wee country score.' The modified Proclaimers anthem, *500 Miles*, was a constant solace to Northern Ireland fans who watched their team play a record 1,298 minutes – that's thirteen-and-a-half games over a period of two years and five days – without finding the back of the net once.

The drought began after David Healy scored the only goal for Northern Ireland against Malta in a World Cup qualifier on 6 October 2001. The barren streak cost manager Sammy McIlroy his job before it was ended – by Healy – in the 56th minute of a 4-1 defeat at Windsor Park against Norway on 18 February 2004. Healy, Northern Ireland's all-time top scorer, said afterwards: 'It was good to get that monkey off our back.'

Such suffering would not impress Stirling Albion fans who, in 1981, watched their beloved Binos get relegated from the Scottish First Division after scoring their last goal of the season in a 1-0 win against Dunfermline on 31 January. Not even extra penalty-taking sessions could end this dismal run. The most remarkable aspect of this debacle is that manager Alex Smith, who had won the Division Two title with the club in 1977, kept his job.

Albion finally broke their duck after 14 matches and 1,292 minutes on 8 August 1981 in a 4-1 loss to Falkirk, though the turnaround in the club's fortunes was far from instant: in October 1981, the Binos' away support had fallen to six. But on 8 December 1984, Stirling recorded the biggest win in the senior game in Britain in the twentieth century, beating Selkirk 20-0 in the Scottish Cup. Smith was still in the dugout then and admitted later: 'I must have lost count, I thought it was 19-0.' He may just have been flabbergasted that Albion could score 20 in one match when they had managed only 18 in their entire First Division season in 1980–81.

⚽ Which player has had the **longest goalscoring streak?**

If we're talking sheer quantities of goals, Middlesbrough centre-forward George Camsell's streak takes some beating. Between 16 October 1926 and 1 January 1927, 'the pitman turned poacher supreme', in the words of the *Middlesbrough Evening Gazette*, was never off the scoresheet, scoring 29 goals in 12 games. In that astonishing run, he scored all five goals

SUN SOCCERCARD No 223

G. CAMSELL (England)

as Boro beat Manchester City 5-3 away from home on Christmas Day, four against Portsmouth, Fulham and Swansea City, and a hat-trick against Port Vale. He finally failed to get his name on the scoresheet in a 0-0 draw against Chelsea on 15 January.

To be fair to Camsell, it is worth pointing out that his run really extended to 13 games in a row because he scored in a 5-3 win against Leicester City in the FA Cup on 8 January but the inclusion of a domestic cup match, football statistics from across the globe being as inconsistent as they are, would make it virtually impossible to compare like with like. That season, Camsell set a Football League record with 59 goals in a season, a feat that would be better remembered today if a young hotshot called Dixie Dean hadn't scored 60 for Everton the very next season.

Camsell is doubly unlucky because, in the very season he was scoring for fun – for once, the cliché seems appropriate – Wolves forward Tom Phillipson scored 22 goals in a 13-game scoring streak. (This is still a Football League record.)

You may wonder why so many scorers were in such prolific form in this era. Apart from the considerable talents of the strikers concerned, there was the small matter of the new offside law. From 1925, there only needed to be two players between the attacker and the goal when the ball was played. The statistics show just how demoralising this change was for defenders. In 1924–25, 4,700 goals were scored in 1,848 Football League matches. In 1925–26, that figure was 6,373.

Still, some strikers have kept their goalscoring runs going without a change in the law. Phillipson's record is equalled by Peter Dubovsky's 13-match run for his home town side Slovak Bratislava in 1991–92. (Mind you, eight of his 18 goals in that streak were penalties.) The club won the title and Dubovsky joined Real Madrid where he lost the battle for a first-team place with a young Raúl. Still revered as a genius in Slovakia, Dubosvky rebuilt his career at Oviedo but in June 2000, he fell to his death taking pictures of a waterfall in the Thai resort of Ko Samui. He was just 28.

Three players are on record as having a 15-game scoring streak: Tor Henning Hamre (Flora Tallinn, 2003, 21 goals including four penalties); Jaime Riveros (Santiago Wanderers, 2004, 21 goals, including seven penalties) and Juan Pedro Young (Penarol, 1933, 22 goals, no penalties). Pelé has claimed to have been on the scoresheet in 14 or 16 games in a row for Santos, but the precise details are hard to pin down.

Two players who are recorded to have scored in 16 league games are Teodor Peterek and the inevitable Gerd Müller.

Peterek scored 22 goals (including five penalties) in 16 matches for Ruch Chorzow in 1937 and 1938 (his run spanned two seasons). Alongside Gerard Wodarz and Ernst Willimowski, Peterek formed one of the greatest attacking tridents the Polish game has ever seen. They were at their peak when World War II effectively ended their careers. After playing for Bismarckhütter SV, the Nazified version of Ruch Chorzow, Peterek was conscripted into the Wehrmacht, escaping to join the Allies. After the war, he returned to Chorzow and played a few games for his old club. But he was 39 by then and soon hung up his boots for good.

Müller's streak dates from 1969–70. Stattos sometimes overlook it, because inclement weather played havoc with a few matchdays and there were Bayern games that had to be postponed by almost three months, a fact that only shows up in record books which ignore the sequence of the matchdays but list the games chronologically. The run started on 27 September 1969 with a goal against Braunschweig (Brunswick) and ended on 3 March

1970 with a goal against Frankfurt. In those 16 games, Müller scored 23 goals. Two of them came from the penalty spot, something we only bring up because it allows us to mention that Müller holds the Bundesliga record for penalties missed. (He took 63 and missed 12.)

Müller's streak ended on 7 March in the Munich derby and on a tricky, snowy surface. The Bomber had only two chances to score and wasted both. For the remainder of the game, the Yugoslav Željko Perušić marked him closely.

So, 16 was the record – set 75 years ago, tied 43 years ago but broken, just last season, by Lionel Messi . On 11 November 2012, matchday 11 in the Primera División season, he scored twice against Mallorca. He also did this, scoring a brace, on the next five – yes, five – matchdays. He lost momentum and scored only one goal per match in four games on the trot. Then he closed in on Camsell's territory, finding the net four times against Osasuna. And on and on it went. Until 9 March 2013. Messi had therefore scored in 16 consecutive league games, tying with Peterek and Müller (and obliterating the old Spanish record, which had stood at 10 games).

But when Barcelona hosted Deportivo La Coruña on 9 March 2013, Messi sat on the bench for more than an hour before finally coming on. With 130 seconds left on the clock, he dribbled past three defenders, played the ball to Dani Alves and ran into the box. He received Alves's pass seven yards in front of goal and with the keeper moving in on him. There was no time to trap the ball and no space to hit it into. So Messi simply chipped the ball over the goalkeeper and into the net with his first touch. If ever a goal was worthy of setting a new world record, this was it.

Three weeks later, on 30 March 2013, Messi was on target against Celta Vigo to score in Barcelona's 19th consecutive game. He'd scored 30 goals during that run (among them three penalties). Messi then missed Barça's next three league encounters. Upon his return, against Bilbao, he scored nine minutes after coming on deep into the second half. Eight days later, he scored two goals aginst Real Betis to make it 21 in a row. And then, on the final day of the season, he played 90 minutes away at Atlético Madrid – but failed to hit the net.

⚽ Does **home advantage** really exist?

In 2005, reviewing a biography of José Mourinho in the *London Review Of Books*, David Runciman wrote: 'The clearest evidence that mysterious forces are at work on the sports field comes from the unarguable impact of home advantage in almost every kind of sporting contest. There has been a lot of academic work on this phenomenon, but there is nowhere near as much consensus about what is causing it.'

Part of the problem is that the factors which used to account for home advantage – the fatigue of away journeys, discomfort of hotel beds, unfamiliarity with the playing surface, the intimidating power of signs like 'This is Anfield' – have been greatly reduced. As Runciman wrote: 'These days, no big league team should ever arrive at an away game tired, tetchy, homesick (the top players lead such bicoastal, transcontinental, post-nuclear lives that it's not clear what it would mean for them to be homesick anyway); yet winning away from home is still very hard.'

The famous 'This is Anfield' sign. It didn't quite work for Roy Hodgson.

His explanation was twofold. 'Familiarity with one's surroundings, however anonymous they might appear from the outside, seems to enhance confidence in the performance of repetitive physical tasks.' Other studies have suggested that testosterone levels, an important predictor of victory in many sports, rise among players defending their own patch. 'The other thing that improves performance is an audience,' says Runciman. He isn't referring to the vaunted power of certain sections of grounds – notably the Stretford End or the Kop – to inspire their players, influence referees and, as the cliché suggests, suck the ball into goal. For Runciman, the important factor isn't how much noise home fans make – the prawn sandwich scoffers at Old Trafford are often out-sung by the away crowd – but their sheer, reassuring presence. Research has also consistently shown that officials are unwittingly influenced by home crowds.

Such challenges may sound insurmountable. Yet away teams are having increasing success surmounting them. In 2008, Dortmund University published a study which said that until 1987–88, home teams won 55.8 percent of their games. But gradually they began scoring less – while conceding the same number of goals – on their own turf. So between 1987–88 and 2006–07, the home side only won 47.8 percent of games. That trend has continued since. Let's be clear, home sides are still more likely to grab three points than their visitors (who only won 27.1 percent of the time in the top flights in England, Germany, Italy, the Netherlands and Spain in 2011–12, according to Betfair's statistics) but that advantage has been significantly eroded. Typically today, a side in one of those leagues will win around 47.6 percent of their home games.

One unpublished study of home advantage in football in la Liga since it was founded in 1928 has suggested that this factor is important to some clubs but not for others. Only nine teams have won the Spanish title and seven of them – Athletic Bilbao, Atlético Madrid, Deportivo la Coruña, Real Betis, Real Sociedad, Sevilla and Valencia – counted on home advantage. The other two – Barcelona (who have 21 titles) and Real Madrid (32) – don't distinguish between the two types of fixture. They expect to win every match.

In 2010–11, when Pep Guardiola's *Blaugranas* broke records on their way to the title, they won their first ten games away from home and became the first team in the history of la Liga to score in every away game. The difference between their home and away form came down, in essence, to the fact that they drew three more games on the road than they did at Camp Nou.

⚽ What is the **longest move** that has led to a goal?

'**It was only when** there was absolutely nobody left you could pass the ball to that we finally put it into the net.' In these days of tiki-taka, the patient short-passing game perfected by the Spanish, you'd probably expect a Barcelona player to have uttered these words not so long ago. Yet they are more than half a century old and come from a German defender by the name of Hans Bornemann, who was describing the style his club, Schalke 04, made famous when he was a player in the 1930s. So the idea of stringing many passes together to create an opening is pretty old. Yet goals from very long moves do seem to be a product of the very modern era, in which ball possession is so prized. At least every impressive example is of fairly recent origin.

True, there is Carlos Alberto's great goal that capped Brazil's 4-1 win in the 1970 World Cup final, in which eight outfield players touched the ball before their captain fired home. It is often cited as a near-perfect example of a goal that puts the finishing touch on an extended move. But there were only nine passes in this 29-second move – and a bit of virtuoso dribbling from defender Clodoaldo to befuddle three Italians. This is nowhere near what you have to come up with to be in the running for a really, really long move.

Such as the arguably most magical 58 seconds of the 2006 World Cup. The move that led to Argentina's second goal in their 6-0 rout of Serbia and Montenegro involved nine players and ended with a back-heeler from Hernán Crespo to set up the eventual scorer Esteban Cambiasso. An American statistician by the name of David R. Brillinger published a 20-page academic paper on this goal, entitled *A Potential*

Carlos Alberto celebrates his classic goal in the 1970 World Cup Final, following pass number nine from Pelé.

Function Approach to the Flow of Play in Soccer. Brillinger does many strange things in his paper – such as expounding on 'the potential function of Newtonian gravity' – but he does state correctly that the number of passes was 25. There is some disagreement about this, as many sources say there were 24. The controversy seems to surround the very first pass, as Maxi Rodriguez robbed an opponent in possession by poking the ball towards his own defence. Yet he intentionally played the ball to Gabriel Heinze, which means that this was the first pass and Crespo's back-heeler the 25th.

In any case, the exact number of passes doesn't make that much difference, as there have been longer moves. As you might expect, Barcelona have scored after stringing together more passes – 27 – in fewer seconds – 33 – than Argentina. The move that led to this goal at Anfield in 2001 started with a throw-in (which doesn't count as a pass) and ended when Xavi, after a seemingly endless succession of short passes, beat the offside trap with a 30-yard through-ball setting up Marc Overmars to round the goalkeeper and slot home.

Yet even this awe-inspiring display of tiki-taka pales into insignificance compared to a 35-pass move that led to a goal in April 2006. This work of art was created by Fenerbahçe in a combustible Istanbul derby with Galatasaray. Leading 3-0 after 78 minutes, Fener won the ball at the edge of their area. In the next 88 seconds, the team passed the ball around 34 times until Ümit Özat got behind the defence on the left wing. He crossed into the box – pass number 35 – for Nicolas Anelka to score with a first-time shot and make it 4-0. The move involved every outfield player and there were only three moments during the move when an opponent was close enough to the ball to have a reasonable chance of intercepting a pass.

⚽ Who took the **first penalty**?

This is surprisingly hard to answer with any certainty. Many reference books and websites confidently cite names and dates. For example, until recent weeks Wikipedia simply stated: 'The first ever penalty kick was awarded to Wolverhampton Wanderers in their game against Accrington at Molineux Stadium on 14 September 1891. The penalty was taken and scored by Billy Heath as Wolves went on to win the game 5–0.' There was even a footnote that told you the source of this information, the BBC.

Yet when you looked up the BBC website in question ('Funny Old Game – Happened On This Day'), you realised that Wikipedia had left out a vital four words, because the text says that on this date in history 'Wolverhampton Wanderers' John Heath converts the first penalty kick in the Football League in a game against Accrington Stanley'. The words that make all the difference here are, of course, 'in the Football League'. Clark Miller's history of the spot-kick, *He Always Puts It to the Right*, says a player by the name of Farman converted one on 5 September 1891 for Newton Heath against Blackpool in the Lancashire League. Miller doesn't say Farman was the first, merely the first 'in England'.

The International Football Association Board introduced the penalty kick during a meeting at the Alexandra Hotel in Glasgow (bear that in mind) on 2 June 1891, some four months after a scandalous match between Stoke and Notts County in which County defender John Hendry deliberately handled the ball on the goal-line to prevent the equaliser. The man who proposed a new, harsh penalty to become effective the following season (bear that in mind, too) for such unsportsmanlike conduct was, ironically, a goalkeeper – William McCrum, who played for Irish side Milford.

Obviously, there was plenty of time between 2 June and Farman's goal on 5 September to take penalties somewhere on the British Isles. A German book on the history of the spot-kick – *Elfmeter!* by René Martens – credits one J. Dalton as the pioneer. It is a tantalising claim because this player happened to be Canadian, in a select XI touring Ireland. On 29 August 1891, they played Linfield at Ulsterville. As George Glass, the leading Belfast statistician, writes: 'During the match Willie Gordon, the Linfield right back handled the ball in the penalty box. Dalton the Canadian right half took the penalty and scored. This was the first penalty kick taken on Irish soil.'

That John Terry moment in Moscow. The golden rule, when taking the vital penalty in a Champions League final, is not to slip as you kick the ball.

But we have more candidates – and one more country: Scotland. The blog *Association Football Before the 'D'* (meaning the half-circle at the edge of the penalty area that was introduced in 1937) says: 'The first goal from a penalty kick was scored by Alex McCall for Renton FC against Leith Athletic on August 22nd 1891.'

And there is talk of an even earlier penalty. A 2009 discussion on *Scottishleague.net* unearthed a match between Airdrieonians and Royal Albert on 6 June 1891, during which 'the referee awarded [a penalty kick] by mistake because although the penalty rule had been passed three days earlier it wasn't due to become law until [the new season]'. The game in question was the Airdrie Charity Cup final played at Mavisbank and the Airdrieonian who put the penalty away was called McLuggage.

What match has prompted the most red cards?

In October 2012, officials in a junior league match in Paraguay issued 36 red cards after the game between Teniente Farina and Libertad ended in a mass brawl. The trigger for the melee was referee Nestor Guillen's decision to send off two players in the closing minutes. They refused to leave the pitch, continuing to feud until their team-mates joined in. Appalled by the melee, flying kicks and punches, Guillen and his assistants left the pitch and, even though they were in the dressing room when the violence peaked, issued 36 red cards, dismissing every player on the field and on the bench.

You would think that would be a record. It is, but only a joint one. Exactly the same number were issued in March 2011 by Argentinian referee Damian Rubino after a match in the fifth tier between Claypole and Victoriano Arenas finished in much the same violent fashion. The only difference being that fans and coaches joined in this brawl.

As bad, mad and undisciplined as that sounds, it could have been far worse. In February 2010, Hawick United striker Paul Cooper was banned for two years by the Scottish FA after being shown two yellow cards – and five reds – in a Borders League Amateur Match. Cooper was so incensed by his second booking he subjected referee Andy Lyon to a stream of verbal abuse as he left the pitch and persisted even as the red cards mounted. The 39-year-old, nicknamed Santa by his team-mates, did apologise to the official later, admitting: 'I overreacted.'

Red and yellow cards, incidentally, have a very recent history. In the old days, refereees 'put players in their book' and pointed to the touchline for a dismissal. But in the 1966

World Cup things got confusing during the charged game between England and Argentina, when both Charltons were reported as being booked (the ref wasn't too clear about this) and Argentina's Rattin was sent off. English referee Ken Aston suggested that red and yellow cards, based on internationaly recognised traffic light colours, could help matters, and they were duly introduced at the 1970 Mexico World Cup.

⚽ Which is the greatest **relegation escape act** of all-time?

Long before 'the great escape' had become a movie, and a cliché of relegation battles, Lincoln City had shredded their supporters' nerves with a survival story that defied belief. With six matches left in the Second Division in 1957–58, the Imps were five points from safety (in an era when a victory was worth two points), had not won in their last 18 matches and had with dismal consistency just lost nine in a row.

Yet six games – and six victories – later, the Imps survived the drop by one point, at Notts County's expense. The tide turned with Lincoln's 3-1 win away to Barnsley on 8 April. The result was even more astonishing because, only the day before, in their Easter Monday fixture, they had lost at home to the Tykes by the same scoreline. During that defeat, one despondent Lincoln fan scaled the Sincil Bank flagpole to lower the club's colours to half mast. Yet the players were made of sterner stuff. With journeyman striker Ron Harbertson, a late signing from Darlington, scoring nine goals in 11 games, the Imps survived. Their Roy Of The Rovers-style comeback came to a fitting end when Harbertson scored the relegation-averting goal with a 30-yard shot that was so hard it broke the stanchion.

For all of Lincoln's heroics, the world's greatest escapologist, the Hungarian-born American Harry Houdini, would probably prefer the great escape staged by SC Freiburg in 1994. A magician who liked to create a fantastic, mysterious aura around his shows, Houdini would have been thrilled to hear that the German club's survival that year was partly inspired by a phantom goal.

With three games left in the Bundesliga in 1993–94, Freiburg trailed 15th-placed Nuremberg by four points and one goal. After four months without a single league victory, Freiburg went on to win their last three games, two of which were away from home. Under the old two-points-for-a-win rule, this meant that Nuremberg needed one win and one draw from three games to stay up. They got a win (a commanding 4-1 against Wattenscheid) and were drawing the Bavarian derby with Bayern Munich when this happened ...

A corner from the right was flicked on towards the far post of Nuremberg's goal, where Bayern's Thomas Helmer bundled the ball into touch from two yards out. While Nuremberg's keeper Andreas Köpke patted Helmer on the back to console him for missing such a sitter, the linesman raised his flag to signal a goal. Despite fierce protests – and even though the ball rolled many yards into touch – the referee trusted his assistant and gave Bayern the goal.

Nuremberg lost the game 2-1 after missing a late penalty but quickly filed a protest and the German FA annulled the game. The decision infuriated FIFA, which strictly opposed this kind of 'trial by television', but German officials argued that what had already become notorious as the Phantom Goal constituted such a blatant error that the rules of fair play demanded Nuremberg were given another chance. They were. They lost the replay 5-0 and went down on goal difference. Sadly, it was not a phantom goal difference.

⚽ What is the lowest number of penalties a team has scored in a **shoot-out** and still won?

None. That's right – Rangers missed all four spot kicks in the shoot-out against Sporting Lisbon in the second round of the Cup Winners' Cup on 3 November 1971 yet still progressed. The incident has become part of the club's folklore but for non-Gers fans, let's explain how it happened.

Rangers won the first leg at Ibrox 3-2 and, after 90 minutes of the second leg in Lisbon, were behind by the same scoreline. In extra time, both sides found the net so the match finished 4-3 to Sporting. With the sides still level on aggregate, Dutch referee Laurens van Ravens ordered a penalty shoot-out which Sporting won. The Rangers players trudged back to the dressing room in dejection. Rangers star Willie Henderson recalled later: 'There was something in my head about away goals but it seemed we were out.' Indeed, even as the kicks were being taken, Rangers manager Willie Waddell was pointing out to UEFA delegate Andre Ramirez that the shoot-out should never have taken place, that Rangers – having scored three away goals to Sporting's two – were in the third round and that the referee was breaking the rules.

Van Ravens' mistake, it should be noted, was not as inexplicable as it would be today. Until 1970, the away goals rule (created in 1965) only applied to goals scored during regular time. Still, when Van Ravens blundered, the new version of the rule had been in effect for well over a season. As he later recalled: 'After the penalties, I returned to the dressing room. There the UEFA officials told me the good news and the bad news. The good news was that I had controlled an excellent game well. The bad news – Rangers should have won the match.'

With the proper away goals rule enforced, Rangers won the tie. Six months later, in Barcelona, they beat Dynamo Moscow 3-2 to win the Cup Winners Cup. That team are fondly recalled as the Barcelona Bears. Yet even this triumph was not without controversy. Rangers were denied the chance of defending the trophy when hundreds of their fans invaded the pitch. As a riot raged, the trophy was presented to Waddell and skipper John Greig in an office deep beneath the Camp Nou stands. UEFA called the Scottish fans' behaviour 'shocking and ugly' and banned the club from European competition for a year.

⚽ Has any **single club** supplied an entire international team?

In the very first international, a 0-0 draw between England and Scotland on 30 November 1872, Queen's Park supplied all 11 Scottish players. The Scottish selectors had hoped that Royal Engineers striker Henry Renny-Tailyour and the Wanderers star Arthur Kinnaird would turn out for them but both were unavailable so they turned to their leading club to field the whole team. As there was no Scottish League then, the Scottish Cup and the Scottish FA weren't founded until 1873, and neither Rangers or Celtic had been properly established, the selectors may have felt they had little option.

On 30 September 1964, modern football history was made at half-time in a match between Belgium and the Netherlands in Antwerp when Guy Delhasse was replaced in the home side's goal by Jean Trappeniers. After that switch, Belgium played the rest of the match with a national side drawn entirely from Anderlecht. Having 11 Mauves on the pitch

England captain Eddie Hapgood introduces his Arsenal team-mate George Male to Prince Arthur of Connaught and the Italian ambassador before the legendary Battle of Highbury.

made the Diables Rouges marginally more cohesive and Jef Jurion scored the only goal of the game in the 87th minute. Jurion was a gifted winger-turned-playmaker who played in seven positions for Belgium but is, a little unfairly, best known for always wearing spectacles on the pitch.

No club has ever supplied more than seven players in the same England team. Arsenal achieved this record in 1934, with seven players in the startling line-up in the epic, violent 3-2 win over Italy remembered in football history as the Battle of Highbury. The Gunners capped that day were keeper Frank Moss, left-back Eddie Hapgood, right-back George

Male, left half-back Wilf Copping, inside-right Ray Bowden, inside-left Cliff Bastin and centre-forward Ted Drake. Manchester United matched this record briefly on 28 March 2001 in a World Cup qualifier, though Wes Brown and Teddy Sheringham came on as subs, the latter in the 84th-minute.

Arsenal's record has never officially been challenged. The FA dismisses the persistent suggestion that Corinthians twice supplied an entire English team, in 1894 and 1895, against Wales. The problem with this theory, as the authoritative England Football Online website has pointed out, is that in both games the players credited as Corinthians also played regularly – and in some cases primarily – for other clubs too. So the Gunners' record stands in England. Seven is also the modern-era record in Germany, set by Borussia Mönchengladbach in 1971 and later equalled, inevitably, by Bayern.

There is, however, an intriguing footnote to this particular national record. After World War II, the territory known as Saarland, today one of Germany's federal states, was a protectorate and, between 1950 and 1956, a FIFA member. The Saarland national team played 19 official internationals and even took part in the 1954 World Cup qualifiers. In one of football history's great jokes, they had to face West Germany. In both games against the Germans – on 11 October 1953 and 28 March 1954 – Saarland fielded a team in which ten players came from the same club, Saarbrücken FC. The odd man out in both games was midfielder Kurt Clemens, under contract at Saarbrücken's local rivals Saar 05.

Nacional, Dynamo Kiev and Torino have all dominated their national sides to a considerable extent. In the 1970 World Cup, Uruguay fielded eight players from Nacional when they drew 0-0 with Italy in Puebla. Sixteen years later, when the Soviet Union kicked off their World Cup campaign against Hungary, the USSR coach Valeri Lobanovskiy picked eight players from Dynamo Kiev, the club he managed in his day job. In the 70th minute, when Dynamo striker Igor Belanov came off he was replaced by club team-mate Vadym Yevtushenko. Four of the goals in the USSR's 6-0 victory were scored by Dynamo players. In the last 16, against Belgium, the coach selected nine Dynamo stars in his starting eleven but despite a Belanov hat-trick, the USSR lost 4-3 in extra time to a Belgian side graced by such talents as playmaker Enzo Scifo and skipper Jan Ceulemans, who was probably five yards offside when he scored Belgium's second. Back in the USSR, few criticised Lobanovskiy's selection. Dynamo had won the Soviet league and cup in 1985 and the Cup Winners' Cup the month before the World Cup. Their dominance of the national squad was a fair reflection of their team's calibre.

The same logic prompted Vittorio Pozzo, the coach who won Italy's first two World Cups, to turn to Torino to supply all ten outfield players when the *Azzurri* faced Hungary on 11 May 1947. Goalkeeper Lucidio Sentimenti IV (so known because he was the fourth of five football-playing brothers) was the odd man out – and even he played for Turin's other team, Juventus. That Grande Torino side was the greatest team in Italian football history. They won five Serie A titles in a row, racked up enough firsts to fill their own book of records and, in April 1946, after going 6-0 up in 19 minutes away to Roma, kept their margin of victory down to 7-0 because their coach Luigi Ferrero told them there was no need to humiliate the opposition.

Against such a side, in Torino's own stadium, Hungary did well only to lose 3-2. In the 76th minute, a 22-year-old Puskás made it 2-2 with a penalty but 13 minutes later Torino midfielder Ezio Loik scored to win the match for Italy. On 9 May 1949, Loik and 17 of his Torino team-mates would die when their plane crashed into the Superga hill near Turin.

⚽ What was the longest amount of stoppage time added to a game?

In the old days, referees rarely played more than one or two minutes of stoppage time. The World Cup semi-final between France and West Germany in 1982 is a case in point. This was the game in which defender Patrick Battiston lost consciousness after being knocked down by German goalkeeper Harald Schumacher. Even though Battiston was treated on the pitch at length, Dutch referee Charles Corver added just three and a half minutes of injury time.

Yet even in the old days, the referees sometimes remembered to stop their watches. Eight years after the Battiston drama, there was another much-debated foul in another World Cup semi-final. In 1990, Italy and Argentina went into extra time at 1-1 and, for some reason, French referee Michel Vautrot added four minutes to the first period. (Some people claim he simply forgot to look at his watch.) Suddenly Italy's Roberto Baggio went down off the ball. Vautrot stopped play, consulted his Danish linesman Peter Mikkelsen and sent off Argentina's Ricardo Giusti for hitting Baggio in the face, sparking lengthy protests by Giusti's team-mates. In the ensuing melee, this first period of extra time lasted 23 minutes. One World Cup later, Scottish referee Leslie Mottram added 8 minutes and 36 seconds to a hard-fought, but largely uneventful 0-0 between South Korea and Bolivia on 24 June 1994. His reasoning remains a mystery and it can't even have been a malfunctioning watch – Mottram wore two of them.

Yet eight, nine or even ten minutes of injury time are nowhere near the record most sources cite, which is held by Paul Alcock, who added almost 23 minutes to the first half of a game between Bristol City and Brentford in August 2000.

You begin to understand why he did so when you read the the BBC's match report: 'Brentford's Lloyd Owusu suffered a neck injury as three players were stretchered off in the 2-2 draw between Bristol City and Brentford at Ashton Gate.'

Yet it's quite possible that the real record holder is Welshman Clive Thomas. According to Jack Rollin's book *More Soccer Shorts*, he 'once added three quarters of an hour to normal playing time'. The explanation was Thomas's legendary penchant for accuracy. 'It was a Boys Club match on the top of a mountain at Blaengwynfi,' explains Rollin, 'and every time the ball went out of play it rolled down the mountainside.'

Thomas must have painstakingly timed every single break in play, displaying the same meticulousness with which he once disallowed Zico's headed winner from a corner against Sweden in the 1978 World Cup. There was, Thomas decided,

The punctilious Welshman Clive Thomas blows for full time a split second before Zico's phantom winner for Brazil against Sweden.

enough time on the clock for Nelinho to take the corner but in the two seconds that elapsed between the kick and Zico heading home, Thomas blew for full time. (An often-overlooked footnote to this infamous story is that Thomas had added considerable stoppage time to the first 45 minutes during which – to Sweden's chagrin – Reinaldo scored Brazil's equaliser. And it all turned out alright for Brazil, who went on to win the World Cup, in its first ever penalty shoot-out.)

Still, many supporters might prefer such punctiliousness to the more laissez-faire brand of timekeeping which has led to the phenomenon known as Fergie Time: the time referees were popularly believed to add on at Old Trafford if Manchester United were behind because they were terrified of Sir Alex Ferguson. Depending which data you read, Fergie Time is either scientifically proven – one study quoted by *The Guardian* found that injury time at United's home games from 2006–07 to September 2009 was, on average, 65.8 seconds longer if they did not have the lead than when they did – or a media myth fuelled by the paranoia of losing teams. An Opta comparison of injury times in the 2011–12 Premier League revealed that the team that benefitted from the most added time was … Wigan Athletic, with an average playing time at home of 96 minutes 12 seconds.

Research on 750 matches in Spain's la Liga by Natxo Palacious-Huerta, a professor at the London School of Economics, and Luis Garicano and Canice Prendergast, suggests this phenomenon was not limited to northwest England. They found that if a home team was ahead in a close match in la Liga, referees added an average of two minutes. But if a home team was behind in a close match, the average added time stretched to four minutes. So Fergie Time is probably a benefit enjoyed by most managers on their own turf. Indeed, Manchester City's Sergio Agüero scored the goal that snatched the 2011–12 title from United in the 94th minute, prompting the overjoyed home fans to sing 'We won it in Fergie Time!'

⚽ What is the furthest a team has travelled for a domestic cup tie?

The reason this is hard to answer is that you can't take the easy route. You cannot pick a really big country like Australia and simply check if Perth Glory, on the west coast, have ever travelled to Brisbane Roar, on the east coast – 2,240 miles as the crow flies. Because what counts here is not just who played whom but where. The Supercoppa Italiana, for instance, the Italian version of the Charity Shield, has been staged in places as far away from Italy as Washington DC, Tripoli and Beijing.

Then there is one very special case – France. What makes this country's domestic competitions so unusual is that the clubs from the French overseas territories – from such far-flung places as Tahiti, New Caledonia, French Guyana, Guadeloupe, Martinique, Mayotte, Tahiti and Réunion – are considered French teams. Naturally, their clubs cannot compete in the French league, but there are regional championships and the respective winners used to play for a trophy known as the Outremer Champions Cup. It was always staged in France, so that it wasn't unusual for clubs from Réunion or Martinique to fly to Paris to play each other. (This competition was replaced in 2008, by one involving national teams.)

Clubs from the territories still compete in the Coupe de France. This competition is notoriously drawn-out – there are eight rounds before the clubs from the French First Division even enter – precisely because so many teams take part. The winners of the regional cups of the overseas departments and territories join the regular Coupe de France in the seventh round and can be drawn against any club from France.

Over the years, some of the journeys have been so long the footballers must have felt like explorers. The longest one we have found took place in 1976, when Nickel Nouméa from New Caledonia were drawn against third-division club AS Corbeil. Since the match was played in Saint-Ouen, in the suburbs of Paris, the visitors had to cover 10,412 miles. One way, of course. (They lost 3-0.)

The farthest a team from an overseas territory has progressed in this competition is the round of 32, or the ninth round, back in 1994–95. The club in question was La Saint-Louisienne from the Réunion island in the Indian Ocean. In the seventh round, La Saint-Louisienne covered 5,817 miles to reach Melun in France, where they beat Third Division side SA Epinal 3-1. One round later, Ligue 2 club Chamois Niortais travelled 5,829 miles to Saint-Louis to be defeated on penalties by La Saint-Louisienne. It took a Ligue 1 side to stop the minnows' heroic progress: AS Cannes (just 5,428 miles from Réunion) won 2-0 on this island in the Indian Ocean.

Culture

⚽ **Can footballers act and can actors play football?**

In 1920, British director George Berthold Samuelson directed a movie called *The Winning Goal*. No copy has survived and the British Film Institute doesn't even have a proper synopsis. Yet several footballers featured in this movie, the most famous being Jack Cock. The first Cornishman to play for England, Cock was a flamboyant character with a fine tenor voice and the looks of a natural celluloid hero. But he didn't really get to flex his acting muscles as the film was based around the fictional team Blackton Rovers – and Cock appeared as himself.

Then again, maybe players should have followed the example of Cock and Meredith. Because with a very few exceptions – notably Eric Cantona and Vinnie Jones – footballers tend to make fools of themselves when they try to act.

Mind you, footballers trying to act are no worse than, to pluck a name at random out of the air, Sylvester Stallone trying to convince as a footballer. In John Huston's *Escape To Victory* Stallone plays a goalkeeper in the POW team intent on both defeating the Germans (at football) and escaping. An early script had Stallone scoring the winning goal in the match but that scenario was rejected by the footballers involved (Pelé, Bobby Moore, Ossie Ardiles) and thereafter the once and future Rocky Balboa seemed to lose interest in his role.

As perfunctory as Sly's performance may have been, he was a cut above Will Ferrell's caffeine-addicted, hypercom-

LORIMAR PRESENTS A FREDDIE FIELDS PRODUCTION A JOHN HUSTON
SYLVESTER STALLONE
MICHAEL CAINE MAX VON SYDOW
"ESCAPE TO VICTORY"

All proceeds in aid of
INSPIRE (The Eden and Razzett Foundation
helping over 1000 children and adults
with disabilities & their families.
Price of Admission: €10 (including Reception)
Tickets available from Embassy Cinema, Inspire Premis

Thursday 6 August at 8.00p.m.
EMBASSY CINEMA, VALLETTA

petitive youth team coach in *Kicking And Screaming* (2005); while Ferrell, in turn, out-acted John Lynch, who was dismally dull as George Best in the prosaically-titled *Best* (2000). El Beatle is far more interesting as the inspiration for Hellmuth Costard's *Football Like Never Before*, which, through the alchemy of Costard's off-the-wall sensibility, spins a routine fixture between Manchester United and Coventry City into a compellingly odd documentary, setting a precedent for the intriguing but more conventional portrait of Zizou in *Zidane* by Douglas Gordon and Philippe Parreno.

The perils of footballers stepping too far out of their comfort zone are illustrated by *Montana Tap* (originally entitled *Potato Fritz*), described by the critic Joe Hembus as a 'mystery cum comedy cum western'. Released in 1975, Peter Schamoni's film is not very good, but not trashy either, which is why it's not even regarded as a cult classic. Starring Hardy Krüger and Stephen Boyd, the film is chiefly remembered because 1974 World Cup winner Paul Breitner has a supporting role as the US Cavalry's Sergeant Stark. His dialogue had to be rerecorded and even though he's supposed to be a soldier, Breitner sports his trademark afro and beard. At least he didn't fall off the horse.

Seeing Breitner on horseback was nothing compared to the shock that awaited Germans on 9 January 1999. On that Sunday evening, the 403rd episode of the hugely popular crime series *Tatort* was televised. It opens with a scene, set at night, in which a small boy releases his pet rabbit into the garden, then closes the French window and walks into the kitchen. He turns on the gas stove, blocks the knobs so that gas keeps emitting, lights a candle, then walks back into his room and climbs into bed. A few moments later, a neighbour knocks on the French door. The boy's father pulls on a bathrobe and opens the French window. The neighbour steps into the living room. He is cradling the rabbit in his arms. 'I found your rabbit near my front door,' he says. Then he sniffs. 'It smells of gas,' he says. The man in the bathrobe runs into the kitchen, realises what is happening and hastily blows out the candle before turning off the stove.

The neighbour strolls into the kitchen, still holding the rabbit. 'What is going on here? Are you trying to kill us all?' he says in the monotonous tone of someone who knows they can't act and approaches each line as a damage limitation exercise. The father blames incompetent heating engineers. The neighbour shakes his head in a robotic, unnatural manner. 'Sue them,' he says. 'Such people have taken up the wrong profession.' Then he hands over the rabbit. 'Give him an extra carrot,' he says. 'He's saved all our lives.'

The neighbour is none other than Berti Vogts, another 1974 World Cup winner. At that time, he was between jobs. Three years later, he became Scotland manager, a role in which, according to the Tartan Army, he was only slightly more convincing.

And so to the stars. Before Cantona and Jones, the one footballer who could be said to have enjoyed a real movie career was Dundee United inside-left Neil Paterson – a man who was the first amateur to captain a professional side in Britain but never wanted to earn a living from the game. This was a smart call, financially, because he was hired by DC Thomson as a sports journalist, wrote several novels and stories and, in 1953, adapted his own tale *The Kidnappers* for the cinema. Five years later he won an Oscar for his screenplay of John Braine's novel *Room At The Top*. He couldn't make it to the ceremony so he stayed up, at home with his family in Crieff, Perthshire, waiting for a call to tell him whether he'd won.

Eric Cantona's movie career has now lasted longer than his time in football. He made his first appearance in a French comedy in 1995 and has surfaced in more than a dozen films since then, including a fine cameo as the French ambassador at the court of Cate Blanchett in *Elizabeth*, and a starring role as Monsieur Cantona in Ken Loach's *Looking for Eric*.

Vinnie Jones was one of the leading lights in Wimbledon's Crazy Gang (a group of maverick footballers who were, to adapt one of Tommy Docherty's famous remarks, legends in their own minds), and his movie career has built on his hardman image. He played the enforcer Big Chris in *Lock, Stock and Two Smoking Barrels*, and was cast in Guy Ritchie's follow-up *Snatch*. In 2000, he had a lot of screen time as the villainous The Sphinx in *Gone In 60 Seconds*. Although Jones insisted he was inspired by Anthony Hopkins' Hannibal Lecter, the *Daily Mail* said that he recited his one line of dialogue with the 'ease and spontaneity of Sylvester Stallone reciting Book Six of *Paradise Lost*.' A limited repertoire of expressions hasn't stopped Jones appearing in more than fifty movies.

⚽ Who was the first team to wear advertising on their shirts?

Kettering Town is the usual answer. The non-league side turned out against Bath City on 24 January 1976 with the words 'Kettering Tyres' emblazoned in white lettering on their shirts. The four-figure sponsorship deal had been masterminded by club chief executive and manager Derek Dougan, the Wolves icon, but he soon began to reconsider when the FA threatened the club with a four-figure fine, saying it had banned the idea in 1972. After complaining that the 'petty-minded bureaucrats' hadn't put their ban in writing, the Doog gave in – after his idea about changing the lettering to 'Kettering T' had been nixed. He must have wondered what all the fuss was about when the ban was lifted five years later and Liverpool broke new ground by wearing Hitachi-sponsored shirts in 1978.

The Reds were the first to pioneer this commercialisation in England but such deals had been allowed in the Bundesliga since 1974–75. That was a response to the rescue of Eintracht Braunschweig by Günter Mast, the owner of Jägermeister liqueur. The club logo was a lion but after a DM 100,000 payment, the lion was ousted by the Jägermeister deer in time for the side's Bundesliga match against Schalke on 24 March 1973.

Mast may have been inspired by the initiative of Austrian brewer Manfred Mautner Markhof who, just before the start of the 1966–67 season, decided to sponsor Austria Wien. The beer glass trademark of Markhof's Schwechater beer was at the centre of their purple shirts. They were even more surprised to be handed new regulations which stipulated, at the sponsor's insistence, that 'long hair will not be permitted on the field of play. A decent haircut is mandatory for all players.'

In the European game, Austria Wien pioneered what some see as a sacrilegious act and others defend as a necessary commercialisation. But there is a possibility that the Uruguayan giants Peñarol experimented with shirt sponsorship in the mid-1950s. The club cite ANDA in 1984 as their first official sponsor but there is a story that, back in the mid-1950s, their

World Cup-winning hero Obdulio Varela refused to wear a sponsored shirt explaining (according to Galeano's *Football In Sunshine And Shadow*): 'They used to drag us blacks around by rings in our noses. Those days are gone.' According to this story, ten Peñarol players took to the field wearing the new shirt, with advertising, while club legend Varela, in his last season, wore the old, unsullied one.

⚽ Who was the only footballer to sing on the same bill as **The Beatles**?

Colin Grainger, aka The Singing Winger, shared a stage with the Fab Four on 13 June 1963 at Manchester's Southern Sporting Club. Grainger recalled: 'The Beatles were on the verge of becoming superstars but they had to take the booking because they had signed the contract a year before. I remember John Lennon, Paul McCartney and George Harrison as serious young men and professional, but Ringo Starr messed about, playing with Dinky cars on the floor. You knew then they were special, so it was a privilege to be on the same bill.'

Once hailed as one of the fastest men in football, Grainger grew up idolising Al Jolson and Mario Lanza. As he rose through the ranks in the 1950s, he admitted: 'Some of the biggest names in football say I'm a fool for not giving up soccer and concentrating on singing. They know that I can earn £100 for singing a few songs in variety theatres.' (Bear in mind that, by the end of the 1950s, the maximum wage for footballers was just £20 a week.)

Yet Grainger stuck at it, playing for seven clubs – notably Sheffield United and Sunderland – in a 16-year career and winning seven caps. His potted biography in the matchday programme for his last international, against Scotland in

Albert Stubbins of Sgt. Pepper fame cleaning his boots. 'It was such a John name,' Paul McCartney recalled, 'Al-bert Stub-bins. It just sounded right.'

April 1957, noted that he 'has great potentialities as a modern popular singer and has made a record'. When he hung up his boots, he turned to 'crooning' full-time, doing reasonably entertaining impersonations of the likes of Jolson, Engelbert Humperdinck and Elvis Presley.

Grainger may have shared the bill with the Beatles but he didn't make the cover of Sgt. Pepper. That honour was reserved for Albert Stubbins, who appears just behind

Marlene Dietrich, to the right of George Harrison. In his biography of the group, Hunter Davies wrote: 'I had always been slightly disappointed that none of the Beatles were interested in sport at all, least of all football. In the end, John stuck in Albert Stubbins, a folk name from his childhood.' Stubbins, who had scored 83 goals in 146 games for Liverpool, didn't realise he had been honoured until he received a copy of the album with a note: 'Well done Albert, for all those glorious years in football. Long may you bob and weave.' This shouldn't be taken as an informed analysis of Stubbins' playing style.

The other Beatles-related football mystery that will probably never be solved is why, given the apathy described above, Matt Busby is namechecked in a Beatles lyric. The song 'Dig it', on the *Let It Be* album, includes the lines, 'Like the FBI and the CIA/And the BBC/B.B. King/And Doris Day/Matt Busby/Dig it dig it'. The legendary Scot had played for Liverpool before any of the Beatles were born but, as Barney Ronay suggests in his book on managers, he may just be mentioned because by 1970, when the song was written, 'Busby already had the air of an ancient, much valued institution, something stoical and comforting, like the World Service'.

⚽ Do **bogey teams** really exist?

David Runciman, who occasionally writes about football matters in the *London Review Of Books*, would probably suggest that the idea of a bogey team – along with the popular myth that the Manager of the Month award is a curse – merely reflect our inability 'to distinguish between statistically meaningless sequences and the march of destiny'. Over time, whatever fans might like to think, results tend to revert to an average.

And yet there are some strange sequences of results that suggest something irrational is going on. Between early 1990 and late 2006, Spurs played Chelsea no less than 37 times in all competitions, both home and away, but could win only one of these games – and that was a League Cup match. This kind of run can become self-perpetuating with the pre-match build-up in the media planting the thought in Spurs players' minds that they are unlikely to beat Chelsea. Once this idea takes hold, it may be more likely to come true.

Given the clubs' respective fortunes over that period, Spurs' barren streak might not seem that surprising. Spurs won just two trophies in that time (the FA Cup in 1991 and the League Cup in 1999), while Chelsea won seven (two Premier League titles, two FA Cups, two League Cups and the Cup Winners Cup). The Blues also finished above their London rivals in the league 13 times in the 18 seasons affected by this run. What was so intriguing about Spurs' run is that they couldn't win home or away. It is far more common for teams to suffer some kind of block when they return to a particular ground.

Spurs themselves also failed to win in 40 attempts at Anfield between 1912 and 1985. And for thirty years, Borussia Mönchengladbach just couldn't scrape a win away to Bayern Munich. Now, you could say it's hard for anyone to win at Bayern, but Gladbach's winless streak lasted from 1965, the year both teams were promoted to the Bundesliga, until 1995. In many of those 30 years, Borussia had a great team, winning the title five times and reaching five European finals (winning the UEFA Cup in 1975 and 1979). Ironically, when they finally broke their duck they did so with one future Bayern star in the side (Patrik Andersson), one former (Michael Sternkopf) and one future and former (Stefan Effenberg).

These curses may have been lifted, but another jinx is still alive and well. In Mexico, Club Deportivo Guadalajara

(Chivas) and Club Universidad Nacional (Pumas) are two of the best teams, having won 18 league titles between them. On 7 February 1982, a Manuel Negrete goal in the 89th minute secured a win for Pumas away at Chivas's Jalisco ground. They haven't won there since. The streak, which now enters its fourth decade, is even odder since Mexico introduced the Apertura/Clausura system in the mid-1990s, which means the league crowns a winter and a summer champion and teams play each other four times instead of just twice. At the time of writing, Pumas have gone 34 matches away at Chivas without a win.

The strange thing is that the Estadio Jalisco is home to three other Mexican teams, namely Atlas, Oro and Universidad de Guadalajara. The Pumas can defeat any of these sides at the Jalisco – and they can beat Chivas at home. It's just the combination of playing Chivas at the Jalisco that undoes them.

⚽ Why do **Brazil wear yellow shirts with green trim and blue shorts?**

The question sounds absurd. Yellow, green and blue are the colours of the Brazilian national flag, so the choice seems perfectly natural – as indeed it is, but strip and flag were not always in glorious unison.

In 1950, Brazil hosted – and expected to win – the World Cup. For the one and only time, the tournament was played in two group stages so there was no official final as such, but Brazil's clash with Uruguay on 16 July 1950 would decide who won the Jules Rimet trophy. Rimet himself, the French inventor of this tournament, had already written a speech congratulating Brazil on winning. The Brazilian FA had commissioned 22 gold medals with the players' names imprinted on them. Brazilian coach Flávio Costa tried to fight such over-confidence, warning: 'The Uruguayan team has always disturbed the slumbers of Brazilian footballers. I'm afraid that my players will take the field on Sunday as though they already had the championship shield sewn on their jerseys. It isn't an exhibition game. It is a match like any other, only harder.'

Such cautionary words went largely unheeded and, as the players lined up in the Maracanã, in front of a crowd of 200,000 (280 of whom came from Uruguay), the governor of the state of Rio addressed the players with a speech that began: 'You Brazilians, whom I consider victors of the tournament ... you players who in less than a few hours will be acclaimed by millions of your compatriots'.

Such hubris had its just reward. The shock, when Brazil lost 2-1 to Uruguay, was so profound, so seismic, that, as Brazilian novelist Carlos Heitor Cony put it, 'Survivors of that cruel afternoon believed they would never again be happy.' As the sadness turned to anger, a national search for scapegoats began. Goalkeeper Moacyr Barbosa would never be forgiven for conceding Uruguay's winner. Twenty years later, he was spotted out shopping and a woman turned to her son and said: 'Look at him, he's the man who made Brazil cry.' Brazilian journalist Roberto Muylaert revealed in his book on the keeper that, in 1963, Barbosa invited friends to a barbecue where the wood he was burning turned out to be the very goalposts he had stood between in 1950, which had just been rendered obsolete by FIFA regulations.

For a nation that was, in Cony's words, 'drenched with pain', persecuting the keeper could never salve the wound. So Brazilians did what many coaches, players and supporters have done: they blamed the kit. At that time, Brazil wore white shirts with a blue collar. After the defeat, as Alex Bellos

The wrong shirts. Barbosa concedes the fateful goal, scored by Ghiggia.

says in his book *Futebol*, 'they were deemed not sufficiently nationalistic'. For Rio paper Correio da Manhã, the white strip suffered from a "psychological and moral lack of symbolism".'

So a competition was launched to create a kit, drawing on the colours of the national flag, that Brazil could wear in the 1954 World Cup. Ironically, given the media's talk of nationalism and symbolism, the competition was won by Uruguayan illustrator Aldyr Garcia Schlee, who entered for a laugh but ending up defining one of the most famous, romantic strips football has ever known. So you could say that Brazil wear yellow, green and blue because they lost to Uruguay.

This reaction is extreme – but not unusual. Bayern once invented a kit to secure a long-awaited win over Kaiserslautern. In the 1970s and early 1980s, the Roten went ten games without a win there, prompting Breitner to remark that Bayern should spare themselves the journey 'and just send them the points by mail'. In November 1983, business manager Uli Hoeness took drastic action, commissioning a custom-made kit Bayern had never worn before and would never wear again. In these unusual colours, Bayern finally enjoyed some luck at Kaiserslautern's Betzenberg ground, with their keeper Jean-Marie Pfaff saving a penalty and Klaus Augenthaler scoring the only goal for the visitors. Bayern usually played in red or white, but for this match, they wore yellow shirts, blue shorts and white socks. Hoeness believed that Brazil's kit would guarantee success.

Sir Alex Ferguson would have understood. He ditched Manchester United's grey away shirts at half-time, when his team went 3-0 down against Southampton. 'The players couldn't pick each other out,' he explained. 'They said it was difficult to see their team-mates at distance when they lifted their heads. It was nothing to do with superstition.' It didn't make much difference on the day as Southampton won 6-3, but the shirts were never used again.

Don Revie would have understood, too. Watching Real Madrid win the 1960 European Cup final 7-3, he decided, when he became Leeds United manager in 1961, that he wanted his new team to play in the same all-white strip. Such a superstitious soul that he nursed a mysterious fear of ornamental elephants, Revie believed in his vision so much that he wanted the fans to share in it and insisted that Admiral make replica kits, the first such deal in British football.

Real Madrid are so synonymous with the all-white kit that it is often forgotten that they once dared to change their colours. In the 1920s, Real stars Perico Escobal and Félix Quesada watched London's Corinthians while travelling in England. The players were so impressed by the Corinthians' fair play and elegance that, when they returned to Madrid, they persuaded club president Pedro Parages that Real should wear black shorts, just like the Londoners, for the 1925–26 season. Parages was willing to give it a go but after two bad defeats in the semi-finals of the Spanish Cup to Barcelona – including a 5-1 thrashing in Madrid that must have hurt deeply – he decided that the black shorts were bad luck. The team reverted to playing in white and have been, if you consider only their home kit, *los blancos* ever since.

What is the world's longest-running football comic?

Let's clarify our terms. Roy Race, the hero of Melchester Rovers, had his own strip in *Tiger* in 1954 but only starred in his own all-football comic between 1976 and 1995. In other words, for 19 years. That is some feat but Race's organ looks like a one-season wonder when compared to *Los Barrabases*, the Chilean football comic which, in four interrupted incarnations, lasted for 32 years and is still published to mark the really big tournaments.

Created by estate agent Guido Vallejos ('I was hopeless at football so I found it easier to draw it'), *Barrabases* first appeared in August 1954 when Vallejos invested a big commission and some money borrowed from his wife in a printing press. The title, which could roughly be translated as rascals or pranksters, refers to a mischief-making youth team coached by a Mr Pipa. The first run of 10,000 copies, distributed only in Santiago and Valparaiso, sold out and the circulation grew to 100,000 as the

comic went from fortnightly to weekly. The Barrabases even got their radio show in which football presenter Máximo Claveriá commentated on the team's fictitious games.

Like Ajax, the Barrabases traditionally favoured 4-3-3. Unlike Ajax, they relied on a loveable Chilean mongrel, team mascot Rasca, to get them out of many nasty scrapes. In one instalment, Mr Pipa's boys took on Colo-Colo, Chile's most successful and popular team. For this prestige fixture, Pipa sent for reinforcements, drafting in a legendary, super-jumping Scottish-Chilean goalkeeper called Sapo Livington (*sapo* means toad).

The early issues featured, in a rather post-modern conceit, *El Camote* (The Muddle), a sports newspaper for kids, which reported on Barrabases' performance in the local championship. After a tournament in 1960, the paper wrote of 'great discontent among the fans. After sensational victories over Boca Juniors and the Spanish children's national side, Los Barrabases have failed. The president Rucedino Tapilla is saying nothing … Mr Pipa under a cloud.'

The team was the centrepiece of the comic, in their heyday filling at least half the issue. The other pages were filled with short stories about various characters from different sports. The comic's publishing history is a bit hazy but the first incarnation lasted until 1961. Relaunched in 1968, revamped in 1970, the title closed again in 1973 (though not before Chilean footballer Carlos Reinoso bought the licence to launch it in Mexico where he was playing for Club America). After another failed comeback, *Los Barrabases* was back in 1989. The team now had the whole comic to themselves and, though the drawings weren't as good, the new formula worked. Mr Pipa's team celebrated their fiftieth anniversary with a match against Real Madrid's galacticos in 2004 and, even though the title closed in 2006, special editions have since been published to mark the 2010 World Cup and the 2011 Copa America.

Los Barrabases may have shown the most stamina but they were not the first. From 1922 until the outbreak of the Spanish Civil War in 1936, young Catalan football fans thrilled to the humour and drawings in *Xut!* ('Shoot!'), a comic created by artist Valentí Castanya in which the spritely, grandfatherly hero Avi became a symbol of Barcelona football club. Now regarded as a crucial cultural record of Catalona in the 1920s and 1930s, *Xut!* struck such a chord that decades later one *Blaugrana*, Joan Casals, started going to games dressed as Avi. In 1992, after Barcelona had won the European Cup, he famously proclaimed that he would shave his beard off if the club won the competition again. He kept his promise in 2006. His devotion to Castanya's comic is one reason why Barcelona is one of the few clubs not to have a man in a fake animal suit as a mascot.

Avi depicted as a *caganero*, or shitting man. Catalans have a tradition of placing these earthy statuettes amid their nativity cribs.

⚽ Who was the greatest ever comic strip football hero?

A supremely gifted right-winger called Eric Castel. At least that was how he was known in Spain, France and Belgium. In the Netherlands they knew him as Ronnie Hansen, in Germany he was Kai Falke. For simplicity, we'll call him Castel.

Inspired by the imminent opportunity provided by the 1974 World Cup, Franco-Belgian illustrator Raymond Reding created a supposedly one-off football comic strip for the German magazine *Zack*. It centred on Falke, the player-manager of a company team, who was signed by Barcelona. That hugely implausible event aside, the strip had little in common with the most famous English football comic, the usually improbable adventures of Roy of the Rovers.

Reding was an artist whose precise, realistic drawings were rich in detail. His stories were as famed for their impressive renderings of buildings and stadiums as for their football action. Reding was anxious to avoid the kind of over-the-top storylines so popular in other football strips. Castel was outstanding but unlike Melchester Rovers hero Roy Race, he was no superman, did not get shot by a lone gunman and never strengthened his squad by signing two members of Spandau Ballet. Castel's Barcelona played realistic games against real-life clubs. It meant that Castel appealed to adults as much as to kids.

Reding resurrected his hero in 1979 for a full-length album, the first of 15 over the next 13 years. Gradually, Castel's story came to be regarded as the best football strip in the world. In 2004, five years after Reding's death, the Catalan company Ramon Usall published a book on the strip that declared that Castel embodied Catalan values. In his foreword, Joan Laporta, then Barcelona's club president, said: 'Eric Castel was one of the best signings in Barça's history.'

Move over, Messi. Barça's all-time top signing was Eric Castel.

Apart from the Rovers' Roy Race, Castel's rivals in Britain would include Billy Dane, the boy who became a brilliant footballer when he put on a pair of magic boots, found in his gran's attic, worn decades before by legendary striker Charles 'Dead Shot' Keen. This simple premise proved so enduring that *Billy's Boots* were featured in *Tiger*, *Scorcher*, *Eagle*, *Roy of the Rovers*, *Total Football*, in the German comic Kobra and (as Billi Boot) in Bengali magazine *Shuktaara*.

Billy Dane was also an inspirations for *Viz* magazine's Billy The Fish, which for many Brits of a certain age was the most iconic comic strip football hero of all. Fulchester United goal-keeper Billy Thomson found it easier to leap like a salmon because he was half-man, half-fish and *Viz*'s skewering of Roy of the Rovers led to such storylines as Shakin' Stevens join-

ing United. Yet the strip developed a surreal iden-tity of its own, with an invisible striker (Johnny X, who had vanished after his father died) and a Professor Wolfgang Schnell B.Sc., Ph.D. whose use of a calculator, charts and a geometry set to calculate the best trajectory for a shot eerily prefigures today's number-crunching, stat-driven, Optastic punditry.

⚽ Why are **corner flags** so important?

When Cameroon's Roger Milla ran over to the corner flag to celebrate his opening goal against Romania at the 1990 World Cup, the world watched in delight – and a trend was born. That was the moment football players discovered the manifold possibilities of using a corner flag as a prop. Many of them no longer treat it as respectfully as Milla. Some goal-scorers have taken to ripping the flag out of its socket, others give it a flying kick. A nadir was possibly reached when Finidi George unleashed a bizarre urinating-dog celebration after he had scored against Greece at USA 94.

But you wonder if any of these celebrants are aware of the risk involved, because if a corner flag is broken and cannot be repaired or replaced the referee has to abandon the game. Yes, that's how important the corner flags are. If they happen to be missing, the beginning of a game will have to be delayed until they arrive (as happened most famously in the 1974 World Cup final, which referee Jack Taylor couldn't start at the appointed time because the corners were empty). And if anything happens to one of the four flagposts during a game, play has to be stopped. As referee Dennis Wickham explains: 'In a professional match, another flag would likely be found. But corner flags are mandatory under the laws of the game. If a flag cannot be found (or safely assembled) the letter of the law would prevail, and the match would be abandoned.'

The question is: why? Why are the flags deemed so important that you cannot play football without them? After all, they don't do much. They mark the corners of the field of play – but so do the line markings. They are supposed to help the linesman decide whether a ball that goes out of play near the corner has crossed the touchline or the goal line but this isn't a common dilemma for officials and only helps them distinguish a corner or a goal kick from a throw-in. In comparison, the flags that used to mark the halfway line at many grounds have virtually disappeared, making way for fourth officials (who first appeared at a major tournament at the 1998 World Cup), TV cameras and technical areas (introduced into the laws of the game in 1994). These flags were only ever optional in the rules ('Flagposts may also be placed at each end of the halfway line'), even though they help the referee decide whether a player is offside or not. (You're never offside in your own half.)

In a game like field hockey – played on a similar pitch with the same kind of corner rules – the corner flags are nowhere near as sacred (if both teams are happy with this, the referee can start a game without them), even though the ball is a lot smaller and harder to follow. Since there is no immediately obvious, plausible explanation for the disproportionate importance of a corner flag in football, it seems likely we're dealing with a remnant of the game's past.

The answer may be found in the original rules of the Football Association as drawn up in 1863. The very first one said: 'The maximum length of the ground shall be 200 yards, the maximum breadth shall be 100 yards, the length and breadth shall be marked off with flags; and the goal shall be defined by two upright posts, eight yards apart, without any tape or bar across them.' Notice the rule doesn't mention the need for a crossbar or any line markings. That's because there were none for many decades. Only in 1891 did the rules require goal lines and touchlines to be marked. So, for almost three decades, the corner flags were the only marks that told you where the pitch began or ended. Actually, together with the four goalposts they were the only objects that defined the field of play. They may be superfluous today but it's hard to imagine the game without them.

⚽ What exactly is a derby?

Fans across the world use the English term *derby* (generally pronounced *der*-by rather than *dar*-by) for a local rivalry. The oddest, geographically, has to be the inter-continental clash between Galatasaray and Fenerbahçe, as the former are based in the European part of Istanbul, the latter on the Asian side of the Bosphorus strait. The oldest is usually said to be the Trentside one, first played on 23 March 1866, between Nottingham Forest (who had only switched to football from the Gaelic sport of shinty the year before) and Notts County. The match is usually said to have ended 0-0.

Just 300 yards (and the river Trent) separate Forest's City Ground from Notts County's Meadow Lane, while

Galatasaray and Fenerbahçe's stadiums are only nine miles apart. But not every club competing a derby is quite so lucky. Whenever Kaliningrad's Baltika on the Russian coast are promoted to the country's top flight – it last happened in 1995 – the players are probably ambivalent about such success. In the Russian top flight, the club closest to Baltika is Zenit St Petersburg, some 620 miles to the north.

Even that would seem a jaunt to footballers in Perth, on the west coast of Australia. When the optimistically monikered Perth Glory steel themselves for a match with their nearest rivals, they have a 1,322 mile schlep to Adelaide United. However, both Australian clubs prefer to acknowledge other derbies. Perth's players, officials and fans focus on the so-called Distance Derby with Wellington Phoenix, 3,270 miles away in New Zealand.

This derby started as a joke but acquired juice when the clubs vied for third in the A League in 2011–12. Adelaide's fiercest rivalry is the Cross-Border Derby with Melbourne Victory. As the name suggests, this fixture's importance has been fuelled by the fierce, historic rivalry between South Australia (where United are based) and Victoria (home to Victory). The first Cross-Border Derby match was only played in 2005 but the rivalry intensified after an incident the following year when Adelaide's outspoken coach John Kosmina grabbed Melbourne skipper Kevin Muscat by the throat after the player had knocked Kosmina off his chair while trying to collect the ball. The incident inspired the Kosmina-Muscat Cup, awarded to the best team in their league encounters.

All of which might suggest that it doesn't really matter how old a derby is. Or how close the teams are. If fans pine for their own 'El Clasico', the Cross-Border Derby shows you just need to create one.

⚽ How effective is **drinking** as a motivational aid?

During the 1997–98 season, Barnsley's only Premier League campaign, the players went out for a night on the town. As German goalie Lars Leese recalls in his memoir *The Keeper Of Dreams*, he shocked midfielder Darren Sheridan by lighting up a Marlboro Light. Sheridan rebuked Leese, saying he shouldn't be smoking because he was a professional athlete. To which the keeper replied: 'Well, look at yourself.' Sheridan, who was about to down his sixth pint of the evening, had no idea what Leese was talking about.

Brian Clough would have been just as mystified. 'The key to preparation,' he said once, 'is relaxation.' So on the coach to Munich's Olympiastadion before the 1979 European Cup final, he urged the Nottingham Forest players to have a beer. He had tried the same tactic in March that year, the night before the League Cup final. 'We had everything we could possibly have wanted to drink. Bitter, lager, mild, champagne,' recalled striker Garry Birtles. 'There were people who could hardly stand by the time we went to bed.

Clough insisted on it. Archie Gemmill wanted to go to bed. He wouldn't let him.' The experiment succeeded – but only just. Forest were 1-0 down to Southampton at half-time but sobered up in time to win it 3-2. It turned out okay for the European Cup, too, with Forest beating Malmö 1-0.

Even in the 1970s, Clough's methods were unorthodox, but many managers turned a blind eye to players' drinking as long as they were sober on the training ground and on match-days. Max Merkel, the great Austrian coach who won league titles in Austria, Germany and Spain, was once asked if his players were allowed a tipple. He replied: 'During training,

I once put all the drinkers into one team and the teetotallers into the other. The drinkers won the match at a canter. So I said, "Okay, keep on drinking".'

The first recorded evidence of concern that footballers were drinking too much is a ringing defence of the profession by Aston Villa forward Archie Hunter – in 1890. Challenging the 'impression abroad' that 'after every match the members [players] go to the nearest tavern and drink as hard as they can', he insisted they could drink only moderately because to do otherwise would be to damage their career. In the decades since, the careers of countless footballers – not just in Britain – have shown that wasn't quite the case. The roll call of only the most famous victims includes such names as Tony Adams, George Best, Hughie Gallacher, Garrincha, Jimmy Greaves, Ladislao Kubala, Diego Maradona (it wasn't just the cocaine, he was a bottle of whisky a night man), Socrates. And Paul Gascoigne.

Some old-school memoirs invest the players' hard drinking escapades with a tawdry glamour. The dismal reality is reflected more accurately in Ken Gallacher's biography of Jim Baxter. The gifted Scottish playmaker joined Sunderland in 1965 and when the move failed to revive his career, drank even more heavily than he had in Glasgow. As Gallacher notes, his Sunderland team-mates 'would gauge just how bad his night had been by how many times he threw up after his arrival.'

One of the most notorious alcohol-fuelled team bonding sessions took place at the China Jump Club in Hong Kong before England were due to host Euro 96. Although Paul Gascoigne pleaded in his autobiography, 'It was all a laugh, us letting our hair down before the Euro finals', the British tabloids profoundly disagreed, with the *Sun* calling Gascoigne a 'disgraced fool'. The England team had started out with Flaming Lamborghini cocktails and then noticed the 'dentist's chair'. If you sat in it, two barmen would come over and pour bottles of three different spirits down your neck. Teddy Sheringham was unlucky enough to be photographed getting the treatment and looked, as team-mate Stuart Pearce noted, more like Ollie Reed than a professional footballer.

The England players must have thought they had had the last laugh when they celebrated Gazza's sublime goal against Scotland. The England No. 8 passed the ball to himself over Colin Hendry's head and volleyed into the net. As Gazza lay prone on the pitch, his team-mates grabbed some bottles and squirted water into his open mouth, mimicking the dentist's chair incident and creating one of the most memorable goal celebrations in the history of the England team. The joy of that memory is tempered, now, by the knowledge of Gascoigne's terrible, subsequent struggles with alcohol.

It is rare for players to go as far as to have an inspirational tipple in the dressing room. Brazilian goal machine Arthur Friedenreich, whose goal won the Copa America in 1919, acquired a taste for beer and French brandy and liked a quick pick-me-up before he ran out on to the pitch. Hughie Gallacher, the outstanding Scottish forward of the 1920s and 1930s, once defended himself against accusations that he was drunk on the pitch by insisting he had used whisky as mouthwash.

Barcelona's Hungarian idol Ladislao Kubala, the club's all-time top scorer before Messi, once drank so much on a matchday that he could only play after being thrown into a shower and pumped with black coffee. That wasn't untypical: Kubala had been in an alcoholic haze when he arrived in Spain, too drunk to realise the train he thought was taking him to Madrid was heading to Barcelona. He scored 274 goals for the *Blaugranas* and was, according to Alfredo di Stéfano, the best ball juggler in the history of the game. Kubala remains a hero in Catalonia and Hungary even if, as time passes, his legend as a drinker is

The infamous dentist's chair celebration: Gazza gets the bottles from Steve McManaman, Alan Shearer and Jamie Redknapp.

in danger of overshadowing his fame as a footballer. Passing through customs once, he was asked to identify the two bottles of whisky he had declared on the form. The Hungarian star just pointed at his stomach.

This was the kind of lifestyle Sir Alex Ferguson fought against when he took over Manchester United in 1986, fuming that he had inherited a drinking club, not a football club. He soon purged the squad but didn't go quite as far as Arnold Hills, the Temperance Society member who changed the name of Thames Ironworks in 1900 to West Ham United. As a report in the *Morning Leader* noted: 'Mr A. F. Hills is very keen on playing a teetotal eleven next season.'

Hills never achieved his goal. Footballers still drink and defy medical science, coaches and the odds. Alcohol eventually did for Rudi Brunnenmeier, a fabulously gifted footballer who could, a trifle reductively, be known as the German George Best, but his career is as full of picaresque incidents as Kubala's. In the early hours of 1 September 1965, he was trying to weave his way home in Munich without hitting the concrete when he collided with a postman clutching a telegram. The German B team were due to face the Soviet Union later that day and he had been called up after a late injury. Still intoxicated, he made his way to the airport and flew to Cologne. He spent the afternoon in a hotel bed, trying to sleep off his hangover. Then he scored twice against the Soviet Union, hopped on a plane back to Munich and headed for the city's bars.

⚽ What is the point of **dugouts**?

Dugouts were originally dug into the ground so that the coaching staff (and, later, substitutes) sat below ground level. But that is an oddity in itself, for a dugout is perhaps the worst possible vantage point for football, given how often managers complain about their view even when they are sitting on a normal bench on the sidelines.

According to the book *Dugouts*, featuring photographs by David Bauckham of team shelters across Britain, the 'first dugout appeared at Aberdeen's ground, Pittodrie, in the early 1920s. Aberdeen's trainer at the time, Donald Colman, was a boxing and dancing enthusiast, obsessed with his players' footwork, who made meticulous notes during each game. Needing a dry notebook, he had Aberdeen build a sunken covered area at Pittodrie, thereafter known as the "dugout".'

This is a wonderful story, though it remains unclear why Colman's idiosyncratic, impractical and expensive invention should have become popular, especially since clubs didn't need a subs' bench at the time because there were no subs in football – and wouldn't be until the 1960s.

Baseball, on the other hand, has always had subs. Lots of them. And the word 'dugout' first appears in print in connection with baseball. *The Dickson Baseball Dictionary* gives the date as 17 October 1912 in the *New York Tribune*, but there seem to be earlier instances. The Library of Congress database reveals that, six days earlier, a piece in the *Washington Post* about pitcher Richard William 'Rube' Marquard began thus: 'Down in the dugout he sat, his lank legs crossed, his long arms dangling – a listless, indifferent man in whom no emotion was visible.'

When you look at the early baseball photographs in the Library of Congress, you discover a metamorphosis. In the latter years of the nineteenth century, the players not involved in the action sit on normal, spacious and sheltered benches, just like subs in football today. These benches are situated as near to home plate (where the batter stands to face the pitcher) as possible without interfering with play, as players coming from the bench usually do so to bat. Traditionally, the home team sits along the first base line, the visitors along the third base line. Gradually, these benches began to shrink. By 1902, some enclosures were so low players couldn't really sit upright. And by 1908, the first benches had been lowered into the ground so that the players' hips or knees were level with the field of play. In 1912, dugouts were so common that newspapers could use the term without having to explain it. It was also the year that an iconic image of New York Giants manager John McGraw was taken: he leans on the railing, observing the game, while his players sit behind and beneath him, in the dugout.

If even managers like McGraw couldn't see what they want from the dugout, why did clubs lower the benches in the first place? Some say it protected the players from foul balls routinely hit with considerable force down the first or third base line. It's more likely, though, that it was done because it helped club owners make money.

The most expensive seats in a baseball stadium are behind the home plate. If you have two sheds for players there, you are blocking the view for quite a few rows. Some clubs must have begun lowering the roof of the players' shelter to install more seats, until the players complained. That's when another solution was needed – and found. We don't know who first hit upon the idea of digging a hole for players, only that it wasn't Colman. Either he thought of it independently a few years later, or he was inspired by something he had heard or seen. Some Aberdeen legends, most notably Alex Jackson and Jock Hume, had spent some time in the American Soccer League in the early 1920s. Yet *Groundtastic* magazine, in a 2005 feature called 'Pyramid Passion', concluded 'it is more likely the idea came from one of Colman's coaching trips to Norway, where shelters were the norm due to the cold climate'.

⚽ When was the first **fanzine**?

The honour is often bestowed upon the venerable *When Saturday Comes*, concocted by Chelsea fan Mike Ticher while working in a London record shop in late 1985 and put into practice with the help of his work-mate, the Evertonian Andy Lyons, in March 1986. Yet the very first issue already mentioned 'another football magazine that refuses to sit back and watch while football dies', namely *Off The Ball*, published in Birmingham by a West Brom fan called Adrian

Goldberg. Many years later, Goldberg would be working for the BBC, which claimed he had 'founded Britain's first football fanzine'.

It's not true, though. Unbeknownst to them both at the time, Goldberg and Ticher had been beaten to the punch by Mike Harrison, who began putting out the Bradford City fanzine *The City Gent* in November 1984. In his Twitter profile, Harrison calls himself the 'editor of the oldest football fanzine in the UK', which is correct because *The City Gent* is still going strong.

But of course the oldest is not the first. That was a publication with a strong satirical bent called *FOUL*, started by a group of Cambridge University students and published between 1972 and 1976. One of the editors was Chris Lightbown. Many years later he said that *FOUL* came into being because 'football had simply not assimilated any of the social or cultural changes of the sixties. It was in a complete time warp'. In the same year in which Lightbown started *FOUL*, he also created a map for *Time Out* that illustrated football rivalries in London by allocating certain colours to certain clubs and showing in which boroughs these clubs' supporters were predominantly based. The map became somewhat famous nine years later when Desmond Morris published it in *The Soccer Tribe*.

Like all similar magazines that would follow, *FOUL* quickly built up a network of contributors, Eamon Dunphy among them. One reason the fanzine eventually folded was that Mike Langley, the then chief football writer for the *Sunday People*, threatened a lawsuit after a piece on soccer scribes. One of the original editors of the fanzine, Alan Stewart, became an investigative journalist and died when he was 35 after his car hit a landmine in southern Sudan. That was in late 1985, shortly before the fanzine boom kicked off.

⚽ Who coined game of two halves, early doors and sick as a parrot?

In his book *Football Talk*, Peter Seddon says that, on 22 March 1978, after Liverpool had lost the League Cup final replay, defender Phil Thompson gave a post-match interview in which he admitted: 'I'm as sick as a parrot.'

This is, as Seddon carefully puts it, 'the first high-exposure usage of the phrase', though by the following year it was popular enough to appear in *Private Eye* – which is where the Oxford English Dictionary lists its first usage. Yet when John Bond died, at the age of 79, in December 2012, the *Daily Telegraph*, and several fan forums for Norwich City and Southampton, credited him with inventing the term. The *Telegraph* writer noted, 'Sick as a dog would have been the predictable cliché', before adding that they weren't sure if the substitution of the parrot was 'merely a blooper' or reflected 'the gift football has for reinvigorating the language'.

The association between gloom and parrots can be traced back to the Restoration dramatist Aphra Behn, in whose 1682 comedy *The False Count*, the maid tells her mistress, 'You are as melancholy as a sick parrot'. However, Bond or Thompson were more likely drawing, possibly sub-consciously, on Monty Python's iconic Dead Parrot sketch, which had been broadcast in 1969 and reappeared in their first movie *And Now For Something Completely Different*. Or was the Liverpool skipper, as Seddon also suggests, merely shortening the old Scouse saying 'sick as a parrot with a rubber beak'?

The first recorded use of the mysterious phrase 'early doors' in a footballing context is by that linguistic master, Brian Clough. In November 1979, the Nottingham Forest manager reflected in an interview on his relationship with some of his players: 'Early doors, it was vital that they liked me.' However, when popularised by champagne-swilling, jewellery-juggling manager and TV pundit 'Big' Ron Atkinson, it was taken to refer to the beginning of a game.

What exactly does early doors mean? Some say it refers to people who wait outside pub doors waiting for them to open (this may explain why Craig Cash called his cult sitcom *Early Doors*). Others claim that it refers to any situation where people are earlier than is customary – indeed, it is used by restaurant owners to promote 'early doors' pre-theatre menus. Seddon has a more cultured explanation: 'It originates from nineteenth-century theatrical jargon, theatre doors being opened early for patrons willing to pay a premium price to nab the best seats.' These were the so-called 'early doors' tickets.

Atkinson may not have coined 'early doors' but, with his eclectic mash-up of football jargon and the English language, he pioneered a new football language – 'Ronglish', if you will. Among his creations are 'lollipop' (when a player puts one foot over the ball and hits it with the outside of his other foot), 'Hollywood ball' (as in 'He could have played the easy pass but he had to try a Hollywood ball') and 'reducer' (using your most competitive defender to nullify a skilful opponent). After being caught on microphone racially abusing Marcel Desailly, Big Ron became Racist Ron. Yet in his heyday, Ronglish had a poetic resonance. His famous description of a penalty kick – 'Left peg. Back stick. Bish bosh.' – has the compressed eloquence of a Japanese haiku.

The origin of the phrase 'A game of two halves' is even more mysterious. In football parlance, it has become a clichéd way of observing that things can turn around. The ultimate example of a game of two halves is probably Liverpool's epic comeback in the 2005 UEFA Champions League final, having been 3-0 down at half-time. However, a recent discussion on the BBC World Service mooted that the original 'game of two halves' was the 1930 World Cup final in which a squabble over whose ball should be used – the point was not then covered in the tournament regulations – forced FIFA to decree that the Argentinian ball should be used in the first half and the Uruguayan in the second. For the record, Argentina won the half played with their ball 2-1, while the Uruguayan hosts edged the half in which their ball was used 3-1 to win the World Cup.

In Germany, they have their own variation on the game of two halves. Herberger, the most influential German coach of all time, used to remind players: 'A game lasts for 90 minutes'. The favoured German cliché, however, is 'In football, everything is possible'.

⚽ At which ground are visitors least likely to be **insulted**?

Germany's St. Pauli, based in the same part of Hamburg as the Reeperbahn, the famous red-light district, was a fairly normal football club until 1980. But then a street near the harbour gained national prominence, because the city wanted to knock down eight untenanted nineteenth-century houses. They attracted a colourful group of radical squatters – from punk rockers and students to political activists and eco-warriors. Many of them adopted St. Pauli as their team and they gradually transformed the club. This, in brief, is why the fans wave skull-and-crossbones flags, why you don't hear bland pop groups during half-time but street punks Cock Sparrer and why the team runs out to AC/DC's 'Hell's Bells'. And why they play the club anthem of the opposing team.

This is a sign of respect, fair play and signals that you are a guest, not an opponent. The same attitude informs a code of honour amongst the home support at St. Pauli's Millerntor

St. Pauli fans show their support for gay rights during their Bundesliga match with SC Paderborn 07 on 1 April 2013.

ground that blacklists songs and banners that put down the visiting team. Many away fans who visit St. Pauli don't feel bound by this rule and sing anti-St. Pauli songs. These are usually met from all stands with a round of pitiful applause that drips with sarcasm.

Asked what characterises the St. Pauli experience, the club's long-time director of football Helmut Schulte once said: 'Standing up to right-wing tendencies in a peaceful atmosphere, in which the opponent is our friend. Visiting teams and fans are not insulted. We don't take ourselves that seriously. Our fans support the team not when things are going well but when it needs support. These are just some of the special things that have become established here.'

It doesn't always work. On occasion you can hear fans sing songs about St. Pauli's local rivals, the much bigger Hamburg SV, that are not complimentary. But it works more often than not. When Hoffenheim travelled to St. Pauli in 2010, the home fans felt they should somehow make clear that they didn't approve of a club bankrolled by a billionaire. But their code of honour said they couldn't sing or do anything insulting. And so the St. Pauli fans silently unfolded a banner as the Hoffenheim team ran out. It read: 'We don't even ignore you'.

⚽ When was the first **football magazine** published?

On 22 November 1873, the first issue of a publication called *Goal: The Chronicle Of Football* appeared. For the first time, a British publisher had decided that the sport of association football was popular enough to warrant its own periodical. The publication barely lasted a season.

That hasn't stopped countless publishers betting on the same belief over the last 140 years. The first modern football magazine – containing the kinds of snippets, interviews and features we would recognise today – is generally said to be *Charles Buchan's Football Monthly* (1951–74). As a footballer with Sunderland and Arsenal, Buchan had lamented the lack of a 'weekly bible for the game' and, after hanging up his boots, decided to create one. In his first issue, he declared: 'Our object is to provide a publication that will be worthy of our national game and the grand sportsmen who play and watch it.' Stanley Matthews was the cover star of the first issue, in which the Marquess of Londonderry confessed he had become interested in football after hearing miners talk about it down the pits.

However, Buchan's tome was predated by *France Football* (launched in 1946) and *El Gráfico* (an Argentinian sports magazine with a strong focus on football, founded in 1919). Martin Westby, who runs the website Soccerbilia, suggests that the first modern football magazine was actually published in Germany. *Die Fussball-Woche* (The Football Week) was launched on 24 September 1923, though the title was published on newsprint and printed in black and white. The magazine was started in Berlin by a 30-year-old journalist called Kurt Stoof and ran until the end of the war, when the Allies shut down all publications. It took a while to get going again, because Stoof languished in a Soviet prison from 1945 to 1950 but on his release he revived his magazine in West Berlin and it's still going as a local football paper.

Yet *Kicker*, Germany's most famous football magazine, has been around even longer. Now idiosyncratically spelled with a lower-case 'k', *Kicker* is such an institution that calling it

the Bible of German football would be an understatement. As with Stoof's *Die Fussball-Woche*, the history of *Kicker* magazine is complicated because of the years after the war when publications were closed and then relaunched. The original *Kicker* was founded by the German football pioneer Walther Bensemann in 1920 and the first issue was sold on 14 July 1920, more than three years before *Die Fussball Woche*. A magazine in a newspaper format, Bensemann's *Kicker* started as a weekly (it now comes out every Monday and Thursday) and covered every aspect of the game, even history: the cover of the first issue depicted two Karlsruhe teams from the 1890s.

Bensemann had discovered the joys of football while attending a British private school in Switzerland in the 1880s. The cosmopolitan son of a Jewish banker, he was instrumental in getting the game off the ground in Germany. Right from the start, the idea behind *Kicker* was to take a broader view, use foreign correspondents and carry smart, critical editorials. This was, Bensemann decided, the only way to distinguish his magazine from the competition.

Yes, *Kicker* had well-established competition in 1920 from *Fussball*, the official mouthpiece of the South German Football Association published by Eugen Seybold since 1911, and *Der Rasensport* (Field or Lawn Sport), launched in Berlin in 1902, whose subtitle was *Wochenschrift für die Interessen des Fussballsports* ('Weekly in the Interests of the Sport of Football'). Though the focus of *Der Rasensport* was on football, the editorial had a broad remit. In 1912, one issue featured detailed coverage of the season in England's Division Two. Five years later it bemoaned the fact that the 'blasé Berliners' didn't support their teams loudly enough. In 1929, the magazine became part of Stoof's *Fussball Woche*.

⚽ What is the **lowest crowd** for a top flight game?

Juventus have this pretty much sewn up. The *Bianconeri* have, according to polls, twelve million fans in Italy alone. Yet until they got their new stadium in 2011, their home games felt like some post-apocalyptic movie. The main reason for this was the Stadio delle Alpi, a cold (in every sense of the word) stadium with a running track and poor visibility, located on the outskirts of Turin. The club were saddled with this inhospitable home after the 1990 World Cup. For the 57 years before that they had been more happily ensconced downtown at the Stadio Comunale Vittorio Pozzo (formerly the Stadio Mussolini). The fans didn't appreciate the move.

On 27 October 1998, just 561 *tifosi* turned up for a Coppa Italia game between Juventus and Vicenza. With impressive understatement, Juve legend Alessio Tacchinardi, who was on the pitch that day, later said: 'We were tired, but maybe we would have found some energy if there had been more passion from the stands.' Then on 14 December 2001, another cup game, between Juve and Sampdoria, attracted (if that's the right word) 237 fans. The match kicked off at 6pm to suit television ('We won't give up a night match to play on a midweek afternoon again,' said the club's vice-president Roberto Bettega) and it was unusually cold that Wednesday. Still, as Amy Lawrence noted in the *Observer*: 'More than 237 would click through the turnstiles at Old Trafford even if there were an outbreak of bubonic plague – so the question must be asked: just what is Juventus's problem?' Well, as Tacchinardi put it: 'At the Stadio delle Alpi, the fans never really were the 12th man.'

The no-show by the *Bianconeri* unfaithful makes the Premier League's all-time low – 3,039 to watch an Everton side starring Peter Beardsley and Tony Cottee beat Wimbledon 3-1 on 26 January 1993 – look like a blockbuster crowd. However, the lowest-ever attendance for a Football League match is 13, the official tally for the crowd that watched Stockport County draw 0-0 with Leicester City at Old Trafford. There were extenuating circumstances – the game kicked off at 6.30pm and Stockport were forced to play at Old Trafford because their ground had been closed after irate fans had broken the window in the referee's dressing room after their team didn't get a stonewall penalty – and the real figure was probably higher. United had played earlier that day and it is estimated that 1,000 to 2,000 spectators from that match stayed behind to watch the second game for nothing.

Then again, it could have been worse for Juventus. If we ignore matches played behind closed doors (for example as a penalty for the home team), the lowest attendance for a proper top-flight game must be two. Yes, two paying customers attended the match between Universitatea Craiova and UM Timisoara in the Romanian First Division on 27 April 2002. (There were also 27 other onlookers and 50 policemen at the ground.) Like the stay-behinds at Old Trafford, the two hardy ticket buyers in Craiova were treated to a 0-0 draw.

Which footballers are best at acquiring native accents?

A video of Steve McClaren – the one-time England manager dubbed the wally with the brolly – went viral in August 2008, after his new club, Twente, were drawn against Arsenal in the Champions League. He sounded distinctly Dutch and spoke as if English was, at best, his second language, though to be fair, it's not the accent that is so odd but the rhythm and syntax of his speech. Unlike Joey Barton, who famously modified his Scouse tones with an *'Allo 'Allo* style French accent to address the press after he joined Marseille in 2012. The player himself dubbed this language 'Bartonese', a nice touch of self-irony, and it had a rather neat precedent in Chris Waddle's French-Geordie, perfected when he, too, played for Marseille between 1989 and 1992.

Still further back in the history of football's verbal fakery, England won the 1966 World Cup under a manager who was so worried by the hint of Essex in his dulcet tones that he would listen for hours to BBC radio announcers – this was at a time when they all spoke that form of upper class English known as Received Pronunciation – and modulate his tones to sound like them. Sir Alf never quite mastered this new accent. Before the World Cup, on a visit to Pinewood studios, Ramsey had his England players in stitches by saying hello to 007 star 'Seen' Connery.

'Eet ees deeffeecult ... we must try ter be burld." Joey Barton reinvents Franglais at Marseille.

Foreign footballers have a rather better record in adapting to regional British accents – and Danish footballers are the acknowledged masters of the genre. Peter Schmeichel grew distinctly Mancunian during his time at United, while Jan Mølby's perfected his Scouse, the midfield visionary insisted, through all the years he changed next to Sammy Lee in the dressing room. Peter Lovenkrands developed such a striking Glaswegian accent in his six years at Rangers that it has its own appreciation society on Facebook. Didi Hamann's Scouse-German accent is also unforgettable, if not quite on a par with the Danes' efforts. And nobody who heard him intervieweed could forget Jeremy Aliadiere, whose accent at Middlesbrough could go from Cockney sparrow to thoughtful Frenchman in three syllables.

⚽ What was the top **pop hit** by a footballer?

Let's make it immediately clear: this isn't an excuse to celebrate former Brentford centre-half Rod Stewart who played football on the *Top Of The Pops* stage with his band The Faces when 'Maggie May' was a UK number one in October 1971 and has since collaborated on two Scotland World Cup hits.

Though it lingers disturbingly long in our collective pop cultural memory, Hoddle and Waddle's 'Diamond Lights', written by Bob Puzey, only reached number 12 in 1987. Puzey's biggest hit was the Nolans' 'I'm In The Mood For Dancing' but Waddle wasn't in the mood for anything, the master of the stepover looking petrified on the nation's screens. Of the parties involved – Waddle, Hoddle, the producers, the presenters, the dancers in the studio and us, the record-buying public – the only one who didn't seem embarrassed by the whole business was Hoddle. They did at least do better than permed pop-football sensation Kevin Keegan whose 'Heads Over Heels In Love' had stalled at number 31 in 1979 in the UK, though it made the top ten in Germany.

This was no surprise. The Germans had all but invented the spine-chilling genre of singing footballers. In 1965, 1860 Munich's Yugoslav goalkeeper Petar 'Radi' Radenković, reached No 5 in the German charts, selling 400,000 copies of 'Bin i Radi, bin i König' ('Am I Radi, Am I King'). It's as atrocious as you would expect but Radenković did know something about music. His father had made his name as a folk singer under the stage name of Rascha Rodell. He was touring the US when World War Two started and never

Singing goalkeeper Petar 'Radi' Radenkovic sets the bar high for all football pop acts to follow, crooning in full strip with a Bavarian oom-pah band.

returned to Yugoslavia. Petar's brother Milan stayed in America and was known as Milan the Leather Boy after his 1967 garage rock hit 'I'm A Leather Boy'.

Making a record has been a temptation that Franz Beckenbauer, John Charles (who covered 'Sixteen Tons'), Ruud Gullit, Gerd Müller and Johan Cruyff (who, after a few, morale-boosting drinks, rose to the challenge of singing 'Oei! Oei! Oei! Dat Was Me Weer Een Loei') have all felt unable to resist. Gullit's reggae music both solo and with a band called Revelation Time is almost credible. Which is more than can be said for the biggest hit by a footballer – Paul Gascoigne's assassination of 'Fog On The Tyne (Revisited)', a UK number 2 in 1990.

☻ Why were **seven dead cats** buried in a stadium in Buenos Aires?

To put a curse on a club. And it worked a treat.

The saga of what Argentinians call *Los Gatos de Racing* (the Racing Cats) begins in November 1967, when Racing Club de Avellaneda won the Intercontinental Cup in a one-game playoff against Celtic in Montevideo. Investigating the case for *When Saturday Comes* in 2002, Ben Backwell wrote: 'When Racing fans were out celebrating their World Club Championship win against Celtic, Independiente supporters entered the Racing stadium and buried seven black cats around the premises. This, for many Racing fans, is the primary reason for their disastrous performance over the following years.'

Racing Club, who had 15 league titles to their name in 1967, when the cats were buried, didn't win anything – not a trophy of any kind – for the next 35 years, while fierce local rivals Independiente ... well, let's just say they won the Copa Libertadores four times running in the 1970s, the first and still the only club to pull off this feat.

Of course the story about the cats and the curse got out, prompting Racing to start a search for the feline bodies. 'Eventually, six of the cats were found and exhumed, but the seventh could not be located,' Backwell wrote. Even an exorcism carried out by a priest and attended by 10,000 fans couldn't lift the curse – in 1998, things were so bad that the club filed for bankruptcy.

In 2001, Reinaldo Merlo (a River Plate legend who made more than 500 league appearances for the club as a defensive midfielder) became Racing's new coach. According to Backwell, he 'ordered a comprehensive search of the stadium, which

The last Racing team before the curse of the cats, photographed before the brutal 'Battle of Montevideo' (see p.53).

included digging up a moat that had been concreted over'. And that's where they finally found the remains of the seventh cat. Having lifted the curse, Racing won their 16th league title – and their first since 1966 – that very season. Merlo was nicknamed *paso a paso* ('step by step') for his insistence that the club take each game as it comes. Despite the best efforts of Merlo and other club legends such as Alfio Basile, Racing have not, however, had to expand their trophy cabinet since.

As outlandish as all this sounds, it is not that rare in football. In March 2005, Sunderland blamed a ghost after their eight game winning streak was ended by defeat to Reading. They were happily chasing promotion to the Premier League until a spectre – described by one witness as 'a strange black shape' – was glimpsed at the training ground, next to a stream called Cut Throat Dene. One player ran off in terror and striker Marcus Stewart insisted: 'Stephen Elliott is adamant he's seen something.' Although two physios pursued the figure, the mystery was never solved. At least the players weren't spooked for long: they recovered in time to clinch the Championship.

If the crisis had persisted, Sunderland might have been well-advised to call in Aguib Sosso, a West African guru of juju who allegedly helped France win the 1998 World Cup. Malian witch doctor Adama Kone insisted that Sosso 'made wrist bands for the players to ward off the evil spirits'. Indeed, if you look at photos of the French squad celebrating their triumph, you can see the wrist bands.

As it turned out, Sosso's intervention may well have been unnecessary. Before the Seleção had set off for France, centre-back Júnior Baiano had consulted his aunt, a voodoo priestess, who warned him: 'Things may not go well in the squad.' And so it proved, with Ronaldo having a mysterious breakdown on the day of the final. Apparently, he hadn't felt his usual self since he'd failed to clear his bowels before the opening game against Scotland – a ritual, designed to expel fears, initiated by Roberto Rivelino when Brazil won the 1970 World Cup. Here again, Sosso (who died in 2002) tried to take the credit, telling Kone: 'I chanted Ronaldo's name over and over again – and the spell was cast.'

⚽ How common is it for footballers to smoke?

In the mid-1980s, Juventus's iconic owner Gianni Agnelli paid one of his regular visits to the dressing room and was shocked to find Michel Platini sitting on the bench in front of his locker puffing away on a cigarette. Recognising Agnelli's consternation, Platini told him: 'You shouldn't be worried if I smoke as long as Bonini doesn't – because he is also doing the running for me.' (If anything, Platini was doing Massimo Bonini a disservice: the midfielder also did most of the running for Zbigniew Boniek.)

Platini was hardly the only great player to enjoy a smoke. Johan Cruyff's nicotine habit was so ingrained that, as a player for Ajax and Barcelona, he typically had a cigarette in the dressing room before a match, a second at half-time, a third when he returned to the dressing room after the final whistle and a fourth when he emerged from the shower. Hennes Weisweiler, the German coach who had nurtured the swashbuckling Borussia Mönchengladbach side of the 1970s, challenged him over his habit when he was managing Barcelona in 1975 and quickly found himself out of a job. Even as coach, Cruyff smoked around 20 cigarettes a day until his doctors finally made him see reason. Remarking that 'Football has given me everything in life, tobacco almost took it all away,' the Dutchman gave up Camel cigarettes for lollipops.

The commercial synergy between smoking and football stretches back to 1896 when Manchester firm Marcus & Company published the first cigarette cards with footballers on them. This seemed a natural development, as smoking was prevalent in the game at that time. In John Powles's book *Iron In The Blood*, about the origins of West Ham United, he quotes a journalist's dismayed report after one London League match in the late nineteenth century: 'I am not an anti-tobacconist but I do not think it is at all good form for a goalkeeper to be seen smoking a cigarette in goal while a game is in progress, and for a linesman to be seen smoking a pipe.'

After World War I, Manchester United legend Charlie Roberts launched a wholesale tobacconist company and

PICTUREGOER December 13 1952

STANLEY MATTHEWS, Blackpool's quicksilver outside-right, has been capped for England no less than 33 times. Stan takes his training very seriously and soon discovered the cigarette which suited him best. "It wasn't till I changed to Craven 'A,'" he says, "that I learnt what smooth smoking meant."

"The cigarette for me"

SAYS FOOTBALL GENIUS **STANLEY MATTHEWS**

EVERY WEEK crowds warm to the brilliant technical play of master-schemer Stan Matthews—football's greatest name to fans and players alike. Like so many leading sportsmen Stan's a Craven 'A' smoker. "For a really satisfying cigarette that's kind to your throat," he says, "give me a Craven 'A' every time."

P.S. That cork tip really does make a difference, you know. There's a lot more pleasure in a cigarette with an end that's always clean, and dry, and firm between your lips

CRAVEN 'A' *smooth, clean smoking*

Sir Stanley, despite the claims of Craven A, wasn't actually a smoker.

invented a cigarette that he called 'Ducrobel' to honour himself and two former team-mates, Dick Duckworth and Alec Bell. In the 1930s, Everton legend Dixie Deans promoted budget Carreras Clubs while in the 1950s, Stanley Matthews advertised Craven A. In one famous advert, a smiling Matthews holds a cigarette above a caption that notes: 'Stan takes his training very seriously and soon discovered the cigarette which suited him best. "It wasn't till I changed to Craven A," he says, "that I learnt what smooth smoking means."' Luckily for Blackpool, England and Stoke City, Matthews was ahead of his time in his attention to diet and lifestyle and didn't smoke.

Attitudes to tobacco in the English game had already begun to change in the 1920s and 1930s as managers such as

Frank Buckley and Herbert Chapman made their disapproval clear. Yet even as powerful a manager as Chapman had to compromise. In 1928, he smashed the British transfer record to pay £10,890 to buy forward David Jack. It was, Chapman said later, 'one of the best bargains' he ever made. Jack won three league titles with the Gunners and scored 124 goals for them. Not bad given that he smoked 25 a day.

England's World Cup winning brothers, Bobby and Jack Charlton, were smokers. There's a lovely photograph of Jack Charlton on the Leeds United training ground, dragging on a cigarette as if his life depended on it. Jack's indulgence is less surprising than Bobby's. The clean-cut United idol, revered by a generation of English schoolboys, smoked ten cigarettes a day in the 1960s but, as *Woman* magazine noted, 'never before 2pm when training was finished.' Gradually, in England, the message that tobacco is bad for a player's lungs, heart and performance, seemed to sink home. However, when Fabien Barthez joined Manchester United that same year, Sir Alex Ferguson said: 'I know Fabien smokes. He is the third United player to have been hooked on cigarettes since I've been at the club. Before him, there were Jesper Olsen and goalkeeper Les Sealey. In England, it's a rare thing to see a player smoking but, all in all, I prefer that to an alcoholic.'

That seems to be the attitude in the rest of Europe. In Italy, Platini's habit was hardly exceptional. The likes of Carlo Ancelotti, Mario Balotelli, Marcello Lippi and Gianluca Vialli all indulged. When Balotelli was at Manchester City, his manager Roberto Mancini urged the player to kick his habit of five or six ciggies a day. Such consumption would hardly impress such 40-a-day-men as European Cup-winning, Croatian midfielder Robert Prosinecki, or nonchalant genius Socrates who captained the greatest

Brazilian side never to win the World Cup (in 1982) and was also a qualified doctor.

The greatest chain-smoker in the history of the game may well be Gérson, the midfield general in Brazil's beautiful World Cup winning side of 1970. Before the tournament, the coaching staff had begged him to cut down his 60-a-day habit. He tried but admitted later that he'd failed so badly the coaches realised he was a lost cause. Gérson's failure would have been painfully obvious to anyone near the players' tunnels when Brazil were playing because, at the end of each half, he ran off the pitch and gratefully accepted a lit cigarette from one of the coaching staff. None of this prevented him from scoring Brazil's second goal in the final – restoring their lead after Italy equalised – or being so effective in that tournament as a playmaker that some fans argue he was a bigger influence in that team than Pelé.

⚽ What's behind those Stadiums of Light?

Actually, Benfica's famous Estádio da Luz goes by many names. When it was opened, in late 1954, it was known as Estádio de Carnide (after the neighbourhood of Lisbon in which the ground is sited) and was officially called Estádio do Sport Lisboa e Benfica (after the full name of the club), while many fans simply referred to it as 'The Cathedral'.

Just a brisk walk from the stadium, maybe 600 yards north, is a church called Igreja de Nossa Senhora da Luz, which translates as 'Church of Our Lady of the Light'. Listed as a national monument, the church has lent its name to many of the surrounding streets and alleys and to the parish, which is simply called Luz. Soon people began to refer to the ground as Estádio da Luz, which you could indeed translate into English as Stadium of Light, though what gets lost in the process is the precise meaning of 'light' in this context, namely God's eternal presence. (As in Hank Williams' famous gospel song 'I Saw the Light'.)

Estádio da Luz is still commonly used for the new Benfica stadium, which opened in late 2003 on the site of the old one. And the Stadium of Light is also, strangely, the name of a football ground in deeply protestant Sunderland, where the name is a reference to the lights local miners wore on their helmets. Sunderland's reborn stadium opened in 1997, on the site of the closed Monkwearmouth Colliery, and replaced the club's old Victorian ground at Roker Park.

Twenty-eight years before, on BBC television, *Monty Python's Flying Circus* had, with amusing prescience, spoofed football punditry in a sketch reflecting on the latest action in the Philosophers' Football Match at Jarrow United's Stadium of Light. The commentator/interviewer, Eric Idle quizzed John Cleese's nonplussed footballer Jimmy Buzzard after declaring, 'Last night in the Stadium of Light, Jarrow, we witnessed the resuscitation of a great footballing tradition, when Jarrow United came of age, in a European sense, with an almost Proustian display of modern existentialist football virtually annihilating by midfield moral argument the now surely obsolescent *catenaccio* defensive philosophy of Signor Alberto Fanffino.'

The one ground in the world that has most right to be called the Stadium of Light stands in Eindhoven. It's the home of what used to be the company side of the largest manufacturer of lighting on the planet but is known, in a masterful display of literal thinking, as the Philips Stadium.

🌑 Why are Italian fans called **tifosi**?

The term *tifosi* comes from the Italian expression *tifo sportive* which describes the social phenomenon of people develop-ing an extreme passion for an athlete or a team. It has been suggested in Italy that the first part of the term – *tifo* – harks back to the Greek typhus (smoke, steam) but as John Foot notes in his history of Italian football, *Calcio*, it most likely comes from the medical term *tifico* (typhoid), stemming from the Greek word 'typhos'. As Foot writes: 'Sporting fans were linked to a kind of mental epidemic, which was contagious and produced forms of confusion typical of the illness … Like football supporting, typhoid came and went in cycles.'

In a nice autobiographical piece, a blogger called Dan-ielle, a Canadian-born freelance writer living in Italy, says: 'When I was a little girl, the word *tifosi* was almost sacred to me. In my mind it implied a higher bond with the team, more so than just a regular fan. Stereotypical *tifosi* are loud, colourful and often drink alcohol.' Then she adds: 'They are usually sporting a Ferrari shirt.' The *tifosi* she is writing about are diehard Ferrari supporters. In Italy, the word is not exclusively reserved for football fans. Birgit Schönau's book about Italian football culture (also called *Calcio*) suggests that the expression was coined by an Italian sportswriter in the 1920s to describe the feverish atmosphere at some foot-ball grounds. At that time, the potentially lethal typhoid fever, caused by the bacterium *Salmonella typhi*, was still a scourge in Italy's poorer regions. At the same time, Italian football fans in that decade were highly politicised: in 1925, there was a famous, bloody street battle between left-wing Genoa fans and fascist Bologna supporters. (Benito Musso-lini didn't like football much, it wasn't manly enough, but he liked the adulation of the game's fans.)

So *tifosi* didn't originally refer to enthusiastic and exuberant fans, slightly batty in a charming way. That may be how we now associate with the term but it was coined to describe very dangerous people.

⚽ Who was the first football TV commentator?

Probably Hans-Günther Marek, one of the announcers for the Paul Nipkow Berlin TV station at the 1936 Olympics. Nipkow's live coverage of the Games, the first live coverage of an event in the history of television, ran from 10am to noon, 3pm to 7pm and 8pm to 10pm and Marek handled all the important stuff – such as Hitler's entrance and the arrival of the Olympic flame – at the Olympic stadium, where two cameras did their best to capture the action. That important stuff would have included, on 10 August 1936 at 5pm, the football semi-final between Italy and Norway. As the game went into extra time, past the 7pm cut-off, viewers may not have known the outcome: Italy won 2-1 thanks to a 96th-minute strike by Annibale Frossi.

One famous photograph of Marek shows him resplendent in a white suit, poised in front of a microphone, looking every inch the ambitious young Nazi. (In World War II he was last heard of heading up Germany's radio service in Norway.) He probably had more influence than any commentator since on the coverage of the game as, with no monitor to see what his cameramen were doing, he just described what he regarded as the most interesting action, hoping the cameras would follow his lead.

Just over a year later, on 16 September 1937, the BBC broadcast parts of a match between Arsenal and Arsenal

TV pundit and Arsenal manager George Allison debates the isssues of the day for the BBC with Thomas Woodroffe, 1935.

Reserves – even though there were fewer than 10,000 television sets in UK homes at that time. Arsenal manager George Allison introduced his players in that historic broadcast and he was behind the microphone on 9 April 1938 when the BBC broadcast the England v Scotland game. Allison had commentated for BBC Radio for years and was joined by a former naval officer called Thomas Woodroffe who had covered the 1936 Olympics. Scotland won the first televised international 1-0 with a goal by Hearts striker Tommy Walker.

Woodroffe is most famous for observing, after 29 minutes of extra time in the 1938 FA Cup final with the score at 0-0, 'If there's a goal scored now, I'll eat my hat.' Within seconds, George Mutch scored for Preston from the spot. Woodroffe kept his word, in a way: according to *Time* magazine, he ate a hat made of cake.

⚽ Was the soccer war about soccer?

Not really. Certainly the event that ignited the brief conflict between El Salvador and Honduras in 1969 was a World Cup qualifying tie, which is why the Polish writer and tale-teller Ryszard Kapuscinski called his account *The Soccer War* – but the underlying tensions between the neighbouring Central American countries had little to do with football.

The root causes of the war were geography and population. Honduras, with a population of 7.7m, has a territory of 43,278 square miles. El Salvador has almost as many people – 6.2m – but is less than a fifth of the size of Honduras. Inevitably, many Salvadorans spilled over a not terribly well-defined border into Honduran territory – 300,000 of them by 1969. That year, a series of two-year accords that tried to regulate this flow of people ended and was not renewed. The Honduran government also passed a new law reforming the agrarian sector which ejected some Salvadoran squatters from their land. Others fled Honduras fearing persecution. Images of their flight prompted predictably jingoistic rhetoric from Salvadoran politicians.

So when the two countries' teams met in a World Cup qualifier on 8 June 1969 in the Honduran capital, Tegucigalpa, the match had taken on titanic symbolic importance.

Honduras won the first match 1-0. A few rival supporters fought in the stands and the visitors left convinced that they had been cheated, with the winning goal scored in the tenth minute of injury time. By the time the second leg was played a week later, the outrage in El Salvador had become so intense that the police had to hide the Honduran team in a secret location outside the capital, San Salvador. Three Salvadorans died in riots before the match. With the police confiscating booze and weapons on the way into the stadium, the match was almost an anti-climax. Salvador won 3-0. This meant that both teams were level on points and, with neither goal difference or aggregate scores being used as tie-breaker, the two sides would meet again in a play-off.

This was the last thing either country needed. Rocks were thrown at some Honduran fans' cars as they drove back home. The Honduran government exaggerated these incidents, even suggesting that the Salvadorans were holding Hondurans prisoner. Such stories provoked attacks on Salvadoran communities. Soon, as many as 1,400 refugees a day were crossing the border, seeking sanctuary in El Salvador.

With troops skirmishing on the border, the Salvadoran Council of Ministers accused the Honduran government of 'the crime of genocide'. Diplomatic relations were broken off a few days after the play-off, in Mexico City on 26 June, which El Salvador won 3-2.

The football was over but the war was about to begin. On 3 July, a small Honduran plane flew over Salvadoran territory. Eleven days later, three Honduran fighters flew into Salvadoran air space in the morning. By that afternoon, Salvador had struck back, bombing Tegucigalpa airport and sending troops across the border.

The war lasted about 100 hours, long enough to kill somewhere between 2,000 and 6,000 people. Peace didn't officially break out until the warring neighbours signed a treaty in 1980. By then El Salvador was engulfed by a far deadlier conflict: a civil war between the right-wing government and its opposition in which 75,000 Salvadorans died.

Reaching the 1970 World Cup finals was a milestone for El Salvador. But they finished bottom of Group A, having scored no goals and losing all three games. The highlight, if you can call it that, of the campaign came in the second match against hosts Mexico. The Salvadorans had held their own, with midfielder Mauricio Rodríguez hitting the post. Then, just before half-time, they were awarded a free-kick by Egyptian referee Hussaian Kandil. For no obvious reason, Mexican defender Mario Peréz decided to take it, passing the ball to Aarón Padilla who crossed for Javier Valdivia to make it 1-0. As Brian Glanville noted: 'In vain did the El Salvador players argue, weep and lie on the ground. The goal disgracefully stood. Mexico went on to score three more against a demoralised side.'

Twelve years later, Luis Ramírez Zapata scored El Salvador's first goal in a World Cup finals. His celebrations were slightly muted by the fact that his side were already losing 5-0 when he scored and would go on to lose 10-1, a record defeat in a World Cup finals. Such is the misery this Central American nation has endured in World Cups, it is a wonder they still enter.

Acknowledgements

Thanks to Alison Ratcliffe, Andrew Murphy, Martin Mazur. Paolo Menicucci, Jack Simpson, Lesley Simpson, Philippe Auclair, Simon Kanter, Helen Morgan, Jonathan Wilson, Susanne Hillen and Henry Iles.

Photo credits

About the authors

PAUL SIMPSON was launch editor of *FourFourTwo*
magazine. He is the author of the critically acclaimed
Rough Guide to Elvis and currently edits the UEFA
magazine, *Champions*. His favourite football team of
all time is Jimmy Bloomfield's Leicester City.

ULI HESSE is the author of *Tor! The Story of German
Football*, a contributor to *11 Freunde* magazine and is
writing a book on the history of Borussia Dortmund,
the club he supports, through the eyes of its fans. He
has written more than 300 columns for ESPN FC.

Room At The Inn

Series Editor: David Hancock
Managing Editor: Isla Love
Senior Editor: Donna Wood
Senior Designer: Kat Mead
Copy Editor: Sharon Amos
Proofreader: Helen Ridge
Cartography provided by the Mapping Services Department of
AA Publishing
Image retouching and colour repro: Matt Swann
Production: Rachel Davis
Index: Hilary Bird

Produced by AA Publishing
© Automobile Association Developments Limited 2007

Published by AA Publishing (a trading name of Automobile Association
Developments Limited, whose registered office is Fanum House,
Basing View, Basingstoke RG21 4EA; registered number 1878835).

Enabled by [Ordnance Survey] This product includes mapping data licensed from
Ordnance Survey ® with the permission of the Controller
of Her Majesty's Stationery Office.
© Crown copyright 2007. All rights reserved. Licence number 100021153.

A03060

ISBN-13: 978-0-7495-5421-7
A CIP catalogue record for this book is available from the British Library.

Colour reproduction by Keene Group, Andover
Printed and bound in Dubai by Oriental Press

The AA's website address is www.theAA.com/travel

Room At The Inn

Contents

Inn Location Map

Welcome to...
Room At The Inn

Not long ago the thought of staying overnight in a pub would conjure up images of cheaply furnished bedrooms, the smell of stale smoke, food and beer, and basic shared bathrooms at the end of dimly lit corridors. How things have changed over the last decade! Just flicking through this colourful collection of stylish inns, it's clear to see that pubs are becoming our new breed of country hotels and restaurants.

Pubs have had to evolve to survive in an increasingly competitive hospitality business. A growing number are now very much in tune with today's leisure aspirations and lifestyle, successfully combining a relaxing, informal atmosphere with good food, real ales, fine wines and smart ensuite accommodation. The increasingly discerning public now have a stylish alternative to a faceless, budget travel inn, a faded town-centre hotel, or a large, impersonal and often expensive country-house hotel.

The gastropub revolution of the early 90s changed the face of pub food forever. Suddenly, from an industry relying on bought-in 'freezer to fryer' foods, there were chic city boozers and rustic rural pubs with open kitchens and chefs cooking modern British and European dishes from fresh, locally sourced produce. The rise of food-driven pubs has continued unabated as consumer interest about where the food they are eating actually comes from has increased. A growing number of pubs are sourcing their produce from local farmers and suppliers, or even growing their own.

Many of the inns listed in these pages are owned by chef/patrons who have previously plied their trade in top restaurants, or there's a talented and ambitious chef at the stove. You'll find chalkboard or daily printed menus championing local, seasonal produce, be it fish and shellfish from local boats, traceable meats from nearby farms, locally shot game or organic vegetables from local allotment holders. One or two have taken their commitment to support local producers a step further by opening small produce shops in adjoining buildings, and a few even hold their own weekly small-scale farmers' markets in the pub car park.

There have also been major improvements in the range and quality of both wine and beer. Gone are the days when there was only one red and one white wine by the glass and a basic list to choose from. Wines are now carefully selected to match the style of food being created in the kitchen. Chalked-up lists blend Old and New World wines, offer decent tasting notes, some classic vintages and often up to 20 by the glass. You'll also find locally brewed hand-pumped ales as the flowering of independent microbreweries (now over 400) continues apace across the country.

So, having wined and dined well, just climb the stairs to sleep in a cosy and well-equipped bedroom. The furnishings, fabrics, cosseting extras and swish bathrooms once only found in posh hotels are now the norm in the classy inns within these pages. You'll find soothing heritage colours, plasma TV screens, digital radios, fresh coffee, home-made biscuits, goose down duvets and pillows and Egyptian cotton sheets on big beds, and spotless bathrooms kitted out with claw-foot baths, storm showers, fluffy bathrobes, under-floor heating and top toiletries. Bliss!

To aid your rest and relaxation on a weekend away we've included details on places to visit, from National Trust properties and select museums to glorious gardens and timeless villages. Ideas to keep active types amused range from balloon trips and where to play golf to information on local cycle rides and where you can hire a classic car for the day. Upmarket shops are not forgotten, we guide you to the best shopping towns, key antique shops, galleries and clothing boutiques and, perhaps, a local farm shop or deli for those all-important edible goodies and gifts to take home.

The final ingredient to a relaxing weekend away is a good country walk, the best way to get to know the area. So, having tucked into a hearty breakfast you can follow the suggested rural ramble. All of the mapped walks are between 3 and 8 miles long and within easy reach of the inn, some even pass the door. You'll find detailed directions, essential notes on the terrain, and the relevant Ordnance Survey map to take with you.

Walking in Safety

Each of the inns featured in this book has a specially selected walk that will guide visitors around a nearby place of interest. Before you embark on any of the walks, read the righthand panel giving at-a-glance practical information about the walk, including the distance, how much time to allow, terrain, nature of the paths, and where to park your car.

All of the walks are suitable for families, but less experienced family groups, especially those with younger children, should try the shorter walks. Route finding is usually straightforward, but the maps are for guidance only and we recommend that you always take the relevant Ordnance Survey map with you.

The Risks

Although each walk has been researched with a view to minimising any risks to walkers, it is also good common sense to follow these guidelines:

• Be particularly careful on cliff paths and in hilly terrain, where the consequences of slipping can often be very serious.
• Remember to check the tidal conditions before walking on the seashore.
• Some sections of the walk routes are by, or cross, busy roads. Take care here, and remember that traffic is a danger even on minor country lanes.
• Be careful around farmyard machinery and livestock.
• Be prepared for the consequences of changes in the weather, and check the forecast before you set out.
• Ensure everyone is properly equipped with suitable clothing and a good pair of boots or sturdy walking shoes. Take waterproof clothing with you and a torch if you are walking in the winter months.
• Remember that the weather can change quickly at any time of the year, and in moorland and heathland areas, mist and fog can make route-finding much harder. In summer, take account of the heat and sun by wearing a hat, sunscreen and carrying enough water.
• On walks away from centres of population you should carry a mobile phone, a whistle and, if possible, a survival bag. If you do have an accident requiring emergency services, make a note of your position as accurately as possible and dial 999.
• Many of the routes in this book are suitable for dogs, but observing your responsibility to other people is essential. Keep your dog on a lead and under control.

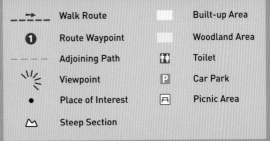

----➤ Walk Route			Built-up Area
1 Route Waypoint			Woodland Area
– – – – Adjoining Path		🚻	Toilet
Viewpoint		P	Car Park
• Place of Interest			Picnic Area
⌄ Steep Section			

The Gurnard's Head
Cornwall

The Inn

An early 17th-century coaching inn standing on the windswept coastal road that runs between St Ives and Land's End, The Gurnard's Head shines out like a beacon of warmth and hospitality amid a patchwork of fields and ancient farms. Brothers Charles and Edmund Inkin have transformed the original building into a fabulous pub with rooms in much the same way that they made The Felin Fach Griffin the must-visit pub of the Brecon Beacons. The Inkins' motto is 'the simple things in life done well', and this extends to all aspects of the running of The Gurnard's Head.

Its stunning location and views of the Atlantic make it popular with walkers, tourists and city dwellers looking for tranquillity. The ensuite bedrooms are simply and tastefully decorated: the handmade beds are so comfortable that the owners regularly get asked if they're for sale, and they're made up with the softest white linen. Each room, like the rest of the pub, is lined with old books and local pictures and maps, which enhances the feeling that guests are staying with old friends.

The Food

Depending on your mood, eat in the cosy bar, the slightly more formal dining room with its contemporary leather chairs, gleaming old oak floors and fine 18th-century stone fireplace, or indeed outside when the uncertainties of a northern English summer allow. Delicious starters include roasted quail with squash mash, caraway and bacon, or ham hock terrine with pear and mustard chutney, while main courses such as Gressingham duck breast served with creamed savoy cabbage, pomme fondant and thyme juices, shoulder and loin of salt marsh lamb with samphire and mint sauce, or line-caught sea bass with roasted Mediterranean vegetables and lemon vierge, reveal a passion for meticulous sourcing of seasonal ingredients.

Puddings, too, have a real feel-good quality with clotted crème brûlée with marinated strawberries and lavender shortbread, or bitter chocolate tart with white chocolate mousse and stem ginger and milk chocolate ice cream, typical of the unusual and irresistible choices. The wine list is both extensive and affordable – in all, spending time here in the South Lakes has never been as pleasurable.

What To Do

Shop

FARFIELD MILL, SEDBERGH

At the foot of the Howgill Fells, a gallery of craft artisans and artists with open studios displaying a selection of work; many accept bespoke commissions. Silversmiths, potters, weavers and contemporary furniture makers are a few of the artists to discuss their works with. The Mill also contains galleries with exhibitions of work from throughout Britain.

Garsdale Road, Sedbergh,
Cumbria LA10 5LW
01539 621958
www.farfieldmill.org

GLASS CRYSTAL ENGRAVING

Unique works from this gallery feature in collections at The Vatican and The White House. Just a handful of master-engravers work in Britain; here, intricate designs based largely on Lake District views are painstakingly hand-engraved or sculpted and individual commissions executed. The town also has several antique galleries.

2A Imperial Buildings, Main Street,
Grange-over-Sands, Cumbria LA11 6DP
01539 535656
www.artcrystal.co.uk

SILLFIELD FARM

Wild boar is the choice delicacy farmed in the hills above Kendal. Free-range pork in all its guises is the result, with speciality bacon, dry-cured and air-cured hams, pies of various styles and a range of sausages available at the farm shop. Another local favourite here is oak-smoked Westmorland cheese.

Endmoor, Kendal, Cumbria LA8 0HZ
01539 567609
www.sillfield.co.uk

Visit

BLACKWELL

A soaring, shapely homage to the Arts and Crafts movement, built for a wealthy merchant on a prime site overlooking Windermere. Beneath the gabled slate roof and round chimney stacks, painstaking restoration and eclectic collecting delivers exquisite furniture, decorative arts and wall-coverings, stained glass and more.

Bowness-on-Windermere,
Cumbria LA23 3JT
01539 446139
www.blackwell.org.uk

DOVE COTTAGE

Once the home of William Wordsworth, the museum here has all the manuscripts and insights you'd expect from a literary shrine. His later home, Rydal Mount, is nearby. While you're here, indulge in the poet's other great passion – walking. An easy trek around tranquil Grasmere, along Loughrigg Terrace, gives outstanding views.

Grasmere, Cumbria LA22 9SH
01539 435544
www.wordsworth.org.uk

LEVENS HALL

The art of the topiarist is explored to the full here in the most varied display of clipped and cosseted box and beech in the country, from geometric forms to shades of Henry Moore sculpture. The beautiful Elizabethan house is graced by rooms with memorable plasterwork and bizarre Cordova leather wall-coverings, fine paintings and remarkable period furnishings.

Kendal, Cumbria LA8 0PD
01539 560321
www.levenshall.co.uk

Activity

OFF-ROAD DRIVING

Tackle former mine roads and pack trails into the higher reaches of the fells with a day's expert tuition in a 4WD vehicle. The rugged terrain, which can include some quite challenging routes encountering water and mud, makes for an adrenalin-packed expedition a world away from the sedate crawl to work on smooth tarmac roads.

Kankku, Victoria Forge, Victoria Street,
Windermere, Cumbria LA23 1AD
01539 447414
www.kankku.co.uk

PONY TREKKING

The Troutbeck Valley and its tributaries percolate to the heart of some of the southern Lakes' most rugged and inspiring landscapes. Treks aimed at beginners explore the lower reaches, while those with more experience may trail ride up onto the high fells on Irish hunters or tough Lakeland ponies.

Limefitt Park, Patterdale Road, Troutbeck,
Cumbria LA23 1NT
01539 431999
www.lakelandponytrekking.co.uk

WINDERMERE YACHTING

Charter a private luxury yacht on England's largest lake, crack open the champagne and sit back and explore at your own pace, with the skipper at the helm and an experienced crew on hand. Alternatively, take tuition while on board, learning the ropes and handling the craft yourself on a full day's experience under sail.

Ferry Road, Ferry Nab, Bowness-on-
Windermere, Cumbria LA23 3JH
01539 552338
www.obsailing.co.uk

The Walk - *Bowness-on-Windermere and Brant Fell*

Enjoy a walk through woodlands with breathtaking views.

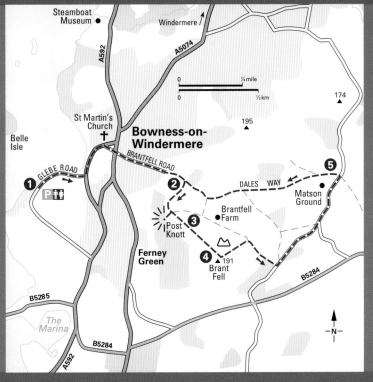

Walk Details

LENGTH: 3.5 miles (5.7km)

TIME: 1hr 15min

ASCENT: 525ft (160m)

PATHS: Pavement, road, stony tracks, grassy paths, 2 stiles

SUGGESTED MAP: aqua3 OS Explorer OL7 The English Lakes (SE)

GRID REFERENCE: SD 398966

PARKING: Car park on Glebe Road above Windermere lake

❶ Take Glebe Road into Bowness. Swing left and, opposite the steamer pier, go right over the main road and turn left. Opposite the Church of St Martin, turn right to go up St Martins Hill. Cross Kendal Road to climb Brantfell Road directly above. At the head of the road, an iron gate leads to Dales Way, which climbs up the hillside. Proceed to the kissing gate by the wood, leading on to lane. ❷ Pass through the kissing gate; turn right ('Post Knott') to follow the lane. Proceed ahead, rising through woods until lane crests height near flat circular top of Post Knott. Bear left; make the final short ascent to summit. Retrace your steps to the track; bear right to the kissing gate, leaving the wood on to open hillside.

❸ Beyond kissing gate take grassy path, rising to rocky shoulder. Cross the shoulder and first descend, then ascend, to ladder stile in top corner of field by fir trees. Cross stile; bear right to ascend up the open grassy flanks of Brant Fell to rocky summit. ❹ Go left (north) from top of fell, descending via a grassy path intercepted by grassy track. Bear right here; follow the track to a stone stile and gate on to the road. Turn left on the road; continue left at the junction to pass the stone buildings and the entrance drive to Matson Ground. Immediately beyond is a kissing gate on the left, waymarked Dales Way. ❺ Go through kissing gate; continue down field to cross the track; pass

through kissing gate into another field. Keep on grassy track until path swings left to emerge through kissing gate on to surfaced drive. Go right along the drive for 30yds (27m) until the path veers off left through trees to follow the fence. An iron kissing gate leads into field. Follow the grassy path, first descending and then rising towards an iron gate in the field corner. Continue to join a grassy track; go through the kissing gate. Cross Brantfell Farm's surfaced drive; keep ahead to another kissing gate leading into field. Follow the path, parallel to the wall, descending the hill to intercept the track, via the kissing gate; regain Point 2. Retrace your route back to Glebe Road.

Where to Go When You Want...

Modern Chic

Albert Arms, Esher 118–21

Bath Arms, Longleat 64–7

Bildeston Crown, Bildeston 210–15

Boar's Head, Ardington 166–9

Bull, Ditchling 108–11

The Clive, Bromfield 246–9

Collyweston Slater, Collyweston 202–5

Crazy Bear, Stadhampton 154–7

Devonshire Arms, Beeley 270–3

Devonshire Fell, Burnsall 278–81

Farmers Inn, West Hatch 26–9

General Tarleton, Ferrensby 300–3

Globe Inn, Wells-next-the-Sea 232–5

Halfway Bridge Inn, Petworth 104–7

Inn at Grinshill 250–3

Miller of Mansfield, Goring-on-Thames 150–3

Olive Branch, Clipsham 262–5

Queen's Head, Belton 258–61

Rose and Crown, Snettisham 228–31

Royal Oak, East Lavant 100–3

Stapleton Arms, Buckhorn Weston 56–9

Swan, Bradford-on-Avon 68–73

Swan Inn, Chiddingfold 122–5

Three Horseshoes Inn, Radnage 174–7

Verzon, Trumpet 194–7

The Weary, Castle Carrock 326–9

Wheatsheaf, Combe Hay 34–7

Wheelwrights Arms, Monkton Combe 30–3

White Horse, Brancaster Staithe 224–7

Rural Splendour

Angel Inn, Hetton 304–7

Boar's Head, Ardington 166–9

Bull, Ditchling 108–11

Cherry Tree Inn, Stoke Row 158–61

Compasses Inn, Lower Chicksgrove 82–5

Dartmoor Inn, Lydford 20–5

Devonshire Arms, Beeley 270–3

Devonshire Arms, Long Sutton 48–51

Drunken Duck, Barngates 316–21

Farmers Inn, West Hatch 26–9

Hawkley Inn, Hawkley 90–3

Howard Arms, Ilmington 198–201

Inn at Grinshill 250–3

Inn at Whitewell 274–7

King's Arms, Didmarton 142–5

Manners Arms, Knipton 254–7

Pear Tree Inn, Whitley 74–7

Peat Spade Inn, Longstock 86–9

Pheasant Inn, Higher Burwardsley 266–9

Punch Bowl, Crosthwaite 330–5

Queen's Arms, Corton Denham 42–7

Queen's Head, Cumbria 322–5

Stagg Inn, Titley 190–3

Three Crowns Inn, Ullingswick 186–9

Three Horseshoes Inn, Radnage 174–7

Verzon, Trumpet 194–7

The Weary, Castle Carrock 326–9

Wensleydale Heifer, West Witton 286–91

Wheatsheaf, Combe Hay 34–7

Wheelwrights Arms, Monkton Combe 30–3

White Swan Inn, Pickering 296–9

Traditional Charm

Abbey Inn, Byland Abbey 282–5

Angel Inn, Hetton 304–7

Beacon, Tunbridge Wells 126–9

Bell at Skenfrith 134–7

Blackwell Ox Inn, Sutton on the Forest 308–11

Blue Lion, East Witton 312–15

Carnarvon Arms, Whitway 94–9

Compasses Inn, Lower Chicksgrove 82–5

Drunken Duck, Barngates 316–21

Eight Bells, Chipping Campden 146–9

George and Dragon, Rowde 78–81

George Hotel, Cranbrook 130–3

George in Rye 112–17

Horse and Groom, Bourton on the Hill 138–41

Hoste Arms, Burnham Market 240–5

Howard Arms, Ilmington 198–201

Inn at Whitewell 274–7

King's Arms, Didmarton 142–5

Kings Head Inn, Bledington 162–5

Lord Poulett Arms, Hinton-St-George 38–41

Museum Inn, Farnham 52–5

Peat Spade Inn, Longstock 86–9

Punch Bowl, Crosthwaite 330–5

Queen's Arms, Corton Denham 42–7

Queen's Head, Cumbria 322–5

Spread Eagle Inn, Stourhead 60–3

Stagg Inn, Titley 190–3

Star Inn, Harome 292–5

Trout Inn, Buckland Marsh 170–3

The Victoria at Holkham, Holkham 236–9

A Taste of History

Sea Air

The Dog to Stay

Index

Acknowledgements

The Automobile Association wishes to thank the following photographers and companies for their assistance in the preparation of this book.

Abbreviations: F/C front cover; B/C back cover

F/C (i) The Collyweston Slater; F/C (ii) The Punch Bowl; F/C (iii) Graham Rowatt; F/C (iv) Keiron Tovell; F/C (v) The George In Rye; F/C (vi) The Punch Bowl; Spine The Punch Bowl; B/C (i) The Bath Arms; B/C (ii) Keiron Tovell; B/C (iii) The Pear Tree Inn; B/C (iv) The Pear Tree Inn; B/C (v) The Drunken Duck; B/C (vi) Carnarvon Arms; 1 The Punch Bowl; 2t Dartmoor Inn; 2c The Bildeston Crown; 2b The George; 5tr Dartmoor Inn; 5ctr Pamela Farrell; 5cbr The Miller of Mansfield; 5br The Devonshire Arms; 9t Dartmoor Inn; 9bl The Bildeston Crown; 9br The Punch Bowl; 10 The Bath Arms; 12-13 The Gurnard's Head; 16-17 Graeme Bexley; 20-23 Dartmoor Inn; 26-27 The Farmers Inn; 30-31 The Wheelwrights Arms; 34-35 Mathew Wyatt; 38-39 Lord Poulett Arms; 42-45 The Queen's Arms; 48-49 The Devonshire Arms; 52-53 The Museum Inn; 56-57 The Stapleton Arms; 58-59 The Spread Eagle Inn; 64-65 The Bath Arms; 68-71 The Swan; 74-75 The Pear Tree Inn; 78-79 The George and Dragon; 82-83 The Compasses Inn; 86-87 The Peat Spade Inn; 90-91 The Hawkley Inn; 94-97 Carnarvon Arms; 100-101 Sussex Pub Company; 104-105 Sussex Pub Company; 108-109 The Bull; 112-115 The George in Rye; 118-119 The Albert Arms; 122-123 The Swan Inn; 126-127 The Beacon; 130-131 The George; 134-135 Joey Ward; 138-139 The Horse and Groom; 142-143 The King's Arms; 146-147 Eight Bells; 150-151 The Miller of Mansfield; 154-155 Abi Taylor; 158-159 The Cherry Tree Inn; 162-163 The King's Head Inn; 166-167 The Boar's Head; 170-171 The Trout Inn; 174-175 Three Horseshoes Inn; 178-179 The Sun Inn; 182-183 The Mistley Thorn; 186-187 The Three Crowns Inn; 190-191 The Stagg Inn; 194-195 The Verzon; 198-199 The Howard Arms; 202-203 The Collyweston Slater; 206-207 Agellus Hotels; 210-213 The Bildeston Crown; 216-217 The Anchor Inn; 220-221 David Watson; 224-225 Pamela Farrell; 228-229 The Rose and Crown; 232-233 The Globe Inn; 236-237 The Victoria at Holkham; 240-243 Keiron Tovell; 246-247 The Clive; 250-251 The Inn at Grinshill; 254-255 The Manners Arms; 258-259 The Queen's Head; 262-263 The Olive Branch; 266-267 The Pheasant Inn; 270-271 Devonshire Country House Hotel & Spa; 274-275 The Inn at Whitewell; 278-279 Devonshire Country House Hotel & Spa; 282-283 The Abbey Inn; 286-289 Graham Rowatt; 292-293 The Star Inn; 296-297 The White Swan Inn; 300-301 The General Tarleton; 304-305 The Angel Inn; 308-309 Penny Hodgson; 312-313 The Blue Lion; 316-319 The Drunken Duck; 322-323 The Queen's Head; 326-327 The Weary; 330-333 The Punch Bowl.

Although every effort has been made to trace the copyright holders, we apologise in advance for any accidental errors. We would be happy to apply the corrections in the following edition of this publication.

In addition, David Hancock would like to thank David Ashby, Elizabeth Carter, Nick Channer, Colin Cheyne, Neil Coates, Sarah Fergusson, Charles Edmondson-Jones, Lesley Mackley, Mark Taylor, Jill Turton, Jenny White, Glyn Williams and Amanda Wragg for their editorial assistance.

The Essentials

Time at the Bar!
12-11.30pm
Food: 12.30-2.30pm, 6.30-9pm

What's the Damage?
Main courses from £9.50

Bitter Experience:
St Austell Tribute,
Skinner's Betty Stogs

Sticky Fingers:
Children welcome, small portions
available

Muddy Paws:
Dogs welcome in the bar

Zzzzz:
6 rooms, £72.50-£82.50

Anything Else?
Patio, garden, car park

The Food

With the Atlantic a mere 500 metres away, it's hardly surprising that locally caught fish is one of the highlights on the menu at The Gurnard's Head. The head chef Matt Williamson works hard to cut down food miles wherever possible, and this means that much of the seasonal produce used in the kitchen has actually been grown or raised on the doorstep. At lunchtime, there's a chalkboard menu offering a handful of options, all of them under £10 and always featuring hearty broths and soups, stews, sandwiches, home-made pork pies and fish and chips.

In the evening, the menu rarely stretches beyond five starters and five main courses. Keen local sourcing is evident in dishes such as smoked Cornish pilchards served with pickled beetroot and horseradish ice cream; The Gurnard's fish stew with new potatoes and aioli; and rabbit and porcini cannelloni – the latter served with Gilly's leaves (a reference to the woman who supplies the pub with salad). All can be washed down with well-chosen wines or beers from the Cornish brewers St Austell or Skinner's.

What To Do

Shop

ST IVES GALLERIES

Reflecting the long history of St Ives as a centre for artists, the town is packed with art galleries and shops selling hand-made artistic goodies. Countless specialist outlets make the town's narrow streets and lanes a treasure trove for those searching for a stunning painting, ceramics, or a one-off piece of pottery, sculpture, jewellery and a wealth of other crafts, to take home.

Tourist Information Centre 01736 769297

www.stives-cornwall.co.uk

VICARAGE FARM SHOP

Specialists in rare-breed pork (Duroc and Large Black) and lamb (Moorits), all raised locally, this well-stocked farm shop also gathers in produce from further afield, including a good range of delicious Cornish farmhouse cheeses. Their own-farm Aberdeen Angus beef is a mainstay; a wide range of unusual preserves and other foods is also available.

Underlane, Helston, Cornwall TR13 0EJ

01326 340484

www.vicaragefarmshop.com

Visit

GOONHILLY SATELLITE EARTH STATION

The very first transatlantic television pictures were received here on this remote Cornish moor on the Lizard Peninsula. Amazingly, Goonhilly Downs is still the world's biggest satellite station; a visitor centre and tour reveal the inside story of the space-age technology in operation here.

Helston, Cornwall TR12 6LQ

0800 679593

www.goonhilly.bt.com

MINACK THEATRE

The unique, open-air, cliff-side setting of the theatre is worth the visit in its own right. An extremely varied programme of plays and events – everything from *Of Mice and Men* to *Robin Hood* to *His Dark Materials* to performances by town bands – ensures that there's something on here virtually every day throughout the summer.

Porthcurno, Lands End, Cornwall TR19 6JU

01736 810181

www.minack.com

ST MICHAEL'S MOUNT

Reached by foot across the causeway at low tide, by boat at high water, St Michael's Mount is an iconic priory-cum-mansion capping a rocky island in Mount's Bay, near Penzance, lived in today by a modern family. An ancient cobbled path leads visitors up to the medieval castle battlements from where the view over Penzance Bay is superb. The craggy garden has a wealth of rare and unusual plants and a hanging sub-tropical garden.

Marazion, Penzance, Cornwall TR17 0HS

01736 710507

www.stmichaelsmount.co.uk

TATE ST IVES

One of Britain's leading abstract and modern art complexes, celebrating the St Ives School and worldwide contemporary art. It incorporates the nearby Barbara Hepworth Museum and Sculpture Garden at Barnoon Hill, once home to the renowned sculptress.

Porthmeor Beach, St Ives, Cornwall TR26 1TG

01736 796226

www.tate.org.uk/stives

Activity

FLYING AT LAND'S END

Flying lessons from Land's End Airport, with flights over the coast and countryside of Penwith, give you the chance to pilot the aircraft (you can even take a friend). Leisure flights are also available. The airport is also the base for scheduled day-return flights to the Isles of Scilly. You can combine a flight-out and boat-back excursion from the island of St Mary's.

Land's End Airport, St Just, Penzance, Cornwall TR19 7RL

For lessons: 01736 788771

www.landsendairport.co.uk

For Isles of Scilly: 0845 710 5555

www.ios-travel.co.uk

GEOLOGY TOURS

Interesting half-day or day trips, led by a professional geologist, can be arranged to introduce non-specialists to the extraordinary geology of the Penwith Peninsula. These trips help to explain the area's natural landscapes as well as exploring its tin-mining heritage.

07887 556245

www.cornwallgeology.co.uk

MARINE DISCOVERY

Appreciate a mariner's view of West Cornwall on a trip into Mount's Bay and along the rugged Penwith peninsula in a semi-rigid inflatable boat. Locations visited include some of the offshore reefs that make this coast so treacherous and a sight of Wolf Rock Lighthouse, built to warn against these hazards. Porpoise, sunfish and huge but harmless basking sharks may be seen.

Penzance Harbour, Cornwall

01736 874907

www.marinediscovery.co.uk

The Walk - The Tinners' Trail from Pendeen

A stroll through Cornwall's tin- and copper-mining country.

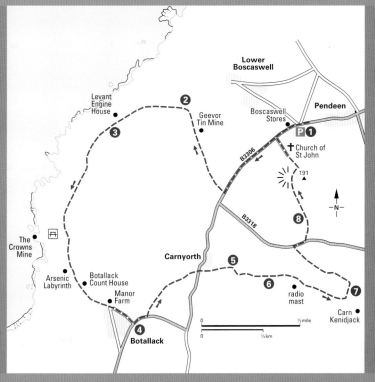

Walk Details

LENGTH: 5 miles (8km)

TIME: 4hrs

ASCENT: 328ft (100m)

PATHS: Coastal footpath; field paths and moorland tracks

SUGGESTED MAP: aqua3 OS Explorer 102 Land's End

GRID REFERENCE: SW 383344

PARKING: Free car park in centre of Pendeen village, opposite Boscaswell Stores, on the B3306

① Turn left out of the village-centre car park and follow the road to reach the entrance of Geevor Tin Mine. Walk down the drive towards the reception building and keep to its left down the road between the buildings, signposted 'Levant'.

② Just beyond the buildings, turn left along the narrow path that soon bears right and becomes unsurfaced track between walls. Turn left at the huge boulder and head towards the very tall chimney stack ahead. Continue across broken ground to the National Trust's Levant Engine House.

③ Follow the bottom edge of Levant car park and then take the rough track to reach Botallack Count House. Keep on past Manor Farm and reach the public road at Botallack. Turn left.

④ Go left at the main road (watch out for fast traffic), then turn left along Cresswell Terrace to reach the stile. Follow the field paths to enter the old mining village of Carnyorth. Cross the main road, then follow the lane opposite. Turn right once you reach the junction, to arrive at a solitary house.

⑤ Keep left of the house, go over the stile and cross the field to the opposite hedge to reach the hidden stile. Follow the path leading through the small fields towards the radio mast. Cross a final stile onto a rough track.

⑥ Go left, then immediately right at the junction. Keep on past the radio mast, then follow the path through gorse and heather to the rocky outcrop of Carn Kenidjack (not always visible when misty).

⑦ At the junction abreast of Carn Kenidjack, go back left along the path past the small granite parish boundary stone, eventually emerging on the road. Turn right and, in about 140yds (128m), go left along the obvious broad track opposite the house.

⑧ Keep left at the junction. By 2 large stones on the left, bear off right along the grassy track. Go left over the big stone stile directly above the Church of St John, built by the mining community in the 1850s, and descend to the main road. Turn right to return to the car park.

Driftwood Spars

Cornwall

Driftwood Spars, Trevaunance Cove, St Agnes, Cornwall TR5 0LE

The Inn

There is a feeling of space and a welcome for all at this solid 17th-century inn, a stone's throw from lovely Trevaunance Cove where good surfing and safe swimming can be enjoyed from the sandy beach. The beams in the ceilings of the two large bars include 'spars' (large poles used for the mast) salvaged from wrecked ships and framed photographs that capture the sea-faring Cornish life of bygone days. Here, a pint of landlord Gordon Treleaven's legendary Cuckoo Ale, brewed in his microbrewery just across the road, is the perfect antidote to a long drive or a hot day on the beach.

The local brew is guaranteed to make your toes tap to the live music played every Friday and Saturday evening. Get there early, grab a barrel seat and be prepared to be treated as one of the locals in this lively and unpretentious environment.

Stay the night here and there are 15 crisp, bright, nautically themed bedrooms to choose from – many have wonderful sea views, all are en suite. There's no doubt that Driftwood Spars is a hidden gem in a beautiful and bustling part of the Cornish coast.

The Essentials

Time at the Bar!
11am-11pm
Food: 12-2.30pm, 6.30-9.30pm (all day in summer)

What's the Damage?
Main courses from £15

Bitter Experience:
Driftwood Cuckoo Ale, Sharp's Own and Doom Bar

Sticky Fingers:
Children welcome; children's menu

Muddy Paws:
Dogs welcome

Zzzzz:
15 rooms, £43-£49

Anything Else?
Terrace, garden, car park

The Food

The Atlantic air causes hearty appetites, so while the bar menu has a something-for-everyone appeal – from light snacks such as red onion and anchovy tartlet topped with parmesan, through salads, baguettes, ploughman's and pies, to good-value mains along the lines of seared loin of swordfish with Mediterranean salsa or lamb steak marinated in rosemary and garlic – look to the Spindrift restaurant to up the culinary stakes. This is where old Cornwall gives way to the new, with oak flooring and chunky wooden tables and chairs, all bathed in a healthy dose of bright sea light.

The ambitious menu features a wealth of seasonal fish and shellfish dishes as well as locally grown produce. Start your meal with delicious black tiger gambas and chorizo or grilled goats' cheese with raspberry and walnut dressing before moving on to whole roasted sea bass stuffed with apricot and hazelnuts and herb butter, or brochette of monkfish marinated in fresh chillies, ginger and Moroccan spices.

Finish with the heavenly white chocolate profiteroles or a Cornish cheese board and you'll be ready for the soft mattress waiting for you upstairs.

What To Do

Shop

ATLANTIS SMOKED FISH

Stop here for high-class smoked fish, meats and cheeses from a long-established local foods business using modern and traditional smoking processes. The goods are on sale in their little shop in Grampound.

Fore Street, Grampound, Truro, Cornwall TR2 4SB

01726 883201

www.atlantisfoods.co.uk

ST AGNES POTTERY

Craft workshop using local clays to produce an eclectic range of functional pottery, exhibition pieces and decorative pots, many finished with glazes developed at the pottery. The pretty town has many other galleries, set beside lanes dropping to Trevaunance Cove.

Vicarage Road, St Agnes, Cornwall TR5 0LT

01872 553445

SPINDRIFT GALLERY

An ultra-modern gallery drawing together the best of contemporary Cornish artists working in oils, watercolours and acrylics. Other exhibitors show their range of ceramics, glass, porcelain and jewellery. Portscatho village has more art galleries, craft and antique shops.

8 The Quay, Portscatho, Truro, Cornwall TR2 5HF

01872 580155

www.spindrift-gallery.co.uk

Visit

CAMEL VALLEY VINEYARD

In the sheltered middle valley of the River Camel, good soils and reliable sun produce international award-winning still and sparkling wines. Daily tours (in season) around the vineyard, plus wine tasting.

Nanstallon, Bodmin, Cornwall PL30 5LG

01208 77959

www.camelvalley.com

GWEEK SEAL SANCTUARY

This long-established rescue and rehabilitation centre provides care for injured seals, most of which are returned to the wild – though some are long-term residents, too traumatised to fend for themselves. Also home to sea-lions and otters.

Gweek, Helston, Cornwall TR12 6UG

01326 221361

www.sealsanctuary.co.uk

NATIONAL MARITIME MUSEUM

Celebrate and investigate Cornwall's long maritime heritage at this quayside museum overlooking one of Britain's greatest natural harbours at Falmouth. There are exhibits on traditional and modern craft and navigation skills. Underwater viewing gallery.

Discovery Quay, Falmouth, Cornwall TR11 3QY

01326 313388

www.nmmc.co.uk

TRERICE

A picture-perfect manor virtually unchanged since Elizabethan times. It houses an excellent collection of furniture, glass, ceramics and an extensive collection of clocks.

Kestle Mill, Newquay, Cornwall TR8 4PG

01637 875404

www.nationaltrust.org.uk

Activity

BISSOE TRAMWAYS CYCLE HIRE

The harbour at Portreath was a major centre for exporting tin ore, carried there on former tramroads and mineral railways. These are now at the heart of a cycle network exploring mid-Cornwall's industrial heritage and peaceful countryside. Hiring a cycle by the hour or the day is the perfect way to explore this half-hidden world.

Old Conns Works, Bissoe, Truro, Cornwall TR4 8QZ

01872 870341

www.cornwallcyclehire.com

PERRANPORTH BEACH

Mile after mile of windswept beaches between Perranporth and Newquay are tailor-made for kite-based adrenalin sports. Buggy-surfing, land-boarding and kite-surfing are just some of the on-beach or in-water activities for which instruction is available. Surf-schools teaching 'traditional' techniques also thrive here.

01637 831383

www.mobiusonline.co.uk

SEGUE CHARTERS

Falmouth Bay and the waters off The Lizard Peninsula are home to a wealth of sealife. Take the opportunity to go cetacean watching: porpoises and perhaps even killer whales, as well as sunfish and basking sharks, are regularly seen during the summer. In a different mode, Segue Charters also operates exciting deep-sea wreck-fishing expeditions or shark angling days; fish of more than 500lbs patrol these waters.

01326 312116

www.seguecharters.co.uk

The Walk - High Cliffs and a High Hill

A bracing walk along the cliffs at St Agnes, then inland to the top of St Agnes Beacon.

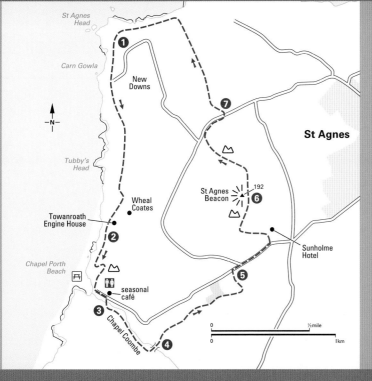

Walk Details

LENGTH: 5 miles (8km)

TIME: 3hrs

ASCENT: 623ft (190m)

PATHS: Good coastal footpaths and inland tracks

SUGGESTED MAP: aqua3 OS Explorer 104 Redruth & St Agnes

GRID REFERENCE: SW 699512

PARKING: St Agnes Head. There are parking spaces along the clifftop track. Start the walk from any one of these

❶ Join the coastal footpath from wherever you park along the cliff top. Follow the stony track across the little promontory of Tubby's Head, the former Iron-Age settlement. Branch off right on to the narrower path about 100yds (90m) before old mine buildings (these are the remains of the Wheal Coates mine). Cross the stone stile and continue on the path to Towanroath mine Engine House.

❷ About 50yds (46m) beyond Towanroath Engine House, branch off right at the signpost and descend to Chapel Porth Beach.

❸ Cross the stream at the back corner of the car park and then follow the path up Chapel Coombe next to the stream. Pass below the mine building and, where the path forks among trees, go left through the wooden kissing gate.

❹ Cross the bridge, then turn right onto the track. Continue along the grassy track and at the point where the track narrows, keep well ahead at the fork. Keep alongside the field and on to the track; now turn left over the wooden stile by the gate onto the track. After around 50yds (46m), reach the junction with the wide track. Turn left and continue to the public road.

❺ Turn right along the public road, and keep ahead at the junction. In 200yds (183m), next to the entrance to the Sunholme Hotel, continue up the stony track on the left. After 50yds (46m), at the junction, go left and follow the path rising to the obvious summit of 629ft (192m) St Agnes Beacon, used traditionally for the lighting of signal fires and celebratory bonfires. The views from the top of the Beacon reach as far as the tors of Bodmin Moor.

❻ From the summit of the Beacon, follow the lower of 2 tracks, heading northwest, down towards the road. Just before you reach the road turn right along the narrow path, skirting the base of the hill, eventually emerging at the road by a seat.

❼ Cross over and follow the track opposite, across New Downs, directly to the edge of the cliffs, then turn left at the junction with the coastal path and return to the clifftop parking spaces.

Dartmoor Inn

Devon

The Inn

Karen and Philip Burgess and their staff imbue this 16th-century roadside coaching inn with warmth and personality. It's set against the backdrop of Dartmoor's spectacular landscape, just a short drive from Lydford Gorge, and is in great walking country. Inside, the relaxed, laid-back, lovingly restored and refurbished interior is made up of a rambling succession of wood- and slate-floored dining rooms, many with their own open fire or wood-burning stove, while a tiny bar dispensing pints of Otter Ale or Dartmoor Best Bitter keeps the pub tradition alive.

This is rural chic at its best, with a French country feel; the soft colours, lamps, and an eclectic mix of furnishings and tasteful bric-a-brac, which is picked up in the three bedrooms upstairs. All are spacious and highly individual. One, decorated in powder blue, is dominated by a lovely cream-painted French provincial-style bed; another has a high-beamed ceiling hung with a chandelier. All of the bedrooms have antique pieces, plus modern and very well-equipped bathrooms, while sofas and Roberts radios are standard issue – TVs, however, are available on request.

The Essentials

Time at the Bar!
11am-3pm, 6-11pm (closed Sun evening, Mon lunchtime)
Food: 12-2.30pm, 6-10pm

What's the Damage?
Main courses from £9.95

Bitter Experience:
Otter Ale, Dartmoor Best Bitter

Sticky Fingers:
Children welcome; children's menu on request

Muddy Paws:
Dogs welcome in the bar

Zzzzz:
3 rooms, £115

Anything Else?
Terrace, car park

The Food

The kitchen at the Dartmoor Inn is committed to using first-class ingredients sourced from the very best suppliers in Devon and Cornwall. Regularly changing menus list some comfortingly familiar traditional dishes alongside a range of imaginative modern ones, with the overall standard of skill, quality of ingredients and presentation being well above average for a country inn. Light bites in the bar may include devilled sprats with a mustard dressing, fish and shellfish cakes with a tomato sauce, and fish and chips served with deliciously different green mayonnaise.

In the evening the choice extends to Cornish crab and saffron risotto with parmesan, or avocado and asparagus salad with pea shoots and balsamic wine vinegar, while main courses may consist of croustade of hake and sea bass with saffron and leeks, and slow-cooked shank of lamb with thyme and shallots. Similarly, chargrilled rib steak with herb butter and Maris Piper chips is a classic done well.

There could be warm caramelized rhubarb cake with clotted cream for dessert, and an exceptionally well-chosen wine list at ungreedy prices proves a happy match to the food. There's a lovely walled patio for summer dining.

Dartmoor Inn, Lydford, Okehampton, Devon EX20 4AY

What To Do

Shop

COUNTRYMAN CIDER

Housed in the 15th-century stables block of a former coaching inn on the Devon side of the Tamar Valley, this traditional cider producer uses apples from local farms to make a range of craft ciders, plus cider brandy and country wines. Mead is also sold at the farm shop. Short tours and tastings are available.

Felldownhead, Milton Abbot, Tavistock,
Devon PL19 0QR
01822 870226

POWDERMILLS POTTERY

A range of unusual and collectible wares produced by craftsmen and women mainly based on Dartmoor and in south Devon. Pottery is made on the premises, plus textiles, baskets and a range of delicious honey and chocolates.

Postbridge, Dartmoor, Devon PL20 6SP
01822 880263
www.powdermillspottery.com

SOUTH WEST CRAFTS

Deep in the heart of Tavistock, a craft gallery concentrating on established artists in the south west as well as displaying work from newcomers. You'll find bronze sculpture by Charlotte Marlow, ceramics by Peter Swanson, hand-made cushions and bags with traditional and contemporary designs by Ann-Marie Stone and fine silver jewellery made by Ann Powell. Wander around town and you'll come across several other art galleries and craft artisans specialising in Dartmoor-related subjects and works.

Church Lane, Tavistock, Devon PL19 8AA
01822 612689
www.southwestcrafts.co.uk

Visit

BUCKLAND ABBEY

Sir Francis Drake's former family home celebrates his life and achievements. The abbey dates from the 13th century and has some fine plasterwork and a series of galleries. Much of it was incorporated into a grand country house by Sir Richard Grenville – another of England's naval heroes – who subsequently sold the building to Drake. The grounds include a large herb garden, a tithe barn and craft workshops.

Yelverton, Devon PL20 6EY
01822 853607
www.nationaltrust.org.uk

DARTMOOR PRISON

It began as a holding point for French captives during the Napoleonic Wars and has seen riots and mutinies, chain-gangs, crime, punishment – and rehabilitation – in its long and disturbing history. Find out more and view fascinating memorabilia such as the original convict 'arrow' suit of the 1850s, at this unusual visitor centre.

Heritage Centre, Princetown,
Devon PL20 6RR
01822 892130
www.dartmoor-prison.co.uk

MORWELLHAM QUAY

Explore the history of the Dartmoor copper mining industry at these renovated quays and old buildings set deep in the Tamar Valley at Great Consols Mine. Interpretive materials re-create the busy site at its height in the 1860s – including a tram trip into one of the old mines.

Tavistock, Devon PL19 8JL
01822 832766
www.morwellham-quay.co.uk

Activity

CANOEING

The Tamar Valley is an Area of Outstanding Natural Beauty and one of the most unusual and highly exhilarating ways to experience it is by Canadian canoe, starting from one of the ports and villages nestling in the wooded valley. Either a full- or a half-day trip (depending on the state of the tide) will probably reward you with a glimpse of a seal or even an otter as you glide past trees, quays and remote cottages well away from any roads.

Canoe Tamar
0845 430 1208
www.canoetamar.co.uk

FALCONRY

Find out all about the feeding and nesting habits of birds of prey and owls before taking the opportunity to fly one of these magnificent creatures yourself. The art of falconry can be savoured on a half- or full-day flying experience on the wild moors of western Dartmoor.

High Willsworth Farm, Peter Tavy,
Tavistock, Devon PL19 9NB
01822 810112
www.totaltravel.co.uk (follow link)

TAVISTOCK TROUT FISHERY

A series of five lakes just outside Tavistock regularly yields enormous rainbow trout to dedicated fly-fishers who know the waters – fish touching 30lbs (14kg) have been caught here. You don't have to be an expert to try your hand: fly-fishing tuition can be arranged for absolute beginners and all the necessary equipment is provided.

Parkwood Road, Tavistock, Devon PL19 9JW
01822 615441
www.tavistocktroutfishery.co.uk

The Walk - On Dartmoor's Highest Tors

An ancient oak woodland and views of Yes Tor and High Willhays at Meldon Reservoir.

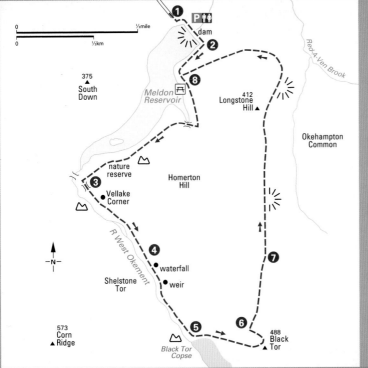

Walk Details

LENGTH: 4.25 miles (6.8km)

TIME: 2hrs 45min

ASCENT: 722ft (220m)

PATHS: Grassy tracks and open moorland

SUGGESTED MAP: aqua3 OS Outdoor Leisure 28 Dartmoor

GRID REFERENCE: SX 563917

PARKING: Car park at Meldon Reservoir (voluntary contributions)

❶ Walk up the stone steps by the toilets, go through the gate and turn left on the tarmac way towards the dam, ('Bridleway to Moor'). Cross over the dam here.

❷ Turn right along the track. The stile on the right leads to the waterside picnic area. Don't cross the stile, but leave the track here to go straight on, following the edge of the reservoir through the side valley and over the footbridge. The narrow path undulates to a steepish descent at the end of the reservoir to meet the broad marshy valley of West Okement River. Corn Ridge at 1,762ft (537m) lies ahead.

❸ Cross the footbridge; take the path along the left edge of the valley, keeping to the bottom of the slope

on the left. The path broadens as it travels uphill and becomes grassy as it rounds Vellake Corner above the river below right.

❹ At top of the hill, the track levels; you can glimpse Black Tor Copse ahead. Follow the river upstream, past the waterfall and weir, right of the granite enclosure, and along the left bank through open moorland to enter Black Tor Copse.

❺ Retrace your steps to emerge from the trees and veer right around the copse edge, walking uphill and aiming for the left outcrop of Black Tor on the ridge above. Walk through the bracken to the tor; there is no definite path here, but it's straightforward. The outcrop on the right rises to 1,647ft (502m).

❻ Return to the grassy area north of tor. Turn right to continue away from the river valley behind, aiming for track visible ahead over Longstone Hill. To find the track go slightly downhill from tor to small stream. Turn left, then right towards 3 granite blocks marking the track.

❼ Intermittent track runs straight across open moor (good views of the quarry ahead). Where Red-a-Ven Brook Valley appears below right, enjoy the view of Row Tor, West Mill Tor and Yes Tor. High Willhays, Dartmoor's highest tor, lies just out of sight to the right. The track veers left around the end of the hill and drops back to the reservoir.

❽ Turn right to rejoin the track back over dam and back to the car park.

The Farmers Inn

Somerset

The Inn

To locate this isolated inn, come off the M5 at junction 25 and take the A358 south for a mile, then head right at the Nag's Head and follow the brown 'inn' signs for two miles down winding narrow lanes, deep into unspoilt Somerset countryside. Taunton is just over the hill, but you wouldn't believe it as you take in the amazing views across the Somerset Levels. Tom and Debbie Lush have injected new life into this rambling 16th-century inn, smartening up the rustic bar with scrubbed oak tables and placing squashy leather sofas around the roaring log fire, and creating a civilised yet relaxed dining area, beyond which you will find a flower-decked terrace with posh benches and brollies just right for sunny days.

Decide to stay the night and you will be hard-pressed to know which of the five bedrooms to choose. Some are large, others are vast, yet all have been kitted out with style and good taste with their antique furnishings, polished wooden floors and gleaming bathrooms with deep claw-foot baths. For a sophisticated continental feel and views across sheep-grazed fields to the Quantock Hills, book the Quantock Room.

The Farmers Inn, West Hatch, Taunton, Somerset TA3 5RS

The Essentials

Time at the Bar!
12-3pm, 6-12pm
Food: 12-2pm (2.30pm Sat-Sun),
7-9pm (9.30pm Thu-Sun)

What's the Damage?
Main courses from £10.50

Bitter Experience:
Otter Ale, Sharp's Doom Bar

Sticky Fingers:
Children welcome; small portions
available

Muddy Paws:
Dogs welcome in the bar

Zzzzz:
5 rooms, £60-£110

Anything Else?
Terrace, garden, car park

The Food

In keeping with the upscale refurbishment of the pub and the addition of the chic bedrooms, both the quality of the food and the style of cooking have improved markedly. You'll find a daily-changing menu that lists imaginative modern British dishes, prepared with some skill, with the focus firmly on seasonal local produce. Start with home-made bread and olives, then follow with butternut squash and root ginger soup, potted smoked trout pâté with soda bread and mixed leaves, or whole grilled sardines served with Napoli sauce and focaccia bread.

If you are in the mood for fish, there may be home-made fishcakes with roasted Mediterranean vegetables, parsley sauce and fries, or pan-fried monkfish with braised leeks and a pancetta, cream and fennel-seed sauce, with meatier mains including rib-eye steak with baked garlic and red onion and rosemary jus, or pan-fried chicken with mushroom and thyme jus.

Finish with the mouthwatering dark chocolate and mint mousse with pistachio anglaise. Otter Ale tapped straight from the barrel and a selection of excellent wines by the glass add to the appeal.

What To Do

Shop

SHEPPY'S CIDER

There was a time when each farm made its own cider in this neck of the woods – no longer, though at Three Bridges, the Sheppys have maintained a tradition that began in the early 1800s. The 370 acres farmed here produce award-winning ciders that you can take home to enjoy. You can sample the wares in the cafe, tour the orchards, and stock up in the shop, which also sells the farm's wonderful home-reared Longhorn meat.

Three Bridges, Bradford-on-Tone, Taunton, Somerset TA4 1ER
01823 461233
www.sheppyscider.com

TAUNTON ANTIQUES MARKET

With more than 130 dealers, this is one of the West Country's biggest markets, and you'll find a huge range of desirables here, from Victorian silver to 20th-century ceramics. Once you've browsed for bargains, you can take a breather in the Market Cafe which sells good coffee and home-made cakes.

27-29 Silver Street, Taunton, Somerset TA1 3DH
01823 289327

Visit

COLERIDGE COTTAGE

Samuel Taylor Coleridge lived here with his family for three years from 1797. In the house you can see his writing ephemera, pictures of friends and family, and letters penned in his distinctive handwriting. His good friends William Wordsworth and his sister Dorothy were regular visitors, and it was on one such occasion that Coleridge and Wordsworth went on one of their nocturnal walks, and Coleridge's *The Rime of the Ancient Mariner* took shape. Walk along The Coleridge Way, starting at the cottage, to see the isolated farm house where he wrote the opium-inspired symbolic poem *Kubla Khan*.

35 Lime Street, Nether Stowey, Bridgwater, Somerset TA5 1NQ
01278 732662
www.nationaltrust.org

HESTERCOMBE GARDENS

The gardens at Hestercombe were designed by Sir Edwin Lutyens and planted by Gertude Jekyll, and you'll see beautiful stonework, an orangery and pergolas. As well as the formal gardens, there are 40 acres of 18th-century landscaped parkland with woodland walks, temples, cascades and breathtaking views across the Vale of Taunton to the Blackdown Hills. The contemporary visitor centre has a plant centre, gift shop and cafe serving good home-made meals.

Cheddon Fitzpaine, Taunton, Somerset TA2 8LG
01823 413923
www.hestercombegardens.com

STUART INTERIORS AT BARRINGTON COURT

Specialising in medieval, Tudor and Georgian interior design, Stuart Interiors are a well-established architectural design company with their showrooms at Barrington Court, a National Trust Elizabethan manor house – be inspired by what they do and steal ideas for your own home. Take a stroll round the Gertrude Jekyll-inspired garden while you're here; it is laid out in a series of walled rooms, including the White Garden, the Rose and Iris Garden and the Lily Garden. There is also a well-stocked arboretum and a kitchen garden that supplies the restaurant with home-grown ingredients. Plants and garden produce are on sale in the shop and make great take-home memories.

Barrington Court, Ilminster, Somerset TA19 0NQ
01460 240349
www.stuartinteriors.ltd.uk

Activity

GOLF

Burnham & Berrow Golf Club has an idyllic 18-hole championship course built into sandy dunes – you'll find the layout challenging, with ravine-like valleys for fairways, and lots of natural hollows and humps. Burnham hosts one of the qualifying events for the British Open Championships, so work on your handicap and you may walk out with the giants!

Burnham & Berrow Golf Club, St Christopher's Way, Burnham-on-Sea, Somerset TA8 2PE
01278 783137
www.burnham-on-sea.com/golf

TAUNTON RACES

If you enjoy the 'sport of kings', why not have a little flutter at the youngest National Hunt racecourse in Britain? The Taunton racecourse is beautifully located, with views out towards the wooded slopes of the Blackdown Hills.

Orchard Portman, Taunton, Somerset TA3 7BL
01823 325035
www.tauntonracecourse.co.uk

The Walk - Woodlands at Blackdown Hills

Prior's Park Wood is at its best with autumn's colours or spring's bluebells.

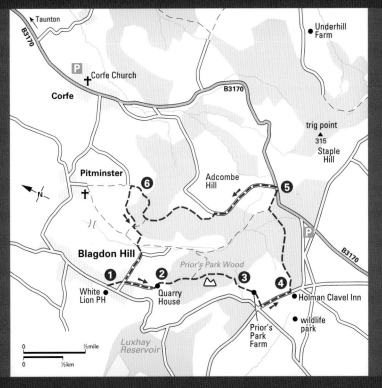

Walk Details

LENGTH: 5 miles (8km)

TIME: 2hrs 40min

ASCENT: 700ft (210m)

PATHS: Rugged in Prior's Park Wood, otherwise comfortable, 7 stiles

SUGGESTED MAP: aqua3 OS Explorer 128 Taunton & Blackdown Hills

GRID REFERENCE: ST 211182

PARKING: Roadside pull-off between post office and White Lion, at Blagdon Hill

❶ The walk starts at the phone boothe opposite the White Lion, a handsome 17th-century inn. Cross the stile and follow along the left edge of the triangular field to another stile into Curdleigh Lane. Cross into ascending Quarry Lane. Bend left between the buildings of Quarry House, on to the track running up into Prior's Park Wood.

❷ From mid-April, Prior's Park Wood is delightful with bluebells and other wild flowers. It is also aglow with the reds and golds of autumn (but possibly muddy) in late October and November. Where the main track bends left and descends slightly, keep uphill on a smaller one. This track eventually declines into muddy trod, slanting up and

leftwards to reach a small gate at the top edge of the wood.

❸ Pass along the wood's top edge to reach the gate. Red-and-white poles mark the line across the next field that leads to another gate. After 50yds (46m) turn right, between the buildings of Prior's Park Farm to its access track and road. Turn left and follow the road with care (this is a fairly fast section) towards the Holman Clavel Inn.

❹ Just before the inn turn left onto the forest track. Where the track ends a small path runs ahead, zig-zagging down before crossing the stream. At the wood's edge turn right up a wider path to the B3170.

❺ At once turn left on the lane ('Feltham'). After 0.5 mile (800m), a

wide gateway on the left leads to an earth track. This runs along the top of Adcombe Wood then down inside it, giving a very pleasant descent.

❻ Once below the wood follow the track downhill for 180yds (165m). Look for a gate with a signpost on the lefthand side. Now go through the gate and follow the hedge on the right to a stile and footbridge, then bend left, below the foot of the wood, to another stile. Ignore the stile leading into the wood on the left, but continue along the wood's foot to the next field corner. Here a further stile enters the wood but turn right, beside the hedge, to the concrete track. Turn left – the track becomes Curdleigh Lane, leading you back into Blagdon Hill once more.

The Wheelwrights Arms

Somerset

The Inn

Just a short drive from Bath and a stone's throw from the banks of the Kennet and Avon Canal, The Wheelwrights Arms sits in the sleepy village of Monkton Combe surrounded by picturesque hills and valleys. Built in 1750 as a house and a workshop by William Harold, a local carpenter, the two buildings were converted into a pub by the Harold family in 1871. Over a century later, the carpentry workshops were transformed into bed-and-breakfast accommodation, but visitors today will find that David Munn has taken The Wheelwrights Arms to a completely different level of luxury since he acquired the place in 2006.

Modern flourishes enhance exposed stone walls, framed paintings and antique furniture, while the old workshops have been carefully restored, creating seven luxury en-suite bedrooms, all with flat-screen TVs, radios, room service and wi-fi internet access. The rooms are light and airy, contemporary and stylish. Individually designed, they are complemented by stunning bathrooms featuring white tongue-and-groove panelling, wooden floorboards, free-standing baths, fluffy white towels and Provencal toiletries.

The Essentials

Time at the Bar!
11am-11pm
Food: 12-3pm, 6-10pm

What's the Damage?
Main courses from £9.90

Bitter Experience:
Butcombe, Greene King IPA

Sticky Fingers:
Children welcome, half portions

Muddy Paws:
No dogs

Zzzzz:
7 rooms, £110-£130

Anything Else?
Garden with patio, car park

The Food

When it comes to the food, 'classic' and 'British' are the watchwords at The Wheelwrights Arms. There are plenty of good old-fashioned English dishes on the menu, which caters for lunchtime snackers as well as diners looking for something a little more substantial. Plenty of West Country produce is in evidence in the wholesome chicken and ham pie, chunky cod, salmon and haddock pie with peas and creamed leeks and a trio of Bath sausages served on mash with rich red wine and onion gravy.

A selection of sandwiches is popular at lunchtimes, and these are a welcome diversion for hungry walkers. They include a steak sandwich with onion marmalade and hand-cut chunky chips, and 'The Wheelwrights' club sandwich' (grilled chicken, bacon, local cheddar, salad, mayo and hand-cut chunky chips), perfect washed down with a pint of Bath Ales Wild Hare or Butcombe Blond, or a glass of wine from the lengthy list. The beef is hung for 30 days, so expect intense flavour from the 8oz hand-carved rib-eyes, cooked just to your liking and served with hand-cut chunky chips, field mushrooms and a delicious sauce of your choice.

What To Do

Shop

AVALON VINEYARD

More than six acres of organic vineyard, where you are free to wander at will or pre-arrange a guided tour. The range of drinks on sale extends beyond grape wines to local cider, fruit wines and mead, which is made from organic honey imported from Brazil.

The Drove, East Pennard, Shepton Mallet, Somerset BA4 6WA

01749 860393

www.pennardorganicwines.co.uk

BATH

There are so many delightful shops in this beautiful city it is impossible to know which to recommend. The best plan is to start near the abbey, where there are yards, lanes and walks with art galleries and specialist jewellery shops; for designer fashion visit Milsom Street or Shire's Yard. Antique galleries and shops pop up everywhere: a good concentration is around The Paragon in Upper Town. Just a short hop from Pulteney Bridge are dozens of craft shops, workshops and galleries on and around Broad Street and Walcot Street. Half the fun is in finding your own favourite.

Bath & NE Somerset

0906 711 2000

www.VisitBath.co.uk

FARRINGTON'S FARM SHOP

An award-winning shop stocking a wide range of largely locally produced, organic products; from meat and game through bakery and preserves to creamery products.

Home Farm, Main Street, Farrington Gurney, Bristol BS39 6UB

01761 451698

www.farringtonsfarmshop.com

Visit

CLAVERTON PUMPING STATION

A remarkable feat of engineering, designed by the engineer John Rennie to help ensure that his Kennet and Avon Canal didn't run dry. A massive waterwheel, powered by the River Avon, can pump 100,000 gallons of river water per hour up to the canal 'pound' (level), nearly 50ft above, to top-up water lost by boats descending the flight of locks to the Avon in Bath.

Ferry Lane, Claverton, Bath, Bath & NE Somerset

01225 483001

www.claverton.org

DYRHAM PARK

Secluded in a vast, wooded estate and deer park, and familiar from the film *The Remains of the Day*, Dyrham Park is an archetypal Cotswold country mansion. Built 300 years ago for the politician William Blathwayt, it has remained virtually unchanged since his day, with grand Delftware, textiles and paintings.

Dyrham, Gloucestershire SN14 8ER

01179 372501

www.nationaltrust.org.uk/dyrhampark

HOLBURNE MUSEUM

In the centre of Bath, this museum is testament to the collecting skills, wealth and eye of Sir William Holburne. The charming house on Great Pulteney Street overflows with fine arts: from miniature masterpieces to Gainsborough paintings; works in silver, glass and porcelain; Renaissance bronzes and art by Turner and Stubbs.

Great Pulteney Street, Bath, Bath & NE Somerset BA2 4DB

01225 466669

www.bath.ac.uk/holburne

Activity

CANOE HIRE

Take to the water in a Canadian-style open canoe, charting a course along the tranquil Kennet and Avon Canal, passing through picturesque villages and remote countryside, heading west towards Bath or east towards distant Devizes. The canoes are easily handled by one or two people, and can be man-handled around locks.

The Lock Inn, 48 Frome Road, Bradford-on-Avon, Wiltshire BA15 1LE

01225 868068

www.thelockinn.co.uk

CAVING & CLIMBING

Formed from million-year-old Ice Age river beds, the Cheddar Gorge caves offer some challenging and exciting activities to those prepared to take the risks. Choose from tackling tight squeezes and hidden glories on a caving expedition in the cathedral-like caverns, or perhaps abseiling into Cheddar Gorge, Britain's largest. And maybe rock-climbing back out, if it takes your fancy. All of the options are tailored to suit beginners and will fill a morning or afternoon.

Rocksport, Cheddar, Somerset BS27 3QF

01934 742343

www.cheddarcaves.co.uk

MENDIP GLIDING CLUB

A trial lesson in a modern glider, launched by ground winch or aerotow, can get you up to 2,000ft (610m) above the Mendips, floating over Cheddar Gorge and the Mendip edge. There is no more glorious way to appreciate the countryside.

New Road, Priddy, Wells, Somerset BA5 3BX

01749 870312

www.mendipglidingclub.uklinux.net

The Walk - *Brunel's Great Tunnel*

A high and hilly walk around Box Hill.

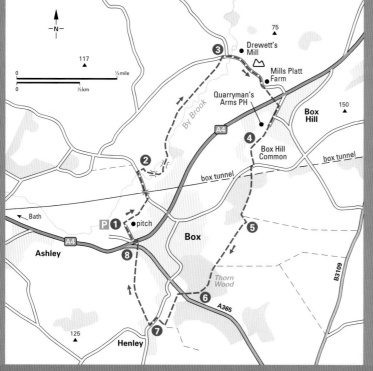

Walk Details

LENGTH: 3.25 miles (5.3km)

TIME: 1hr 45min

ASCENT: 508ft (155m)

PATHS: Field and woodland paths, bridle paths, metalled lanes, 15 stiles

SUGGESTED MAP: aqua3 OS Explorer 156 Chippenham & Bradford-on-Avon

GRID REFERENCE: ST 823686

PARKING: Village car park near Selwyn Hall

INFORMATION: This walk is over the county border in Wiltshire

❶ Facing the recreation ground, walk to the lefthand side of football pitch; join the track in the corner, close to railway line. At lane, turn left, pass beneath the railway, cross the bridge and take arrowed footpath, to right, before 2nd bridge.

❷ Walk by the river, cross the footbridge and turn left. Cross the next footbridge and continue to the stile. Walk through the water-meadows close to the river, go through the squeeze stile and maintain direction. Shortly, bear left to the squeeze stile in the field corner. Follow the righthand edge of field to the stile and the lane.

❸ Turn right, then right again at the junction. Cross the river, pass Drewett's Mill and ascend the lane.

Past Mills Platt Farm, take the arrowed footpath ahead and climb over the stile. Continue uphill to the stile; cross the A4. Ascend the steps to the lane and proceed straight on up Barnetts Hill. Keep right at the fork, then turn right again; pass by the Quarryman's Arms.

❹ Keep left at fork; continue beside Box Hill Common to junction. Take path ahead into woodland. Almost immediately, fork left and follow path close to woodland edge. As it curves right into beech wood, bear left and follow path through gap in wall, then right at junction of paths.

❺ Follow the bridlepath to the fork. Keep left, then turn right at the T-junction and take path left to stile. Cross further stile and descend into

Thorn Wood, following the stepped path to the stile at the bottom.

❻ Continue through scrub to stile; turn right by fence to wall stile. Bear right to further stile, then left uphill to stile and A361. Cross and follow drive ahead. Where it curves left by the stables, keep ahead along the arrowed path to the house. Bear right up the garden steps to drive and continue uphill to T-junction.

❼ Turn left; on entering Henley, take path right, across stile. Follow field edge to stile; descend to allotment and stile. Continue to stile and gate.

❽ Follow the drive ahead, bear left at garage; take path right, into Box. Cross the main road and continue to the A4. Turn right, then left down access road back to Selwyn Hall.

The Wheatsheaf

The Inn

Run by Adele and Ian Barton and expertly managed by their children, it's hardly surprising that The Wheatsheaf feels like such a family-run affair. Located in idyllic countryside just 15 minutes from Bath, this impressive 16th-century pub has been stripped back to its original stone walls and flagstone floors, but enhanced by more contemporary furnishings. Inside, it's all solid oak tables, comfortable sofas and Lloyd Loom chairs but, when the weather allows, the tables dotted around the stunning terraced gardens are highly sought-after. Set on two levels, the grassed garden has the most tranquil views of the nearby hills and it's little wonder that the pub is so favoured by walkers and local shooting parties.

Walk down the stone steps from the garden and you'll find a detached stone building housing three lovely bedrooms, all with state-of-the-art shower rooms. The bedrooms are contemporary with the same calm colours as the dining room and chunky teak furniture. In each, there are crisp linen sheets, White Company products, a 30-channel plasma TV screen and amusing paintings of local cows.

The Wheatsheaf, Combe Hay, Bath, Somerset BA2 7EG

The Food

Since opening in 2006, The Wheatsheaf has gained a formidable reputation for its food. The kitchen sources local produce, all of it in its rightful season. Although there's a lunchtime bar menu featuring walker-friendly Montgomery cheddar cheese and chutney sandwiches, steak baguettes and the pub's famous ploughman's, just as many foodies are attracted by a la carte dishes such as Scottish king scallops with boudin noir and sweet potato, fillet of turbot with chive creamed potato and salsify, or fillet of Buccleuch Estate beef with horseradish creamed potato and onion bhaji.

Of course, no visit to The Wheatsheaf would be complete without trying desserts such as the seductive dark chocolate fondant with Tonka bean ice cream, or ploughing through one of the two cheeseboards on offer - one English and the other entirely French. Although Butcombe beers and local Cheddar Valley cider are on tap, the Euro-centric wine list may feature too many vinous distractions. The pub's regular summer barbecues are an added attraction, with lobster and langoustines making an extravagant change from the normal burgers and steaks.

The Essentials

Time at the Bar!
12-3pm, 6-11pm (closed Mon)
Food: 12-2.30pm, 6-9.30pm
(10pm Sat)

What's the Damage?
Main courses from £16.50

Bitter Experience:
Butcombe and IPA

Sticky Fingers:
Children welcome

Muddy Paws:
Dogs welcome in the bar

Zzzzz:
3 rooms, £95-£120

Anything Else?
Terrace, garden, car park

What To Do

Shop

NB GALLERY
A specialist gallery concentrating on British arts and crafts using only natural materials, including glass, textiles and a wide range of jewellery. All items are displayed among a regularly changing series of exhibitions that could include abstract paintings and a stream of new work from on-site craftspeople and artists. See tapestry artist and gallery owner Kimberley Jackson weaving tapestries in her workshop.
4 Church Walk, Trowbridge,
Wiltshire BA14 8DX
01225 719119
www.NBgallery.co.uk

CHEDDAR GORGE
CHEESE COMPANY
Watch the traditional cheddar-making at the dairy before buying some in the on-site shop, which also sells a range of biscuits and chutneys to serve with the cheese.
The Cliffs, Cheddar Gorge,
Somerset BS27 3QA
01934 742810
www.cheddargorgecheese.co.uk

JON THORNER FARM SHOP
Foodies will love the huge range of mostly locally sourced foodstuffs available here, including more than 50 cheeses; Mendip beef, pork and lamb; smoked goods; game from local estates and a selection of exotic specialist meats. For over 30 years Jon Thorner has worked closely with West Country farmers and food producers to ensure only top-quality produce is sold in his Pylle and Street farm shops.
Pylle, Shepton Mallet, Somerset BA4 6TA
01749 830138
www.jonthorners.co.uk

Visit

MUSEUM OF COSTUME
This fascinating museum is housed in The Assembly Rooms, designed by John Wood the Younger in 1771, and is one of Bath's finest public buildings, recalling the Georgian city in its opulent, carefree heyday. The museum houses one of the largest and most prestigious collections (more than 30,000 objects) of fashionable dress for men, women and children since the time of Elizabeth I with a serious nod to modern fashion history. The regularly changing special exhibitions entice fashion design students from all over the country.
Bennett Street, Bath,
Bath & NE Somerset BA1 2QH
01225 477785
www.museumofcostume.co.uk

TYNTESFIELD
A stunning 19th-century country house and estate situated on a ridge overlooking the beautiful Yeo Valley and run by the National Trust. It was built in 1864 for a wealthy merchant, William Gibbs, and is memorable for its extraordinary Gothic-revival architecture, most notably the spectacular array of towers, turrets and chimneys that adorns the building. Its true worth is slowly being revealed as restoration progresses. Inside the house are collections of Victorian decorative arts and furnishings as well as artefacts giving detailed insight into below-stairs life in High-Victorian England. Outside you will find a complete walled kitchen garden as well as parkland estate.
Wraxall, North Somerset BS48 1NT
0870 458 4500
www.nationaltrust.org.uk/tyntesfield

Activity

CYCLING
Hire a bicycle and tackle the more challenging roads, byways and tracks of the Mendip Hills or the complex web of lanes threading the low-lying Somerset Levels. Either way, you'll discover the countryside and villages around Cheddar and north Somerset.
Cheddar Cycle Store, Valley Line Industrial Park, Wedmore Road, Cheddar,
Somerset BS27 3EE
01934 741300
www.cheddarcyclestore.co.uk

SOMERSET WILDLIFE TRUST
The Trust has dozens of reserves throughout Somerset and arranges frequent events, varying from hands-on conservation to animal watches, walks and talks. One of the largest is Ubley Warren, a former lead-mining area with many relics of this old industry, plus specialist plants and grand views. The area is accessed from Blackmoor Nature Reserve, Charterhouse.
01823 652400
www.somersetwildlife.org

SPA TREATMENT
Britain's only natural thermal spa (the water is a constant 45°C) is adjacent to the Roman foundations. Here you can enjoy modern spa-based treatments in the spirit of the Roman days. Do as the Celts and Romans did and enjoy various therapies and pamper yourself in style in the steam rooms and baths, including the magnificently refurbished Georgian bath.
The Hetling Pump Room, Hot Bath Street, Bath, Bath & NE Somerset BA1 1SJ
01225 335678
www.thermaebathspa.com

The Walk - *Cotswolds Meet Mendips at Wellow*

A green valley walk, tracing a legacy of abandoned industry and failed technology.

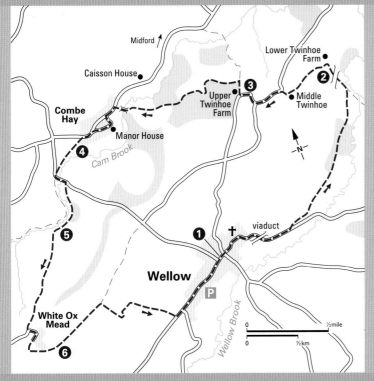

Walk Details

LENGTH: 6.5 miles (10.4km)

TIME: 3hrs 30min

ASCENT: 984ft (300m)

PATHS: Byways, stream sides and some field paths, 12 stiles

SUGGESTED MAP: aqua3 OS Explorer 142 Shepton Mallet

GRID REFERENCE: ST 739583

PARKING: Street parking in village centre, or large car park below Peasedown road

① Head past the church and walk under the viaduct. Immediately after Wellow Trekking, the track starts just above the road. Where it becomes unclear, cross to the hedge opposite; continue above it. The new track runs through the wood, then down to the valley floor. Where the bridleway sign points right, turn left to pass under the railway bridge.

② Just before Lower Twinhoe Farm, turn left onto the signposted track. At the hilltop, the track fades into thistly ground. Bear right, before Middle Twinhoe, to small gate. Turn right along farm's driveway to lane. Turn left, then right around farm buildings and left towards Upper Twinhoe. Just before the farm, a signed track descends to the right.

③ After 130yds (118m) turn left through the double gate and along the field top. The path slants down through woodland towards Combe Hay. From the woodland edge follow the lower edge of the field to the stone bridge into Combe Hay village. Follow the main road left, to pass the Manor House.

④ After the last house of Combe Hay, find gap in wall on left. Bear right, down to Cam Brook; follow to road bridge. Cross and continue with stream down to right through field and wood. Follow the stream across another field to the stile, then along foot of short field to gateway.

⑤ Don't go through the gateway, but turn up the field edge to reach the stile on the right. Slant up left across the next field to the nettled way between thorns. At the top bear right on the rutted track to the lane. Turn uphill to White Ox Mead; follow the lane to the stile. Slant up to another stile; turn up the tarred track to where it divides near to the shed without any walls.

⑥ Keep ahead on the rutted track along the hill crest. Ignore the waymarked stile to pass under some electric cables. Here a small metal gate on the right leads to the hoof-printed path down beside the fence. At the foot of the field turn left, then turn left again (uphill), and head round the corner to the gate. Turn left across the field top and walk down the edge to the street leading back into Wellow village centre.

Lord Poulett Arms

Somerset

The Inn

Set in a village full of scenic charm, the handsome Lord Poulett Arms bears the character of many years of service. Unstuffy and relaxed, the imaginatively restored interior mixes Osborne & Little with Farrow & Ball, while flagstones, wooden floors, polished antique tables, several open fires and evening candles create a classy, comfortable look. The balance between the pub (the bar delivers Branscombe brewery ales straight from the cask and is popular with locals and their dogs) and food is just about right.

Bedrooms have style and simple good taste, juxtaposing exposed stone with contemporary wallpapers, while handsome beds and quality fabrics take centre stage. A Victorian roll-top and an old slipper bath are placed eccentrically in two of the rooms; another has its private bathroom across the corridor – dressing gowns are provided. Thoughtful touches include home-made biscuits, organic apple juice, cafetières, fresh milk and Roberts radios.

The Food

You wouldn't expect such a modern twist on food in so classic an interior, but the kitchen delivers an eclectic menu. All sorts of influences show up among starters – grilled Capricorn goats' cheese with pickled rhubarb and almonds, or brown crab and smoked haddock fishcake with sweet chilli mayonnaise – while mains include pan-roasted tenderloin of pork with Chantenay carrots, baby leeks and a Somerset cider brandy sauce.

The kitchen uses the best in raw materials. Herbs are grown organically in the garden while other ingredients are as local as can be: port-braised hare, for example, served with parsnip purée; and free-range meat that comes from trusted suppliers on the Somerset/Dorset border. Everything is handled with aplomb. Puddings include bread and butter pudding with vanilla ice cream and a raspberry purée, locally made ice creams and a fine selection of West Country cheeses, and there's a decent wine list, too. This is the kind of idyllic country inn that woos urbanites from the glamour of the city.

The Essentials

Time at the Bar!
12-3pm, 6.30-11pm. Food: 12-2pm, 7-9pm

What's the Damage?
Main courses from £9

Bitter Experience:
Branscombe Vale Branoc, guest ales

Sticky Fingers:
Children welcome, smaller portions available

Muddy Paws:
Dogs welcome in the bar

Zzzzz:
4 rooms, £88

Anything Else?
Garden, car park

What To Do

Shop

THE OLD FORGE FOSSIL SHOP

A large and spacious shop stocked with a unique range of fascinating fossils and minerals from all over the world. A complete service is available, including restoration work, cleaning, reformulating and casting. The shop also sells amber jewellery and unusual gifts.

15 Broad Street, Lyme Regis,
Dorset DT7 3QE
01297 445 977
www.fossilshop.net

THE SOMERSET GUILD OF CRAFTSMEN

Situated in the picturesque old Wessex capital of Somerton, the guild is one of the oldest in the country and enables members to sell their work to customers looking for something that is individual.

Market Place, West Street, Somerton,
Somerset TA11 7LX
01458 274653
www.somersetguild.co.uk

MARTOCK GALLERY

A small, friendly business stocking prints by most of the country's leading artists and also offering a complete framing service.

Water Street, Martock, Somerset
01935 823 254
www.martockgallery.co.uk

DODGE & SON

Antique dealers and interior furnishers for nearly a century: exceptional antiques, garden furniture, reproductions and interior fabrics and sofas.

28-33 Cheap Street, Sherborne,
Dorset DT9 3PU
01935 815151
www.dodgeandson.com

Visit

FORDE ABBEY & GARDENS

Completed in 1148, Forde Abbey flourished as a Cistercian monastery for 400 years until the Dissolution, when it began its career as a private residence. A unique opportunity to see both the monastic and state rooms, as well as 30 acres of spectacular award-winning gardens.

Forde Abbey, Chard, Somerset TA20 4LU
01460 220231
www.fordeabbey.co.uk

THE PHILPOT MUSEUM

This award-winning little museum offers a great insight into the history of Lyme Regis as a port, the geology of the Jurassic coast and the development of geology as a science, as well as links with famous writers connected with this area such as Henry Fielding, Jane Austen and John Fowles.

Bridget Street, Lyme Regis, Dorset DT7 3QA
01297 443 370
www.lymeregismuseum.co.uk

MONTACUTE HOUSE

A superb Elizabethan house built of the local golden Ham Hill Stone; its architecture is an exquisite pastiche of Gothic tradition and new Renaissance ideas that were arriving from the continent at the time of its completion in 1601. The house is filled with historic treasures and a fantastic collection of 17th-century textile samples and artworks on loan from the National Portrait Gallery. It was also the location for the film of Jane Austen's *Sense and Sensibility*.

Montacute, Somerset TA15 6XP
01935 823289
www.nationaltrust.org.uk

Visit

BARRINGTON COURT GARDEN

Gertrude Jekyll influenced the creation of this beautiful formal garden, laid out in a series of walled rooms that surround a fine Tudor manor house. Stroll through the White Garden and on into the Rose and Iris Gardens.

Barrington Court, Ilminster,
Somerset TA19 0NQ
01460 241938
www.nationaltrust.org.uk

Activity

GOLF

The Windwhistle Golf Club offers a well-designed 18-hole course.

Cricket St Thomas, Chard,
Somerset TA20 4DG
01460 30231
www.windwhistlegolfclub.co.uk

SAILING

Saltsail Charters offer sailing with a qualified, experienced skipper on day trips, weekends or longer on a well-equipped cruiser/racer yacht.

Saltsail Charters, Weymouth, Dorset
01297 32169
www.saltsailcharters.co.uk

HORSE RIDING

Horseback riding tailored to suit all levels and abilities.

Hill View Riding Centre, Sunnyside Farm,
Crewkerne, Dorset
01460 72731

FOSSIL HUNTING TOUR

Take a walk along Dorset's Jurassic coast with geology expert Chris Pamplin and discover what has been moving and shaking on Planet Earth for the last 400 million years.

www.fossilwalks.com

The Walk - *From Thorncombe to Forde Abbey*

The going is fairly easy through this area renowned for its soft fruit.

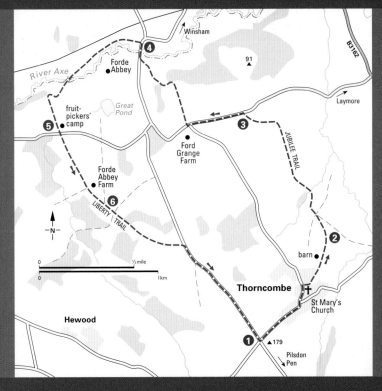

Walk Details

LENGTH: 5 miles (8km)

TIME: 2hrs 30min

ASCENT: 443ft (135m)

PATHS: Field paths, country lanes, 18 stiles

SUGGESTED MAP: aqua3 OS Explorer 116 Lyme Regis & Bridport

GRID REFERENCE: ST 373029

PARKING: At crossroads south-west of Thorncombe

INFORMATION: This walk is over the county border in Dorset

❶ From the crossroads turn left (north-east) and walk down into Thorncombe. Turn left up Chard Street and take the footpath on the right through the churchyard. Now bear right down the lane, then left on the gravel track beside the wall, opposite Goose Cottage. Cross the stile into the field, pass barn on left, then go straight on down the hedge. ❷ Cross the stile in the corner; go straight across the field. Cross the stile and bear diagonally right, down to the corner of the next field. Cross the stile, then cross the 2nd stile on your right. Ford the stream and bear left, up the field. Cross the stile on the left; continue up. Cross another stile on the right; bear right round the edge of the field. The track veers

right through the hedge. Cross 2 more stiles; continue straight on. By the trough turn left over a pair of stiles; go straight ahead up the field edge. Go through the gate and bear right, towards the house. ❸ Emerge through the gate on to the road; turn left. At the junction turn right on to the path; head for the woods. Turn left before the edge of the woods; at the corner go right, through the gate. Head diagonally left to the bottom corner, opposite Forde Abbey gates. Cross stile; turn right on the road to cross River Axe. ❹ Turn immediately left on to the footpath; follow it past the back of the Abbey. At the far corner cross a footbridge over the river; bear right towards the lone cedar, then left up

the slope to stile ('Liberty Trail'). Cross, then walk along top of the woods. Cross stile; bear left across the fields towards another cedar. ❺ Meet the road by the fruit-pickers' camp. Go across, through a gate and up the field. Towards the top righthand corner bear right through the gate; keep on this line. Cross a pair of stiles in the corner, pass Forde Abbey Farm on the left and keep straight on by the hedge. Cross the stile and walk down track. ❻ At the junction of tracks keep straight on. Where the track forks bear left, go through the gate and left across the field. Cross the stile in the hedge; turn right up the road. Follow the road for 0.5 mile (800m) to return to your car.

The Queen's Arms

Somerset

The Queen's Arms, Corton Denham, Somerset DT9 4LR

The Inn

Drive down winding narrow lanes through stunning countryside to find this 18th-century pub hidden away in a sleepy village. The simple stone façade and the slate sign by the door stating 'We like muddy boots and dogs' set the informal feel of this revamped and revitalised village local. The slate- and wood-floored bar is patrolled by the resident labrador and is filled with a refreshing mix of farm workers, walkers and the local gentry. Here, you can sink into a deep leather armchair by the glowing fire, sup a pint of local Butcombe ale and tuck into one of the irresistible home-made pork pies – bliss after an invigorating country walk.

Bedrooms are all contemporary rustic chic where great care has been taken with the fabrics – think squashy, rose-patterned bedspreads, Egyptian cotton bedlinen and silk curtains. Even the beanbags are suede. Bathrooms are swish, modern affairs – choose from a rainstorm shower, cast iron bath (lilac!) or a twin-headed shower for showering à deux. Only the most hard of heart will fail to be enchanted by the views of the church, sheep-grazed fields and distant rolling hills.

The Food

The contemporary-style lunch and dinner menus change weekly to reflect the availability of local produce which includes succulent lamb reared in the village, Old Spot pork from the Piddle Valley, fish from the Dorset coast and organic vegetables.

Lunch is a hearty affair and could consist of English sausages served with hearty chive mash and red onion gravy, a ploughman's lunch with Montgomery cheddar, or a wholesome bowl of broth packed with pearl barley, ham and vegetables. Robust British dishes are simply cooked and presented to allow the flavours to shine through. In the evening, start with chicken liver pâté with Cumberland sauce, followed by classic jugged hare, roast local partridge with game sauce, or pork tenderloin stuffed with figs.

Puddingophiles should really consider the pressing need for building in a healthy country walk in the rolling Somerset countryside to their stay at The Queen's Arms. Only this could possibly justify the steamed syrup sponge with home-made custard or gooey chocolate pudding with chocolate chip ice cream.

The Essentials

Time at the Bar!
12–3.30pm, 6–11pm (all day weekends)
Food: 12-3pm, 6-10pm (9.30 Sunday)

What's the Damage?
Main courses from £8.40

Bitter Experience:
Butcombe, Timothy Taylor Landlord

Sticky Fingers:
Children welcome in bar and overnight; children's menu

Muddy Paws:
Dogs welcome in bar & bedrooms

Zzzzz:
5 rooms, £75–£120

Anything Else?
Terrace, car park

What To Do

Shop

DODGE & SONS

Dodge & Sons have been trading in antiques for more than 80 years – they also have a modern interior design shop selling fabrics by Colefax and Fowler and Jane Churchill, and Zoffany wallpapers. With more than 100 similarly independent shops, you'll find everything from hand-made chocs, Georgian silverware and modern art to kitchenware and delis.

28-33 Cheap Street, Sherborne,
Dorset DT9 3PU
01935 815151
www.dodgeandson.com

EAST LAMBROOK MANOR GARDENS NURSERY

Known as 'the home of English cottage gardening', Lambrook was created in the 1930s by owner Marjorie Fish who would dig up plants and give them to interested visitors. In time, she set up a nursery, and people came from far and wide to buy her rare 'gems'. You can now choose from more than 800 specialist plants. In the award-winning tea shop everything is home-made and locally sourced.

South Petherton, Somerset TA13 5HH
01460 240328
www.eastlambrook.co.uk

SWAN GALLERY

Specialist art gallery established in 1982 where you'll find a wealth of antique works of art from the 18th, 19th and 20th centuries. This is the place for antique maps and prints, original oils and watercolours.

51 Cheap Street, Sherborne,
Dorset DT9 3AX
01935 814465
www.swangallery.co.uk

Visit

MONTACUTE HOUSE

An Elizabethan manor house glittering with thousands of tiny windows, Montacute stands in 300 acres of parkland and incorporates part of the National Portrait Gallery. Here you'll find 17th-century textile samplers, fine 17th- and 18th-century furniture, and the smallest ensuite bathroom you've ever seen – Lord Curzon installed a bijou bath behind a wood panel in his bedroom in the early 1900s. Outside are two 'pudding houses', from a time when guests at dinner parties would savour their dessert in the garden.

Montacute, Somerset TA15 6XP
01935 823289
www.nationaltrust.org

HAYNES MOTOR MUSEUM

This museum houses the UK's largest collection of iconic cars, from Fords to Ferraris. There are 350 cars and bikes in 10 exhibition halls: the Red Room has 50 beautiful red sports cars from around the world. Don't miss the nostalgic 1950s and 60s classics, Bentleys, Rollers and super-modern cars. Buy memorabilia from the shop and top off your afternoon by indulging in a West Country cream tea in the cafe.

Sparkford, Yeovil, Somerset BA22 7LH
01963 442784
www.haynesmotormuseum.com

THOMAS HARDY'S HOUSE

Hardy was born in 1840 in this idyllic cob and thatch cottage built by his grandfather and almost unaltered since the family left. He lived here until he was 22 and in this period wrote *Under the Greenwood Tree*, in which he describes the cottage in detail, and *Far From the Madding Crowd*. He would sit at a window seat in a small room upstairs to write, overlooking his beloved Black Down. The traditional cottage garden has superb displays of lupins, lavender and lilies.

Higher Bockhampton, Dorchester,
Dorset DT2 8QJ
01297 561900
www.nationaltrust.org

Activity

RACING AT WINCANTON

Saturday meetings provide some of the best jump racing of the National Hunt season, featuring some of the country's top horses. Thursday racing includes Irish Day with pints of the black stuff and live Irish music – with seven bars you won't need to go thirsty.

Wincanton, Somerset BA9 8BJ
01963 32344
www.wincantonracecouse.co.uk

HORSE RIDING

You are deep in Thomas Hardy's fictionalised Wessex here, and what better way to discover his beloved county than on horseback. Go back in time to explore the woodland bridleways, gently rolling clay pastures and patchwork-quilt fields vividly depicted by Hardy in his novel *Tess of the D'Urbevilles*.

Pound Cottage Riding Centre, Luccombe
Farm, Milton Abbas, Blandford Forum,
Dorset DT11 0BD
01258 880057

The Walk - *Cadbury Castle as Camelot?*

South Cadbury's hill fort gives wide views of Somerset and a glimpse of pre-history.

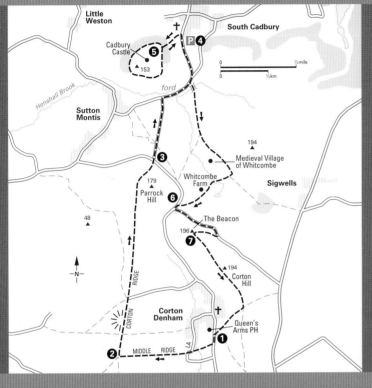

Walk Details

LENGTH: 6.75 miles (10.9km)

TIME: 3hrs 30min

ASCENT: 1,000ft (300m)

PATHS: Well-used paths, 6 stiles

SUGGESTED MAP: aqua3 OS Explorer 129 Yeovil & Sherborne

GRID REFERENCE: ST 635224

PARKING: The Queen's Arms car park, or Cadbury Castle car park (free), south of South Cadbury (point 4)

1 From The Queen's Arms turn left on the road, between high banks for 110yds (100m) to the stile ('Middle Ridge Lane'). Keep left of the trees to the field gate, with stile beyond leading into lane. Go onto the stony track that climbs to the ridgeline.

2 Turn right; walk along Corton Ridge with the hedge on your right and the view on your left. After 650yds (594m) Ridge Lane starts on the right, but go through the small gate on the left to continue along the ridge. After the small gate, the green path bends around the flank of Parrock Hill. With Cadbury Castle now on your left, ignore the 1st green track down to the left. Shortly the main track turns down left into the hedge end and a waymarked

gate. From this point a hedged path leads you down to reach the road.

3 Cross into the road ('South Cadbury'). Shortly turn right, again for South Cadbury; follow the road around the base of Cadbury Castle to reach the adjacent car park.

4 Turn right out of the car park to the 1st house in South Cadbury. The track leads up to Cadbury Castle. The ramparts and top of the fort are access land; stroll around at will.

5 Return past car park. After 0.25 mile (400m), pass a side road on the left, to a stile signposted 'Sigwells'. Walk down to reach the stile and footbridge. Cross then follow left edge of field, then uncultivated strip. Track starts ahead, but take stile on right to follow field edge next to

it, to gate with 2 waymarkers. Faint track leads along top of following field. At end turn down into hedged-earth track which leads out past Whitcombe Farm to rejoin road.

6 Turn left to junction below Corton Denham Beacon. Turn left to slant uphill for 0.25 mile (400m). The track on the right leads to open hilltop and summit trig point.

7 Head along the steep hill rim to stile with dog slot. Continue along top of slope (Corton Denham below). Pass modern 'tumulus' (small, covered reservoir). Above, 5 large beeches slant to the waymarked gate. A green path slants down again, until a gate leading to tarred lane; follow this to reach the road below and The Queen's Arms.

The Devonshire Arms

Somerset

The Inn

The impressive Devonshire Arms is at odds with its rural village setting, but the coat of arms displayed prominently over the porticoed front door gives a clue to the building's origins – this was once a hunting lodge belonging to the Dukes of Devonshire. Inside, a colour scheme of light wood (stripped floorboards, chunky tables), terracotta, stone and leather sets a rather elegant tone, but despite the urbane, sophisticated look you are made to feel very welcome. A log fire crackles in the bar in winter, fronted by leather sofas for cosy laid-back lounging, but in fine weather head out to the sheltered courtyard or the large terraced garden for peerless alfresco eating.

The bedrooms are full of thoughtful touches that reflect the owner-managed approach. Digital TV, cafetières with fresh coffee and tasteful, neutral colour schemes are common to all, as are quality beds and bed-linen. The rooms at the front with views over the village green are the most spacious, but smaller rooms overlooking the garden are equally charming. Bathrooms are a mix of bath and shower – there's even a Victorian roll-top – and all are impressively maintained.

The Essentials

Time at the Bar!
12-3pm, 6-11pm
Food: 12-2.30pm, 7-9.30pm
(9pm Sunday)

What's the Damage?
Main courses from £12.95

Bitter Experience:
Teignworthy Reel Ale, Bath Ales SPA

Sticky Fingers:
Children welcome

Muddy Paws:
Dogs welcome in the bar

Zzzzz:
9 rooms, £75-£120

Anything Else?
Terrace, garden, car park

The Food

Tasty, consistently well-cooked food draws people from miles around. Lunch in the bar can be as simple as cream of parsnip and stilton soup served with hunks of locally baked granary bread, or chargrilled beef salad with horseradish dressing, while other highlights include ploughman's of Keen's cheddar and Somerset brie, or a traditional bangers and mustard mash with red onion gravy. Impressive, too are the refreshingly low prices with a set lunch coming in at under £10.

The cooking offers a well judged mix of the familiar and the gently inventive, best seen at dinner (served in the elegant dining room) in dishes like crab crème brûlée with fennel and rocket salad, and mains of roasted wood pigeon with bacon, caramelized button onions and thyme jus, or slow-cooked shoulder of Somerset lamb.

Puddings are a must, whether a ginger sticky toffee pudding with lime leaf ice cream or crème fraîche and black pepper pannacotta with strawberry sorbet. The wine list features some interesting bottles.

What To Do

Shop

THE COURTHOUSE

Craftspeople from Somerset and beyond display and sell a range of hard and soft craftworks, including pottery, textiles and paintings.

Market Place, West Street, Somerton, Somerset TA11 7LX

01458 274653

www.somersetguild.co.uk

HECKS CIDER

One of the longest established smaller producers, Hecks Cider makes a range of ciders from Somerset orchards, together with cider brandies and aperitifs and the rare perry cider (made from pear juice). The mill shop stocks locally made cheeses and preserves.

9-11 Middle Leigh, Street, Somerset BA16 0LB

01458 442367

www.hecksfarmhousecider.co.uk

MUCHELNEY POTTERY

John Leach is the latest in an acclaimed family lineage of potters and designers to produce both functional and decorative pottery at this rural retreat with gallery.

Muchelney, Langport, Somerset TA10 0DW

01458 250324

www.johnleachpottery.co.uk

SOMERSET LEVELS BASKET & CRAFT CENTRE

Making the most of local materials, artisans utilise the copious willow carrs of The Levels to produce basketware, furniture, sculpture and houseware. Rush, seagrass and cane products add a global feel.

Lyng Road, Burrow Bridge, Bridgwater, Somerset TA7 0SG

01823 698688

www.somersetlevels.co.uk

Visit

FLEET AIR ARM MUSEUM

Discover the little-known history of the Fleet Air Arm – part of the navy's airforce. A Fairey Swordfish and a Concorde, for example, at this busy airbase bring operations to life – from WWI to the present day.

Yeovilton, Ilchester, Somerset BA22 8HT

01935 840565

www.fleetairarm.com

PEAT MOORS CENTRE

A look at how culture, lifestyle and industry – including peat digging over thousands of years – have shaped the Somerset Levels. At the heart of the centre is a reconstruction of Glastonbury Lake Village, an Iron Age settlement.

Shapwick Road, Westhay, Glastonbury, Somerset BA6 9TT

01458 860697

www.somerset.gov.uk/cultureheritage

WELLS CATHEDRAL

The West Front of the cathedral has the largest collection of medieval statuary in Britain. Within is a treasure trove of architectural gems and stained glass; look out, too, for the astronomical clock with its jousting knights. The clever swans on the moat of the adjoining Bishop's Palace have been trained ring a bell when they want to be fed.

Cathedral Green, Wells, Somerset BA5 2UE

01749 832210

www.wellscathedral.org.uk

Activity

BIRDWATCHING

The Levels are one of England's prime wild bird sites. The RSPB has several reserves, the largest is at Greylake: 5,000 acres of flood-plain grassland, ditches, reeds and open water with hides in place for birdwatching. You'll see mainly waterbirds, but with many other species, resident or passing. Regular events and walks also introduce visitors to the land mammals that make a home here.

Greylake RSPB Reserve, Bridgwater, Somerset

01458 252805

www.rspb.org.uk

CYCLING

Langport is at the heart of the Somerset Levels, an area with a wealth of peaceful lanes ideal for easy cycling through wildlife-rich countryside and characterful ancient villages. The River Parrett Centre is the ideal starting place.

Bow Bridge Cycles, Westover, Langport, Somerset TA10 9RB

01458 250350

www.southsomerset.gov.uk (follow links)

MIDDLEMOOR WATER PARK

This 20-acre lake has facilities for waterskiing, wakeboarding, jetskiing and other waterborne activities. Tuition is available for beginners; equipment can be hired by more experienced users.

The Causeway, Woolavington, Bridgwater, Somerset TA7 8DN

01278 685578 www.middlemoor.co.uk

The Walk - *In Praise of Apples at East Lambrook*

A gentle ramble around the fields and fragrant apple orchards of Somerset.

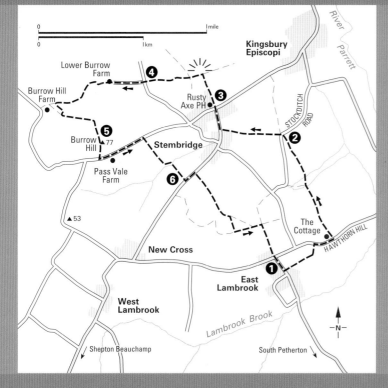

Walk Details

LENGTH: 4.75 miles (7.7km)

TIME: 2hrs 30min

ASCENT: 350ft (110m)

PATHS: Little-used field paths (some possibly overgrown by late summer), 24 stiles

SUGGESTED MAP: aqua3 OS Explorer 129 Yeovil & Sherborne

GRID REFERENCE: ST 431190

PARKING: Street parking in East Lambrook village

1 Head into the centre of the village, eventually turning left onto the track. After passing one field, the track leads left to the lane (Hawthorn Hill). Turn right to The Cottage, where the gate with the stile leads into the orchard on your left. Follow the left edge and the next field. Cross the following field, keeping 70yds (64m) from the left edge, to the gate. Bear right to the stile-with-footbridge and the orchard. At the far end the gate leads onto Stockditch Road.
2 Turn left for 40yds (37m), onto an overgrown track. The edge of another orchard leads to 2 stiles and a footbridge. Follow the left edges of 2 fields to the road; turn right to reach the Rusty Axe pub.

3 Keep ahead, onto the track, past the houses. On crossing the crest, turn left on the green track. At the next field follow the hedge on left (ignoring the waymarker for a different path). Two stiles lead into a long field with the stumps of a former orchard. Keep to left of house to join the quiet country lane.
4 Cross into the tarred driveway of Lower Burrow Farm; follow waymarkers between the farm buildings. Bear left, slanting uphill, to the gateway. Cross the next field to the double stile. Inside the next field bear right to the gate and stile. Burrow Hill Farm is one field ahead. Turn left, up the side of the field and across top to the gate. Go up field to poplars and summit of Burrow Hill.

5 Drop to the lane at Pass Vale Farm and then turn left for 0.25 mile (400m) to the waymarked field gate on the right. Follow the left edges of 2 fields to the footbridge with the brambly stile. Turn left beside the stream to another brambly stile and turn right to lane.
6 Turn left to the gate on the right ('East Lambrook'). Follow the left edges of 3 fields, then bear left over the stile and footbridge to the 2nd bridge beyond. In the next large field, follow the waymarkers down the righthand side and across the far end to the orchard. Do not cross the obvious stile out of the orchard but turn right, to its far end, where the lane leads you back into East Lambrook and your car.

The Museum Inn

Dorset

The Inn

Farnham is a sleepy village, enticingly lost within the rolling folds of Cranborne Chase and filled with timeless thatched cottages. At its heart is the part-thatched Museum Inn, which owes its name to the 17th-century archaeologist General Pitt-Rivers who took over Gypsy School nearby to house one of his museums. The current 'curators', Vicky Elliot and Mark Stephenson, restored and revived the inn in 2001 and business has been brisk ever since. Original features in the three civilised beamed rooms around the bar have been retained, so expect yellow-washed walls, flagstone floors, crackling log fires and scrubbed tables, which perfectly set the scene in which to enjoy some superlative bar food, local ales and top-notch wines with a dozen by the glass.

Style and attention to detail can be seen in the eight bedrooms. Each is individually decorated with warm colours and quality fabrics, and offers easy chairs and comfortable beds for a sound night's sleep. Big bathrooms have power showers over baths, while added touches include magazines, home-made biscuits and organic chocolate.

The Essentials

Time at the Bar!
12-3pm, 6-11pm
Food: 12-2pm (2.30pm Sat, Sun), 7-9.30pm (Sun 9pm)

What's the Damage?
Main courses from £14

Bitter Experience:
Ringwood Best, Hop Back Summer Lightning

Sticky Fingers:
Children welcome at lunchtime

Muddy Paws:
Dogs welcome

Zzzzz:
8 rooms, £95-£150

Anything Else?
Terrace, car park, conservatory

The Food

The kitchen is the domain of Clive Jory, who takes sourcing quality local produce very seriously. He uses only traditionally reared meats and free-range poultry, game from neighbouring estates and local organic vegetables. Dine informally in the bustling bar or head for the more formal Shed restaurant, which is open evenings and weekends only – booking is essential. Typical starters include chicken liver and mushroom parfait with sticky onion marmalade, smoked haddock chowder or potted brown shrimps served with rocket salad and grilled bruschetta.

To follow, there may be a hearty and satisfying Portland fish stew with saffron potatoes, simply grilled lemon sole, or well-executed modern dishes like herb-crusted rack of Dorset lamb with fondant potato, ratatouille and aubergine purée, or local estate venison with butternut squash mash and a sour cherry jus. To finish, the dark chocolate brownie served with lashings of bitter chocolate sauce and coffee ice cream is irresistible. Upmarket sandwiches like Longhorn steak, mushroom and onion are available only at lunchtime.

What To Do

Shop

ELLWOOD BOOKS
Four rooms of beautiful books, including rare and secondhand, fiction and non-fiction, local interest, history and poetry.

38 Winchester Street, Salisbury,
Wiltshire SP1 1HG
01722 322975
www.ellwoodbooks.com

HARE LANE POTTERY
Jonathan Garratt is one of Britain's foremost terracotta potters and his passion for plants informs many of the innovative shapes. Local clay is refined on site and all the work is fired exclusively with wood to give distinctive dark colours and real character. Also available: glazed tableware and garden sculpture.

Hare Lane, Cranborne, Wimborne Minster,
Dorset BH21 5QT
01725 517700

NUGGS 1268
In this beautifully restored Tudor building you will find specialist foods, culinary gifts, excellent wines, oils, vinegars and cookware.

51 Blue Boar Row, Salisbury,
Wiltshire SP1 1DA
01722 417600

WALFORD MILL CRAFT CENTRE
A converted mill in a quiet riverside setting with a Crafts Council shop and exhibition gallery, featuring the best in contemporary British design. Join a workshop and try your hand at silk weaving, stained glass and machine embroidery. Wide variety of art and craft events.

Stone Lane, Wimborne Minster,
Dorset BH21 1NL
01202 841400
www.walford-mill.co.uk

Visit

KINGSTON LACY
This elegant 17th-century country mansion was the home of the Bankes family for more than 300 years and is set in formal gardens with extensive wooded parkland. There are impressive Old Master paintings by Van Dyck, Titian and Brueghel, Egyptian artefacts and the famous dramatic Spanish Room with walls hung in gilded leather.

Wimborne Minster, Dorset BH21 4EA
01202 883402
www.nationaltrust.org.uk

SALISBURY CATHEDRAL
Building of the cathedral was begun in 1220 and largely completed in just 38 years, and Salisbury is unique among English medieval cathedrals for having no substantial later additions. You can also see one of only four remaining copies of the original *Magna Carta* here, as well as viewing Europe's oldest working clock dating from 1386.

Salisbury, Wiltshire
www.salisburycathedral.co.uk

STOURHEAD HOUSE & GARDENS
Built in the 1720s, this fine Palladian mansion houses a collection of Chippendale furniture, magnificent paintings and an exquisite Regency library. Surrounding the mansion is one of the finest landscape gardens in the world: winding lakeside paths lead past classical temples and follies, set against a backdrop of beautiful and exotic trees, revealing vistas that have captured the imagination of visitors for more than two centuries.

Stourton, Warminster, Wiltshire BA12 6QD
01747 841152
www.nationaltrust.org.uk

Activity

CHARTER A YACHT
Sail anywhere between the Isle of Wight and Weymouth and explore the Jurassic coast on a fully equipped 39ft Bavaria yacht, owned and skippered by sailing team Russ and Jenny Upton. Novices can build up their sailing miles for RYA courses while experienced sea dogs can be more hands-on.

One Day Yacht Charter, 5 Thames St,
Poole Quay, Poole, Dorset BH15 1JN
07921 833115
www.charter-oneday.com

FLY FISHING
Catch your own dinner on a day on the lakes at Christchurch Angling Club. Two put-and-take lakes (rainbow trout) and one catch-and-release lake (brown and rainbow trout). Open all year; dry and wet fly.

Christchurch Angling Club, White Sheet
Trout Fisher, Holt, nr Wimborne, Dorset
01202 871703

WATERSKIING & WAKEBOARDING
Waterskiing for all ages and abilities with professional and friendly guidance. The training bar on the side of the boat helps beginners gain confidence. Wakeboarding is the latest extreme sport: a combination of waterskiing, snowboarding and surfing.

New Forest Water Park, Ringwood Road,
Fordingbridge, Hampshire SP6 2EY
01425 656868
www.newforestwaterpark.co.uk

The Walk - Roaming the Woods at Ashmore

A gentle amble through plantations of mixed woodland to a village highpoint.

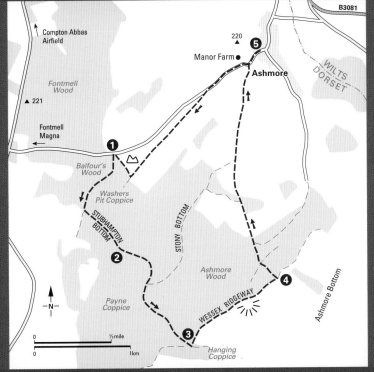

Walk Details

LENGTH: 5.75 miles (9.2km)

TIME: 3hrs

ASCENT: 427ft (130m)

PATHS: Forestry and farm tracks, woodland and field paths, 1 stile

SUGGESTED MAP: aqua3 OS Explorer 118 Shaftesbury & Cranborne Chase

GRID REFERENCE: ST 897167

PARKING: At Washers Pit entrance to Ashmore Wood

❶ With your back to the road, walk past the gate; follow the forestry road as it curves past Washers Pit Coppice on the left and Balfour's Wood on the right. After 0.5 mile (800m) ignore crossing bridleway and stay ahead on track. You're now in Stubhampton Bottom, following the winding valley through the trees.
❷ Where the main track swings up to the left, keep ahead, following the blue public bridleway marker, on the rutted track along the valley floor. The path from Stony Bottom feeds in from the left – keep straight on. Where an area of exposed hillside appears on the left, follow the blue markers on to the narrower track to the right, which runs down through woodland parallel and

below the forestry road. At Hanging Coppice, a fingerpost shows where the Wessex Ridgeway path feeds in from the right – again, keep ahead. The path soon rises to emerge again at the corner of the field.
❸ Turn left at the fence (following blue marker); walk uphill. Follow the path along the edge of forest, with good views to south-east of rolling hills and secretive valleys.
❹ After 0.75 mile (1.2km), turn left at a marked junction of tracks and walk through the woods. Cross the track and keep straight on, following the marker, to meet the track. Go straight on, following signs for Wessex Ridgeway, and passing under a beech tree. Go through the old gate. Continue up the track

for about 1 mile (1.6km), through farmland and across exposed open hilltop, with the houses of Ashmore appearing. At the end of the track turn right; walk into the village to pass by the duck pond.
❺ Retrace the route but stay on the road out of the village, passing Manor Farm (right) and heading downhill. Just before the road narrows, bear left through the gate (blue marker). Walk along the top of the field, pass the gate on the left and bear down to the right to lower of 2 gates at far side. Cross the stile and walk ahead on the broad green track. Go through the gate into the woods; immediately turn right, following the steep bridleway down the side of the hill to the car park.

The Stapleton Arms

Dorset

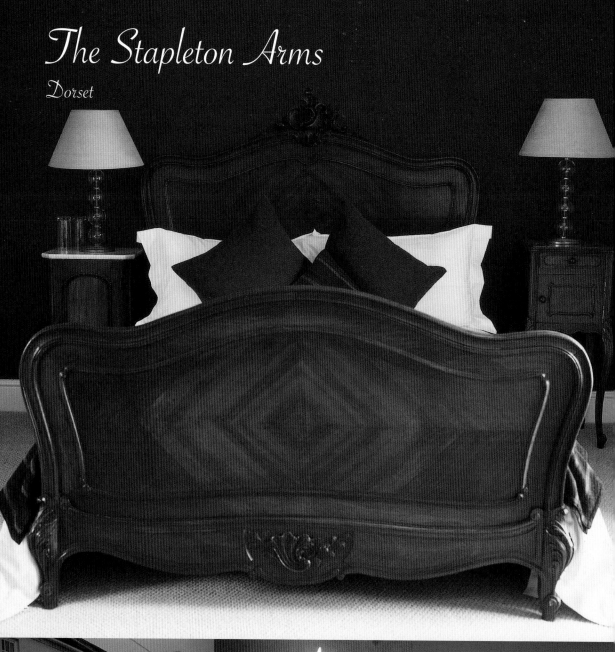

The Stapleton Arms, Church Hill, Buckhorn Weston, Dorset SP8 5HS

The Inn

They revamped the Queen's Arms down near Sherborne and made a huge success of it, so Rupert and Victoria Reeves set about repeating their winning formula at this once run-down inn in Buckhorn Weston. Naturally, the result is stunning and they have managed to breathe new life into the place. Chic, modern decor has been introduced in the slate-floored bar area, yet the pub remains a true local, one where drinkers and diners mix happily. Expect big scrubbed tables, an eclectic mix of chairs, contemporary colours and squashy leather sofas, which invite you to relax with the papers and a pint of Butcombe Bitter. The adjoining dining room has huge mirrors on deep blue-painted walls.

A peaceful night's sleep is guaranteed in one of the four quirky, classy bedrooms. Individually designed, they mix contemporary and antique furnishings, plus all have plasma TVs, DVD players, internet access, cotton sheets on big wooden beds, and huge tiled bathrooms with storm showers and posh smellies. Breakfast on Dorset bacon, free-range eggs, home-made bread and jams, then walk it off by striding across open fields.

The Food

Food is simple, modern and innovative, and the daily changing menus are prepared using quality local and seasonal produce, most from within 25 miles of the pub. Fish is delivered daily from the Dorset coast; salads and vegetables are grown on Roswells Farm near Ilminster; and meats are sourced from Dorset farms. A hand-made pork pie at the bar or a lunchtime sandwich of rare roast beef with horseradish sauce, or even a fisherman's platter – a feast for two – suits peckish drinkers. But for something more substantial, look to the main dishes: whole plaice with lime and caper butter or tagliatelle with wild mushrooms, chorizo, peas and parmesan are typical mouthwatering choices.

The evening menu extends to guinea fowl, partridge and mushroom terrine with spicy tomato chutney, followed by hake with chive mash and tomato hollandaise or duck with marmalade and pepper sauce. For pudding, try the warm plum tarte tatin with stem-ginger ice cream or the intriguing 'four spoons of chocolate'. Wash it all down with tip-top ales, real cider, Luscombe organic juices or some interesting wines.

The Essentials

Time at the Bar!
11am-3pm, 6-11pm; Sat 12-11pm;
Sun 12-10.30pm
Food: 12-3pm, 6-10pm

What's the Damage?
Main courses from £8.50

Bitter Experience:
Timothy Taylor Landlord, Butcombe

Sticky Fingers:
Children welcome; children's menu

Muddy Paws:
Dogs welcome

Zzzzz:
4 rooms, £80-£120

Anything Else?
Patio, terrace, car park

What To Do

Shop

ONE CRAFT GALLERY

This Grade II listed building, previously a saddlers, is co-operatively run and looks onto the market place with its market cross and 15th-century 'shamble'. It is home to items crafted by local artists, many of them internationally renowned. Ceramics, jewellery, millinery, knitwear, paintings and prints are among some of the arty delights.

1 High Street, Shepton Mallet,
Somerset BA4 5AA
01749 343777
www.1craft.co.uk

PARKERS MENU

Parkers is a family-run catering business established in 1902 and now run by Jane, a great-granddaughter of the original owners. Their Taste of the West award-winning take-home meals are hand-made in small batches from locally sourced, seasonal ingredients – try the fish pie (made from a secret family recipe), raspberry pavlova, Dorset apple cake, shepherds pie and goats' cheese tarts. While you're here, don't miss the walk down Gold Hill, the steep cobbled street made famous by the Hovis boy in the 1980s bread adverts.

2 Swan Yard, Shaftesbury, Dorset DT9 3AX
01935 814527
www.parkersmenu.co.uk

FERNSTROM & FARRELL DELI

This friendly deli and grocery is filled with breads, cakes and masses of other locally sourced, home-made goodies.

2 High Street, Wincanton, Somerset BA9 9JP
01963 31549

Visit

FLEET AIR ARM MUSEUM

All the iconic planes are under one roof here: World War I Sopwith Camels and Fokkers; the World War II Fairey Swordfish. The Leading Edge exhibition demonstrates how advances in design and technology allowed the British Aircraft industry to lead the world, and includes the second Concorde prototype, Hawkers and De Havillands. There's a Restoration Hangar where you can watch the latest renovation project, a well-stocked shop where you can buy kits, books, DVDs and prints, and a cafe from which – on a clear day – you can watch next door's Royal Naval Air Station planes going through their paces.

Ilchester, Somerset BA22 8HT
01935 840565
www.fleetairarm.com

LYTES CAREY MANOR

Set deep in rural Somerset, this manor house with its Tudor great hall and 14th-century chapel was the home of medieval herbalist Henry Lyte. Originally the garden was laid out in a series of 'rooms' with topiary, mixed borders and a herb garden where the plants that Lyte cultivated are still grown.

Lytes Carey Manor, Charlton Mackrell,
Somerton, Somerset TA11 7HU
01458 224471
www.nationaltrust.org.uk

SHAFTESBURY ABBEY MUSEUM & GARDEN

On the site of Saxon England's foremost Benedictine nunnery, founded by King Alfred in 888 AD, the abbey is a magical series of buildings lying in a peaceful walled garden. King Canute is said to have loved Shaftesbury and probably restored the Saxon buildings – Catherine of Aragon also stayed here. The museum vividly brings to life the history of the Abbey, through fascinating collections of excavated carved objects, medieval floor tiles and carved stonework. The plants you'll see would have been used by the nuns to flavour food, heal the sick and dye cloth. A medieval orchard has been planted, spanning the 15th to the 19th century.

Park Walk, Shaftesbury, Dorset SP7 8JR
01747 852910
www.shaftesburyabbey.co.uk

Activity

GLIDING

Fancy the idea of soaring soundlessly for an hour or two above the glorious Wiltshire and Dorset countryside? Try your hand at the controls, or just relax and enjoy the ride and the view.

Dorset Gliding Club, The Park, Kingston
Deverill, Warminster, Wiltshire BA12 7HF
01380 859161
www.bwnd.co.uk

HORSERIDING IN BLACKMORE VALE

Enjoy the gently rolling pastures of Thomas Hardy's Wessex on horseback. This is traditionally dairy country, hence the patchwork quilt fields and the hedgerows bordered by the high arc of chalk hills. As described by Hardy in *Under the Greenwood Tree,* this is quintessential rural England.

Pound Cottage Riding Centre, Luccumbe
Farm, Milton Abbas, Blandford Forum,
Dorset DT11 0BD
01258 880057

The Walk - *A Stroll Around Cucklington*

Up hill and down dale, taking in a church with over a thousand years of history.

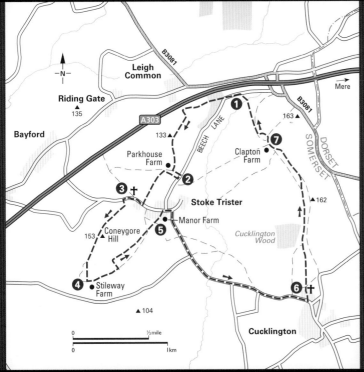

Walk Details

LENGTH: 5.5 miles (8.8km)

TIME: 2hrs 45min

ASCENT: 600ft (180m)

PATHS: Little-used field paths, which may be overgrown, 11 stiles

SUGGESTED MAP: aqua3 OS Explorer 129 Yeovil & Sherborne

GRID REFERENCE: ST 747298

PARKING: Lay-by on former main road immediately south of A303

INFORMATION: This walk is over the county border in Somerset

❶ With your back to the A303, turn right on the lane to where the track runs ahead into the wood. At the far side, the fenced footpath runs alongside the main road. Turn left up the path, then right into the fenced-off path that bends left to Parkhouse Farm. After the passage to the left of the buildings, turn left again to the lane.
❷ Turn back right, following the field edge back by the farm track. Go through the gate; turn left through the gate. Heading towards Stoke Trister church, follow the left edge of the field; go straight up 2nd field, turning right along lane to church.
❸ Continue to the stile. Go uphill past the muddy track, but turn right alongside the hedge immediately

above. Follow around Coneygore Hill, over the stile, then to 2nd; go straight down to Stileway Farm.
❹ Turn left by the top of the farm buildings. Continue into the field track but immediately take the gate above; pass along the base of 2 fields, to the gate by the cattle trough. Head uphill, with the hedge to the left, to the steeper bank around Coneygore Hill. Turn right and follow the banking to the stile. Keep on to the gap between the bramble clumps; slant down right to reach the gate in the corner leading on to the green track and then to the lane near Manor Farm.
❺ Turn downhill past the thatched cottage and red phone box; bear right for Cucklington. There are

field paths on the left, but use the lane to cross the valley and climb to Cucklington. The gravel track on the left leads to Cucklington church.
❻ Pass left of the church; cross 2 fields, passing above Cucklington Wood. In the 3rd field slant to the right to join track to Clapton Farm.
❼ After the Tudor manor house the track bends right, uphill. Turn left between the farm buildings to the gate, then turn left down the wooded bank. Turn right, along the base of the bank, to the gap in the hedge. Bear left past the power pole to the field's bottom corner. Cross 2 streams; bear left to cross a 3rd and the stile beyond. Go straight up to the stile by the cattle trough and rejoin the lane you parked on.

The Spread Eagle Inn

Wiltshire

The Spread Eagle Inn, Stourton, Warminster, Wiltshire BA12 6QE

The Essentials

Time at the Bar!
11am-11pm
Food: 12.30-2.30pm daily,
7-9pm Mon-Sat
(Sun dinner residents only)

What's the Damage?
Main courses from £9

Bitter Experience:
Wessex Kilmington Best, Butcombe

Sticky Fingers:
Children welcome, small portions
available

Muddy Paws:
No dogs

Zzzzz:
5 rooms, £110

Anything Else?
Garden, car park

The Food

In this one-road village it's hard to miss the Spread Eagle – although being close to the entrance to Stourhead House and Garden is helpful (and convenient for the many visitors to this National Trust property). The inn is now in the hands of Stephen Ross, who comes with impeccable credentials as hotelier and restaurateur. Refurbishment has certainly brought out the best in this handsome building with stone floors, painted beams and big windows looking out onto a shady courtyard. The civilised bar is a generous, comfortable room, hung with 19th-century prints and horse brasses, and warmed by a large, blazing log burner in winter.

The best of the five traditional bedrooms are large rooms with window seats and verdant views; others are more compact but equally immaculate, painted in soft colours and offering crisp white linen, plump duvets and pillows on very comfortable beds. In addition, expect flat-screen TVs and the odd sloping floor – this is an 18th-century building after all. Admission to Stourhead (in season) is included in the room price, a very pleasant added extra.

The Inn

The cooking here is first class, the kitchen offering a menu that is neither too long nor over-ambitious, with food that is simple, straightforward and reliant on prime seasonal and local produce. Lunch in the bar, in particular, emphasises local ingredients. Typical offerings are pressed coarse country pâté served alongside fruit chutney, pickled walnuts and toast; farm-shop ham, free-range egg and chips; ploughman's of West Country cheeses; and something more elaborate like slow-roasted Barbary duck leg teamed with smoked bacon and butterbean and sausage stew.

Dinner in the restaurant is a more formal affair: in winter a log fire blazes and candles cast a glow on the rich red walls, while in summer the evening light streams through big windows. Here, a meal could start with smoked haddock and prawn fishcakes with remoulade sauce, go on to estate venison casserole with juniper, red wine, rosemary and shallot dumplings, or cod fillet with wilted red chard and tomato and shallot dressing, and finish with rum and raisin cheesecake.

What To Do

Visit

LONGLEAT HOUSE & SAFARI PARK

Set within 900 acres of Capability Brown landscaped parkland, Longleat House is one of the best examples of high Elizabethan architecture in Britain and one of the most beautiful stately homes open to the public in the whole country. The drive through the safari park, opened in 1966, was the first of its kind outside Africa: giraffe, zebras, lions, rhino and monkeys all have right of way here.

Longleat, Warminster, Wiltshire BA12 7NW
01985 844 400
www.longleat.co.uk

SHERBORNE ABBEY

Founded by St Aldhelm in 705 AD, the abbey has developed from a Saxon cathedral to the worshipping heart of a monastic community and, finally, to one of the most beautiful of England's parish churches. For many it is still the 'cathedral of Dorset', and our Benedictine heritage lives on in the daily offering of prayer and praise.

The Parish Office, 3 Abbey Close, Sherborne, Dorset DT9 3LQ
01935 812452
www.sherborneabbey.com

WILTON HOUSE

This 460-year-old building with its history, architecture, art treasures and 21 acres of gardens and parkland attracts visitors from all over the world. The south front and state rooms remain a testimony to the popularity of the Palladian style of architecture in the middle of the 17th century.

Wilton, Salisbury, Wiltshire SP2 0BJ
01722 746714
www.wiltonhouse.com

Shop

DAUWALDER'S OF SALISBURY

Britain's largest provincial stamp shop also sell coins, banknotes, cigarette cards, old bonds and share certificates, and small collectibles – including die-cast cars and railways.

92/94 Fisherton Street, Salisbury, Wiltshire SP2 7QY
01722 412 100
www.worldstamps.co.uk

THE GALLERY AT FISHERTON MILL

Built in 1880 as a grain mill, Fisherton Mill is now one of the south's largest independent art galleries, comprising three floors of dazzling works of art including painting, sculpture, furniture, ceramics, textiles, metalwork and contemporary craft. There is also an outdoor seasonal exhibition area, studio workshops and a cafe.

108 Fisherton Street, Salisbury, Wiltshire SP2 2QY
01722 415 121
www.fishertonmill.co.uk

THE JERRAM GALLERY

The gallery hosts a regularly changing selection of paintings, watercolours and engravings in wood from 1860 to 1950 as well as the work of contemporary artists.

7 St John Street, Salisbury, Wiltshire SP1 2SB
01722 412310

Activity

CROP CIRCLE SPOTTING

Crop circles have been appearing in the area for years. The finest have been seen in the Marlborough Downs and Pewsey Vale.

Pewsey Vale, Wiltshire
www.cropcircles.org

PAINTING CLASSES

Graham Oliver has led painting classes for 17 years in his gallery and is a regular demonstrator to art societies. His series of exercises in watercolour is ideal for beginners.

Graham Oliver Gallery, 97a Brown Street, Salisbury, Wiltshire SP1 2BA
01722 503610
www.grahamolivergallery.co.uk

HIRE A CLASSIC CAR

Grab a picnic hamper and take your pick of 1960s classics such as E-types, Jag Mk2, Healey, MGB, Rover P5B. Based in the Nadder Valley just a few gear changes away from beautiful Cranborne Chase, you could drive to the New Forest.

Wiltshire Classics, Westfield Park, Dinton, Salisbury, Wiltshire SP3 5BT
01722 716328
www.wiltshireclassics.co.uk

HORSE RIDING

The Riding Centre at Grovely has been established for more than 50 years and offers unparalleled riding experiences, ranging from tuition, both group and private, through to participation in beautiful woodland treks and rides over rolling chalk downs with wide tracks, Roman roads and grassy droves.

Grovely Riding Centre, Water Ditchampton, Wilton, Salisbury, Wiltshire SP2 0LB
01722 742 288
www.grovely.info

The Walk - *Alfred's Tower at Three County Corner*

An expedition through Somerset, Dorset and Wiltshire, to Stourhead and Alfred's Tower.

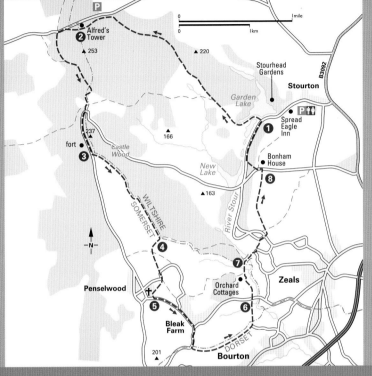

Walk Details

LENGTH: 8.5 miles (13.7km)

TIME: 4hrs

ASCENT: 950ft (290m)

PATHS: Some tracks and some small paths and field edges, 7 stiles

SUGGESTED MAP: aqua3 OS Explorer 142 Shepton Mallet

GRID REFERENCE: ST 776339

PARKING: The Spread Eagle car park, or Penselwood church; some verge parking at Bleak Farm

1 From The Spread Eagle, the track bends right and heads into the wooded valley with Alfred's Tower ahead, reaching open ground at the hilltop, with road ahead. Turn left, in the grassy avenue, to Alfred's Tower.
2 Join the road ahead for 220yds (201m), down to the sunken path on the left ('Penselwood'). Follow this, ignoring paths on both sides, on to track down to the major junction. Bear right to the lane, then right again, on the road ('Penselwood'), which leads over the hilltop with its hill fort. Descend until some open ground appears on the left.
3 Cross the stile; head downhill with Castle Wood left, and young trees right. Move into the wood to join the track along its edge. At the

corner of the wood, a waymarked gate on the right leads into fields.
4 Follow the left edge of 1st field to 2 gates on the left; keep ahead to the gate and a 2nd gate beyond. A track leads out to road. Turn right to sharp righthand bend, where a gate starts the field path to Penselwood church.
5 Go through the churchyard to the road beyond. Turn left through Bleak Farm village, then left onto the sunken track, ending at the top of the tarred lane. Turn left through the white gate ('Pen Mill Hill'). Head down to the kissing gate in the dip; follow the track past the pond to reach the road.
6 Cross into the path ('Coombe Street'). Pass below Orchard Cottages, then turn left over 2 stiles.

Cross the stream in the dip to the stile below the thatched cottage. The woodland path bends right to the footbridge over the River Stour.
7 From here to Point 8 is marked ('Stour Valley Way'). Go on to the tarred lane; turn left. Keep ahead into a hedged way to the stile. Go up and round left to another stile. The lane beyond leads to the T-junction; go across and turn left onto the bridleway. Go through the gate to follow the left edge of the field into the hedged track, to emerge opposite Bonham House.
8 Turn left; at the 2nd signpost bear right to the road below. Follow the road to the right, to the rustic rock arch. Take the track on the left ('Alfred's Tower') back to the inn.

The Bath Arms

Wiltshire

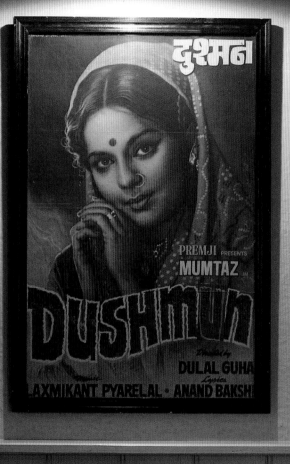

The Inn

Standing smack beside one of the entrances to Longleat House, the estate-owned Bath Arms is an impressive, creeper-clad stone inn fronted by 200-year-old pollarded lime trees. Since taking it over in 2006, Christoph Brooke has worked wonders in restoring the fortunes of this grand building, employing interior designer Miv Watts to stamp her eclectic style throughout, using furnishings and fabrics imported from Rajasthan.

Big, bright paintings line the walls in the locals' bar, with its roaring log fire, bare-board floor, and local Wessex Brewery beers on tap. Next door, in the red-walled dining room, distinctive rugs and tables, unusual wall lamps, antique chandeliers, an ornate stone fireplace and a painting of Lord Bath set the scene for savouring some classic pub food.

The bedrooms are all quirky and colourful, relecting aspects of Lord Bath's style and kitted out with plasma screens, DVDs and big wooden beds, and individually decorated as befits their names: the exotic Geisha, the rather risqué Karma Sutra, or Man with its purple and lime green walls. Book a room in The Lodge for views down the long sweeping drive to the big house.

The Food

Using local suppliers is at the heart of the inn's ethos, and every effort is made to source raw ingredients from small producers within a 50-mile (80km) radius of Horningsham. The emphasis is on traditional preserving methods – smoking, curing and pickling – and using local game and rare-breed meats. Vegetables come from the inn's kitchen garden.

Don't expect fusion or Mediterranean cooking or elaborately described menus here – both are simple and very traditionally British in style and execution.

The daily lunch menu is served in the bars, restaurant, terrace and garden, and may take in pea and mint soup, lamb hotpot, crayfish salad, goats' cheese and tomato risotto, and a beef sandwich with horseradish. Kick off a memorable dinner in the dining room with seared scallops with sauce vierge, followed by chump of lamb on crushed potatoes and ratatouille, or grilled sea bass with baby spinach and squid sauce, and finish with chocolate tart or a plate of West Country cheeses.

The Essentials

Time at the Bar!
11am-11pm
Food: 12-2.30pm, 7-9.30pm

What's the Damage?
Main courses from £8.50

Bitter Experience:
Wessex Ales

Sticky Fingers:
Children welcome; children's menu

Muddy Paws:
Dogs welcome in the bar

Zzzzz:
14 rooms, £80-£130

Anything Else?
Terrace, garden, car park

What To Do

Shop

BEAU ARTS

In a fine Georgian building near the abbey, this long-established gallery displays work of major 20th-century painters, sculptors and ceramicists.

12/13 York Street, Bath, Somerset BA1 1NG
01225 464850
www.beauxartsbath.co.uk

THE WHITE COMPANY

For everything white for the house, from luxurious lifestyle accessories to pure linen and knitwear.

15 Northgate Street, Bath,
Somerset BA1 5AS
01225 445284
www.thewhitecompany.com

OIL & VINEGAR

A culinary treasure trove with hand-made pasta, oil and balsamic vinegars from Italy, virgin olive oils from Spain, and spicy sauces and chutneys from around the world.

8 Abbey Church Yard, Bath,
Somerset BA1 1LY
01225 338655

JOHN ANTHONY

Cutting-edge fashion store selling top designer clothes, including Armani and Paul Smith.

26-28 High Street, Bath, Somerset BA1 1RG
01225 424066
www.john-anthony.com

SHANNON

Sue Shannon has gathered unusual Scandinavian furniture and home accessories in the country – choose from Wenger, Jacobsen and Aalto in her eponymous shop.

Shannon, 68 Walcot Street, Bath,
Somerset BA1 5BD
01225 424222
www.shannon-uk.com

Visit

LACOCK ABBEY

Built in 1232 and converted into a country house around 1540. The Photographic Museum commemorates the pioneering work of William Fox Talbot, a former resident. The woodland garden is stunning in the spring and there's an intimate Victorian rose garden with a summerhouse. The abbey stars in several Harry Potter films.

Lacock, Chippenham, Wiltshire SN15 2LG
01249 730459
www.nationaltrust.org

STOURHEAD HOUSE & GARDENS

Stourhead is one of the finest landscape gardens in the world. Lakeside paths lead past classical temples and follies, set against a backdrop of exotic trees. Mr Darcy's famous lake scene was shot here at the Temple of Apollo, in the BBC's adaptation of *Pride and Prejudice*. Climb King Alfred's Tower, a fine 164ft (50m) folly, and from the top you can scan three counties. Sitting majestically above the garden is Stourhead House, a grand Palladian mansion filled with Chippendale furniture, Georgian paintings and an exquisite Regency library.

Stourton, Warminster, Wiltshire BA12 6QD
01747 841152
www.nationaltrust.org

STOURTON GARDENS

Stroll along the many grassy paths that lead through the varied and colourful shrubs which include scented azaleas, camellias and over 250 varieties of hydrangeas, and don't miss the ferny secret garden. Buy unusual plants in the shop.

Warminster, Wiltshire BA12 6QF
01747 840417

Activity

EAST SOMERSET RAILWAY

The Strawberry Line running through the serene Mendip Hills has one of the steepest gradients on any preserved line: the steam engine has to work hard, though you don't. Just sit back and enjoy the countryside: why not have Sunday lunch on the magnificent Mendip Belle, and experience elegant travel from a bygone age?

Cranmore, Shepton Mallet,
Somerset BA4 4QP
01749 880417
www.eastsomersetrailway.com

LONGLEAT SAFARI PARK

Stroll down the drive from the Bath Arms and within minutes you could be on safari. Get up close and personal with the lions, rhinos, giraffes and monkeys in a purpose-built 4x4, or take a boat trip to Gorilla Island, where Nico and Samba have their own mini-stately home and satellite telly! A family of Californian sea lions bobs about in the lake, accompanying you on your voyage. Worth seeing, too, is the butterfly garden, with hundreds of exotic species, some that are fully as big as your hand.

Warminster, Wiltshire BA12 7NW
01985 844400
www.longleat.co.uk

The Walk - Woodland and Wildlife at Longleat

Glorious woodland and parkland walking at a famous country estate.

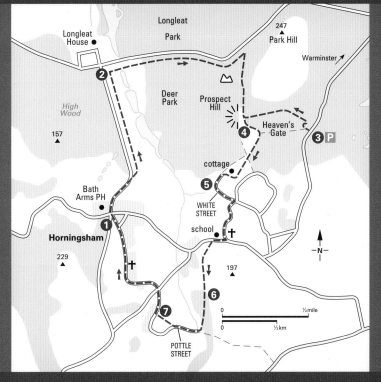

Walk Details

LENGTH: 5.25 miles (8.4km)

TIME: 2hrs 30min (longer if visiting attractions)

ASCENT: 508ft (155m)

PATHS: Field, woodland and parkland paths, roads, 4 stiles

SUGGESTED MAP: aqua3 OS Explorer 143 Warminster & Trowbridge

GRID REFERENCE: ST 810417

PARKING: The Bath Arms car park or Heaven's Gate car park, Longleat estate

❶ From The Bath Arms go straight across at the crossroads, walk down the estate drive and pass through the gatehouse arch into Longleat Park. With the house ahead, walk beside the metalled drive with lakes and weirs to the right. At T-junction in front of house, keep ahead to visit the house and follow the path left to reach the other tourist attractions.

❷ For main route, turn right and walk beside the drive, heading uphill through the Deer Park. Begin to climb steeply, then take metalled drive right beyond the white barrier. Ascend Prospect Hill and reach Heaven's Gate viewpoint. Retrace your steps back to the car park.

❸ Cross the road and follow the path into the trees. Disregard the straight track left, bear right, then left along a wide worn path through mixed woodland to double gates and reach viewpoint at Heaven's Gate.

❹ Facing Longleat, go through the gate in the lefthand corner. Shortly, at a crossing of paths, turn right, then keep right at fork and head downhill through woodland to metalled drive by thatched cottage. Turn right, keeping ahead where drive bears left; shortly follow path left, heading downhill close to woodland edge to pass between the garage and cottage to the lane.

❺ Turn left on White Street to the crossroads; turn right downhill. Ascend past the church to the T-junction; turn right. Turn left opposite the school; follow the bridlepath up the track and between sheds to a gate. Bear left with track, pass through 2 gates; bear slightly right to stile on woodland edge.

❻ Follow the path through the copse then bear off right diagonally downhill to stile and gate. Turn left along the field edge to reach the track. Turn right, go through the gate beside thatched cottage and follow the metalled lane (Pottle Street). In 200yds (183m), cross the stile on the right and cross the field to the stile and rejoin the lane.

❼ Turn right and follow quiet lane to crossroads. Proceed straight across and follow the road through Horningsham village, passing the thatched chapel, to crossroads opposite The Bath Arms.

The Swan

Wiltshire

The Inn

Judge Jeffreys once held court in this historic 16th-century pub with rooms, but, rest assured, new owners Stephen and Penny Ross offer a far friendlier welcome. The first thing you notice about this Grade II listed building is the stunning, flagstoned hall, which runs the entire length of the ground floor. The Swan is right in the centre of Bradford-on-Avon; it was renovated in 2006 and the bedrooms have been given a fresh new look.

Each room has been individually designed and the style of decor chosen seems to effortlessly mix contemporary chic with original features. Colour schemes tend to be cream, mushroom or mulberry, with many of the walls featuring striking framed black-and-white photographs or gilt-edged mirrors. High ceilings, exposed beams and original fireplaces are a constant reminder of the building's history, but these are offset by modern touches such as power showers, deep baths and plasma screens. Egyptian cotton sheets cover the comfortable beds, and muslin drapes make for a stylish and airy alternative to the usual net curtains.

The Essentials

Time at the Bar!
10am-11pm
Food: 12-2.30pm (3pm Sun),
6.30-9.30pm

What's the Damage?
Main courses from £8.50

Bitter Experience:
Greene King IPA, Old Speckled Hen

Sticky Fingers:
Children welcome, small portions
available

Muddy Paws:
Dogs welcome on outside terrace

Zzzzz:
12 rooms, £95-£140

Anything Else?
Terrace, car park

The Food

With their wooden floors, leather sofas and ox-blood walls, the two lounges at the front have a clubby feel to them and are perfect for an aperitif before moving into the dining room with its enormous fireplace and fresh flowers on bare tables. Although former chef Stephen Ross has long retired from the professional kitchen, the menus bear all the hallmarks of his accessible British food with its French bistro accent. Local suppliers are proudly listed on the menu and they include Hobbs House Bakery and Eades of Bath.

Start, perhaps, with courgette and tarragon soup, or Looe Bay spider crab and artichoke salad. Lighter meals include a ploughman's with Keene's cheddar and walnut bread; if you want something more substantial, look out for braised shin of local beef with horseradish and root vegetables, or Old Spot pork and apricot pudding with Somerset cider. Make room for classic comfort puds of the sticky toffee and crumble variety. To drink, there's real ale or a carefully chosen wine list that includes 12 by the glass.

What To Do

Shop

BAY TREE GALLERY

Vibrant exhibition galleries showing the works of a wide range of contemporary artists working in sculpture, pottery, jewellery, painting, photography, printing and other crafts. There is a ceramics workshop attached to the gallery.

48 St Margaret's Street, Bradford-on-Avon, Wiltshire BA15 1DE
01225 864918
www.baytreegallery.co.uk

BRISTOL

Explore the winding streets and lanes of the older part of the city and you'll find designer shops and galleries, antiques, boutiques and myriad specialist shops. The areas near to the harbour, along Whiteladies Road, the Old Corn Exchange, St Nicholas Markets and the chic streets of Clifton, at the edge of the extensive Clifton Downs, are all good places to browse for more unusual items. Look out for pieces of Bristol Blue Glass, or perhaps even visit the craft works.

0906 711 2191
www.visitbristol.co.uk

STAINED GLASS

A working stained glass studio complemented by an exhibition gallery highlighting its uses – from leaded glass to Tiffany-style pieces, sculpture to furnishings.

Alan Sparks Stained Glass Studio & Gallery
Pound Lane, Bradford-on-Avon, Wiltshire BA15 1LF
01225 868146
www.stainedglassonline.co.uk

Bristol Blue Glass
14 The Arcade, Broadmead, Bristol BS1 3SA
0117 922 6833
www.bristol-glass.co.uk

Visit

THE AMERICAN MUSEUM

This excellent museum houses a collection of American decorative and folk art dating back to the very first days of European colonisation of the eastern seaboard, plus some Native American art. The collections are enhanced by period settings in a maze of rooms and galleries. To complete the all-American effect, the grounds are planted with varieties of North American trees and shrubs.

Claverton Manor, Bath, Somerset BA2 7BD
01225 460503
www.americanmuseum.org

BOWOOD HOUSE

An early Georgian country house, designed in part by Robert Adam, and the family home of the Marquis of Lansdowne. His predecessor was a Viceroy of India, hence the collections of sub-continental costumes, sculptures and artefacts. Plus watercolours and jewellery, the famous Lansdowne Marbles collection and Georgian costume.

Derry Hill, Calne, Wiltshire SN11 0LZ
01249 812102
www.bowood.org

ROMAN BATHS & PUMP HOUSE

Britain's most spectacular Roman remains in the historic centre of Bath. Interpretive displays leave no stone unturned in explaining the importance of the hot springs to the Romans and the significance of the Temple of Sulis Minerva. Take the waters at the Pump House next door and visit the restaurant for a very civilised lunch.

Pump Rooms, Bath, Somerset BA1 1LZ
01225 477785
www.romanbaths.co.uk

Activity

BALLOONING

Enjoy a balloon flight in early morning or mid-evening, drifting over the Avon Valley towards the Cotswolds or wherever the wind decides to take you.

Bath Balloons, 8 Lambridge, London Road, Bath, Somerset BA1 6BJ
01225 466888
www.bathballoons.co.uk

CYCLING

Enjoy the network of gentle cycle rides along the tow path of the Kennet and Avon Canal into Bath or eastwards along the tranquil valley of the Avon. Lanes link in to some of the area's glorious country manors. Alternatively, join the Colliers Way near Dundas Aqueduct, riding this old railway through dimpled countryside where the classic *Titfield Thunderbolt* was filmed.

The Lock Inn, 48 Frome Road, Bradford-on-Avon, Wiltshire BA15 1LE
01225 868068
www.thelockinn.co.uk

NARROWBOAT TRIP

Hire a short, self-drive traditional narrowboat in the city of Bath and cruise one of England's most beautiful canals for a full or half-day. Potter along the spectacular section near Bradford-on-Avon and wrestle with the intricacies of operating locks and stopping for a pub lunch, or you could take a hamper and moor wherever you fancy for a relaxing picnic. Boats are also available for hire at Hilperton, near Trowbridge.

Bath Narrow Boats, Sydney Wharf, Bathwick Hill, Bath, Somerset BA2 4EL
01225 447276
www.bath-narrowboats.co.uk

The Walk - *A Miniature Bath at Bradford-on-Avon*

Combine a visit to this enchanting riverside town with a relaxing canal-side stroll.

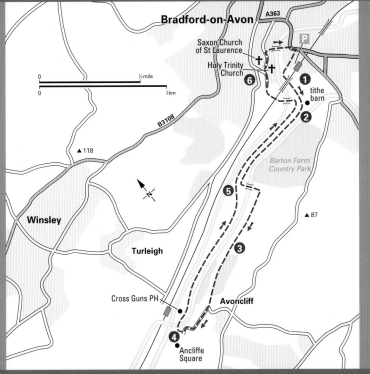

Walk Details

LENGTH: 3.5 miles (5.7km)

TIME: 1hr 45min

ASCENT: 164ft (50m)

PATHS: Tow path, field and woodland paths, metalled lanes

SUGGESTED MAP: aqua3 OS Explorers 142 Shepton Mallet;156 Chippenham & Bradford-on-Avon

GRID REFERENCE: ST 824606 (on Explorer 156)

PARKING: Bradford-on-Avon station car park (charge)

❶ Walk to the end of the car park, away from the station, and follow the path to the left beneath the railway and beside the River Avon. Enter Barton Farm Country Park and keep to the path across the grassy area to the information board. Here you can visit craft shops housed in former medieval farm buildings and marvel at the great beams and rafters of Bradford-on-Avon's magnificent tithe barn, the 2nd largest in Britain. With the packhorse bridge to the right, keep ahead to the right of tithe barn to the Kennet and Avon Canal.

❷ Turn right along the tow path. Cross the bridge over the canal in 0.5 mile (800m) and follow the path right to the footbridge and stile.

Proceed along the righthand field edge to the further stile, then bear diagonally left uphill away from the canal to the kissing gate.

❸ Follow the path through the edge of the woodland. Keep to the path as it bears left uphill through the trees to reach the metalled lane. Turn right and walk steeply downhill to Avoncliff and the canal.

❹ Don't cross the aqueduct at this point, instead pass by the Mad Hatter Tea Rooms, descend the steps on your right and pass beneath the canal. Keep right by Cross Guns and join the tow path towards Bradford-on-Avon. Continue for 0.75 mile (1.2km) to reach the bridge you passed on your outward route.

❺ Bear off left downhill along the metalled track and follow it beside the River Avon back into Barton Farm Country Park. Now cross the packhorse bridge and the railway line to reach Barton Orchard.

❻ Follow the alleyway to Church Street and continue ahead to pass Holy Trinity Church and the Saxon Church of St Laurence, the jewel in Bradford-on-Avon's crown and not to be missed. Founded by St Aldhelm, Abbot of Malmesbury in 700 AD, this building dates back to the 10th century. Now cross over the footbridge and walk straight through St Margaret's car park to reach the road. Turn right, then right again back into the station car park where the walk began.

The Pear Tree Inn

Wiltshire

The Essentials

Time at the Bar!
11am-11pm
Food: 12-2.30pm, 6.30-9.30pm
(10pm Fri-Sat); 7-9pm Sun

What's the Damage?
Main courses from £9.95

Bitter Experience:
Wadworth 6X, Moles Tap Bitter,
Stonehenge Ales

Sticky Fingers:
Children welcome, children's menu

Muddy Paws:
Dogs welcome in the bar

Zzzzz:
8 rooms, £105

Anything Else?
Terrace, garden, car park,
conservatory

The Pear Tree Inn, Top Lane, Whitley, Melksham, Wiltshire SN12 8QX

The Inn

A former working farm dating back to 1750, the impressive mellow stone Pear Tree is set back off the aptly named Top Lane in four acres of glorious gardens, where fragrant lilacs and cottage roses border manicured lawns. Martin and Debbie Still have cleverly maintained a truly local feel in the rustic bar while at the same time seriously developing the food and accommodation side of the business. A refreshing lack of formality and pretension prevails throughout. Rug-strewn flagstone floors, worn wooden tables and a crackling log fire draw you into the bar for pints of Pigswill from Stonehenge Brewery. Most people come here to eat in the intimate dining room and bright garden room, both furnished with old farming implements and simple wooden tables.

Comfort and style sum up the eight contemporary bedrooms, split between the inn and a beautifully converted barn. All sport goose-down duvets on big beds, deep easy chairs, plasma screens, and Fired Earth tiled bathrooms with power showers over baths and posh smellies. For mullioned windows, exposed beams and rural views stay in the inn.

The Food

The heart of the business lies in the kitchen, which produces everything from fresh ingredients. The Stills are passionate about using local produce and they constantly champion organic and free-range meats and vegetables from local farms. This commitment has seen them team up with Lady Venetia Fuller to develop the Organic Farm Shop, Cafe and Bakery at nearby Atworth, where you can stock up on some quality goodies before you head home.

Daily lunch and dinner menus, the superb-value set lunch menu and a good choice of sandwiches serve both dining room and bar. Cooking is honest and the style modern and imaginative. From a typical winter dinner menu, try the likes of crispy pork belly with rocket, fennel and caper salad and baked lemon dressing, or warm squid salad with chorizo, rocket and fennel to start, followed by Stokes Marsh Farm beef fillet with dauphinois, pancetta and shallot-stuffed mushroom and red-wine butter, or sea bass with tomato and herb sauce. Leave room for pudding, perhaps rice pudding with mulled fruits and home-made jam. The short list of wines is arranged by style, with 14 by the glass.

What To Do

Shop

NESTON PARK FARM SHOP

Buy organic, humanely reared meat from the Neston Estate and local farms, plus freshly made soup, home-made cakes and pastries at this fabulous farm shop.

Bath Road, Atworth, Melksham, Wiltshire SN12 8HP

01225 700881

www.nestonparkfarmshop.com

THE GALLERY ON THE BRIDGE

There are several antique shops in Castle Combe, which is a warren of honey-stoned cottages, with typical thick Cotswold walls and stone roofs. Start at The Gallery on the Bridge, which sells fine art, local crafts and interesting collectibles.

The Street, Castle Combe, Wiltshire SN14 7HU

01249 782201

BRADFORD ON AVON

A stroll around the pretty Georgian town reveals Elise in The Shambles selling quality leather goods, the Earth Collection on Market Street offers a range of environmentally friendly clothing, while One Caring World on Silver Street is an Ethical Trading Centre with an organic vegetarian cafe and health food shop. For specialist cheeses, wines, meats and preserves why not call into The Cheeseboard on Silver Street, and for handcrafted Italian ceramic and glass visit Un Po di Piu on The Shambles.

Elise 01225 309303

Earth Collection 01225 868876

www.theearthcollection.com

One Caring World 01225 866590

The Cheeseboard 01225 868042

www.cheeseboardboa.co.uk

Un Po di Piu 01225 867663

Visit

BOWOOD HOUSE

Bowood is a perfectly proportioned Georgian mansion, standing in 2,000 acres of gardens and parkland landscaped by Capability Brown. In Robert Adam's orangery is a collection of paintings, busts and a sculpture gallery, which includes some of the famous Lansdowne Marbles. A magnificent collection of jewels is on display, along with Georgian costumes. In the grounds are a formal Italianate terraced garden, a Doric temple, a grotto, cascades and an arboretum.

Calne, Wiltshire SN11 0LZ

01249 812102

www.bowood.org

THE COURTS GARDEN

The Courts is a delightful English country garden with many interesting and unusual plants, imaginative use of colour, topiary and ornaments. Stroll through the peaceful water gardens planted with irises and lilies – there's also an arboretum, a kitchen garden and a very pretty orchard.

Holt, Bradford-on-Avon, Wiltshire BA14 6RR

01225 782875

www.nationaltrust.org.uk

MUSEUM OF COSTUME

One of the finest collections of clothes and accessories, dating from the late 16th century to the present day – there are more than 30,000 pieces. Check out Biba, Dior, Chanel, Muir and McQueen! Lady Ottoline Morell's evening dresses, shoes and bags are stunning.

Museum of Costume, Bennett Street, Bath, Somerset BA1 2QH

01225 477173

www.museumofcostume.co.uk

Activity

NARROWBOAT TRIP

The *Barbara McLellen* is a traditional barge painted with castles and roses, and it winds along the Kennet and Avon canal through picturesque countryside and across the monumental Avoncliff aqueduct en route to Bath. Avoncliff is a fascinating industrial hamlet, where grist and fuller mills remain from the 16th century.

The Kennet and Avon Canal Trust, The Wharfe, Frome Road, Bradford-on-Avon, Wiltshire

01380 721279

www.katrust.org

STEAM TRAIN RIDE

Treat yourself to Sunday lunch while you chug through the glorious Avon Valley towards Bath, and discover parts of the countryside you would never see any other way. The Station Buffet in Bitton is good, too, and known all over the county for its tasty home-made cakes. Take tea here and you'll have everything you need to complete a day steeped in old-style travel nostalgia.

Avon Valley Railway, Bitton Station, Bath Road, Bitton, Bristol BS30 6HD

0117 932 5538

www.avonvalleyrailway.co.uk

The Walk - A Walk with Good Manors at Holt

A stroll from a Wiltshire industrial village to a 15th-century moated manor house.

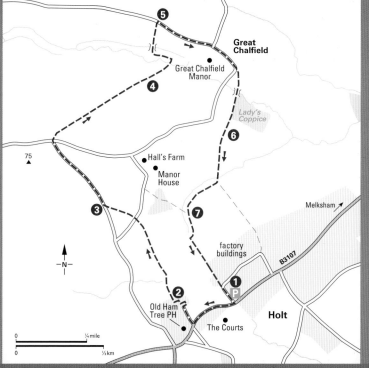

Walk Details

LENGTH: 3 miles (4.8km)

TIME: 1hr 30min

ASCENT: 147ft (45m)

PATHS: Field paths, metalled track, country lanes, 8 stiles

SUGGESTED MAP: aqua3 OS Explorer 156 Chippenham & Bradford-on-Avon

GRID REFERENCE: ST 861619

PARKING: Holt Village Hall car park

❶ Turn left out of the car park, then right along B3107 through village. Just before Old Ham Tree pub and the village green, turn right along Crown Corner. At the end of the lane take the waymarked path left along the drive. Follow the fenced path beside 'Highfields' to the stile.
❷ Keep to the right along the edge of the field, then keep ahead in the next field towards the clump of fir trees. Continue following the worn path to the right, into a further field. Keep left along the field edge to the stile in the top corner. Maintain direction to a ladder stile and cross metalled drive and stile opposite. Bear diagonally left through field to hidden stile in hedge, level with the clump of trees to the right.

❸ Turn right along the lane. At the junction, turn right towards Great Chalfield and go through the kissing gate almost immediately on the left. Take arrowed path right, diagonally across large field towards Great Chalfield Manor, visible ahead.
❹ Cross stile and bear half-right downhill to stile. Cross the stream via the stepping stones, then the stile, and bear diagonally left across the field to the gate. Cross the bridge and keep ahead beside hedge to the metalled track by the barn.
❺ Turn right, then right again when you reach the lane, passing in front of Great Chalfield Manor. At the sharp righthand bend, go through the gate ahead and bear right, then half-left across the field to cross

the footbridge over the stream. Continue straight on up the field beside the woodland to reach the gate in the field corner.
❻ Follow the lefthand field edge to the gate, then follow the path straight ahead towards the chimney on the skyline. Go through the gate, bear immediately right to the gate in the hedge and turn right along the path around the field edge.
❼ Ignore the stile on the right; continue to the field corner and the raised path beside water. Go through the gate and turn left along the field edge to reach the further gate on left. Join the drive past Garlands Farm and pass between small factory buildings to the road. Turn right back to the car park.

The George and Dragon

Wiltshire

The Inn

In truth, the plain yellow, pebble-dashed façade of the George and Dragon may not set the heart racing with anticipation, as it looks like just another boozer. Things improve at the back, where there is a delightful summer garden and the higgledy-piggledy nature of the building indicates great age and character. Step inside the rustic bar, however, and you are transported back to 1645, to a world of wooden floors, simple benches and farmhouse chairs, old school tables and a log fire blazing on the hearth in the large and impressive stone fireplace. Equally unfussy is the black-and-white timbered dining room, decorated with displays of home-made chutneys, leaving the food to take rightful centre stage.

Wonky floors, wood panelling and wall timbers are prominent within the three individual bedrooms: Country, Funky and Classic. Think cool wall coverings, plasma screens, feature fireplaces, White Company goose-down duvets on big beds, iPod attachments on Logic clock-radios, and Cowshed toiletries and fluffy white bathrobes in gleaming tiled bathrooms. The Classic even has an old claw-foot bath in the bedroom.

The Essentials

Time at the Bar!
12-3pm, 7-10pm (4pm Sat & Sun)
Closed Sun eve & Mon
Food: 12-3pm (4pm Sun), 7-10pm
(6.30-10pm Sat).

What's the Damage?
Main courses from £10.50

Bitter Experience:
Butcombe, Ringwood Fortyniner

Sticky Fingers:
Children welcome; small portions

Muddy Paws:
Dogs welcome in the bar

Zzzzz:
3 rooms, £65-£85

Anything Else?
Garden, car park

The Food

Fish is the speciality here. It comes fresh from Cornwall, and the ever-changing chalkboard menu has been wowing the landlocked Wiltshire diners for years, with dishes ranging from creamy baked potted crab and smoked haddock and chive risotto to grilled sardines with lemon oil. Straightforward grills, such as whole Dover sole and skate wing with caper butter, are mixed with more enterprising ideas, like roast monkfish with green peppercorn cream, wild sea bass with pesto mash and crispy bacon, and lobster linguine with chilli tomato sauce.

If you don't fancy fish, and red meat is more to your taste, then you may find carpaccio of beef with mustard sauce or devilled kidneys for starters, and chargrilled sirloin steak with blue cheese and herb crust, or roast rack of lamb with mustard mash among the main courses. The short list of simple, traditional puddings might include hot apple and sultana crumble, and Eton mess. The set Sunday lunch (served until 4pm) is excellent value and, to drink, you'll find local Butcombe ale on tap and a raft of wines by the glass.

What To Do

Shop

BELOW STAIRS
Looking for original 19th- and 20th-century items? Head for this antique shop with five showrooms selling kitchenalia, enamel advertising signs, garden furniture, and a huge selection of lights. The Swan Inn just outside Hungerford is a good spot for lunch, serving organic food in beautiful rural surroundings.

103 High Street, Hungerford,
Berkshire RG17 0NB
01488 682317
www.belowstairs.co.uk

VINTAGE TO VOGUE
Vintage to Vogue specialises in 1850s to 1950s shoes, hats, lace, costume jewellery and formal wear. Another vintage outlet, Jack and Danny's, sells not just clothes but also musical instruments.

28 Milsom Street, Bath,
Bath & NE Somerset BA1 1DG
01225 337323
Jack & Danny's
3 London Street, Bath,
Bath & NE Somerset BA1 5BU
01225 469972
www.jackanddannys.net

Visit

NUMBER ONE ROYAL CRESCENT
As you might guess, Number One was the first house to be built in Royal Crescent, John Wood's masterpiece of Palladian design. A dining room, elegant drawing room, feminine bedroom and Georgian kitchen have been restored and furnished to create a picture of life in 18th-century Bath.

1 Royal Crescent, Bath,
Somerset BA1 2LR
01225 428126

HOLBURNE MUSEUM OF ART
One of the country's most impressive small museums, Holburne was created by local sailor William Holburne, who was widely known for his collection of silver and old masters, but also collected porcelain, glass and furniture. Exhibits include the famous Kneeling Venus Italian bronze, once owned by Louis XIV.

Great Pulteney Street, Bathwick, Bath,
Bath & NE Somerset BA2 4DB
01225 466669

AVEBURY STONE CIRCLE
A World Heritage Site, Avebury is one of the most important megalithic monuments in Europe, and it is a magical place to visit at any time of year. Wander around the stones, set at the heart of a prehistoric landscape. Some of the world's most significant archeological finds are exhibited in the Museum Galleries, where you can discover Avebury restorer and 'Marmalade Millionaire' Alexander Keiller's passion for archaeology.

Avebury, Marlborough, Wiltshire SN8 1RF
01672 539250
www.nationaltrust.org.uk

CAEN HILL LOCKS
This famous flight of locks is one of the great wonders of the canal era. Completed by John Rennie in 1810, in order to carry the Kennet and Avon Canal to a height of 237ft (72m), the flight consists of 29 locks in all, extending over 2 miles (3.2km). There's canal-side parking near Rowde, west of Devizes, and you can walk the length of the locks via the tow path.

www.waterscape.com

Activity

BALLOONING
Enjoy a balloon flight in early morning or mid-evening, drifting serenely over the Avon Valley towards the Cotswolds or wherever the wind and fancy takes you.

Bath Balloons, 8 Lambridge, London Road,
Bath, Bath & NE Somerset BA1 6BJ
01225 466888
www.bathballoons.co.uk

BOWOOD GOLF & COUNTRY CLUB
This championship course is set in the heart of the Marquis of Lansdowne's estate. Built on Capability Brown's landscaped grounds, the 18-hole course will challenge and delight you in equal measure. Visitors are welcome – you can hire everything you need for a round or two from the Pro Shop, and even take a lesson from one of the PGA professionals.

Derry Hill, Calne, Wiltshire SN11 9PQ
01249 822228
www.bowood-golf.co.uk

CYCLE THE KENNET & AVON CANAL TOW PATH
The 40-mile canal-side route runs from Bristol to Devizes, mostly along canal tow paths and, of course, you cycle (or walk) as much or as little of it as you choose. If you are starting from Bath you can hire bikes at The Bath & Dundas Canal Co, where you'll also get information about what to look out for en route – one of the first sights is the Dundas aqueduct. From here to Hilperton is one of the prettiest parts of the route.

Brass Knocker Basin, Monkton Combe,
Bath, Bath & NE Somerset BA2 7JD
01225 722292
www.bradenford.co.uk

The Walk - *Exploring Bowood Park*

A visit to one of Wiltshire's grandest houses from Calne town centre.

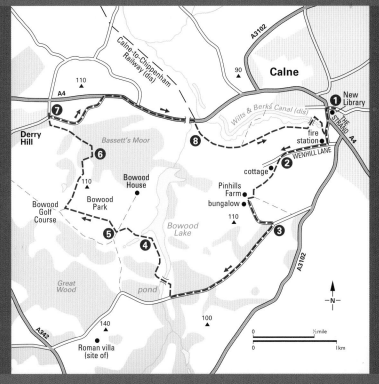

Walk Details

LENGTH: 7 miles (11.3km)

TIME: 3hrs 30min

ASCENT: 360ft (110m)

PATHS: Field, woodland and parkland paths, metalled drives, pavement beside A4, former railway line, 3 stiles

SUGGESTED MAP: aqua3 OS Explorer 156 Chippenham & Bradford-on-Avon

GRID REFERENCE: ST 998710

PARKING: Choice of car parks in Calne

❶ Locate the new library on The Strand (A4); walk south along New Road to the roundabout. Turn right along Station Road; take the footpath left opposite the fire station. Turn right at Wenhill Lane; follow it out of the built-up area.
❷ Near the cottage, follow the waymarker left and walk along the field edge. Just beyond the cottage, climb the bank and keep left along the field edge to the bridge and stile. Keep to the lefthand field edge and bear left to the stile. Follow the path right, through rough grass around Pinhills Farm to the stile opposite bungalow and turn left along drive.
❸ At the junction, turn right along the drive; continue for 1 mile (1.6km). Near the bridge, take the footpath right, through the kissing gate and walk through parkland beside the pond. Cross the bridge, go through the gate; turn right by Bowood Lake.
❹ Follow the path left to the gate and cross the causeway between lakes to the gate. Keep straight on up track; follow left, then right to cross driveway to Bowood House.
❺ Beyond gate, keep ahead along field edge, then follow path left across Bowood Park. Keep left of trees and field boundary to the gate. Turn right along the drive beside Bowood Golf Course. Where drive turns sharp right to the cottage, keep straight into woodland.
❻ Follow the path left, downhill through the clearing (often boggy) along the line of telegraph poles. Bear right with the path back into the woodland and follow it uphill beside the golf course. Turn right into the break in the trees; now go through the main gates to Bowood House into Derry Hill.
❼ Turn immediately right along Old Lane. At the A4, turn right along the pavement. Shortly, cross to the opposite pavement and continue downhill. Pass beneath footbridge and take the drive immediately right.
❽ Join former railway line at Black Dog Halt. Turn left and follow it back towards Calne. Cross the disused Canal and turn right along the tow path. Where the path forks keep right to Station Road. Retrace your steps to the town centre.

The Compasses Inn
Wiltshire

The Inn

There's a timeless feel to this attractive 16th-century thatched inn, set in rolling Wiltshire countryside. It's quite remote, but locating it via a series of tortuously narrow lanes off the A30 is fun. Once here you won't want to leave this quintessential country pub; there's even an old cobbled path leading up to a low latch door. Duck on entering and find a charmingly unspoilt bar, which has a low-beamed ceiling, partly flagstoned floor and an interesting assortment of traditional furniture arranged in secluded alcoves. Various old-fashioned advertising posters and a collection of primitive-looking farm tools and tackle from times past cover the open-brick walls, and you can toast your toes by a blazing log fire in winter.

Step outside and climb the covered stair to reach the four cottagey bedrooms, one tucked beneath the heavy thatch with a big wooden bed and low beams – watch your head! Expect flat-screen TVs, biscuits with your coffee, and good en-suite facilities, two with showers only. The pub owns the sweet little cottage next door, which you could rent and use as a base from which to really explore this beautiful area.

The Compasses Inn, Lower Chicksgrove, Tisbury, Salisbury, Wiltshire SP3 6NB

The Food

You'll find the menu chalked up on boards in the bar, with additional specials written on the canopy of the wood-burning stove in the inglenook. Dishes change daily, reflecting the seasons and the availability of the local farm produce that owner Alan Stoneham is keen to support. Typically, start with smoked duck and red onion tart, a big bowl of mussels cooked in bacon, cream, garlic and white wine, or the day's soup, perhaps mushroom and rosemary. The classic main dishes take in a hearty steak and kidney pie with suet pastry, lamb shoulder slow-roasted with red wine, molasses and soy sauce, or a warm salad of scallops, crayfish and chorizo.

Portions are more than generous and you won't leave dissatisfied. If you have room, do try the chocolate brownie that arrives with scoops of blackcurrant ice cream. Mini onion loaves filled with rib-eye steak and onions, salads and ham, egg and chips provide great lunchtime fare. Quaff a pint of Wadworth 6X, one of 12 wines by the glass or, if whisky is your tipple, there's a raft of malts to choose from.

The Essentials

Time at the Bar!
12-3pm, 6-11pm
Food: 12-2pm, 6.30-9pm

What's the Damage?
Main courses from £10

Bitter Experience:
Chicksgrove Churl, Wadworth 6X

Sticky Fingers:
Children welcome; children's menu

Muddy Paws:
Dogs welcome

Zzzzz:
6 rooms, £85-£90

Anything Else?
Terrace, garden, car park

What To Do

Shop

CRANBORNE STORES

The Marquis of Salisbury has had a passion for rearing rare breeds of pig for many years – and now you can buy the resulting pork, along with free range beef and lamb, in the estate stores. Own-cured bacon, home-made sausages and estate game can be taken home, too, along with local cheeses, home-baked pies and terrines. No small wonder the Cranborne Stores is one of Rick Stein's 'food heroes'.

1 The Square, Cranborne, Dorset BH21 5PR
01725 517210
www.cranbornestores.co.uk

HARE LANE POTTERY

Jonathan Garratt has rapidly established himself as one of the country's leading terracotta potters/garden artists. His passion for plants informs many of his innovative designs for wall pots, planters and more unusual containers for particular plants. Local clay is fired with wood to create distinctive dark colours, and Jonathan's 'Garden punctuation' takes traditional ideas from sculpture and 'knits' these pieces into the plants and pots. There's a handsome 18th-century courtyard garden and as you'd expect, a gallery where you can buy a unique pot or two to take home.

Hare Lane, Cranborne, Dorset
01725 517700
www.jonathangarratt.com

Visit

WILTON HOUSE

Wilton House stands magnificently in 21 acres of landscaped parkland, and is the home of the 18th Earl of Pembroke. Over 460 years old, the house was rebuilt by Inigo Jones in the Palladian style, and is one of the treasure houses of Britain – see the stunning state rooms and the world-famous collection of paintings by Van Dyck, Rubens, Reynolds and Breughel. The Tudor Kitchen, Victorian Laundry and Pembroke Palace Dolls House are well worth visiting, and outside, the Rose Garden, Palladian Bridge and the Millennium Fountain are all within easy walking distance. Make a day of it and have lunch in the restaurant, and stock up on plants in the garden centre.

Wilton House, Salisbury, Wiltshire SP2 0BJ
01722 746714
www.wiltonhouse.co.uk

MOMPESSON HOUSE

A perfect example of Queen Anne architecture, Mompesson is an elegant, spacious 18th-century house just outside of Salisbury city centre, with fine Georgian features, intricate plasterwork and a monumental oak staircase. There's a world-class collection of Turnbull drinking glasses, and many superior porcelain pieces. The delightful walled garden has a pergola and traditional herbaceous borders. The house doubled as the redoubtable Mrs Jennings' London residence in Emma Thompson's production and screenplay of Jane Austen's novel *Sense & Sensibility*.

The Close, Salisbury, Wiltshire SP1 2EL
01722 335659
www.nationaltrust.org.uk

Activity

GOLF

Enjoy a round of golf at Rushmore Golf Club, an 18-hole championship parkland course set within one of England's most historic estates on the Wiltshire/Dorset border.

Rushmore Park Golf Club, Tollard Royal, Salisbury, Wiltshire SP5 5QB
01725 516328
www.rushmoregolfclub.co.uk

HORSE RACING AT SALISBURY

One of the oldest race courses in England, there's been horse racing here at Salisbury since the 16th century. The historic course is set in the Wiltshire downland, with a great view of Salisbury Cathedral.

Netherhampton, Salisbury, Wiltshire SP2 8PN
01722 326461
www.salisburyracecourse.co.uk

HOT- AIR BALLOONING

What better way to explore the rolling Wiltshire Downs than from a hot-air balloon? Soar above the countryside and float among the clouds, as a miniature model world appears below you.

Aerosaurs Balloons, 5 Rivers Leisure Centre, Salisbury, Wiltshire SP1 3NR
01404 823102
www.ballooning.co.uk

The Walk - *Along the Unspoilt Nadder Valley*

Architecture, history and varied scenery on woodland pathways.

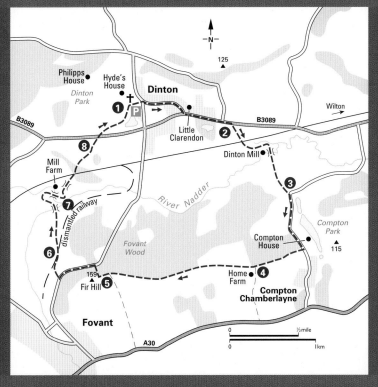

Walk Details

LENGTH: 5.25 miles (8.4km)

TIME: 3hrs

ASCENT: 360ft (110m)

PATHS: Tracks, field and woodland paths, parkland, 15 stiles

SUGGESTED MAP: aqua3 OS Explorer 130 Salisbury & Stonehenge

GRID REFERENCE: SU 009315

PARKING: Dinton Park National Trust car park

1 Leave the car park, cross and follow the lane to the B3089. Turn left, pass Little Clarendon, and continue for 0.25 mile (400m). Take the path on the right by bus shelter.
2 Follow track to kissing gate and cross railway line to further gate. Keep to track; bear left alongside stream to Dinton Mill. Pass left, cross the footbridge over River Nadder and follow drive to lane.
3 Turn right and follow metalled lane into Compton Chamberlayne. Take the footpath right, opposite the entrance to Compton House. Ascend, pass the round gate and continue along the track to Home Farm and the junction of tracks.
4 Turn right, follow the track left around buildings and remain on the

track (views of regimental badges etched into chalk). Walk beside woodland; near the field corner, follow path into trees and continue close to woodland fringe. Pass the reservoir to reach the track.
5 Turn right; walk downhill to the lane. Turn left, then, at the sharp left bend, take path right and enter field (stile left). Bear half-right to stile. Cross the track, pass through kissing gate and walk across rough grassland, then bear left to gate.
6 Turn right along the field edge, go through the kissing gate and bear left down the righthand side of the field. At waymarker, follow the path left, downhill to the stile. Descend through the scrub, cross the footbridge, then stile, and walk

ahead to further stile. Bear left along riverbank, cross stile and continue to bridge over mill stream.
7 Pass before Mill Farm on the path. Cross the footbridge and stile; bear diagonally right towards the railway. Cross the railwayline via stiles; bear slightly right to the stile and woodland. Walk through to the stile and keep ahead, to the rear of the barn, to the stile. Continue ahead to stile; cut across the pasture, keeping to the right of the 2nd telegraph pole to stile and road.
8 Cross the stile opposite into Dinton Park; turn right alongside the hedge. Bear left along the path, pass the pond and head towards the church. Go through the 1st gate on the right and return to the car park.

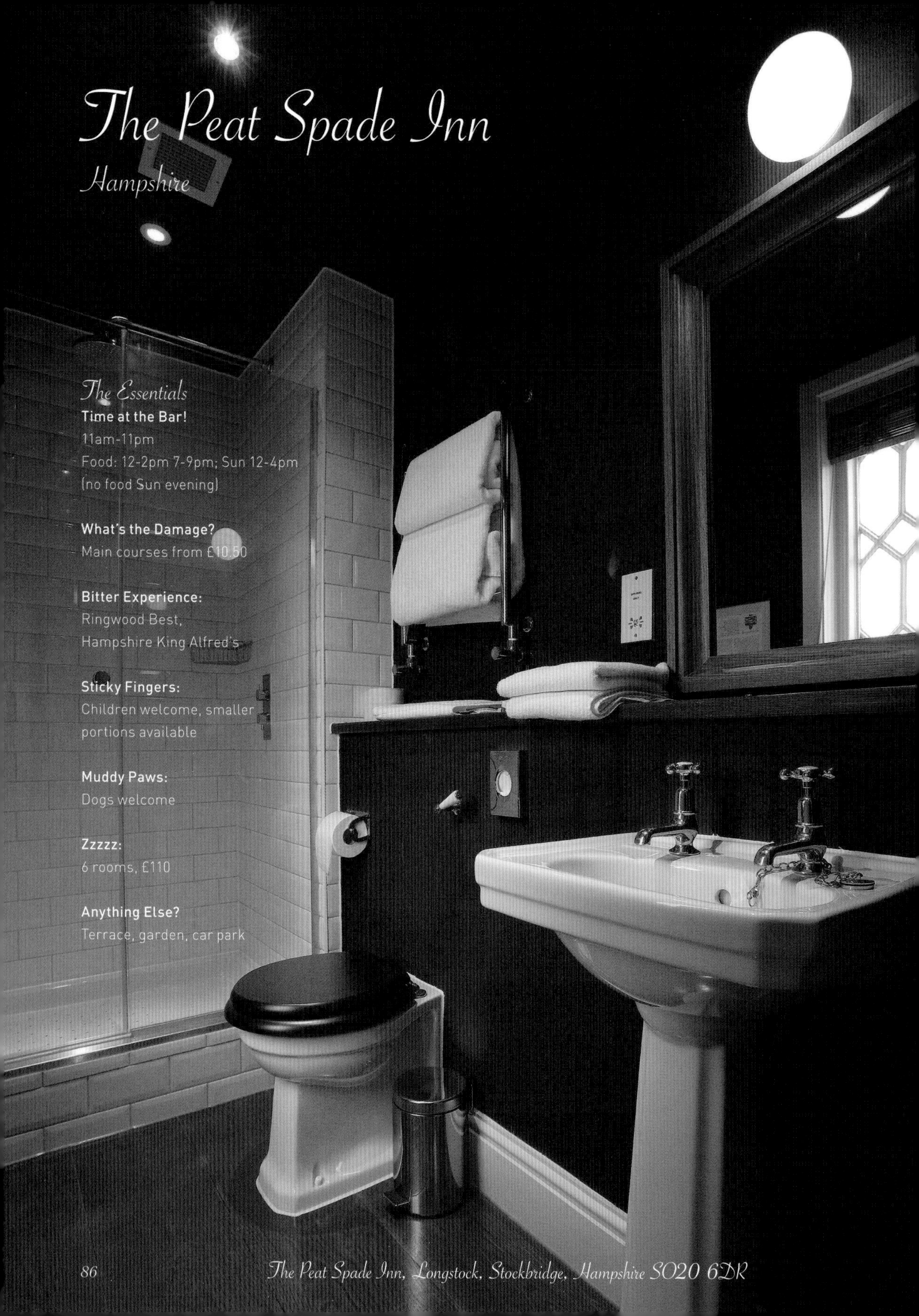

The Peat Spade Inn

Hampshire

The Essentials

Time at the Bar!
11am-11pm
Food: 12-2pm 7-9pm; Sun 12-4pm
(no food Sun evening)

What's the Damage?
Main courses from £10.50

Bitter Experience:
Ringwood Best,
Hampshire King Alfred's

Sticky Fingers:
Children welcome, smaller
portions available

Muddy Paws:
Dogs welcome

Zzzzz:
6 rooms, £110

Anything Else?
Terrace, garden, car park

The Peat Spade Inn, Longstock, Stockbridge, Hampshire SO20 6DR

The Inn

Following months of searching for their perfect country inn, Andrew Clarke and Lucy Townsend snapped up the Peat Spade in summer 2005, quickly seeing the potential of the striking, red-brick and gabled Victorian pub. It overlooks a peaceful lane and idyllic thatched cottages in the Test Valley village of Longstock, only yards from the famous trout stream that attracts fishermen from all over the world. Here, they have created a classy country inn, one where you will find a relaxed atmosphere in the cosy fishing and shooting themed bar and dining room, a simple menu listing classic English food, and six sumptuous bedrooms. If you fancy fly-fishing, then Lucy can arrange a day with a ghillie on the Test, with a picnic hamper provided for lunch. The on-site fishing shop stocks all you'll need.

Book well ahead as the rooms have found favour with shooting parties and fishing folk, and you can see why – all have big beds with down pillows and duvets, deep easy chairs, flat-screen TV with DVD, wireless internet connection, and tiled bathrooms with glorious power showers and local Longbarn toiletries.

The Food

Naturally, given Andrew's background as head chef at Winchester's Hotel du Vin, good pub food is driving the business. As much local produce as possible is sourced, including free-range pork from Greenfields Farm near Andover and fruit and game from the Leckford Estate, while villagers bring in herbs, apples and vegetables from their allotments in return for a pint. The short simply described menu changes daily and lists some great pub classics.

Start with potted shrimps with toasted sour dough or game terrine with Cumberland sauce, then move on to braised faggots with green split-pea puree, rib-eye steak with chips and béarnaise sauce, Lancashire hotpot with pickled red cabbage, or halibut with Jerusalem artichokes and wild mushrooms. Finish with walnut and date pudding with caramel sauce, chocolate and cherry brownie with crème fraîche, or a plate of English cheeses served with quince paste. To drink, try a pint of Ringwood Fortyniner or one of eight wines by the glass from the carefully prepared list. Dine alfresco on the sheltered rear terrace on sunny summer days.

What To Do

Shop

DAIRY BARN FARM SHOP

Award-winning farm shop stocked with home-produced beef, lamb and pork from native British rare and minority breeds of livestock, home-made sausages (gluten free) and dry cured bacon, plus a full range of local produce including cheese, organic vegetables and bread, chutneys, jams and woollen goods.

North Houghton, Stockbridge,
Hampshire SO20 6LF
01264 811405
www.dairybarn.co.uk

RIVER TEST SMOKERY

One of the best-known traditional trout smokeries in the country. Bring your catch here to be smoked or buy their cold-smoked trout and salmon, or smoked trout chowder.

Watch Estate, Coley Lane, Chilbolton,
Hampshire SO20 6AZ
01264 860813
www.rivertest.net

WYKEHAM GALLERY

For paintings, watercolours and sculpture by contemporary artists, alongside pictures from 1880-1940 head for the Wykeham Gallery in Stockbridge, where the wide high street straddles the River Test and is lined with traditional tea rooms, picture and craft galleries. Here you'll also find Courcoux & Courcoux, one of Britain's leading provincial galleries for contemporary art. For unusual ideas for your home and garden go to Garden Inn, and for stylish crafts take a look in Broughton Crafts.

High Street, Stockbridge,
Hampshire SO20 6HE
01264 810364
www.wykehamgallery.co.uk

Visit

HOUGHTON LODGE GARDENS

Twelve acres of tranquil gardens bordering the lovely River Test.

Houghton, Stockbridge,
Hampshire SO20 6LQ
01264 810502
www.houghtonlodge.co.uk

MOTTISFONT ABBEY

Originally a 12th-century Augustinian priory, Mottisfont Abbey has a drawing room decorated by Rex Whistler and a walled garden with one of the finest collections of roses in the country. You can stroll through the elegant grounds beside a clear chalk stream, a tributary of the River Test.

Mottisfont Abbey, Mottisfont, Romsey,
Hampshire SO51 0LP
01794 340757
www.nationaltrust.org.uk

WHITCHURCH SILK MILL

This lovely old mill in the country town of Whitchurch has been producing silk since 1830. The oldest working silk museum in the country, it operates on Victorian machinery. The shop stocks silk items and gifts.

28 Winchester Street, Whitchurch,
Hampshire RG28 7AL
01256 892065
www.whitchurchsilkmill.org.uk

WINCHESTER

Join a tour and explore the city's historic streets on foot. From the cathedral, stroll through the close to the famous college, then through the watermeadows beside the River Itchen. Don't miss the Great Hall, home to the legendary Round Table.

Tourist Information 01962 840500
www.visitwinchester.co.uk

Activity

CYCLING

Pick up the packs of cycling routes available from local tourist information centres and explore the beautiful Test Valley on two wheels. Routes vary in length, terrain and difficulty so there is something for everyone. For an easy ride, cycle the old railway line from Stockbridge to Mottisfont.

www.hants.gov.uk/cycling

FISHING

Book a day's fly-fishing tuition with a local ghillie on the River Test, Britain's finest trout stream. Lucy at the Peat Spade will arrange everything, right down to the picnic hamper for lunch.

RACING AT SALISBURY

One of the oldest courses in England, there's been horse racing at Salisbury since the 16th century – it's a very picturesque flat-racing course set in the Wiltshire downland, with a spectacular view of Salisbury Cathedral.

Netherhampton, Salisbury,
Wiltshire SP2 8PN
01722 326461
www.salisburyracecourse.co.uk

The Walk - Murder in Harewood Forest

In search of Deadman's Plack, the spot where King Edgar murdered Athelwold.

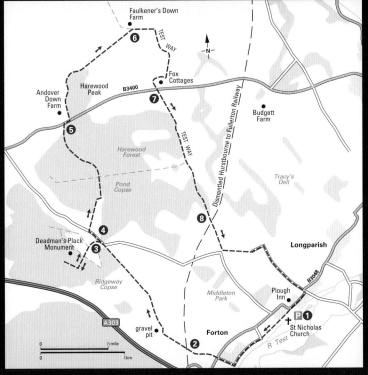

Walk Details

LENGTH: 7.5 miles (12.1km)

TIME: 3hrs 30min

ASCENT: 295ft (90m)

PATHS: Field, woodland paths and tracks, sections of Test Way

SUGGESTED MAP: aqua3 OS Explorer 144 Basingstoke, Alton & Whitchurch

GRID REFERENCE: SU 426439

PARKING: Car park at St Nicholas Church or by village hall

❶ Walk through the churchyard; exit via the gate; follow Test Way across water-meadow. Go through 2 gates. Turn left along the lane into Forton. Take sharp righthand bend by barn to T-junction. Pass through the gate opposite to the field path; bear right along the track.

❷ Cross the old railway; follow the track between fields. At the copse, leave track. Bear left with waymarker along field edge. Shortly, cross track to follow the path along lefthand edge of the field at base of shallow valley. At copse, keep left and continue to reach gate and lane.

❸ To see Deadman's Plack, turn left before gate. Follow the path uphill into woodland. Ignore 2 tracks on right. Take 3rd path. Where it

forks, keep right; follow the path for 300yds (274m), take the path on the right leading to the monument.

❹ Retrace your steps back to lane. Turn left; after 50yds (46m), cross the stile in hedge on right; follow path between fields, by woodland. Bear left by birch trees to join main track through Harewood Forest. Keep ahead at crossing of paths by conifer tree. Eventually join the gravel drive leading to the B3400.

❺ Turn right then left up the drive to Andover Down Farm. Keep to the right of the farm and industrial site. Bear left at gates to the house; follow the track right. Head downhill towards Faulkner's Down Farm.

❻ At the farm, bear right along metalled drive, ('Test Way' – 'TW').

Proceed downhill. Turn right ('Private Road, No Thoroughfare') on to a track between fields. Go through gap in the hedge ('TW'). Follow lefthand field edge to stile near cottages. Bear left through the gate; follow the drive to the B3400.

❼ Cross the road and stile opposite. Follow the grassy track ('TW') beside arable land. Gently climb, then descend, to join a stony track. Shortly, bear left ('TW') along the narrow path to a metalled track.

❽ Turn left, cross the railway. Keep left at the fork on to a gravel track. Follow it left. Shortly reach a junction of tracks. Turn right ('TW') to reach Longparish. At village lane, turn right, passing the Plough Pub, back to the church or village hall.

The Hawkley Inn

Hampshire

The Inn

Beware: approach the village of Hawkley from the west and you will experience tortuously steep and narrow lanes; instead head for Petersfield and follow signs off the B3006 north of the town to locate this friendly and unpretentious village local, tucked away well off the beaten track in unspoilt rolling countryside. First impressions are deceptive, for the simple and unassuming opened-up rustic front bar is not smart – but this is the charm of the place and the locals love it. You'll find big scrubbed pine tables topped with chunky candles, a 'listed' very worn carpet, the odd battered armchair, posters on nicotine-stained walls, and a mad moose head above the crackling log fire. Step into the rear dining room and you enter the 21st century, with its sandstone flagged floor and modern art on the walls.

Upstairs bedrooms are positively space age in comparison: sleigh or colonial four-poster beds have thick goose-down duvets and Italian Beltrami cotton sheets, there are plasma screens, free wi-fi/broadband access, and top-notch Hudson Reed-designed bathrooms. These classy rooms come as a big surprise and are hugely comfortable.

The Hawkley Inn, Pococks Lane, Hawkley, Liss, Hampshire GU33 6NE

The Essentials

Time at the Bar!
Food: 12-3pm, 5.30-11pm;
Sun 12-5pm, 7-10.30pm

What's the Damage?
Main courses from £7.50

Bitter Experience:
Eight changing guest ales

Sticky Fingers:
Children welcome in bar until 8pm

Muddy Paws:
Dogs welcome

Zzzzz:
6 rooms, £65-£95

Anything Else?
Terrace, garden, no car park

The Food

Chalkboards list the hearty range of traditional pub dishes. Everything
is freshly prepared in the kitchen, from the filled rolls and generous
ploughman's at lunchtime to the rustic evening meals that may take in the
likes of curried parsnip soup, minted lamb casserole, spaghetti bolognese
or pesto, cottage pie, grilled duck breast with green peppercorn sauce,
or the delicious Sussex beef stew, served with spring greens, carrots and
lashings of creamy mash.

Real ale aficionados regularly beat a path to the Hawkley Inn to sample
the mind-boggling and ever-changing choice of ales (from local
microbreweries) that flows through the 12 hand pumps on the bar. So,
wash your casserole down with a pint of Goddards Special, or the full-
bodied and malty Ballards Wassail, or perhaps a tankard of the dark,
coffee-like Espresso from the Dark Star brewery in Sussex. Arrive on a
Friday night and a local band may be playing, or a festival of local ale may
be in full swing. In summer, sit and enjoy an alfresco pint at slate-topped
tables on the front veranda or in the peaceful rear garden.

What To Do

Shop

BOSHAM WALK ART & CRAFT CENTRE

Overlooking Chichester Harbour, an Area of Outstanding Natural Beauty, Bosham is the perfect setting for this art and craft centre on the Sussex coast. Here you can wander around 20 shops and an art gallery to see where local artists and resident and visiting craftspeople make, display and sell their products. Or join one of the regular workshops for children and adults.

Bosham Lane, Bosham, Chichester,
West Sussex PO18 8HX
01243 572475
www.bosham-walk.co.uk

NICHOLAS MOSSE & BURLEIGH POTTERIES

Nicholas Mosse and Burleigh Potteries use traditional hand skills so that each piece you buy is both beautiful and unique. Nicholas Mosse (based in southern Ireland) concentrates on hand crafting and decorating techniques developed in the 18th and 19th centuries, while Burleigh (from Stoke-on-Trent), is famous for blue-and-white earthenware. Situated next door to the ruins of Cowdray House.

River Ground Stables, Cowdray Park,
Midhurst, West Sussex GU29 9AL
01730 810880
www.mosse-burleigh.co.uk

Visit

GILBERT WHITE'S HOUSE

Take a stroll round picturesque Selborne village and visit The Wakes Museum, much-loved home of 18th-century naturalist Gilbert White who, with his brother, cut the nearby Zigzag Path that climbs above the village. Opposite his house is the church, which has a window dedicated to him, depicting St Francis feeding the birds.

Selborne, Hampshire GU34 3JH
01420 511275
www.gilbertwhiteshouse.org.uk

HINTON AMPNER HOUSE & GARDENS

Garden lovers should make a trip to this elegant country house, best known for its masterpiece of 20th-century garden design. Manicured lawns and fine topiary combine formality of design with informality of planting, and the gardens are full of scent and colour. The house has an outstanding collection of furniture, paintings and *objets d'art*.

Alresford, Hampshire SO24 0LA
01962 771305
www.nationaltrust.org.uk

UPPARK

Imagine Uppark during the great days of the British Empire when Queen Victoria was on the throne and the mother of HG Wells was housekeeper here. Look out for a Grand Tour collection of paintings, furniture and ceramics in the elegant Georgian rooms. From its setting on the South Downs there are breathtaking views to the coast.

South Harting, Petersfield,
West Sussex GU31 5QR
01730 825857
www.nationaltrust.org.uk

Activity

THE HANGERS WAY

This spectacular 21-mile (34-km) trail runs from Alton to the Queen Elizabeth Country Park south of Petersfield. Hardly a moment passes without a superb view. One of the route's highlights is Shoulder of Mutton Hill – the view from the top was described by the Edwardian poet Edward Thomas as 'sixty miles of South Downs at one glance'.

0800 028 0888
www3.hants.gov.uk/longdistance/
hangers-way.htm

JANE AUSTEN – THE EARLY YEARS GUIDED TOUR

Our most famous romantic novelist continues to enthral nearly 200 years after her death. As well as visiting her home at Chawton you can tour The Vyne near Basingstoke where she attended balls, visit Winchester Cathedral where she is buried or book a half-day tour illustrating her early life - she was born in the tiny Hampshire village of Steventon, near Basingstoke.

Hidden Britain Tours, 28 Chequers Road,
Basingstoke, Hampshire RG21 7PU
01256 814222
www.hiddenbritaintours.co.uk

WATERCRESS LINE

Experience history in motion as you travel by steam or heritage diesel through 10 miles of glorious countryside between Alton and Alresford. Learn how to drive a steam train on a day's Footplate Experience Course, or join one of the regular real ale trains.

Mid Hants Railway, Alresford,
Hampshire SO24 9JG
01962 733810
www.watercressline.co.uk

The Walk - *Looking for Edward Thomas*

Explore The Hangers - beech-clad hills and vales that inspired Hampshire's great poet.

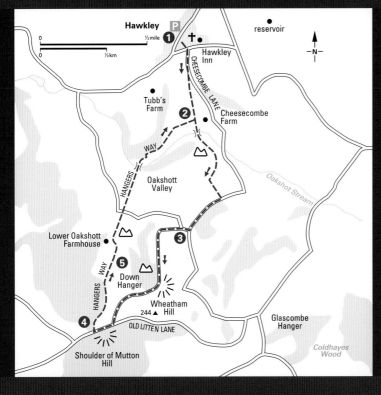

Walk Details

LENGTH: 3 miles (4.8km)

TIME: 2hrs

ASCENT: 682ft (208m)

PATHS: Field and woodland paths, rutted, wet and muddy tracks (in winter) and short stretches of road, 29 stiles

SUGGESTED MAP: aqua3 OS Explorer 133 Haslemere & Petersfield

GRID REFERENCE: SU 746291

PARKING: By village green and church in Hawkley

❶ With your back to Hawkley church, walk left beside the green to the road junction. With Hawkley Inn to your left, cross straight over and head down Cheesecombe Farm Lane ('Hangers Way'). Shortly, bear off right along the concrete path. Descend to the stile and keep straight on at the fork of paths, with Cheesecombe Farm on your left.
❷ Cross Oakshott Stream and keep left along the field edge beside woodland. Steeply ascend to the stile, keep right to a further stile, then turn left beside the fence and drop down to the track. Turn right, to reach the lane, then right again for 55yds (50m) to take the waymarked right of way beside Wheatham Hill House.

❸ Climb the long and steep chalky track up through Down Hanger (be warned, this track habitually gets very wet and muddy), with views unfolding east along the South Downs. At the top of Wheatham Hill, turn right at the T-junction of tracks along Old Litten Lane. In 300yds (274m), take Hangers Way right over the stile. To look at the Edward Thomas memorial stone and appreciate the glorious South Downs views, continue along the track for 200yds (183m) and turn left with the waymarker. Pass beside the wooden barrier and then drop down to the clearing on Shoulder of Mutton Hill.
❹ On the return route, follow a short section of Hangers Way, this is a 21-mile (34km) long-distance trail that traverses the countryside of East Hampshire, from the Queen Elizabeth Country Park to Alton. Follow the Hangers Way trail as it descends through the edge of the beech woods and steeply down across lush meadowland, eventually joining the drive to Lower Oakshott Farmhouse and the road.
❺ Turn right, then go left over the stile and follow the clearly defined Hangers Way path through the Oakshott Valley, crossing stiles, plank bridges and some delightful meadows to reach the junction of paths before Cheesecombe Farm. Turn left to reach the stile and then retrace your steps back to Hawkley village green and your car.

Carnarvon Arms

Berkshire

The Inn

Four months of careful refurbishment in 2005 saw the Carnarvon Arms, a rambling old coaching inn near the gates of Highclere Castle, reopen as a 'fine dining, traditional country inn' – one with a warm, contemporary and tasteful look. Today's incarnation has fresh, natural colours on the walls, bare boards and subtle lighting throughout; there are deep sofas in relaxing lounge areas, and a stylish, yet traditional feel to the extended bar. What's more, you'll find three real ales on tap, a raft of wines by the glass, and a bar menu listing traditional pub dishes.

The high-vaulted dining area is equally informal, sporting painted beams, rug-strewn boards, polished tables, an ornate fireplace, and Egyptian motifs inspired by Highclere Castle's Egyptian collection – brought back to the south of England from the Valley of the Kings by the fifth Earl of Carnarvon. Bedrooms are furnished and decorated with style and panache: all are comfortable and homely, featuring pale wood furnishings, plasma screens, internet access, and smart tiled bathrooms with top toiletries and power showers.

The Essentials

Time at the Bar!
11am-11pm
Food: 12-3pm, 6.30-9pm
(Fri-Sat 9.30pm), Sun 12-4pm,
6.30-8.30pm

What's the Damage?
Main courses from £7.95

Bitter Experience:
Fuller's London Pride,
Shepherd Neame Spitfire

Sticky Fingers:
Children welcome, children's menu

Muddy Paws:
No dogs

Zzzzz:
23 rooms, £79.95-£89.95

Anything Else?
Garden, car park

The Food

The fine dining side of the operation comes courtesy of executive chef Robert Clayton, whose skilled cooking, based on modern British cuisine, has seen him head up several Michelin-star kitchens, notably the Priory Hotel in Bath. Using local butcher meats, game from the Highclere Estate, fish from Brixham, and other ingredients from quality suppliers, Clayton's menus change with the seasons, although the odd dish changes on a whim to add interest.

The main menu is also available in the bar and you can order just a starter, perhaps scallops with asparagus and parmesan and balsamic dressing, or crispy braised duck leg with celeriac mash. Or go the whole hog and tuck into pan-fried turbot with confit fennel and red wine sauce, or shoulder of lamb with red wine sauce, followed by vanilla bean panna cotta with berry compote, or citrus bread and butter pudding. Conversely, if you fancy fish and chips or steak and ale pie in the dining room, then that's fine, too. The bar menu also offers sandwiches and classic pub dishes like homemade burger with red onion marmalade.

What To Do

Shop

ANTIQUES
Hungerford is the place to visit for antiques. The town has been well known for its antiques trade for many years, and today there are two sizeable centres, housing 80 individual dealers, several general antique shops and many specialists. All of the outlets are great hunting grounds for dealers, collectors and browsers of fine furniture, clocks, silverware, ceramics, pottery and an endless range of decorative and utilitarian collectibles.

Hungerford High Street, Berkshire
www.hungerford.co.uk

WEST BERKSHIRE BREWERY
The West Berkshire Brewery is a real rural success story. It was back in 1995 that local builder Dave Maggs and his wife Helen decided to start their own micro brewery. It became so successful that they had to find larger premises in Yattendon. Today the brewery benefits from an extended brewhouse, new equipment and has a shop selling a good range of the company's excellent ales plus local ceramics and crafts.

Yattendon, Thatcham, Berkshire RG18 0UE
01635 202968
www.wbbrew.co.uk

Visit

HIGHCLERE CASTLE
Berkshire's largest house dates back to the first half of the 19th century and was designed for the third Earl of Carnarvon by Charles Barry, the architect of the Houses of Parliament. It was later home to the fifth Earl who opened Tutankhamun's tomb in 1922. The castle contains objects from other sites in Europe and is one of the county's major tourist attractions, and a popular wedding venue.

Highclere, Newbury, Berkshire RG20 9RN
01635 253210
www.highclerecastle.co.uk

SANDHAM MEMORIAL CHAPEL
This small red-brick chapel was built in the 1920s to house a series of fascinating but disturbing murals by the artist Stanley Spencer, inspired by his experiences in World War I. Influenced by Giotto's Arena Chapel in Padua, Spencer took five years to complete what is arguably his finest achievement. The chapel is in the care of the National Trust and it stands in a mature orchard enjoying beautiful views towards Watership Down.

Harts Lane, Burghclere, Newbury,
Berkshire RG20 9JT
01635 278394
www.nationaltrust.org.uk

THE VYNE
It was in 1956 that the National Trust added this grand country house to their collection of historic treasures. Built by William Sandys, Henry VIII's Lord Chamberlain, between 1518 and 1527, The Vyne includes a Tudor chapel, a Palladian staircase and a variety of fine old panelling and furniture. There's also the chance to enjoy a woodland stroll in the grounds where you can discover the Herbaceous borders, a wild garden and an example of one of the earliest summer houses.

Sherborne St John, Basingstoke,
Hampshire RG24 9HL
01256 883858
www.nationaltrust.org.uk/thevyne

Activity

BALLOONING
What better way to see and appreciate the English countryside than from a hot-air balloon? One of the longest established hot-air balloon operators in the country, based near the M4, specialises in providing passengers with breathtaking views over rural Berkshire, Wiltshire and Oxfordshire. A variety of balloons take to the skies – from the smallest three-passenger size to the largest, which is capable of carrying 11 people.

01635 201007
www.floatingsensations.co.uk

FLY FISHING
Experience a day's fly fishing at one of the exclusive sites (Wherwell Priory or Mottisfont Abbey) along the beautiful River Test, one of England's finest chalk streams. Day rods can be booked on the river and private tuition for the day can be arranged on the Wallop Brook at Nether Wallop Mill.

Fishing Breaks, The Mill, Heathman Lane,
Nether Wallop, Stockbridge,
Hampshire SO20 8EW
01264 781988
www.fishingbreaks.co.uk

KENNET HORSE BOAT COMPANY
Enjoy the pace and tranquillity of a bygone era on this horse-drawn canal cruise along the Kennet and Avon canal to the west of the market town of Newbury. The boat journey offers some stunning scenery and an unmissable trip into the past as you discover the fascinating history of this restored waterway.

01488 658866
www.kennet-horse-boat.co.uk

The Walk - High Above Highclere Castle

A hilltop grave and a decorated chapel are just two of the features of this walk.

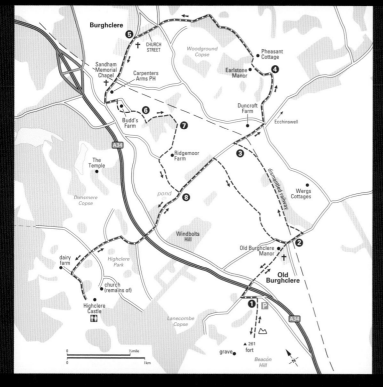

Walk Details

LENGTH: 6.5 miles (10.4km)

TIME: 3hrs

ASCENT: 767ft (234m)

PATHS: Tracks, field and woodland paths, some roads, 6 stiles

SUGGESTED MAP: aqua3 OS Explorers 144 Basingstoke, Alton & Whitchurch; 158 Newbury & Hungerford

GRID REFERENCE: SU 463575 (on Explorer 144)

PARKING: Beacon Hill car park off A34

INFORMATION: This walk is over the county border in Hampshire

❶ Climb Beacon Hill at the start or finish. Leave the car park via the access road. Cross A34 bridge to T-junction. Take footpath opposite, downhill to gate. Walk along field edge to Old Burghclere. Pass beside church wall and Old Burghclere Manor to lane. Proceed ahead, cross railway bridge and take path left.

❷ Keep to the lefthand field edge. Enter woodland. Shortly, bear left on to the track bed. Turn right. Follow the track to the bridge.

❸ Bear left up the chalky path to the track. Turn right over the bridge. Descend to the lane, turn left then right, ('Ecchinswell'). In 50yds (46m), take the waymarked bridleway left. Keep to the path until the gravel drive. Turn left.

❹ Follow the track to Earlstone Manor. Proceed through or close to woodland for 1 mile (1.6km) to road. Turn right, then left along Church Street in Burghclere, ('Sandham Memorial Chapel').

❺ Turn left by the church; keep to the road, passing the Memorial Chapel and Carpenters Arms, before turning left along a metalled dead-end lane. Pass the cottage; take the footpath right between the gardens to stile. Skirt round Budd's Farm across 3 fields via 3 stiles; join the path through the trees to stile.

❻ Turn right along the field edge, following it left in corner. Descend to fingerpost. Follow lefthand path into woodland. If the route is boggy, keep to the field edge, looking out

for gap and path right into woodland. Cross to the stile keep ahead across field. Bear right through gap to field.

❼ Ignore path to left. Continue, with woodland on right, to waymarker. Turn right towards Ridgemoor Farm. Pass pond to gate and track. Turn right, then where it bears right, go left on the sunken path to the track. To visit Highclere Castle, turn right to the road; cross the A34; enter parkland; follow drive to house. Retrace steps; keep ahead.

❽ Turn left to the crossroads, then right. Head uphill; keeping to the undulating track for 0.5 mile (800m) to Old Burghclere. Turn left along the lane; then right along the drive to Old Burghclere Manor. Retrace your outward steps to the car park.

The Royal Oak

West Sussex

The Inn

With Goodwood Racecourse just up the hill and the cathedral city of Chichester only about two miles (3km) away, pub entrepreneur Nick Sutherland was destined to succeed when he bought this tiny 200-year-old village inn. Within a year he had extended the dining area and converted the rear barn and cottage into bedrooms, and the once sleepy local morphed into a thriving and very stylish gastropub-with-rooms. From the pretty raised terrace, step into the open-plan bar and dining area to find a buzzy atmosphere and a rustic chic feel, with crackling log fires, fat cream candles on scrubbed tables, leather sofas, and local ales tapped from the cask.

Money has been lavished on the bedrooms, so expect a contemporary look and great attention to detail, with big comfy beds, leather chairs, magazines and luxurious bathrooms, plus plasma screens, CD/DVD players and PlayStations. Two smart cottages across the road are let out as B&Bs during the week, with self-catering packages available at weekends. So why not book a chef to cook a private dinner for you?

The Royal Oak, Pook Lane, East Lavant, Chichester, West Sussex PO18 0AX

The Essentials

Time at the Bar!
12-11pm
Food: 12-2.30pm, 6-9.30pm

What's the Damage?
Main courses from £11

Bitter Experience:
Harvey's Sussex Best, Ballard's
Best, guest ale

Sticky Fingers:
Children welcome, children's menu

Muddy Paws:
Dogs welcome in the bar

Zzzzz:
8 rooms, £110-£195

Anything Else?
Terrace, garden, car park

The Food

The food draws people from all over, the modern British menu offering classy renditions of pub classics, plus more obvious restaurant dishes such as seared scallop and king prawn salad with lime and shallot dressing, or confit duck leg with red wine and Puy lentil sauce. In general, main courses strike a more robust, traditional note, say fresh haddock cooked in deliciously light beer batter and served with minted pea puree and chips, salmon fishcake with parsley and caper sauce, and fillet steak served with roasted tomatoes, field mushrooms and a peppercorn sauce. You'll also find lunchtime sandwiches, and home-made comfort puddings, perhaps mulled wine trifle, warm orange bread and butter pudding with Marsala custard, and a classic crème brûlée.

Everything is prepared from quality raw ingredients, with the London markets of Billingsgate, Smithfield and Covent Garden the source of much of the produce, although crab comes from Selsey and the pork is reared in Sussex. Local Ballard's and Harvey's ales and some top-notch French classics feature on the good-value wine list.

What To Do

Shop

ADSDEAN FARM SHOP

Foodies will want to take home free-range home-produced pork and beef, lamb from the farm next door, home-cured meats and seasonal game such as pheasant, partridge and venison – sourced from regular shoots on the farm.

Funtington, Chichester,
West Sussex PO18 9DN
01243 575212
www.adsdeanfarm.co.uk

CHICHESTER

A market cross stands at the meeting of West, North, East and South Streets in this historic cathedral city, each of which is packed with interesting shops, many privately owned. There is a good mixture of stylish boutiques and brand chain stores within Chichester's ancient streets – designer fashion labels, organic luxury chocolates and French pastries are just some of the quality commodities that await the 'professional shopper'. A good choice of upmarket restaurants, organic cafes and gastropubs enhances the experience.

01243 534677
www.chichester.gov.uk

WINE & FOOD TRAIL

Uncover some of southern England's best-kept culinary secrets on this tour of sites specialising in local and regional produce. Use the Wine Trail map to plot your route and combine a visit to a vineyard with a trip to a farmers market or a cheese producer.

01444 259265
www.atasteofsussex.co.uk
www.buylocalfood.co.uk

Visit

ARUNDEL CASTLE

There has been a fortification here since the 11th century, though most of the present building is Victorian. Today the castle remains the ancestral home of the Dukes of Norfolk. Within its great battlemented walls you'll find fine furniture dating from the 16th century, tapestries, clocks and portraits by prestigious artists such as Van Dyck and Gainsborough, among others.

01903 883136
www.arundelcastle.org

LANCING COLLEGE CHAPEL

This Gothic chapel stands high on the South Downs and can be seen for miles around. Founded in 1868 and dedicated in 1911, the nave is an incredible 90ft (27.5m) to the apex of the vault. The newly installed stained-glass window is dedicated to the memory of Bishop Trevor Huddleston, a pupil at Lancing in the late 1920s.

Lancing, West Sussex BN15 0RW
01273 465949
www.lancingcollege.co.uk

WEST DEAN GARDENS

Features of these fabulous historic gardens, once owned by the poet Edward James and laid out along classic 19th-century lines, include a 300ft (91m) pergola, an arboretum, a restored walled kitchen garden with 13 glasshouses, plus a gallery and a visitor centre. Regular events held throughout the year include a popular Chilli Festival.

West Dean, Chichester,
West Sussex PO18 0QZ
01243 818210
www.westdean.org.uk

Activity

BOAT TOUR

Chichester's vast natural harbour has 50 miles (80km) of shoreline and 17 miles (27km) of navigable channel, making it great for a leisurely boat trip, especially as the harbour is a haven for wildlife.

Solar Boat Tours, Itchenor, Chichester,
West Sussex PO20 7AW
01243 513275
www.conservancy.co.uk

RACING AT GOODWOOD & FONTWELL

For racegoers the place to be is Goodwood. One of the south's loveliest and most famous racecourses rises and falls around a natural amphitheatre, with the horses dashing along the ridge to create one of the greatest spectacles in the racing world. For one week every summer it becomes Glorious Goodwood, when thousands of punters come to one of the most colourful events of the sporting and social calendar. Regular meetings are also held at Fontwell Racecourse a few miles east along the coast.

Goodwood Racecourse
01243 755022
www.goodwood.co.uk
Fontwell Racecourse
01243 543335
www.fontwellpark.co.uk

SEA FISHING

Head out beyond Chichester Harbour for some serious sea fishing – half- or full-day trips, or an evening outing for mackerel. Rods and bait are supplied.

Something Fishy Charters, 12 The Parade,
East Wittering, West Sussex PO20 8BN
01243 671153

The Walk - *Espying the Spire at Chichester*

Enjoy a walk around the ancient treasures of a cathedral city.

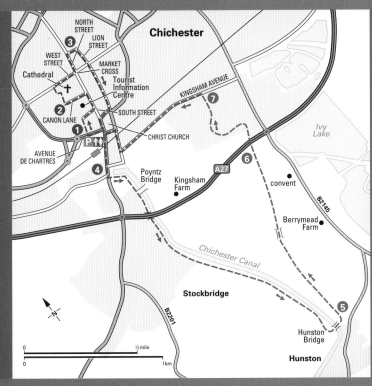

Walk Details

LENGTH: 4.5 miles (7.2km)

TIME: 2hrs

ASCENT: Negligible

PATHS: Urban walkways, tow path and field paths, 4 stiles

SUGGESTED MAP: aqua3 OS Explorer 120 Chichester, South Harting & Selsey

GRID REFERENCE: SZ 857044

PARKING: Fee-paying car park in Avenue de Chartres

1 Leave the car park. Cross the footbridge over Avenue de Chartres. Head towards the city centre. Turn right at city map and left into South Street. Bear left into Canon Lane, just beyond the tourist information centre. Turn right into St Richard's Walk then approach the cathedral.

2 Swing left at cloisters and left again (keep stone wall left). Make for West Door. Pass the Bell Tower to reach West Street; bear right. Opposite is pub. Proceed on West Street. At Market Cross, turn left into North Street. Bear right beyond Council House into Lion Street.

3 Walk to St Martin's Square (opposite is St Mary's Hospital). Turn right; proceed to East Street (Corn Exchange on left.) Go over

into North Pallant. Walk to Pallant House. Keep ahead into South Pallant. Follow the road round to the right, passing Christ Church on your left. Turn left at the next junction, head for the traffic lights; continue south into Southgate.

4 Cross railway; then swing left to reach canal basin. Follow tow path to Poyntz Bridge; continue to the next bridge, carrying A27. Continue over next footbridge and follow path to road. Confusingly, the bridge is labelled Poyntz Bridge on OS maps.

5 Bear left briefly to the stile by the car park entrance. Cross into field. Keep field boundary on immediate right and make for footbridge and stile. Continue ahead, with trees and bushes on left. Make for stile

in field corner; cross the next field, maintaining direction. Aim for the stile in the wooded corner and just beyond it is the busy A27.

6 Cross with extreme care over to the footpath opposite. Turn right at the junction; follow the tarmac path to the recreation ground. Cross to far side of the green, keeping the cathedral spire straight ahead. Look for Cherry Orchard Road, with post-box and telephone box on corner.

7 Bear left at the crossroads into Kingsham Avenue; follow avenue into Kingsham Road. Turn right at T-junction, pass bus station and, on reaching the one-way system, cross at the lights. Bear right into Southgate, then left into Avenue de Chartres. The car park is on the left.

The Halfway Bridge Inn

West Sussex

The Inn

Interested in following the polo set at Cowdray Park or attending the races at Goodwood? Then this rambling, red-brick 18th-century coaching inn right beside the A272 is the place to stay. Six stunning rooms, four of which are suites, are located in a magnificent converted Sussex barn, just staggering distance from the pub. Think quality, a contemporary stylish feel and attention to detail, with big comfy beds, leather chairs, superb fabrics, excellent lighting, luxurious bathrooms kitted out with power showers and top toiletries, and up-to-the-minute 'toys for the boys' – plasma screens, CD/DVD players and Game Boys – to keep you amused.

Taste and style extend to the pub and the series of cosy, interconnecting rooms that radiate out from the central bar. Modern colours and furnishings combine well with the traditional old beams, wooden floors, and no fewer than five log fires (one in an old kitchen range) to create a casual and relaxed atmosphere for drinking or an intimate dinner. There are tables on the lawn and a flower-festooned rear terrace for those days when the weather is right for alfresco dining.

The Food

Traditional pub dishes are given a uniquely modern twist and everything is freshly prepared from quality raw ingredients. London is the source of much of the quality produce – Billingsgate Market for fish, Smithfield Market for meat and Covent Garden for exotic vegetables – although the menu does champion Selsey crab, Sussex pork, lamb from the Goodwood Estate, and locally grown soft fruits and vegetables.

After an appetiser of scallops with Puy lentils and Provençale sauce, tuck into steak and kidney suet pudding with braised red cabbage, whole lemon sole served with red chilli butter, or opt for rack of Sussex lamb with redcurrant and mint jus. If you have room, try the warm chocolate fondant with home-made chocolate and thyme ice cream, or a classic baked rice pudding with butterscotch sauce.

Light lunches in the bar take in seafood bisque and hearty sandwiches, perhaps crab or roast beef with horseradish. Expect to find local Arundel Gold and Harvey's Sussex Bitter on hand pump and a select list of wines offering 15 by the glass, including champagne.

The Essentials

Time at the Bar!
Food: 12-2.30pm, 6.30-9.30pm

What's the Damage?
Main courses from £10.95

Bitter Experience:
Skinner's Betty Stogs,
Ballard's Best

Sticky Fingers:
Children welcome, half portions
of main menu available

Muddy Paws:
Dogs welcome in the bar and garden

Zzzzz:
6 rooms, £120-£160

Anything Else?
Terrace, garden, car park

What To Do

Shop

RICHARD GARDNER ANTIQUES

Over the years Petworth has become a mecca for antiques and fine arts, attracting visitors from far and wide. Among the town's many businesses is the award-winning Richard Gardner Antiques where six large showrooms display a wide range of stock, including bronzes and glass, furniture, porcelain, sculpture, silver, Chinese pottery, Staffordshire figures and more.

Market Square, Petworth,
West Sussex GU28 0AN
01798 343411
www.richardgardnerantiques.co.uk

SPRIGGS FLORIST

One of the country's leading florists, Spriggs's stock of unusual plants and flowers is delivered direct from the Dutch flower markets. Quirky containers and a range of glassware and candelabras are available, and a choice of superb silk orchid plants can be despatched by post.

Lancaster House, Golden Square, Petworth,
West Sussex GU28 0AP
01798 343372

Visit

BIGNOR ROMAN VILLA

Rediscovered in 1811, this Roman house was built on a grand scale. It is one of the largest known and has the longest mosaic in Britain (82ft/25m) in its original position.

Bignor, Pulborough,
West Sussex RJ20 1PH
01798 869259
www.bignorromanvilla.co.uk

NUTBOURNE VINEYARDS

Wander through the vineyards, learn how grapes are grown in this often chilly and inhospitable country, and then visit the historic windmill to taste and buy some of the award-winning wines.

Gay Street, Nutbourne, Pulborough,
West Sussex RH20 2HH
01798 815196
www.nutbournevineyards.com

PARHAM HOUSE & GARDENS

This magnificent Elizabethan mansion is one of the great treasures of Sussex, recalling the days of lavish weekend house parties, servants living a separate life below stairs and the days of gracious living. The wonderful setting, deer park and views of the South Downs enhance Parham's beauty and little has changed here since Tudor times. The house has been open to the public since 1948.

Storrington, Pulborough,
West Sussex RH20 4HS
01903 744888
www.parhaminsussex.co.uk

PETWORTH COTTAGE MUSEUM

The Petworth Cottage Museum provides a glimpse of rural life around 1910. It has a scullery with a stone sink and 'copper' for washing clothes and boiling water; the bedroom includes an iron bedstead, a washstand and a hand-made bedspread. Care has been taken in the garden to choose plants that would be found in this setting during the Edwardian era.

346 High Street, Petworth,
West Sussex GU28 0AU
01798 342100
www.petworthcottagemuseum.co.uk

Activity

BALLOONING

For that once-in-a-lifetime flying experience, take to the air and soar across the Sussex countryside in a hot-air balloon. The take-off point is north of Petworth.

01428 707307
www.hotair.co.uk

BIRDWATCHING

Bring your binoculars and explore the nature trail that winds through the RSPB reserve at Wiggonholt to viewing hides overlooking the watermeadows in the Arun Valley.

Wiggonholt, Pulborough,
West Sussex RH20 2EL
01798 875851
www.rspb.org.uk

BOAT TRIP

Enjoy a boat trip on the tranquil, tree-lined Chichester Ship Canal, an inland waterway between London and Portsmouth until 1855. It was designed by John Rennie and opened in 1822.

Canal Basin, Canal Wharf, Chichester
West Sussex PO19 8FR
01243 771363
www.chichestercanal.org.uk

COWDRAY PARK

Built by the Earl of Southampton in the early years of the 16th century, Cowdray House was one of the great palaces of Tudor England. Sadly, it was destroyed by fire in 1793 and today is no more than a romantic ruin. Its setting, however, is truly splendid and the adjoining park is used for sporting activities.

The Estate Office, Cowdray Park, Midhurst,
West Sussex GU29 0AQ
0845 056 0553
www.cowdray.co.uk

The Walk - Tennyson Country at Black Down

Follow in the footsteps of Alfred, Lord Tennyson on this gloriously wooded, high-level walk.

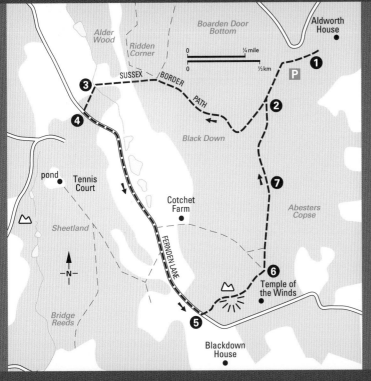

Walk Details

LENGTH: 4.5 miles (7.2km)

TIME: 2hrs

ASCENT: 315ft (95m)

PATHS: Woodland paths and tracks, some minor roads

SUGGESTED MAP: aqua3 OS Explorer 133 Haslemere & Petersfield

GRID REFERENCE: SU 922306

PARKING: Free car park off Tennyson's Lane, near Aldworth House to the south-east of Haslemere

1 Turn left out of the Tennyson's Lane car park and then left again to join the Sussex Border Path. Keep left at the junction and swing right at the fork.

2 Follow the long distance border trail to the triangular green and veer right here. Keep left at the fork, still on the Sussex Border Path, and pass over the crossroads. Veer left just beyond it at the fork and drop down to the rhododendron bushes. Turn sharp left here and follow the path through the tunnel of trees.

3 Bear left at the drive and when, after a few paces, the drive curves to the right, keep ahead through trees to join the road.

4 Turn left towards the entrance to Sheetland. Avoid the turning and

follow the lane for about 1 mile (1.6km), passing the entrance to Cotchet Farm on your left. Continue along Fernden Lane.

5 Make for the signposted bridleway on the left and after a few paces you will reach the National Trust sign ('Black Down'). Keep left here and follow the sunken path as it climbs between the trees, quite steeply in places. On higher ground, follow the path as it winds pleasantly along between the bracken and silver birch. Walk along to the seat, which takes advantage of the magnificent view, partly obscured by trees. Keep the seat and the view on your right and walk along to the seat at what is known as the Temple of the Winds.

6 Do not retrace your steps but instead take the path running up behind the seat to the junction. Don't turn left at this point; instead head north on the bridleway. Avoid the path you will see running off sharp right and the flight of steps and veer left or right at the waymarked fork. Both paths soon merge again.

7 Continue ahead and veer right at the next fork. Keep ahead at the next junction, now following part of the Sussex Border Path again. Alfred, Lord Tennyson would have found inspiration for his writing in this countryside near his home at Aldworth. Veer to the right at the fork, still following the long distance trail, and head back towards the road by the car park entrance.

The Bull
East Sussex

The Essentials

Time at the Bar!
11am-11pm
Food: Mon-Fri 12-2.30pm, 7-9.30pm;
Sat 12-3pm, 7-9.30pm; Sun 12-6pm

What's the Damage?
Main courses from £9.50

Bitter Experience:
Harvey's Sussex, Timothy Taylor
Landlord, Welton's Horsham

Sticky Fingers:
Children welcome; children's menu

Muddy Paws:
Dogs welcome in the bar

Zzzzz:
4 rooms, £80-£100

Anything Else?
Terrace, garden, car park

The Inn

Ditchling Beacon is a key landmark for walkers and cyclists tackling the famous South Downs, which tower above the village. And the 16th-century Bull, a former coaching inn, is the place to head for following a day on the Downs. It's been restored with passion (and a contemporary touch) by Dominic Worrall, yet still retains its historic charm and character. Head for the bar and you'll find feature fireplaces with glowing log fires, sagging ceiling timbers, bare floorboards and a mix of simple benches, carved settles and farmhouse chairs at big scrubbed tables. Quirky *objets d'art*, modern art on the walls and vases of lilies on the bar add a touch of class.

There are four individually decorated bedrooms, all named after their principal colour. Ruby, for example, as you might guess, has bright red walls, plus white-painted timbers, Thai silk curtains, a plasma TV/DVD player, a big leather sleigh bed with Egyptian cotton sheets and a claw-foot bath in the fully tiled bathroom. Welcome extras include fresh flowers, fat cream candles and digital radios.

The Food

Local is the watchword when it comes to food and drink. You'll find top-notch ales from Harvey's (Lewes) and Welton's (Horsham) breweries on hand pump, and very quaffable fizz from Ridge View Vineyard up the road. Menus change daily and make good use of lamb from Foxhole Farm on the edge of the village, seasonal game, including venison, from the Balcombe Estate, Sussex pork and beef, south coast fish, and asparagus from nearby Little Horsted Farm. This translates to classic mains like roasted sausages with mash and onion gravy, haddock in Harvey's ale batter with hand-cut chips and mushy peas, and beef fillet with chips and black pepper jus.

More contemporary dishes run to whole roasted lemon sole with crushed olive new potatoes and lemon caper butter, and loin of pork with apricot crumble, sage mash and mustard sauce. Precede these with king prawn open ravioli with rocket and pesto, or vegetable and mozzarella terrine, and finish with Sussex pond pudding with lemon and lime anglaise or a plate of local cheeses. For a snack, share a camembert, roasted in its box and served with grape chutney and crusty bread.

What To Do

Shop

ABODE
Stylish and well-designed contemporary, vintage and antique home furnishings and accessories sourced from both local and international designers.
32 Kensington Gardens, Brighton, East Sussex BN1 4AL
01273 621116 www.abodeliving.co.uk

ANANDA
Reclaimed hardwood furniture in colonial and contemporary styles imported from Java – home accessories, kilims and folk art.
24 Bond Street, Brighton, East Sussex BN1 1RD
01273 725307 www.ananda.co.uk

BILL'S PRODUCE STORE
Unique cafe and shop specialising in fresh organic fruit and vegetables, flowers and plants and a mind-boggling array of goodies in an amazing deli section.
56 Cliffe High Street, Lewes, East Sussex BN7 2AN
01273 476918

BONNE BOUCHE CHOCOLATES
If you love hand-made, high-quality chocolates, then don't miss this shop tucked down an alleyway.
3 St Martins Lane, Lewes East Sussex BN7 1UD
01272 472043

BOW WINDOWS BOOKSHOP
Bookworms will find it hard to leave the creaking shelves of Bow Windows Bookshop where the stacks of old fine and rare books on all subjects never fail to enthrall.
175 High Street, Lewes, East Sussex BN7 1YE
01273 480780 www.bowwindows.com

PARTERRE
Parterre on the High Street sells upmarket garden-related products ranging from Amazonas hammocks and Roger Lascelles clocks to Muck Boots and stylish Fermob garden furniture from France.
170 High Street, Lewes, East Sussex BN7 1YE
01273 476305
www.parterredesign.co.uk

Visit

CHARLESTON FARMHOUSE
Set in the midst of rolling countryside, 17th-century Charleston Farmhouse is inextricably linked with the bohemian world of the artists Vanessa Bell and Duncan Grant. The house was also a meeting place for other unconventional members of the Bloomsbury Group, including Virginia Woolf and EM Forster. Decorated furniture and murals.
Charleston, Firle, Lewes, East Sussex BN8 6LL
01323 811265
www.charleston.org.uk

DITCHLING MUSEUM
Situated in the old school, Ditchling's museum celebrates rural life through the decades. Tools, country crafts and costumes are displayed and, among many famous artists celebrated here, are the calligrapher Edward Johnston, who created the typeface and logo for the London Underground, and the cartoonist Rowland Emett.
Ditchling Museum, Church Lane, Ditchling, East Sussex BN6 8TB
01273 844744
www.ditchling-museum.com

ROYAL PAVILION
Don't miss this former seaside residence of King George IV, 'the most extraordinary palace in Europe', with its myriad domes and minarets. View the music room, the banqueting room and royal bedrooms, then stroll through the restored Regency gardens.
4/5 Pavilion Buildings, Brighton, East Sussex BN1 1EE
01273 292820
www.royalpavilion.co.uk

Activity

PARAGLIDING & HANG GLIDING
Wheel effortlessly like a bird high above the Sussex countryside following a day (or longer) course at exclusive training sites on the South Downs with one of the experienced team from the Sussex Hang Gliding and Paragliding School.
Tollgate, Lewes, East Sussex BN8 6JZ
01273 858170
www.sussexhgpg.co.uk

HORSE RIDING
Trot or canter along the South Downs Way and savour the views across the Weald on horseback during a half- or full-day's hack.
Ditchling Common Stud, Burgess Hill, West Sussex RH15 0SE
01444 871900
www.ditchlingcommonstud.co.uk

The Walk - Delightful Downs at Ditchling

A gloriously wooded, high-level walk exploring the South Downs.

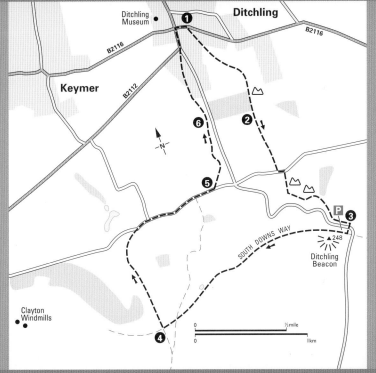

Walk Details

LENGTH: 5.5 miles (8.8km)

TIME: 2hrs 30min

ASCENT: 600ft (183m)

PATHS: Field paths, bridleways and a stretch of road, 11 stiles

SUGGESTED MAP: aqua3 OS Explorer 122 South Downs Way – Steyning to Newhaven

GRID REFERENCE: TQ 326152

PARKING: Free car park at rear of village hall in Ditchling

❶ Turn right out of the car park; follow the B2116. Pass Charlton Gardens; bear right, joining path ('Downs'). Cross 3 pastures via 5 stiles; follow the broad path through woodland. Keep right at the fork by the bridleway waymark post; pass by the house. Keep ahead alongside the beech hedge where the concrete track runs off right.

❷ Pass Claycroft House. Follow the path between the trees and houses. At the road, turn left and proceed to the bridleway on the right, pointing towards South Downs Way. Follow path, swing left at the junction; climb the steep escarpment. Keep view of Weald on left and, further up, path runs by road. Look for South Downs Way sign ahead. Turn right.

❸ Pass by the car park and over Ditchling Beacon. Go through the gate. Look for trig point left. Head west along South Downs Way, pass the dew pond. Make for the junction of paths. Keymer is signed to the right and Brighton to the left.

❹ Follow the path north towards Keymer, soon descending quite steeply. Keep right at the fork, making for gate out to lane. Bear left to the junction, then turn right past turning for Keymer on the left. Walk towards Ditchling; join Sussex Border Path at next stile on the left.

❺ Cross the field to the stile; enter woodland. Follow the path through the trees, then go straight over the drive and alongside barns and loose boxes. Cross grass to line of trees,

curve right and briefly follow track to several stiles and a footbridge. The path makes its way across the elongated field towards the trees.

❻ Cross stile, avoiding another stile leading out to road; continue across pasture, keeping to left of houses. Make for far left corner of field; look for opening in hedgerow. Follow path round to right, alongside row of houses. Cross stile on right and follow path to road. Bear left by the grassy roundabout. Take path to right of sign for Neville Bungalows. Cut between the trees, hedges and fences, following the narrow path to road. Bear right towards Haywards Heath and Lindfield and walk back to the centre of Ditchling, turning right into Lewes Road for car park.

The George in Rye

East Sussex

The George in Rye, 98 High Street, Rye, East Sussex TN31 7JT

The Inn

For Alex and Katie Clarke, bringing this down-at-heel 16th-century coaching inn in the centre of Rye back to life was a labour of love. And locals and visitors adore it. Since its launch in the autumn of 2006, they have adopted its stunning interior and smart courtyard with enthusiasm. At its heart is the George Tap, a classic pub, complete with heavy ships' timbers in the ceiling, a roaring winter fire and lots of nooks and crannies. Harvey's Sussex Ale and Biddenden cider are on draught, and eight wines from vineyards in Kent and Sussex feature on the short modern wine list.

Along rambling corridors and under steeply pitched roofs, urban cool bedrooms come in all shapes and sizes, from intimate standard rooms to lavish junior suites, and while the beds themselves may be either antique or modern, they are all made up with Italian Frette linen sheets. Tivoli clock radios, flat-screen TVs, power showers (if it's not a roll-top bath) and Aveda smellies are all standard issue.

The Food

The George Tap gives on to a casual, good-looking dining room and both share an unfussy day menu of chicken liver pâté, potted shrimps, club sandwiches, home-made beef burger or grilled rib-eye steak with chunky chips, and Rye Bay scallops with chilli and herb butter. Breakfast and afternoon tea are further pluses. But the restaurant moves up a gear in the evening with a menu that criss-crosses the Mediterranean, picking up chorizo, tabbouleh and Turkish flatbread along the way. Pear, apple and beetroot salad with lemon dressing is a zingy wake-up call, or there could be chargrilled sardines with aioli and local leaf salad.

The main course roast pork loin with warm potato salad and braised spinach is meltingly tender comfort food, while, in contrast, roasted sea bass with saffron fondant potato and braised leeks is a classic combination of textures and flavours. The dessert menu may be short, but it includes an outstanding chocolate, almond and armagnac cake, a fine tarte au citron and a good plate of tasty English cheeses.

The Essentials

Time at the Bar!
11am-11pm
Food: 12-3pm, 6.30-10pm

What's the Damage?
Main courses from £12

Bitter Experience:
Harvey's Best, Copper Ale, Rother
Valley Level Best, Greene King Old
Speckled Hen

Sticky Fingers:
Children welcome

Muddy Paws:
Dogs welcome in the bar

Zzzzz:
24 rooms, £125-£225

Anything Else?
Terrace, no car park

What To Do

Shop

GLASS ETC

Apart from a wealth of decorative and functional glass products, Glass Etc in Rope Walk sells a range of antique and retro furniture, and deals in architectural ironmongery and kitchenalia. Throughout the rest of Rye's quaint old streets you'll find antiquarian bookshops, retail outlets specialising in sporting equipment, jewellers and shops offering fresh local produce.

Glass Etc, 18-22 Rope Walk, Rye,
East Sussex TN31 7NA
01797 226600
www.visitrye.co.uk

STORMONT STUDIO

The Stormont Studio holds a collection of more than 400 works of art by nationally and regionally important artists including Whistler, Bell, Burra, Grant, Epstein and Hitchens. For exhibitions of contemporary paintings, prints, photography, ceramics, sculpture and textiles, visit Rye Art Gallery where you can browse and buy.

Ockman Lane, Rye, East Sussex TN31 7JY
01797 222433
Rye Art Gallery
Easton Rooms, 107 High Street, Rye,
East Sussex TN31 7JE
01797 222433
www.ryeartgallery.co.uk

Visit

BODIAM CASTLE

One of the most evocative castles in Britain, moated Bodiam was built in 1385, as both a defence and comfortable home. The exterior is virtually complete and the ramparts rise dramatically out of the moat.

Bodiam, Robertsbridge,
East Sussex TN32 5UA
01580 830436
www.nationaltrust.org

CHAPEL DOWN WINERY

Discover England's leading wine producer and enjoy a range of tours and tastings to learn about the history of English wine. Wander around the vineyards and herb garden, take lunch on the bistro terrace and visit the Wine and Fine Food Store to buy some wine and quality English produce to take home – cheeses, smoked meats, chutneys, pies and much more.

Tenterden Vineyard, Smallhythe,
Kent TN30 7NG
01580 752501
www.englishwinesgroup.com

GREAT DIXTER

This was the home of gardening writer Christopher Lloyd who, over many years, transformed the garden into a plantsman's dream. With its medieval buildings, natural ponds and striking yew topiary, Great Dixter is one of the most exciting, colourful and constantly changing gardens of modern times. The house is equally fascinating, with its magnificent great hall, the largest surviving example of a timber-framed hall in Britain.

Northiam, Rye, East Sussex TN31 6PH
01797 252878
www.greatdixter.co.uk

Activity

BIGGEST LITTLE RAILWAY IN THE WORLD

Visit one of Kent's favourite tourist attractions and take a ride on the world-famous Romney, Hythe and Dymchurch Railway. The line skirts atmospheric Romney Marsh, which has been a haunt of artists and writers for centuries. Evoking the great days of steam travel, the RHDR offers daily services from Easter until the end of September.

RHDR, New Romney Station, New Romney,
Kent TN28 8PL
01797 362353
www.rhdr.org.uk

BIRDWATCHING

Explore the seashore, saltmarsh, shingle and gravel pits of Rye Harbour Nature Reserve via a network of level footpaths and discover the birdlife – four hides offer the chance to see summer and winter migrants at close quarters.

Rye Harbour Nature Reserve,
East Sussex TN36 4LU
www.naturereserve.ryeharbour.org

THE 1066 COUNTRY WALK

Follow in William the Conqueror's footsteps through 31 miles (50km) of glorious Sussex countryside from Rye to Pevensey. The perfect way to learn about the Norman invasion.

Rye Tourist Information Centre, Strand
Quay, Rye, East Sussex TN31 7AY
01797 226696
www.1066country.com

The Walk - *Wide Skies and Lonely Seas at Rye*

This remote coastal walk offers excellent opportunities for birdwatching.

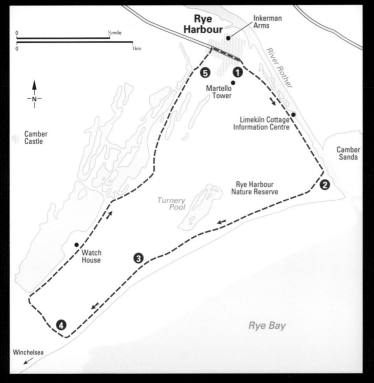

Walk Details

LENGTH: 4.5 miles (7.2km)

TIME: 2hrs

ASCENT: Negligible

PATHS: Level paths and good, clear tracks, no stiles

SUGGESTED MAP: aqua3 OS Explorer 125 Romney Marsh, Rye & Winchelsea

GRID REFERENCE: TQ 942190

PARKING: Spacious free car park at Rye Harbour

❶ Keep the Martello Tower and the entrance to the holiday village on your right and enter Rye Harbour Local Nature Reserve. In late May and June the shingle here is transformed by a colourful array of flowers. Salt marsh, vegetation along the river's edge and grazing marsh add to the variety and the old gravel pits now represent an important site for nesting terns, gulls, ducks and waders. The Rother can be seen on the left, running parallel to the path. Head for Limekiln Cottage Information Centre and continue on the firm path, with the Rother still visible on the left. Camber Sands (a popular holiday destination) nudges into view beyond the river mouth.

❷ Follow the path to the beach, then retrace your steps to the point where the permissive path runs off to the left, cutting between the wildlife sanctuary areas where access is not allowed. Pass the entrance to the Guy Crittall hide on the right. From here enjoy superb views over Turnery Pool. Continue west on the clear path as it gradually edges nearer the shore.

❸ Ahead now is the outline of the old abandoned lifeboat house and, away to the right in the distance, the unmistakable profile of Camber Castle. Keep going on the clear path until you reach the waymarked footpath on the right, running towards the line of houses on eastern edge of Winchelsea.

❹ Take this footpath and head inland, passing the small pond on the right. Glancing back, an old lifeboat house can be seen. Turn right at the next junction, pass by the Watch House and continue on the track as it runs alongside several lakes. Pass to the left of some dilapidated farm outbuildings and keep going along the track. Lakes are still seen on the lefthand side, dotted with trees, and silent fishermen can often be seen along here. Begin the approach to Rye Harbour; on the left is church spire.

❺ On reaching the road in centre of village, turn left to visit the parish church before heading back along the main street. Pass Inkerman Arms and return to the car park.

The Albert Arms

The Inn

Money has been lavished on this impressive, white-painted pub on the corner of Park Street and Esher's busy high street; it's one of a handful of thriving eateries developed by Jonathan Dunne that includes a cafe around the corner and a fine dining restaurant a few doors away. Swing open the doors to the pub and you are immediately hit by style, be it the sleek mahogany bar, the polished oak flooring in the elegant dining room, or the large plasma TV screen in the lively bar area, which draws punters in for the racing and rugby at weekends. Live weekend jazz, private dining rooms and regular wine courses add to the appeal of this classy town-centre inn.

Simple rooms are just a short stroll away in a peaceful mews building, well removed from the hustle and bustle of both pub and high street. Although quite small, all six rooms have been carefully designed and equipped with style and taste. Expect superior beds with quality linen, 30-channel TV, mini hi-fi system, internet access, and über-trendy wet rooms.

The Food

Vast menus offer an eclectic choice, from traditional favourites such as calves' liver and bacon, grilled Dover sole, rack of lamb with garlic sauce, or the pub's speciality 28-day matured Angus steaks – grilled T-bone or sirloin with pepper sauce – to fish stew, roasted quail on tagliatelle with pesto, or sea bass cooked in chilli, lime and wine sauce.

Starters and puddings have a slightly retro feel. You can take in a classic prawn cocktail or crab claws in garlic butter, and if you've room to squeeze in a pudding, then try the home-made profiteroles with chocolate sauce. On Sundays a big crowd pleaser is the Albert's famous roast – sirloin of beef served with Yorkshire pudding and all the trimmings.

The mind-boggling range of drinks includes more than 30 wines available by the glass, eight tip-top ales from local microbreweries (including Hogs Back TEA and Surrey Hills Shere Drop), and a raft of spirits. If you like the wine you quaffed with your meal, then why not buy a case to take home with you along the road at Jonathan's wine store or on line at the Albert Wine Company, where you have 700 to choose from.

The Essentials

Time at the Bar!
10.30am-11pm
(Thu-Sat 10.30am-12 midnight)
Food: 12-2.45pm, 7-10pm,
Sun 12-4pm (no food Sun evening)

What's the Damage?
Main courses from £10.50

Bitter Experience:
Fuller's London Pride, Surrey Hills
Shere Drop, Brakspear, guest beers

Sticky Fingers:
Children welcome, children's menu
Sunday lunch only

Muddy Paws:
No dogs

Zzzzz:
10 rooms, £110-£150

Anything Else?
Car park (but not directly linked)

What To Do

Shop

KINGSTON ANTIQUES MARKET

Eighty independent dealers are housed in the Antiques Market, a great place to start a day of full-blown retail therapy in Kingston. The world-famous Bentalls department store is just down the road (for that Missoni or Nicole Farhi something) and Kingston Ancient Market is the place for locally grown and produced fruit, vegetables and meat.

29-31 London Road, Kingston upon Thames, Surrey KT2 6ND

0208 549 2004

www.kingstonantiques.co.uk

KEW GARDENS

Kew's Victoria Plaza is home to the Garden Shop selling a huge range of plants, shrubs and bulbs. Pick up cherry oil, preserves, organic ginger and chocolate fudge at The Cook Shop. The Bookshop, on the same site, stocks a fantastic variety of titles for gardeners at every level.

Royal Botanic Gardens, Kew, Richmond, Surrey TW9 3AB

020 8332 5655

www.kew.org

GARSON FARM SHOP

Garson Farm has over 40 different Pick Your Own crops between May and Sep. The shop, housed in renovated old farm buildings, prides itself on its meats and dairy products, fresh fruit, vegetables, cakes and ice creams. And if you're a keen gardener, visit the garden centre, which sells plants, garden tools, BBQs, furniture and clothing. There's also a restaurant on-site.

Winterdown Road, Esher, Surrey KT10 8LS

01372 464389

www.garsons.co.uk

Visit

THE HOMEWOOD

Recently acquired by the National Trust, this modernist masterpiece was designed and built as a 'party house' for his parents by Patrick Gwynne when he was only 24. It's a perfect example of form and function working in harmony – dramatically stark from the outside, but pure luxury inside. The dressing room at the top of the stairs is simply a stroke of genius.

Portsmouth Road, Esher, Surrey KT10 9LJ

01372 476424

www.nationaltrust.org.uk

CLAREMONT HOUSE & LANDSCAPE GARDENS

This stunning Palladian mansion was built in the 1700s by Capability Brown for Clive of India – it's now a private school, but it opens for visitors at the weekends. While you are here, take the chance to wander round the National Trust's landscaped gardens, and don't miss the unique turf amphitheatre rising magnificently above the lake.

Portsmouth Road, Esher, Surrey KT10 9JG

01372 467841

www.nationaltrust.org.uk

HAMPTON COURT PALACE

An amazing place, just as a royal palace should be. Come to see the magnificent state apartments of William III and Henry VIII, the starkly imposing Tudor kitchens, the hammerbeamed great hall, and fine Renaissance works of art in the Picture Gallery, or lose yourself in the famous Maze and the 60 acres of beautiful riverside gardens.

Hampton Court, Surrey KT8 9AU

0870 752 7777

www.hrp.org.uk

Activity

BROOKLANDS MUSEUM

Brooklands has the distinction of being the first purpose-built motor racing circuit in the world – now it's a museum and venue for any number of events – if you're a Jaguar or Morris and Austin nut, there are regular 'enthusiasts days out'. Their pride and joy is the Napier Railton collection, Grand Prix and Campbell exhibitions – so you can dream about being the next Stirling Moss to your heart's content. There's a shop selling motoring memorabilia and the Sunbeam Tea Room, too.

Brooklands Road, Weybridge, Surrey KT13 0QN

01932 857381

www.brooklandsmuseum.com

SANDOWN PARK RACES

Enjoy a day at the races – Sandown Park run both flat and National Hunt racing fixtures throughout the year. The views from the racecourse are spectacular, and you can spot famous London landmarks such as The London Eye and the Gherkin from a place in the stands.

Portsmouth Road, Esher, Surrey KT10 9AJ

01372 464348

www.sandown.co.uk

THAMES PASSENGER BOAT

View some of the most historic landmarks of London and, in the summer months, alight to explore the various sites along the way by taking a scheduled, fully licensed passenger boat between Richmond, Kingston and Hampton Court.

Turks Launches, Town End Pier, 68 High Street, Kingston, Surrey KT1 1HR

020 8546 2434

www.turks.co.uk

The Walk - *Anyone for Real Tennis?*

Learn about the game of kings on a walk through the regal landscape of Hampton Court.

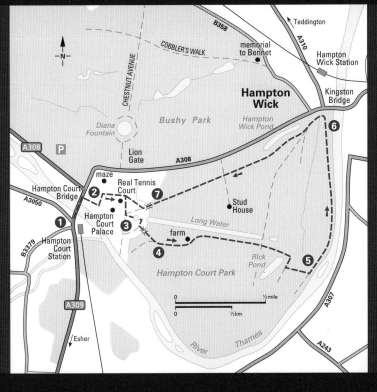

Walk Details

LENGTH: 4.75 miles (7.7km)

TIME: 1hr 45min

ASCENT: Negligible

PATHS: Gravel, tarmac and riverside tracks

SUGGESTED MAP: aqua3 OS Explorer 161 London South

GRID REFERENCE: TQ 174697 Hampton Court rail

PARKING: Car park in Hampton Court Road

❶ Cross Hampton Court Bridge, turn right through the main gates to Hampton Court Palace and walk along the wide sweeping drive. Just before reaching the palace turn left through the gatehouse and then walk under the arch.

❷ Turn right just before the tea room. Walk through the gateway and along the path through the gardens. At the end, on the right, is the real tennis court building. Pass through another gateway and then turn sharp right to walk alongside the real tennis court and past the entrance to it. King Henry VIII played real tennis here, as did Charles I. Today, Prince Edward and his wife Sophie are members of the 700-strong members-only club.

❸ Take the central gravel path in front of the palace and walk past the fountain, then walk towards the railings overlooking Long Water, an artificial lake nearly 0.75 mile (1.2km) in length. Head towards the footbridge on the right and go through the wrought-iron gates.

❹ After 220yds (201m) the footpath bears left and joins the tarmac track. Follow this, turning left by some farm buildings, after which the path runs parallel to Long Water. Where the lake ends, continue ahead at the crossing of tracks and bear right to skirt the left side of Rick Pond. Turn left through the metal gate, walk along the enclosed footpath and through the gate to reach the River Thames.

❺ Turn left along this riverside path and follow it for 0.75 mile (1.2km) to Kingston Bridge. Here, join the road leading to the roundabout.

❻ At the end of the row of houses turn left through the gateway. Immediately after the cattle grid bear right along the grassy path running along the left side of the boomerang-shaped Hampton Wick Pond. Follow the straight path for about 0.75 mile (1.2km) back to Hampton Court Palace.

❼ Bear right to cross the footbridge and follow the footpath back to the real tennis court, from where you can retrace your steps to the gatehouse and the start of the walk over Hampton Court Bridge and back into Hampton Court Road.

The Swan Inn
Surrey

The Inn

Like the phoenix of old, the Swan has risen out of the ashes of a disastrous fire that destroyed much of the first floor of this 14th-century, tile-hung coaching inn in 2004. The impressive reincarnation has seen the once traditional interior transformed to create a cool, modern bar with wooden floor, chunky scrubbed tables and chairs, subtle spotlighting and a long, sleek bar lined with gleaming beer pumps and huge vases of lilies.

A trendy, minimalist space it may be, with the adjoining dining room quite formal and upmarket, but this has not obscured the Swan's original function as a cracking village pub: the atmosphere is relaxed and you can still call in for a pint of Hogs Back TEA, sit back and peruse the papers.

It was an upstairs function room that bore the brunt of the fire and from this space 11 contemporary bedrooms have been created, all with 21st-century mod cons. Expect to find decor in muted, earthy colours, plasma TV screens, individual stylish furnishings and lavish bathrooms kitted out with posh basins, power showers and top toiletries.

The Food

The Swan's chef Darren Tidd's bar menu successfully balances the traditional and modern, with decent sandwiches, ham, egg and chips, and calves' liver and bacon featuring alongside fishcakes with smoked salmon and chive sauce, pork medallions with bubble-and-squeak and mustard cream sauce, and duck leg confit.

The kitchen turns out dishes with ease and confidence in the well laid-out dining room: anything from starters like seared foie gras with warm Sauternes butter sauce, or leek and gruyère tart with dressed leaves and balsamic dressing, to interesting main dishes of asparagus and roasted pepper risotto with pesto and parmesan, and braised lamb shank on celeriac puree with sun-dried tomato and mint sauce.

If you have room for a pudding, why not try the roasted figs with nougat ice cream or the warm chocolate and hazelnut brownie. Alternatively, opt for a plate of French cheeses with a glass of Warres 1988 vintage port. The prettily landscaped terraced garden, decked out with flower-filled urns, teak tubs, terracotta pots and upmarket benches and brollies, makes a perfect alfresco dining option for balmy days.

The Essentials

Time at the Bar!
11am-11pm (Sun 10.30pm)
Food: 12-2.30pm (3pm Sat-Sun),
6.30-10pm

What's the Damage?
Main courses from £8.45

Bitter Experience:
Fuller's London Pride,
Hogs Back TEA

Sticky Fingers:
Children welcome, small portions available

Muddy Paws:
Dogs welcome in the bar if on leads

Zzzzz:
11 rooms, £70-£140

Anything Else?
Terrace, garden, car park

What To Do

Shop

GUILDFORD HIGH STREET

The cobbled High Street has a wide range of shops behind traditional frontages, criss-crossed with lanes and alleyways lined with the nation's favourites and an eclectic mix of individual shops. Heals on Tunsgate is the place for quality contemporary furniture and stylish accessories. On the fashion front, you'll find a trendy Fat Face store, Karen Millen for womenswear and footware, Amanda Graham in the Tunsgate Centre for designer ladies fashion specialising in Basler and Hauber, and Barbour for quality country clothing and accessories.

Amanda Graham
12 Tunsgate, Guildford, Surrey GU1 3QZ
01483 306543

Barbour
Tunsgate, Guildford, Surrey GU1 3QZ
01483 538365 www.barbour.com

Fat Face
9-13 Market Street, Guildford, Surrey
01483 449695 www.fatface.com

Heals
Tunsgate, Guildford, Surrey GU1 3QU
01483 796500 www.heals.co.uk

Karen Millen
120 High Street, Guildford, Surrey GU1 3HQ
01483 451621 www.karenmillen.com

SECRETTS FARM SHOP

A delightful farm shop crammed with fruit and veg picked in the market garden each day. An extensive delicatessen offers 300 cheeses, cooked meats, salads and delicious individual dishes prepared in the kitchens. Garden furniture and barbecues are on sale.

Hurst Farm, Chapel Lane, Nilford,
Godalming, Surrey GU8 5HU
01483 520500
www.secretts.co.uk

Visit

HATCHLANDS PARK

The National Trust runs this elegant 18th-century mansion set in stunning landscaped parkland. Robert Adams designed much of the interior, which also houses the world's largest collection of keyboard instruments, many of which are associated with Purcell, JC Bach, Chopin and Elgar. Music recitals and concerts are run regularly both at lunchtime and in the evening. There's also a very pretty formal garden designed by Gertrude Jekyll.

East Clandon, Guildford, Surrey GU4 7RT
01483 222482
www.nationaltrust.org.uk

JANE AUSTEN'S HOUSE

Jane Austen lived in this handsome 17th-century house for the last eight years of her life, and penned *Mansfield Park* and *Persuasion* here. The rooms she lived and wrote in are perfectly preserved, and if you walk round the pretty garden, you'll see beautiful plants of the period. Her mother and sister are buried in nearby Chawton churchyard.

Chawton, Alton, Hampshire GU34 1SD
01420 83262
www.janeaustenmuseum.org.uk

PETWORTH HOUSE

This vast late 17th-century mansion is set in a beautiful park, landscaped by Capability Brown and immortalised in Turner's paintings. Works by Turner and Van Dyck, sculpture, furniture and carvings can be seen in the gallery, one of the finest collections in the country.

Petworth, West Sussex GU28 0AE
01798 343929
www.nationaltrust.org.uk

Activity

HOT-AIR BALLOONING

Float over three counties with your loved one and nothing but a bottle of champagne to keep you company (apart from the pilot, of course). The wind takes you wherever it will, but you're guaranteed to see some of the most beautiful countryside in rural southern England.

Horizon Balloons, Blacknest Industrial
Park, Blacknest, Alton,
Hampshire GU34 4PX
01420 520505
www.horizonballooning.co.uk

WINKWORTH ARBORETUM

Lose yourself in the tranquil hillside woodland, wander among the award-winning collection of thousands of rare shrubs and trees, and imagine yourself in New England in the fall – Winkworth is most famous for autumn hues, but magnolias, cherries, azaleas and bluebells ensure year-round colour.

Hascombe Road, Godalming,
Surrey GU8 4AD
01483 208477
www.nationaltrust.org.uk

The Walk - *The Lost Canal at Alfold*

Take a walk through the wild woods along a derelict canal tow path.

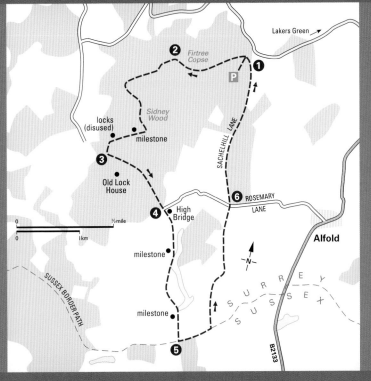

Walk Details

LENGTH: 4.75 miles (7.7km)

TIME: 2hrs

ASCENT: 164ft (50m)

PATHS: Old canal tow path, field and forest paths, muddy after rain

SUGGESTED MAP: aqua3 OS Explorer 134 Crawley & Horsham

GRID REFERENCE: TQ 026350

PARKING: Forestry Commission car park between Alfold and Dunsfold

❶ From the car park, walk back towards the road for 35yds (32m) until you see the track on the left, marked by a concrete post with a small Wey South Path waymark near the top. Turn left; then keep right at the fork 300yds (274m) further on. Cross the tarmac drive at the public bridleway signpost and follow the waymarked path around the edge of Firtree Copse.

❷ Wey South Path meets the canal at the gate. Turn left, and follow the tow path for 1 mile (1.6km). Notice the gentle slope as you pass the Arun 13/Wey 10 milestone; it's the only clue that this was once the site of a 6-lock flight.

❸ A gravelled track now crosses the canal at Sydney Court. Leave the tow path here and turn left, following the waymarked route across the bridleway crossroads to reach High Bridge.

❹ Zig-zag right and left across Rosemary Lane; rejoin the old tow path. After 0.5 mile (800m) look out for the Arun 11.5/Wey 11.5 milestone, and continue for 150yds (137m) until the Sussex Border Path crosses the canal.

❺ Turn left, and follow the Sussex Border Path for 350yds (320m) until the track bends sharply right. Turn left through a metal field gate, and follow the hedge on the right. A 2nd gate leads past a cottage; now, follow the public bridleway signpost that points your way through 2 fields, and through another gate on

to a path leading out to Rosemary Lane. You can turn right here, to make a 0.5 mile (800m) diversion to The Crown at Alfold.

❻ Otherwise, cross over the lane and follow waymarked bridleway for 0.5 mile (800m). Now turn left at public footpath signpost then, just past prominent sign ('Riding by permit only'), turn right to walk along waymarked footpath through woods. Fork right a short way further on and then continue over 2 stiles and follow path just inside woodland edge until it bears left and then meets Wey South Path at waymark post. Turn left, and follow path to Sidney Wood car park road, before turning left again for a short distance to return to your car.

The Beacon

Kent

The Inn

With open fires to toast your toes in winter and the famous far-reaching view best appreciated over drinks on the terrace, The Beacon seems to have found the ultimate recipe for all year-round appeal.

The gorgeous late Victorian building impresses with a sense of space and wealth of ornate period details – in particular the magnificent stained glass, oak panelling and decorative ceilings – while the clubby bar scores highly in terms of creature comforts, with attentive service, good beer and an impressive range of wines by the glass.

Bedrooms, reached via a grand wooden staircase, are comfortable. There's antique furniture and a posh bathroom with a roll-top slipper bath in the pretty Georgian Room; the more spacious Colonial Room has bold African prints and a stunning outlook over the surrounding countryside; while the third room, a single, works perfectly with its fresh contemporary styling and light, uncluttered feel. All are equipped with plump cushions, comfortable beds and a relaxed, peaceful air. The Beacon is a perfect weekend bolt hole with the Weald of Kent on its doorstep.

The Beacon, Tea Garden Lane, Rusthall, Tunbridge Wells, Kent TN3 9JH

The Essentials

Time at the Bar!
11am-11pm
Food: 11am-2.30pm

What's the Damage?
Main courses from £9.50

Bitter Experience:
Harvey's Sussex Best, Timothy Taylor
Landlord, Larkin's Traditional

Sticky Fingers:
Children welcome

Muddy Paws:
Doge welcome in the bar

Zzzzz:
3 rooms, £68.50-£97

Anything Else?
Terrace, garden, car park

The Food

Light floods through big windows into the spacious, formally laid dining room, which does well with its food, as long as you're not looking for culinary fireworks. Slow cooking is a favoured method, whether lamb shank or belly pork, and there are easy British classics like haddock fillet battered in Harvey's ale with hand-cut chips and mushy peas.

Alternatives include cheese fondue with crusty bread, crudités and tiger prawns, or dishes that come with the occasional Mediterranean or Asian twist – roasted red onion and butternut squash in a puff pastry parcel with lemon and mint pesto, say, or scallops and tiger prawns with chilli noodles.

If you prefer to have a meal in the bar, you can order the likes of rib-eye steak with chips, and lambs' liver and bacon served with rich onion gravy. And if you can't resist ordering the apple sticky toffee pudding for afters, and manage to polish off all the accompanying butterscotch ice cream, you can always make amends with a stroll in The Beacon's delightful wooded grounds to the chalybeate spring, which is similar to the one that made nearby Royal Tunbridge Wells famous.

What To Do

Shop

ANTIQUE SHOPPING IN ROYAL TUNBRIDGE WELLS

Pop along to the Pantiles, famed for its colonnaded streets, for some of Kent's best-known antique shops. Antique and modern jewellery is at Chapel Place Antiques, for a quality range of Georgian, Victorian and Edwardian furniture call into Pantiles Antiques, and if you're interested in Chinese antiques, try Yiju. Elsewhere, Up Country has a good selection of country furniture and rural artefacts, while the Architectural Stores on St John's Road has antique fireplaces, stained glass and salvage pieces.

Chapel Place Antiques
9 Chapel Place, Tunbridge Wells TN1 1YQ
01892 546561

Pantiles Antiques
31 The Pantiles, Tunbridge Wells TN2 5TD
01892 531291

Yiju
27 The Pantiles, Tunbridge Wells TN2 5TN
01892 517000 www.yiju.co.uk

Up Country
The Old Corn Stores, 68 St John's Road,
Tunbridge Wells TN4 9PE
01892 523341
www.upcountryantiques.co.uk

Architectural Stores
55 St John's Road, Tunbridge Wells TN4 9TP
01892 540368
www.architecturalstores.com

YALDING ORGANIC GARDENS

Tour the gardens then browse around the shop where you can buy books on organic gardening, unusual ornamentals and herb and vegetable plants in season.

Benover Road, Yalding, Maidstone,
Kent ME18 6EX
01622 814650
www.gardenorganic.org.uk

Visit

HEVER CASTLE

Situated deep in the countryside outside the small town of Edenbridge and probably best known as Anne Boleyn's childhood home, 13th-century Hever Castle is arranged around a courtyard complete with a romantic-looking drawbridge. With its award-winning gardens, lake, topiary, rose garden, yew and water mazes, the setting is completely irresistible.

Hever, Edenbridge, Kent TN8 7NG
01732 865224
www.hevercastle.co.uk

PENSHURST PLACE

Sir Philip Sidney, one of the great heroes of the Elizabethan era, was born here in 1554 and his descendants are still in residence. Visit the staterooms en route to the baron's hall and then enjoy the Tudor walled gardens, the toy museum and the woodland trail before relaxing with a well-earned cup of tea in the garden tea room.

Penshurst, Tonbridge, Kent TN11 8DG
01892 870307
www.penshurstplace.com

CHARTWELL

The former home of great British statesman Sir Winston Churchill is filled with reminders of the renowned prime minister, from his hat and uniforms to gifts presented by Stalin and Roosevelt. An exhibition gives you an insight into his life at Chartwell and you can view his studio and stroll through the gardens, which have glorious views across the Weald.

Mapleton Road, Westerham, Kent TN16 1PS
01732 866368
www.nationaltrust.org.uk

Activity

CYCLING

Head off to Bedgebury Forest near Goudhurst for easy cycling along 6 miles (10km) of surfaced track or, for the more adventurous, 7 miles (12km) of challenging single track for mountain bikes. You can hire bikes at the visitor centre bike shop (01580 879694).

Park Lane, Goudhurst, Kent TN17 2SL
01580 879920
www.forestry.gov.uk

HERITAGE WALKING TRAIL

Pick up a leaflet on the Royal Tunbridge Wells Heritage Walking Trail and amble through 400 years of history. The trail commemorates notable figures from Britain's past connected with the town.

Tourist Information Centre, Old Fish Market,
The Pantiles, Tunbridge Wells,
Kent TN2 5TN
01892 515675
www.visittunbridgewells.com

BEWL WATER

At the largest lake in the Southeast you can pedal or walk the 12.5 mile (20km) cycle route around the reservoir (map and bike hire is available at the visitor centre), buy a permit and fish for trout, or join day courses and learn to sail and windsurf on the lake.

Lamberhurst, Kent TN3 8JH
01892 890661
Outdoor Centre 01892 890716
www.bewlwater.org
www.bewlwindsurfing.co.uk
www.cuckmere-cycle.co.uk

The Walk - Royal Passion at Hever

Memories of King Henry VIII and Anne Boleyn on this circular walk.

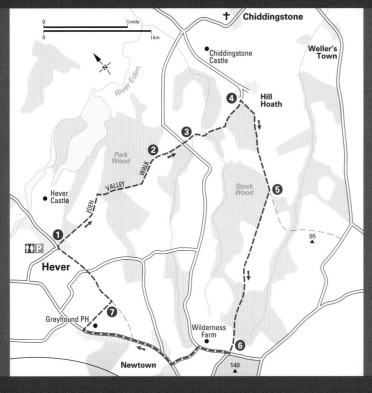

Walk Details

LENGTH: 3.5 miles (5.7km)

TIME: 2hrs

ASCENT: 279ft (85m)

PATHS: Paths, grassy tracks and field edges, some roads, 6 stiles

SUGGESTED MAP: aqua3 OS Explorer 147 Sevenoaks & Tonbridge

GRID REFERENCE: TQ 476448

PARKING: Car park by Hever Castle

1 Walk under the lychgate and go through the churchyard following the Eden Valley Walk. The path goes downhill, across the bridge and soon becomes a narrow lane parallel to the road, offering occasional glimpses of the lake at Hever Castle. The lake looks natural but it was actually created by William Waldorf Astor when he bought the castle in 1903. The path now bends round, goes through woodland, across another bridge and finally opens out.

2 When you come to the house, climb the gate following the Eden Valley Walk (follow it all the way to Point 4). Pass another house, then take the track on the righthand side, which winds round the edge of the meadow to woodland. When you come to the tarmac road, cross it and pop over the stile.

3 Continue along enclosed track, which can get very muddy, crossing 2 more stiles and gradually heading uphill. Another stile leads you past deer fencing and through the gate on to the tarmac road at Hill Hoath.

4 Now turn back to right and go through the large gate, so that you seem to be doubling back on yourself. This leads to a broad, grassy track. Walk ahead (don't be tempted into crossing stile on the left) and walk between trees, passing the lake on your lefthand side. Soon enter much thicker woodland and the track becomes narrower, but is still clear to follow.

5 At the branching of footpaths, bear right. Be warned, this can be very muddy. Continue down the track, passing another 2 areas of woodland until you reach the road.

6 Turn right here and walk to Wilderness Farm, then take the road that leads to the left opposite the farm. At another road turn right and walk up, past the road that leads to the right. Continue ahead to take the footpath on the right that runs alongside the Greyhound pub.

7 When you come to a fork by 2 stiles turn left, then walk around the edge of the field and past the pond. Continue ahead to the lane, where you turn left, then take the footpath on the right. Follow this back into Hever and return to the car park.

The George Hotel

Kent

The Inn

Old-world charm with modern trimmings is a good way to describe this inn, one of Cranbrook's most historic landmark buildings. An open-plan bar/brasserie kitted out with pale wood (floor and tables) and leather sofas (ideal for sinking into with a pint of Harvey's Best) creates a welcoming first impression. It contrasts nicely with the full suit of armour standing guard at the bottom of a magnificent 14th-century staircase with the impressive half-timbered, chandeliered restaurant beyond. There's a relaxed and informal atmosphere that comes through in a pleasant mix of local drinkers and long-distance diners.

Climb that ancient staircase and you will find that no two bedrooms are the same, although some have exposed brick and timber, bulging walls and the odd wonky floor in common. All have been refurbished to an exacting standard and decorated with an eye for detail. While the best room in the house has a striking antique four-poster bed, others blend ancient features with a more modern feel, and the bathrooms, in particular, are very up to date and equipped with all the comforts such as fluffy white towels, bathrobes and complimentary bath products by Gilchrist & Soames.

The Food

The restaurant may date from the 16th century and come with a big inglenook, mullioned windows and lots of exposed timber, but the look and style is very contemporary, with undressed oak tables, bare floorboards and high-backed leather chairs. This is a place where food takes centre stage. The menu (served in both the restaurant and the brasserie) is an ambitious collection of upmarket pub dishes with brasserie leanings: think twice-baked goats' cheese soufflé served with a crisp salad and shallot and balsamic dressing; chunky shepherd's pie made with locally reared lamb and accompanied by honey and mustard roasted carrots; and Harvey's beer-battered cod with hand-cut chips and creamed peas.

A range of influences combine with local sourcing, and the food is pitched exactly right for the surroundings: what the kitchen delivers is fresh, honestly prepared dishes with bags of flavour. Desserts are a mixture of old favourites like zesty lemon meringue pie served with vanilla ice cream or more of-the-moment interpretations like hot chocolate fondant with white chocolate ice cream and a raspberry shake.

The Essentials

Time at the Bar!
11am-11pm
Food: 12-3pm, 6-9.30pm

What's the Damage?
Main courses from £9.50

Bitter Experience:
Harvey's Sussex Ale, Adnams

Sticky Fingers:
Children welcome, children's menu

Muddy Paws:
Dogs welcome in the bar

Zzzzz:
12 rooms, £80-£125

Anything Else?
Small terrace, car park

What To Do

Shop

RYE ART GALLERY

Comprising two historic buildings, the permanent collection of fine art on display in this town-centre gallery includes works by Lowry, Epstein and Eric Gill. The Gallery Trust was founded in 1957 by flower, landscape and interiors artist Mary Stormont who eloped to Rye in 1957 with landscape and portrait artist Howard Stormont. The ever-changing themed and general exhibitions cover many fields of the creative arts including painting, glasswork, sculpture, metalwork and prints – many for sale.

107 High Street, Rye, East Sussex TN31 7JE
01797 222433
www.ryeartgallery.co.uk

THE WEALD SMOKERY

An ultra-traditional smokery, using oak shavings and sawdust to hot or cold smoke the raw material in kilns or over open fires. The farm shop sells a comprehensive choice of products over the entire meat, fish and fowl range, including smoked venison, trout and cuts of pork, much of it sourced locally.

Mount Farm, Flimwell,
East Sussex TN5 7QL
01580 879601
www.wealdsmokery.co.uk

Visit

BIDDENDEN VINEYARDS

Around 22 acres of vines bask in the sunshine in the Kentish Weald. Nine different types of grape are planted, with more than a nod towards German varietals. Indulge in a self-guided tour before sampling a range of red, white, rosé and sparkling wines. The vineyard shop also sells a range of ciders produced from Kent apples.

Gribble Bridge Lane, Biddenden,
Kent TN27 8DF
01580 291726
www.biddendenvineyards.com

KENT & EAST SUSSEX RAILWAY

An atmospheric evocation of rural branch lines in Edwardian times. The railway line runs through some pretty villages in the Rother Valley, linking Tenterden and Bodiam in over 10 miles (16km) of (largely) steam-hauled nostalgia. Hands-on driving experiences are available.

Station Road, Tenterden, Kent TN30 6HE
0870 6006074
www.kesr.org.uk

LEEDS CASTLE

The classic English castle, in the midst of a huge lake-cum-moat is familiar from many films that have featured its medieval splendour. It is used today as a venue for major political conferences and all the trappings are thus in-situ, from magnificent tapestries and fine furnishings to paintings and centuries-worth of ephemera, including a collection of (canine!) dog-collars. There's also themed gardens, a maze and a vineyard.

Maidstone, Kent ME17 1PL
01622 765400
www.leeds-castle.com

Activity

CLAY PIGEON SHOOTING

Instruction for novices is available at the school and all the equipment is on-hand for the use of more experienced shooters.

West Kent Shooting School, Paddock Wood,
Kent TN12 7DG
01892 834306
www.wkss.demon.co.uk

HEADCORN AIRFIELD

Book a pleasure flight across the Weald, the South Downs and the south coast from here, or take a trial lesson with an experienced instructor. You can try flying a light aircraft or even a small helicopter. The Lashenden Air Warfare Museum is also based here, with World War II ephemera and a V1 flying bomb.

Headcorn, Ashford,
Kent TN27 9HX
01622 891539
www.headcornaerodrome.co.uk

HONNINGTON EQUESTRIAN CENTRE

Beginners and improvers can book riding lessons or take part in short pony treks on this large country estate near Tunbridge Wells.

Vauxhall Lane, Southborough,
Tunbridge Wells, Kent TN4 0XD
01892 531154
www.honnington.com

The Walk - *Sissinghurst, A Gardener's Delight*

A lovely, easy walk to the famous garden created by Vita Sackville-West.

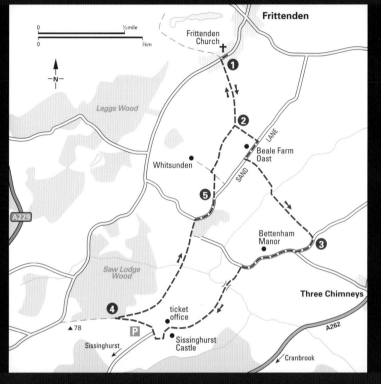

Walk Details

LENGTH: 3 miles (4.8km)

TIME: 2hrs

ASCENT: 33ft (10m)

PATHS: Well-marked field paths and woodland tracks

SUGGESTED MAP: aqua3 OS Explorer 137 Ashford

GRID REFERENCE: TQ 814409

PARKING: On street in Frittenden

❶ With your back to Frittenden church, turn right, then turn left down the pathway by the hall. Cross the stile and walk straight ahead over the field, through the gate and across another field. Go through the kissing gate, then straight ahead again – it's clearly marked. At the gap in the hedge cross the little wooden bridge and head to the telegraph pole. Branch left.

❷ Nip over the stile, go across the next field, over another stile and on to the tarmac lane to turn right past Beale Farm Oast. At the next house, turn left and walk up the track until you pass the old barn. Turn right just after the barn, continue ahead over 2 more stiles and eventually cross footbridge to the right of a clump of trees. Walk a few paces left, continue in the same direction up the edge of the field then turn left again to cross another bridge. Scramble through some scrub and follow the path ahead to another stile and on to the road.

❸ Turn right, then turn right again at the road junction. You pass Bettenham Manor, turn left up the bridleway, over the bridge, then pass Sissinghurst Castle, keeping the building on your left. Walk up to the oast houses, then bear left around them, past the ticket office and up the driveway. Turn left, then right, and walk by the side of the car parks to the stile. Cross into field, then bear right in a few paces to cross a stile by some cottages.

❹ Turn right and walk back past the cottages, then bear left along the path through the trees. Continue ahead along the tree-lined track. Now cross the stream and keep following the bridleway. When you come to the road, cross over and walk up Sand Lane.

❺ Eventually reach the stile on the lefthand side, cross and then head diagonally across the field to another stile in the fence ahead of you. Continue diagonally, passing a dip in the field. Keep the church spire ahead and proceed to cross another stile. The path is clear ahead, then veers to the telegraph pole where you go left, heading for the church spire. Cross the bridge and walk back into the village.

The Bell at Skenfrith

Monmouthshire

The Inn

Loving refurbishments by owners Janet and William Hutchings have brought this stone-built inn just on the Welsh border firmly into the 21st century without losing its venerable charm. Flagstone floors, bare beams and three working fireplaces remain, but everything is fresh and light from the yellow-and-cream public areas to the bedrooms, where pale walls and beautiful fabrics create a feeling of space and calm. Here, the air of quality and style extends to little luxuries such as jars of home-made biscuits, waffle bath robes and Cath Collins toiletries. The front bedrooms overlook the River Monnow, while those at the back look across the garden to fields and hedgerows. The exceptional attic suites have views of both.

A footpath starts beside the pub; many guests come here to explore the enchanting landscape that cradles Skenfrith. A gentle stroll takes you to the Norman castle opposite and on into the pretty village. After that, sink into a sofa, thumb through the magazines and warm your toes by the fire before turning your attention to the menu or the extraordinary wine list.

The Food

A blackboard lists suppliers, including Neal's Yard Dairy (for the cheeses) and meat from local farms. The substantial kitchen garden produces most of the fruit and vegetables, while William provides the game. His other major contribution is the remarkable wine list. There are lots of half bottles, plus a long list of champagnes. His ongoing love of cognac is reflected in a superb selection, expertly annotated.

The cooking draws its inspiration both from abroad and from the familiar canon of traditional and classic recipes. You could begin your meal with thyme-roasted scallops, braised oxtail and a red wine reduction followed by Monmouthshire lamb with spiced couscous, Mediterranean vegetable ratatouille, wilted spinach and wild mushroom cream, or perhaps fillet of Brecon beef with fondant potato, caramelised shallots and bacon lardons with wilted spring greens and a port wine sauce. Lunchtime brings snacks (Spanish ham and grilled goats' cheese baguette; open sandwich of salmon, crème fraîche and parsley pesto) alongside the main menu. Puddings range from hot chocolate fondant with pistachio anglaise and white chocolate sorbet to simple, comforting apple crumble at lunchtime.

The Essentials

Time at the Bar!
11am-11pm
Food: 12-2.30pm, 7-9.30pm (9pm Sun)

What's the Damage?
Main courses from £14.50

Bitter Experience:
Freeminer Bitter,
Timothy Taylor Landlord

Sticky Fingers:
Children welcome, children's menu;
age 12 and above only in restaurant
in evening

Muddy Paws:
Dogs welcome in bar

Zzzzz:
8 rooms, £105-£185

Anything Else?
Terrace, garden, car park

What To Do

Shop

BOOKS AT HAY-ON-WYE

More than 30 bookshops fight for space in virtually every building, from the castle to the old fire station. Countless volumes line shelves in shops and on pavements. The little border town also has many galleries and craft shops.

Hay-on-Wye, Herefordshire
Tourist Information Centre 01497 820144
www.hay-on-wye.co.uk

TACK ROOM GALLERY

Changing exhibitions of works by new and established artists and artisans. Ceramics, lithographs, prints, pots and etchings featuring works by, among others, Eric Gill.

Stabes, Craft Centre, Bridges,
Wonastow Road, Monmouth,
Monmouthshire NP25 5AS
07779 680114
www.monmouth-pottery.co.uk

Visit

ABBEY DORE COURT

Set in the beautiful Golden Valley, Abbey Dore Court has a walled garden, arboretum and river walk. The Cistercian abbey is both parish church and archaeological site.

Hereford, Herefordshire HR2 0AD
01981 240419
www.abbeydorecourt.co.uk

CIDER FARM

Walk the paths and tracks through the orchards, view the farm's herd of alpacas and finish off with a cream tea. Ciders and perry are sold from the cask or bottled.

Broome Farm, Peterstow, Ross-on-Wye,
Herefordshire HR9 6QG
01989 567232
www.rosscider.com

CLEARWELL CAVES

A jigsaw of nine caverns, created over 4,000 years by miners following veins of iron ore and deposits of ochre (still used in paints and cosmetics): an eye-opening way to experience an unknown face of the Forest of Dean.

Near Coleford, Gloucestershire GL16 8JR
01594 832535
www.clearwellcaves.com

HEREFORD CIDER MUSEUM & KING OFFA DISTILLERY

Discover the history and heritage of traditional cider-making through demonstrations and displays of the ancient craft; from pip to pomona, scratting to scrumpy.

21 Ryelands Street, Hereford HR4 0LW
01432 354207
www.cidermuseum.co.uk

LLANTHONY PRIORY

Deep in the Black Mountains, this secluded priory retains the sense of tranquillity sought by Augustinian canons more than 700 years ago. Nearby are the tiny, ancient church at Capel-y-ffin and the adventurous mountain road to Hay-on-Wye. The priory is 10 miles (16km) west of Skenfrith in the Honddu valley.

Llanthony, Monmouthshire

SUGAR LOAF VINEYARDS

The south-facing slopes of the Sugar Loaf mountain support this 5-acre vineyard specialising in white-grape varieties but also producing red and sparkling wines. Try all the award-winning wines.

Dummar Farm, Pentre Lane, Abergavenny,
Monmouthshire NP7 7LA
01873 858066
www.sugarloafvineyards.co.uk

Activity

LLANTHONY RIDING & TREKKING

Day or half-day pony treks in the Black Mountains meander along ancient tracks up to windswept hilltops with far-reaching views.

Court Farm, Llanthony, Abergavenny,
Monmouthshire NP7 7NN
01873 890359
www.llanthony.co.uk

MONMOUTH CANOE & ACTIVITY CENTRE

Glide along in a canoe or kayak amidst the hanging woodlands and limestone pinnacles of the beautiful Wye Gorge. Tackle deep pools and easy rapids as miles of tranquil, wildlife-rich countryside slip past.

Castle Yard, Old Dixton Road, Monmouth,
Monmouthshire NP25 3DP
01600 713461
www.monmouthcanoehire.20m.com

WYE VALLEY AVIATION

Drift silently on the wind above the cider orchards and hop yards of south Herefordshire, or perhaps careen above the trees of the Wye gorge and the edge of the Forest of Dean. Balloon flights last about an hour (dawn or sunset) and you'll cover perhaps 15 miles (24km), celebrating at the end of your flight with a glass of bubbly!

Bridstow, Ross-on-Wye,
Herefordshire HR9 6AJ
01989 763134
www.wyevalleyaviation.co.uk

The Walk - Beside the River Wye

A peaceful walk with fine views around Coppet Hill.

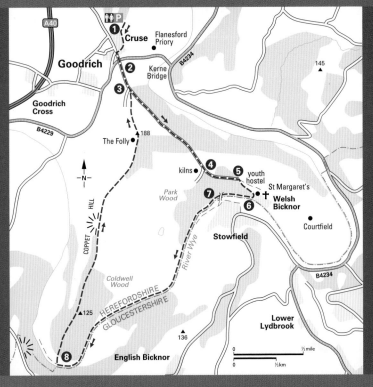

Walk Details

LENGTH: 6.75 miles (10.9km)

TIME: 3hrs

ASCENT: 855t (260m)

PATHS: Quiet lanes, riverside meadows, woodland paths, 2 stiles

SUGGESTED MAP: aqua3 OS Explorer OL14 Wye Valley & Forest of Dean

GRID REFERENCE: SO 575196

PARKING: Goodrich Castle car park open daily 9:30am to 7pm

INFORMATION: This walk is over the county border in Herefordshire

❶ From the car park, walk back to the castle access road junction and turn left. In about 125yds (114m) cross the bridge over the B4229.
❷ Go up a further 400yds (366m). Ignore another road branching off to the right, and continue for a few paces – there are 3 low wooden posts to your left.
❸ Opposite, between 2 roads, the sign ('Coppet Hill Nature Reserve') indicates the return route. Go 0.5 mile (800m) up this dead end, to a cattle grid. Here, at brow, woods give way to parkland. Go ahead for 275yds (251m) to the single horse chestnut tree at a right turn.
❹ Continue for 400yds (366m), bending left and dipping down, along the road. It curves right slightly,

while the gravel track goes up the ramp and slightly left.
❺ Curve right. Ignore the pillared driveway but go down the youth hostel's driveway. At its entrance gate take the footpath that runs initially parallel to it. Go down the wooden steps and then walk along the sometimes muddy path to reach a T-junction beside the River Wye.
❻ Turn right, following the Wye Valley Walk (turn left to visit the church first). Within 0.25 mile (400m) you'll reach the old, iron girder railway bridge, which carries the Wye Valley Walk over the river, but stay this side, passing beneath the bridge. After walking 125yds (114m) look out for 6 wooden steps down to your left at the fork.

❼ Take the steps, to remain close to the river. Continue for about 1.25 miles (2km). Enter Coldwell Wood to walk beside the river for a further 0.25 mile (400m). On leaving, keep by the river in preference to the path that follows the woodland's edge. In about 350yds (320m) you'll reach a stile beside a fallen willow.
❽ Turn right ('Coppet Hill'). Soon begin the arduous woodland ascent. Eventually you'll have some fine views. The path levels, later rising to The Folly, then goes down (not up!) to the triangulation point. Follow the clear green sward ahead, which becomes a narrow rut and then a stepped path, down to the road, close to Point 3. Retrace your steps back to the castle car park.

The Horse and Groom

Gloucestershire

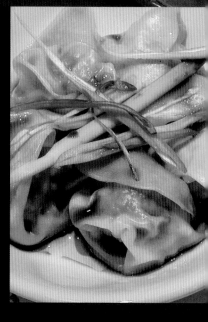

The Inn

Set high on a hill, this honey-coloured Cotswold stone former coaching inn is still a watering place of the highest order. The polished oak floorboards, exposed stonework, large open fireplace and walls hung with horse-related and village life prints and paraphernalia reflect brothers Tom and Will Greenstock's passion and flair for innkeeping. A more upbeat, almost continental, bar houses well-kept real ales and also Tom's short but highly varied wine list, while a grassed garden rises to the rear, providing a great area in which to soak up summer sunshine and admire the far-reaching views. A welcoming atmosphere pervades throughout and makes this a place to enjoy at a leisurely and relaxed pace.

Upstairs you will find five light and airy bedrooms with styles that range from an elegant period double to one with a more contemporary design with French doors opening onto a pretty landscaped garden; all have flat-screen TVs and DVD players. All of the rooms are en-suite with pretty bathrooms, huge soft towels and lots of cosseting toiletries.

The Food

The kitchen is Will's domain and he is determined to build on the family's well-earned reputation for delivering fine food (the boys' parents own the Howard Arms at Ilmington – see separate entry). The menu on the large blackboard in the bar may change daily to make the most of what is fresh and available – indeed, in season, many vegetables come straight from the garden. Butternut squash soup with curry oil makes for a great winter warming start, as do Thai pork dumplings with a lemon grass dipping sauce.

Meaty mains include Dexter beef pasty with onion gravy, roast leg of Cotswold lamb with apricot stuffing, or pan-fried Gressingham duck breast on sautéed pak choi with garlic, chilli and plum sauce, while fish can come in the guise of pan-roast skate wing with prawn, caper and preserved lemon butter. Deserts are legendary – get your order in quickly – the River Café's chocolate nemesis is a favourite, closely followed by pear, apple and blueberry flapjack crumble served with lashings of organic vanilla ice cream. James White organic juices are on offer for drivers and children, and some of the best coffee west of Naples is served here.

The Essentials

Time at the Bar!
11am-11pm (closed Sun evening)
Food: 12-2pm (2.30pm Sat-Sun), 7-9pm (9.30 Fri-Sat)

What's the Damage?
Main courses from £9.50

Bitter Experience:
Everard's Tiger, Greene King Old Speckled Hen

Sticky Fingers:
Children welcome

Muddy Paws:
Dogs in garden only

Zzzzz:
5 rooms, £70-£125

Anything Else?
Garden, car park

What To Do

Shop

BECKFORD SILK

Skilled craftspeople design, dye and print a huge range of silks at this modern workshop outside Tewkesbury. Silk scarves, dressing gowns and ties are sold and there's access to the whole workshop.

Beckford, Tewkesbury,
Gloucestershire GL20 7AU
01386 881507
www.beckfordsilk.co.uk

DAYLESFORD ORGANIC

A selection of cheeses made in the on-site creamery; venison and lamb from the family estate; bakery products made at the shop; fresh, seasonal, locally grown vegetables and one of the best delicatessens in the Cotswolds. Crafts and countryware produced by local people are also sold here.

Daylesford, Kingham,
Gloucestershire GL56 0YG
01608 731700
www.daylesfordorganic.com

LAVENDER FARM

More than 50 acres of lavender colour the slopes of the Cotswolds above the Vale of Evesham. The flowers are steam-distilled to produce a wide range of oils, soaps and cosmetics. The farm shop also acts as a gallery for local crafts, pottery and paintings.

Hill Barn Farm, Snowshill, Broadway,
Worcestershire WR12 7JY
01386 854821
www.snowshill-lavender.co.uk

SUSAN MEGSON GALLERY

A Stow on the Wold gallery concentrating on glassware from all over the world.

Tourist Information Centre 01451 831082

Visit

SNOWSHILL MANOR

Charles Paget Wade was the ultimate eccentric collector. His eclectic tastes fill every room of this beautiful Cotswold manor house: Japanese armour, toys, clocks, antiques of every hue, domestic ephemera, musical instruments, bicycles. The manor grounds are homage to the Arts and Crafts movement, with a series of garden 'rooms'; terraced organic gardens offer grand vistas of the Cotswolds.

Snowshill, Broadway,
Gloucestershire WR12 7JU
01386 852410
www.nationaltrust.org.uk

SUDELEY CASTLE

Once home to Catherine Parr. Connoisseur tours of some of the private parts of the castle include viewings of old masters, while exhibitions in the Long Room recall Tudor and Victorian times. The gardens include topiary, a Tudor knot garden and sculpture.

Winchcombe, Gloucestershire GL54 5JD
01242 602308
www.sudeleycastle.co.uk

TEWKESBURY ABBEY

The medieval town of Tewkesbury stands at the confluence of the rivers Severn and Avon. The former Benedictine abbey was decimated during the Dissolution; nonetheless the surviving church is larger than many cathedrals. Inside is fine medieval stained glass and some notable sculptured tombs. There are regular guided tours.

Church Street, Tewkesbury,
Gloucestershire GL20 5RZ
01684 850959
www.tewkesburyabbey.org.uk

Activity

COTSWOLD COUNTRY CYCLES

Hire a mountain bike or a high-geared hybrid cycle and discover many miles of quiet lanes linking the glorious villages of the north Cotswolds and the verdant Vale of Evesham. This is the most environmentally friendly way to visit local manor houses, or perhaps the National Trust's fabulous Fleece Inn at nearby Bretforton.

Longlands Farm Cottage, Chipping Campden, Gloucestershire GL55 6LJ
01386 438706
www.cotswoldcountrycycles.com

COTSWOLD FALCONRY CENTRE

Falcons, owls, hawks, eagles and vultures can be found here: a veritable cornucopia of raptors to study and a plethora of falconry displays to enjoy. There's a strong conservation message here, too. Experience days offer training and handling skills with the chance to 'fly' a variety of the birds, including owls and even eagles.

Batsford Park, Moreton-in-Marsh,
Gloucestershire GL56 9QB
01386 701043
www.cotswold-falconry.co.uk

SALFORD TROUT LAKES

Greenhorns can learn the rudimentary skills of the graceful art of fly fishing by pre-booking some tuition at these peaceful, spring-fed lakes. Tackle hire is available; the more experienced fly angler may expect good sport from stocks of brown and rainbow trout between March and October.

Rectory Farm, Salford, Chipping Norton,
Oxfordshire OX7 5YZ
01608 643209
www.salfordtroutlakes.co.uk

The Walk - *A Taste of India at Sezincote*

Discovering the influences of India through the Cotswold home of Sir Charles Cockerell.

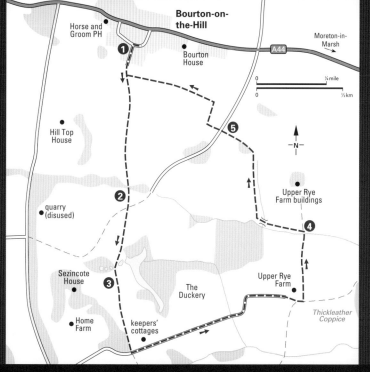

Walk Details

LENGTH: 3 miles (4.8km)

TIME: 1hr 15min

ASCENT: 85ft (25m)

PATHS: Tracks, fields and lanes, 7 stiles

SUGGESTED MAP: aqua3 OS Explorer OL45 The Cotswolds

GRID REFERENCE: SP 175324

PARKING: In the street below Bourton-on-the-Hill church, parallel with the main road

❶ Walk up the road from the telephone box with the church to your right. Turn left down a signposted track between walls. Go through the gate into the field and then continue forward to pass through 2 more gates.

❷ Cross over the stile, followed by 2 kissing gates among the trees. This is the Sezincote Estate. Its architecture and design were inspired, like many other buildings in the early 19th century, by the colourful aqua-tints that were brought to England from India by returning artists, such as William and Thomas Daniell. Built on the plan of a typical large country house, in every other respect it is thoroughly unconventional and

owes a lot to Eastern influence, not least in the large copper onion dome that crowns the house and the garden buildings. Go straight ahead, following the markers and crossing the drive. Dip down to the gate among the trees, with ponds on either side. Go ahead into the field, from where Sezincote House is visible to the right.

❸ Walk into the next field and go right to the end, aiming for the top righthand corner. Pass through the gate to reach narrow road and turn left. Walk down this road, passing keepers' cottages to your left, and through a series of gates. The road will bottom out, curve left and right and then bring you to Upper Rye Farm. Pass to right of the

farmhouse, go through the gate and, immediately before the barn, turn left along the track and the road.

❹ After the 2nd cattle grid, go left over the stile. Follow the edge of the field to the footbridge. Go over it and turn right. Now follow the righthand margin of the field to reach the stile in the far corner. Cross this to follow the path through woodland until you come to stile and field, and continue on same line to another stile.

❺ Cross the track to another stile and walk on. After few paces, with Bourton-on-the-Hill plainly visible before you, turn right and follow path to next corner. Turn left and pass through 3 gates. After 3rd one, walk on for few paces and turn right through gate to return to the start.

The King's Arms

Gloucestershire

The Inn

The southern edge of the Cotswolds is all rolling countryside, with a heritage that is rich in the English passion for horses: Badminton, Gatcombe Park and Cheltenham are all nearby (as is the M4, although you'd never know it). And just the thing after a hard day in the saddle is this 17th-century coaching inn, which sits squarely on Didmarton's high street. The inn offers a traditional terracotta-tiled and beamed back bar with dark wooden tables and chairs and an impressive collection of ale pump badges. The more contemporary front bar has cool neutral colours, a cosy settle, window seats, a log fire and a collection of modern prints on the walls. It all feels very inviting.

Upstairs are three stylish doubles and a single bedroom, all with en-suite shower rooms and TV, while across the yard the coaching stable has been converted to make three self-catering cottages in the full English country style: roofs open to the ridge with exposed beams, crisp white linen and super comfy beds.

The Food

A favourite foodie haunt, the inn has won a swathe of awards for its food, cask ales and fine wines. Fresh game is a notable speciality, and the seasonal menu and blackboard specials change weekly. At lunchtime you can drop in to enjoy a hearty selection of sandwiches or classics such as Old Spot sausages, mash and onions, or calves' liver with bacon and mash; if you feel like something lighter, why not go for the likes of wild mushroom and red pepper tagliatelle.

Against a backdrop of warm red walls and high-backed padded chairs, evening meals in the restaurant are more elaborate. Garlic bruschetta, sautéed scallops and wild mushroom salad could then lead on to roast haunch of Badminton venison on butter onion mash with a red wine and juniper jus. Or for something less robust, the pan-seared sea bass fillet on a sweet tomato and prawn risotto is pure comfort eating. Don't skip desserts, they are well worth saving room for, especially the mouthwatering chocolate chip Italian meringue served with a toffee sauce.

The Essentials

Time at the Bar!
11am-11pm, Sun 12-10.30pm
Food: 12-2.30pm, 6-9.30pm;
Sun 12-9pm

What's the Damage?
Main courses from £8.95

Bitter Experience:
Uley Bitter, Otter Ale,
Hook Norton Hooky

Sticky Fingers:
Children welcome,
smaller portions available

Muddy Paws:
Dogs welcome in the bar

Zzzzz:
4 rooms, £80

Anything Else?
Terrace, garden, car park

What To Do

Shop

CHESTERTON FARM SHOP

A farm shop specialising in supplying meat from rare breeds, including beef from Shorthorn and Dexters cattle and pork from Berkshire and Tamworth pigs. The shop also supplies locally caught game, other meats from the home farm and a variety of Cotswold farm vegetables and fruits.

Chesterton Farm, Cirencester, Gloucestershire GL7 6JP

01258 642160

www.chestertonfarm.co.uk

TOP BANANA ANTIQUES

The heart of Tetbury old town is rich with antique shops and galleries, many collectively trading under the Top Banana marque. More than 60 dealers trade in most specialities, from clocks and furniture to fabrics, china and silver, sporting memorabilia, Victoriana and even French *objets d'art*.

1 New Church Street, Tetbury, Gloucestershire GL8 8DS

0871 2881102

www.topbananaantiques.com

Visit

BERKELEY CASTLE

This is the oldest inhabited castle in England, with treasures and fittings amassed over the centuries contributing to the sense of history – which includes the supposedly gruesome dispatch of King Edward II and a Civil War siege. Pleasantly terraced Elizabethan gardens enhance the setting within this small Severnside village.

Berkeley, Gloucestershire GL13 9BQ

01453 810332

www.berkeley-castle.com

RODMARTON MANOR

An imposing multi-gabled, Cotswold stone country house built a century ago to celebrate the Arts and Crafts movement. The furnishings and fittings are similarly influenced by those zealous artists and artisans. Formal gardens include a kitchen garden, rockery and topiary.

Cirencester, Gloucestershire GL7 6PF

01285 841253

www.rodmarton-manor.co.uk

ULEY BREWERY

One of the longest-surviving microbreweries in the Cotswolds, based in a listed, traditional tower brewery dating from the 1830s. A good range of standard, special and seasonal beers are made here using traditional methods and the best regional ingredients. Tours are by prior arrangement only; bottled beers available, draught beers on tap in the village's Old Spot pub.

31 The Street, Uley, Dursley, Gloucestershire GL11 5TB

01453 860120

www.uleybrewery.com

WESTONBIRT NATIONAL ARBORETUM

One of the largest in Europe, where the specimen trees represent all continents except Antarctica. Spread over 600 acres, there are miles of footpaths through glades and beneath 'champion' trees, the greatest of their species; in all, more than 18,000 trees. At their best in autumn; spring colour comes from the shrubs and woodland flowers.

Tetbury, Gloucestershire GL8 8QS

01666 880220

www.forestry.gov.uk/westonbirt

Activity

COTSWOLD GLIDING CLUB

A trial flight offers novices an introduction to the sport of gliding; if you're hooked, then further lessons may be tacked on, or a full day's course arranged for more hands-on experience in this eerily silent, but strangely addictive sky-based world.

Aston Down Airfield, Cowcombe Lane, Chalford, Stroud, Gloucestershire GL6 8HR

01285 760415

www.cotswoldgliding.co.uk

COTSWOLD WATER PARK

More than a hundred lakes between Cirencester and Cricklade, formed in disused gravel pits, are now home to a comprehensive variety of water-based activities, from the relatively sedate cycling and walking to adrenalin-rich waterskiing and sailboarding. Tuition and short experience courses are available.

www.waterpark.org

SLIMBRIDGE WETLAND CENTRE

Founded by Sir Peter Scott, Slimbridge is HQ of the Wildfowl & Wetlands Trust. This huge reserve of reedbeds, marsh and pasture beside the Severn Estuary has myriad species of resident birds and attracts scores of migrants. Particularly famous for water birds: a series of viewing points, hides and a tower allow visitors to appreciate the bird world to the full. The events and site tours that take place here range from brown hare watches to wildflower safaris.

Slimbridge, Stroud, Gloucestershire GL2 7BT

01453 890333

www.wwt.org.uk

The Walk - On the Fringe of the Cotswolds

A pastoral ramble around the village of Sherston.

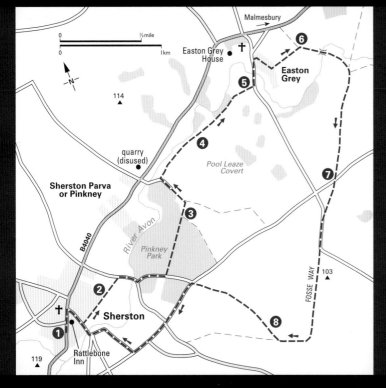

Walk Details

LENGTH: 6.5 miles (10.4km)

TIME: 3hrs

ASCENT: 131ft (40m)

PATHS: Field and parkland paths, tracks, metalled lanes, 11 stiles

SUGGESTED MAP: aqua3 OS Explorer 168 Stroud, Tetbury & Malmesbury

GRID REFERENCE: ST 853858

PARKING: Sherston High Street; plenty of roadside parking

INFORMATION: This walk is over the county boundary in Wiltshire

❶ On the High Street, walk towards village stores, pass Rattlebone Inn; turn right into Noble Street. Pass Grove Road; take footpath left up the steps. Cross the cul-de-sac; follow the footpath to the gate then to the rear of the houses to the gate.

❷ Bear diagonally right across the field to the gate and lane. Turn right, cross over the river and turn left ('Foxley'). At end of the woodland on the left, take the footpath left through the gate. Follow the track across Pinkney Park to the gate.

❸ Keep ahead, bearing left beside the wall to the gate. Follow the track ahead towards farm buildings; where drive curves left, turn right into farmyard. Keep right to join the path to the stile. Turn left around

the field edge to the stile; keep to lefthand field edge to stile in corner.

❹ Bear half-right across the field; follow the path along the field edge above Avon to the stile. Cross a further stile; walk beside fence (Easton Grey House left), and head downhill to the gate and lane.

❺ Turn left into Easton Grey. Cross the river bridge, turn right uphill to the footpath ahead on reaching the entrance gates on right. Cross gravelled area, go through the gate and ahead to the stile. Continue across the next field; descend to follow track into the next field.

❻ Turn right along field edge; bear off right downhill through scrub to footbridge. Keep ahead beside ruin to gate. Cross stile and continue to

further stile and gate. Follow track downhill to stile; turn right along track (Fosse Way). Continue for 0.5 mile (800m) to road.

❼ Cross over; follow the byway to another road. Bear left and keep ahead where the lane veers left. Follow the rutted track for 0.5 mile (800m), then cross the arrowed stile on right. Head across field to gate and bear diagonally right across the large paddock to the stile.

❽ Join the track, cross racehorse gallop and go through the lefthand gate ahead. Walk through scrub to another gate; keep to track ahead to road. Turn left and continue to the crossroads. Proceed straight on to next junction; keep ahead, following the lane back into Sherston.

Eight Bells
Gloucestershire

The Inn

Chipping Campden is one of the loveliest small towns in the Cotswolds and the streets are lined with ancient houses, each with their own distinctive embellishments. Once you've had your fill of the antique shops, a quick detour off the high street brings you to this charming 14th-century inn. It was built to house the team of stonemasons working on the nearby church and, as the name suggests, they stored the bells here, too. A suntrap rear terrace looks onto the local almshouses and St James's church – and the bells can often be heard.

Within, flagstones and tiles give way to soft carpet; there are oak beams, large gilt mirrors and fireplaces at every turn. It has the feel of a real local – the bar is strewn with dried hops and dangling tankards waiting to be filled with Old Hooky or Butty Bach. Seven good-sized bedrooms are tucked into this ancient building and the decor blends the old and the new with considerable style. One room necessitates ducking under a huge oak beam, several overlook the terrace, and some come with super king-sized beds.

Eight Bells, Church Street, Chipping Campden, Gloucestershire GL55 6JG

The Food

There is plenty of comfortable seating, with a more formal candle-lit dining area next door to the bar (there is even a priest hole beneath the floor, currently not in use!) At lunch, pork and leek sausages with apple mash and stilton sauce, and fillet of beef stroganoff are typical, as well as brie, bacon and cranberry sandwiches and fluffy three-egg omelettes. In the evening, the choice broadens considerably, with plenty of Cotswold produce featuring on menus that have Mediterranean and Asian touches.

Expect dishes such as gammon steak with a spiced Catalan bean cassoulet or oven-baked fillet of Scottish salmon with Mediterranean vegetable risotto. Similarly, there could be monkfish tail wrapped in Parma ham with tagliatelle, vermouth cream sauce and roasted Mediterranean vegetables, followed by passion fruit cheesecake and orange sauce or English cheeses with home-made apple and cinnamon chutney and highland oatcakes. A solid wine list features all the major world wine-growing regions as well as interesting artisan wine makers. There are fruit wines to choose from, too, such as damson, plum, sloe and elderberry.

The Essentials

Time at the Bar!
12-11pm (10.30pm Sun)
Food: 12-2pm (2.30pm Fri-Sun), 6.30-9pm
(9.30pm Fri-Sat, Sun 7-9pm)

What's the Damage?
Main courses from £10

Bitter Experience:
Hook Norton Old Hooky, Goff's Jouster, Butty Bach

Sticky Fingers:
Children welcome, children's menu

Muddy Paws:
Dogs welcome on a lead in the bar

Zzzzz:
7 rooms, £55-£125

Anything Else?
Terrace, garden, no car park

What To Do

Shop

DAYLESFORD ORGANIC FARM SHOP

Quite the most luxurious farm shop you're ever likely to come across: Daylesford Organic has award-winning cheeses from the creamery, breads, pastries, cakes and biscuits from the bakery and fresh meat from their Staffordshire estate. A foodie's heaven: bring a big basket and a big appetite – you can eat here, too!

Daylesford, Kingham,
Gloucestershire GL56 0YG
01608 731700
www.daylesfordorganic.com

THE ROPE STORE STUDIO GALLERY

Catering for the first-time buyer or the serious collector, this gallery has a wide range of contemporary artwork by new and established artists, designers and makers. Monthly exhibitions of paintings are shown alongside jewellery, glass, ceramics and sculpture and serve to put this gallery well at the forefront of the contemporary art scene in the Cotswolds.

The Shambles, Stroud,
Gloucestershire GL5 1AS
01453 753799
www.ropestoregallery.co.uk

STUART HOUSE ANTIQUES

On your very doorstep is this well-established antique shop, famous for its fine collection of porcelain and Royal Doulton, Toby jugs and Staffordshire figurines. There's enough to keep the keenest collector occupied for hours.

High Street, Chipping Campden,
Gloucestershire GL55 6HR
01386 840995
www.cotswoldstay.co.uk

Visit

HIDCOTE MANOR GARDENS

One of England's greatest gardens, this Arts and Crafts masterpiece features a series of outdoor 'rooms', each with its own character. Wander among ancient roses, plants and trees from around the world, all set against a stunning panorama across the Vale of Evesham.

Hidcote Bartrim, Chipping Campden,
Gloucestershire GL55 6LR
01386 438333
www.nationaltrust.org.uk

ROYAL SHAKESPEARE THEATRE

This is one of the world's most iconic theatrical sites set in the beautiful Warwickshire countryside, on the banks of the River Avon. Take in one of the many performances in the Swan and Courtyard Theatres. The birthplace of William Shakespeare is steeped in culture and history, so why not explore the Shakespeare Trail, visiting the family home in Henley Street, Mary Arden's house in nearby Wilmcote, Anne Hathaway's Cottage in Shottery, and Hall's Croft near Stratford's parish church?

Waterside, Stratford-upon-Avon,
Warwickshire CV37 6BB
01789 403444
www.rsc.org.uk

WARWICK CASTLE

The ancestral home of the Earls of Warwick and the 'King Maker', this is the finest medieval castle in England dating from the days of William the Conqueror. There are attractions including displays of jousting and falconry.

City of Warwick, Warwickshire CV34 4QU
0870 442200
www.warwick-castle.co.uk

Activity

COTSWOLD COUNTRY CYCLES

Cycles – and even tandems – available for daily hire, with detailed cycling routes and maps provided so that you can enjoy the quieter backroads of the Cotswolds.

Longlands Farm Cottage, Chipping
Campden, Gloucestershire GL55 6LJ
01386 438706
www.cotswoldcountrycycles.com

COTSWOLD GLIDING CLUB

What better way to appreciate the beauty of this part of England than from the air? Benefit from expert instruction in first-class two-seater gliders: trial lesson, day or week courses available.

Aston Down Airfield, Cowcombe Lane,
Chalford, Gloucestershire GL6 8HR
01275 760415
www.cotswoldgliding.co.uk

POTTERY WORKSHOP

Discover the pleasure of pottery-making and learn to throw a pot and handle the potters' wheel, or try your hand at ceramic painting.

Honeybourne Pottery, 3 High Street,
Honeybourne, Evesham,
Worcestershire WR11 7PQ
01386 832855
www.honeybournepots.co.uk

PRESCOTT SPEED HILL CLIMB

The Bugatti Owners' Club was founded in 1929 by enthusiasts. Prescott Hill Climb is the club's home, where members and spectators get a glimpse of what many believe to be motor sport at its most skilful and testing.

Prescott Hill, Gotherington,
Gloucestershire GL52 9RD
01242 673136
www.prescott-hillclimb.com

The Walk - *Chipping Campden, Olimpick Playground*

From a beautiful wool town to Dover's Hill, the site of centuries-old Whitsuntide festivities.

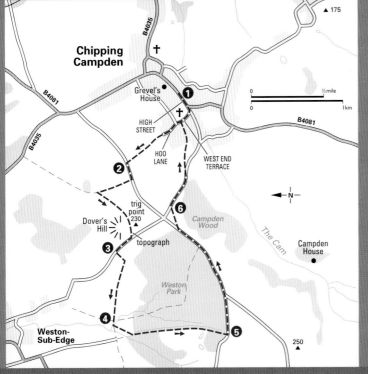

Walk Details

LENGTH: 5 miles (8km)

TIME: 2hrs

ASCENT: 280ft (85m)

PATHS: Fields, roads and tracks, 8 stiles

SUGGESTED MAP: aqua3 OS Explorer OL45 The Cotswolds

GRID REFERENCE: SP 151391

PARKING: Chipping Campden High Street or main square

1 Turn left from the Noel Arms, continue to the Catholic church. Turn right into West End Terrace. Where this bears right, keep ahead on Hoo Lane. Follow this up to the right turn, with farm buildings on your left. Continue uphill over the stile to the path; keep going to reach a road.

2 Turn left for few paces then right to cross to the path. Follow this along the field edge to the stile. Go over to Dover's Hill. Follow the hedge to the stile with extensive views ahead. Turn left along the escarpment edge, which drops away to your right. Pass a trig point then a topograph. Now go right, down slope, to a kissing gate on the left. Go through to road. Turn right.

3 After 150yds (137m) turn left over the stile into the field. Cross and find the gate in the bottom righthand corner. Head straight down the next field. At the stile go into another field and, keeping to the left of the fence, continue to another stile. Head down the next field, cross the track then find the adjacent stiles in the bottom lefthand corner.

4 Cross over the 1st stile. Walk along the bottom of the field. Keep the stream and the fence to your right and look for the stile over in the far corner. Go over, crossing the stream, then turn left, following a rising woodland path alongside stream. Enter the field through the gate and continue to meet the track. Stay on this track, passing through

gateposts, until you reach the country lane. Turn left.

5 After 400yds (366m) reach a busier road. Turn left for 450yds (411m). Shortly before the road curves left, drop down right on to the field path parallel with the road. About 200yds (183m) before the next corner go half-right down the field to eventually reach the road.

6 Turn right, down the road. Shortly after the cottage on the right, go left into the field. Turn right over the stile and go half left to the corner. Pass through the kissing gate, cross the road among the houses and continue ahead to meet West End Terrace. Turn right to return to your car in the centre of Chipping Campden, where the walk began.

The Miller of Mansfield

Oxfordshire

The Inn

When Paul Suter bought the Miller back in 2005 it was in a sorry state. He lavished money on the historic ivy-clad coaching inn and the finished result is very impressive. What's more, it's in a pretty riverside village, an amble from the Thames Path and smack between the Chilterns and the Berkshire Downs, both classic walking areas. Be prepared for a quirky interior, from the chic bar with its black-lacquered wood floor, leather club chairs and suede bar stools and sand-blasted beams to the smart and airy rear restaurant and the 11 decidedly funky bedrooms.

The bedrooms ramble across the first floor of the 18th-century building and all combine the old (antique fireplaces, rustic wooden floors) with an element of funky 21st-century chic (extravagant marble-tiled bathrooms, Perspex Philippe Starck chairs and bold silk fabrics). Expect vibrant wall coverings, like the metallic Cole & Son floral wallpaper in room seven, and strong colours, notably the lime green-upholstered antique French beds in room two. Added touches include plasma TV screens, fluffy robes and Molton Brown toiletries.

The Essentials

Time at the Bar!
11am-11pm; Sun 12-10.30pm
Food: 12-3pm, 6-9.30pm

What's the Damage?
Main courses from £8.95

Bitter Experience:
Marlow Rebellion, West Berkshire
Good Old Boy

Sticky Fingers:
Children welcome, small portions

Muddy Paws:
Dogs welcome in bar & bedrooms

Zzzzz:
11 rooms, £110-£175

Anything Else?
Garden terrace, car park

The Walk - *Pangbourne, Fashionable Riverside Resort*

Visit the River Pang and a National Trust meadow on this easy-going walk.

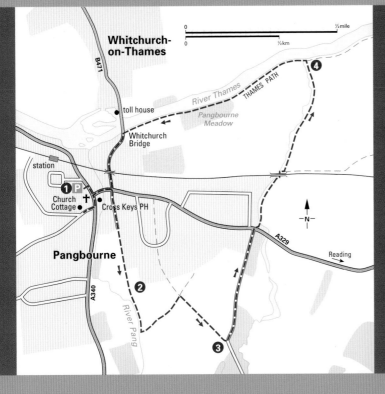

Walk Details

LENGTH: 3 miles (4.8km)

TIME: 1hr 30min

ASCENT: Negligible

PATHS: Field and riverside paths, stretches of road, section of Thames Path, 4 stiles

SUGGESTED MAP: aqua3 OS Explorer 159 Reading, Wokingham & Pangbourne

GRID REFERENCE: SU 633765

PARKING: Car park off A329 in Pangbourne, near railway bridge

INFORMATION: This walk is over the county border in Berkshire

① From the car park turn right to the mini-roundabout; walk along to church and adjoining cottage. Retrace your steps to the main road, keep Cross Keys pub on your right and turn right at the mini-roundabout. Cross the Pang; bear right at the next major junction into The Moors. At the end of the drive continue ahead on the waymarked footpath. Pass alongside various houses and patches of scrub; then go through the tunnel of trees. Further on is a gate with map and information board. Beyond the gate the River Pang can be seen.
② Follow the riverside path. Make for the footbridge. Don't cross it, instead, turn sharp left and walk across open meadow to the stile in

the far boundary. Once over, keep alongside the hedge on left and, as you approach a World War II pill box, turn right at path intersection and cross the footbridge. Head for another footbridge on the far side of the field and then look for 3rd bridge with white railings, by the field boundary. Cross the bridge and stile beyond it; then head across the field to the far boundary.
③ Exit to the road and bear left. Follow lane between hedges and oak trees and proceed to A329. Go diagonally right to footpath by sign ('Purley Rise') and follow the path north towards distant trees. Turn right at the next bridge; follow the concrete track as it bends left to run beneath the railway line. Once

through it, bear right to stile; then follow track along left edge of field, beside rivulet. Ahead on horizon are hanging woods on north bank of Thames. Pass double gates and bridge on left; continue on footpath as it crosses the gentle lowland landscape. Cross stile; walk across the next field to reach river bank.
④ On reaching River Thames, turn left and head towards Pangbourne. Follow Thames Path to Pangbourne Meadow and up ahead now is Whitchurch Bridge. As you approach it, begin to veer away from the river bank towards the car park. Keep left when you get to road, pass beneath railway line and turn right at next junction. Bear right again at mini-roundabout and return to car park.

The Crazy Bear
Oxfordshire

The Inn

It's a fitting name for a fairly quirky place, but then the Crazy Bear likes to pride itself on being quirky. This 16th-century coaching inn succeeds in weaving its ancient features into a modern look, creating the kind of wonky charm that goes down well with weekenders as well as a crowd as diverse as the proximity to Oxford can conjure up. The place has a genius all of its own, boldly mixing colour and texture in slate floors, exposed stone walls, fake fur carpets, crushed velvet and leather, adding a sprinkling of Asian artefacts and a life-sized stuffed bear for good measure.

But it's in the bedrooms where contemporary interior design and wild imagination have free reign. Arranged higgledy-piggledy throughout the inn and garden, every bedroom is different, but you can choose a theme – art deco, cottage rooms, garden rooms, suites or the opulent infinity suites. Beds are gorgeous, dressed with snowy white linen and frequently, eccentrically, with a bath at the end of them (there may even be a juke box, too), while snazzy bathrooms are state-of-the-art impressive.

The Crazy Bear, Bear Lane, Stadhampton, Oxfordshire OX44 7UR

The Essentials

Time at the Bar!
12pm-12am
Food: 12-9.45pm

What's the Damage?
Main courses from £11.50

Bitter Experience:
Greene King Old Speckled Hen, IPA

Sticky Fingers:
Children welcome, children's menu

Muddy Paws:
No dogs

Zzzzz:
18 rooms, £95-£380

Anything Else?
Terrace, garden, car park

The Food

The Crazy Bear scores highly in terms of creature comforts – diners rave about its pleasant garden and funky bar area. It also does well with its food – you'd be mad not to eat here. There's not only an English restaurant serving all-day breakfasts (with some upmarket choices such as duck eggs benedict or smoked haddock kedgeree if you're not in the mood for a full English), as well as classic prawn cocktail, tournedos Rossini, chargrilled calves' liver and Sunday roasts, but the inn also includes an authentic Thai brasserie.

Here, oriental standards – chicken satay, spring rolls, steamed pork and prawn dumplings, various salads and red and green curries – sit alongside slow pot-roasted ox cheek, steamed baby squid, whole crispy sea bream and braised salmon with Chinese rosé wine, ginger, lime, coriander and soy sauce. If you find it impossible to choose, check out the eight-to-twelve plate tasting menus. Flexibility is the keyword here, though – for the best of both worlds, head for the bar where both the English and Thai menus are offered.

What To Do

Shop

OXFORD COVERED MARKET

The quality of the fare at this famous market brings foodies from all over the country. Everything is under one roof: fish, cheese, vegetables and flowers. Rick Stein's Food Hero Mr Feller has been working here since 1979, and now it's a family affair – selling organic pork, beef, lamb, home-made sausages and burgers.

M Feller Organic Butchers, 54-55 Oxford Covered Market, Oxford, Oxfordshire OX1 3DY
01865 251164
www.mfeller.co.uk

SARAH WISEMAN GALLERY

This is a large, light, airy space exhibiting and selling a wide and contemporary collection of paintings, glass, ceramics, photography and jewellery, made by both established and new artists. Take home a future investment!

40-41 South Parade, Summertown, Oxford, Oxfordshire OX2 7JL
01865 515123
www.wisegal.com

BICESTER SHOPPING VILLAGE

For the ultimate designer shopping experience, head for this stylish complex, one of the best retail outlets in the country. The Shopping Village is home to top designer names such as Christian Dior, Ralph Lauren and Ted Baker. Clothes, shoes, jewellery, household items, lingerie and accessories can all be found here at bargain prices, and there are plenty of places to eat.

50 Pingle Drive, Bicester, Oxfordshire OX26 6WD
01869 323200
www.bicestervillage.com

Visit

BLENHEIM PALACE

Home to 11th Duke of Marlborough and birthplace of Sir Winston Churchill, there's a full day's worth of things to do and see at Blenheim Palace, with its 2,100 acres of parkland designed by Capability Brown, sweeping lawns, formal gardens and a magnificent lake. The Baroque palace has staterooms, carvings, painted ceilings and treasures collected over 300 years. You'll need to break for refreshment at the cafe, restaurant or ice cream parlour, which also sells Blenheim Palace wines and champagne.

Woodstock, Oxfordshire OX20 1PX
01993 811091
www.blenheimpalace.com

WATERPERRY GARDENS

Waterperry is famous for its magnificent herbaceous borders designed by Alan Bloom – but there's also the Mary Rose garden, a tranquil river walk where you might spot darting kingfishers, and a formal and alpine garden. Make sure you have enough space in the car, as the shop produces and sells the largest range of plants in the country. Buy art and crafts here, too, from the gallery housed in a restored 18th-century barn.

Wheatley, Oxfordshire OX33 1JZ
01993 811091
www.waterperrygardens.co.uk

OXFORD

This ancient and picturesque university city dating back to the 8th century sits comfortably on the rivers Cherwell and Thames. With so much to see and do, from taking a tour around the colleges and visiting some fascinating museums to enjoying some first-class shopping, you'll need a day, if not more, to get a real flavour of the city. Highlights include The Oxford Story, the University of Oxford Botanic Garden and the Ashmolean Museum of Art and Archaeology.

www.oxfordcity.co.uk

Activity

PUNT ON THE CHERWELL

What better way to spend a lazy summer day than messing about on the river? At the Cherwell Boat House you can start or end your sojourn with a good lunch on the terrace overlooking the river.

Cherwell Boat House, Bardwell Road, Oxford, Oxfordshire OX2 6SR
01865 515978
www.cherwellboathouse.co.uk

WATCH A CLASSIC FILM

If you're a fan of the classics rather than the blockbusters, The Ultimate Picture Palace is for you – it's Oxford's only remaining independent cinema, showing European and cult movies, and there are regular late-night screenings – a great way to round off the evening.

The Ultimate Picture Palace, Jeune Street, Oxford, Oxfordshire OX4 1BN
01865 245288

HOT-AIR BALLOONING

Take off from South Park or Cutteslowe Park close to Oxford and glide peacefully over the city's dreaming spires, the Thames and surrounding countryside.

Adventure Balloons
01253 844222
www.adventureballoons.co.uk

The Walk - A Very Special Abbey at Dorchester

A stroll around an ancient settlement with some superb views.

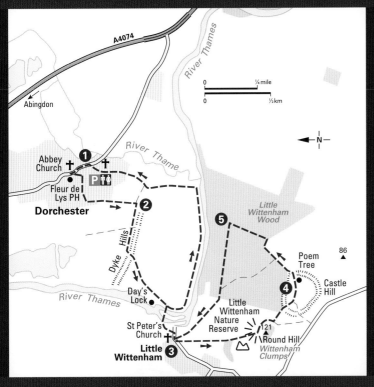

Walk Details

LENGTH: 4.5 miles (7.2km)

TIME: 1hr 45min

ASCENT: 115ft (35m)

PATHS: Field and woodland paths and tracks, stretch of Thames Path and main road with pavement

SUGGESTED MAP: aqua3 OS Explorer 170 Abingdon, Wantage

GRID REFERENCE: SU 578939

PARKING: Parking area in Bridge End at southern end of Dorchester

❶ From parking area walk towards the centre of Dorchester, keeping the abbey church on right. As you approach Fleur de Lys, turn left into Rotten Row and walk to Mayflower Cottage and Pilgrims. Take the path between the 2 properties and pass beside the allotments. At the row of cottages, veer left to follow the track. Swing right after 60yds (55m) at the sign for Day's Lock. Pass between the fencing and out across the large field. Ahead is the outline of Wittenham Clumps. At the low embankment of Dyke Hills, turn right in front of the fence.

❷ Follow the path along field edge, pass over the track and continue. The path, enclosed by hedge and fencing, heads south towards the Thames river bank. Go through gate and follow path, now unfenced, to footbridge at Day's Lock. Cross river to Lock House Island and head for St Peter's Church, Little Wittenham.

❸ Turn left just beyond it, at the entrance to the manor. Keep right at immediate fork, go through the gate and begin steep climb to viewpoint on Round Hill at top. Veer left as you approach the seat, pass 2nd seat and keep left at next fork, heading for Castle Hill. Head towards gates at foot of the hill, avoid stile and go through gate, up flight of steps and into trees. At T-junction, turn left.

❹ Emerge from trees and pass the commemorative stone, keeping it on your right. Descend the grassy slope to the gate and pass through trees to the field. Continue on perimeter, with woodland left. Pass the stile, continue along the field edge and round to the right in corner. Swing left to join the nature trail; follow it through Little Wittenham Wood.

❺ At a barrier and T-junction in heart of the wood, turn left and follow the path back to Little Wittenham. Recross the Thames, then turn right to follow the river downstream. On reaching the confluence of Thames and Thame, swing left and head north towards Dorchester. As Thame bends right, keep ahead to the gate. Keep to the right of Dyke Hills to another gate and skirt field to track (Wittenham Lane). Pass the Catholic Church of St Birinus to reach the car park.

The Cherry Tree Inn

Oxfordshire

The Inn

Perfectly placed for visiting Henley-on-Thames and exploring the Chiltern Hills, this collection of 400-year-old brick-and-flint farm cottages, now enjoying new life as a popular inn, is well worth locating. The Cherry Tree stands in sleepy Stoke Row and is best reached from junction 6 of the M40. Following extensive refurbishment by Paul Gilchrist and chef Richard Coates, who have worked wonders in bringing this old village local bang up-to-date, there's a confident blend of ancient and modern inside.

A plethora of old beams, worn flagstones and crackling log fires provide a warm, welcoming atmosphere in the bar areas and prove to be the classic backdrop to a wealth of stylish contemporary furnishings – expect to find a palette of soothing earthy colours, soft lighting and squashy sofas. Chunky wooden tables and high-backed chairs lend a sense of occasion to the dining room.

You will not be disappointed with the food or the chic bedrooms in the converted barn. The rooms mirror the contemporary theme of the pub, with stylish furnishings and a host of cosseting extras: plasma screens, fresh Illy coffee, mineral water, bowls of fruit and Molton Brown goodies in the smartly tiled bathrooms. The bedrooms are

The Essentials

Time at the Bar!
12-11pm, Sun 12-10.30pm
Food: 12-3pm (Sun 4pm), 7-10pm;
no food Sun evening

What's the Damage?
Main courses from £10.50

Bitter Experience:
Brakspear Bitter and Special

Sticky Fingers:
Children welcome, children's menu

Muddy Paws:
Dogs welcome in the bar

Zzzzz:
4 rooms, £95

Anything Else?
Terrace, garden, car park

The Food

Simplicity, quality, fresh, seasonal and local are the five key words that sum up the philosophy of the food operation at The Cherry Tree, alongside uncomplicated presentation and value for money. Cooking is classic European with a modern twist, as seen in grilled sea bass with roast vegetable couscous and a tomato and chilli dressing, and roast confit duck leg with cassis and green peppercorn sauce.

You could start with the likes of tempura fried squid and courgette with red chilli oil and rocket, or smoked haddock fishcakes with lime hollandaise, then tuck into main courses of roast belly of Old Spot pork with creamed mash, smoked black pudding and cider jus, or braised shank of Chiltern lamb with garlic and herb mash and honey roast vegetables.

The menu recommends a beer with some courses: for a change, try a bottle of Leffe Blond with your skate wing with clam, caper and parsley jus. Pasta, steak sandwiches and wild boar sausages are typical lunch dishes, best enjoyed alfresco in the big garden on warm days. Pudding lovers should try the chocolate and cherry pudding with white chocolate ice cream

What To Do

Shop

FARMERS MARKETS

South Oxfordshire's monthly markets, which are held in Henley, Didcot, Thame and Wallingford, offer everything from fish, meats, sausages and pies to a mouth-watering choice of cheeses, home-made jams, fruits, vegetables, herbs and spices.

Tourist Information Centre, King's Arms Barn, Kings Road, Henley-on-Thames, Oxfordshire RG9 2DG
01491 578034
www.visit-henley.org.uk

HENLEY-ON-THAMES

As well as boating, Henley is known for its quality and variety of shops. Near the town hall is Henley's exhibition centre, which features all manner of artists and collections. The town's four main thoroughfares are lined with shops specialising in antiques, rare books and gifts, in addition to shoe shops, jewellers, and gift and interiors boutiques.

Henley Tourist Information (as above)

Visit

CHILTERN VALLEY WINERY & BREWERY

Situated in an area of outstanding natural beauty, Old Luxters Vineyard is home to Chiltern Valley Wines. The first vines were planted back in 1982 on the slopes of the Chiltern Hills and since the first harvest two years later, the company has produced an increasing range of fine award-winning English wines.

Hambleden, Henley-on-Thames, Oxfordshire RG9 6JW
01491 638330
www.chilternvalley.co.uk

GREYS COURT

The historic National Trust house and the village owe their name to Lord de Grey, who fought at Crecy and became one of the original Knights of the Garter. Greys Court contains a Tudor donkey-wheel well house and the Archbishop's Maze. There are glorious views from the house over the surrounding parkland, and regular events held here include open-air theatre, black-tie picnics and evening walks.

Rotherfield Greys, Henley-on-Thames, Oxfordshire RG9 4PG
01494 755564
www.nationaltrust.org.uk

RIVER & ROWING MUSEUM

The history of rowing, as well as that of the River Thames and Henley, are brought to life through the use of interactive displays and fascinating exhibits housed at this stunning riverside building.

Mill Meadows, Henley-on-Thames, Oxfordshire RG9 1BF
01491 415600
www.rrm.co.uk

THE WARBURG RESERVE

Named after an Oxford botanist and acquired in 1967, the Warburg Reserve is the jewel in the local Wildlife Trust's crown. During daylight hours the air is filled with the song of countless birds and the ground is a richly textured carpet of wild flowers in spring and summer. Orchids and bluebells and more than 900 species of fungi thrive here and a visitor centre puts the site's natural elements into perspective.

Bix, Henley-on-Thames, Oxfordshire
01491 642001
www.bbowt.org.uk

Activity

BALLOONING

Enjoy a birds-eye view of the Thames, Henley and the rolling Chiltern countryside from the basket of a hot-air balloon as it drifts peacefully through the sky from its Henley launch site.

Hot Air Balloons, 7 The Green, Middle Assendon, Henley-on-Thames, Oxfordshire RG9 6AT
01491 574101
www.henleyballoons.com

BOATING

There is no shortage of opportunities to go boating on the Thames. Hobbs of Henley offer cruises and boats for hire, whether it's row boats, canoes, steamers or motor boats. One of the most popular is a passenger cruise, following the Thames through some of the region's prettiest countryside.

Hobbs of Henley, Station Road, Henley-on-Thames, Oxfordshire RG9 1AZ
01491 572035
www.hobbs-of-henley.com

MIDSOMER MURDERS TRAIL

This world-famous and highly successful TV series now has its own trail. Key locations are part of the route, hidden away in deepest Buckinghamshire and the Vale of Aylesbury. Along the trail, which can be picked up at any point, you discover a world of snug cottages, village greens and quaint old pubs – and maybe the odd corpse or two!

www.visitbuckinghamshire.org

The Walk - *A Maharajah's Gift at Stoke Row*

Discover the link between India and a quiet village in the Chilterns.

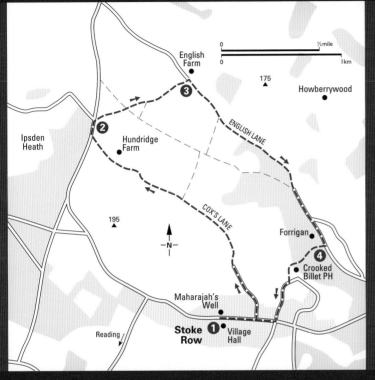

Walk Details

LENGTH: 5 miles (8km)

TIME: 2hrs

ASCENT: 164ft (50m)

PATHS: Field and woodland paths and tracks, road (busy), 8 stiles

SUGGESTED MAP: aqua3 OS Explorer 171 Chiltern Hills West

GRID REFERENCE: SU 678840

PARKING: Roadside parking in Stoke Row; two spaces in village hall car park when hall is not in use

1 From the car park turn right and walk past the village stores. Enclosed in an exotic cupola you'll see the Maharajah's Well, which was a gift to the village from the Maharajah of Benares in 1863. Turn left into Cox's Lane and follow it as it curves to the left. Soon it dwindles to a track. Continue to the waymark, avoid the footpath on the right and keep ahead on the right of way. The track narrows to a path now, running between trees and hedgerows. Pass the stile and footpath and eventually you reach the outbuildings of Hundridge Farm. Join the track running through woodland and make for the road.

2 Turn right along the road for several paces, then swing right at the footpath sign into the wood. Follow the path between the trees and cross the drive. Make for the stile ahead and then go diagonally right in the field, using the waymark posts to guide you. Look for the stile in the corner and cross the lane to the further stile on the opposite side. Head diagonally right inside the field and look for the stile by the hard tennis court. Pass alongside beech hedge to the drive; turn left. As drive sweeps left to house, go forward over cattle grid to field. Continue with the boundary on your left and on reaching the corner, go straight on along the track.

3 Turn right at English Farm and follow the narrow track known as English Lane. Go past the footpath and stile on righthand side. Follow the track along edge of woodland. Continue to the junction and keep ahead through trees. Pass timber-framed cottage on lefthand side and house on right called Forrigan. Keep ahead for about 100yds (91m) and swing right at sign ('Stoke Row').

4 Cross the stile and cut through the wood to a 2nd stile. Emerge from woodland at a gate and cross pasture to a further patch of woodland. Negotiate next stile within sight of Crooked Billet and go up the gentle slope towards the pub. Turn right at the road, pass the footpath on right, followed by Rose Cottage, and head for the crossroads in centre of Stoke Row. Turn right and return to the start.

The Kings Head Inn
Oxfordshire

The Inn

A more delightful or typically English spot must surely be hard to find, and facing the well-kept village green with its meandering brook and border-patrolling ducks, the Kings Head looks like the quintessential Cotswold pub. It dates back to the 15th century and stands smack on the Gloucestershire border in the picture-perfect village of Bledington.

Step through the old-fashioned latch door into the original low-beamed and stone-walled bar, find an ancient settle by the crackling log fire in the huge stone inglenook and cosy up with a foaming pint of Hooky, brewed in nearby Hook Norton. You can eat a meal here seated at a rustic oak table or head next door to the informal dining room, decked out with solid oak furniture on flagstones.

Archie and Nicola Orr-Ewing have worked their magic on this former cider house, creating a classy rural atmosphere. Comfort, charm and style also sum up the 12 elegant bedrooms, which are split between the pub and a converted barn, and they have all been tastefully kitted out by Nicola with plump cushions on big beds, fresh flowers, CD and video players, and posh toiletries in the fully tiled bathrooms.

The Essentials

Time at the Bar!
11.30am-3pm, 6-11pm (all day Fri-Sat)

What's the Damage?
Main courses from £9.95

Bitter Experience:
Hook Norton Hooky, guest beers

Sticky Fingers:
Children welcome, children's menu

Muddy Paws:
Dogs welcome in the bar

Zzzzz:
12 rooms, £70-£125

Anything Else?
Courtyard, garden, car park

The Food

Fresh local produce, notably free-range and organic ingredients and game from local estates, features on the ever-changing menus. The Aberdeen Angus beef is sourced from the Orr-Ewing family farm in Fifield and is hung for 21 days to enhance its unique flavour, so why not try the chargrilled fillet, served with green salad and pommes frites?

Modern influences on traditional English dishes can be seen in lamb cutlets with garlic roasted potatoes and redcurrant and mint salsa, chargrilled chicken with herb and shallot butter, or venison with bubble and squeak and sage and mustard butter.

Starters take in potted shrimps with lemon butter and devilled lambs' kidneys, while home-made puddings run to chocolate caramel brownie with vanilla ice cream or apple and plum crumble – or there could be some unusual English cheeses, perhaps Cotswold organic brie made at Kirkham Farm in Stow-on-the-Wold. Lighter lunchtime bar meals are listed on the chalkboard. In addition to a choice of four real ales, you can sample some first-rate wines from local independent merchants (ten are available by the glass), and a good range of bottled ciders.

What To Do

Shop

BURFORD GARDEN COMPANY
A huge range of interior furnishings, garden plants and products, on a 15-acre site just outside the town. Follow the signs on the A40. There's also an organic food shop and restaurant. Burford itself is renowned for its picturesque main street lined with gift shops, antique shops, old inns and tea rooms.

Shilton Road, Burford,
Oxfordshire OX18 4PA
01993 823117
www.burford.co.uk

OLD FARM FARM SHOP
Established in 2004, this growing farm shop sells home-reared lamb, beef and Old Spot pork, as well as a host of locally produced goodies, from jams, honey, cheese (Brie made in Lower Slaughter), ice cream, yoghurts and apple juice.

Dorn, Moreton-in-Marsh,
Gloucestershire GL56 9NS
01608 650394
www.oldfarmdorn.co.uk

RED RAG GALLERY
Art lovers will enjoy Stow's Red Rag Gallery, a cluster of rooms lined with contemporary art and paintings. Then there's Foundation, selling stylish clothes and shoes. With its winding streets lined with shops, Stow-on-the-Wold has something for everyone.

5-7 Church Street, Stow-on-the-Wold,
Gloucestershire GL54 1BB
01451 832563
www.redraggallery.co.uk

The Square
Stow-on-the-Wold,
Gloucestershire GL54 1AB
01451 832453
www.shopfoundation.com

Visit

CHASTLETON HOUSE
Chastleton House is both a national monument and a family home. Filled with a mixture of unusual and everyday objects, furniture and textiles collected since its completion in 1612, the house has been continuously occupied by one family for 400 years. The gardens recall typical Elizabethan and Jacobean designs, and it was here in 1865 that the rules of modern croquet were codified.

Chastleton, Moreton-in-Marsh,
Oxfordshire GL56 0SU
01608 674355
www.nationaltrust.org.uk

HIDCOTE MANOR GARDEN
Designed and created by the horticulturalist Major Lawrence Johnston, Hidcote is the perfect embodiment of the Arts and Crafts style of garden landscaping. The garden is arranged as a series of outdoor rooms, each with a different character and separated by hedges and walks of many different species. Also of note are Hidcote's rare shrubs and trees and magnificent herbaceous borders.

Hidcote Bartrim, Chipping Campden,
Gloucestershire GL55 6LR
01386 438333
www.nationaltrust.org.uk

ROLLRIGHT STONES
On the sides of the road between Great and Little Rollright village. The Rollright Stones are two curious Bronze Age clusters of stones that assumed their identity in medieval myth – some say they are a conquering king and his men turned to stone.

www.rollrightstones.co.uk

Activity

COTSWOLD FALCONRY CENTRE
Experience the Eagle Day (for two people) at Batsford Park and learn the correct way to handle an eagle, before taking a 4x4 trip into the Cotswolds to fly one for yourself.

Batsford Park, Moreton-in-Marsh,
Gloucestershire GL56 9QB
01386 701043
www.cotswold-falconry.co.uk

GLOUCESTERSHIRE WARWICKSHIRE RAILWAY
Dubbed as 'the friendly line in the Cotswolds', this diesel and steam railway is run wholly by volunteers. Since 1981 these dedicated enthusiasts have restored more than 10 miles (16km) of railway line, together with platforms, buildings, steam and diesel locomotives and rolling stock. In addition to a scheduled service, the GWR hosts various galas and enthusiasts' events throughout the year, and there's also the chance to learn to drive a diesel locomotive.

The Railway Station, Toddington,
Gloucestershire GL54 5DT
www.gwsr.com

WALKING
The Cotswold Way runs for just over 100 miles (161km), starting in the city of Bath and finishing in the lovely old Cotswold market town of Chipping Campden. En route it follows the Cotswolds' western escarpment, with its breathtaking views and picturesque honey-stoned villages. Follow linear stretches of the route or devise your own manageable half-day circular walk along the way.

www.nationaltrail.co.uk/cotswold
www.cotswold-way.co.uk

The Walk - The Rollright Stones

An ancient and mythical site near Chipping Norton.

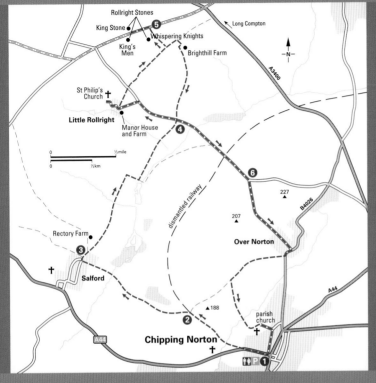

Walk Details

LENGTH: 8 miles (12.9km)

TIME: 4hrs

ASCENT: 295ft (90m)

PATHS: Field paths and tracks, country roads, 9 stiles

SUGGESTED MAP: aqua3 OS Explorer 191 Banbury, Bicester & Chipping Norton

GRID REFERENCE: SP 312270

PARKING: Free car park off A44, in centre of Chipping Norton

① Follow the A44 downhill. Pass Penhurst School, then veer right, through the kissing gate. Skirt the lefthand edge of the recreation ground and aim for the gate. Descend to the bridge and, when the path forks, keep right. Go up slope to 3 stiles and keep ahead along right edge of field. Make for gate and drop down to double gates in corner.
② Cross the track just beyond the gates. Walk towards Salford, keeping the hedge left. Continue into village. Turn right by patch of grass ('Trout Lakes – Rectory Farm').
③ Follow track to righthand bend. Go ahead here, following field edge. Make for gate ahead. Turn right in next field. About 100yds (91m) before field corner, turn left. Follow

path across to opening in boundary. Veer left, then right to skirt field. Cross the stream. Maintain direction in the next field to reach the road.
④ Turn left, then left again for Little Rollright. Visit the church, then retrace route to D'Arcy Dalton Way on left. Follow path up field slope to road. Cross over. Continue between fields. Head for trees and approach stile. Don't cross it; instead, turn left and skirt field, passing close to Whispering Knights.
⑤ At the road, turn left to visit the Rollright Stones. Return to Whispering Knights, head down the field to the stile and cross it to reach another. Continue along the grassy path. Turn right at the stile towards Brighthill Farm. Pass

beside the buildings to the stile. Head diagonally right down the field to a further stile. Keep the boundary on your right and head for the stile in bottom right corner of the field. Make for the bottom right corner of the next field. Go through the gate and skirt the field; turn left at road.
⑥ Keep right at the fork and head towards Over Norton. Walk through the village to T-junction. Turn right. When road swings to left by Cleeves Corner, join track ('Salford'). When hedge gives way, look for a waymark on the left. Follow path down the slope, make for 2 kissing gates; follow path alongside wall to reach church. Join Church Lane. Follow it as far as T-junction. Turn right and return to the town centre.

The Boar's Head

Oxfordshire

The Inn

Bruce and Kay Buchan's handsome half-timbered pub stands in a timeless estate village beneath Ardington Down. Dating back some 400 years and enjoying a lovely spot beside the parish church, it successfully combines being a welcoming village local, a first-class food pub offering top-notch bar and restaurant meals, and a classy inn with three contemporary-styled bedrooms. Log fires blaze in the three light and airy interconnecting rooms – you'll find Ridgeway walkers and local drinkers in the simply furnished bar area, while chunky candles and fresh flowers adorn old pine tables, and tasteful paintings line sunny yellow walls in the two intimate dining rooms.

The idyllic village setting, as well as the pub's proximity to the city of Oxford, the Cotswolds and miles of downland walks, makes it a perfect place to stay. You can relax in one of the three stylishly decorated bedrooms, all with soothing Farrow & Ball colours, thick down duvets, fresh coffee, chocolates and mineral water, and Nutrogena smellies in smart, tiled bathrooms. If you book Room One, you'll be able to luxuriate in the enormous bathroom with its free-standing claw-foot bath.

The Essentials

Time at the Bar!
12-3pm; 6-11pm
Food: 12-2pm; 7-9.30pm

What's the Damage?
Main courses from £12

Bitter Experience:
Hook Norton Hooky; West Berkshire
ales; Butts ales

Sticky Fingers:
Children welcome

Muddy Paws:
Dogs allowed in the bar only

Zzzzz:
3 rooms £85-£130

Anything Else?
Garden, patio, car park

The Food

Bruce Buchan offers an accomplished home-grown style of cooking, and his short, innovative menus make good use of seasonal local produce, notably game from the estate, and lamb and pork from surrounding farms, while fish is delivered daily from Cornwall. In addition, bread, ice creams and pasta are made in the kitchen. His restaurant menu goes in for an ambitious and inventive style with some unusual flavour combinations, as seen in a starter of seared foie gras with brioche and rhubarb, and a main course of roast venison with sweet and sour onions. The daily choice may also take in red mullet with ratatouille and chorizo and lamb rump with butter beans and seared kidneys. For pudding, try the irresistible hot pistachio soufflé with iced chocolate cream.

By contrast, the philosophy when it comes to bar food is to keep everything simple. The succinct blackboard choice may list squid tempura with chilli dressing, spaghetti carbonara and sea bass served with rosti and hollandaise. Expect a decent wine list favouring the vineyards of France and some tip-top ale from the West Berkshire brewery.

What To Do

Shop

WANTAGE

The town's focal point is its wonderful and traditional Market Place overlooked by a splendid statue of King Alfred presented to the town in 1877. A bustling market is held here every Wednesday and Saturday, and lining the square are many independent retailers. Just round the corner in Newbury Street is Gus Mills Gallery, stocking original artwork, prints, cards, ceramics, glass and wood carving.

Gus Mills Gallery, Newbury Street, Wantage
Oxfordshire OX12 8BS
01235 770353

ARDINGTON VILLAGE

Ardington is a prime example of a classic estate village. Take a stroll round it and you'll find a butchers shop, a village stores and a tea room. Many of the old farm outbuildings have been converted into craft shops, workshops, offices, a picture gallery and a pottery, helping to boost the local economy, raise the village's profile and provide much-needed employment for local people.

01235 833200

www.lockinge-estate.co.uk

BROOKLEAS FISH FARM

This small trout farm is fed by the waters of Ginge Brook from neighbouring downland. It's possible to catch a trout to take home here, or simply visit the small farm shop and smokery to buy their delicious fresh or oak-smoked trout, smoked trout paté and locally caught crayfish.

Ludbridge Mill, East Hendred, Wantage,
Oxfordshire OX12 8LN
01235 820500

Visit

KELMSCOTT MANOR

Kelmscott is best known for its connection with William Morris, founder of the Arts and Crafts Movement and remembered for his furnishing designs, rich with flowers, leaves and birds, still popular on fabric and wallpaper. He called the village 'a heaven on earth', and his country home was Kelmscott Manor. Morris is buried in the local churchyard.

Kelmscott, Lechlade,
Gloucestershire GL7 3HJ
01367 252488
www.kelmscottmanor.co.uk

ASHDOWN HOUSE

Now in the care of the National Trust, this fine 17th-century house was built as a hunting lodge by the first Lord Craven. Tall and ornate, Ashdown is reminiscent of a child's dolls' house. Located on the windswept downs between Lambourn and Ashbury and at the heart of spectacular walking country, this extraordinary Dutch-style house is one of the Trust's more unusual acquisitions.

Lambourn, Newbury, Berkshire RG17 8RE
01793 762209
www.nationaltrust.org.uk

GREAT COXWELL BARN

This large monastic stone barn dates from the 13th century and is a remnant of the Cistercian Grange at Coxwell. William Morris said the barn was 'as noble as a cathedral'. It is 152ft (46m) long and 44ft (13m) wide, and has a fine stone-tiled roof and an interesting timber structure.

Great Coxwell, Faringdon, Oxfordshire
01793 762209
www.nationaltrust.org.uk

Activity

RIDGEWAY WALKING

The Ridgeway runs very close to Ardington and is perfect for space, solitude and views to far horizons. Here you can blow away the cobwebs, exploring a dramatic landscape of chalk downland and mysterious ancient long barrows. This is Britain's oldest road and the well-signposted, easy-to-follow trail follows it for 85 miles between Avebury in Wiltshire and Ivinghoe Beacon in the Chilterns.

01865 810224
www.nationaltrail.co.uk/ridgeway

WILLIAMS F1

Book a tour of the Williams Formula One state-of-the-art conference facility, which has the added bonus of a superb Grand Prix collection – the largest privately owned collection of F1 racing cars. The venue is the prestigious Wantage-based headquarters of one of the world's most successful F1 teams, with facilities to stage a range of activities from pit-stop challenges to corporate race days, from small meetings to product launches.

01235 777900
www.williamsf1conferences.com

FARMOOR RESERVOIR

The largest single area of water in Oxfordshire is the location for excellent trout fishing (day tickets available) and a noted site in the county for birdwatching, especially at Pinkhill Meadow Nature Reserve beside the Thames. You can explore the 4-mile (6km) 'countryside walk' around the reservoir.

Oxford, Oxfordshire OX2 9NS
01865 865551
www.farmoor.iofm.net

The Walk - Alfred's Greatness Remembered

Visit the statue of a revered British king before heading for downland country.

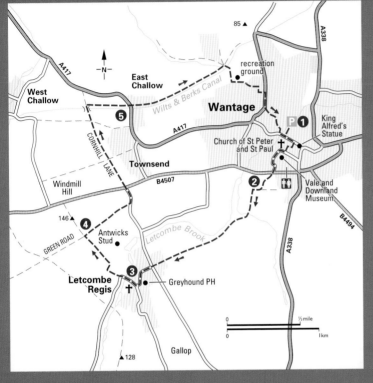

Walk Details

LENGTH: 6 miles (9.7km)

TIME: 2hrs 45min

ASCENT: 150ft (46m)

PATHS: Pavements, tow path, field paths and tracks, 1 stile

SUGGESTED MAP: aqua3 OS Explorer 170 Abingdon, Wantage

GRID REFERENCE: SU 397881

PARKING: Long-stay car park off Mill Street

1 Keep to the right edge of the car park and look for the pedestrian exit. Turn left into Mill Street and walk up into Market Place. Make for the statue of King Alfred, then follow signs for the museum. Approach the parish Church of St Peter and St Paul; turn left into Church Street. The museum is opposite you at the next junction. Turn right here, avoid Locks Lane and follow Priory Road to the left. Head for Portway and cross to footpath to left of The Croft.

2 Follow the clear tarmac path as it runs between the fences and playing fields. At length you reach the housing estate; continue ahead into Letcombe Regis and make for the junction with Courthill Road. Keep it on your left and go straight ahead through the village, passing the Greyhound pub and the thatched cottage dated 1698.

3 Turn right by church ('Letcombe Bassett and Lambourn') and, when the road bends sharp left, go straight ahead. After a few paces the drive bends right. Keep walking ahead along the path between banks of vegetation, following the path as it curves right, then swings to the left. Pass Antwicks Stud over to the right and then climb gently between the trees and bushes.

4 Turn right at the next intersection and follow tree-lined track to road. Turn left and make for the junction. Cross, pass alongside the house and follow Cornhill Lane. Begin the gentle descent, cross the track and continue down the slope. Avoid the turning on the right and keep ahead to the footbridge crossing the Wilts and Berks Canal. Turn right and continue, following the tow path.

5 Cross the A417 and then continue towards Wantage. Follow the drive, then take the parallel path on the right, running alongside a section of restored canal. On reaching tarmac drive, turn right and walk along to the row of houses. Turn left at path junction, pass the recreation ground and follow path as it curves right. Turn left into Wasborough Avenue, then, after lock-up garages, left into St Mary's Way. Turn right and swing left into Belmont. Keep right at the fork, heading for Mill Street. Keep left and the car park is on the left.

The Trout Inn

Oxfordshire

The Inn

The setting – smack on the banks of the infant River Thames – is straight out of *Wind in the Willows*, and you can imagine Ratty and Toad enjoying a pint of Ramsbury Gold on the riverside. Narrow boaters, fishing folk and Thames Path walkers rarely pass it by: the lure of a refreshing drink in the garden or in the stone-flagged bar, with its roaring winter fire, old settles and fishing paraphernalia proves too tempting, whatever the weather.

Since the arrival of practised hoteliers Gareth and Helen Pugh in 2006, and with the subsequent refurbishment of the restaurant and six bedrooms, this 17th-century inn now offers first-class food and accommodation.

Rooms really have been given the boutique hotel treatment – all are individually designed with quality fabrics, soft Farrow & Ball colours, antique furnishings, big lamps and mod cons like flat-screen TVs, DVD and CD players and clock radios. Room Five has a brass bed, Room Four a claw-foot bath, Room Six a big sleigh bed and private terrace, while all have fresh coffee and posh bathrooms with Molton Brown smellies.

The Trout Inn, Tadpole Bridge, Buckland Marsh, Faringdon, Oxfordshire SN7 8RF

The Essentials

Time at the Bar!
11.30-3.30pm, 6-11pm
(closed Sun evening in winter)
Food: 12-2pm, 7-9pm

What's the Damage?
Main courses from £9.95

Bitter Experience:
Youngs Bitter, Ramsbury Ales

Sticky Fingers:
Children welcome, children's menu

Muddy Paws:
Dogs welcome

Zzzzz:
6 rooms, £100-£130

Anything Else?
Garden, car park

The Food

Chef Robbie Ellis is passionate about sourcing the best produce from top local suppliers, and his innovative daily menus reflect the seasonal larder. Nearby shoots provide pheasant, wild duck and partridge – the latter roasted and served with dauphinois potatoes, braised red cabbage and a redcurrant jus. Faringdon and Abingdon butchers supply Cotswold lamb, perhaps a roast rump served with herb lentils, gratin potatoes and red wine jus, and Angus sirloin steak, which comes traditionally with chips, salad and béarnaise sauce. Soft fruits and vegetables are from Buscot Park down the road, and the day's fish delivery from Cornwall may yield baked whole black bream with sauté potatoes and a warm green bean and rocket salad.

To start, there may be scallops with pan-fried chorizo, pureed shallots and rosemary jus, or carpaccio of seared beef with horseradish crème fraîche. Round off with rich chocolate tart with mango sorbet or a plate of local cheeses, say Cerney goats', Stinking Bishop and Cotswold Blue. The wine list has some classic vintages from small vineyards and offers excellent tasting notes.

What To Do

Shop

BURFORD

The long main street of this lovely Cotswold town descends steeply down the hill and is lined with pretty grey-gabled houses, tea shops and a wide variety of craft and antique shops, clothes boutiques and art galleries, and much more, including a traditional English butchers (WJ Castle & Jesse Smith), who has prize-winning sausages.

Gateway Antiques
Cheltenham Road, Burford,
Oxfordshire OX18 4JA
01993 823678
www.gatewayantiques.co.uk

Boxroom Antiques
59 High Street, Burford,
Oxfordshire OX18 4QA
01993 824268

WJ Castle & Jesse Smith Butchers
High Street, Burford,
Oxfordshire OX18 4RG
01993 822113
www.jessesmithbutchers.co.uk

TRADITIONAL CHRISTMAS SHOP

This specialist shop is about much more than tinsel and glitter with a Christmas theme. Here you will find dozens of real collectors' items that are stocked throughout the year. A variety of Good Luck incense-burning character vessels rub shoulders with figures from Tchaikovsky's *Nutcracker*, there are carved wooden Nativity sets and a small collection of Russian nesting dolls. A large selection of the Christmas Tree decorations is German, mainly hand-crafted in wood, porcelain and brass.

High Street, Lechlade,
Gloucestershire GL7 3AD
01367 253184
www.thechristmasshop.org

FOXBURY FARM SHOP

Former National Producer of the Year winner, Foxbury Farm Shop stocks the full range of farm meats – beef, lamb, Gloucester Old Spot pork, chicken and duck – as well as cooked meats, milk, bread and locally grown vegetables, plus cheeses, delicious chutneys and local wines and bottled beers.

Burford Road, Brize Norton,
Oxfordshire OX18 3NX
01993 867385
www.foxburyfarm.co.uk

Visit

BUSCOT PARK

This late 18th-century neo-classical mansion contains the fine paintings and furniture of the Faringdon Collection Trust. Within the grounds are an Italianate water garden and a large walled garden. The church at Buscot has some fine examples of stained glass from the firm of Morris and Co, founded by Arts and Crafts man William Morris in 1861.

Estate Office, Buscot Park, Faringdon,
Oxfordshire SN7 8BU
0845 345 3387
www.nationaltrust.org.uk

THE PENDON MUSEUM

The museum at Long Wittenham reproduces in miniature scenes of the English countryside around 1930 – an evocative depiction of a bygone era. Exquisitely modelled cottages, farms, fields and chalky lanes recall the quiet charm of the Vale of White Horse. The museum also has railway relics and a reconstructed GWR signal box.

01865 407365
www.pendonmuseum.com

MINSTER LOVELL HALL & DOVECOTE

One of the prettiest and most unspoilt old villages in the area; there's an attractive 15th-century church, a stone bridge over the River Windrush, and the imposing and extensive ruins of Minster Lovell Hall, steeped in history and legend. The medieval dovecote nearby survives intact.

www.english-heritage.org.uk

Activity

OXFORD WALKING TOUR

Thomas Hardy's Jude likened Oxford to 'the heavenly Jerusalem'. Its history, beauty and tradition are admired throughout the globe, and the city ranks in importance alongside Rome, Athens and Paris. The best way to appreciate the ancient colleges and historic buildings of this world-class city is on a walking tour. Numerous facts about Oxford and its university life are provided by experienced guides.

01865 250551
www.visitoxford.org

CYCLING

Leave the car behind and explore Oxfordshire's back lanes and byways the healthy way. The Hanson Way, part of the National Cycle Network, heads north from Abingdon to Radley, Kennington and Oxford. Alternatively, cycle south to the picturesque village of Sutton Courtenay; in the churchyard you'll find the grave of controversial writer George Orwell.

Pedal Power, 92 The Vineyard, Oxford Road,
Abingdon, Oxfordshire OX14 3PB
01235 525123

The Walk - From Buscot To Kelmscott

A chance to see the home of 19th-century craftsman and designer William Morris.

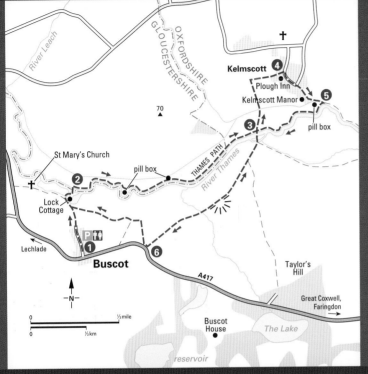

Walk Details

LENGTH: 4.75 miles (7.7km)

TIME: 2hrs

ASCENT: 82ft (25m)

PATHS: Riverside paths, fields, village lanes, 7 stiles

SUGGESTED MAP: aqua3 OS Explorer 1 70 Abingdon, Wantage & Vale of White Horse

GRID REFERENCE: SU 231976

PARKING: National Trust car park (free) in Buscot, signed 'Buscot Weir'

① Turn left. Walk back into Buscot to admire the arcaded pump. Retrace your steps and continue along the road, signed to the weir. The road becomes a track. Follow it round the edge of Village Field and cross the bridge. Keep right, to pass Lock Cottage. Follow the footpath over the weir. Bear left and continue, crossing the lock gate.

② Turn right, cross the stile and follow the path beside the river. Soon bear left and cross the bridge, with a view left to the main weir. Turn right; follow the Thames Path beside the meandering river. Cross the stile and continue past 2 wartime pill boxes and a gate. Go through a pair of gates. The roofs of Kelmscott appear ahead. Go

through gateway and on towards the bridge, passing through the trees.

③ Pass bridge, go through gate. Turn left up the field. At the far side, cross stile and 2 footbridges. Bear left and ahead up hedge (yellow waymarker). At the end turn right along path (possibly overgrown). Follow this into Kelmscott village.

④ Turn right to pass Plough Inn. Bear left along the road, passing Memorial Cottages and Manor Cottages. Keep right to reach Kelmscott Manor. Keep ahead on the track, pass World War II pill box. Turn right just before the river.

⑤ Cross the bridge. Go through the gate to join the Thames Path National Trail. Cross the stile and continue, passing pill box on left. Go

through gate by footbridge; turn left over bridge. Bear left then right over 2nd bridge. Cross stile and walk up track. Soon cross ditch; now head diagonally right across the field. At corner cross the stile and footbridge by the fingerpost. Turn right. Keep ahead up edge of field, with views of Buscot House, left. Follow track downhill, and bend right. Turn left over footbridge. Continue on path diagonally right across next 2 fields.

⑥ Go through gate by road. Turn right up drive. Look out for yellow waymarker and take footpath off left. Soon cross stile and veer left along edge of field. Cross stile and footbridge at other end, walk across Village Field. Turn left to retrace your route back to start in Buscot.

Three Horseshoes Inn

Buckinghamshire

The Inn

After a decade in the London hothouses of Le Gavroche and the Connaught Hotel, in 2005 chef Simon Crawshaw swapped the city for this 18th-century red-brick pub deep in the Chiltern Hills. He hasn't looked back. Lost down narrow leafy lanes, with valley views across rolling fields, the place draws walkers for ale and sandwiches, and foodies for accomplished modern cooking. Step through the latch door to find a cracking snug bar, replete with blackened beams, a flagstone floor and a blazing log fire in the original brick fireplace – the perfect spot for a post-walk pint of locally brewed Marlow Rebellion. Rooms ramble beyond, and from the split-level rear restaurant the view of the duck pond and its gradually sinking red telephone box will keep you amused between courses.

The quirky, individually decorated bedrooms are named after local shoots; all are done out in calming Farrow & Ball colours, with plump down duvets on big brass and wooden beds, an eclectic mix of furnishings, fluffy towels and Molton Brown toiletries in the tiled bathrooms.

The Essentials

Time at the Bar!
12-3pm, 6-11pm; closed Mon lunch and Sun from 8pm
Food: 12-2.30pm, 6.30pm-9.30pm

What's the Damage?
Main courses from £10.50

Bitter Experience:
Marlow Rebellion, Wells Bombardier

Sticky Fingers:
Children welcome

Muddy Paws:
Dogs welcome in the bar only

Zzzzz:
4 rooms, £85-£95; single £65

Anything Else?
Garden, car park, views

The Food

Everything is freshly prepared on the premises from local ingredients, and Simon's daily menus are varied and versatile to please both the booted walkers who call by at lunchtime for soup and sandwiches and the evening diners who travel miles to sample his innovative modern cooking. In the bar, tuck into tomato, lettuce and potato soup, served with olive and pesto bread, and a thick sandwich filled with roast Oxfordshire beef, wild rocket and horseradish, or you may like to try the home-made beef burger or, perhaps, wild mushroom and tarragon risotto. If you have time to linger, opt for the excellent-value set lunch menu, perhaps starting with chicken liver parfait with home-made piccalilli and following with steak and kidney pie.

The cooking style moves up a gear in the evening, with the short, imaginative menu offering the likes of seared scallops with chorizo and cauliflower fritter ahead of lamb rump with aubergine caviar and black olive jus or pan-fried cod with crushed peas and shrimp butter. Lemon cheesecake with confit of pineapple makes a tangy choice for afters. Don't miss the popular monthly live jazz and tapas evening.

What To Do

Shop

THE ANTIQUES TRAIL

Pick up a map and guide to buying antiques in the Thames Valley and you'll find a range of choice from the conventional to the positively quirky. The extent is best represented by the Swan at Tetsworth, near Thame. In this 40-room Grade II-listed Elizabethan coaching inn, you'll find antiques from more than 70 dealers. There's even an award-winning restaurant.

The Swan at Tetsworth, Thame, Oxfordshire OX9 7AB
01844 281777
www.theswan.co.uk

BURGERS

Head for Burgers, Marlow's long-established tea room on The Causeway, to enjoy the civilised ritual of afternoon tea after some serious shopping in the High Street, West Street and Spittal Street with their mixture of quality shops and independent retailers.

Tourist Information Centre, 31 High Street, Marlow, Buckinghamshire SL7 1AU
01628 483597
www.visitbuckinghamshire.org

THE GRANARY DELICATESSEN

Foodies will want to seek out this fantastic deli for its mind-boggling stock of 150 cheeses, ranging from top-grade parmesans and continental soft cheeses to a huge choice of English farmhouse cheeses. Watlington also has a very fine cookshop (The Galley) and a quality old-fashioned butchers (Calnan Brothers).

30 High Street, Watlington, Oxfordshire OX49 5PY
01491 613583
www.granarydeli.co.uk

Visit

HUGHENDEN MANOR

Looking at this striking Georgian house and its glorious rural setting, it's easy to see why Benjamin Disraeli chose Hughenden as his country seat in 1848. Now the property of the National Trust, the house holds letters from Queen Victoria, who regarded Disraeli as her favourite prime minister.

High Wycombe, Buckinghamshire HP14 4LA
01494 755565
www.nationaltrust.org.uk

WEST WYCOMBE HOUSE

If this National Trust treasure looks familiar, that's because it featured in the film version of Oscar Wilde's *The Importance of Being Earnest*, starring Judi Dench. The house dates back to the 18th century and was built for Sir Francis Dashwood, founder of the Dilettanti Society and the notorious Hellfire Club. Have a look at the nearby caves, open to Trust members.

West Wycombe Park, West Wycombe, Buckinghamshire HP14 3AJ
01494 513569
www.nationaltrust.org.uk

STONOR HOUSE & PARK

Home of Lord and Lady Camoys and occupied by the Stonor family for 800 years, the house dates back to 1190 but features a Tudor façade. View fine works of art, including paintings by old Italian masters, visit the medieval Catholic chapel, wander through the walled Italianate garden and explore the surrounding deer park.

Stonor, Henley-on-Thames, Oxfordshire RG9 6HF
01491 638587
www.stonor.com

Activity

GLIDING

Get away from it all in a lofty world of summer thermals and endless views by booking a trial lesson at the Booker Gliding Centre, one of Britain's top sites. The flight includes membership of the club for the day, so you can use all the facilities, and the lesson allows you plenty of time to get the feel of piloting a glider.

Wycombe Air Park, Marlow, Buckinghamshire SL7 3DP
01494 442501
www.bookergliding.co.uk

RED KITE-SPOTTING

This striking bird of prey was reintroduced to Britain in the 1990s and today the Chilterns are home to England's largest population, with around 200 pairs breeding in the area. Use the Red Kite Walks leaflet to guide you on a series of rambles exploring their haunts, or visit the cafe in Charwood Garden Centre, near Stokenchurch, to watch live CCTV images of a pair of kites nesting and rearing their chicks (April to mid-July).

High Wycombe Tourist Information Centre
Pauls Row, High Wycombe, Buckinghamshire HP11 2HQ
01494 421892
www.visitbuckinghamshire.org
Charwood Garden Centre
Wycombe Road, High Wycombe, Buckinghamshire HP14 3XB
01494 483761

The Walk - Disraeli's Des Res at West Wycombe

Visit Hughenden Manor, home of famous British statesman Benjamin Disraeli.

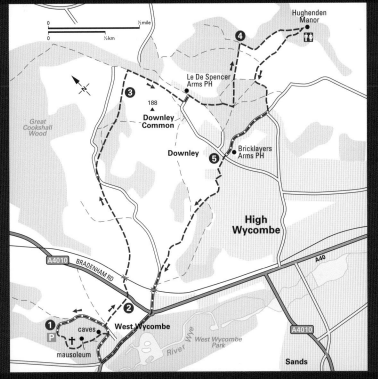

Walk Details

LENGTH: 7 miles (11.3km)

TIME: 2hrs 45min

ASCENT: 280ft (85m)

PATHS: Field, woodland and parkland paths, some roads, 5 stiles

SUGGESTED MAP: aqua3 OS Explorer 172 Chiltern Hills East

GRID REFERENCE: SU 826952

PARKING: Car park by church and mausoleum at West Wycombe

❶ From the car park pass to the immediate right of the church. Continue to the mausoleum and line up with the A40 below. Take the grassy path down hillside, avoiding path on right, and walk to fork. Keep right to steps; descend to the road. Bear left and pass Church Lane on right. Take next path on right; keeping to field righthand boundary. Look for stile and maintain same direction to the stile by the road. ❷ Cross over, making for the gate; pass under railway. At field keep ahead, keeping right of fence. Follow path to stile; cross track and continue up the slope. Make for 2 stiles by gate and barns. Join lane, swing right at the waymark and follow ride through woodland.

Eventually reach a stile with the path crossing the field beyond. ❸ On reaching the track, turn right and cut through the wood. Veer left at fork and head for road. Bear left into Downley. Turn left for pub or right to continue. Pass houses; when track bends left, keep ahead briefly, veering left at the waymark. Cross the common, following the path through clearings and into trees. At the National Trust sign, turn sharp left and follow the path through woods. Avoid path on left following white arrows. Pass the gate and continue ahead, up a fairly steep slope to the junction. ❹ Keep right; follow path to track. Swing left to visit Hughenden Manor or right to continue. Follow path

through parkland, making for trees. Bear immediately left, up the slope. Look for the house; turn right at the road. Pass the Bricklayers Arms and go straight ahead at junction. ❺ Keep ahead through trees to housing estate. Go forward for several paces at road, bearing right at 1st footpath sign. Follow path as it bends left and leads to junction. Swing left for several steps; veer right by houses, heading through trees to galvanised gate. Take the sunken path to right of the gate, follow it to fork and continue ahead. Head for lane and follow it towards West Wycombe. Cross Bradenham Road; proceed into village. Turn right into West Wycombe Hill Road. Head uphill to the car park.

The Sun Inn

Essex

The Sun Inn, High Street, Dedham, Essex CO7 6DF

The Essentials

Time at the Bar!
11am-11pm
Food: 12-2.30pm (Sat-Sun 3pm),
6.30-9.30pm (Fri-Sat 10pm)

What's the Damage?
Main courses from £10.50

Bitter Experience:
Adnams Broadside, Crouch Vale

Sticky Fingers:
Children welcome

Muddy Paws:
Dogs welcome

Zzzzz:
5 rooms, £85-£130

Anything Else?
Terrace, garden, car park

The Inn

As country pubs go in this historic part of the world, the 16th-century Sun Inn presents a pretty typical look, with beamed ceilings, exposed timbers, several open fires and plenty of panelling. But it sets itself apart as a laid-back pub serving local ales; as a great place for lingering meals in a rambling, atmospheric restaurant; and, with its classy rural-chic bedrooms, as the perfect weekend getaway. In summer the terrace is an additional lure.

Half-timbered walls, beams, wonky wood floors and some imaginative auction-room finds make up the five character bedrooms on the first floor. They come with super-sized beds, crisp white linen, plump pillows and extras like CD players, alongside the ubiquitous TV, mineral water and morning newspaper. Bathrooms are compact, but put together with the same modern eye for detail and have great showers (only one can fit a bath in).

The Food

Behind all the ancient beams and timbering is a kitchen with a young, modern attitude, working away and producing a breezy line-up of appealing modern Mediterranean dishes with a strong Italian accent. Short and to the point, the seasonal repertoire is built around top-notch produce (the greengrocers next door, selling locally grown fruit and veg, is owned by the inn). Purple sprouting broccoli and duck egg frittata with mixed salad leaves and pecorino, and grilled squid with borlotti beans, grilled red chilli, rocket and lemon could appear alongside unfussy mains such as Colne Valley lamb with roast green pumpkin and fennel, grilled polenta and salsa rossa, or local sea bass accompanied by potatoes, ceps, rosemary and spinach.

Desserts offer rich pickings: a glorious coffee, walnut and hazelnut cake with melted chocolate and cream, perhaps, or a deliciously creamy panna cotta with baked rhubarb. English cheeses served with fruit and chutney make a savoury alternative, especially if the 30 wines offered by the glass and the interesting wine list tempt you.

What To Do

Shop

LONG MELFORD

If you love browsing antique shops, book shops and small, independent boutiques, then head for pretty Long Melford, which is a renowned antique centre. Highlights of your visit may include the Lime Tree Gallery, which specialises in contemporary art and glass; Instep for quality Italian shoes and handbags; Swags and Bows for opulent fabrics, beautiful soft furnishings and design-led goods for the home; and Sue and Roger Kistruck's Posting House Pottery for individual handmade stoneware. Don't miss Long Melford Antiques Centre and its extensive range of antique furniture, silver, pictures and *objet d'arts*, or to rest and refuel at The Lounge, a stylish café serving great coffee and lunches.

Lime Tree Gallery
Hall Street 01787 319036
www.limetreegallery.com

Instep
Hall Street 01787 313403

Swags & Bows
Hall Street 01787 379860

Posting House Pottery
Hall Street 01787 311165

Long Melford Antiques Centre
Chapel Maltings, Little St Marys
01787 379287

The Lounge
Little St Marys 01787 379279

DEDHAM ART & CRAFT CENTRE

A large selection of furnishings, jewellery, books and clothing, plus paintings and work by local artists. The centre was originally a congregational chapel built in 1738.

High Street, Dedham, Essex CO7 6AD
01206 322666
www.dedhamartandcraftcentre.co.uk

Visit

SIR ALFRED MUNNINGS ART MUSEUM

The well-proportioned Tudor and Georgian Castle House is where the artist Sir Alfred Munnings lived and painted for 40 years. He called it 'the house of my dreams'. Noted for painting racehorses and equestrian scenes, Munnings is probably best known for capturing on canvas the spirit and essence of the East Anglian countryside as it was in the early 20th century. Many examples of his work are on view, as is his original studio.

Dedham, Colchester, Essex CO7 6AZ
01206 322127
www.siralfredmunnings.co.uk

LAYER MARNEY TOWER

England's tallest Tudor gatehouse has magnificent views, gardens, wildlife walks and 120 acres of parkland. The tea room serves both light lunches and tea and cakes, and the shop stocks a good range of souvenirs, cards, gifts and local produce. The site is a venue for rallies and theatre productions.

Colchester, Essex CO5 9US
01206 330784
www.layermarneytower.co.uk

BRIDGE COTTAGE

Situated just upstream from Flatford Mill, the 16th-century thatched Bridge Cottage houses an exhibition on John Constable – several of his paintings depict the cottage. There is a tea garden, shop, information centre and boat hire, and walks across National Trust land through the Dedham Vale.

Flatford, East Bergholt, Suffolk CO7 6UL
01206 298260
www.nationaltrust.org.uk

Activity

PAINTERS' TRAIL

The Painters' Trail is a 70-mile circular route exploring an area of Suffolk renowned for its links with famous artists – among them Constable, of course. Discover this corner of East Anglia on foot or by cycle – the trail takes you to the heart of the English countryside, and the Dedham Vale area.

Tourist Information Centre, 1 Queen Street, Colchester, Essex CO2 2PG
01206 282920

VINEYARD NATURE TRAIL

Explore 40 acres of vines, wild flower meadows, lakes and woodlands at Carter's Vineyard at Boxted. Follow the nature trail, take a tour of the vineyard and winery, and taste several English wines.

Carter's Vineyards, Green Lane, Boxted, Colchester, Essex CO4 5TS
01206 271136
www.cartersvineyards.co.uk

WALKING TOUR OF COLCHESTER

Discover the people, places and drama of Britain's oldest recorded town on a walking tour with one of Colchester's qualified guides. Go on patrol with a Roman soldier as he describes his duties on the streets; then return to 1648 with Master Barton and Mistress Turner as they re-enact the time when Colchester was under siege.

Tourist Information Centre, 1 Queen Street, Colchester, Essex CO2 2PG
01206 282920
www.colchesterwhatson.co.uk

The Walk - East Bergholt, Constable Country

A gentle walk through the landscape that inspired one of England's greatest artists.

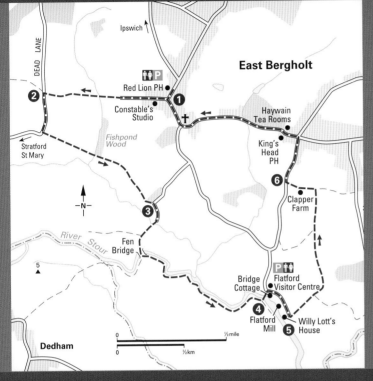

Walk Details

LENGTH: 3.75 miles (6km)

TIME: 1hr 30min

ASCENT: 246ft (75m)

PATHS: Roads, field paths and riverside meadows, 9 stiles

SUGGESTED MAP: aqua3 OS Explorer 196 Sudbury, Hadleigh & Dedham Vale

GRID REFERENCE: TM 069346

PARKING: Free car park next to Red Lion, East Bergholt

INFORMATION: This walk is over the county border in Suffolk

❶ Turn right out of the car park, past the Red Lion pub and post office. Turn right along the lane, note Constable's studio on the left. Continue walking past the chapel and cemetery, through the gate and down lefthand side of the meadow to cross the footbridge. Climb the path on the far side for views of Stour Valley, church towers at Dedham and Stratford St Mary.

❷ Turn left at the junction of paths to walk down Dead Lane, sunken footpath ('Dedham Road'). At the foot of the hill, turn left on to field-edge path. The path goes right then left to cross the stile on the edge of Fishpond Wood. Walk beside the wood for a few paces, then climb the stile into the field and walk beside a hedge to your right. Follow the path, which switches to the other side of the hedge and then back again before bending left around the edge of woodland to reach Fen Lane.

❸ Turn right along the lane, crossing the cart bridge and ignoring footpaths to the left and to the right as you continue towards wooden-arched Fen Bridge. Cross this bridge and turn left beside the River Stour towards Flatford on the wide open pasture of flood plain.

❹ Cross bridge to return to north bank of river beside Bridge Cottage. Turn right here, passing restored dry dock on way to Flatford Mill.

❺ Pass Willy Lott's House and turn left past car park. An optional loop, on National Trust permissive path, leads right around outside of Gibbonsgate Field beside newly planted hedge. Otherwise, keep left on the wide track and go through gate to join another National Trust path through Miller's Field. Stay on this path as it swings left and climbs to the top of field, then go ahead through the kissing gate, crossing 2 stiles to the T-junction of footpaths. Turn left along the edge of the meadow and continue down drive of Clapper Farm to Flatford Road.

❻ Turn right along the road. At the crossroads, turn left passing by the King's Head pub and Haywain Tea Rooms on way back to East Bergholt. Stay on pavement on right side of road to walk through churchyard and return to the start.

The Mistley Thorn

Essex

The Inn

People come here from all over, and you can see at once why the Mistley Thorn is popular. It's a solid early 18th-century building overlooking the magnificent Robert Adam-designed Swan Basin, and the estuary views guarantee an instant holiday feel. The low-key contemporary interior (soft colours, modern art) blends comfortably with period features, and there's a relaxed yet orderly feel to the place. For informal eating and drinking in what can be thought of as a gentrified pub, it's nothing short of a find.

Upstairs in the five large bedrooms the style owes a lot to New England, with simple decor and the use of lots of crisp white on walls and beds – which are ultra-comfortable king- and super-king-size topped with plump pillows. There are quirky touches also, with high ceilings sporting the odd chandelier. The two best rooms have estuary views; all have TVs, DVD and CD players and positively gleaming modern bathrooms, while home-made biscuits and ironing boards are just two of many thoughtful touches.

The Food

Chef/proprietor Sherri Singleton's feeling for comfort food is finely tuned, and she sends out smoked haddock chowder, home-made burgers and chicken fricassee for lunch. The cooking is not formulaic, however, and the starting point is tip-top ingredients – from Mersea Island oysters to locally caught pollack to lamb and beef reared nearby. Dinner expands the choice, adding twice-baked Oxford Blue soufflé, or crispy duck salad with Asian leaves, almonds and sweet ginger dressing, and free-range chicken breast with Aspall's cyder-mustard sauce, to calamari with lime, coriander and chilli, and Harwich lobster with lemon butter.

It is completely impossible to resist the home-made bread (and the accompanying olive oil for dipping), so it's fortunate that lightness of touch pervades the cooking. The presentation is appealing, too, especially when it comes to desserts: chocolate and amaretto torte is delicious – be sure to order it when it's on the menu. Service is friendly and professional, and the wine list reflects the care taken elsewhere.

The Essentials

Time at the Bar!
11am-3pm, 6.30-11pm
Food: 12-3pm, 6.30-9.30pm;
Sat 12-10pm; Sun 12-9pm

What's the Damage?
Main courses from £8.95

Bitter Experience:
Adnams Bitter, Mersea Island Ales

Sticky Fingers:
Children welcome, children's menu

Muddy Paws:
Dogs welcome in bar and bedrooms

Zzzzz:
5 rooms, £90-£105

Anything Else?
Small terrace, car park

What To Do

Shop

ARNA FARRINGTON GALLERY & CERAMIC STUDIO

View and buy some of the best arts, crafts and design by established artists and emerging new talent at this contemporary gallery.

High Street, Thorpe le Soken, Colchester, Essex CO16 0EA

01255 862355

www.arnaandfarrington.co.uk

HALL FARM SHOP & CAFE

Opened in 2001, the shop has rapidly expanded from selling just prize-winning beef and lamb to offering an extensive range of local foods from small producers across East Anglia. Cakes, preserves and pickles, fine cheeses and wines, local milk and free-range eggs, and delicious olives and oils. Much of the produce on sale in the farm shop is used in the smart new cafe situated in a converted 16th-century cattle byre, which looks out across Dedham Vale to Dedham church.

Stratford St Mary, Colchester, Essex CO7 6LS

01206 322572

www.hallfarmshop.co.uk

H GUNTON

A long-established family grocer, Guntons is now a high-class deli selling fine East Anglian products, such as locally reared meat, salt from Maldon and even olive oil from olives grown and pressed down the road – plus they have a huge selection of local and continental cheeses. Coffee is roasted on the premises: try a cup in the cafe.

81-83 Crouch Street, Colchester, Essex CO3 3EZ

01206 572200

www.guntons.co.uk

Visit

THE BETH CHATTO GARDENS

Beth Chatto has transformed this six-acre site over the last 40 years into a stunning informal garden. Alliums, verbascums and flowering grasses now inhabit what was once a dried-up river bed, while shade-loving plants illuminate the woodland. You can buy most of the plants at the well-stocked shop.

White Barn House, Elmstead Market, Colchester, Essex CO1 2JQ

01206 822007

www.bethchatto.co.uk

PAYCOCKE'S

A fine half-timbered 15th-century merchant's house run by the National Trust, Paycocke's has intricate woodwork and panelling – testimony to the wealth of the East Anglian wool and lace trade. There's a lovely cottage garden, too.

West Street, Coggeshall, Colchester, Essex CO6 1NS

01376 561305

www.nationaltrust.org.uk

OLD HARWICH

Once a bustling port, Old Harwich has a rich nautical history. Start your journey at The Redoubt, the 180ft (55m) circular fort built in 1808 to defend Harwich against a Napoleonic invasion – part of it is now a military museum, and battle enactments are held in summer months. The Harwich Society, which restored and maintain the fort, run guided tours starting from the Ha'penny Pier Visitor Centre on the quay. It's a town of great character, with cobbled criss-cross streets and narrow alleyways.

Harwich Redoubt Fort, Behind 29 Main Road, Harwich, Essex CO12 3LT

Activity

BOAT TRIP ALONG THE RIVER STOUR

Enjoy a trip through picturesque water meadows on *Rosette*, an elegant Edwardian launch. It starts at Sudbury – begin your journey with coffee and home-made cakes at The Granary on the quayside. The boat stops in a couple of pretty villages, and in Henny, where the Henny Swan pub is great for food and is right by the river.

The Granary, Quay Lane, Sudbury, Essex CO10 2AN

(Leaves at 11.30am, Sun only)

CYCLE THE PAINTER'S TRAIL

Hire a bike and explore scenes and skies painted by John Constable in this Area of Outstanding National Beauty. The length of the routes varies, but all are on well-established paths and quiet roads. Start at Manningtree station – but don't forget to pick up your Route Pack from Colchester Tourist Information Centre.

Colchester TIC: 01206 282920

www.realessex.co.uk/countryside

Bike hire at Colchester in Action Bikes: 01206 541744

THE ELECTRIC PALACE CINEMA

For all you fans of Cinema Paradiso! Built in 1911, this independent cinema is one of the oldest and least altered in the country, so it's a complete nostalgia-fest! It still has its silent screen, original projection room and rococo frontage. It's now run as a community cinema, showing films every weekend.

Kings Quay Street, Harwich, Essex CO12 3ER

01255 55333

www.electricpalace.com

The Walk - *Manningtree, England's Smallest Town*

Where Matthew Hopkins, the notorious Witchfinder General, was born and buried.

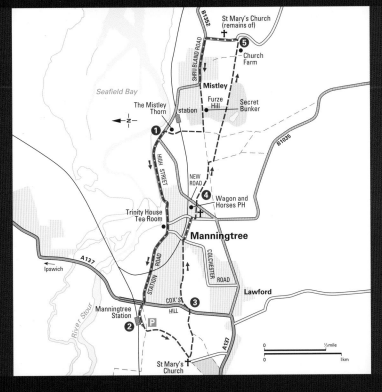

Walk Details

LENGTH: 7 miles (11.3km)

TIME: 3hrs 30min

ASCENT: 98ft (30m)

PATHS: Field paths, footpaths, tracks and sections of road, may be boggy, 5 stiles

SUGGESTED MAP: aqua3 OS Explorer 184 Colchester, Harwich & Clacton-on-Sea

GRID REFERENCE: TM 093322

PARKING: The Mistley Thorn car park, or pay-and-display at Manningtree Station; free at weekends

❶ From The Mistley Thorn, turn left into the High Street; follow The Walls by the River Stour to Manningtree. Turn left into the High Street. Walk for about 1 mile (1.6km) along Station Road.

❷ Turn right at Dedham following the fingerpost ('Lawford') on the steep, grassy path to St Mary's Church. Go through the black gate, keep the church on your right, cross the stile over the church wall. Turn left and, at the wooden post, follow the yellow waymark half right across the meadow. Cross the earth bridge over Wignell Brook, go left uphill keeping line of trees on your right. Just before the house at the top of the hill, cross the stile and bear left to Cox's Hill, on to the A137.

❸ Cross Cox's Hill, turn left and after 40yds (37m), at the fingerpost ('Essex Way'), turn right. Walk downhill with the trees on your left and the pond on your right. Pass the housing estate on the left and cross the plank bridge over the stream. Follow the gravel path through the Owl Conservation Area. Ignoring the concrete path on the left, turn half-right on to cross-field path towards the playing fields. Cross Colchester Road, and at the T-junction turn right into Trinity Road, ignoring the signs for Essex Way. At the Evangelical church turn left between houses to New Road, Wagon and Horses pub is on the left.

❹ Cross New Road and follow the yellow waymarked footpath between backs of houses. At T-junction turn left on to the wide bridleway. After 70yds (64m) follow the waymark half-right and rejoin Essex Way. Continue, crossing the earth bridge over the brook and 2 stiles. Just after the 2nd stile, follow the track between 2 concrete posts into the wooded slopes of Furze Hill. Emerge from the woods, go ahead keeping to the field-edge path to Church Farm. Turn left on to Heath Road.

❺ Cross the road to the low wall to the remains of St Mary's Church. Continue north and turn left on to the B1352 and into Shrubland Road, which becomes a green lane. Cross the 1st stile on the right and walk under railway. Turn left into Mistley Green, which joins the High Street.

The Three Crowns Inn

Herefordshire

The Essentials

Time at the Bar!
12-3pm, 7-11pm (closed Mon)
Food: 12-2.30pm, 7-10pm

What's the Damage?
Main courses from £14.95

Bitter Experience:
Wye Valley Butty Bach, Timothy
Taylor Landlord

Sticky Fingers:
Children welcome, small portions
available

Muddy Paws:
No dogs

Zzzzz:
1 room, £95

Anything Else?
Terrace, garden, car park

The Three Crowns Inn, Ullingswick, Herefordshire HR1 3JQ

The Inn

It's not easy to find the Three Crowns, tucked away in the depths of the Herefordshire countryside, but it's certainly worth it when you get there. Flagstone floors, scrubbed wooden tables, log fires, hops hanging from black beams and the smell of wood smoke in the air – in other words, all the essentials of a good country pub – are here. A recent extension houses an unfussy slate-floored dining room, furnished with specially commissioned English oak chairs and tables.

Upstairs is one stylish bedroom where urban chic (pale carpets, soft Italian leather sofa) meets country cottage (sloping ceiling, distant views of the Sugar Loaf Mountain). Bed linen on the contemporary iron and wood bed is white Egyptian cotton, and the mattress, with different springs on each side, is perfect for mismatched partners. The huge bathroom is straight out of *Country Living* magazine with its opulent red marmoleum floor, two basins on black stands and contemporary roll-top bath. Watch a DVD, listen to digital radio or enjoy the peace – there are no other guests and your neighbours are sheep.

The Food

Locals meet here to enjoy a pint of well-kept Hobsons; others are here for Brent Castle's consistently well-judged no-frills food. Apart from the excellent fish, ingredients are local (many come no further than Brent's own garden) and largely organic. A daily changing menu is chalked up on a blackboard and may include a starter of roast woodcock with a risotto of its liver and winter vegetables, or stir-fried mussels with black beans, ginger and spring onions. Main courses could be crisp belly of Shortwood Farm pork with Three Crowns black pudding, red cabbage and mustard mash, or grilled sole with capers and beurre noisette.

There is an impressive selection of local cheeses, and puddings include winter fruit compote with rice-pudding ice cream and chocolate fondant with pistachio ice cream and griottine cherries. The menu is sensibly priced and the blackboard lunch menu represents particularly good value for money at £12.95 for two courses and £14.95 for three. But think seriously about coming for dinner and staying the night to avoid negotiating those country lanes.

What To Do

Shop

DUNKERTONS ORGANIC CIDER

The Dunkerton family has been farming this smallholding for nearly 30 years using traditional methods, including a 1930s press and mill – you can watch the process during autumn. The orchard is 100 percent organic, planted with ancient varieties. Buy their bottled award-winning cider, or take your own container and buy it on draught. Due to the scarceness of the perry pear, they produce the only organic sparkling perry in the country.

Pembridge, Leominster, Herefordshire HR6 9ED 01544 388653 www.dunkertons.co.uk

THE LITTLE BIG CHEESE SHOP

This shop in Ludlow stocks an impressive range of local cheeses – take home some Monkland or the delicious Long Mynd goats' cheese. Ludlow is a gourmet's heaven, with a huge variety of independent food shops in the town, including Farmer's, a back-to-basics high-quality grocer, with boxes of wild mushrooms and local organic fruit and vegetables piled high.

124 Corve Street, Ludlow, Shropshire
Farmer's
Mill Street, Ludlow, Shropshire

OLD MERCHANT'S HOUSE ANTIQUE CENTRE

This Grade II listed building right in the heart of Leominster is home to more than 25 dealers offering a wide selection of china, glass, sci-fi collectibles, jewellery, books, pictures, silver, furniture and more.

10 Corn Square, Leominster, Herefordshire HR6 8LR 01568 616141

Visit

BROADFIELD COURT & GARDENS

This Domesday manor house is set in four acres of a quintessentially English garden, with a David Austin rose garden, yew hedges, courtyards and an old walled kitchen garden. There's a shop and award-winning cafe where you can get a cracking roast on a Sunday – and enjoy a glass of classic wine from the local vineyard.

Bowley Lane, Bodenham, Hereford, Herefordshire HR1 3LG 01568 797483

BROCKHAMPTON ESTATE

At the heart of this huge estate lies Lower Brockhampton, a romantic timber-framed manor house dating back to the late 1300s. It is surrounded by a moat and you enter via a timber-framed gatehouse. There's a ruined chapel and miles of walks through park and woodland, home to a rich variety of wildlife.

Bromyard, Herefordshire HR6 9PW 01885 488099 www.nationaltrust.org.uk

CROFT CASTLE

'See 14 counties on a clear day' is the claim at the National Trust's Croft Castle. This handsome 14th- and 15th-century pink-stoned castle has a fine Georgian gothic staircase and ceilings, and an avenue of 350-year-old Spanish chestnuts. Wander through the restored walled garden and vineyard, admire the ornamental rose beds and ancient plants, and indulge your gardening whims in the well-stocked shop.

Yarpole, Leominster, Herefordshire HR6 9PW 01568 780246 www.nationaltrust.org.uk

Visit (continued)

ST MARY'S CHURCH

Follow the brown signs down winding country lanes to locate this gem of a church surrounded by fields and orchards. It contains some of the finest early medieval wall paintings in Britain, with frescos from the 12th century.

Kempley, Dymock, Gloucestershire

Activity

BALLOONING

Lift off from the impressive surroundings of Eastnor Castle and glide silently across the Herefordshire countryside for this experience of a lifetime.

www.virginballoonflights.co.uk

CYCLE THE CIDER ORCHARDS

Hire a couple of bikes and wend your way through old cider orchards, quiet river valleys and some of Herefordshire's beautiful black-and-white villages. There will always be several tea rooms and pubs to visit en route.

Petchfield Farm, Elton, Ludlow, Shropshire SY8 2HJ 01568 770755 www.wheelywonderfulcycling.co.uk

LUDLOW RACES

Ludlow is a National Hunt course, retaining much of its Edwardian charm, although the welcome is absolutely up to date – Ludlow likes to think of itself as 'the friendliest course in the country'. Treat yourself to lunch in a private viewing box overlooking the track and surrounding countryside.

Bromfield, Ludlow, Shropshire SY8 2BT 01584 856221 www.ludlow-racecourse.co.uk

The Walk - Two Churches in the Frome Valley

Secluded churches and special wild service trees are set amid pastures on this easy ramble.

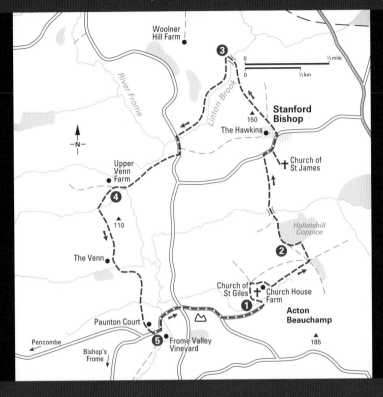

Walk Details

LENGTH: 4.75 miles (7.7km)

TIME: 2hrs 30min

ASCENT: 475ft (145m)

PATHS: Field paths, dirt tracks, lanes and minor roads, 14 stiles

SUGGESTED MAP: aqua3 OS Explorer 202 Leominster & Bromyard

GRID REFERENCE: SO 679502

PARKING: Roadside just before grassy lane to Acton Beauchamp's church – please tuck in tightly

❶ Leave the churchyard by the iron gate in the top corner. Soon, enter the orchard. Skirt round to the right, passing the outbuildings of Church House Farm and then down to pass behind the tall barns. Now the orchard track ascends. When you are 110yds (100m) beyond the power lines, at the corner of the plantation, turn left (blue waymarker), to walk between the orchard rows. At the end turn left. In roughly 160yds (146m), well before the power lines and just before the trees that are shielding the pond, go right. Soon you'll have the hedge on your left; reach the gate and the stile made from 3 railway sleepers.

❷ Once you are through Halletshill Coppice drop straight down to the footbridge. Now go straight up the bank, swapping hedge sides, to reach the minor road. Turn right. Take the opportunity to visit the church. You will notice that the stonework is of a similar vintage to that in Acton Beauchamp – Norman and 13th-century. Return to the road and turn right. At the entrance to The Hawkins take the stile, then follow the waymarkers across the track to skirt this farm. Now head down over the pastures to cross the footbridge over Linton Brook.

❸ Turn left, walking beside Linton Brook for just over 0.5 mile (1km), to the road. Turn left for 160yds (146m). Turn right. Now the driveway to Upper Venn Farm runs for 0.5 mile (800m). Just before the farm buildings, move left, to reach a stile roughly 70yds (64m) along the edge of the field from the farm.

❹ Cross the field diagonally, to the gate in the left hedge. Turn left across the field, aiming slightly uphill, beside the residual mature oaks. You'll find the stile beyond the electricity pole. Pick up the rough track to The Venn. Admire its cream walls and exposed timbers and then turn away, along the drive. Follow this down to the minor road.

❺ Turn left, passing Frome Valley Vineyard on a sharp bend. At the crossroads go straight over. Climbing this quite steep lane, the Church of St Giles comes into view. Take the 1st turning on the left to return to your car.

The Stagg Inn

Herefordshire

The Essentials

Time at the Bar!
12-2.30pm, 6-11pm; closed Mon
Food: 12-2pm, 6.30-9pm; no food Sun
evening or all day Mon

What's the Damage?
Main courses from £11.90

Bitter Experience:
Hobsons Choice, Hobsons Town Crier

Sticky Fingers:
Children welcome, small portions
available

Muddy Paws:
Dogs welcome in the bar

Zzzzz:
6 rooms, £85-£120

Anything Else?
Terrace, garden, car park

The Inn

The Stagg is all you hope a village pub will be – and more. Hops and pub jugs hang from the beams in the bar, where you'll be welcome whether you are a walker with muddy boots and a wet dog, a local, calling in for a pint, or simply someone who is hungry and in search of a good meal. Beyond the bar are three uncluttered dining rooms. There are three beamed bedrooms in the pub: no gimmicks here, just classic country rooms with sensible bathrooms, polished rug-scattered floors, antique furniture, and brass beds made up with feather duvets and pillows and white cotton bedlinen.

If you're worried that a room in a pub might be too noisy, a short walk up the road takes you to the Vicarage (a gracious, mostly Georgian, country house) where there are three more bedrooms. The hall opens into a sitting room complete with grandfather clock and wood-burning stove, and up the oak staircase are the enormous, elegantly traditional bedrooms. Views are either of the church at the front, or the garden with croquet lawn, terrace and free-range hens at the back.

The Food

A board in the bar lists all the local food producers who supply the Stagg kitchens – evidence of the emphasis placed on quality, fresh ingredients. Seasonality, too, is obvious in Steve Reynolds's consistently precise cooking. The fairly priced menu is uncomplicated – comfort food with a light touch. Starters may include home-smoked haddock fish cake, and the mains tend to be meaty: Herefordshire beef fillet with béarnaise sauce and chips, or rack of lamb with baby shepherd's pie, though there will be a fish dish such as succulent sea bass fillet with mushroom duxelle and herb oil with dauphinois potato, and a vegetarian option.

A whole menu is devoted to local and Welsh cheeses, and make sure you leave room for puddings such as treacle tart with local clotted cream or three crème brûlées of vanilla, elderflower and lemon. Offerings on a blackboard bar menu include devilled kidneys and Berkshire Black pork sausages – wash them down with a glass of locally brewed beer or cider, or choose a wine from the sensibly priced and helpfully annotated wine list.

What To Do

Shop

LEOMINSTER MARKET

The town is known for its Friday market, with its closely packed stalls in Corn Square. Also of note are the many antique shops, ranging from high quality to cheap and cheerful bric-a-brac. Regular antique auctions are held at the Fine Art sales rooms.

Leominster Tourist Information Centre,
1 Corn Square, Leominster,
Herefordshire HR6 8LR
01568 616460
www.visitherefordshire.co.uk

MONKLAND CHEESE DAIRY

Watch Little Hereford cheese being made by hand, then enjoy a ploughman's lunch in the cafe, washed down with local cider, beer or apple juice. Complete your visit by taking home a selection of local cheeses, wines, beers and chutneys from the farm shop. The cheeses are also on sale in the Mousetrap Cheese Shops in Leominster, Hereford and Ludlow.

The Pleck, Monkland, Leominster,
Herefordshire HR6 9DB
01568 720307
www.mousetrapcheese.co.uk

THE OLD CHAPEL GALLERY

Here you'll find an eclectic range of the best of British contemporary arts and crafts, including cards, prints, original paintings, ceramics, glass, jewellery, ironwork, furniture, wearables, sculpture and much more. The gallery was converted from a redundant Victorian chapel in 1989.

East Street, Pembridge,
Herefordshire HR6 9HB
01544 388842
www.oldchapelgallery.co.uk

Visit

BERRINGTON HALL

Occupying a magnificent setting above a wide valley with views to the Brecon Beacons, Berrington Hall dates back to the late 18th century. It was built by Henry Holland and is set in parkland laid out by Capability Brown. The external appearance is somewhat austere but inside is a different story, with decorated ceilings and a striking staircase.

Leominster, Herefordshire HR6 0DW
01568 615721
www.nationaltrust.org.uk

HEREFORD MUSEUM & ART GALLERY

In this splendid Victorian Gothic building you'll find exhibits like a Victorian school desk with slates and a dressing-up box: there are hands-on displays for all ages and regular programmes of events and activities, as well as changing exhibitions of paintings, prints, photography and crafts.

Broad Street, Hereford,
Herefordshire HR4 9AU
01432 260692
www.herefordshire.gov.uk

HERGEST CROFT GARDENS

A riot of colour dazzles the eye at Hergest. Here are four gardens for all seasons, from spring bulbs to autumn shades. Wherever you look there are roses, brilliant azaleas, plus an old-fashioned kitchen garden growing unusual vegetables. There are also more than 60 champion trees in one of the finest collections of trees and shrubs in the country.

Kington, Herefordshire HR5 3EG
01544 230160
www.hergest.co.uk

Activity

GROVE GOLF CENTRE

You can spend all day here trying out the two linked 9-hole golf courses or the 20-bay floodlit driving range. There's also a very well-stocked golf shop, buggies available and equipment for hire. Continue that competitive edge in Grove's ten pin bowling centre and round things off with something to eat at the Hickory Restaurant.

Ford Bridge, Leominster,
Herefordshire HR6 0LE
01568 610602
www.grovegolf.co.uk

RALLYING

After some instruction, you are free to experience driving rally cars on a loose gravel surface with timed laps against the clock. Enjoy the thrill and excitement as a passenger while a professional hits competition speed over a rally stage on this action-packed day in the Welsh mountains.

Phil Price Rally School, Coed Harbour,
Llangunllo, Knighton, Powys LD7 1TP
01547 550300
www.philprice.co.uk

WALK, DRIVE OR CYCLE

Discover the delightful black-and-white villages of North Herefordshire on this 40-mile (64-km) circular trail set out in a clockwise direction – you can join at any point. En route you step back into a bygone age, discovering a wealth of ancient timber-framed buildings and historic churches.

Leominster Tourist Information Centre,
1 Corn Square, Leominster,
Herefordshire HR6 8LR
01568 616460
www.visitorlinks.com

The Walk - Overlooking Wales at Hergest Ridge

Up to a glorious ridge for a glimpse of another country - Wales.

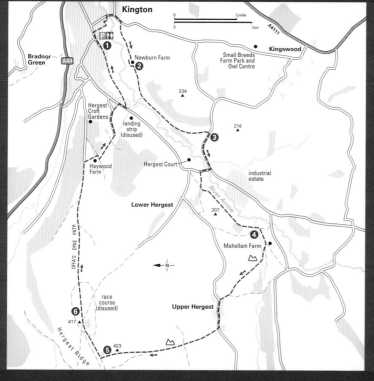

Walk Details

LENGTH: 7.5 miles (12.1km)

TIME: 3hrs 30min

ASCENT: 1,115ft (340m)

PATHS: Meadows, field paths, excellent tracks, 14 stiles

SUGGESTED MAP: aqua3 OS Explorer 201 Knighton & Presteigne

GRID REFERENCE: SO 295565

PARKING: Mill Street car park (east and west sides of Crabtree Street)

❶ Walk down the High Street. Take alley on right, between hairdresser and shop. Zig-zag to Bridge Street. Turn right. Cross River Arrow. Take the driveway to Newburn Farm.

❷ Walk through the farmyard. Go round 3 sides, then take the gate into the field. After the area planted with trees, take the stile to the righthand field edge, under huge oak limbs. Walk for over 0.5 mile (800m) through meadows, curving left to the stile and steps down to the road.

❸ Turn right, and right again to cross Hergest Bridge. After 100yds (91m) take the left fingerpost. Along right field edge, cross the stile into trees. On the track, bend left. Cross the meadow to line of sweet chestnuts. Over difficult stile

turn right, along an awkward path across a steep, wooded bank. After 325yds (297m) stile puts you into another meadow. Cross footbridge. Drop slightly to skirt woodland and reach marker post. Cross 2 more stiles in this pasture. Go ahead and fractionally right for 80yds (73m) to single-plank stile and waymarker (possibly obscured). Another, more substantial, double-stiled footbridge stands 40yds (37m) ahead. Bear left, to find, in 100yds (91m), steps down to the metal footbridge.

❹ At the road on caravan site turn right. Just 30yds (27m) after gates find stile (perhaps overgrown), right. Almost immediately, take the 2nd stile beside the huge oak. At the track beside Mahollam Farm bear

right, downhill. Do not stay on green lane, but go right, finding another metal footbridge. Ascend steeply, soon in farmland. Cross fields to road. Turn right. Go left for 400yds (366m), to gate. Now go straight up to trig point on Hergest Ridge.

❺ The path leads to the pool. Turn right. Continue for 1.5 miles (2.4km). Once on the road again, 30yds (27m) after sign, 'Kington – centre for walking', turn right. Round Haywood Farm, continue to the cattle grid. Along road look for fingerpost by 'No. 31'. Go down this field. Turn away from Kington for 120yds (110m); turn sharply left, '16 Tatty Moor'. Cross the meadows to the recreation ground. Join Park Avenue, which becomes Mill Street

The Verzon

Herefordshire

The Inn

This Georgian country house has been lovingly transformed into a stylish hotel. The bar and brasserie, in particular, achieve the balance of being both chic and sophisticated yet comfortably informal. Exposed brickwork provides the background for contemporary artwork, and background music is as soft as the leather chairs. In summer, everyone spills out onto the terrace to enjoy the stunning views over the Herefordshire countryside and Malvern Hills beyond.

An impressive modern chandelier dominates the stairs leading up to the eight bedrooms, which are named after local cider apples. All the rooms are large, unashamedly luxurious and each has its own individual style. In one there is a modern oriental four-poster, in another a celebrity-style leather bed, and there are free-standing baths in two rooms.

Neutral furnishings are combined with bold Osborne & Little wallpapers, designer and antique furniture, original fireplaces, wood floors and thick carpets. Hand-made Vi-Spring mattresses, Hungarian goose-down pillows, feather duvets and fine Egyptian cotton bedlinen make an early night irresistible.

The Essentials

Time at the Bar!
11am-11pm
Food: 12-2.30pm, 7-9.30pm (Sun 9pm)

What's the Damage?
Main courses from £12

Bitter Experience:
Wye Valley Butty Bach

Sticky Fingers:
Children welcome; half portions of main menu

Muddy Paws:
Dogs welcome on the terrace only

Zzzzz:
8 rooms, £80-£150

Anything Else?
Terrace, garden, car park

The Food

Eat in the bustling bar or calmer brasserie – in both, the atmosphere is informal yet the service is attentive and unobtrusive. Whether you just fancy a light snack or have a heartier appetite, the menu is spot on. At lunch time, British classics such as a miniature game pie with Savoy cabbage rub shoulders with an Asian-style beef and noodle salad. A tapas-type platter of cured meat, smoked fish, cheese and chutneys is good for sharing, and sandwiches are substantial.

The dinner menu might offer some trendy surprises such as roast kangaroo with vanilla and balsamic cabbage, but there is also steak and black pudding mash or chargrilled aubergine cannelloni.

Puddings range from the comforting (vanilla and cinnamon rice pudding with apple crumble) to the luxurious (chocolate and allspice panna cotta, pistachio layer cake and coffee ice cream). There is a good wine list and, as you'd expect in this part of Herefordshire, the bar serves local beers, ciders and perry.

What To Do

Shop

LITTLE VERZONS FRUIT FARM

Buy organic seasonal fruity fare at this family-run business, including home-made apple juice and mouthwatering apple pies. But the outright speciality is the range of eye-catching and unusual hanging baskets – take a couple home with you and and you'll be the envy of your neighbours.

Hereford Road, Ledbury,
Herefordshire HR8 2PZ
01531 670816

THREE CHOIRS VINEYARD

A must for all discerning wine lovers, Three Choirs is England's leading award-winning single-estate vineyard. Choose from white, rose or red – and sample them both in the restaurant before you buy. The Cats Whiskers ale is also brewed on the premises.

Newent, Gloucestershire GL18 1LS
01531 890223
www.three-choirs-vineyards.co.uk

WOBAGE MAKERS GALLERY

Wobage Farm Craft Workshops overlook South Herefordshire. Pottery, wood items and jewellery are produced by nine makers and exhibited in the 18th-century barns.

Upton Bishop, Ross-on-Wye,
Herefordshire HR9 7QP
01989 780495

Visit

HELLENS HOUSE

Tudor England lives again. Flagstone floors, suits of armour, wood panelling and a tale of thwarted love. There are no ropes to keep you at arm's length – the owners want you to get up close and personal. Concerts, poetry readings and workshops are regular events. Wander the walled knot garden, with its rare 17th-century dovecote.

Much Marcle, Ledbury,
Herefordshire HR8 2LY
01531 660504
www.hellensmanor.com

EASTNOR CASTLE

This is a proper Gothic picture-book castle, looming in the Malvern Hills. Much of the interior was designed by Pugin – the drawing room, with its stained glass, tiles and ornate fittings is in the High Gothic revival style. The setting is perfect for outdoor theatre – Shakespeare is regularly staged on the terraces overlooking the lake.

Ledbury, Herefordshire HR8 1RL
01531 633160
www.eastnorcastle.com

ELGAR MUSEUM

Sir Edward Elgar was born in this picture-postcard cottage looking out onto the Malvern Hills, and lived here most of his life. You can see a collection of priceless manuscripts, scores, concert programmes and press cuttings – and albums of informal family snap shots too. A fascinating insight into the great composer's life.

Crown East Lane, Lower Broadheath,
Worcester, Worcestershire WR2 6RH
01905 333224
www.elgarfoundation.org

Activity

BALLOONING

The Wye Valley countryside is spectacular, so why not explore it from the air? You'll drift along at tree-top height, then soar effortlessly to thousands of feet above the earth – an unforgettable day out, which is always rounded off nicely with a glass or two of celebratory champagne.

Wye Valley Ballooning, Bridstow,
Ross-on-Wye, Herefordshire HR9 6AJ
01989 673134
www.wyevalleyaviation.co.uk

GLIDING

Take a single flight in a two-seater glider with an instructor, or go up three times on a day course and eventually progress to controlling the flight yourself.

Shobdon Airfield, Shobdon,
Herefordshire HR6 9NR
01568 708908
www.shobdon.com

LEDBURY GHOST WALK

Not for the faint-hearted – Ledbury has more than its fair share of ghosts. Meet by the Market House at 8pm and prepare to be scared out of your skin. You'll encounter characters from the past, notably a serving wench who was fatally wounded in the Civil War. The walk takes in the oldest, most historic parts of this black-and-white town, and one or two pubs as well.

Market House, Ledbury, Herefordshire
Elisabeth Galvin (guide): 01531 650414

The Walk - Hereford's Lost Canal

Along an old waterway, now being restored, at Ashperton.

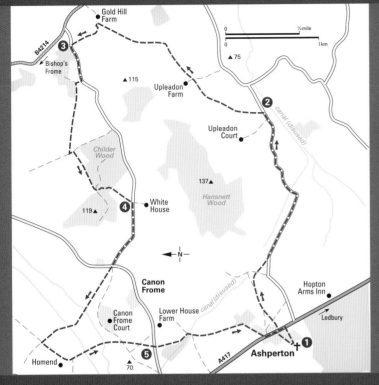

Walk Details

LENGTH: 7.75 miles (12.5km)

TIME: 3hrs 30min

ASCENT: 260ft (79m)

PATHS: Field and woodland paths, minor roads, at least 35 stiles

SUGGESTED MAP: aqua3 OS Explorer 202 Leominster & Bromyard

GRID REFERENCE: SO 642415

PARKING: St Bartholomew's Church, Ashperton

❶ From the car park take 'forty shillings' gate, behind the houses. (For 10 paces this path is in a garden.) Join the track to the A417. Turn left, then right, beside the driveway. Follow the fingerpost across meadows for 600yds (549m). Find gate by cricket net. Veer right. Cross driveway down field. Join Haywood Lane near house. Turn left. Follow this for 1 mile (1.6km). Find the stile on the left just beyond the gate, 100yds (91m) after the driveway to Upleadon Court.

❷ Cross arable fields and ditch, then Upleadon Farm's driveway. Aim for the far lefthand corner. Skirt the woodland to the left, later striking left (waymarked) up huge field. At Gold Hill Farm go right of tall shed.

Behind this, turn left, then briefly up and right. Follow boundary to road.

❸ Turn left for 0.25 mile (400m). Where the road turns left continue for 0.5 mile (800m), initially beside the wood. Over rotting plank turn left but in 25yds (23m) turn right. After 500yds (457m) enter trees. On leaving them strike half-right for White House.

❹ Turn right along road. At junction, take footpath opposite (ditch on right). Beware of hitting your head on horizontal tree trunk just after single-plank footbridge. Walk 700yds (640m) across fields, over 3 footbridges and under power lines, passing through gap to stile, but do not cross – note 3 waymarkers on its far side. Turn left, heading

towards old orchards. Just beyond Homend find stile in far lefthand corner, shielded by ash and elder. Turn left, soon moving right to double gates flanking wide concrete bridge. After avenue keep ahead, eventually veering right. Go 550yds (503m), crossing driveway to Canon Frome Court, then another track, finally reaching road by spinney.

❺ Cross road; walk to canal. Turn left. In 140yds (128m) turn right, over canal. Veer left and uphill, finding large oak in top lefthand corner. Keep this line despite field boundary shortly curving away. At copse turn right, later moving left into indistinct lane. Village hall heralds A417. Turn left, along pavement, then right to church.

The Howard Arms

Warwickshire

The Inn

Ilmington is a typically pretty Cotswold village and the mellow stone
Howard Arms a real delight, suitably rambling like any self-respecting
400-year-old building should be. Five arched and bay windows overlook the
well-kept village green and there's a pretty rear garden that comes into its
own when used for alfresco meals in summer.

Inside, the inn has been carefully remodelled and the result is a popular,
hugely civilised modern dining pub that manages to retain full period charm
and character, with a flagstone bar, wooden beams, an open-plan dining
room and bags of informal atmosphere.

Robert and Gill Greenstock are ex-hoteliers, and past experience clearly
shows in the style and furnishings of the three charming bedrooms
upstairs. Each one is highly individual – a beamed ceiling and antique
country-style furnishings in one; bright American patchwork quilts and
painted furniture in another; and a lavish half-tester, rich fabrics and
antique pieces in the third. Compact modern bathrooms and the luxury of
total peace and quiet are further pluses, and after a good night's sleep, you
can look forward to a superb breakfast.

The Essentials

Time at the Bar!
11am-3pm, 6-11pm,
Sun 12-3.30pm, 6.30-10.30pm
Food: 12-2pm, 7-9pm

What's the Damage?
Main courses from £10.50

Bitter Experience:
Everard's Tiger,
Hook Norton Hooky

Sticky Fingers:
Children welcome

Muddy Paws:
Guide dogs only

Zzzzz:
3 rooms, £120-£138

Anything Else?
Terrace, garden, car park

The Food

The style of food suits this inn well: down to earth, first-class ingredients and unfussy presentation. A blackboard above the vast inglenook fireplace in the dining area lists the weekly-changing menu, on which local produce features prominently – whether it is game, vegetables and soft fruit, or Hereford beef and Warwickshire lamb from a butcher in Stratford-upon-Avon. And so it continues with oak-smoked organic salmon with warm potato cake and sour cream, or creamed leeks and goats' cheese tart, followed, perhaps, by chargrilled port escalopes with apple and sage compote and cider sauce.

Fresh fish is a strong suit, too, delivered daily from Cornwall – say, grilled lemon sole with lime, chilli and parmesan butter, or lightly crumbed fillet of sea bass served with baby spinach and saffron aïoli. And pub favourites such as battered haddock with pea purée and home-made tartare sauce, or beef, ale and mustard pie make regular appearances.

The home-made puddings are not to be missed either, the repertoire running to toffee meringue, steamed spotted dick with custard, and spiced apple and sultana flapjack crumble.

What To Do

Shop

GUILD OF WORKSHOPS
For hand-crafted jewellery, pottery and stoneware visit the Guild of Workshops in Chipping Campden's Sheep Street. This classic Cotswold town also has antiques, individual gift shops, classy lifestyle shops, boutiques and artisan food stores.

Sheep Street, Chipping Campden, Gloucestershire
www.chippingcampden.co.uk

VINEGAR HILL
Vinegar Hill is a simply delicious 'lifestyle emporium', offering individual home furnishings, accessories, gifts, jewellery and much more. The changing stock is chosen with an eye for the quirky and the unusual.

1 Meer Street, Stratford-upon-Avon, Warwickshire CV37 6QB
01789 415191
www.vinegar-hill.co.uk

WHICHFORD POTTERY
Tucked away in the fold of a pretty Warwickshire valley, this traditional pottery specialises in making classic English flowerpots by hand. Choose from small or large ornate urns or flowerpots with contemporary designs, and be inspired by the plantings in the courtyard garden. Visit the craft shop and make your own pots by joining an adult pottery workshop.

Whichford, Shipston-on-Stour, Warwickshire CV36 5PG
01608 684416
www.whichfordpottery.com

Visit

HIDCOTE MANOR & KIFTSGATE COURT GARDENS
Hidcote is one of England's great gardens, designed and created in Arts and Crafts style and arranged as a series of outdoor rooms, each with a different character. At Kiftsgate Court, set on the edge of the Cotswold escarpment, there are views across the Vale of Evesham and rare plants collected by three generations of women gardeners.

Hidcote Manor Garden
Hidcote Bartrim, Chipping Campden, Gloucestershire GL55 6LR
01386 438333
www.nationaltrust.org.uk

Kiftsgate Court Garden
Hidcote Bartrim, Chipping Campden, Gloucestershire GL55 6LN
01386 438777
www.kiftsgate.co.uk

THE SHAKESPEARE TRAIL
Stratford-upon-Avon is the birthplace of our most celebrated playwright. The Shakespeare Trail takes in his birthplace in town, a wonderful half-timbered property, New Place/Nash's House in Chapel Street, Halls Croft in Old Town, Anne Hathaway's Cottage in Shottery, and Mary Arden's House in nearby Wilmcote.

www.visitstratforduponavon.co.uk

SNOWSHILL MANOR
Charles Paget Wade's fascinating collection fills this Cotswold Tudor manor house. Musical instruments, clocks, toys, weavers' and spinners' tools, and Japanese armour.

Snowshill, Broadway, Gloucestershire WR12 7JU
01386 852410
www.nationaltrust.org.uk

Activity

BALLOONING
Take off from Stratford and the winds may carry you over the River Avon to Warwick Castle, or across the Cotswold edge to the historic town of Chipping Campden. Choose Stow-on-the-Wold as your launch site and you will glide peacefully across the rolling Cotswold landscape and its picture-book honey-stone villages, that look even more perfect from the air.

Heart of England Balloons
01789 488219
www.heartofenglandballoons.co.uk

CYCLING
Hire a mountain bike or high-geared hybrid cycle and discover the many miles of quiet lanes linking the villages of the north Cotswolds and the verdant Vale of Evesham. This is the green and environmentally friendly way to visit the wealth of local manor houses – or perhaps the National Trust's fabulous Fleece Inn at Bretforton.

Cotswold Country Cycles, Longlands Farm Cottage, Chipping Campden, Gloucestershire GL55 6LJ
01386 438706
www.cotswoldcountrycycles.com

CLASSIC CAR HIRE
Choose your car, choose your destination, collect the keys and go. Great Escape's classic twin-cam Alfa Romeo Spider and 7.2 litre V8 Jensen Interceptor are two entirely different ways to explore the Cotswolds, the Malvern Hills and the Welsh Borders.

Great Escape Classic Car Hire, Feckenham, Worcestershire
01527 893733
www.greatescapecars.co.uk

The Howard Arms, Lower Green, Ilmington, Shipston-on-Stour, Warwickshire CV36 4LT

The Walk - The Houses of Welford-on-Avon

A lovely village walk where black-and-white thatched cottages line the streets.

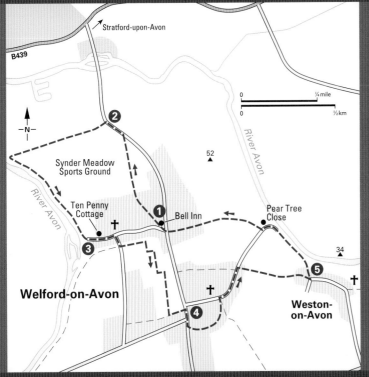

Walk Details

LENGTH: 3 miles (4.8km)

TIME: 1hr

ASCENT: 49ft (15m)

PATHS: Village footpaths and field paths, 3 stiles

SUGGESTED MAP: aqua3 OS Explorer 205 Stratford-upon-Avon & Evesham

GRID REFERENCE: SP 148522

PARKING: Near the Bell Inn, Welford-on-Avon

1 From your parking place near the Bell Inn, come out on to the main road in Welford village and go left down a footpath at the side of the parking area. At the end of the footpath, near Daffodil Cottage, go right along the footpath past the back of the houses until you come to the end of Church Lane, by Applegarth House. Continue through the gate and follow the green path at the back of more houses to reach the main road once again, then go left along the pavement for 100yds (91m).

2 Go left again into the entrance gate of Synder Meadow Sports Ground. Walk along the track, then go over 2 stiles to continue along the footpath down to the River Avon.

At the river, go left and follow the bank for 500yds (457m).

3 Go over the stile at end of field and left up Boat Lane, lined with beautiful old thatched black-and-white cottages. Look out for Ten Penny Cottage. Near top of lane is St Peter's Church; go right here along Headland Road. When you are opposite Mill Lane, turn left along footpath at back of houses. You will pass by extension to graveyard of St Peter's Church and in about 400yds (366m) come to junction of paths. Go left and walk up to High Street to emerge opposite Maypole Wine Stores, near the famous maypole. There has been a maypole here since the 14th century and the children dance around it each year.

4 Turn right along the pavement for a few paces, then cross and go down another waymarked footpath, past more thatched cottages. Walk through Pool Close to Chapel Street (the chapel is on the left). Go right along Chapel Street, then right again down Millers Close towards Weston-on-Avon.

5 At the crossroads bear left to descend to the bridlepath set just above the River Avon. Follow it as it arcs left, then continue to Duck Lane by another thatched house, 'Pear Tree Close'. At the next residential drive, go right up the hedged path and walk up to the High Street, where you will emerge at the junction with Church Street. The Bell Inn is on the right.

The Collyweston Slater

Lincolnshire

The Inn

The village of Collyweston gives its name to the stone slates that are quarried in the area: the extraordinarily weathered and textured roofs are one of the most distinctive features of the historic towns and villages hereabouts. The Collyweston Slater, however, has moved on from being the village boozer and taken the contemporary dining pub route, although the sympathetic remodelling retains the old fabric and character of the 17th-century inn and offers tables for drinkers, too. The open-plan interior is spacious and rambling, with lots of oak and slate and exposed timbers, while leather chairs and several real fires add to the comfort factor. Warmer weather can be enjoyed at tables on the front terrace.

Upstairs, the impeccable bedrooms are crammed full of creature comforts. What is offered here is very much in tune with modern times – guests can expect to find everything from a suite offering a king-size bed and double Jacuzzi bath to a decent-sized and comfortable single. In between there are contemporary doubles with crisp white linen, soft, neutral colours, bright and gleaming modern bathrooms and pretty village views.

The Essentials

Time at the Bar!
10am-3pm, 5-11pm
(Sat 10am-11pm, Sun 11.30am-5pm)
Food: 12-2pm, 5-9pm
(12-6pm Sunday)

What's the Damage?
Main courses from £8.95

Bitter Experience:
Everards Original & Slaters Ale

Sticky Fingers:
Children welcome, children's menu

Muddy Paws:
No dogs

Zzzzz:
5 rooms, £65-£85

Anything Else?
Terrace, car park, pétanque court

The Food

On the food front there's plenty of ambition and the scope of the cooking is wide, with the kitchen coming up with some intriguing twists on classic ideas. To start, there might be honey and mustard chargrilled chicken with spiced red slaw, ham hock terrine with home-made piccalilli, or devilled whitebait with lemon and cracked black pepper mayo. Main courses are in a similar vein: braised lamb shank might be teamed with parsnip mash and honey roast root vegetables, and vegetarians can home in on a minted pea risotto with aged parmesan.

The choice of desserts runs to sherry and apricot trifle, and the selection of British cheeses usually includes a Colston Bassett blue stilton. At lunchtime there's a good-value set-price menu at one, two or three courses, and Sunday lunch keeps tradition alive with classic prawn cocktail, roast beef with all the trimmings, and sticky toffee pudding. Another plus is the flexible approach – you can eat where you like in the pub. The atmosphere is warm, welcoming and buzzy.

What To Do

Shop

EAST NORTHAMPTONSHIRE

East Northamptonshire has a growing reputation for an array of independent speciality shops selling items that are quirky and unusual. There are antiques, memorabilia, books, both new and old, and a range of delicious delicacies. Many of the nearby towns and villages have specialist local food shops, grocers, bakers, butchers, greengrocers, cheese shops and delicatessens worth seeking out.

www.east-northamptonshire.gov.uk

DOVECOTE BUTTERY

Located at Newton 3 miles north of Kettering, Dovecote Buttery is where you can pick your own soft fruit from late May until early August, and fresh asparagus between April and June. The farm shop specialises in preserves, homemade cakes, fresh eggs, bread and a great deal more. The buttery with its attached gift shop serves hot and cold lunches, traditional Sunday roast and cream teas.

Dovecote Buttery and Farm Shop,
Dovecote Farm, Newton, Kettering,
Northamptonshire NN14 1BW
01536 742227
www.dovecotefarm.co.uk

ANTIQUES IN UPPINGHAM

Head for the civilised little town of Uppingham if you love browsing antique shops and are after a bargain. There's plenty to choose from, including the Rutland Antiques Centre, where 60 dealers offer furniture, jewellery, books, linen, clocks and collectibles.

Rutland Antiques Centre, Crown Passage,
Uppingham, Rutland
01572 824011

Visit

LYVEDEN NEW BIELD

Started in 1595 by Sir Thomas Tresham as a monument to his Catholic faith, Lyveden remains virtually unchanged since his death in 1605. With its striking architectural detail, water garden, terraces and spiral mounds, this fascinating Elizabethan lodge is an obvious attraction.

Oundle, Peterborough,
Northamptonshire PE8 5AT
01832 205358
www.nationaltrust.org.uk

KIRBY HALL

One of the region's great Elizabethan houses, Kirby Hall was begun in 1570 and completed by Sir Christopher Hatton, a favourite at the court of Queen Elizabeth I. The finely carved decoration is quite exceptional, illustrating the birth of new concepts about architecture and design. Much of the house is a ruined shell, but the Great Hall and state rooms remain intact. The gardens, one of Kirby Hall's main features, have been restored by English Heritage.

Corby, Northamptonshire NN17 3EN
01536 203230
www.english-heritage.org.uk

OAKHAM

Rutland's attractive county town has a good sense of country bustle about it, one or two interesting antique shops, and a fine Norman Great Hall of a 12th-century fortified manor house. Visit the Museum of Rutland Life, in a superb 18th-century cavalry riding school.

Rutland Country Museum, Catmose Street,
Oakham, Rutland LE15 6HW
01572 758440

Activity

RIVERSIDE WALKS

Enjoy an easy walk through meadows and along the River Nene, starting perhaps at Barnwell Country Park just outside the historic town of Oundle. The wealth of wildlife you can spot makes this much more than a pleasant waterside stroll. Expect to see grey herons or even otters along the way, the latter now making a welcome return to the British countryside.

Tourist Information Centre, 14 West Street,
Oundle, Northamptonshire PE8 4EF
01832 274333
www.east-northamptonshire.gov.uk

GOLF

Enjoy a round at the home of the 'Oundle Putter'- the popular name for a long-established tournament. Founded in 1893, Oundle Golf Club is where you can play a testing 18-hole, 6265yds, par 72 course.

Benefield Road, Oundle,
Northamptonshire PE8 4EZ
01832 273267
www.oundlegolfclub.com

RUTLAND WATER

You can try energetic sports such as windsurfing, rock-climbing or canoeing, hire a dinghy, bicycle or fishing boat or just relax by the water and watch the action around the 25-mile shoreline. A range of crafts is available to hire (book in advance), or you can launch your own. The Anglian Water Birdwatching Centre at Egleton features 20 hides.

Rutland Watersports 01780 460154
www.anglianwaterleisure.co.uk
Anglian Birdwatching Centre
01572 460154
www.rutlandwater.org.uk

The Walk - A Stroll Around Rutland Water

A short but scenic introduction to Rutland Water's aquatic charms.

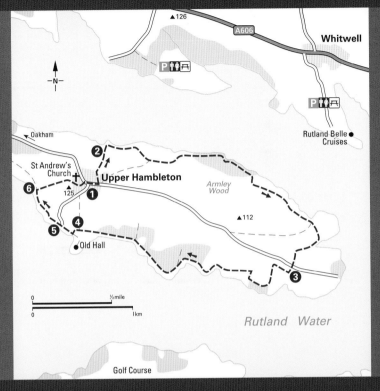

Walk Details

LENGTH: 4.5 miles (7.2km)

TIME: 2hrs 30min

ASCENT: 311ft (95m)

PATHS: Wide and firm the whole distance

SUGGESTED MAP: aqua3 OS Explorer 234 Rutland Water

GRID REFERENCE: SK 900075

PARKING: Roadside parking in Upper Hambleton

❶ From St Andrew's Church in the centre of Upper Hambleton, walk east on the long and level main street as far as the red pillar box. Turn left through the gate for the grassy lane ('public footpath') that leads straight through the gate and down the middle of the sloping field.

❷ Go through the gate at the bottom and turn right on to the wide track that runs just above the shore. This popular and peaceful route around Hambleton peninsula is also shared by cyclists, so be alert. Follow it from field to field, and through Armley Wood, with views across Rutland Water. You gradually swing around the tip of Hambleton peninsula with views towards the dam at the eastern end.

❸ When you arrive at the tarmac lane (gated to traffic at this point, as it simply disappears into water a little further on!), go straight across to continue on the same unmade track. It turns right and for a short distance runs parallel with the road before heading left and back towards the water's edge and an area of mixed woodland.

❹ Approaching Old Hall, the handsome building perched just above the shore, turn left to reach its surfaced drive, then go right and walk along it for 160yds (146m) to reach the cattle grid.

❺ At this point you can return directly to Upper Hambleton by following the lane back uphill; otherwise veer left to continue along the waterside track, with views across to Egleton Bay and the corner of Rutland Water that is reserved for wildlife, and is consequently out of bounds to sailing boats.

❻ After 500yds (457m) look for an easily missed stile in the hedge on your right, and the public footpath that heads straight up the field. (If you overshoot here, or want to extend the walk by 0.5 mile/800m, carry on along the track to the far end and return along the lane to the village.) Aim for the apex of the field, where successive stiles lead to a narrow passageway between the hedge and fence that eventually brings you out in the churchyard in the centre of the village.

The Westleton Crown

Suffolk

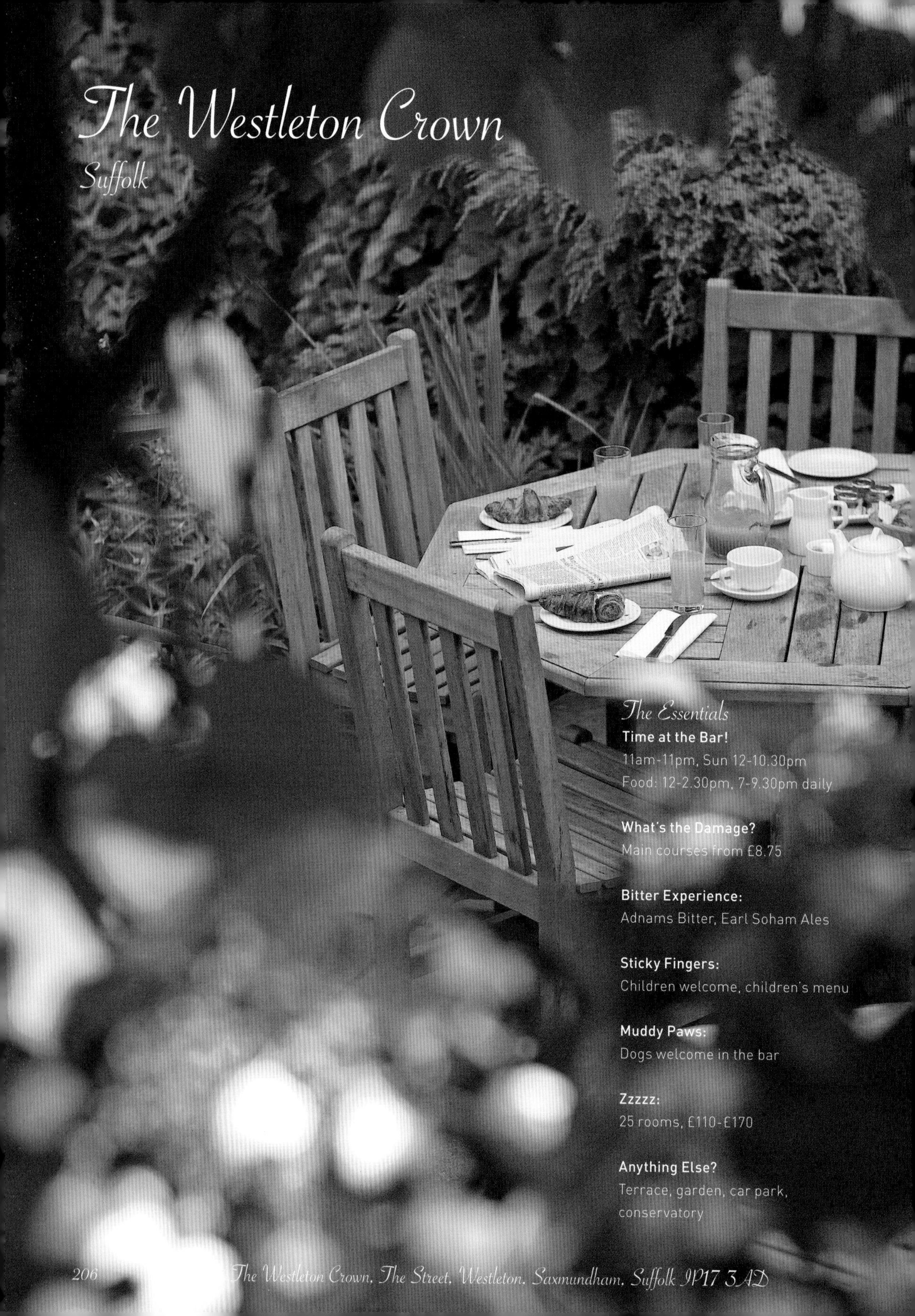

The Essentials

Time at the Bar!
11am-11pm, Sun 12-10.30pm
Food: 12-2.30pm, 7-9.30pm daily

What's the Damage?
Main courses from £8.75

Bitter Experience:
Adnams Bitter, Earl Soham Ales

Sticky Fingers:
Children welcome, children's menu

Muddy Paws:
Dogs welcome in the bar

Zzzzz:
25 rooms, £110-£170

Anything Else?
Terrace, garden, car park, conservatory

The Westleton Crown, The Street, Westleton, Saxmundham, Suffolk IP17 3AD

The Inn

Halfway between the trendy Suffolk havens of Aldeburgh and Southwold, the Crown sits rather aptly for such a stylish, historic building in an Area of Outstanding Natural Beauty, among the reed-fringed creeks, tidal marsh and low, heath-backed cliffs of Suffolk's Heritage Coastline. With the ornithological delights of the RSPB's flagship Minsmere Reserve and nearby Dunwich Heath just two miles away, it's superb countryside for exploring on foot or by pedal power.

The enthusiastic owners have a definite taste for the finer things in life and this comes across in dramatic fashion at the Crown. Losing none of their soul or age-old charm, the luxurious yet simply elegant bedrooms – like the rest of this seductively relaxing building – exude all the sophistication and comforts of contemporary living: think Egyptian cotton sheets, sprung mattresses, chrome four-posters, cafetières and home-made biscuits. Downstairs, it's log fires, eclectic 'befriended' furniture, stripped boards – a real sense of rural chic. So kick off your shoes – be they high heels or walking boots – and relax.

The Food

Whether dressing up for dinner in the smart conservatory or dining room, or in comfy clothes for a light bite in the bar, the single menu covers it all: from simple treats like crispy whitebait, hearty steak and kidney pudding or homely collar of bacon and chive mash, to the epicurean heights of seared scallops, pan-fried beef fillet with fig tarte tatin or roasted loin of venison with griottine cherries.

With an eye for presentation and flavours, Richard Bargewell's cooking is definitely style and substance, using fresh local ingredients from some super producers to great effect. One of his signature themes is to re-create loved retro dishes from his childhood such as arctic roll and Black Forest gateau, though, as to be expected, they have a culinary twist that improves on the originals.

Each pudding dish has a recommended sticky dessert wine by the glass. How about white chocolate fondant with dark chocolate ice cream, accompanied by berry-laden Quady's Californian Elysium Black Muscat?

What To Do

Shop

NORWICH

Once inside the city you can spend all day exploring its medieval streets and browsing its shops. Stroll along to Chapelfields where the shopping mall is worth closer inspection. Also visit the family-owned Jarrolds department store.

Tourist Information Centre, The Forum, Millennium Plain, Norwich, Norfolk NR2 1TF
01603 727927
www.visitnorwich.co.uk

FRIDAY STREET FARM SHOP & TEA ROOM

Visit this popular farm shop, which offers an impressive selection of home-grown or locally sourced products, including cheeses, poultry, fish, fresh flowers and a variety of gifts. Pick your own strawberries and round off your shopping trip with a visit to the tea room for lunch or afternoon tea.

Farnham, Saxmundham, Suffolk IP17 1JX
01728 602783

ST PETER'S HALL & BREWERY SHOP

Built in 1280 and extended in 1539, the impressive manor and surrounding farm buildings were refurbished in 1996 to provide the rather grand setting for a unique microbrewery and individual bar and restaurant. Sample the full range of St Peter's ales in the magnificent hall, enjoy a talk about the history of the brewery in the visitor's centre, and visit the shop to buy some excellent ale .

St Peter South Elham, Bungay, Suffolk NR35 1NQ
01986 782322
www.stpetersbrewery.co.uk

Visit

SUTTON HOO

Described as 'page one of English history', Sutton Hoo is the place to visit for famous treasures, including a warrior's helmet, shield and gold ornaments in the remains of a burial chamber of a 90-ft (27-m) ship. A permanent display in the special Exhibition Hall reveals how Anglo-Saxon nobles lived, went to war and founded a new kingdom in East Anglia. The site includes magnificent estuary views, heathland walks and various woodland trails.

Tranmer House, Sutton Hoo, Woodbridge, Suffolk IP12 3DJ
01394 389700
www.nationaltrust.org.uk

LEISTON ABBEY

For hundreds of years this impressive 14th-century abbey was used as a farm and its church became a barn. A Georgian house was built into its fabric and this is now used as a religious retreat. The rest of the abbey is in ruins, but remains of the choir and transepts of the church and the ranges of the cloisters still stand.

Leiston, Suffolk
www.english-heritage.org.uk

SAXTEAD GREEN POST MILL

The present mill dates from 1854 and is one of the finest examples of a traditional Suffolk post-mill. Climb the steep staircase and find the machinery in working order.

Saxtead Green, Framlingham, Suffolk
01728 685789

Activity

WIZARD BALLOONS

See the sprawling East Anglian landscape and its evocative coastline from a totally different perspective – an exhilarating hot-air balloon ride. The rides launch from sites across Suffolk and Cambridgeshire and are available from spring through until autumn.

01379 898989
www.wizardballoons.co.uk

BIRDWATCHING AT MINSMERE

With its wide variety of habitats – encompassing woodland, heathland, reed beds, salt marsh, estuaries, shingle beaches and low cliffs – the Suffolk Coast is one of Britain's prime destinations for birdwatching. The RSPB Reserve at Minsmere shelters nesting avocets, marsh harriers and bitterns.

Westleton, Suffolk IP17 3BY
01728 648281
www.rspb.org.uk

SUFFOLK COAST PATH

The spectacular 50-mile (80-km) Suffolk Coast Path runs along between Felixstowe and Lowestoft. Many famous landmarks crop up along the way, including Orford Ness and the charming little town of Southwold. The final section offers walkers a charming mixture of low sandy cliffs, some handsome stretches of the Suffolk Broads and a panoply of church towers.

Felixstowe Tourist Information Centre, 91 Undercliff Road, Felixstowe, Suffolk IP11 2AF
01394 276770
www.suffolkcoastal.gov.uk

The Walk - Aldeburgh, Home of Benjamin Britten

A waterside walk on the trail of the great 20th-century composer.

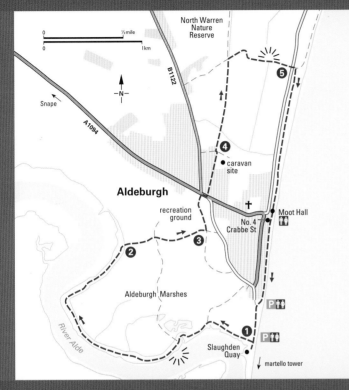

Walk Details

LENGTH: 5.75 miles (9.2km)

TIME: 2hrs 30min

ASCENT: Negligible

PATHS: River and sea wall, meadows, old railway track, 6 stiles. Note: Dogs not allowed on beach between May and September

SUGGESTED MAP: aqua3 OS Explorer 212 Woodbridge & Saxmundham

GRID REFERENCE: TM 463555

PARKING: Slaughden Quay free car park

❶ Start the walk at Slaughden Quay (yacht club). Walk back briefly in the direction of Aldeburgh and turn left along the river wall on the north bank of the River Alde – notice the views to your left of the Martello tower. Stay on the river wall for 2 miles (3.2km) as the river swings right towards Aldeburgh.

❷ When the river bends left at the stile, go down the wooden staircase to your right and keep straight ahead across the meadow with the water tower ahead. Go through the gate and bear half-left across the next meadow to cross the footbridge. Follow the waymarks, bearing half-right, then keep straight ahead across the next field to another footbridge. After crossing the 3rd footbridge, the path runs alongside allotments and goes through the gate to the lane.

❸ Turn left by brick wall; cross the recreation ground. Continue past the fire station to road. Turn right for 75yds (69m) then go left on the signposted footpath almost opposite the hospital entrance. Follow the path via the housing estate, cross the road. Continue with the caravan site on your right.

❹ When you see the stile on the right, leading to the track across the caravan site, turn left and immediately right on the permissive path that follows the old railway trackbed. Stay on this path for 0.5 mile (800m) climbing steadily between farmland to the left and woodland and marshes to the right. Turn right at the junction of paths and cross stile to open meadows. Stay on this path, crossing North Warren nature reserve with Sizewell power station to your left.

❺ Cross the road and turn right along the concrete path running parallel to the beach. As you approach Aldeburgh, pass the fishermen's huts and fishing boats on the shingle. Pass Moot Hall and continue along Crag Path past the model yacht pond, lifeboat station and pair of lookout towers. Stay on this esplanade between houses and beach with Martello Tower ahead. At end of Crag Path, bear right across car park and walk around old mill to return to Slaughden Quay.

The Bildeston Crown

Suffolk

The Bildeston Crown, 104 High Street, Bildeston, Ipswich, Suffolk IP7 7EB

The Inn

Seven hundred years on from its construction, the Bildeston Crown is attracting more than its fair share of the county's gastronomic acclaim – thanks to new custodians. The pretty village setting of timber-framed houses and the simplicity of the Crown's beamed ochre-painted exterior belie its multi-million pound transformation into a luxurious bolthole. Revealing its history at every twist and turn, the charming building now revels in opulence and warmth, no expense having been spared in complementing the original period features with every modern essential you could wish for.

In the bedrooms – which come in all shapes and sizes due to the building's extreme age – designers have been allowed to run wild with tactile textures, chic fabrics and bold colour schemes. Every opportunity has been taken to indulge and spoil the guests: think deep-pile carpets, huge mirrors, big fluffy cushions, sumptuous drapes, bathrobes and iPods piping tunes into the bathrooms. A hearty breakfast sets you up for a good browse around the nearby landmarks of Lavenham and Kersey, full of quintessential Suffolk charm and quaint tea shops for a civilised stop-off in the mid-afternoon.

The Food

The Bildeston Crown's restaurant is where it is all happening. Chef/patron Chris Lee (with wife Hayley running front of house) is cooking at the top of his game. He's virtually self-taught, but in just three years he has gained respect from food critics as well as his peers. His free-wheeling culinary exuberance is as exciting as the sheer quality of his cooking (made doubly enjoyable by being excellent value for money, too).

Descriptions of the dishes give little indication of the ensuing masterpieces. In the case of Pork Head to Toe, the down-to-earth name barely describes the indulgent creation. It consists of no less than eight cuts of pork, each cooked separately and individually garnished: cheeks and ears from one end, finishing with trotters at the other, down to the perfectly crisp, salty crackling presented in an extraordinary strip 10in (25cm) long. To match the dazzling decadence of the food and the interior, you can expect to find all the usual luxury restaurant accompaniments, including a well-chosen wine list, full of the great and godly, as well as the unusual.

The Essentials

Time at the Bar!
11am-11pm
Food: 12-3pm, 7-10pm daily

What's the Damage?
Main courses from £10

Bitter Experience:
Mauldons Ales, Adnams Bitter

Sticky Fingers:
Children welcome, small portions
available

Muddy Paws:
Dogs welcome in the bar

Zzzzz:
10 rooms, £170

Anything Else?
Terrace, garden, car park

What To Do

Shop

LONG MELFORD & LAVENHAM

If you love browsing, then take the opportunity to embark on a fascinating antiques and crafts tour of Suffolk. The village of Long Melford has at least 16 antique shops, along with many independent retail businesses, galleries, tearooms and pubs, while the historic town of Lavenham has more of the same plus Debenhams department store. From there you can try your luck at the Old Town Hall Antiques and Collectors Centre in Needham Market.

Lavenham Tourist Information Centre, Lady Street, Lavenham, Suffolk CO10 9RA
01787 881320
www.southandheartofsuffolk.org.uk

MARKETS

Many of the towns in Suffolk still operate markets on a regular twice-weekly basis – Stowmarket and Sudbury host them on Thursdays and Saturdays, Hadleigh holds them on Fridays and Saturdays. There are regular Farmers Markets here, too, as well as at Lavenham, Long Melford, Needham Market and Rickinghall. Specialist book markets and antique fairs are also held in the area.

Contact any of the Tourist Information Centres for more details.

WILDLIFE ART GALLERY

A fine gallery specialising in 20th-century and contemporary wildlife art, featuring work from many of Britain's best wildlife artists, past and present, including Robert Gilmour and Bruce Pearson.

97 High Street, Lavenham, Suffolk CO10 9PZ
01787 248562
www.wildlifeartgallery.com

Visit

FRAMLINGHAM CASTLE

Enchanting Framlingham Castle offers spectacular views over the delightful reed-fringed Mere to the countryside beyond. But there is much more to this ancient stronghold than its splendid setting. Throughout its colourful history it has been a fortress, an Elizabethan prison, a poor house and a school. While there, do the wall walk, explore the outer courts and don't miss the 17th-century poor house.

01728 724189
www.english-heritage.org.uk

ICKWORTH HOUSE, PARK & GARDENS

Visit this unusual Georgian pile in its landscape park and you'll discover an eccentric house created by an equally eccentric aristocrat. Characterised by curved corridors and a central rotunda, Ickworth was built by the 4th Earl of Bristol in 1795. His collections of paintings include works by Titian, Gainsborough and Velazquez. An Italianate garden lies to the south, set in a Capability Brown park.

The Rotunda, Horringer, Bury St Edmunds, Suffolk IP29 5QE
01284 735270
www.nationaltrust.org.uk

LAVENHAM GUILDHALL

This fine 16th-century timber-framed building overlooks and dominates the market place in this remarkably preserved medieval village. View exhibitions on local history, farming, industry and the medieval woollen cloth trade.

Market Place, Lavenham, Suffolk CO10 9QZ
01787 247646
www.nationaltrust.org.uk

Activity

CYCLING

East Anglia is known as 'England's Cycling Country' – and for very good reasons. The terrain tends to be gently undulating, rather than dramatically steep – perfect for pedal power. A network of quiet lanes allows you to cycle in peace and admire the scenery. There are two signposted cycle routes in the region, with accompanying leaflets from tourist information centres.

Suffolk Cycle Breaks, Bradfield Hall Barn, Alder Carr Farm, PO Box 82, Needham Market, Suffolk IP6 8BW
www.cyclebreaks.co.uk

GOLF

With its huge skies, gently undulating countryside and excellent facilities for golfers, both amateur and professional, Suffolk is the ideal setting for the much-loved game of golf. Many of the clubs in the area have restaurants, swimming pools and other leisure facilities. With its fishing lakes, garden centre, 9-hole golf course and coffee shop, Stonham Barns at Stonham Aspal is a prime example.

Pettaugh Road, Stonham Aspal, Stowmarket, Suffolk IP14 6AT
01449 711755
www.stonhambarns.co.uk

HORSE RIDING

At Swifts Manor Riding School in nearby Preston St Mary you can book individual lessons with a qualified instructor in the indoor or outdoor school or explore the peaceful bridleways that run through the Suffolk countryside on a hack or picnic ride (4-5 hours).

Preston St Mary, Sudbury, Suffolk CO10 9NL
01449 740862

The Walk - The Wool Town of Lavenham

A walk through picturesque medieval streets built on the back of the wool industry.

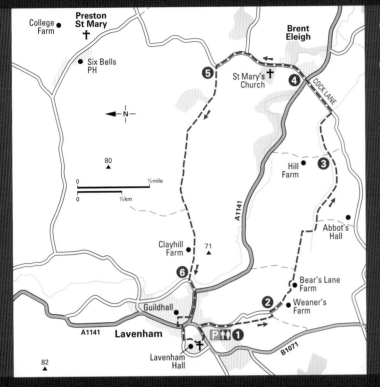

Walk Details

LENGTH: 5.5 miles (8.8km)

TIME: 2hrs 30min

ASCENT: 197ft (60m)

PATHS: Field-edge paths and tracks, some stretches of road

SUGGESTED MAP: aqua3 OS Explorers 196 Sudbury, Hadleigh & Dedham Vale; 211 Bury St Edmonds & Stowmarket

GRID REFERENCE: TL 914489 (on Explorer 196)

PARKING: Church Street car park, Lavenham

❶ Turn right out of the car park and walk down the hill into town. At the 1st junction, turn right along Bear's Lane. Continue for 0.25 mile (400m) until the last house, then take the footpath to the right across fields. After 0.25 mile (400m) reach the field boundary. Turn left across a small footbridge and follow the ditch to rejoin the road.

❷ Turn right, walk past Weaner's Farm, then turn left at the footpath sign just before the barn. Stay on this path as it swings around Bear's Lane Farm, then turn left on to the wide track beside the hedge. Walk along this track as it descends to the valley bottom. When the track bends right towards Abbot's Hall, keep straight ahead and fork to the right

on the grassy path that runs along beside the stream.

❸ Emerging from the poplar grove, arrive at a concrete drive and turn right and immediately left. The path swings round to the right to the road, Cock Lane. Turn left and stay on the road as it climbs and then descends to the crossroads.

❹ Cross the A1141 into Brent Eleigh. When the road bends, with the village hall and the half-timbered Corner Farm to the right, keep ahead to climb to St Mary's Church. Visit the church to see the 13th-century wall paintings and 17th-century box pews. Proceed, climbing up the same road.

❺ When the road swings sharp right, look for the path on the left.

Stay on the path for 1.25 miles (2km) as it winds between tall hedges. Pass Clayhill Farm and descend into the valley, crossing the white-painted bridge.

❻ Turn left at the junction and walk into Lavenham along Water Street, with its fine timber-framed houses. After De Vere House, turn right up Lady Street, passing the tourist office on the way to the market place. Turn left down narrow Market Lane to arrive at the High Street opposite picturesque Crooked House. Turn briefly left and then right along Hall Road. Before the road bends, look for a footpath on the left, then walk through the meadow to reach Lavenham church. The car park is across the road.

The Anchor
Suffolk

The Anchor, Main Street, Walberswick, Southwold, Suffolk IP18 6UA

The Inn

Sleepy except on high days and holidays, the celebrity hamlet of Walberswick still has more than enough charm and sophistication to compete with its big sister, Southwold – a mere 'taxi ride' away by rowing boat over the river Blyth. Overlooking the beach-hut-dotted horizon, the sea is only a wander away out of the back gate of this 1920s Arts and Crafts building and through the allotments (look out for your dinner ingredients growing there on your way past). Great for sandy feet and easy access, the courtyard-style rooms around the landscaped gardens are spacious, bright and airy.

A facelift is planned for the Anchor over the next year, but the convenient accommodation still makes a comfortable and pleasant base to explore this part of north-east Suffolk, which is full of nature reserves, wildlife and winding paths through forest and heath – don't forget your bike. The focus of The Anchor is very much on the laid-back bar and restaurant, warmly welcoming the hotchpotch of drinkers and diners, locals and tourists, with its easy-going yet foodie ambience.

The Essentials

Time at the Bar!
11.30-4pm, 6-11pm
Food: 12-2.30pm, 6.30-9pm,
Sat-Sun 12-9pm

What's the Damage?
Main courses from £10

Bitter Experience:
Adnams Bitter, Broadside and Seasonal Ale

Sticky Fingers:
Children welcome, small portions available

Muddy Paws:
Dogs welcome in the bar

Zzzzz:
7 rooms, £45

Anything Else?
Terrace, garden, car park

The Food

The smell of malt in the air, blown over from Southwold's artisan brewery, gives a clue that this is Adnams country. Few (if any) hostelries keep a better pint of their golden ales than this delightful family-orientated establishment, devoted to the good life. It's run with passion and personality by Sophie and Mark Dorber: her zealous dedication to local ingredients and skill in the kitchen is more than matched by his erudite capacity for all things 'grape'n'grain'.

The short perfectly seasonal menu, pairing each flavour-packed dish with a different suggestion for beer and wine by the glass, illustrates Sophie and Mark's ambition – perhaps you would care to try mozzarella and spinach arancini risotto cakes with Brooklyn Lager from New York or Endrizzi Italian Pinot Grigio; rib-eye steak with hand-cut chips, field mushrooms and red wine jus with Rochefort 10 Belgian Trappist Ale or Portuguese Douro Red Quinta do Crasto. 'Unfussy forceful flavours with attitude' aptly describes the modern British pub food served here, as well as the 80-bin wine list and 15-odd speciality beer selection.

What To Do

Shop

ADNAMS WINE CELLAR & KITCHEN STORE

Adnams may know a thing or two about brewing beer but they are also a respected wine merchant, and their full range of wines can be viewed, tasted and purchased at their fabulous shop behind the Crown Inn in Southwold.

Victoria Street, Southwold, Suffolk
01502 727244
www.adnamswines.co.uk

SOUTHWOLD

Stylish Southwold still evokes an atmosphere of Edwardian England and seaside gaiety, making it the perfect spot for a bit of leisurely shopping and browsing. The town has an excellent range of shops offering antiques, crafts and unusual gifts, and there are various art galleries and tearooms as well as a number of pubs selling ales produced at the local Adnams Sole Bay Brewery. Markets, dating back to the 13th century, are held on Mondays and Thursdays.

Tourist Information Centre, 69 High Street,
Southwold, Suffolk IP18 6DS
01502 724729
www.visit-southwold.co.uk

SOUTHWOLD GALLERY

Visit the Southwold Gallery where paintings from over 30 top artists are on show. There are a wide variety of styles from traditional, contemporary and surreal to the quirky and miniature. The artists capture the East Coast with its big skies, dramatic shores, eccentric characters and rich artistic history.

64a High Street, Southwold, Suffolk
01502 723888
www.southwoldgallery.co.uk

Visit

BUNGAY CASTLE VISITOR CENTRE

While the town's distinctive architecture reflects its changing fortunes over the years, one landmark remains reassuringly timeless. Built in 1165, Bungay Castle was all but destroyed in 1174 when it was besieged by Henry II. All that remains today are the ruins of two semi-circular towers, flanked by the gatehouse. There's a newly built visitor centre tracing the history of the town and castle.

01986 896156
www.visit-sunrisecoast.co.uk

DUNWICH MUSEUM

What is fascinating about Dunwich's infrastructure is not what is there today, but what has gone. Dunwich was once a thriving city, with an important boat-building industry and harbour, home to an impressive fleet of royal ships. Take a look around Dunwich's little museum and you will get some idea of its fascinating and mysterious past.

Dunwich, Southwold, Suffolk
01728 648796

SOMERLEYTON HALL

Situated ten minutes from Lowestoft, Somerleyton Hall was rebuilt in the mid-19th century on the basis of an Elizabethan house and designed in the Anglo-Italian style. Inside are carvings by Grinling Gibbons as well as big-game trophies, which confirm the sporting interests of the Somerleyton family. There are guided tours of the Hall, which has 12 acres of beautiful gardens, including an 1846 yew hedge maze.

0871 222 4244
www.somerleyton.co.uk

Activity

BROADS NATIONAL PARK

A mecca for outdoor enthusiasts, this corner of the holiday region is a gem. The area encompasses rich aquatic broadland, miles of glorious rivers, maritime heritage and breezy, award-winning beaches. From the River Blyth at Southwold to the River Waveney, there's a choice of activities, including jetskiing, yachting, cruising, windsurfing, canoeing and fishing.

www.visit-sunrisecoast.co.uk

THE GREAT OUTDOORS

Whether you're a cyclist, a wildlife enthusiast, a golfer or a tennis player, Suffolk's Sunrise Coast, as it has been dubbed by the tourism industry, offers something for everyone. You could even have a go at kite boarding, take to the water to try scuba diving, explore the area on horseback, complete a llama trek accompanied by an experienced guide, or even learn to fly.

www.visit-sunrisecoast.co.uk

SEA & RIVER TRIPS

Cruise serenely up the River Blyth to view wildlife or hop on board *Sea Blast* for a 30-minute high-speed trip out to sea off Southwold.

Coastal Voyager
07887525082
www.coastalvoyager.co.uk

The Walk - The City That Fell into the Sea

Conjure up visions of lost 13th-century Dunwich as you stand on the cliffs gazing out to sea.

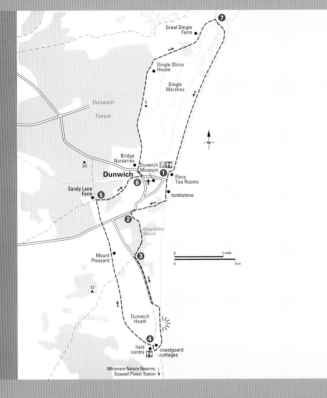

Walk Details

LENGTH: 8 miles (12.9km)

TIME: 4hrs

ASCENT: 262ft (80m)

PATHS: Farm tracks, heathland paths, quiet roads, shingle beach

SUGGESTED MAP: aqua3 OS Explorers 212 Woodbridge & Saxmundham; 231 Southwold & Bungay

GRID REFERENCE: TM 478706 (on Explorer 231)

PARKING: Dunwich Beach free car park

① From the beach car park walk up the road and keep left at the junction. When the road bends, turn left on to the footpath that climbs through the woods to the ruins of Greyfriars Friary. Turn left along the cliff top, go over a set of wooden steps and bear right through the trees on the waymarked path. At the end of the path, turn right along a track to reach the road.

② Turn left off the road after 100yds (91m) on the track to Dairy House. Keep straight ahead as the track enters Greyfriars Wood and continues to the road.

③ Turn left and proceed along the road for 0.5 mile (800m), passing 2 caravan sites on the left. As soon as you enter National Trust land, turn left on to the path that is waymarked with white arrows.

④ Walk around the National Trust's Coastguard Cottages and take the track beside Heath Barn field centre, then bear right on to a sandy path that climbs through the heather. Keep on the path, bearing left and right at the crossing track to follow the Sandlings Walk nightjar waymarks. At the bridleway, keep ahead on the farm track passing Mount Pleasant farm. Cross the road and keep ahead on the concrete lane to Sandy Lane Farm.

⑤ Turn right for 0.5 mile (800m) on the shady lane to St James's Church, built in the 19th century when Dunwich's other churches were falling into the sea, along with the rest of the 13th-century port. For a short cut, keep straight ahead here to return to Dunwich.

⑥ Turn left at the road and, in 100yds (91m), go right at Bridge Nurseries. Keep to the right around the farm buildings and stay on this track for 1.5 miles (2.4km) beside Dunwich Forest before turning seawards. Pass through the gate to enter the covert and fork right at the junction around Great Dingle Farm, then follow the path through the reed beds towards the sea.

⑦ Turn right at the junction, with the old drainage mill to your left, and follow the flood bank across Dingle Marshes. Turn right to return to Dunwich along the beach or take the path behind the shingle bank.

Crown & Castle
Suffolk

The Food

In the relaxed atmosphere of the Trinity, stripped wooden floorboards, polished tables and original artwork set the scene in which to relish quality modern food that draws on Suffolk's rich larder. Casual lunches may include Carlingford oysters, moules marinières, or a plate of good artisanal Spanish cured meats, as well as rump of Suffolk lamb with barberry, saffron and pistachio pilau and yogurt.

At dinner a typical meal could take in chicken liver parfait or Orford smoked trout with new potato and beetroot salad, then local skate with brown shrimps, sautéed cucumber and nut brown butter or, perhaps, rump of Suffolk lamb with rosemary mash and creamy courgette sauce, with desserts running from crème caramel with apricot compote via New York-style baked cheesecake with berry compote to a classic glazed lemon tart. It's all serious stuff, from a kitchen where simple techniques are responsible for much of the output, complemented by a front of house that operates smoothly and is run by pleasant staff who are good at their job.

The Inn

When Ruth and David Watson decided to take over this run-down former hotel, they realised they faced quite a challenge. Undaunted, they set about creating their vision of a modern, stylish inn – one where a friendly and informal atmosphere is crucial.

The location, adjacent to a Norman castle keep in a pretty coastal village with stunning views across the Ore estuary, was certainly on their side. Now it's a real treat to stay here. In winter, a roaring fire greets guests in the roomy entrance hall where deep sofas beckon; the bar and Trinity restaurant are suitably laid back; and there's a terrace for summer alfresco dining.

All of the 18 bedrooms are perfect, but which do you choose? Should it be in the main house, especially one with an estuary view? Or maybe a garden room to make the most of having your own private patio?

Whichever you go for, you will find that all of the rooms are decorated in light and refreshingly simple style. The entire place is clearly stamped with the Watsons' trademark attention to quality and detail – seen in the colours, fabrics, large comfy beds and the luxury towels and toiletries in the bathrooms.

The Essentials

Time at the Bar!
11am-3pm, 7-11pm
Food: 12-2pm, 6.45-9pm

What's the Damage?
Main courses from £12.50

Bitter Experience:
Greene King IPA and Old Speckled Hen

Sticky Fingers:
Children welcome (9 years and over in the evening)

Muddy Paws:
Dogs welcome in the bar

Zzzzz:
18 rooms, £90-£140

Anything Else?
Residents' garden, car park, terrace

What To Do

Shop

GARNETT'S GARDENS

An award-winning farm shop and retail nursery specialising in local fresh meat and organic and seasonal produce – including those perennial favourites strawberries and asparagus. In addition to local apple juice, locally made cakes, jams, honey and chutney, the business offers home-grown raspberries, leeks, courgettes, runner beans and spray chrysanthemums. After browsing and buying, relax over a Fairtrade coffee or a chilled apple juice.

Hacheston, Woodbridge, Suffolk
01728 724589

SNAPE MALTINGS

Delightfully situated amid the salt marshes of the River Alde, Snape Maltings offers far more than the famous concert hall, focal point of the Aldeburgh Festival, which was the brainchild of composer Benjamin Britten and tenor Peter Pears in the late 1960s. Shops, galleries and restaurants also occupy centre stage in the converted industrial buildings, with a tremendous range of quality antiques and collectibles offered by more than 40 dealers.

Snape, Aldeburgh, Suffolk IP17 1SR
www.snapemaltings.co.uk
01728 688303

Visit

MELFORD HALL

This romantic turreted Tudor mansion has links with Beatrix Potter. The writer was related to the Hyde-Parker family, owners of Melford Hall, and was a frequent visitor. Queen Elizabeth I was entertained here in 1578. Take a tour of the house, see the Regency library and the panelled Great Hall, and take a stroll in the park, with its striking specimen trees.

Long Melford, Sudbury, Suffolk CO10 9AA
01787 376395
www.nationaltrust.org.uk

SUTTON HOO

Described as 'page one of English history', Sutton Hoo is the place to visit for Anglo-Saxon treasures, including a warrior's helmet, shield and gold ornaments in the remains of a burial chamber of a 90ft ship. A permanent display in the special Exhibition Hall reveals how the ancient nobles lived, went to war and founded a new kingdom in East Anglia. The site includes magnificent estuary views, heathland and woodland trails.

Tranmer House, Sutton Hoo, Woodbridge, Suffolk IP12 3DJ
01394 389700
www.nationaltrust.org.uk

WOODBRIDGE TIDE MILL

Situated in a busy quayside beside the River Deben, this unique building looks over towards the historic site of the Sutton Hoo ship. The machinery of the 18th-century mill has been completely restored and is activated when the mill is open and the tides are suitable.

Tide Mill Way, Woodbridge, Suffolk IP12 1AP
01473 626618

Activity

THE LADY FLORENCE

Enjoy a glorious lunch or dinner cruise on the Lady Florence, a wartime Admiralty supply ship, as she sails upriver from Orford Quay towards Aldeburgh, Iken and Snape. The River Cruise Restaurant is designed to provide a rare and highly enjoyable fine-dining experience, while the detailed on-board commentary explains how the elements have shaped this eerie stretch of Suffolk coast.

07831 698298
www.lady-florence.co.uk

ORFORD NESS

One of Britain's loneliest and most atmospheric coastal sites, mysterious Orford Ness is the largest shingle spit in Europe. A National Trust ferry conveys visitors from Orford Quay to the Ness and, once there, visitors often spend all day exploring this former military test site on foot; a 5-mile (8-km) pedestrian route loops round Orford Ness and there are displays to help put it into historical context.

Quay Office, Orford Quay, Orford, Woodbridge, Suffolk IP12 2NU
01394 450057 (info line)
www.nationaltrust.org.uk

THE WINE TRAIL

Tour 16 of East Anglia's thriving vineyards, beginning at Carter's at Boxted near Colchester and finishing at Wissett Wines near Halesworth, in a small valley 12 miles inland from the coast. Wines can be tasted and bought.

Carter's Vineyard, Green Lane, Boxted, Colchester, Essex CO4 5TS
01206 271136
www.cartersvineyards.co.uk

The Walk - Down by the River at Woodbridge

Along the River Deben from a riverside town, with views of a working tide mill.

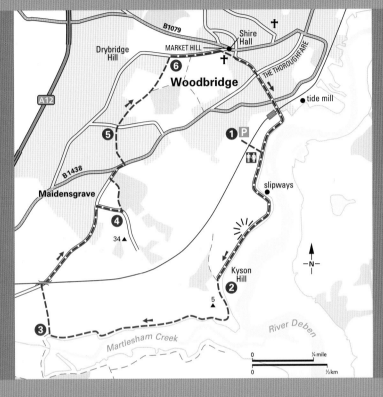

Walk Details

LENGTH: 4 miles (6.4km)

TIME: 1hr 30min

ASCENT: 164ft (50m)

PATHS: River wall, riverside paths, town streets, some steps

SUGGESTED MAP: aqua3 OS Explorer 197 Ipswich, Felixstowe & Harwich or 212 Woodbridge & Saxmundham

GRID REFERENCE: TM 271485

PARKING: The Avenue car park, Woodbridge

❶ Leave the car park on The Avenue and cross the railway line to the boatyard at the end of the lane. Turn right along the river wall, passing the slipways of Deben Yacht Club. Continue on an easy section of the walk, on the tarmac path with views over meadows to the right, to enter the National Trust's Kyson Hill.

❷ Turn left at the 3-way junction; descend to the beach. Walk along the foreshore under oak trees. (At high tide you may have to turn right instead, picking up the route at Point 4.) Keep right at the railings, follow the path to Martlesham Creek, scramble up the embankment and follow the riverside path.

❸ Turn right at the end of the creek and walk around the sewage works

to Sandy Lane. Turn right beneath the railway bridge and stay on this road as it climbs for 700yds (640m). At the top of the rise, turn right on to Broom Heath.

❹ When the road bends round to the right, turn left past the gate leading to Woodland Trust woods (the short cut rejoins from the right here). Stay on the path on the outside of the woods to return to Sandy Lane by the telephone box. Turn right here and right at the main road, then cross the road and climb steps on the far side after 50yds (46m). Keep ahead to the end of the footpath and cross the road to Portland Crescent.

❺ Continue to descend the hill and climb up the other side. Continue on Fen Walk, enclosed by black railings

with graveyards either side. Fork left at a junction of paths to descend the grassy slope with views of the church tower ahead. Keep ahead and climb the steps leading to Seckford Street.

❻ Turn right and continue to Market Hill. The alleyway on the righthand side leads to the churchyard. Turn left through the churchyard on to Church Street, emerging alongside the site of the old abbey, now a private school. Walk down Church Street and cross over The Thoroughfare, the pedestrian street on the lefthand side. Continue along Quay Street and cross station yard to the footbridge over the railway line. Turn left to visit the Tide Mill or right to return to the start.

The White Horse

Norfolk

The Inn

Behind an unprepossessing façade, the White Horse hides quite a surprise. Drinkers may like the modern style of the front bar with its tiled floors, scrubbed pine and walls adorned with old photographs (as much as the welcoming atmosphere and tip-top beers from East Anglian brewers), but it's diners heading for the rear conservatory restaurant who get to enjoy one of the most hauntingly beautiful views in north Norfolk – across salt marsh to the coast and Scolt Head Island.

All of the eight bedrooms in the cleverly designed extension face the marsh. Designed in a wave to give each a private patio, they are light, spacious and comfortably furnished, with a beach-hut theme and soft colour scheme. The roof is grassed over so that the main house back bedrooms, as well as the dining room and its adjoining summer sun deck, have uninterrupted natural views. The pick of these bedrooms is the spacious, split-level Room at the Top (complete with viewing telescope). Street-facing rooms are ideal for families, as two rooms have a connecting door.

The Food

In the conservatory-dining room, the natural decor displays beachcomber finds and contemporary paintings to great effect. In the evening, candles on simply laid wood tables further soften the look. The emphasis of the menu is on fresh locally caught fish. The kitchen favours Mediterranean techniques, so lunch might consist of baked sardines on toasted ciabatta or Brancaster Staithe mussels cooked in a white wine, cream and parsley sauce, washed down with something lively from the wine list. But British classics such as deep-fried fillet of cod with pease pudding are not neglected.

Dinner might mean risotto of local brown shrimps with parmesan crisp, or tempura of tiger prawns with sweet chilli sauce, rock salt and lemon, preceding roast fillet of halibut with pappardelle of courgette and carrot, and a smoked paprika sauce. There are meat options in the form of fillet of Norfolk pork with apple tarte tatin, mashed potatoes and cider sauce, say, and very good steak and chips. Hazelnut and ricotta torte with honey ice cream and orange syrup is a good way to finish.

The Essentials

Time at the Bar!
11am-11pm
Food: 12-2pm, 6.30-9pm

What's the Damage?
Main courses from £9.25

Bitter Experience:
Woodforde's Wherry, Adnams Bitter, London Pride

Sticky Fingers:
Children welcome; children's menu

Muddy Paws:
Dogs welcome in the bar

Zzzzz:
15 rooms, £50-£75

Anything Else?
Terrace, car park

What To Do

Shop

BURNHAM MARKET

Not only will you find a traditional post office, butchers, bakers, hardware shop and a fish shop, but the upmarket village of Burnham Market has 30 highly original independent and specialist shops. For designer clothing, visit Anna, Gun Hill Clothing or Ruby & Tallulah; for stylish furniture and gifts for the home, pop into Norfolk Living; and for contemporary art, take a look at the Fairfax Gallery.

www.burnhammarket.co.uk

WALSINGHAM FARMS SHOP

A beautiful old barn in the heart of Little Walsingham has been converted to house a fabulous, state-of-the-art food emporium, its mission to sell food from Norfolk farms. Visit the butchery for local meat, see the kitchen where ready-made pies and patés are prepared, and browse the shop and buy some Hill House Farm beef, local wines and beers and fresh vegetables, and locally ground flour.

Guild Street, Walsingham,
Norfolk NR22 6BU
01328 821877
www.walsinghamfarmsshop.co.uk

REAL ALE SHOP

You'll find the Real Ale Shop in the midst of a classic North Norfolk malting barley farm, which supplies the brewers with their prime ingredient. The business is a unique off-licence offering more than 40 ales, all bottle-conditioned, from nine Norfolk brewers.

Branthill Farm, Wells-next-the-Sea,
Norfolk NR23 1SB
01328 710810
www.therealaleshop.co.uk

Visit

TITCHWELL NATURE RESERVE

On the stunning north Norfolk coast, Titchwell Marsh is one of the RSPB's most visited reserves. A firm path along three nature trails takes you to hides where you have the opportunity to see many species of ducks, waders, geese and seabirds, notably breeding avocets and terns, bitterns and marsh harriers. 300 species have been recorded and around 50 have bred. Learn more in the visitor centre.

01485 210779
www.rspb.org.uk

BLICKLING HALL

Dating back to the 17th century, Blickling Hall is one of Britain's great Jacobean houses. The magnificent Long Gallery houses one of the finest private collections of rare books in the country, and also on view are splendid Mortlake tapestries depicting the stories of Abraham, finely detailed plasterwork ceilings, and an impressive collection of furniture and paintings from different periods. Look out for the orangery, secret garden and woodland dell.

Blickling, Norwich, Norfolk NR11 6NF
01263 738030
www.nationaltrust.org.uk

HOUGHTON HALL

A spectacularly grand Palladian mansion set in charming parkland. Expect lavish staterooms, furnished by William Kent, and see the collection of 20,000 model soldiers and other militaria. Don't miss the restored walled garden.

Houghton, King's Lynn, Norfolk PE31 6JU
01485 528569
www.houghtonhall.com

Activity

RACING AT FAKENHAM

Fancy a flutter, then head for Fakenham Racecourse, a popular National Hunt Racecourse situated in the picturesque countryside just 9 miles (14km) from the coast at Holkham. The course has existed since 1905 and its racing season runs between October and May.

01328 862388
www.fakenhamracecourse.co.uk

CYCLING

Explore the gently rolling country lanes and byways and unspoilt villages of north-west Norfolk by bike. A selection of 1- or 2-hour cycle routes or all-day rides are available from Bircham Windmill, where you can hire mountain bikes, trailer bikes and tandems.

Great Bircham, King's Lynn, Norfolk PE 6SJ
01485 578393
www.birchamwindmill.co.uk

WALKING THE COAST

Officially opened by the Prince of Wales in 1986, the 93-mile (150-km) Peddars Way and North Norfolk Coast Path are two long-distance trails, which join together to form one continuous route. The trail begins near Thetford and follows lonely ancient tracks and Roman roads all the way to the sea near Hunstanton. The scenery en route accurately reflects the well-known description of North Norfolk as 'a long way from anywhere'.

The Walk - From Brancaster to Branodunum

Enjoy the scent of the sea as you walk from Brancaster to its Roman fort.

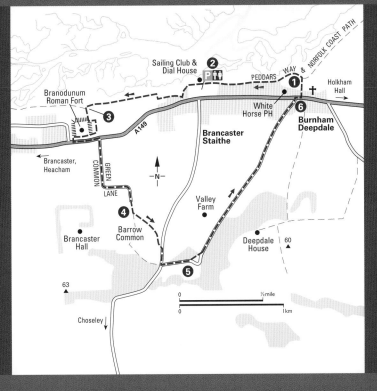

Walk Details

LENGTH: 4.5 miles (7.2km)

TIME: 2hrs 15min

ASCENT: 148ft (45m)

PATHS: Winding paths and tracks, with some paved lanes, 2 stiles

SUGGESTED MAP: aqua3 OS Explorer 250 Norfolk Coast West

GRID REFERENCE: TF 793443

PARKING: The White Horse car park or in lay-by on A149 on edge of Brancaster Staithe

❶ From the garden and car park of the White Horse, join the path and continue to a small boatyard. Follow the trail through the wooden huts, staying on the coast path to Sailing Club and car park.

❷ Walk towards the harbour into the area owned by the Sailing Club and, just before the slipway, you will see the National Trail marker on your left. Shortly, go through the kissing gate and stroll along the boardwalk edging the marshes. Continue for 0.75 mile (1.2km).

❸ Turn left and leave the coastal path, passing through a kissing gate to enter a large field. This is Rack Hill, the area that houses the Roman fort. Follow the lefthand side of the field until you reach the top, then turn right and continue to the first five-bar gate and kissing gate on your left. Cross the gravel drive, go through another gate and continue ahead through the field. At the top, turn left parallel with the A149, exiting the field via a kissing gate in the field corner. Cross the A149 and walk up Green Common Lane, passing the felled tree stumps blocking vehicular access. The track bends left, then sharp right at a field entrance, uphill between hedges.

❹ At a waymarked gate further up the hill, enter Barrow Common nature reserve. Follow the main path ahead, then at a junction of three paths take the middle path and remain on this to a peaceful paved lane. Turn right, and follow the lane down a fairly steep (for Norfolk!) hill. Turn left at the junction and walk straight on to reach a wood.

❺ Head left at the footpath that cuts through a copse to emerge back on the paved lane. When you reach the lane, turn left along it. Just past Valley Farm, enter the field on your left and walk parallel with the road along the permissive path. Rejoin the lane at Burnham Deepdale and continue to the A149.

❻ Cross over the A149 and turn right. After a few paces turn left along The Drove, opposite garage and post office. At the end of the lane is a sign for the coast path. Follow a narrow, tree-lined track that emerges on to the marshes and the main Norfolk Coast Path.

The Rose and Crown

Norfolk

The Inn

Like the Queen at nearby Sandringham, many a London resident holidays in these chic parts of North Norfolk (aka Chelsea-on-Sea). Cocking a cosmopolitan hat in the direction of urbane Burnham Market, the Rose and Crown is a thriving village local in a more tranquil rural retreat just down the coast. Welcoming to families, wet dogs and, in places, dirty boots – whether they belong to locals or weekenders – its soul-warming lack of pretension and touch of esoteric quirkiness sing out. But that's not to say the Rose and Crown doesn't have more than its fair share of style and natural good taste. Besides the inn itself, the great outdoors is the real pull. A goose's honk from the East Coast's number one RSPB reserve, Snettisham Beach is a paradise for walkers, with footpaths meandering through one of Norfolk's last great wildernesses.

Upstairs and to the rear of the inn, the 16 stylish bedrooms are simple and contemporary, with colour schemes of blue and white reflecting the serene coastal feel. Unfussy, chintz-free luxuries such as crisp white linen, plump pillows and power showers do the cosseting, along with Molton Brown toiletries and wireless internet connection.

The Food

Dating from the 14th century – imagine inglenooks, olde-worlde country ephemera, open fires and woodburners – this rambling building with no less than three bar rooms and another trio of principal eating areas, lends itself to flexible dining inside and out. The sun-trap walled garden and spacious terrace are popular. Along with a continental approach of encouraging younger diners to try 'proper food', the wooden climbing frame works up kiddies' appetites outside the top family-style garden room.

Chef Andrew Brice's extensive eclectic menu uses local produce imaginatively. 'Classics' – old pub favourites of proper fish and chips or butchers' sausages and mash – sit alongside new-wave dishes such as confit lamb ravioli and chargrilled globe artichokes on spring pea velouté or hot-sour salad of griddled scallops and sweet roast pork. After 12 years' hard work, Anthony and Jeanette Goodrich and their dedicated team have created the epitome of a proper dining pub, relaxed and friendly yet professional and well run.

The Essentials

Time at the Bar!
10-11.30pm
Food: 12-2pm, 6.30-9pm;
Sat-Sun 10-2.30pm, 6.30-9.30pm

What's the Damage?
Main courses from £8.25

Bitter Experience:
Adnams Bitter, Fuller's London Pride,
Woodforde's Wherry, guest ales

Sticky Fingers:
Children welcome, children's menu

Muddy Paws:
Dogs welcome in the bar

Zzzzz:
16 rooms, £85-£95

Anything Else?
Garden, car park, conservatory

What To Do

Shop

CARTER FARM SHOP

Carter Farm produces asparagus and other specialist fruit and vegetables, and the farm shop opened in 2006 to provide a local outlet for the farm's produce. That's not all, for there's a thriving deli, organic meats, cheeses, local wines and beers, and smoked fish and seafood products. The gallery next door features changing exhibitions.

32 Lynn Road, Great Bircham, King's Lynn, Norfolk PE31 6RJ

01485 578502

www.carterfarmshop.co.uk

DERSINGHAM POTTERY & GALLERY

June Mullarkey makes her hand-thrown pots in stoneware and porcelain using a wide range of colours and textures, while Ben Mullarkey's colourful acrylic, oil and watercolour paintings of lively Norfolk scenes line the walls of this popular gallery.

46 Chapel Road, Dersingham, King's Lynn, Norfolk PE31 6PN

01485 540761

NORFOLK LAVENDER VISITOR CENTRE

This is England's premier lavender farm located at Caley Mill, which stands in its garden of lavender, roses and herbs. The Lavender Shop stocks an extensive range of English lavender and other fragrant products, while the Gift Shop offers a wide choice for all occasions. The Conservatory has a varied selection of plants and gifts for the gardener. There are guided tours.

Heacham, Norfolk PE31 7JE

01485 570384

www.norfolk-lavender.co.uk

Visit

CASTLE ACRE PRIORY

The extensive ruins of the Cluniac Priory, built by William the Conqueror's son-in-law, include the fine arcaded west front of the 11th/12th-century church, a chapel and a 15th-century gatehouse. It stands next to the awe-inspiring ruins of a great castle and the unspoilt village is worth closer inspection.

www.english-heritage.org.uk

HOUGHTON HALL

Built for Robert Walpole and obviously designed to impress, Houghton Hall is a spectacularly grand Palladian mansion set in charming parkland. Expect to see lavish staterooms, decorated and furnished by William Kent. A museum houses an important collection of 20,000 model soldiers and other militaria. Don't miss the restored walled garden.

Houghton, King's Lynn, Norfolk PE31 6JU

01485 528569

www.houghtonhall.com

SANDRINGHAM

If you've seen Buckingham Palace and Clarence House, you'll want to add Sandringham to your list of royal residences. Situated within 60 acres of glorious gardens, the house – once described as the most comfortable in England – was built in 1870 by the Prince and Princess of Wales, later Edward VII and Queen Alexandra. The ground-floor rooms are open to the public, and in the grounds you can view a range of vintage Royal motor vehicles.

The Estate Office, Sandringham, Norfolk PE35 6EN

01553 612908

www.sandringhamestate.co.uk

Activity

BIRDWATCHING

The RSPB's Snettisham reserve gets you close to the wild heart of The Wash, and two of Britain's best wildlife spectacles can be experienced at Snettisham: tides that are especially high force thousands of birds to leave the mudflats where they feed, and settle close to the hides overlooking the lagoons. Visit the reserve at dawn in midwinter to see thousands of pink-footed geese flying inland from The Wash.

RSPB Snettisham

01485 542689

www.rspb.org.uk

CYCLING

Explore the gently rolling country lanes and byways and unspoilt villages of north-west Norfolk by bike. A selection of 1- or 2-hour cycle routes or all-day rides are available from Bircham Windmill, where you can hire mountain bikes, trailer bikes and even tandems. It's OK; there aren't many steep hills!

Great Bircham, King's Lynn, Norfolk PE 6SJ

01485 578393

www.birchamwindmill.co.uk

WALKING TOUR OF KING'S LYNN

Nine hundred years of maritime trading history are preserved in the historic core of King's Lynn. All the fine houses, medieval churches and guildhalls, secret courtyards and hidden alleys can be uncovered if you join one of the expert-led guided tours of the town.

King's Lynn Tourist Information, The Custom House, Purfleet Quay, King's Lynn, Norfolk PE30 1HP

01553 763044

www.visitnorthnorfolk.com

The Walk - A Royal Stroll Around Sandringham

Take in a stately home, a country park and nature reserves on forest pathways.

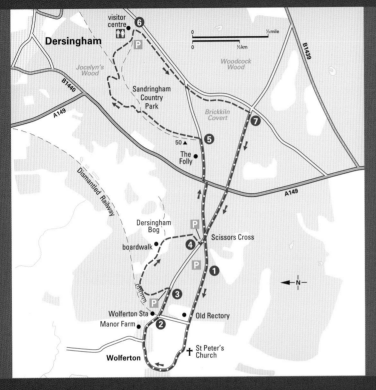

Walk Details

LENGTH: 6.25 miles (10.1km)

TIME: 2hrs 45min

ASCENT: 131ft (40m)

PATHS: Marked forest trails and country lanes

SUGGESTED MAP: aqua3 OS Explorer 250 Norfolk Coast West

GRID REFERENCE: TF 666279

PARKING: Car park on road to Wolferton, or Scissors Cross car park

❶ From the Wolferton road car park turn left towards Wolferton. The walled gardens of the Old Rectory mark the end of mixed woodland. Continue ahead at the junction, past St Peter's Church. The road bends to the right and here you will see cottages (1881) bearing the motto 'Ich Dien' and fleurs-de-lis. Just after Manor Farm is Wolferton Station on the left, which is not currently open to the public.

❷ After Wolferton Station, follow the road to the left and go up the hill to the car park for Dersingham Nature Reserve and a gate beyond.

❸ Go through the gate and take the track to your left, ('Wolferton Cliff and wood walk'). This reserve comprises valley mire and heath, as well as some fairly recent woodland. Follow the track to the 330yd (302m) circular boardwalk around the bog. When you have finished viewing the bog, continue along the track, into the woods again, to reach the Scissors Cross car park.

❹ Turn left out of the car park, then take the lefthand fork, crossing the A149 and passing a house named The Folly. After a few paces you will see a lane to your left ('Scenic Drive'). Just beyond this is a footpath that runs along parallel to the Scenic Drive.

❺ Take this footpath through Sandringham Country Park. There are lots of picnic places here. Follow the yellow trail when it leaves the lane and winds towards Jocelyn's Wood, then continue to the visitor centre. If you want to take time out to visit Sandringham House, this is the best point at which to do it.

❻ From the visitor centre, head for the lower car park and pick up the yellow trail again, which follows the main road, but is tucked away behind the trees of Scotch Belt. Eventually cross the lane and pick up the path once more on the opposite side as it passes through Brickkiln Covert.

❼ At the crossroads, where the footpath ends, turn right down a quiet lane with wide verges, still in woodland. Cross the A149 to reach Scissors Cross. Take the fork on your left and you will be back at the car park where the walk began.

Following on from the success of the Victoria Hotel at Holkham, the Holkham Estate bought The Globe in 2005 and set about sensitively refurbishing the building. It's an old coaching inn that overlooks a pretty, leafy Georgian square known as The Buttlands and remains decidedly pubby, in marked contrast to the chic Victoria. Big round tables take pride of place in the broad bay windows of the simple front bar with its gleaming hand pumps – locals and holidaymakers are drawn in for pints of Adnams and Woodforde's ales. There are evocative photographs on the plain walls, and a wood-burning stove belts out heat on cold winter days. Bare boards lead into the rear dining area and a seaside feel prevails as befits its location.

Well-thought-out upstairs bedrooms are simple but light and airy and modern: rugs on polished oak floors, big metal-framed beds with down duvets and scatter cushions, subtle spotlighting, cane chairs and simple wooden furnishings. Digital TVs, phones and spotless tiled bathrooms are standard throughout.

The Food

In keeping with the ethos of the Holkham Estate, food at the Globe makes good use of the abundant seasonal produce to be found along the coast: say, crab and bass landed at Wells quay, local cheeses and asparagus, and venison and game from the estate. The printed menu lists a good range of classic pub favourites. Tuck into thick-cut Norfolk ham and mustard sandwiches, freshly battered haddock with chips and home-made tartare sauce, and Holkham-reared steaks from the chargrill.

Look to the daily chalkboard for something a little more imaginative, such as wild garlic soup or potted shrimps with watercress and cucumber salad for starters. For the best seasonal local produce, opt for the Norfolk tasting plate – Norfolk Dapple cheese, local salami, smoked mackerel and Arthur's pork pie – or go for the excellent roast belly pork, served with apple mash, fine beans and cider gravy, or the seared sea bass on tomato and fennel compote. Leave room, if you can, for warm chocolate pudding or a selection of Holkham ice cream. Wines are first class and include ten by the glass.

The Essentials

Time at the Bar!
11am-11pm (12-10.30pm Sun)
Food: 12-2.30pm, 7-9pm

What's the Damage?
Main courses £8.50

Bitter Experience:
Woodforde's Wherry, Adnams Bitter

Sticky Fingers:
Children welcome, children's menu

Muddy Paws:
Dogs welcome in the front bar

Zzzzz:
7 rooms, £65-£130

Anything Else?
Courtyard, no car park

What To Do

Shop

HOLT

Wander the back alleys of this timeless market town for galleries, boutiques, delis and individual shops. Don't miss the edible goodies in Byfords Deli & Cafe or in Bakers & Larners store. For local arts and crafts, head for Bircham Gallery in the Market Place.

Byfords
Shirehall Plain, Holt, Norfolk NR25 6BG
01263 711400
www.byfords.org.uk

Bakers & Larners
8-12 Market Place, Holt, Norfolk NR25 6BW
01263 712323
www.bakersandlarners.com

Bircham Gallery
14 Market Place, Holt, Norfolk NR25 6BW
01263 713312
www.birchamgallery.com

BIRDSCAPES GALLERY & PINKFOOT GALLERY

Paintings, prints and sculptures from over 30 nationally known Norfolk-based wildlife artists.

Manor Farm Barns, Glandford, Holt,
Norfolk NR25 7JP
01263 741742
www.birdscapesgallery.co.uk

Pinkfoot Gallery
High Street, Cley-next-the-Sea NR25 7RB
01263 740947
www.pinkfootgallery.co.uk

PICNIC FAYRE

Award-winning deli set in an old forge, crammed with local cheese, speciality breads, fruit and vegetables and a great antipasti bar – so load up the car and head off along the coast.

Old Forge, Cley-next-the-Sea NR25 7AP
01263 740587
www.picnic-fayre.co.uk

Visit

HOLKHAM HALL

Holkham Hall is home to the Earls of Leicester and the Coke family and has been in that family's ownership for almost 400 years. Situated within a beautiful deer park, this classic 18th-century Palladian-style mansion is a living treasure house of artistic and architectural history. With the stunning architectural grandeur of the Marble Hall, the magnificent staterooms and the vast and well-equipped kitchen quarters, there is certainly plenty to see.

Holkham, Wells-next-the-Sea,
Norfolk NR23 1AB
01328 710227
www.holkham.co.uk

WELLS & WALSINGHAM LIGHT RAILWAY

Visit the longest narrow-gauge steam railway in the world and see the unique Garratt Locomotive 'Norfolk Hero' built specially for this line. Travel through the tranquil and scenic East Anglian countryside from Wells to Walsingham, famed for centuries as a centre of pilgrimage, explore the village and visit the shrine before catching the train back to Wells. Have a look at the charming restored signal box where refreshments are available.

www.wellswalsinghamrailway.co.uk

THURSFORD COLLECTION

A fascinating organ collection, with a Wurlitzer cinema organ, fairground organs, barrel and street organs among its treasures.

Thursford Green, Fakenham,
Norfolk NR21 0AS
01328 878477
www.thursford.com

Activity

CYCLING

Cycling is one of the great ways of exploring this stunning, windswept stretch of British coastline. One of the finest routes is the North Norfolk Coast Cycleway, offering quiet lanes, dramatic views and plenty more besides on its 59-mile (95-km) journey from Cromer to King's Lynn.

Wells & Holkham By Cycle, Beach Road,
Wells-next-the-Sea,
Norfolk NR23 1DR
07879 032241 or 07747 012616
www.cyclenorfolk.co.uk

GUIDED BIRD WALKS

The reserves and bird sanctuaries on this stretch of coast make this an obvious destination for ornithologists. Here you can join a local expert and discover the birdlife that abounds in Norfolk.

01263 821604

SEAL TRIPS

Visit the seals in their natural environment on a boat trip to Blakeney Point, a famous breeding ground for terns and waders. The seal colony numbers 400 common and grey seals and, if weather conditions are suitable, the boat can land and you can visit the Information Centre.

Temples, Morston Quay, Norfolk
01263 740791

The Walk - The Magical Marshes of Blakeney

Walk along the sea defences to some of the finest bird reserves in the country.

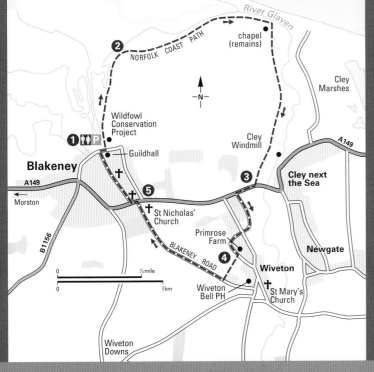

Walk Details

LENGTH: 4.5 miles (7.2km)

TIME: 2hrs

ASCENT: 98ft (30m)

PATHS: Footpaths with some paved lanes, can flood in winter

SUGGESTED MAP: aqua3 OS Explorer 251 Norfolk Coast Central

GRID REFERENCE: TG 028441

PARKING: Carnser (pay) car park, on seafront opposite Blakeney Guildhall and Manor Hotel

① From the car park head for the wildfowl conservation project, a fenced-off area that is home to ducks, geese and widgeon. A species list has been mounted on one side, so you can see how many you can spot. From here, take the path ('Norfolk Coast Path') out towards the marshes. This raised bank is part of the sea defences, and is managed by the Environment Agency. Eventually, you will walk with salt marshes on both sides.
② At the turning, head east. Carmelite friars once lived around here, although there is little to see of their chapel, the remains of which are located just after you turn by the wooden staithe (landing stage) to head south again. This part of

the walk is excellent for spotting kittiwakes and terns in the late summer. Also, look for Sabine's gull, manx and sooty shearwaters, godwits, turnstones and curlews. The path leads past Cley Windmill (1810) which last operated in 1919. It is open to visitors and you can climb to the top for a wide-ranging view across the marshes. Follow signs for the Norfolk Coast Path until you reach the A149.
③ Cross the A149 to the pavement opposite, turn right. Take the 1st left after crossing the little creek. Eventually reach the cobblestone houses of Wiveton and a crossroads; go straight ahead.
④ Take the grassy track opposite Primrose Farm, and continue to the

T-junction. This is Blakeney Road, turn right along it and proceed. Alternatively, if you are in need of refreshments, turn left and walk a short way to reach the Wiveton Bell pub. The lane is wide and ahead you will see the 13th-century St Nicholas Church. Its 2 towers once served as navigation beacons for sailors, and the east one is still floodlit at night.
⑤ On reaching the A149 you will see 2 lanes opposite you. Take the High Street fork on the left to walk back through the centre of Blakeney village. Keep a lookout for the 14th-century Guildhall undercroft at the bottom of Mariner's Hill. Keep ahead to return to the car park where the walk began.

The Victoria at Holkham

Norfolk

The Inn

Standing at one of the entrances to Holkham Hall, one of Britain's most majestic stately homes, and just a stroll from Holkham's expansive sandy beach, the estate-owned Victoria was built in the 1800s to house the entourage of visiting aristocracy. Lovingly restored in 2001 by Tom and Polly Coke, this imposing and hugely individual brick inn is the place to stay along Norfolk's glorious north coast. Bedrooms have a shabby chic feel with bold colours, beautiful fabrics, ornately carved furnishings from Rajasthan, and quirky bathrooms with roll-top baths and classy toiletries. Book The Marsh room, where you can laze in the bath and soak up the view across Holkham Nature Reserve. For a total get-away-from-it-all experience, stay in one of the beautifully restored lodges in the heart of the estate.

The smart colonial theme extends downstairs into the informal bar, decked out with carved furniture, huge sofas, amazing Indian artefacts and a vast table adorned with fat candles and a huge bowl of fruit. The adjoining dining room has an elegant, contemporary feel, with modern art on the walls.

The Essentials

Time at the Bar!
10am-11pm
Food: 12-2.30pm, 7-9pm

What's the Damage?
Main courses from £12

Bitter Experience:
Woodforde's Wherry,
Fuller's London Pride

Sticky Fingers:
Children welcome; children's menu

Muddy Paws:
Dogs welcome in the bar

Zzzzz:
14 rooms, £120-£220

Anything Else?
Terrace, garden, car park

The Food

The modern British menus focus on fresh, local produce, notably beef and seasonal game reared on the estate, and fish and seafood from along the coast. In the classic tap room and adjoining bar you can tuck into spiced pumpkin soup, potted shrimps with green salad, or a delicious plate of antipasti – smoked estate venison, Suffolk salami, local Binham Blue cheese and marinated olives – the perfect lunch with a cracking pint of Woodforde's Wherry.

Cooking and menu choice move up a gear in the dining room. From the seasonally changing menu, begin with terrine of rabbit, apple and pistachio with celeriac remoulade, or work your way through a bowl of linguine with Thornham mussels, garlic and herb cream. Accomplished main courses may take in pan-fried cod with shellfish chowder, loin of estate venison with braised cabbage, root vegetable casserole and confit shallots, or a classic Holkham rib-eye steak served with béarnaise sauce, chips and salad. Round off with praline parfait with roasted almond ice cream. Drink or dine alfresco in the sun-trap courtyard.

What To Do

Shop

ANCIENT HOUSE GALLERY

Here you'll find pottery made on the estate, an eclectic mix of paintings, jewellery, ceramics and local foodstuffs. A short stroll from the village you'll find Bringing the Outside Inn, a studio featuring landscape photography and attractive coastal artefacts.

Ancient House Gallery
01328 711285
Bringing the Outside Inn
01328 713093

MADE IN CLEY

Head east along the coast to Made In Cley at Cley-next-the-Sea for hand-thrown stoneware pottery, prints and contemporary jewellery made on the premises. At Wells-next-the-Sea you'll find dynamic Big Blue Sky Gallery and, at nearby Wighton, the School House Gallery, with work by East Anglian artists.

Made in Cley
01263 740134
www.madeincley.co.uk
Big Blue Sky
01328 712023
www.bigbluesky.uk.com
The School House Gallery
01328 820457

NORFOLK LIVING

For stylish furniture and gifts for the home, pop into Norfolk Living in Burnham Market. The village has 30 highly original independent and specialist shops. For designer clothing, visit Anna, Gun Hill Clothing or Ruby & Tallulah, and for contemporary art, take a look at the Fairfax Gallery. There's also a post office, butchers, bakers, hardware shop and a fish shop.

www.burnhammarket.co.uk

Visit

HOLKHAM HALL

Walk up the drive from the Victoria to visit Holkham Hall, home to the Earls of Leicester and the Coke family for almost 400 years. Stroll through the deer park to find the classic 18th-century Palladian-style mansion with magnificent staterooms and vast kitchen quarters. Waymarked walks and a nature trail to explore in the park; an excellent cafe in the lavender-fringed courtyard of the old stables.

Holkham, Wells-next-the-Sea,
Norfolk NR23 1AB
01328 710227
www.holkham.co.uk

HOUGHTON HALL

Built for Robert Walpole and obviously designed to impress, Houghton Hall is another Palladian mansion set in charming parkland. The lavish staterooms were decorated and furnished by William Kent. A museum houses an important collection of 20,000 model soldiers and other militaria.

Houghton, King's Lynn, Norfolk PE31 6JU
01485 528569
www.houghtonhall.com

LANGHAM GLASS

Watch as molten crystal is transformed into glass using traditional methods; then create your own glass masterpiece alongside the expert glassmakers.

Sculthorpe Boulevard, Tattersett Business Park, Fakenham, Norfolk NR21 7RL
01485 529111
www.langhamglass.co.uk

Activity

BIRDWATCHING

This stretch of the North Norfolk coast offers some of the best birdwatching in Britain. If you have binoculars but are not too sure what you're looking at, then call Andy Stoddart, an experienced, locally based birder, who will guide you on a half- or full-day walk.

01263 711396
www.northnorfolkbirds.co.uk

HOLKHAM BEACH

Cross the road from the Victoria and walk down Lady Anne's Drive to find one of the most unspoilt and beautiful stretches of sand in the country. Soak up the sheer sense of space at low tide and walk for miles along the vast beach, then laze in the dunes or explore the paths that criss-cross the marsh and pasture of Holkham's Nature Reserve.

SEAL TRIPS

Visit the seals in their natural environment on a boat trip to Blakeney Point, also a famous breeding ground for terns and waders. The seal colony numbers 400 common and grey seals. The boat will land at the point for up-close viewing, weather permitting.

Temples, Morston Quay, Norfolk
01263 740791

The Walk - A Medieval Shrine at Walsingham

A stroll to one of the most important medieval shrines in England.

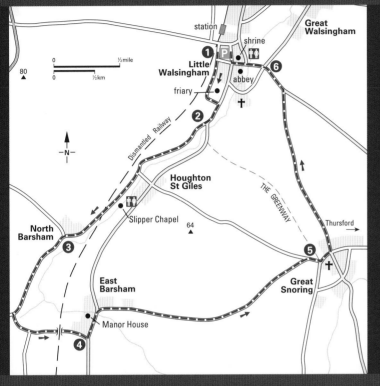

Walk Details

LENGTH: 7.75 miles (12.5km)

TIME: 3hrs 45min

ASCENT: 164ft (50m)

PATHS: Mostly country lanes

SUGGESTED MAP: aqua3 OS Explorer 251 Norfolk Coast Central

GRID REFERENCE: TF 933368

PARKING: Pay-and-display car park, Little Walsingham

1 From the car park, head for the exit sign, and turn left down the hill. Go straight across at the junction, walking down narrow Coker's Hill. The remains of a Franciscan friary can be seen off to your left, incorporated into a private house. When you reach the open fields, go left and down a hill, then turn right and continue down the road.

2 Take the righthand fork, with the stream on your lefthand side. This road is part of the old pilgrim route, when folk left their shoes in Houghton St Giles in order to walk the last stretch barefoot as a mark of their sincerity and extreme piety. Pass Slipper Chapel on your left (built in the 1300s and partly destroyed during the Reformation),

and then walk past the remains of the now dismantled railway to enter North Barsham.

3 At the junction, keep to the left; take the lane ('West Barsham') to the junction in the copse. Take the lane to the left, up the hill with the fir plantation on the right. Descend the hill, passing more of the dismantled railway, eventually reaching East Barsham.

4 Turn left at the T-junction and walk past the White Horse Inn. Just after the red-brick manor house, turn right into Water Lane ('Great Snoring'). Look out for partridges, yellowhammers and finches fluttering among the hedgerows.

5 At the junction, take the righthand turn towards Thursford.

(It is possible to take The Greenway to Walsingham shortly after this point, but be warned that this route can be extremely boggy.) Continue ahead into Great Snoring, and turn left by the large red-brick house, then quickly reach open fields again. After a little more than 1 mile (1.6 km), bear left towards Little Walsingham and continue to a patch of shady woodland.

6 At the crossroads, continue straight ahead, and go ahead again at the next crossroads, to walk past an Anglican shrine. Go up the hill to the pumphouse topped by a brazier that is lit on state occasions. Turn right by the shrine shop, and then turn immediately left to reach the car park where the walk began.

The Hoste Arms

Norfolk

The Hoste Arms, The Green, Burnham Market, King's Lynn, Norfolk PE31 8HD

The Essentials

Time at the Bar!
10am-11pm
Food: 12-2pm, 7-9pm

What's the Damage?
Main courses from £10.95

Bitter Experience:
Woodforde's Wherry, Greene King
Abbot Ale, Adnams Bitter

Sticky Fingers:
Children welcome, children's menu

Muddy Paws:
Dogs welcome in the bar, lounge
area and some bedrooms

Zzzzz:
37 rooms, £122-£193

Anything Else?
Terrace, garden, car park

The Food

Paul Whittome's handsome, pale yellow 17th-century inn overlooks both the village green and parish church of this upmarket Georgian village. Passion, dedication and unstinting investment over the years have transformed it into a rare combination of stylish pub, restaurant and chic hotel, one that appeals as much to celebrities, well-heeled locals and city folk up for the weekend, as it does to tourists and local fishermen popping in for a pint. Tardis-like, the Hoste extends back from its rustic, unpretentious bar – still the village local where you can flick through the daily papers and down a few pints of Wherry – and the adjoining, rather tasteful brasserie-style dining areas, with their dark wood panelling and blazing log fires, to the plush rather clubby leather sofa-filled conservatory lounges and a magnificent alfresco dining terrace.

Rooms are split between the inn and converted buildings to the rear and have been individually designed by Jeanne Whittome, with the unique Zulu Wing reflecting her South African heritage. Expect strong colours, bold designer fabrics, four-posters or vast leather sleigh beds, and luxurious, state-of-the-art bathrooms with big baths, bathrobes and top toiletries. Perfect after a day exploring the coastal salt marshes and sand dunes.

The Inn

An eclectic cooking style draws its inspiration from Asia, Europe and, specifically, modern British innovations. The influences may be global but the extensive and imaginative menu focuses on fresh Norfolk produce with a policy of sourcing ingredients – notably fish and seafood – within a 20-mile (32km) radius. Start with a plate of Brancaster oysters, served tempura style or with garlic and parsley butter, or a spicy salmon fishcake with sweet chilli sauce. For main course, opt for sesame-crusted sea bass with Thai spiced potatoes and coriander dressing, rack of lamb with cauliflower mash and glazed beetroot and port jus, or try the beef fillet, served with roasted plum tomatoes, field mushrooms and hand-cut chips.

Lighter meals take in various salads, pastas and risottos, and lunchtime sandwiches may include Letzer's smoked salmon with lemon and chive crème fraîche. For pudding, there may be banana tarte tatin and liquorice ice cream, a savoury like Welsh rarebit with Parma ham and poached egg, or a plate of cheese featuring local Binham Blue. Indulge in the notable, well-chosen wine list and you will find some quality French offerings alongside plenty of New World wines.

What To Do

Shop

BURNHAM MARKET

Step out of the Hoste, stroll through the market place and neighbouring streets and savour the traditional village atmosphere. You'll find more than 30 independent and specialist shops, from an exciting deli (Humble Pie) and lifestyle shops selling vibrant and stylish accessories for the home and garden (Norfolk Living) to trendy clothes shops (Anna, Pukka Clothing, Ruby & Tallulah) and select galleries (Fairfax Gallery), bookshops (Brazen Head Bookshop) and antique shops.

www.burnhammarket.co.uk

CARTER FARM SHOP

Carter Farm produces asparagus and other specialist fruit and vegetables, and the farm shop opened in 2006 to provide a local outlet. There's also a thriving deli, organic meats, cheeses, local wines and beers, and smoked fish and seafood products.

32 Lynn Road, Great Bircham, King's Lynn, Norfolk PE31 6RJ
01485 578502
www.carterfarmshop.co.uk

SAMPHIRE FOOD SHOP

If you're heading to Blickling's magnificent Jacobean Hall, then call in at this fantastic farm shop in the barn next to the car park. Fill your basket with cheeses, crab from the coast, seasonal fruit and vegetables, wonderful pork pies, and rare-breed meats. They'll even make you a great picnic to enjoy in the grounds of Blickling Hall.

The Estate Barn, Blickling, Aylsham, Norfolk NR11 6NF
www.samphireshop.co.uk

Visit

BLICKLING HALL

Dating back to the 17th century, Blickling Hall is one of Britain's great Jacobean houses. The Long Gallery houses one of the finest private collections of rare books in the country; also on view are splendid Mortlake tapestries depicting the stories of Abraham, finely detailed plasterwork ceilings, and an impressive collection of furniture and paintings from different periods. Look out for the orangery, secret garden and woodland dell.

Blickling, Norwich, Norfolk NR11 6NF
01263 738030
www.nationaltrust.org.uk

GREAT BIRCHAM WINDMILL

One of the last remaining windmills in Norfolk, this striking example stands on that Norfolk rarity, a hill, so expect fine views across rolling fields towards the coast once you have climbed the five floors. Sails turn on windy days and you can visit the adjoining bakery, take tea in the cafe and hire a bike.

Great Bircham, King's Lynn, Norfolk PE31 6SJ
01485 578393
www.birchamwindmill.co.uk

SANDRINGHAM

In 60 acres of glorious gardens, the house – once described as the most comfortable in England – was built in 1870 by the Prince and Princess of Wales, later Edward VII and Queen Alexandra. Don't miss the vintage royal motor vehicles.

The Estate Office, Sandringham, Norfolk PE35 6EN
01553 612908
www.sandringhamestate.co.uk

Activity

GOLF AT BRANCASTER

The Royal West Norfolk Golf Club at Brancaster exudes a unique sense of tradition, history and character. Rated amongst the top 50 clubs in Ireland and Great Britain, Royal West Norfolk is a testing links course, laid out in a grand manner and characterised by extraordinary sleepered greens, cross-bunkers and salt marshes.

01485 210087

NORFOLK NATURE TOURS

Enjoy a relaxing walk through the North Norfolk countryside with an expert local guide and develop your knowledge of natural history and your identification skills. There are one-day wildlife or orchid walks, or join one of the two- to three-day wildlife workshops.

01263 587736
www.norfolknature.co.uk

SEAL TRIPS

Visit the seals in their natural environment on a boat trip to Blakeney Point, also a famous breeding ground for terns and waders. The seal colony numbers 400 common and grey seals and, if the weather conditions are suitable, you can visit the Information Centre in the Old Lifeboat House.

Temples Boats, Morston Quay, Morston, Norfolk
01263 740791

The Walk - The Burnhams

In the footsteps of Lord Admiral Nelson around the Norfolk marshes.

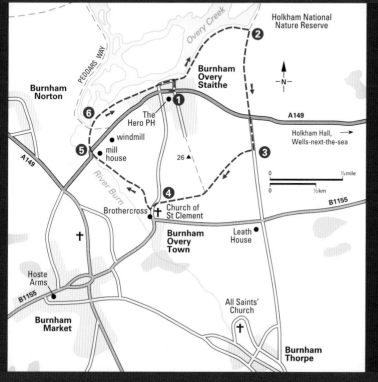

Walk Details

LENGTH: 4 miles (6.4km)

TIME: 2hrs

ASCENT: 49ft (15m)

PATHS: Waymarked paths and some paved lanes, 1 stile

SUGGESTED MAP: aqua3 OS Explorer 251 Norfolk Coast Central

GRID REFERENCE: TF 844441

PARKING: On-street parking on main road in Burnham Overy Staithe

❶ From The Hero pub, turn right, then immediately left down East Harbour Way to Overy Creek. Turn right next to the black-painted house, go through the gate and bear left along the waterfront. Eventually, the path reaches the T-junction.

❷ At the T-junction, turn right, through the gate, into the marshy meadow of long grass. This area is an English Nature Reserve (part of Holkham National Nature Reserve). The sand dunes, salt marshes and mudflats are home to a wide variety of birds and plants, including sea aster and plovers. Cross the stile, then follow the grass track to the A149. Cross to the tarmac lane opposite, and follow this until you have passed 2 fields on your right.

❸ Go through the gap at the entrance to the 3rd field, which is marked with a yellow arrow on a post. Keep right to the waymarker pointing left, across the middle of the field. Keep ahead, through the gaps in the hedges, to reach the dirt lane. Cross this and go down the track opposite, walking towards the Norman tower of Burnham Overy's Church of St Clement.

❹ Turn left at end of the track on to Mill Road, then go right up the track called Marsh Lane. Go through the gate and continue into the field, so that the River Burn is off to your left, with the round Saxon tower of Burnham Norton visible in the distance to your left and Burnham Overy windmill straight ahead. Go

through the gate by the Mill House, complete with its own mill pond and mill race (1820).

❺ Taking great care, cross the A149, keeping the pond on your left, then cross the signed footpath over the stile into the next field and follow the hedge on the right. Away to your right you will be able to see Burnham Overy windmill (privately owned and not open to the public).

❻ Cross over a stile by a gate, then, at the junction of paths, turn right and head across the field towards the road. Just before the road, follow the path along the field edge parallel with the road, soon to join the pavement in the field corner. Continue back to The Hero pub and the start of the walk.

The Clive

Shropshire

The Inn

As you drive along the A49 just north of Ludlow, The Clive is impossible
to miss. It is a striking building – a farmhouse in the 18th century, more
recently a pub for estate workers, then a bar/brasserie/restaurant
operation known as the Cookhouse. Now refurbished and renamed,
new owners have added accommodation to the mix. The bar is a bright
modern area, with glass-topped tables, chrome and leather chairs and
contemporary artwork, and leads to a more traditional space with beams
and brick and stone walls where you can relax on sofas by an enormous
fireplace. On warmer days, take your drinks out onto a sheltered terrace.

Behind the main building a group of old barns set around a courtyard has
been converted into 15 stylish yet uncluttered bedrooms, all of which have
beams and gleaming slate-floored bathrooms but are simply furnished in a
style that is more Scandinavian-inspired than English country. The ground-
floor rooms have pale wooden floors and overlook the courtyard, while the
thickly carpeted and comfortable rooms on the first floor have skylights in
the roof, so the only thing missing is a view.

The Essentials

Time at the Bar!
11am-11pm
Food: 12-2.30pm, 6.30-9.30pm;
Sat-Sun 12-9.30pm

What's the Damage?
Main courses from £9.95

Bitter Experience:
Hobsons Best

Sticky Fingers:
Children welcome, small portions
available

Muddy Paws:
Dogs welcome in outside areas

Zzzzz:
15 rooms, £75-£97.50

Anything Else?
Grassed area, courtyard

The Food

Children are welcome here, and the menu indicates dishes that are available in small portions. Families may prefer to eat in the less formal area adjoining the bar than in the more elegant restaurant, though that is not to say the restaurant is stuffy or pretentious – far from it. The cooking is a reasonably priced, happy mix of good old British staples with Mediterranean touches, with the emphasis on fine local ingredients. A typical lunch menu might include a salad of pesto tomatoes with buffalo mozzarella, olives and rocket, perhaps lightly battered cod with chips and peas or braised lamb and beans with roasted aubergine, and there is always a roast on Sunday.

In the evening, everything cranks up a notch. The dinner menu might offer sweet and spicy beef carpaccio with wild mushroom millefeuille, and braised and roasted rabbit with grilled black pudding. Puddings range from apple and raisin pie with hot custard to a tulip of dark chocolate mousse with green tea ice cream. The bar menu offers grills and pizza or baguettes with substantial and imaginative fillings.

What To Do

Shop

LUDLOW

Shopping in Ludlow is an altogether different retail experience. There is a welcome absence of familiar chain stores and high-street names and in their place you will find many small individual shops and family-owned businesses, representing shopping with a personal touch. Quality culinary produce attracts top chefs, and the conspicuous presence of various artisans add a sense of colour and individuality to what has been described as England's finest market town and centre for local produce.

Myriad Organics
22 Corve Street 01584 872665
www.myriadorganics.co.uk

Deli on the Square
4 Church Street 01584 877353

Mousetrap Cheese Shop
6 Church Street 01584 879556
www.mousetrapcheese.co.uk

Farmers Produce Market
1 Mill Street 01584 873532
www.cittaslow.org.uk

LUDLOW FOOD CENTRE

This unique market place for quality, locally produced food and drink stands adjacent to The Clive, so there's no excuse for not stocking up on local artisan goodies before you head home. Inside the impressive building you'll find fresh seasonal produce from local growers, organic meats, farmhouse cheeses, Herefordshire cider and apple juice, hand-made pickles and chutneys, in addition to in-house butchery, bakery, dairy and jam-making enterprises.

Bromfield, Ludlow, Shropshire SY8 2JR
01584 856000
www.ludlowfoodcentre.co.uk

Visit

STOKESAY CASTLE

Set in a green valley amid rolling countryside, 11th-century Stokesay Castle is one of English Heritage's rare treasures. The Great Hall remains unchanged since it was built in 1291, and one of Stokesay's most impressive features is its breathtaking Elizabethan fireplace, complete with elaborately carved overmantel. Across the courtyard stands the striking Jacobean gatehouse, constructed in 1620.

Stokesay, Craven Arms, Shropshire SY7 9AH
0870 333 1181
www.english-heritage.org.uk

WALCOT HALL ARBORETUM

There are 30 acres of garden and rare trees to savour in this glorious country-house setting. Walcot Hall is home to the Parish family, who have lived here for almost half a century, and the Tudor house is surrounded by a vast amphitheatre of hills set on the edge of the Clun Forest. The arboretum is one of the finest in Britain.

Lydbury, Shropshire SY7 8AZ
01588 680570
www.walcothall.com

ACTON SCOTT WORKING FARM MUSEUM

A vivid introduction to traditional rural life, with plenty of rare breeds, and crops cultivated using old rotation methods; all the work is done by hand or horse power, with period farm machinery. There are craft demonstrations of spinning, pottery and butter-making.

Acton Scott, Church Stretton, Shropshire SY6 6QN
01694 781306
www.actonscottmuseum.co.uk

Activity

SEVERN VALLEY RAILWAY

Travel through 16 miles (26 km) of glorious countryside along the River Severn on this much-loved preserved steam railway. Begin at Kidderminster or Bewdley and then journey at a sedate pace to the lovely old hilltop town of Bridgnorth where there is time for afternoon tea and a stroll through its ancient streets before making the return trip. Wallow in nostalgia and enjoy outstanding views from the window.

www.svr.co.uk
01299 403816

WALKING THE WELSH MARCHES

The opportunities for walking in the Welsh Marches are endless and there are regular guided walks through the Carding Mill Valley and around Ludlow and Cleobury Mortimer. For something more adventurous, try the Mortimer Trail, which runs for 30 miles (48 km) through the heart of the Marches between Ludlow and Kington. Break your journey midway, enjoying an overnight stop at the aptly-named Riverside Inn at Aymestrey.

01584 875053
www.visitsouthshropshire.co.uk

LUDLOW RACES

Ludlow is a National Hunt course, retaining much of its Edwardian charm – although the welcome is absolutely up to date – Ludlow likes to think of itself as 'the friendliest course in the country'. Treat yourself to lunch in a private viewing box overlooking the track and surrounding countryside.

Bromfield, Ludlow, Shropshire SY8 2BT
01584 856221
www.ludlow-racecourse.co.uk

The Walk - Over the Edge from Stokesay

A walk that takes in a 13th-century house set in gorgeous hills.

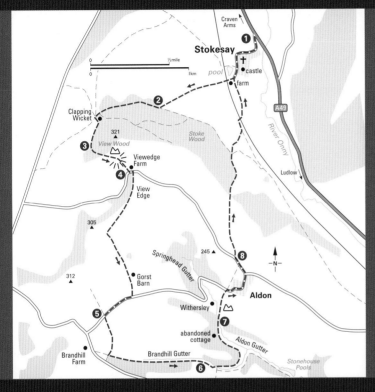

Walk Details

LENGTH: 6.25 miles (10.1km)

TIME: 2hrs 30min

ASCENT: 909ft (277m)

PATHS: Mostly excellent, short stretch eroded and uneven, byway from Aldon to Stoke Wood occasionally floods, 12 stiles

SUGGESTED MAP: aqua3 OS Explorers 203 Ludlow; 217 The Long Mynd & Wenlock Edge

GRID REFERENCE: SO 437819 (on Explorer 217)

PARKING: Lay-by on A49 north of Stokesay turn

① Take the footway from the lay-by to lane that leads to Stokesay Castle. Walk past the castle; take the 2nd footpath on the right, at far side of the pool. It skirts the farm, then crosses the railway. Keep ahead through 3 meadows on the worn path, with a series of stiles providing further guidance.

② Enter Stoke Wood, proceed to the track; turn right. Leave the wood at a stile at the far end and walk past the house, Clapping Wicket, then turn sharp left up the field in front of the house. Turn right at the top, walking by the edge of View Wood.

③ Join the track that leads into the wood, then emerges from it to run alongside the edge. It soon plunges back into the trees, climbing quite

steeply, then levelling out to reach lane by Viewedge Farm.

④ Turn left for few paces, then join footpath on right. Turn right by field edge and walk to top of knoll, continuing in same direction across fields to waymarker that sends you sharp left across adjacent field. Join track at far side and continue past Gorst Barn to lane. Turn right.

⑤ Turn left on footpath, crossing 3 pastures to concealed stile, which gives on to bridleway. Turn left down Brandhill Gutter. Eventually go through gate on right, but immediately turn left to continue in same direction. Keep close to stream or dry streambed on left.

⑥ After passing through the gate, the bridleway becomes narrow,

uneven and eroded for while but soon improves. It eventually crosses stream (next to stile) and starts to swing northwards, into Aldon Gutter. Beyond the abandoned cottage, the bridleway passes to right of pheasant pens – watch carefully for waymarkers here.

⑦ 200yds (183m) after the cottage, the bridleway bears right, climbing up the steep valley side to meet the lane at the top. Turn right to pass through the hamlet of Aldon, then left at the T-junction.

⑧ Join byway on right at slight bend in lane (no sign or waymarker). This lovely hedged track leads between fields, then through Stoke Wood, beyond which it descends to Stokesay and the walk start point.

The Inn at Grinshill

Shropshire

The Inn

The area around Grinshill is popular walking country and the Inn at Grinshill makes a great base for exploring. The original Georgian building has been extended over the years and since 2001, when Kevin and Victoria Brazier moved in, has been transformed from a rather run-down boozer into a smart and comfortable inn. With an open fire and real ale on tap, the Elephant and Castle Bar (named after the original pub) still has a pubby atmosphere, complete with background music of the easy listening variety – though there is live music on a Friday night. The restaurant is uncluttered and decorated in cool neutral colours with one end open to the kitchen.

The six sound-proofed bedrooms are pretty and unfussy. All are similarly decorated in pale creamy colours and furnished with a mixture of antiques and contemporary painted furniture. Deep double-ended baths, power showers and fluffy towels are common to all bathrooms, and all the rooms are equipped with DVD players, broadband connection and state-of-the-art flat-screen TVs, cunningly disguised as mirrors.

The Inn at Grinshill, The High Street, Grinshill, Shrewsbury, Shropshire SY4 3BL

The Essentials

Time at the Bar!
11am-3pm, 6-11pm; Sun 12-4pm
Food: 12-2.30pm, 6.30-9.30pm
(closed Sun evening)

What's the Damage?
Main courses from £9

Bitter Experience:
Hanbys Drawell, Theakston XB,
guest ale

Sticky Fingers:
Children welcome, small
portions available

Muddy Paws:
Dogs welcome in the bar only

Zzzzz:
6 rooms, £50-£120

Anything Else?
Terrace, garden, car park

The Food

Whether you eat in the child- and dog-friendly bar, the restaurant with entertaining views of the kitchen or, on a warm day, out on the terrace with views over the Shropshire countryside, the menu has something for everyone. There are pub favourites such as sausages with leek mash and gravy, beer-battered cod with chips and mushy peas, and chilli con carne.

Some dishes are what you would expect on a modern British-style menu: seared scallops with black pudding and rarebit croûte, and confit of duck leg with crushed potato and rosemary gravy; while others sound quaintly old-fashioned, such as Chateaubriand with a bouquetière of vegetables, and mornay and chasseur sauces and peas bonne femme. Puddings might include chocolate fondant with cinder toffee cream, and baked egg custard tart with apple compote. The Early Bird menu served at lunch and early evenings is good value at £11.95 for three courses and coffee.

What To Do

Shop

ELEY'S OF IRONBRIDGE

Eley's is the home of traditional pork pies made by the age-old method of hand-raising. They sell sausages and apple pies, too – all home-made on the premises using local high-quality ingredients.

13 Tontine Hill, Ironbridge,
Shropshire TF8 7AL
01952 432504

COOKING MARVELLOUS

Domestic goddesses will love Cooking Marvellous, where you can source every kitchen gadget known to woman. Work your way down Shrewsbury high street, which is a million miles from being a bland shopping experience: you'll find hats, Japanese groceries, ironmongers, Shropshire cheese, contemporary art and designer togs. All tastes are catered for: Wyle Cop is a haven for fashionistas and culinary divas alike.

3 Wyle Cop, Shrewsbury,
Shropshire SY1 1UT
01743 368199
www.cookingmarvellous.com

MAWS CRAFT CENTRE

The former factory buildings of tile manufacturer Maws & Co in the heart of the Ironbridge Gorge have been refurbished and now comprise residential units and 20 individual workshops housing a wide variety of art, craft and design specialists. You'll find traditional crafts - furniture making, pottery, upholstery, jewellery - alongside a sculptor and puppet shop.

Ferry Road, Jackfield, Telford,
Shropshire TF8 7LS
01952 883030
www.mawscraftcentre.co.uk

Visit

ATTINGHAM PARK

The National Trust runs this elegant 18th-century mansion with Regency interiors, ambassadorial silver collection, Italian furniture and Grand Tour paintings. Costumed guides bring the house to life, and there's a chance to see how the servants lived 'below stairs'. There's also a magnificent picture gallery by John Nash. Outside, explore the deer park landscaped by Repton, with riverside walks and woodland sculpture trails. Within the estate, Home Farm (run by NT tenants), is one of the country's few completely organic farms.

Shrewsbury, Shropshire SY4 4TP
01743 708162
www.nationaltrust.org

IRONBRIDGE GORGE

Ironbridge is the birthplace of Industry – follow in the footsteps of the millions who have journeyed here since 1779 to marvel at the world's first cast-iron bridge. Built by Abraham Darby III and recognised as a great symbol of the Industrial Revolution, the extraordinary structure still dominates the pretty town that takes its name. There are ten award-winning museums along the valley beside the River Severn: start at the Jackfield Tile Museum with its gas-lit galleries exhibiting colourful and diverse tiles, some of which have been rescued and restored. The period room settings give a real insight into the lives of the townspeople in the 18th century.

Visitor Information Centre,
Ironbridge, Shropshire
01952 884391
www.ironbridge.org.uk

Activity

CYCLING

Hire mountain bikes from Broseley House near Ironbridge and explore the Shropshire countryside for yourself. You'll be given maps and help with planning your routes. Don't miss the beautiful black-and-white historical towns of Much Wenlock and Bridgnorth.

1 The Square, Broseley, Nr Ironbridge,
Shropshire TF12 5EW
01952 882043
www.broseleyhouse.co.uk

GOLF

Hawkestone Park has two 18-hole championship golf courses set in English Heritage Grade 1 landscape, and a par-3 six-hole academy course for the learners. Sandy Lyle is a local lad and cut his golfing teeth here, later nurturing and perfecting his game on the greens and fairways.

Weston-under-Redcastle, Shrewsbury,
Shropshire SY4 5UY
www.hawkstone.co.uk

HAWKSTONE PARK FOLLIES

This extraordinary park has grottoes, tunnels, labyrinths and deep woods, crags, cliffs and 200-year-old buildings. The magical landscape includes the Swiss Bridge, a rustic wooden affair swinging unnervingly over a deep chasm, continue round The Cleft, a winding path between two cliffs narrowing into a chilly dark tunnel – but be sure to end up at the top of The Monument, from where you'll see 13 counties on a clear day.

Weston-under-Redcastle, Shrewsbury,
Shropshire SY4 5UY
01939 200611
www.hawkstone.co.uk

The Walk - *Drama on High Ground*

Dramatic cliffs and views around the village of Clive.

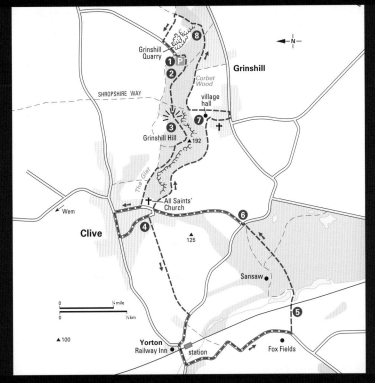

Walk Details

LENGTH: 5.25 miles (8.4km)

TIME: 2hrs

ASCENT: 540ft (165m)

PATHS: Rocky, woodland and field paths, mostly well used, 5 stiles

SUGGESTED MAP: aqua3 OS Explorer 241 Shrewsbury

GRID REFERENCE: SJ 525237

PARKING: Car park in Corbet Wood, next to Grinshill Quarry

1 Join the bridleway near the stone building on the east side of the car park, fork right to pass below the car park. Go on at junction, passing a sycamore tree, then a slab of rock. **2** At junction by another slab, keep to the bridleway (blue arrow), descending to where the wall rises on the right, at right angles to the bridleway. Follow the wall up to the Shropshire Way. Don't join it, instead turn left by the post with carvings of a butterfly, ascend to the viewpoint. **3** With view behind you, ascend to path. Follow this to left, keep left at fork. Continue to summit. With view behind you take lefthand path. Keep left at fork. Path joins walled track (Glat), to All Saints' Church at Clive. You could turn left here, but to see

Clive, turn right then left on main street and left again on Back Lane. **4** Turn right on the footpath, which begins as green lane, then crosses sheep pasture to the road. Turn right past Yorton Station, left under the railway and left again. Soon after passing the house (Fox Fields) join the footpath on the left, cross the field, then the railway. **5** Push through the trees to track. Turn right for a few paces, then left between 2 pools to parkland. Follow lefthand boundary, pass Sansaw, go through the iron kissing gate next to the wooden field gate. Where Sansaw's garden wall turns left, keep straight on to another wooden field gate. Cross the driveway and continue across parkland to road.

6 Turn left, then immediately right, towards Clive. Turn right opposite Back Lane on the walled bridleway, go below the churchyard and round Grinshill Hill to Jubilee Oak and the village hall. **7** Turn right along track, passing church to main street. Turn left and left again on Gooseberry Lane. Pass other side of village hall, rejoin walled bridleway and walled grassy track. Turn right past the houses. **8** At the fork, go left then up the steps to cross the stone step stile. Ascend through woodland, soon bearing right and climbing steeply to a fenced area. Turn right on the broad path to the junction, turn left on the track, left at the road, past Grinshill Quarry to the car park.

The Manners Arms

Leicestershire

The Inn

This Georgian red-bricked hunting lodge has played host to an array of guests in its colourful past. Set on the Belvoir Estate, which belongs to the Duke of Rutland, it is now a country inn and has been since the 1950s, welcoming the poacher, the gamekeeper and all manner of country folk, as well as walkers, day trippers and the odd tourist. The bar beckons with real ales, log fires and polished floorboards, while every Thursday there's live music – anything from acoustic guitar to lively Irish jigs.

Across the vestibule is a slightly rakish dining room – rich red walls, mahogany and rattan furniture, humorous hunting prints – with a conservatory opening on to a terrace beyond, a perfect spot for warm weather alfresco drinks, afternoon tea and full-scale dining. At the end of a busy day you may wish to stay the night in one of the eight bedrooms. And very comfortable they are, too, with either shower or bath, plus period furniture and artefacts that wouldn't look out of place in nearby Belvoir Castle.

The Food

This is where Lincolnshire, Nottinghamshire and Leicestershire meet, and where Colston Bassett stilton is king: order it in the bar as part of a ploughman's, alongside Somerset brie, vintage Lincolnshire cheddar and a pork pie; or tuck into a home-made burger and chips or one of various sandwiches. The food on offer here is just what you might expect: hefty portions of simple, unpretentious pub classics with a few more adventurous dishes thrown in.

The main focus of culinary attention is in the restaurant. Ingredients are mostly sourced locally – this part of the East Midlands is very rural and supplies terrific produce, especially game. The cooking style shows a wider influence, with dishes ranging from mousseline of Belvoir Estate pike with spring cabbage and bacon as a starter, to oven-roasted loin of Belvoir venison served with dauphinois potatoes, salsify and a ragout of wild mushrooms and port reduction.

To finish, there are good things like fruit crumbles, treacle tart and crème brûlée. Coffee can be taken in the conservatory or on the terrace.

The Essentials

Time at the Bar!
11am-11pm
Food: 12-3pm, 6-9pm; Sat-Sun 12-9pm

What's the Damage?
Main courses from £12.95

Bitter Experience:
Hardy & Hanson's Olde Trip, Belvoir Beaver Bitter

Sticky Fingers:
Children welcome, small portions available

Muddy Paws:
Dogs welcome in bedrooms

Zzzzz:
10 rooms, £70-£145

Anything Else?
Terrace, garden, car park, conservatory

What To Do

Shop

COLSTON BASSETT STORE

All inglenooks, beams and drawers stuffed with sweets, this recently renovated store has everything you'd expect from a village shop. Yes, you can buy a paper and post a letter but it's also a gourmet's paradise, with a fine deli counter groaning with 40 different British and French cheeses and award-winning antipasti and olives, plus a traditional bacon counter, fresh breads from the village bakery, and a range of 80 wines and 40 bottled beers. This is the place to buy a slab of stilton – it's made in the village.

Church Gate, Colston Bassett, Nottinghamshire NG12 3FE
01849 81321
www.colsonbassettstore.com

NEWARK ANTIQUES CENTRE

Newark is the antiques and collectibles capital of the country. Visit the antiques quarter in town, or time your stay to coincide with one of the biggest fairs in the UK, with more than 4,000 stallholders on an 84-acre site, in 44 marquees.

Lombard Street, Newark, Nottinghamshire NG24 1XP
01636 643979
Fairs: 01636 702326
www.dmgantiquefairs.com

YE OLDE PORK PIE SHOPPE

You'll be spoilt for choice in Melton, but start your search at Dickinson & Morris's shop, where they've been baking since 1851. They're the oldest and the last remaining makers of authentic pork pies.

10 Nottingham Street, Melton Mowbray, Leicestershire LE13 1NW
01664 482068
www.porkpie.co.uk

Visit

BELVOIR CASTLE

Belvoir has been the grand residence of the Duke and Duchess of Rutland for a thousand years. It is now home to the 11th Duke and his family. It has one of the most stunning ornate interiors of any building its age, housing an outstanding collection of French furniture, Italian sculpture and paintings by Gainsborough, Holbein and Reynolds. There's also an insight into 'below-stairs' life, with kitchens and a bakery, plus a school room and nursery. The fifth Duchess designed the gardens herself, inspired by her Italian Grand Tours – they feature a series of summer houses. There's also a restaurant, and ice-cream parlour with home-made ice cream.

Belvoir, Grantham, Leicestershire NG32 1PE
01476 871000
www.belvoircastle.com

LYDDINGTON BEDE HOUSE

This beautiful building was originally a wing of a medieval palace belonging to the Bishops of Lincoln – it then became an almshouse for 12 poor 'bedesmen' and two women, all 'free of lunacy, leprosy and French Pox'. The bedrooms are intriguing, with tiny windows and fireplaces. The Bishop's Great Chamber has got an ornate carved ceiling, and there's also a very pretty herb garden.

Lyddington, Rutland LE15 9LZ
01572 822438
www.english-heritage.co.uk

Activity

RUTLAND WATER CYCLEWAY

There are 23 miles (37km) of traffic-free cycling round Rutland Water, but all routes take in the countryside and woodland around the lake – the view across the water to the Hambleton Peninsular is spectacular. There are several places to stop and have a cup of tea.

Rutland Cycling, North Shore, Whitwell car park, Rutland Water LE15 8BL
www.rutlandcycling.co.uk

NARROWBOAT TRIP

Explore the River Soar on a narrow boat: head south towards Leicester through surprisingly remote countryside teeming with wildlife. Pause for lunch at The Mulberry Tree, an award-winning pub right on the riverside, run by a former Raymond Blanc-trained chef.

Sileby Mill Boatyard, Mill Lane, Sileby, Loughborough, Leicestershire LE12 7UX
01509 813583

TANDEM SKYDIVING

Experience the thrill of free-falling through the sky for 30 seconds at 120mph (75 kmph) from 12,000ft (3660m) while attached to an experienced instructor. On the way down you will learn how to steer and help land the parachute and, if you can bear to look, take in the amazing views.

British Parachute Schools, Langar Airfield, Langar, Nottinghamshire NG13 9HY
01949 860878
www.bpslangar.co.uk

The Walk - *King of the Castle*

A fairytale castle and a lost canal at Woolsthorpe by Belvoir.

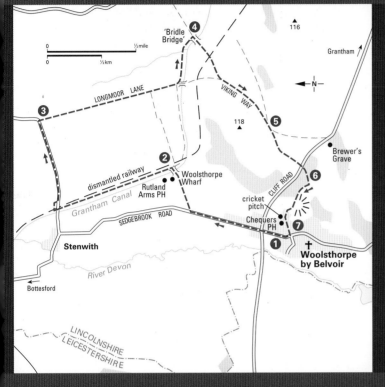

Walk Details

LENGTH: 4.75 miles (7.7km)

TIME: 2hrs 30min

ASCENT: 558ft (170m)

PATHS: Tow path, field and woodland tracks and country lane

SUGGESTED MAP: aqua3 OS Explorer 247 Grantham

GRID REFERENCE: SK 837342

PARKING: Main Street in Woolsthorpe by Belvoir

PARKING: This walk is over the county border in Lincolnshire

❶ Walk northwards out of Woolsthorpe by Belvoir on the pavement of Sedgebrook Road, a continuation of Main Street, towards Bottesford. Turn right into the wide-verged lane for the Rutland Arms pub (signposted) and go over the canal bridge at Woolsthorpe Wharf.
❷ Turn left. Follow the straight, grassy bank of Grantham Canal until Stenwith Bridge (No. 60). Go underneath and right, for the short path up and on to the road. Turn left. Follow this over the old railway bridge and out along the wide lane of oak trees. At the far end it bends left, and here turn right.
❸ Follow the initially hedged and unmade Longmoor Lane for 0.75 mile (1.2km). At the far end turn left

before the bridge, to join gravel tow path, and walk along this to wooden arched bridge ('Bridle Bridge').
❹ Cross bridge. Head across middle of arable field. Go over course of old railway again and continue up lefthand side of sloping field. At top turn left on to well-walked track.
❺ Follow track with views towards hills surrounding Grantham. Where track kinks left, after fenced section, go straight on/right across the wide field – follow the direction of the public footpath signpost and aim for the hedge opening at the very far side of the field. Go across Cliff Road for track into woodland.
❻ Just before private tip, turn left to enter the field via the stile. Turn right and follow the field edge along

and then down the grassy slope back to Woolsthorpe. There are excellent views across the head of the Vale of Belvoir to Belvoir Castle opposite. At the bottom go over the stile behind the cricket scorebox, along edge of pitch (football ground to left), and down the drive of the pub to reach village centre.
❼ To extend the walk to Belvoir Castle, turn left into Main Street then right into Belvoir Lane. At the end of the cul-de-sac go over a small brick bridge and continue straight ahead across the fields towards the hilltop fortification. Using the same route to return, the complete journey is a further 2 miles (3.2km) and involves a further 100ft (30m) of ascent.

The Queen's Head

Leicestershire

The Queen's Head, 2 Long Street, Belton, Leicestershire LE12 9TP

The Inn

Don't be fooled by the plain white-painted exterior of this traditional-looking village inn. A thorough revamp has created a light, modern, good-looking interior. In the locals' bar, the pale wood furniture, sanded wood floor, chocolate leather chairs and state-of-the-art stainless-steel hand pumps dispensing local ales are easy on the eye. The neutral good looks of the brasserie and restaurant are upmarket enough for a smart meal a deux, yet casual enough for eating out with friends.

The Queen's Head puts a chic country spin on the gastropub formula that is something of a find: especially as it's only a few miles and an easy drive along country roads from junction 23 of the M1.

Upstairs, six equally contemporary bedrooms vary in size, but are spotlessly clean and comfortable, decorated in calm and muted colours. There is nothing busy or overdone about them, just good mattresses, crisp linen, the odd sofa (in the largest rooms) and free internet connection. Smart, modern and well-maintained bathrooms are a mix of bath or showers.

The Food

Whether you're planning to eat in the bistro or the restaurant, an unpretentious atmosphere is created by a cheerful absence of formality in the front-of-house approach. The menu displays real passion, aiming to make good food widely available, and achieve it with the help of sound ingredients, sensitive cooking and a fair pricing policy (note the excellent-value set menu available for lunch and dinner at £13 for two courses, £17 for three).

Lunch can be pub staples of steaks, home-made burgers, fish and chips, or the more imaginative slow-cooked neck of lamb with aromatic couscous, apricots and lamb jus, and sea bass with crisp potatoes and fennel salad. At dinner, pumpkin risotto with aged parmesan, brill with anna potatoes, roasted ceps, foie gras and cauliflower panna cotta, or fillet of beef with slow-cooked ox cheek and black-truffle mash are all bankable options. And dessert? How do you say no to pan-fried prune soufflé and spiced bread ice cream? Or if puds aren't your thing you could go for the Colston Basset stilton served with a glass of port.

The Essentials

Time at the Bar!
12-3pm, 6.30-11pm, Sun 12-5pm, closed Sun eve
Food: 12-2.30pm, 7-9.30pm; Sun 12-4.30pm

What's the Damage?
Main courses from £7.50

Bitter Experience:
Marston's Pedigree, Fuller's Discovery

Sticky Fingers:
Children welcome, children's menu

Muddy Paws:
Dogs welcome in bar

Zzzzz:
6 rooms, £65-£100

Anything Else?
Terrace, garden, car park, children's play area

What To Do

Shop

ATOMIC

Atomic stocks 20th-century design classics – chairs, tables, lighting – by giants like Corbusier, Panton and Van der Rohe – in contrast to the 19th-century buildings of the adjacent Lace Market. It's part of the voguish Hockley Village, where you'll also find cutting-edge clothes and contemporary furniture shops.

Atomic, Plumptre Square, Nottingham, Nottinghamshire NG1 1JF
0115 941 5577
www.atomicinteriors.co.uk

LEICESTER ANTIQUES WAREHOUSE

Leicester is a mecca for antique hunters. Start out at the Antiques Warehouse where there are more than 100 dealers under one roof: the Lost World Salvage Yard sells unique architectural finds, and Corry's Antiques specialises in French and English carriage clocks.

Clarkes Road, Wigston, Leicester Leicestershire LE18 2BG
0116 288 1315

SELDOM SEEN FARM

The Symingtons have been farming this 200-acre site for 30 years – it's worth the journey for the view alone. Their free-range geese have endorsements from Rick Stein, and the Famous Three Bird Roast is legendary. Pick your own fruit, too: there are ten types of strawberry, plus raspberries and tayberries. The shop sells homemade chutneys and jams, as well as jellies, rape- and raspberry-blossom honey, and blackberry vinegar.

Billesdon, Leicestershire LE7 9FA
0116 259 6742
www.seldomseenfarm.co.uk

Visit

CALKE ABBEY

A baroque mansion owned for hundreds of years by the eccentric Harpur family. You won't find a highly restored interior here, but a fascinating and informal picture of a grand country house in decline. It's cluttered with years of family ephemera, with quirky touches like the stunning 18th-century Chinese silk bed. Outside, there are 600 acres of parkland, a walled kitchen garden and restored orangery.

Ticknall, Derbyshire DE73 7LE
01332 863822
www.nationaltrust.org.uk

ECOHOUSE

Britain's original and leading showhome and organic garden, the EcoHouse showcases hundreds of environmental products and energy-efficient solutions for the home. Worktops have been made from juice cartons, and bedroom furniture from reclaimed wood, and solar panels and wind turbines heat and power the home.

Western Park, Hinckley Road, Leicester, Leicestershire LE3 6HX
0116 254 5489
www.gwll.org.uk/ecohouse

WOOLLATON HALL

Designed by Robert Smythson and completed in 1588, Woollaton is a Grade 1 listed Tudor building set in 500 acres of parkland. It houses a natural history museum, an industrial museum, a steam engine house and the Yard Gallery – a vibrant exhibition space with a changing programme. Discover the story of life below stairs.

Nottingham, Nottinghamshire NG8 1AE
0115 915 3900

Activity

DONINGTON PARK

Take a spin round the track of one of the famous racing circuits in a Ferrari, Porsche or Lotus, and think yourself into Jenson Button's famous boots. Donington also houses the world's largest collection of Grand Prix racing cars driven by the likes of Fangio, Moss, Prost, Senna and Stewart.

Derbyshire DE74 2RP
01332 811048
www.donington-park.co.uk

GREAT CENTRAL RAILWAY

Spend a day steeped in nostalgia on a steam train – travel in one of GCR's traditional dining cars and have a slap-up lunch while trundling through the Leicestershire countryside. If you have a Thomas the Tank Engine fixation, you can learn to drive a steam locomotive, too: get the overalls on, mount the footplate and away you go.

Loughborough, Nottinghamshire LE11 1RW
01509 230726

The Walk - Panoramic Views from West Leake Hills

An enjoyable walk with great views.

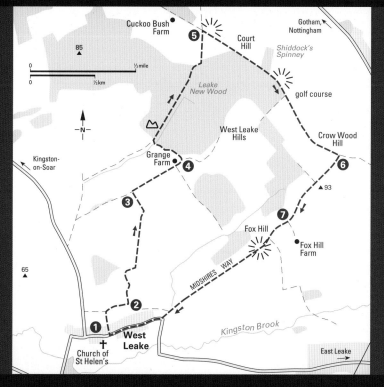

Walk Details

LENGTH: 4.25 miles (6.8km)

TIME: 2hrs

ASCENT: 246ft (75m)

PATHS: Field-edge paths, farm lanes and forest tracks

SUGGESTED MAP: aqua3 OS Explorer 246 Loughborough

GRID REFERENCE: SK 527264

PARKING: Roadside parking near West Leake church

1 Walk across the road from the church, halfway along West Leake's main street, to cross the stile opposite. Go between the houses and directly across open field. Cross stile at far side. Turn right to follow the field-edge path to the end.

2 Go through to next field. Turn left. Now follow the route alongside the hedge, past vegetation-choked pond (often dry in summer), and out across the middle of subsequent fields on the obvious farm track. Far away to left are cooling towers of Ratcliffe-on-Soar power station.

3 When you arrive at the wide gravel track, turn right and follow this as far as dilapidated open barn, called Grange Farm on map, with the hedge behind.

4 Go left before the hedge and after 275yds (251m) turn right for the bridleway route (waymarked with blue arrows) up steep hillside between trees. At the top this becomes clear, straight path through attractive mixed woodland of Leake New Wood. When you reach the far side go through the gate and across to the far side of field.

5 Turn right. Walk along initially open hilltop, with views left over Trent Valley. Continue along this easy, panoramic route via Court Hill for almost 1 mile (1.6km). Beyond the trees of Shiddock's Spinney, the golf course appears on your left. At fork of paths keep right so that you end up alongside arable field on your right, not fairway on your left.

6 At Crow Wood Hill you reach the bend of the semi-surfaced lane. Turn right and follow its southwesterly route across the open fields of Fox Hill, with wide views out towards the red-tiled roofs of East Leake.

7 When the drive turns into Fox Hill Farm go straight on along clear field-edge track ahead, and ignoring the path off to the left follow this long, straight route all the way back down to West Leake. The vista now stretches out towards the south, where the wooded ridges of Charnwood Forest (especially Beacon Hill and Bradgate Park) dominate the skyline. At the road junction at the bottom go straight on for the centre of the village.

The Olive Branch

Rutland

The Inn

Clipsham is famous for its avenue of 150 clipped yew trees, but for many the impressive Olive Branch pub-with-rooms is now the main reason for stopping here.

While retaining all its pubby personality – namely space for just having a drink, and a casual relaxed style, which takes in both decor and service – the Olive Branch is very much a foodie destination with both wine and food taken very seriously by enthusiastic owners Ben Jones and Sean Hope. It's certainly not your usual ex-boozer turned chi-chi gastropub. Plain wooden tables, chairs and pews, pale pastel walls, wooden tops from

posh-denomination wine boxes, roaring log fires, soft lamplight – they all blend together in a tasteful jumble to create a comfortable, laid-back atmosphere.

Stroll across the lane to Beech House to find the pub's six stunning bedrooms. They were extensively refurbished in 2006, so expect contemporary fabrics, big beds with Egyptian cotton sheets and goose-down duvets, plasma screens and DVD players, individual bathrooms kitted out with baths and storm showers, and extras like internet access, fresh coffee, home-made biscuits and Roberts radios.

The Essentials

Time at the Bar!
12-3pm, 6-11pm (all day Sat & Sun)
Food: 12-2pm, 7-9.30pm; Sun 12-3pm

What's the Damage?
Main courses from £12.50

Bitter Experience:
Grainstore Olive Oil, Truman's Triumph

Sticky Fingers:
Children welcome, children's menu

Muddy Paws:
Dogs welcome in the bar

Zzzzz:
6 rooms, £80-£160

Anything Else?
Garden, car park

The Food

Wine is obviously a passion at the Olive Branch, and chalkboards almost cover the bar area detailing choices such as keenly priced house specials, mixing classic labels with up-and-coming producers from around the world. Impressed with the wine you chose with your meal? Then take away a case or two from the pub's wine shop. Chalkboards also detail lunchtime sandwiches and the good-value set lunch, while the bar groans with locally brewed ales on hand-pump and specially imported cognacs and armagnacs.

The daily lunch and dinner menus feature a map of all the local producers that supply the pub: there could be Grasmere Farm pork and stilton pie with home-made piccalilli to start; then roast Ellet Farm chicken with baked sweet potato, pesto mayonnaise and chilli dressing; turbot with white wine and girolle fricassee; or chargrilled rib-eye steak with chips and béarnaise sauce. To finish, choose from chocolate tart teamed with blood-orange sorbet, lemon cheesecake or local cheeses. First-class breakfasts to set you up for the day, and summer Saturday barbecues are a huge hit.

What To Do

Shop

STAMFORD

The finest stone town in England is home to a huge range of specialist shops, including elegant and funky clothes boutiques, antiquarian bookshops and quirky antique shops. Everything you could want is here, from designer furniture to sheet music, plus the added incentive of 40 refreshment stops.

Tourist Information Centre, St Mary's Street, Stamford, Lincolnshire PE9 2DL

01780 755611

www.stamford.co.uk

YE OLDE PORK PIE SHOPPE

Melton Mowbray is synonymous with pork pies, and a shopping tour of the town reflects this long-standing tradition. Dickinson & Morris's pork pie shop has been in Melton Mowbray since 1851. In the original shop, craft bakers prepare delicious Melton Mowbray pork pies in the time-honoured way. Next door you can buy hand-linked sausages and quality bacon.

10 Nottingham Street, Melton Mowbray, Leicestershire LE13 1NR

01664 562341

www.porkpie.co.uk

NORTHFIELD FARM SHOP

Visit this award-winning farm shop for home-reared rare and traditional breed meats, including Dexter beef hung for 3-4 weeks, game shot around the farm, home-cured bacon, and an excellent range of local cheeses, locally baked bread, vegetables, cooked meats and local bottled beers.

Whissendine Lane, Cold Overton, Oakham, Rutland LE15 7QF

01664 474271

www.northfieldfarm.com

Visit

BURGHLEY HOUSE

Burghley is one of the largest and grandest houses of the first Elizabethan age, and in the 21st century one of the most high profile. To celebrate its starring roles in films such as *Pride & Prejudice* and *The Da Vinci Code*, Burghley is hosting a costume exhibition and a mystery tour through the 17th-century Italian paintings on show.

Stamford, Lincolnshire PE9 3JY

01780 752451

www.burghley.co.uk

ROCKINGHAM CASTLE

Standing on the edge of an escarpment with stunning views over five counties, Rockingham Castle was the brainchild of William the Conqueror. The present, mainly Tudor building is known for its fine architecture, striking furniture and splendid works of art, including a remarkable collection of 20th-century paintings. Charles Dickens was a frequent visitor and was inspired to feature Rockingham as one of the settings in *Bleak House*.

Rockingham, Market Harborough, Leicestershire LE16 8TH

01536 770240

www.rockinghamcastle.com

WOOLSTHORPE MANOR

This small 17th-century manor house was the birthplace and family home of Sir Isaac Newton and where he formulated some of his major works between 1665 and 1667. Explore Newton's ideas in the hands-on Science Discovery Centre.

Woolsthorpe-by-Colsterworth, Grantham, Lincolnshire NG33 5NR

01476 860338

www.nationaltrust.org.uk

Activity

WALKING TOUR

To embark on a walking tour of Stamford is to take a journey into the past. The town's reputation and prosperity were established as a direct result of the coaching era. Many of the houses you see while exploring the ancient streets were built by wealthy merchants and lawyers. In later years it achieved national fame when the BBC chose it as the main setting for its production of *Middlemarch*.

Tourist Information Centre, St Mary's Street, Stamford, Lincolnshire PE9 2DL

01780 755611

www.stamford.co.uk

CYCLING

Pedal beside tranquil Rutland Water and you'll enjoy cycling as it was always meant to be and, indeed, used to be – well away from traffic and with the sights and sounds of the countryside all around you. This is Europe's largest man-made reservoir, located at the heart of England's smallest county. The track never strays far from the water's edge, making it an ideal environment for cycling.

Whitwell Leisure Park, Rutland Water, Oakham, Rutland LE15 8BL

01780 460705

www.rutlandcycling.co.uk

BALLOONING

Experience the freedom and tranquillity of floating across the sky with a bird's-eye view of Rutland Water, Oakham Castle and the surrounding countryside. Balloons launch from a lakeside site near Edith Weston or from Stamford Meadows near Stamford.

www.virginballoonflights.co.uk

The Walk - *The Miniature Charm of Rutland*

Explore the open countryside and parkland around Exton.

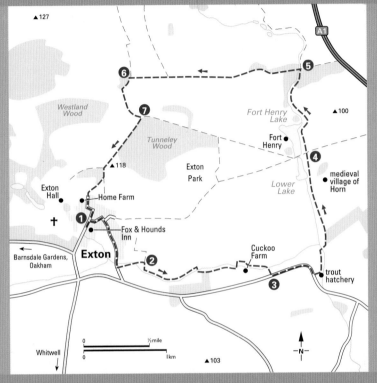

Walk Details

LENGTH: 6.5 miles (10.4km)

TIME: 3hrs

ASCENT: 425ft (130m)

PATHS: Mainly field paths and firm farm tracks, 12 stiles

SUGGESTED MAP: aqua3 OS Explorer 234 Rutland Water

GRID REFERENCE: SK 924112

PARKING: Roadside parking in the centre of Exton

❶ With your back to the pub leave the Green on your far righthand side on Stamford Road and, at the end, turn right. This becomes Empingham Road and, at the point where the houses finish, continue over the stream and turn left on to the public footpath.

❷ Just before the fence at the end climb over the stile on the right (not the stile straight ahead). Drop down across the end of the field. Turn left to make for the stile in the fence ahead. Cross it, then follow the wide, grassy track along the shallow valley for 1 mile (1.6km), at one point climbing into the field on the left to avoid Cuckoo Farm. Finally the track clambers up through fields on the right to reach the lane.

❸ Turn left and walk on the verge until just beyond the bend, then go left on the footpath ('Fort Henry and Greetham'). Follow this above the trout hatchery, then head diagonally right via the small concrete bridge to the fence at the top. Turn left to Lower Lake, then go ahead/right on the surfaced drive for a few paces, climb over the stile to the left of the old bar gate, and then walk out across the pasture above the water.

❹ At the far side turn right on to the lane and then, in a few paces, turn left for the footpath signposted 'Greetham'. Follow this footpath alongside Fort Henry Lake and then on along the corridor between the woodland. At the far end climb up the stairs to reach the lane.

❺ Turn left and walk up through woods and, when the semi-surfaced drive bears left, go straight on through newly planted trees. Wide, unmade track now heads out across open fields for 1 mile (1.6km).

❻ At trees on the far side turn left on to the track that descends and bears left. Here go straight on via stile and wooden plank footbridge and head up diagonally left towards the top of the field. Go over the stile and turn left on to the farm track.

❼ At the junction turn right on to straight, metalled lane. Bear left at fork before woods and follow this back to Exton. Follow signs around Home Farm, then turn left at end of West End and right by stone shelter into High Street and return to Green.

The Pheasant Inn
Cheshire

The Inn

Records indicate The Pheasant was already a pub in 1650, though it was also once a farm; yet further back in time still lies the origin of the name Burwardsley – clearing in the woods. Thankfully, some things don't change. Stand at the front door today, taking in the glorious views across the Cheshire plain to the Welsh mountains, and you will see broad-leaved woodland all around and hear birds calling from field and forest. This is great walking country, and The Pheasant is located in the middle of one of the biggest walks in the county, the Sandstone Trail.

Recent months have seen a successful revamp inside this gorgeous inn. The original beams, wooden floors and vast fireplace survive intact, but there's an updated vibe evident in the squashy leather sofas in one snug corner, the well-chosen background jazz and the framed prints. Service is young and friendly. The 12 bedrooms – located in the main building and in the stable wing – are boutique-hotel standard, with attractive soft furnishings, flat-screen TVs, wireless internet access and their share of good views and peace and quiet. Outside is a sunny terrace with tables and chairs, perfect for fair-weather drinking and dining.

The Essentials

Time at the Bar!
11am-11pm, 12-9pm (Sat 10pm),
Sun 12-8.30pm

What's the Damage?
Main courses from £8.50

Bitter Experience:
Weetwood Best, Eastgate and Old Dog

Sticky Fingers:
Children welcome, children's menu

Muddy Paws:
Dogs welcome

Zzzzz:
12 rooms, £65-£130

Anything Else?
Terrace, garden, car park

The Food

The Pheasant operates as a destination dining pub as well as a stop-off for hungry walkers. Sandwiches can either be simple (Cheshire cheese on bloomer bread) or elaborate (Goosnargh duck with hoi sin sauce in a tortilla wrap). Raw materials are sourced, where possible, from local farms and waters or the nearby Cholmondley Estate, and translate into the likes of Caesar salad with corn-fed chicken and poached egg; beef and Old Spot sausages; suckling pig with baked apple; steak, Weetwood ale and mushroom pie; minted lamb Henry or grilled fillet of Anglesey sea bass. There's plenty of choice for vegetarians with salads, risottos and pastas, such as pappardelle with wild rocket, roasted butternut squash and red onions.

Top marks awarded, too, for the entirely local cheese board offering Blacksticks Blue, Mollington Cheshire, Burland Green brie and Whitehaven. Comforting home-made desserts include apple and sultana crumble with custard, or there are several flavours of Gog's Cheshire Farm ice cream including mouthwatering strawberries and cream, honeycomb, and banoffi. The incidentals – great coffee and hot chocolate served with biscotti; 12 wines by the glass from a decent list – show good attention to detail. Real-ale drinkers will always find four excellent beers, including guest appearances, available on the hand pump.

What To Do

Shop

CHESTER ROWS
The famous 'Rows' – double-level shopping arcades largely dating from Victorian times with some medieval survivals – have a wealth of top-class shops and galleries, tea shops and bistros. Antique fairs, markets and auctions are another attraction. The city centre has a Roman amphitheatre, a cathedral and the Grosvenor Museum.
www.visitchester.com

DAGFIELDS CRAFTS CENTRE
More than 200 dealers and a score of craft workshops come together at Dagfields, a countryside centre selling collectibles, furniture, ceramics and paintings.
Walgherton, Nantwich, Cheshire CW5 7LG
01270 841336
www.dagfields.co.uk

THE HOLLIES FARM SHOP
Fresh produce of virtually every edible variety is available here, from organic vegetables to preserves, Lancashire and Cheshire cheeses (and many from beyond), smoked fish, bacon and meats from the Cheshire Smokehouse.
Forest Road, Little Budworth, Cheshire CW6 9ES
01829 760414
www.theholliesfarmshop.com

HS BOURNE CHEESE
Hand-made cheeses from a pedigree herd of Friesians. The traditional Farmhouse Mature and organic Cheshire from HS Bourne is augmented by oak-smoked and blue varieties. There's farm butter, too.
The Bank, Malpas, Cheshire SY14 7AL
01948 770214
www.hsbourne.co.uk

Visit

ANDERTON BOAT LIFT
Like a Meccano set on steroids, the Anderton Boat Lift links canal and river, hoisting narrow boats 50ft (15m) vertically, negating the need for locks. Take a boat trip for a ride in this Cathedral of the Waterways; an exhibition centre explains all.
Lift Lane, Anderton, Northwich, Cheshire CW9 6EW
01606 786777
www.andertonboatlift.co.uk

BEESTON CASTLE
Perched on a precipitous outlying crag of Cheshire's Sandstone Ridge, the skeletal remains of Beeston Castle, known as The Castle of the Rock, hide tales of treasure and sieges. Views over eight counties.
Beeston, Tarporley, Cheshire CW6 9TX
01829 260464
www.english-heritage.org.uk/northwest

JODRELL BANK
Home to one of the world's most famous telescopes, the Jodrell Bank Science Centre offers eye-opening views of the solar system in a 3D theatre and lots of space info. Firmly down to earth is the surrounding renowned arboretum.
Holmes Chapel, Macclesfield, Cheshire SK11 9DL.
01477 571339
www.manchester.ac.uk/jodrellbank/viscen

TATTON PARK
The mansion has grand furniture, paintings, and more than 50 acres of formal gardens including topiary, a Japanese garden, a walled garden and a fernery.
Knutsford, Cheshire WA16 6QN
01625 534400/534435
www.tattonpark.org.uk

Activity

CARDEN PARK GOLF
The contemporary courses are spread across a 750-acre estate, with two championship courses, one designed by Jack Nicklaus (handicap certificate needed), plus a 'fun' par-3 course.
Chester, Cheshire CH3 9DQ
01829 731600
www.deveregolf.co.uk

CATTON HALL
Archery is just one of the outdoor adrenalin-based activities available on the Catton Hall estate; others include clay-pigeon shooting, falconry and paintball. Advance booking essential.
Bradley Lane, Frodsham, Cheshire WA6 7EX
01928 788295
www.cattonhall.co.uk

CYCLE IN DELAMERE FOREST
Miles of accessible tracks criss-cross Delamere Forest, a mix of mature broadleaf woods and fir tree plantations dappled with meres and viewpoints. Minor roads link to villages on the Sandstone Ridge offering further options for a day's cycling. Cycle hire available on site.
Forest Visitor Centre, Linmere, Cheshire
01625 572681

The Walk - Views of Beeston Castle

A walk atop a prominent sandstone ridge from Burwardsley.

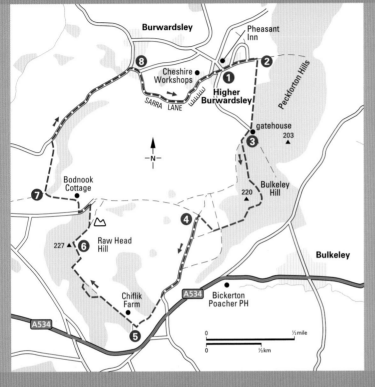

Walk Details

LENGTH: 5.5 miles (8.8km)

TIME: 2hrs

ASCENT: 919ft (280m)

PATHS: Field and woodland paths, plus some lane walking, 9 stiles (gradually being replaced by gates)

SUGGESTED MAP: aqua3 OS Explorer 257 Crewe & Nantwich

GRID REFERENCE: SJ 523566

PARKING: The Pheasant Inn car park, or verges at the end of the tarmac on Coppermines Lane, off A534

❶ From The Pheasant go right then up the hill. Keep right at the fork. The lane becomes unsurfaced at the Crewe and Nantwich boundary.
❷ Just before the boundary sign go right over the stile and follow the clear path down edge of field. Keep straight on to meet narrow lane and go up left. On the crest, opposite the gatehouse, go right on the track.
❸ Go left up steps into the wood; continue less steeply. Where path splits, left branch follows brink of steep slope. Keep fairly close to this edge as path levels. Go through gap in the fence then descend ahead, through the plantation, to kissing gate by iron gate. Go diagonally right on the clear track across the field to rejoin Coppermines Lane.

❹ Walk down Coppermines Lane to a sharp lefthand bend, then over a stile beside an arched sandstone overhang. Cross field, then ascend edge of wooded area. Cross fields to edge of another wood. Go up right, joining track towards Chiflik Farm.
❺ Go through kissing gate by farm and up fenced path. The path generally runs below the top of the steep slope, gradually climbing to the trig point on Raw Head Hill.
❻ The path goes right and into a slight dip. Go left down steps, then back right, slanting through steep plantation. Go left down narrow lane for 300yds (274m). Opposite the track and footpath sign, descend right on clear ground under tall trees. At the bottom cross the stile

and go up towards Bodnook Cottage. Just below this bear left and into the wood. Follow the much clearer path, roughly level then slightly left and downhill among spindly beech trees.
❼ Cross the stile at edge of wood, then another to its right. There's no path, so aim directly for the stile below large tree, 50yds (46m) left of house. The path is clearer through the next field. At the end cross the stile and follow the road ahead.
❽ On the edge of Burwardsley village turn right up the 1st lane. Go right again up Sarra Lane, then fork left at 'Unsuitable for Motor Vehicles' sign. Follow the lane through a narrow section past Cheshire Workshops. Just beyond, the road forks, leading back to pub.

Devonshire Arms

Derbyshire

The Inn

Arrive down a road that winds across the Chatsworth Estate delivering glorious views, tantalising glimpses of the great house and one hell of a humpback. The ancient, estate-owned inn is a great place to stay. A recent, bold renovation allows thick stone walls, open fires, stone floors, oak beams and lots of dark wood to create a timeless feel, while, in an interesting juxtaposition of styles, the sleek, glass-fronted brasserie extension with its bright colours and contemporary furniture, is firmly in the 21st century.

All four bedrooms are exemplary: they may not be large, but they are suitably stylish with the Duchess of Devonshire's trademark love of rich colour, and a smattering of botanical watercolours painted by the Duke's sister, Lady Emma Tennant. Each of the rooms is named after local dales: the eccentric Peak Dale boasts a roll-top bath in the room itself, while Cuckoostone Dale is a pleasant suite that could work well as a family room. Big, comfortable beds, flat-screen TVs, dressing gowns and peace and quiet are common to all.

Devonshire Arms, Devonshire Square, Beeley, Matlock, Derbyshire DE4 2NR

The Food

There's a welcome informality to eating here: try the bar for the buzz or the brasserie for a calmer experience. During the day, there's a walker-friendly selection of wholesome favourites such as honey-roasted ham sandwich, home-made burgers and toasted steak sandwich with fried egg and chips, which can be washed down with local real ales. This hits the spot – but the varied menu also suits most tastes. Asian-influenced dishes – roast chicken breast with pineapple rice, red curry, sultanas and toasted coconut – complement the Med-leaning likes of moules marinieres or chargrilled tuna steak with ratatouille and hard-working Brit classics such as bangers, mash and crispy onions, or ploughman's with pork pie, local cheeses and tin loaf.

Desserts, too, are well worth saving room for and continue the robust theme (sticky toffee pudding with vanilla ice cream, say, or warm rice pudding with orange syrup and raisins), while wines offer economy and character. In short, the wonderful food offers a perfect balance of old and new – just like the surroundings.

The Essentials

Time at the Bar!
11am-11pm
Food: 12-3pm, 6-9.30pm

What's the Damage?
Main courses from £8.95

Bitter Experience:
Three guest ales

Sticky Fingers:
Children welcome, children's menu

Muddy Paws:
Dogs welcome

Zzzzz:
4 rooms, £110-£165

Anything Else?
Garden, car park

What To Do

Shop

BLUE JOHN STONE

Unique to north Derbyshire, this variety of fluorite was polluted by hydrocarbons when formed, producing the translucent blue/purple mineral that is often made into jewellery. The ultimate collector's item.

Castleton, Hope Valley, Derbyshire
Tourist Information Centre 01433 620679

CHATSWORTH FARM SHOP

A cornucopia of organic and local produce, much of it produced and cured on the Chatsworth Estate. A bakery, an extensive butchery (including water buffalo), a substantial delicatessen with more than 80 British cheeses; game, smoked goods and top-notch foods.

Chatsworth, Bakewell,
Derbyshire DE45 1PP
01246 565300
www.chatsworth.org

CHEESE SHOP

Stilton, together with Buxton Blue and Dovedale Blue, is produced at the dairy in Hartington, in the Upper Dove valley south of Buxton. Made from local milk, the cheese is available at the creamery shop.

Hartington, Derbyshire
01298 84935
www.hartingtoncheese.co.uk

DAVID MELLOR CUTLERY

Literally at the cutting edge of modern design, innovative and traditional cutlery is produced at this award-winning factory. Design classics on display in the museum.

The Round Building, Hathersage, Sheffield,
Derbyshire S32 1BA
01433 650220
www.davidmellordesign.co.uk

Visit

CASTLETON CAVES

This little Peak District village is the capital of accessible caverns in the UK. There are four different systems to visit, the most unusual of which is Speedwell Cavern, at the foot of the Winnats Pass, where the visit is made by tub-boat on an underground waterway. At other caverns such as Treak Cliff, Blue John Stone is still worked, to be painstakingly crafted into jewellery.

Treak Cliff Cavern, Castleton, Derbyshire
01433 620571
www.bluejohnstone.com

CHATSWORTH HOUSE

One of the great treasure houses and stately homes of England, Chatsworth is the seat of the Duke of Devonshire. The house devours superlatives: furniture, tapestries, sculptures, porcelain and a collection of old masters unrivalled outside major museums. The landscaped grounds sport cascades and the impressive Emperor Fountain amidst gardens modelled by Capability Brown.

Bakewell, Derbtshire DE45 1PP
01246 565300
www.chatsworth.org

HADDON HALL

A sublime English fortified manor house built in the 1380s and essentially mothballed since the Duke of Rutland forsook it as his main residence 300 years ago. Set in woodland on a promontory above the river Wye, this fairytale marvel has featured in countless period films and television adaptations.

Bakewell, Derbyshire DE451LA
01629 812855
www.haddonhall.co.uk

Activity

BALLOONING

Usually taking off from Bakewell Showground, voyages can glide over the Wye valley, across heather-burnished moors or over the White Peak towards Castleton – the wind is your engine and navigator.

Dragon Balloon Company,
Mam House Farm, Castleton, Hope Valley,
Derbyshire S33 8WA
01433 623007
www.dragonballoon.co.uk

NORTHFIELD FARM RIDING & TREKKING

At the point where three counties meet, this is the ideal setting for an adventurous exploration of the countless miles of old salters' ways, packhorse trails and ancient roads that thread the moors and drop into deep, secluded valleys. A great way to get to know the Peak District, the riding centre is based on the edge of Flash, England's highest village.

Flash, Buxton, Derbyshire SK17 0SW
01298 22543
www.northfieldfarm.co.uk

PEAK CYCLE HIRE

At the heart of the White Peak, old railways and back lanes form an ideal network of cycling trails. The High Peak and Tissington Trails offer effortless riding on railway track beds through magnificent countryside. Radiating from these arteries are wild flower-rich lanes and byways to atmospheric villages like Monyash and Youlgreave and some of the most unspoiled limestone dales to be found in the National Park.

Parsley Hay, Buxton, Derbyshire SK17 0DG
01298 84493
www.peakdistrict.org

The Walk - Chatsworth Park and Gardens

Past gardens and through parkland created by gardening guru Capability Brown.

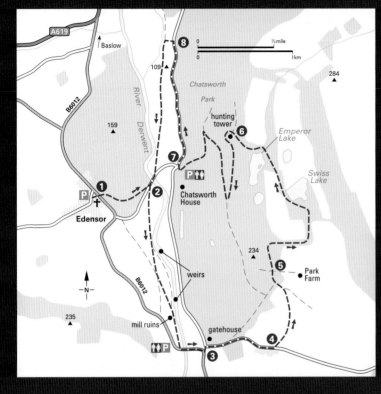

Walk Details

LENGTH: 7 miles (11.3km)

TIME: 3hrs

ASCENT: 459ft (140m)

PATHS: Good paths and forest trails

SUGGESTED MAP: aqua3 OS Explorer OL24 White Peak

GRID REFERENCE: SK 251699

PARKING: Edensor village

❶ From Edensor village cross over the B6012; take the footpath at the righthand side of the large tree. Walk across the parkland to join the main drive to Chatsworth House near the bridge. Cross over the road; continue on the footpath, walking downhill on the other side to the river bank.
❷ Follow the River Derwent past a couple of weirs and the remains of the old mill to the next bridge that carries the B6012 over the river. To the left of the bridge, a metal kissing gate allows access to the road. Cross the bridge.
❸ Ignore the left turn into the drive past the gatehouse to the estate and take the next left along the side of the gatehouse. Continue up the hill,

past house on right and then farm. Cross stile on left to the footpath ('Robin Hood and Hunting Tower').
❹ Cross the field and over the next stile; go diagonally left, uphill following waymarkers on the well-defined path. When this meets made-up track turn left, cross the wall into the estate by the high stile and continue to the crossroads.
❺ Keep ahead, following the track as it passes Swiss Lake on the right and then loops round Emperor Lake on the left. The path will come to another, faint, crossroads. On the left is the Hunting Tower.
❻ Continue on the path as it loops left around the tower, ignoring turn off to the right. The path heads downhill, past what appears to be

the remains of an old viaduct with water cascading from the end, then doubles back, still going downhill, eventually reaching the car park at Chatsworth House.
❼ Go past the wooden hut at the car park entrance; turn right on to estate road heading north. Follow the road past several wooden sculptures until you are within sight of the gates at the end of the estate.
❽ Near here turn left across the park to the gate that leads eventually to Baslow. Don't go through the gate but turn left on to the trail that follows the river back to Chatsworth. Turn right on to the road, cross the bridge, then go immediately right on the track, which leads back to Edensor village.

The Inn at Whitewell

Lancashire

The Essentials

Time at the Bar!
10am-11pm
Food: 12-2pm, 7.30-9.30pm

What's the Damage?
Main courses from £7.50

Bitter Experience:
Two guest ales

Sticky Fingers:
Children welcome, small portions

Muddy Paws:
Dogs welcome in bar and bedrooms

Zzzzz:
23 rooms, £96-£162

Anything Else?
Terrace, garden, car park,
wine shop

The Inn

Whichever way you approach this place, you're convinced you're lost, and that the sat nav is telling you lies, but finally the glorious Inn at Whitewell looms, and you know you've arrived at one of the best-kept secrets in the country. The Forest of Bowland is the most breathtaking countryside in the north-west of England, and the inn nestles on the banks of the River Hodder; the views are spectacular from almost every room. The welcome is as warm as the night is chilly: huge fires in ornate iron grates, polished flagstones and grainy oak furniture, the *Dandy* and *Beano* sit in the paper rack alongside *Lancashire Life*, and black dogs wander around.

A lot of thought, time and good taste has gone into furnishing the 23 bedrooms. All are different, but every one is of an extraordinarily high standard, with Colefax and Fowler fabrics, antiques and top-spec bathrooms – some of which have massive salvaged brass baths with jet sprays. Beds are generally testers or four-posters. The carpets and towels are thick and luxurious, and if you're not feeling quite pampered enough, most of the rooms have peat fires flickering away through the night.

The Food

The restaurant splits into several bar areas, any of which you can sit in to eat. A blackboard menu offers daily specials of simply cooked local produce – smoked fillet of trout with beetroot salad and horseradish relish is earthy but sweet, and roast breast of Goosnargh duckling with bubble and squeak, black-pudding sausage and red wine jus is delicious and substantial. Roast loin of Bowland lamb with minted pease pudding is about as from down-the-road as you can get, and arrives with crunchy vegetables.

The puddings change every day, and are described on the board as 'nursery-like'. You won't have tasted a treacle tart quite like this one – deep, rich, and how do they make it so it just dissolves in your mouth? The Inn's philosophy hits all the right notes: great food and wine in luxurious yet unpretentious surroundings. This is the kind of place you want all to yourself, while at the same time dying to tell the world about it.

What To Do

Shop

LEAGRAM ORGANIC DAIRY
The lush pastures of the Hodder Valley and the sheep-walks of the fells produce rich cows' and sheeps' milk, ideal for both ultra-traditional Lancashire farmhouse and a range of specialist cheeses. This dairy near Chipping is one of a number of craft-producers in the Bowland area, but the only one where cheese-making can be viewed.
High Head Farm, Green Lane, Chipping, Preston, Lancashire PR3 2TQ
01995 61532
www.cheese-experience.com

PRESTON ANTIQUES CENTRE
The pleasant drive to Preston ends at the North-West's largest antiques gallery, where more than 40 dealers exhibit over three floors. There's a heavy concentration on furniture here, but a decent range of other specialisms and more general dealers cover much of the spectrum, from ceramics and glass to sculpture, paintings and fine art.
Horrock's Yard, Newhall Lane, Preston, Lancashire PR1 5NQ
01772 794498
www.prestonantiquescentre.com

SAMLESBURY HALL
The remaining parts of this medieval hall (built 1325) are an unforgettable confection of black-and-white half-timbered decoration at its finest. Take a tour of the hall before visiting the stunning long gallery, now host to an eclectic mix of antique outlets selling wares that fit well into the period feel.
Preston New Road, Samlesbury, Preston, Lancashire PR5 0UP
01254 812010
www.samlesburyhall.co.uk

Visit

GAWTHORPE HALL
An unusual building, once home to the Kay-Shuttleworth family, major players in the Lancashire textile industry. This heritage is reflected in the extensive costume and textile collections held here, enhanced by furniture and portraits on loan from the National Portrait Gallery.
Padiham, Burnley, Lancashire BB12 8UA
01282 771004
www.nationaltrust.org.uk

GLASSON SMOKEHOUSE
Lancaster's handkerchief-sized port is busy with coasters, yachts and narrowboats reaching the end of the Lancaster Canal. It's a restful place, with shops, inns and – the *piece de resistance* – the Glasson Smokehouse, with Morecambe Bay potted shrimps and wild Lune salmon to be enjoyed. Easy walks meander to ruined Cockersand Abbey and the pretty Lune Estuary.
West Quay, Glasson Dock, Lancashire LA2 0DB
01524 751493
www.glassonsmokehouse.co.uk

LANCASTER
A scenic drive through the Trough of Bowland leads to Lancashire's former county town. The priory and castle (guided tours only, it's still a prison!) loom over the old town with its galleries and museums; on the riverside quays, the Maritime Museum recalls fortunes made from cotton and slavery. A little further north is the imposing Leighton Hall and the RSPB reserve at Leighton Moss, famed for bittern, marsh harriers and deer.
Tourist Information Centre 01524 32878
www.citycoastcountryside.co.uk

Activity

BALLOONING
It is said that JRR Tolkien based the Hobbits' idyllic homeland, The Shire, on the countryside he had encountered in the middle Ribble Valley. Balloon flights from Stonyhurst College, at the heart of this area, drift across the valley towards the Yorkshire Dales or north up the Hodder Valley and across the Forest of Bowland, reaching heights of 6,000ft (1830m). Beware – something so enjoyable could be Hobbit-forming! Advance booking is essential.
01952 292020
www.virginballoonflights.co.uk

CYCLING
Energetic routes follow byways and moorland tracks onto the heights of the Forest of Bowland or Stocks Forest; less ambitious cyclists can follow lanes along the peaceful Ribble Valley in the shadow of Ingleborough. Explore the pretty Wenning Valley or cycle to Ingleton and enjoy its attractions.
Dalesbridge Activity Centre, Austwick, Settle, North Yorkshire LA2 8AZ
0845 370 0558
www.countrylanes.co.uk

WALK TO THE CENTRE OF BRITAIN
Tiny Dunsop Bridge is the nearest village to the very centre of Britain: the actual spot is above Whitendale Beck, a glorious 4-mile (6-km) hike from the village car park through prime bird-watching and bilberry-picking country.

The Walk - The Forest of Bowland

Down in the Hodder Valley.

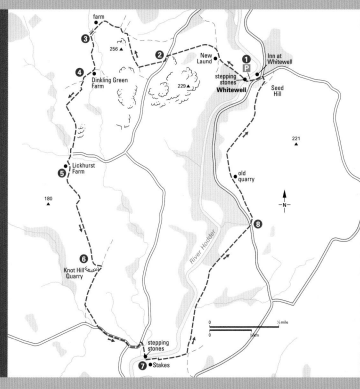

Walk Details

LENGTH: 7 miles (11.3km)

TIME: 2hrs 30min

ASCENT: 853ft (260m)

PATHS: Field paths, farm tracks and quiet lane, 8 stiles

SUGGESTED MAP: aqua3 OS Explorer OL41 Forest of Bowland & Ribblesdale

GRID REFERENCE: SD 658468

PARKING: Roadside parking near Inn at Whitewell or below church

1 From the lower parking area follow the riverbank left to stepping stones. Climb just right of the woods and straight through the farmyard of New Laund. By the old cheese press go left on the curving track below the slopes, then up the field. Bear left to the gate into the lane. Go a few paces left to the stile on right.

2 Cross rough pasture, aiming just left of house, then go right on a surfaced track, swinging round into another little valley. Go left to the farm, then right, through the farmyard and down to a footbridge.

3 Turn left, past the chicken coops, to stile on right. Cross field corner to 2nd stile, then ahead to Dinkling Green Farm. The gap to the right of the cow shed leads to the farmyard.

4 Halfway down the yard go right, between buildings, to the ford. Keep left past the plantation, follow the next field edge, then go through a gate in the dip. Follow the hedge round, then cross it and go over the rise. Bear right, down to the beck, then up the lane to Lickhurst Farm.

5 Turn left into the farmyard, then bear right and straight on down the track. When it swings right, go left before the next gate, then straight ahead on the intermittent track.

6 Just before Knot Hill Quarry, turn left, past the limekiln, to the junction. Go right and down to lane. Go left, then left again, round bend and down. Cross bridge on right and head towards Stakes farm, crossing the river on stepping stones.

7 Turn left and climb above the river. At the next junction go left, descend steeply, then swing right, slightly above River Hodder, to the stile. Follow the fence to stile, then bear left to ford. Go up rough track and keep climbing past right edge of plantation. Keep straight on across open field to stile in furthest corner.

8 Across the road, a few paces to the left, is a gate. Bear left to the iron gates. Contour around the hill, just above the fence, to reach more gates. After 100yds (91m) go down through the aluminium gate. The track swings right. Just past Seed Hill turn left and descend the steps by the graveyard. From here, a short steep lane descends back to the start of the walk.

The Devonshire Fell

North Yorkshire

The Inn

The former Victorian club for gentlemen mill-owners is now owned by the Duke of Devonshire and stands on the edge of his great Yorkshire estate. Given the lineage, and the stunning Dales National Park setting, one would expect polished antiques and plenty of classic country-house trim, but it is modern good looks that hold sway here. Enter straight into the lounge bar, where the polished floorboards and vivid colour scheme of lilac, pink, turquoise and purple is as eye-catching as the bold contemporary artworks that are displayed throughout.

The bedrooms are highly individual and each one is named after a local village. While one room is quite small, it is stylish, with views to the fells and to the roof – which is covered in Astroturf with fake sheep. Others are larger but equally distinctive and are painted in bright yellows, muted salmon or mustard tones, even black and white, with matching checked or patterned fabrics, comfy beds (local craftsmen make the furniture), flat-screen TVs, DVD players and gorgeous bathrooms. Guests are welcome to use the stunning pool and spa facilities, pictured here, at the sister country-house hotel a couple of miles away at Bolton Abbey.

The Devonshire Fell, Burnsall, Skipton, North Yorkshire BD23 6BT

The Food

There's a relaxed, casual feel to the easy, open-plan lounge bar; a mood enhanced by plain, well-spaced tables and a big wood-burning stove. There is a small, more formal conservatory restaurant, which has wide-ranging views of Wharfedale, but the straight-to-the-point menu is the same in both. The modern repertoire picks up on Mediterranean influences, say grilled plum tomatoes with mozzarella bruschetta or chicken liver, pancetta and fig salad to start, and mains of grilled pepper-coated tuna steak with roast vine tomatoes, but doesn't neglect traditional British favourites, often inspired by what is available locally (wild rabbit and forest mushroom terrine, for example, and Masham pork sausages with chive mash and onion jus).

Beware of the home-made bread: it is delicious and very moreish. Those who make it all the way to dessert may be able to find room for rice pudding with coconut and lemon grass, a delicious crème caramel with amaretto biscuit, and warm chocolate fondant with honeycomb ice cream. The atmosphere is helped by the informal and friendly service that sets a busy pace without making people feel at all rushed.

The Essentials

Time at the Bar!
11am-11pm
Food: 12-2.30pm, 6-9pm

What's the Damage?
Main courses from £9.95

Bitter Experience:
Timothy Taylor Landlord, Black Sheep

Sticky Fingers:
Children welcome, children's menu

Muddy Paws:
Dogs welcome

Zzzzz:
12 rooms, £125-£175

Anything Else?
Garden, car park

What To Do

Shop

PJK GALLERY

Exhibitors are carefully selected to keep a balance of both classic and contemporary paintings, many of which are inspired by the Dales. Other fine arts and crafts are drawn from artists working locally, nationally and internationally, including ceramics and sculpture. Skipton Antiques Centre is nearby.

Mount Pleasant, High Street, Skipton, North Yorkshire BD23 1JZ
01756 793164

WEETON'S OF HARROGATE

Yorkshire to the core, this exclusive delicatessen sells rare-breed meats, venison and other game; cheeses galore; Yorkshire cider; Swaledale lamb; Vale of York sloe gin; in-shop bakery pies. Small producers are well represented, including organic farms.

23/24 West Park, Harrogate, North Yorkshire HG1 1BJ
01423 507100
www.weetons.com

WRIGHT WINE AND WHISKY

This enticing emporium in the back streets of Skipton groans under the sheer volume of collectible beverages. At least 600 malts are stocked, from all over Scotland but with particular emphasis on the Spey Valley and Islay producers; some very rare singles put in an appearance here. Wines from 17 countries complement this shrine to grain, with more than 900 bins represented, again with rare vintages often available.

The Old Smithy, Raikes Road, Skipton, North Yorkshire BD23 1NP
01756 700886
www.wineandwhisky.co.uk

Visit

KEIGHLEY & WORTH VALLEY RAILWAY

One of England's first and favourite preserved railways, charting a course up the winding Worth Valley to Haworth, with its Brontë connections, museum, antique shops and countryside locations; and beyond to Oxenhope, in the South Pennines. The film *The Railway Children* was filmed here.

The Railway Station, Haworth, Keighley, West Yorkshire BD22 8NJ
01535 645214
www.kwvr.co.uk

MALHAM COVE

The combination of the incredible cliffs of Malham Cove, the great chasm and falls of Gordale Scar and the limestone pavements between the Cove and lovely Malham Tarn thrill first-time visitors every year. Self-guided walks start from the visitor centre at Malham.

Malham Cove Information Centre, Malham, Skipton, North Yorkshire BD23 4DA
01729 830363
www.yorkshiredales.org

RIPLEY CASTLE

Centuries-worth of acquisition by the Ingilby family means that rare china, paintings and armour set off this Elizabethan castle to perfection. It's also renowned for its gardens, particularly the spring bulbs, the hot-house and the National Hyacinth Collection. Quirkily, there's a famous collection of rare vegetables grown here by Garden Organic (formerly the Henry Doubleday Research Association).

Ripley, Harrogate, North Yorkshire HG3 3AY
01423 770152
www.ripleycastle.co.uk

Activity

DALES PARAGLIDING

Boost your adrenalin levels by floating, twisting and turning above the scenic southern reaches of Yorkshire's hills and dales. A full day's paragliding can be tailored to your experience – and the weather. Advance booking is essential.

Active Edge, Glasshouses, Pateley Bridge North Yorkshire
0845 129 8286
www.dhpc.org.uk

FLY FISHING

Even if you've never tried it before, book an idyllic day's angling – this gentle sport guarantees a shallow learning curve and maximum enjoyment. You get one-to-one tuition from one of the best-known names in English fly-fishing circles, Stuart Minnikin – who has access to many prime stretches of the Yorkshire Dales' renowned trout rivers, lakes and reservoirs. It is possible to meet on-site or at The Devonshire Fell.

01535 635464
www.yorkshire-dales-flyfishing.com

YORKSHIRE DALES FALCONRY & WILDLIFE CONSERVATION CENTRE

A centre for the study, rescue and rehabilitation of birds of prey as well as being a falconry school, this fascinating conservation centre is stocked with birds from many corners of the world. Try some basic handling experience and tuition, or brave a full day's flying experience, hunting with the hawks in their natural environment.

Crows Nest Road, Giggleswick, Settle, North Yorkshire LA2 8AS
01729 822832
www.falconryandwildlife.com

The Walk - River and Woodland at Bolton Abbey

Over moorland and alongside the River Strid to visit the romantic priory.

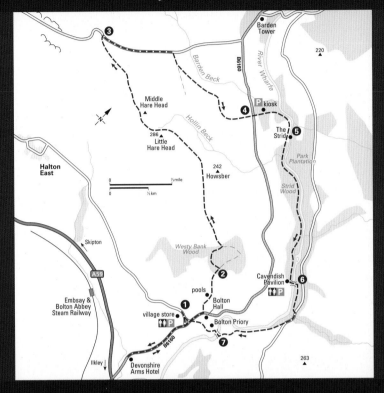

Walk Details

LENGTH: 6.75 miles (10.9km)

TIME: 2hrs 30min

ASCENT: 870ft (265m)

PATHS: Field and moorland paths, then riverside paths, 4 stiles

SUGGESTED MAP: aqua3 OS Explorer OL2 Yorkshire Dales – Southern & Western

GRID REFERENCE: SE 071539

PARKING: Main pay-and-display car park at Bolton Abbey

1 Leave the car park at its north end and go past the Village Store and the telephone box. Turn right, walk down the left side of the green; turn left. Pass under the archway. Opposite battlemented Bolton Hall, turn left on to the track through the signed gate. At the top of the track, go through the gate on the right with the bridleway sign. Walk half-left to pass the corner of some pools. Continue through the gate beyond; now turn right towards another gate into the wood.

2 Go through the gate and follow the signed track through the wood to another gate out into the field. Follow the blue waymarkers, many of them painted on the rocks, across the fields. The path eventually

ascends a small hill, with wide views. Descend to the gate, and 20yds (18m) beyond, take the path downhill to the right to the gated stone stile on to the road.

3 Turn right along the road. After 200yds (183m) go right through the gate by the sign 'FP to B6160'. Follow the path across the fields, crossing the stile to reach the wall. Turn right, following the wall and then follow the yellow waymarked posts. Eventually descend to the stone stile on to the road.

4 Turn left and walk along the road for 300yds (274m), then turn right into the car park and pass beside the Strid Wood Nature Trails Kiosk. Follow the signposted paths ('The Strid') down to the river bank; now

turn right to reach the narrowest part of the river at The Strid.

5 From The Strid, continue along the riverside path until you reach an information board and gateway near Cavendish Pavilion. Go through the gate, turn left by the cafe and go over the footbridge.

6 Immediately at the end of the bridge turn right ('Bolton Abbey'). Follow the path that runs parallel with the river, eventually descending to reach the bridge beside the stepping-stones and priory.

7 Cross the bridge and walk straight ahead up the slope and steps to the gateway – known as the Hole in the Wall. Go through the gateway, then keep ahead beside the green to reach the car park.

The Abbey Inn

North Yorkshire

The Abbey Inn, Byland Abbey, Coxwold, York, North Yorkshire YO61 4BD

The Food

Meals are served in a warren of ground-floor rooms filled with mismatched tables, oak chairs, settles, flagged floors and oriental carpets. An old Yorkshire range features in one room and tapestries in another reinforce the medieval theme. A predominantly British, seasonal menu and a specials board feature starters like smoked Gressingham duck with basil and garlic croutons and Cumberland sauce or smoked salmon and crayfish roulade served with lemon crème fraîche. Food goes up a notch with the mains. Try a meltingly slow-braised lamb shank, served with mashed potatoes and gravy or stuffed chicken breast with mashed and roast potatoes and a redcurrant jus.

There is a vegetarian option at each stage, lovely chewy rye bread and vegetables that in early spring happily embrace hearty local swede, parsnip and cauliflower cheese. Desserts are trusty favourites: sticky toffee pudding with butterscotch sauce and clotted cream, and steamed sponge pudding with vanilla ice cream. With coffee and a sloe gin or elderberry port to finish, you will have dined like the Abbot.

The Inn

Set in a lovely valley of the Hambleton Hills, Byland Abbey doesn't have the glamour or scale of Yorkshire's grander ruins like Fountains or Rievaulx, but in its day it was one of the most impressive churches in Europe and even now it retains a striking presence. The Abbey Inn, opposite the ruins, was built by the monks of Ampleforth in 1845 and has provided hospitality for passing pilgrims ever since it was converted from a farmhouse at the turn of the century. Today it is the first and only pub to be owned by English Heritage.

Not many hotel rooms give you a view down the nave of a 12th-century Cistercian ruin, but that's what you get from Prior's Lynn, one of three comfortable rooms with four-poster or half-tester beds, antique country furniture and spacious, luxurious bathrooms. The garden is a pleasant spot to drink in the history, along with a pint of excellent Byland Brew, a real ale brewed exclusively for the Abbey Inn.

The Essentials

Time at the Bar!
11.30am-3pm, 6.30-11pm, closed Sun eve & Mon lunchtime
Food: 12-2pm, 6.30-9pm, Sun 12-3pm

What's the Damage?
Main courses from £12

Bitter Experience:
Black Sheep Bitter, Byland Brew

Sticky Fingers:
Children welcome. No children's menu; small portions available

Muddy Paws:
No dogs

Zzzzz:
3 rooms from £95-£155

Anything Else?
Patio, car park

What To Do

Shop

'MOUSEMAN' THOMPSON FURNITURE

Robert 'Mouseman' Thompson was Yorkshire's greatest 20th-century Arts and Crafts furniture maker, and his great grandsons are carrying on the tradition, crafting beautiful pieces from aged English oak, all with the trademark mouse carved somewhere on the item. As well as tables, chairs and dressers, you can take home book troughs, lamps and breadboards. The visitor centre has rooms set in the 1930s where you can see original furniture made by Thompson, and there's a good cafe and gift shop, too.

Kilburn, North Yorkshire YO61 4AH

01347 869100

www.robertthompsons.co.uk

HUNTERS OF HELMSLEY

Nestled in the lush Wolds, Helmsley is a historic, thriving market town with many independent shops. Start at Hunters, a great deli where you can fill your basket with Bliekers Smokehouse Yorkshire Dales venison, duck and Nidderdale trout, hand-made goats' cheeses, or locally made pork and apple pies. There are two floors of preserves, pickles, posh crisps and handmade chocolate. Call in, too, at Pern's Butchers to fill up with home-cured bacon, puddings and pies 'made by the ladies behind the counter'!

13 Market Place, Helmsley, North Yorkshire YO62 5BL

01439 771307

www.huntersofhelmsley.co.uk

Pern's

18 Market Square, Helmsley, North Yorkshire YO18 5BL

01439 770249

www.thestaratharome.co.uk/butchers

Visit

SHANDY HALL

Coxwold is an idyllic village in the fold of a rolling valley, and Shandy Hall was the home of Laurence Sterne, who wrote *Tristram Shandy* here in the 1760s. Originally a medieval priest's house, the Hall is architecturally as eccentric as its former owner, and the still-lived-in interior is a jumble of books, pictures and memorabilia. In the study, where Sterne did most of his writing, is the largest collection of first editions of his work in the world. The old kitchen has a magnificent 18th-century fireplace.

Shandy Hall, Coxwold, North Yorkshire YO61 4AD

www.shandean.org

RIEVAULX ABBEY

'Everywhere peace, everywhere serenity, and a marvelous freedom from the tumult of the world' was written over eight centuries ago but describes Rievaulx today. Set in a magical, tranquil valley, the former monastery is northern England's most atmospheric and complete ruined abbey. It was founded in 1132 , it grew into one of the wealthiest monasteries in medieval England, and was the first northern Cistercian monastery.

Rievaulx Abbey, Helmsley, North Yorkshire YO62 5LB

www.english-heritage.org

CASTLE HOWARD

Standing magnificently in the Howardian Hills, Castle Howard is best approached down The Avenue, a straight 5-mile road lined with lime and beech trees. Designed by Vanbrugh, it's been home to the Howards for three centuries, and was the location for Granada Television's *Brideshead Revisited*. View the impressive Italian picture collection, porcelain by Meissen, Derby and Sevres, and a dramatic sculpture collection, before exploring the 1000 acres of stunning parkland and walled gardens.

York, North Yorkshire YO60 7DA

01653 648529

www.castlehoward.co.uk

Activity

GLIDING AT SUTTON BANK

Soar 2000 feet over stunning countryside, taking in the verdant North Yorkshire moors, the gentle Vale of York, and the Kilburn White Horse. If you book a Trial Lesson, you can take the controls – alongside the pilot - or just sit back and enjoy the ride. The cafe serves a cracking Sunday roast.

Yorkshire Gliding Club, Sutton Bank, Thirsk, North Yorkshire YO7 2EY

0845 597237

www.ygc.co.uk

NORTH YORKS MOORS RAILWAY

NYMR run authentic steam trains along 18 miles (29km) of stunning track through the heart of the North York Moors National Park from Pickering to Grosmont. Alight in Goathland, which doubled for Harry Potter's Hogwarts station, and is also *Heartbeat*'s Aidensfield. Another stop on the way is Levisham, where there are peaceful walks through leafy woods by the river. Why not pull out all the stops and treat yourself to lunch in the Pullman dining car.

Pickering, North Yorkshire YO18 7AJ

01751 472508

The Walk - Monuments to Monks and Astronomy

A walk that takes in an observatory and the romantic ruins of Byland Abbey.

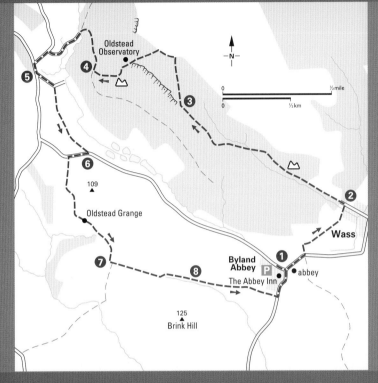

Walk Details

LENGTH: 5 miles (8km)

TIME: 2hrs 30min

ASCENT: 623ft (190m)

PATHS: Woodland tracks, field paths, 11 stiles

SUGGESTED MAP: aqua3 OS Outdoor Leisure 26 North York Moors – Western

GRID REFERENCE: SE 548789

PARKING: Signed car park behind Abbey Inn in Byland

① From the car park, walk towards the abbey ruins; turn left along the abbey's north side. At the public footpath sign, go left through gateway, then right through waymarked gate, just before 2nd set of gateposts. After the 2nd gateway bear half-left to waymarked gate behind a bench. Go through 2 more gates, then on to a metalled lane.

② Turn left. At the top of the lane, go through the gate ('Cam Farm, Observatory'). The path climbs, then leaves the wood edge to rise to terrace. After stile take left path, following Cam Farm. At junction of 3 paths, turn right, climbing up track, which levels out to big, open space.

③ Turn right, then, just before waymarked metal gate, turn left along wood edge. Follow the path to Oldstead Observatory. Go to left of Observatory, down slope to the track descending steeply to signpost.

④ Turn right ('Oldstead'). Follow the track as it curves left to become a metalled lane. Turn left at the T-junction, then turn left again on to the road by the seat. Just before the road narrows sign, turn left.

⑤ Go through the gateposts and over cattle grid. As avenue of trees ends, take the waymarked footpath to the right, uphill. Climb to the stile, bending to the left beside woodland to a stile, marked by a fingerpost. Continue past waymarker and over waymarked stile. The footpath goes between the hedge-and-wire fence, then over the stile on to the road.

⑥ Turn right, then, just beyond road sign indicating bend, take track to left by 'Oldstead Grange' sign. As you near house, turn left towards barns; wind your way through farmyard to stile by metal gate. Bear right downhill, then bend slightly to the right to the waymarked stile.

⑦ Over stile turn left; through wood to 'Byland Abbey' signpost. Follow path as it bends left by another sign; go over stile; down field with hedge on left to another signpost. Go over the stile beside metal gate and along a field with a hedge on the right.

⑧ Cross 2 stiles, then bear slightly left to stile. Go half-left to signpost by metal gate. Follow fence, then on to road by stile. Turn left, then left again past Abbey Inn to the start.

The Wensleydale Heifer

North Yorkshire

The Inn

Standing proudly in the stunning North Yorkshire landscape, this handsome, whitewashed 17th-century coaching inn has been treated to a classy and unusual renovation. The pristine picket fence guides you in to a clubby, welcoming lounge with a roaring log fire, leather sofas and tartan carpets. Sit back and enjoy a pint of Black Sheep bitter with a copy of *Yorkshire Life*, or mosey through to the newly transformed bar, a shrine to contemporary chic, with sea-grass flooring and subtle lighting.

Each of the nine themed ensuite bedrooms has a highly individual flavour, although all have luxuries as standard – Egyptian cotton bedlinen, plasma screens and Molton Brown goodies in the bathrooms. The Heifer Room has a black and white cow skin headboard, a 'grass' carpet and hundreds of tiny twinkling stars in the ceiling and the fresh black-and-white tiles in the bathroom bring to mind an upmarket milking parlour. And for chocoholics, the Chocolate Room is a dream come true – not only is the décor in delicious shades of caramel and cream, the dressing table drawer is bursting with all your favourite bars.

The Essentials

Time at the Bar!
11am-11pm
Food: 12-2.30pm, 6-9.30pm

What's the Damage?
Main courses from £10.50

Bitter Experience:
Black Sheep, Copper Dragon ales

Sticky Fingers:
Children welcome; children's menu

Muddy Paws:
Dogs welcome

Zzzzz:
9 rooms, £110-£140

Anything Else?
Patio, garden, car park

The Food

Locally sourced produce guarantees high-quality fare, which includes lamb from West Burton, beef from Bainbridge, cheese from Swaledale, vegetables from Bedale, and eggs from the village; but this is primarily a fish restaurant. Tian of Whitby crab, new potato and caper salad with chive dressing is melt-in-the-mouth, as is the sesame tempura of tiger prawns with hoi sin dipping sauce, or the chilli salt squid with sweet chilli salsa.

Fish stew, new potatoes, parsley and olive oil is deep and earthy, and Whitby cod with crackling Black Sheep batter, posh peas and fat chips is utterly exceptional – and it arrives on a newspaper plate. A meaty alternative may include duck leg confit with cabbage and bacon mash and redcurrant jus. For lunch, try the famous hot fish ciabatta or a bowl of steaming mussels cooked in white wine and garlic butter. It's a good job you're in hiking territory, since you'll need to walk off the lavender and honey crème brûlée with fig and orange compote – even more so if you choose the dark chocolate parfait with succulent warm cherries.

What To Do

Shop

ARTHAUS GALLERY
Lithographs and sculptures by renowned artist MacKenzie Thorpe are the main draw at this specialist gallery in Richmond. The town is home to a range of creative arts outlets; Phoenix Fine Arts has a rolling programme of exhibitions.
13b Finkle Street, Richmond,
North Yorkshire DL10 4QA
01748 823224
www.mackenziethorpe.net

Phoenix Fine Arts
11 Finkle Street, Richmond,
North Yorkshire DL10 4QA
01748 822400

SWALEDALE WOOLLENS CENTRE
Making the most of the local Swaledale sheep, with a hint of Welsh Blackface and Herdwick, fleeces are spun in a worsted mill in Bradford before returning to hand-knitters in the northern Dales. Result? Real Yorkshire luxury, with hand-crafted sweaters and other garments in traditional patterns.
Stawbeck, Muker, Richmond,
North Yorkshire DL11 6QG
01748 886251
www.swaledalewoollens.co.uk

WENSLEYDALE CREAMERY
This dairy is the only major producer of Wensleydale cheese, including smoked and blue varieties, as well as the original. Watch it being made from the viewing gallery before buying from the on-site shop. A museum recalls the days of small-scale making on remote farms.
Gayle Lane, Hawes,
North Yorkshire DL8 3RN
01969 667664
www.wensleydale.co.uk

Visit

AYSGARTH FALLS
The River Ure tumbles through a wooded gorge over a long series of falls and shoots, featured in the film *Robin Hood – Prince of Thieves*. Spectacular in flood, this section of river is also beautiful at low water due to the wealth of plant and wildlife here. Ranger-guided walks start from the National Park Centre at the old Aysgarth Station.
Aysgarth, Hawes, North Yorkshire
01969 663424
www.yorkshiredales.org.uk

BOLTON CASTLE
An eye-catching lump of a castle dominating the middle of Wensleydale. Famed as one of the places of incarceration of Mary, Queen of Scots, it was besieged in the Civil War but still remains only partially ruined, its solid walls defying the elements and sheltering a medieval herb garden and a vineyard. Five storeys high, with tableaux and rooms furnished in medieval style.
Leyburn, North Yorkshire DL8 4ET
01969 623981
www.boltoncastle.co.uk

WENSLEYDALE RAILWAY
An old cross-Dales railway, long defunct, has seen a renaissance in recent years, with services aimed at the local community, as well as visitors, taking traffic off the roads. Old-fashioned diesel units link Leyburn to Castle Bolton and Bedale – a glorious way to appreciate the countryside.
Leeming Bar Station, Leases Road,
Leeming Bar, North Yorkshire DL7 9AR
08454 505474
www.wensleydalerailway.com

Activity

DALES MOUNTAIN BIKING
There's plenty of opportunity for energetic off-road cycling on the green lanes, bridleways and old mine roads that lace the hills above Arkengarthdale and Swaledale. Alternatively, simply meander along the lanes threading through picturesque hamlets and up onto the higher moors of the northern Dales. Bikes can be delivered to the Wensleydale Heifer.
West Hagg, Fremington, Richmond,
North Yorkshire DL11 6AU
01748 884356
www.dalesmountainbiking.co.uk

KILNSEY RIDING & TREKKING CENTRE
Short and easy first-timer rides close to base beside the river Wharfe, or longer treks on the Kilnsey Park estate. Individual tutoring for beginners to horse riding is also offered at an outdoor facility in the hamlet of Conistone.
Conistone-with-Kilnsey, Grassington,
North Yorkshire BD23 5HS
01756 752861
www.kilnseyriding.com

THORP PERROW BIRDS OF PREY
Learn the basics of handling before taking a Hawk Walk through the estate grounds, flying a Harris hawk or buzzard under the tutelage of a falconer. Longer, more detailed courses are run; a more passive experience is simply to admire the collection of more than 70 birds of prey and watch flying displays held several times daily. The centre is based in a renowned arboretum.
Bedale, North Yorkshire DL8 2PR
01677 425323
www.thorpperrow.com

The Walk - *Villages, Falls and Follies*

A diverse walk from West Burton to visit the famous Aysgarth Falls.

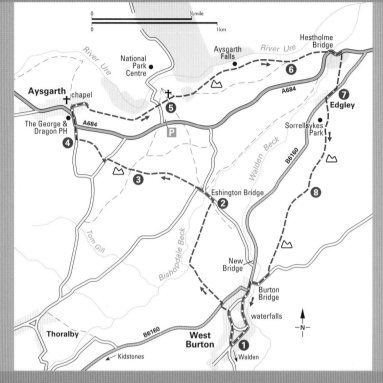

Walk Details

LENGTH: 4 miles (6.4km)

TIME: 1hr 30min

ASCENT: 394ft (120m)

PATHS: Field and riverside paths and tracks, 35 stiles

SUGGESTED MAP: aqua3 OS Outdoor Leisure 30 Yorkshire Dales – Northern & Central

GRID REFERENCE: SE 017867

PARKING: Centre of West Burton, by (but not on) the Green

① Leave the Green near the shop. Opposite 'Meadowcroft' go left ('Eshington Bridge'). Cross the road, turn right, then left, go through the gate and down the steps. Pass the barn, go through the gateway and across the field. Go through the gap in the wall with the stile beyond then bend right to the stile on to the road.

② Turn left, go over the bridge and ahead up the narrow lane. As it bends left go ahead through a stile ('Aysgarth'), then on through a gated stile. Proceed to a gap in fence near the barn, then through the gate. Bend left to gate in field corner, then go through gateway and on to stile. Turn right; descend to signpost.

③ Proceed to the stile in the field corner. Follow the signpost uphill

to the gateway; go through stile on right. Cross field half left to go through gated stile to lane. Turn left, then almost immediately right through stile ('Aysgarth'). Go through 3 stiles to reach the road.

④ Turn right into village, past the George and Dragon. At the left bend, go ahead towards the chapel, then right at the green; follow lane. Go through stile by Field House to another stile, turning left along the track. Follow the path through 8 stiles to reach the road.

⑤ Go ahead into the churchyard, pass right of church; go through 2 stiles, through woodland, then over a stile. Follow path downhill towards the river, descending the steps to a gate, then the stile. When

the footpath reaches the river bank, take the signed stile to the right.

⑥ Follow the path over 2 stiles to signpost, bending right across field to road. Turn left over bridge, turning right into woodland a few paces beyond ('Edgley'). Cross the stile and field to gate to the road.

⑦ Turn right. About 150yds (137m) along, go left over the stile ('Flanders Hall'). Walk below follies on ridge to footpath sign, cross the track; go uphill to stile with steps.

⑧ Opposite the stone barn go right, through the gate; go downhill through 2 gates, then over 3 stiles to the lane. Turn right. Go over the bridge to join the road to the village. Turn left, back to West Burton village green and your car.

The Star Inn

North Yorkshire

The Inn

With its sandstone cottages, village green, duck pond and thatched pub, Harome looks and feels like no other Yorkshire village. And nowhere else will you find a corner shop stocked with gourmet takeaways and fine deli items, as well as spuds and the daily papers. That's because the shop is owned by the pub and the pub happens to be the multi-award-winning Star at Harome. Duck as you enter the low beamed, 14th-century long house, and settle in among the polished brass and candlelight, which stays the right side of cute. Eat in the bar off an oak table or in the dining room before retreating up rickety stairs to the comfy old chairs and sofas in the eaves to nibble on cheese, nuts, chocolate and sweetmeats.

Bedrooms are in luxuriously kitted-out cottages in the village. They come complete with plump pillows, starched sheets and sumptuous throws. Plasma screens, spa baths, double showers – and in one room your very own snooker table – help make for a perfect weekend away.

The Food

The food at The Star is robust, seasonal, packed with flavour and what chef Andrew Pern calls 'British with a twist'. In winter, this might mean local partridge with braised chestnuts, curly kale and white truffle, followed by baked ginger parkin with hot-spiced syrup and rhubarb ripple ice cream. In summer, it could be crab and lobster salad with celeriac coleslaw followed by roast local suckling pig served with apple and black pudding. To finish, you might choose a refreshing summer fruit soup with a rose-petal sorbet.

The menus change daily, depending on the season and local sourcing. For breakfast, there's an exceptional do-it-yourself hamper delivered in a wicker basket to your cottage. It comes bursting with organic fruit juices, home-made muesli, dry-cured bacon, duck, venison and pork sausage, Bury black pudding, Yoadwath Mill smoked salmon, organic free-range eggs and lots more. If you get peckish in the night or need something for afternoon tea, there are home-made biscuits, flapjacks and caramel slices. The only problem is gastronomic overdose.

The Essentials

Time at the Bar!
11.30am-3pm, 6.15-11pm (all day Sun) closed Mon
Food: 11.30-2pm, 6.30-9.30pm, Sun 12-6pm

What's the Damage?
Main courses from £14.95

Bitter Experience:
Black Sheep, Skipton, Cropton

Sticky Fingers:
Children welcome

Muddy Paws:
No dogs

Zzzzz:
11 rooms, £130-£210

Anything Else?
Garden, car park, corner shop

What To Do

Shop

JORVIK GLASS

Glass-blowing demonstrations liven up the galleries of fine-art glass, decanters, decorative and functional pieces and unusual dichroic jewellery for which the gallery is well known. The shop is in the stableyard at Castle Howard.

Castle Howard, York,
North Yorkshire YO60 7DA
01635 648555
www.jorvikglass.co.uk

PERNS OF HELMSLEY

Locally sourced, origin-traceable foods make this first-class delicatessen in Helmsley Market Place well worth seeking out. Beef and pork from local farms in Harome and Kilburn; game (including fallow and roe deer venison) from nearby farms and estates; home-cured hams and dozens of regional and specialist cheeses, plus a panoply of other high-quality foodstuffs.

18 Market Place, Helmsley,
North Yorkshire YO18 5BL
01439 770249

WOLDS WAY LAVENDER

Six acres of purple haze colour the landscape on the edge of the Yorkshire Wolds, producing ample lavender blooms to be distilled into oils, then used to make soaps and cosmetics on sale at the farm shop. There's also a herb farm here.

Deer Park Farm, Wintringham, Malton,
North Yorkshire YO17 8HW
01439 770012
www.woldswaylavender.co.uk

Visit

NUNNINGTON HALL

A picturesque – and haunted – Tudor country manor house with memorable tapestries, fine porcelain and a huge, oak-panelled hall among its attractions – including the Carlisle collection of miniature rooms, each furnished and dressed to reflect a particular period of English history. The rare 17th-century walled garden has a collection of clematis.

Nunnington, York, North Yorkshire YO62 5UY
01439 748283
www.nationaltrust.org.uk

RIEVAULX ABBEY

The first abbey to be founded in the north of England by the seclusion-seeking Cistercian order of monks, it remains a tranquil and atmospheric place in the peaceful Rye Valley outside Helmsley. Above the ruins is Rievaulx Terrace, a Georgian landscaped promenade amidst glorious woodland.

Helmsley, North Yorkshire YO62 5LB
01439 798228
www.english-heritage.org.uk/yorkshire

RYEDALE FOLK MUSEUM

Buildings rescued from the North Yorkshire Moors now reflect the area's history. Cottages, shops and agricultural buildings recall harder times in the challenging countryside. The village of Hutton-le-Hole is one of the most picturesque in the National Park; a good base in spring for the famous Farndale Daffodils, or the walk to Lastingham's early Norman church.

Hutton-le-Hole, Pickering,
North Yorkshire YO62 6UA
01751 417367
www.ryedalefolkmuseum.co.uk

Activity

CYCLING IN DALBY FOREST

Thousands of acres of pinewoods and stands of broadleaf woodland criss-crossed by cycle tracks and challenging, unmanaged routes. Easier options include a network of graded forestry roads and lanes linking some of the villages. Sturdy mountain bikes make the going easier; instruction is available.

Purple Mountain Bike Centre,
The Courtyard, Low Dalby, Pickering,
North Yorkshire YO18 7LT
01751 460011
www.purplemountain.co.uk

KIRKBYMOORSIDE GOLF CLUB

A very unusual par-69 course, which mixes holes in a traditional parkland setting with challenging sections on the moorland fringes. Professional tuition is available for beginners and improvers; a handicap certificate is not required.

Manor Vale, Kirkbymoorside,
North Yorkshire YO62 6EG
01751 431525
www.kirkbymoorsidegolf.co.uk

PONY AND TRAP DRIVING

Your chance to exchange multiple horsepower for one horsepower. Take the rare opportunity to learn the basics of driving a pony and trap along these peaceful byways. Enjoy a beautiful old-fashioned drive north across the Moors to Great Fryup Dale and a maze of lanes above the River Esk. If you prefer to saddle up instead, then small groups (up to four) can take guided treks deep into the National Park.

Hollinequest, Great Fryup Dale, Leaholm,
Whitby, North Yorkshire YO21 2AS
01947 897470
www.hollinequest.co.uk

The Walk - Castle Howard, a Famous Stately Home

A walk around the estate of Castle Howard, designed in 1699 by John Vanbrugh.

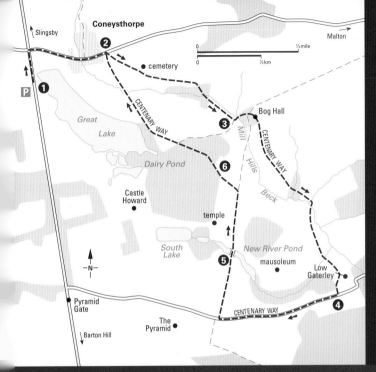

Walk Details

LENGTH: 5.25 miles (8.4km)

TIME: 2hrs

ASCENT: 256ft (68m)

PATHS: Field paths and estate roads, 1 stile

SUGGESTED MAP: aqua3 OS Explorer 300 Howardian Hills & Malton

GRID REFERENCE: SE 708710

PARKING: Roadside car park near lake north west of Castle Howard, near crossroads

1 From the roadside car park at Great Lake, to the north-west of Castle Howard, walk to the crossroads and then turn right towards Coneysthorpe. Walk all the way through the village, and just beyond the 'Slow' sign go right through the tall white gate in the wall, following the sign ('Centenary Way').

2 Go half-left, crossing the track, and head towards the further telegraph pole. Pass the cemetery on your left, walking now along the track. Through the gateway, go right along the edge of the field and, when you reach the double gate, turn right again, now walking along the edge of the wood. Continue along the track to reach the bridge.

3 Do not cross the bridge, instead turn left to walk along the track, following the track as it bends to the right through farm buildings, following the Centenary Way sign. The track passes through wood, winds left to cross bridge and then right. At farm buildings follow the Centenary Way sign off to the right.

4 At the T-junction, turn right along the metalled lane. The Pyramid will now come into view on your lefthand side. As you approach nearer to The Pyramid, you will reach a staggered crossroads where Centenary Way is signed to your left. Turn right here and descend to the bridge over a dammed stream, with the mausoleum on your right and Castle Howard on your left.

5 Cross the bridge and continue up the track, with the Temple of the Four Winds on your left. The path goes over the ridge, then turns left to the park wall. Follow the wall as it bends to the left and go over the stile beside the white gate and continue along the track.

6 After about 30yds (27m), just beyond the gate on your left marked 'Private No Public Right of Way', go left off the gravel track down the grassy path. Follow this to another gravel track, where you turn left to reach the signpost. Turn right here and follow the track back to the tall white gate in Coneysthorpe. Turn left here, and retrace your route back to the car park to the north-west of Castle Howard.

The White Swan Inn

North Yorkshire

The Inn

This 16th-century former coaching inn stands in the centre of Pickering, a perfect launching pad for days out on the moors and the Yorkshire coast. And if by coaching inn, you imagine the romantic ideal of old beams, oak panelling, flagstone floors, log fires and four-poster beds, then the White Swan ticks all the boxes. Take an aperitif in a cosy bar, eat in a low-beamed, blood-red dining room, then sleep in a four-poster bed in a traditional and immaculate bedroom.

If you have a more contemporary ideal, then you could ask for a room in the stable block. Gorgeous crisp white linen sheets offset a modish neutral palette with shaggy rugs, suede cushions, new art, sleek bathrooms, under-floor heating and LCD/CD and DVD technology. Also in the stable block is the Club Room: a comfortable, contemporary lounge where residents can help themselves to drinks from the honesty bar and relax by a glowing fire with a pile of books and magazines - it's a regular home from home. For the really energetic, the Club Room has its own pool table.

The Food

You can eat from the same menu in the bar, the lounge or the atmospheric dining room with its oak tables and polished stone flags. It features impeccable Yorkshire credentials: meat comes primarily from rare-breed farmer Tim Wilson at nearby Levisham who, when he is not selling from his London shop Ginger Pig, supplies the White Swan with top-quality cuts: braised shoulder of Swaledale lamb, rib of Levisham beef, for example.

Also on the menu is slow-roasted belly pork served with red cabbage, mustard mash and apple sauce made with apples from Ampleforth Abbey's orchard. Fresh from the coast come the raw materials for Whitby fishcakes and crab linguine.

The cheese board, too, is entirely sourced from the region: Yorkshire Blue, Richard III Wensleydale, even mozzarella from Yorkshire's own buffalo herd near Thirsk. Besides some 12 wines by the glass described as 'safe and familiar', the cellar is strong in wine from interesting small producers, including fine Burgundies, vintage ports and, notably, some 50 top-quality Bordeaux from St Emillion, their speciality.

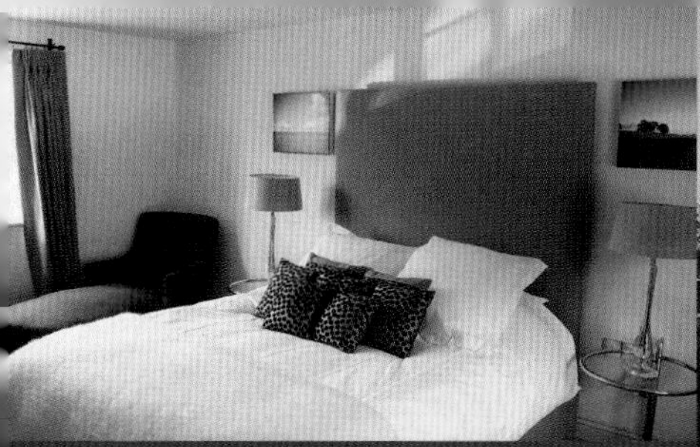

The Essentials

Time at the Bar!
11am-11pm
Food: 12-2pm, 6.45-9pm

What's the Damage?
Main courses from £10.95

Bitter Experience:
Black Sheep, Timothy Taylor Landlord

Sticky Fingers:
Children welcome: cots, Z-beds, sofa beds available and children's menu

Muddy Paws:
Dogs allowed in bar and lounge and in some rooms at small charge

Zzzzz:
21 rooms, £130-£245

Anything Else?
Terrace, car park

Room At The Inn, North Yorkshire

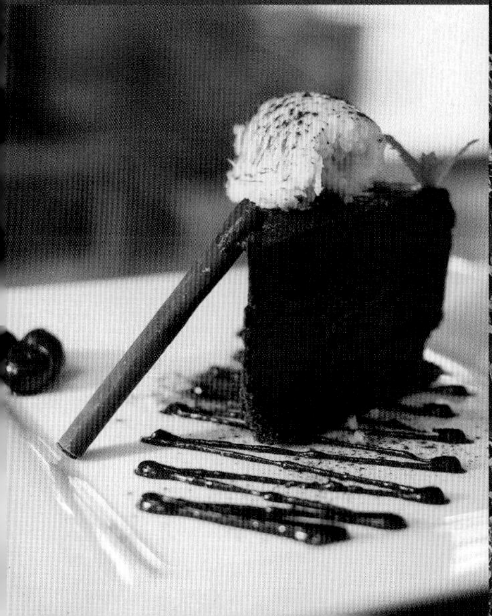

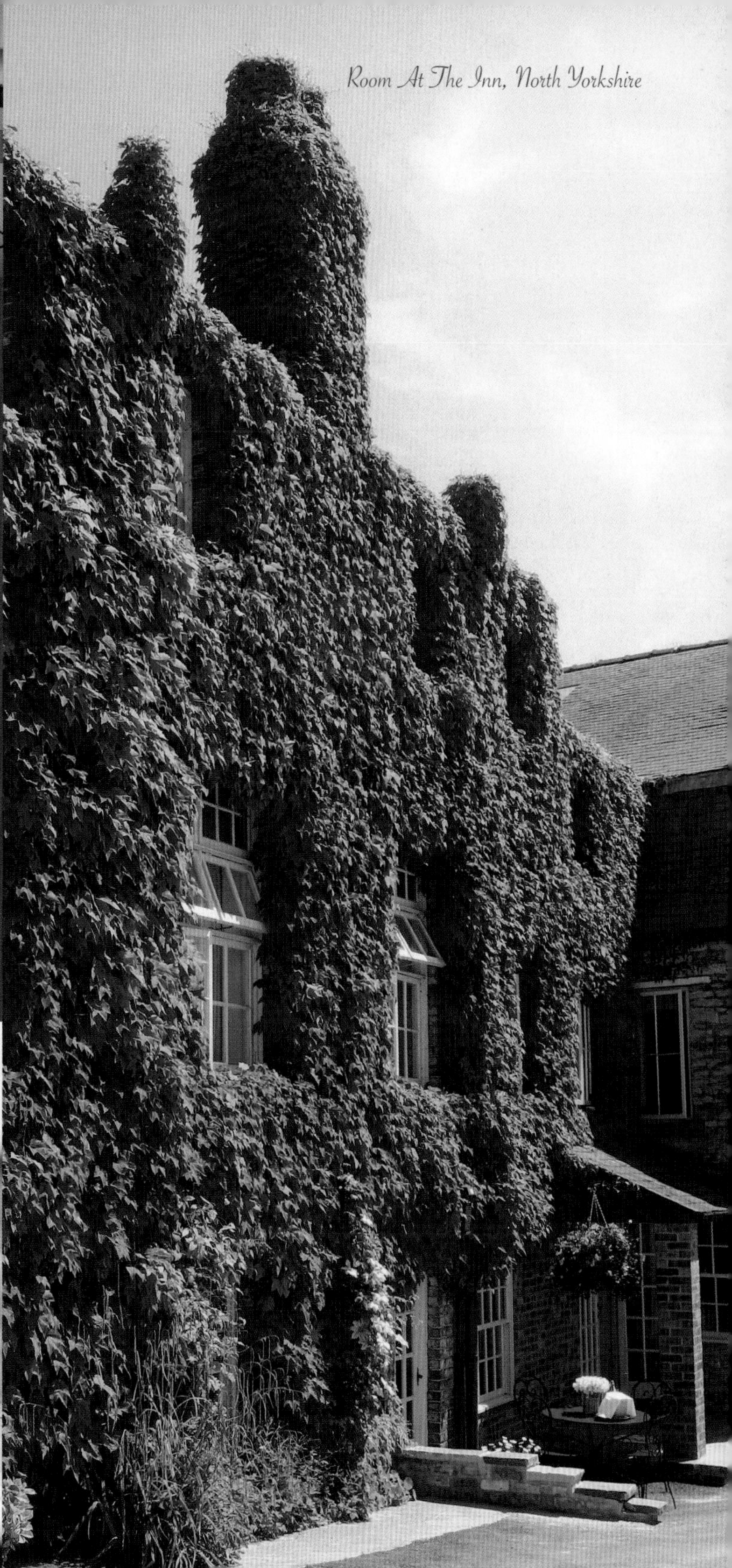

What To Do

Shop

CROPTON BREWERY

A dozen or more real ales plus seasonal specials are produced at this thriving microbrewery tucked away behind the New Inn. You can follow the brewing process via the visitor centre; stock up from their range of bottle-conditioned beers or try the additive-free beers available on-tap at the pub.

Woolcroft, Cropton, Pickering,
North Yorkshire YO18 8HH
01751 417330
www.croptonbrewery.co.uk

PICKERING ANTIQUE CENTRE

More than 40 dealers congregate here, ensuring the widest possible choice of antiques for punters. There is sure to be Georgian furniture and silver, Victorian ceramics and glass; enamelware, classic radios and paintings.

Southgate, Pickering,
North Yorkshire YO18 8BL
01751 477210
www.pickeringantiquecentre.co.uk

WHITBY VICTORIAN JET WORKS

Jet is a rare, mineralised form of wood – from the Jurassic araucaria tree – that occurs in thin layers and nodules only around Whitby. It can be carved, polished and worked into jewellery and became hugely popular in Victorian times, reflecting the Queen's obsession with all things black during her extended period of mourning after the death of her beloved husband, Prince Albert. Craft artisans still create highly individual pieces.

123b Church Street, Whitby,
North Yorkshire YO22 4DE
01947 821530
www.whitbyjet.co.uk

Visit

CASTLE HOWARD

An iconic stately home famous as the setting for television's *Brideshead Revisited*. Opulent collections of paintings (including two Holbeins), antique furniture, sculpture and porcelain vie with water features, temples, a rose garden and a thousand acres of landscaped parkland.

Castle Howard, York,
North Yorkshire YO60 7DA
01653 648333
www.castlehoward.co.uk

NORTH YORKSHIRE MOORS RAILWAY

One of the longest-preserved lines in Britain. The sound of steam trains chugging through Newtondale is evocative of the heyday of the rural railway. Hop off at remote stations to visit unspoiled villages such as Goathland; picturesque walks lead to treasures such as the Birch Hall Inn at Beck Hole, a shop-cum-pub from days long gone by.

Pickering, North Yorkshire YO18 7AJ
01751 472508
www.nymr.co.uk

WHITBY ABBEY

The haunting skeleton of Whitby Abbey broods above the harbour, at the top of 199 steps; galleries unearth its long history. Nearby St Mary's Church is fitted out with furnishings created by 18th-century mariners. Explore the old town and harbour along lanes and ginnels little-altered since Captain Cook embarked on his voyages; his home is now a museum charting his life.

Whitby, North Yorkshire YO22 4JT
01947 603568
www.english-heritage.org.uk/yorkshire

Activity

DEEP SEA FISHING

Experience a day's deep sea or wreck fishing on a boat from Whitby Harbour. Several operators offer a variety of trips, which include all equipment and basic tuition. The *Sea Urchin* also operates evening wildlife cruises on which basking sharks, porpoises, seals and even whales are regularly seen.

Sea Urchin, Whitby Harbour,
North Yorkshire
07855 439380
www.whitby-sea-fishing.co.uk

EXTREME DRIVING

Located in the depths of Langdale Forest, a range of challenging off-road driving circuits and courses are designed to push both your driving skills and the 4WD vehicles to the limit. Quagmires, climbs, gullies, boulder-fields – all are designed to bring out the explorer or rally driver in you and boost your adrenalin levels.

Moorland Adventure Sport,
Bickley Rigg Farm, Bickley, Langdale End,
Scarborough, North Yorkshire YO13 0LL
01723 882335
www.moorlandadventuresport.co.uk

HORSE RIDING

Beginners can learn the basics of horse riding with personal one-to-one lessons or as part of a small group. More experienced riders can enjoy hacking; trekking is organised through woodland and on to local villages, and there's a programme of short dusk rides for the romantically minded.

Friars Hill Stables, Sinnington,
North Yorkshire YO62 6SL
01751 432758
www.friarshillstable.co.uk

The Walk - St Cedd's Monastery

Visit the ancient site of St Cedd's monastery at Lastingham.

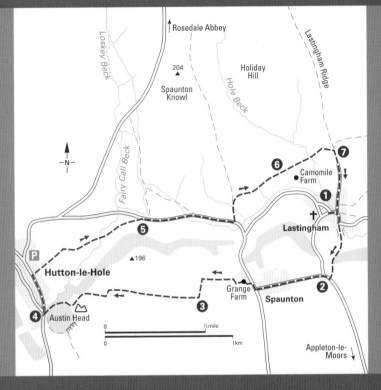

Walk Details

LENGTH: 4.5 miles (7.2km)

TIME: 2hrs

ASCENT: 463ft (141m)

PATHS: Farm tracks and field paths, 8 stiles

SUGGESTED MAP: aqua3 OS Outdoor Leisure 26 North York Moors – Western

GRID REFERENCE: SE 729905

PARKING: Village street in Lastingham. There is alternative parking in car park at north end of Hutton-le-Hole

❶ Begin the walk by the Green and follow the signs ('Cropton, Pickering and Rosedale'), past the red telephone box. Where the road swings to the left, go right to wind over the small bridge and beside the stream. Ascend to the footpath sign, and go right, uphill, through the gate and woodland to reach the handgate leading on to the road. Turn right, signposted 'Spaunton'.

❷ Follow the road through Spaunton, and bend right at the end of the village, then turn left by the public footpath sign over the cattle grid into the farmyard. Waymarked track curves through the farm to reach another footpath sign, where the track bends left. At the barn, the track bends left again.

❸ After about 200yds (183m), follow public footpath sign right and walk on to another sign as track bends left. After 100yds (91m) take footpath to right, down hill into woodland. Where path divides, take left fork down to stile on right, going off track and down steep grassy path into valley. Descend beside stream to stile by gate, which takes you on to road in Hutton-le-Hole.

❹ Turn right up main street. Turn right at yellow waymark by Beckside Gift Shop. Go through gate beside Barn Hotel car park entrance and ahead through garden and to right of sheds to stile. Go ahead over 3 stiles to kissing gate before footbridge. Follow path through woodland to gate and follow grassy track to road.

❺ Turn right and follow the road for 0.5 mile (800m) and turn left at footpath sign just before road descends to stone bridge. Follow grassy path, going over stile, to footpath sign just before farm.

❻ Follow direction indicated by signpost to left, bending alongside wall beside clump of trees and descending into valley. Cross over stream to stile and kissing gate. Continue walking with wall on righthand side to another kissing gate and stile, which leads to carved stone with cross and 3-pointed sign.

❼ Take none of directions indicated by the sign, but turn right, downhill through the gate and on to the metalled road. Follow the road downhill back into Lastingham.

The General Tarleton

North Yorkshire

The Inn

If you're looking for a cosy hideaway that's conveniently close to the A1 and within striking distance of Harrogate and the rural delights of the Yorkshire Dales, then this 18th-century coaching inn, set in open country on the edge of the village of Ferrensby, fits the bill nicely. Chef/ patron John Topham, former head chef at the famous Angel Inn across the Dales, has transformed the General Tarleton, making it a real foodie destination, whether for casual meals in the rambling, low-beamed bar brasserie or in the more formal atmosphere of the smart dining room. Elsewhere, expect an informal, pubby feel in the bar, helped along by a log fire and some cosy alcoves – and should you pop in wanting just a lunchtime sandwich and a pint of Black Sheep ale, you'll be made very welcome.

The purpose-built block housing the inn's 14 rooms may not look attractive but the rooms certainly are. Refurbished in contemporary style – lots of wood, bold fabrics, good-quality linen on big beds – they all have plasma screens, wi-fi internet access, and slate-floored bathrooms with Molton Brown toiletries.

The Essentials

Time at the Bar!
12-3pm, 6-11pm (10.30pm Sun)
Food: 12-2.30pm, 6-9.15pm

What's the Damage?
Main courses from £9.95

Bitter Experience:
Timothy Taylor Landlord, Black Sheep

Sticky Fingers:
Children welcome, children's menu

Muddy Paws:
Dogs welcome in some bedrooms

Zzzzz:
14 rooms £97-£120

Anything Else?
Terrace, garden, car park

The Food

John Topham offers a varied choice of modern British dishes on an imaginative brasserie-style menu with the emphasis firmly on local and regional produce. From interesting snacks/starters like his trademark rustic fish soup, little 'moneybags' – seafood in a pastry bag with lobster sauce – or Whitby crab and organic salmon fishcake with rocket and lemon oil, move on to confit of Dales lamb with garlic and thyme jus, cod in Black Sheep batter, steak and ale pudding with a suet crust, and seafood thermidor – monkfish, salmon, scallops, sole, cod and tiger prawns in a mustard sauce.

If you fancy a more formal three-course affair, then book a table in the restaurant where main course options may take in Goosnargh corn-fed duck with braised savoy cabbage and pancetta and thyme jus, and plaice with saffron and mussel sauce. Go for old favourites at dessert, good things such as rhubarb crumble with home-made vanilla ice cream, or warm Valrhona chocolate fondant. Similarly, the wine list is well chosen and includes a range of 20 by the glass.

What To Do

Shop

BETTY'S TEA SHOP

Betty's is a Yorkshire institution specialising in luxury cakes and confectionery. Recover here with a pot of tea and something delicious after a day's shopping in Harrogate where galleries and antique shops jostle for position in the Georgian arcades and terraces.

1 Parliament Street, Harrogate, North Yorkshire HG1 2QU
01243 502746
www.bettysandtaylors.co.uk

MACKENZIES YORKSHIRE SMOKEHOUSE

Hot or cold oak smoking is applied to a cornucopia of meats, fish and fowl; most of the ingredients are from traceable sources in North Yorkshire. Venison and trout, cheeses and dry-cured bacon are just some of the hamper-fillers at the farm near the domes of Blubberhouses radar station.

Wood Nook Farm, Hardisty Hill, Blubberhouses, North Yorkshire LS21 2PQ
01943 880369
www.mackenziesyorkshiresmokehouse.co.uk

TOMLINSON ANTIQUES

The largest collection of antique furniture galleries (more than 75,000sqft) in England, with forests-worth of wood transformed into desirable *objets d'art*. There are thousands of items to be viewed, with an ever-changing stock from small collectibles to major pieces; Georgian masterpieces to elegant Arts and Crafts work; plus items of Art Deco flamboyance.

Moorside, Tockwith, York, North Yorkshire YO26 7QG
01423 358833
www.antique-furniture.co.uk

Visit

FOUNTAINS ABBEY & STUDLEY ROYAL

A World Heritage Site, secluded in the manner favoured by the founding Cistercian monks in 1132. Immense abbey ruins complement the intricate Georgian water garden. Nearby is Fountains Hall, an Elizabethan manor with eye-catching temples, cascades and lakes in a large, wooded estate in glorious countryside.

Fountains, Ripon, North Yorkshire HG4 3DY
01765 608888
www.nationaltrust.org

HARLOW CARR GARDENS

These gardens are the bastion of the RHS in the north of England. Around 60 acres of show gardens, informal gardens and trial gardens, woodland and water gardens, plus Gardens Through Time, an exploration of trends and tastes over the centuries. Frequent events and plant sales add to the colour.

Crag Lane, Harrogate, North Yorkshire HG3 1QB
01423 565418
www.rhs.org.uk

RIPON CATHEDRAL

One of England's lesser-known cathedrals contains some of the finest misericords to survive from medieval times. Easily pre-dating these is the oldest crypt in northern Europe, secreted beneath the inspiring, soaring architecture of the main building. The compact city of Ripon has museums, galleries and some pleasant canalside walks.

Minster Road, Ripon, North Yorkshire HG4 1QS
01765 602072
www.riponcathedral.org

Activity

MICROLIGHT FLYING

Take to the skies in a variety of craft; some are fixed-wing while others come in flexi-wing options. This is probably the nearest you can get to the pioneering days of aviation – open cockpits come as part of the experience. Trial flights last around an hour, more than enough time to take over the controls for a spell if you dare!

Airsports Training, Rufforth Airfield East, York, North Yorkshire YO23 3QA
01904 738877
www.airsportstraining.co.uk

TURKISH BATHS & HEALTH SPA

The Laconium steam room, the hottest of three, will sort out the men from the boys at the lavishly restored Victorian spa complex in Harrogate. A full day's pampering, including the latest in beauty and relaxation therapies and detox treatments, is available.

Royal Baths, Parliament Street, Harrogate, North Yorkshire HG1 2WH
01423 556746
www.harrogate.gov.uk/turkishbaths

WARREN GILL SHOOTING GROUND

Both experienced guns and complete beginners can vent their frustrations at clay pigeons scuttling across field or sky near Masham. One-to-one tuition in this increasingly popular sport is the best and safest way to learn how to handle a shotgun. Various kinds of trap are used to imitate the behaviour of real prey, including a tower launch facility.

Fearby Cross, Masham, Ripon, North Yorkshire HG4 4NE
01765 689232
www.warrengill.co.uk

The Walk - A Medieval Walk from Fountains Abbey

From the ruins of Fountains Abbey to the medieval manor of Markenfield Hall.

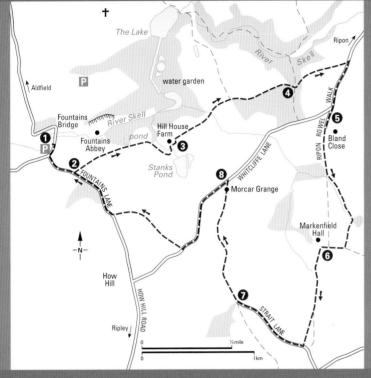

Walk Details

LENGTH: 6.5 miles (10.4km)

TIME: 3hrs

ASCENT: 328ft (100m)

PATHS: Field paths and tracks, a little road walking, 8 stiles

SUGGESTED MAP: aqua3 OS Explorer 298 Nidderdale

GRID REFERENCE: SE 270681

PARKING: Car park at west end of Abbey, or at visitor centre

❶ From the car park turn right uphill ('Harrogate'). At fork go left ('Markington, Harrogate'). Just after the road bends right, cross the stile beside gate with bridleway signs.

❷ Follow grassy path just inside ancient Abbey Wall, past small pond. Go through waymarked gate and follow track as it curves round to right through another gate, then left round farm buildings of Hill House Farm. Go through the small gate near the farmhouse.

❸ Turn right, then follow the footpath signs to go left at the end of the large shed and then right. Go through the metalled gate on to the track. At the end of the hedge proceed down the field to the gate into the wood. Follow the track, passing the ruined archway, to descend to the crossroads.

❹ Go straight on ('Ripon'). Track climbs to gate with Ripon Rowel Walk sign. Follow track beside line of trees to gate on to Whitcliffe Lane. Turn right. At the top of the rise, keep ahead on metalled road.

❺ Go over cattle grid by Bland Close, then straight ahead with hedge on right to reach the stile. Continue along the waymarked track, eventually with woodland to right. Go over stile near the metal gate and follow track as it goes right to reach gate. Turn right to farm buildings by Markenfield Hall.

❻ Follow the wall to the left, going through the metal gate and straight ahead down track, through the gate.

Follow the track, then the waymark sign, across the field to the stile by the gate. Turn right up narrow Strait Lane, to emerge into the field.

❼ Follow waymarked path beside field. Go through gate in field corner and continue ahead with hedge to right. Go through 4 more gates and follow the track as it curves towards farm buildings. Go over the stile into farmyard of Morcar Grange. Keep ahead to metalled Whitcliffe Lane.

❽ Turn left; follow lane as it bends left, then right. At next corner, look for stile on right by gate. Cross field half-left and cross 3 stiles, following waymarked path towards buildings. Go over the stile; pass between the buildings to reach the metalled road. Turn back to the car park.

The Angel Inn

North Yorkshire

The Inn

Beyond Skipton towards Grassington you're deep into the Yorkshire Dales, where patchwork fields criss-crossed with limestone walls shelter sheep, through picturesque Rylstone where WI ladies famously de-robed for a charity calendar, and into Hetton, where there's a church, a couple of farms – and the Angel Inn.

Over the years, the inn has evolved into a glorious dining pub. With parts of the building 500 years old, there are plenty of quiet corners: the snug is oak beamed with deep pink carpets, panelled walls and modern suede chairs; or opt for the more traditional feel of the bar, with its gleaming black range, richly grained oak tables, comfy settles and flagged floor.

Five bedrooms comprise studios and suites in a converted stone barn across the way, uniquely designed and furnished by owner Juliet Watkins with her exceptional eye for detail; fabulous bathrooms, luxurious Osborne & Little fabrics, *objets d'art* scattered liberally around the rooms – ancient papyrus pictures from the Nile delta, antique carved French figures – create a winning meld of old and new.

The Essentials

Time at the Bar!
12-2.30pm, 6-10.30pm (11pm Sat);
from April 12-3pm, 6-11pm
Food: 12-3pm, 6-9pm

What's the Damage?
Main courses from £8.95

Bitter Experience:
Timothy Taylor Landlord, Black Sheep

Sticky Fingers:
Children welcome; children's menu

Muddy Paws:
Dogs welcome in bedrooms

Zzzzz:
5 rooms, £155-£180

Anything Else?
Terrace, small garden, car park

The Food

On a warm day, the best spot to enjoy lunch is outside under the awning, looking out over Rylstone Fell; in winter, choose the cosy informality of the bar or the grander restaurant resplendent in rich golds and reds. Top-class ingredients are carefully sourced, and come to the table with thought and imagination; the Angel's signature 'little moneybag' is a filo parcel stuffed with fish from Fleetwood sitting in a creamy lobster sauce, while home-made black pudding with foie gras, spiced roasted pear and Puy lentils is earthy and dense. Roasted chump of Yorkshire lamb with crushed Jerusalem artichokes, trompette mushrooms and truffled jus does justice to locally reared sheep, and warm oak-smoked organic salmon with celeriac remoulade and bois boudran sauce is sweetly moist.

Vegetarians are handsomely rewarded with crisp tomato and olive tart with Yorkshire feta, or baked sweet potato gnocchi with ricotta, baby spinach and wild mushrooms. It's as well to start planning a yomp through the Dales at this point, as the desserts are unmissable: witness rhubarb brûlée with lavender biscuits, or the Angel's famous sticky toffee pudding with butterscotch sauce and chantilly cream. Wines are mainly French and the list is both sophisticated and surprisingly affordable.

What To Do

Shop

HARROGATE ANTIQUES

This handsome town is as famous today for its antiques as for its spa. The elegant Georgian and Regency terraces almost burst at the seams with nearly 20 galleries and dealers, some specialising in furniture, others offering a broader spectrum of collectibles. The main concentration of galleries is off Parliament Street.

www.harrogateantiques.com

TOWNEND FARM

Changing farming practices in the Dales mean that farmers have fresh opportunities to try new products. The Limestone Country Beef Project sees rare beef breeds replacing sheep; meat from Blue Gray Cross Galloways and White Shorthorns are among the specialities at this farm shop, joining smoked venison and cheeses, hams, bacon and preserves, along with seasonal organic vegetables.

Scosthrop, Airton, Skipton,
North Yorkshire BD23 4BE
01729 830902
www.malhamdale.com/townend

Visit

PARCEVALL HALL GARDENS

Camellia and rose gardens sheltered by woodland. The site, high above Burnsall, also suits the collections of Himalayan and Asian plants, and lends itself to water features tumbling over the rocks. In all, there are 24 acres of peaceful terraces and pathways.

Skyreholme, Skipton,
North Yorkshire BD23 6DE
01756 720311
www.parcevallhallgardens.co.uk

SETTLE & CARLISLE RAILWAY

England's most scenic railway cuts a swathe through the western Dales. Part of the national network, normal scheduled services are enhanced by specials and regular steam-hauled excursions, passing through spectacular scenery and across Ribblehead Viaduct.

09065 660607
www.settle-carlisle.co.uk

SKIPTON CASTLE

The castle is a maze of period rooms, halls and yards. It dominates the market town of Skipton from its wooded crag at the head of the Market Place.

Skipton, North Yorkshire BD23 1AW
01756 792442
www.skiptoncastle.co.uk

YORKSHIRE COUNTRY WINES

A former flax mill on the River Nidd now processes a different harvest; it makes locally sourced hedgerow as well as cultivated fruits and flowers into wine.

Riverside Cellars, The Mill, Glasshouse,
Harrogate, North Yorkshire HG3 5QH
01423 711947
www.yorkshirecountrywines.co.uk

Activity

FALCONRY

Meet the spectacled owls, hawks and eagles before joining a half- or full-day course on flying them to and from the hand. Fly goshawks or Harris hawks on the shorter course or brave the magnificent sea eagles on a full-day's falconry in the shadow of Pen-y-Ghent.

Greengates Farm, Brackenbottom, Horton-in-Ribblesdale, North Yorkshire BD23 0EW
01729 860316
www.hawkexperience.co.uk

SPORTS BALLOONING

This is hot-air ballooning, but on a smaller scale, with room for just a couple of fliers and the pilot. Flights from Skipton or Settle across the Dales take off around dawn or mid-evening. If you want to help inflate, pilot and land the aircraft, go for the 'hands-on' experience.

Airborne Adventures,
Old Burton Croft, Rylstone, Skipton,
North Yorkshire BD23 6LW
0870 755 4447
www.airborne.co.uk

TREKKING

Short rides on placid ponies for novices or challenging full-day treks for the saddle-wise. Treks meander through the spectacular scenery of Malhamdale and the western Dales, along miner's tracks, across moors and past old lead-mining works. The good-natured Dales Ponies used are a rare and hardy native breed, little-known outside the area.

Yorkshire Dales Trekking Centre,
Holme Farm, Malham, Skipton,
North Yorkshire BD23 4DA
01729 830352
www.ydtc.net

The Walk - Along the Canal from Gargrave

A lovely walk following the route of the Leeds and Liverpool Canal.

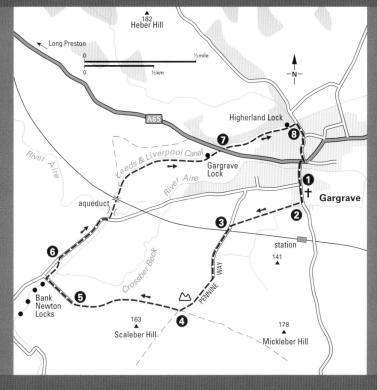

Walk Details

LENGTH: 3.5 miles (5.7km)

TIME: 1hr 30min

ASCENT: 114ft (35m)

PATHS: Field paths and tracks, then canal tow path, 4 stiles

SUGGESTED MAP: aqua3 OS Outdoor Leisure 2 Yorkshire Dales – Southern & Western

GRID REFERENCE: SD 931539

PARKING: Opposite the church in Gargrave or in village centre

1 Walk along the road keeping the church tower on your left. Once you have passed Church Close House, which is on your right, turn right, following the Pennine Way signpost, then cross over the stone stile found in the wall on your left.

2 Follow the side of the wall, along the Pennine Way path, which is partly boarded and partly paved here. Go ahead across the field to the waymarked stile, then turn half-left to another stile. Walk towards the top lefthand corner of the field to a stile that leads to Mosber Lane near the railway bridge.

3 Turn left, going over the bridge over the railway, then follow the track through the gateway and climb the hill. After the cattle grid, go half-

right off the track and across the field to meet another track, which leads to a signpost.

4 At the signpost, turn right, soon to walk below the wire fence to reach the waymarked gate in the crossing fence. Go ahead, walking across the field to reach a pair of gates. Take the waymarked lefthand one and then continue walking ahead, at first with the fence on your right. Follow the track through 2 gateways into the lane.

5 Follow the lane between the wall and the fence to descend to the canal by Bank Newton Locks. Cross over the bridge and turn right along the tow path. The tow path passes through the gate and then goes on to reach the road.

6 Go ahead along the roadside, cross the bridge over the canal and then turn left down the winding path under the bridge and continue along the tow path. Pass over the small aqueduct crossing the river, then walk under the railway bridge to reach Gargrave Lock.

7 Beyond the lock, opposite the Anchor Inn, go under the road bridge and then continue along the tow path to reach Bridge 170, at Higherland Lock. Carry on to the road by the signpost.

8 Turn right along the road, and follow it through the village, past Gargrave Village Hall. At the main road turn right, cross over the road and then go left over the bridge back to the church and your car.

The Blackwell Ox Inn

North Yorkshire

The Inn

Sutton on the Forest is a peaceful village ten miles north of York, with a stock of pretty Georgian houses in mellow brick, a church where the author Laurence Sterne was vicar, a minor stately home in Sutton Park – and the Blackwell Ox Inn, an ambitious roadhouse on the edge of the village.

Comfortable and traditional is the theme throughout. The public bar serves snacks around the log fire, while the more formal dining room has a profusion of brocades and tassels at the window, plumped-up cushions and severely starched white linen on the table.

Five spacious bedrooms done out in neutral shades of cream and taupe have brass bedsteads or four-posters. The silk bedspreads are dressed with quilted throws, cushions and crisp cotton sheets. Each room has a television with DVD player and a well-equipped and stylish ensuite bathroom. There is even a roll-top bath within the four-poster bedroom. From the bar loos upwards, every corner of The Blackwell Ox is as neat and clean as a new pin.

The Food

Seasonal produce and local sourcing is celebrated across a menu of six starters and six mains. Beef comes from Inman's of North Rigton; Spilman's of Helperby supply the shoulder of lamb for slow roasting; rare-breed pork and suckling pig comes from nearby Cold Kirby and almost every Yorkshire cheesemaker must be represented here. Head chef Steven Holding declares a love for the big rustic flavours of south-west France and Catalan Spain, but throughout the menu his Yorkshire accent is unmistakeable.

So, a hearty French onion soup is served with Richard III Wensleydale; confit of duck and cassoulet sit beside a lovely haddock and chips with the crispest beer batter this side of Whitby. Roast lamb is given a potato gratin and served with an olive and rosemary jus. Local pork is matched with chorizo and garlic sausage. Desserts follow a similar Anglo/Euro pattern with choices such as apple crumble and custard or crème brulee; warm chocolate pudding and clotted cream alongside tarte tatin. For the most part, service is efficient, the cooking is assured, portions are generous, and value is strong.

The Essentials

Time at the Bar!
12-3pm, 6-11pm (all day Sun)
Food: 12-2pm, 6-9.30pm,
Sun 12-7.30pm

What's the Damage?
Main courses from £8.25

Bitter Experience:
John Smiths, Black Sheep

Sticky Fingers:
Children welcome: no special menu but the kitchen will simplify and adapt the main menu

Muddy Paws:
No dogs

Zzzzz:
5 rooms from £85-£95

Anything Else?
Garden, car park

What To Do

Shop

BALLOON TREE FARM SHOP

'The further food travels, the more it loses' is the guiding principle of this multi-award-winning farm shop. Farm-raised Longhorn cattle and Gloucester Old Spot-cross pigs are among the rare-breed meats; and there's a well-stocked deli with cheese and dairy produce, locally made preserves and honey.

Stamford Bridge Road, Gate Helmsley, York, North Yorkshire YO41 1NB
01759 373023
www.theballoontree.co.uk

LUND GALLERY

A chic and airy gallery in a former village dairy offering a balanced mix of ceramics, painting and sculpture created by established and contemporary artists. The gallery is noted for its regularly changing exhibitions. Easingwold also has a number of antique and craft shops in which to browse.

Alne Lane, Easingwold, North Yorkshire YO61 3PA
01347 824400
www.lundgallery.co.uk

RED HOUSE ANTIQUES

The ginnels, lanes and cobbled streets of the compact city centre house both specialist and general dealers. Red House Antiques Centre is a good place to start, with 60 dealers based in a Georgian mansion. And all of this in the shade of the magnificent Minster, just a few steps away. York also has a good range of galleries selling contemporary crafts.

Dunscombe Place, York, North Yorkshire YO1 2EF
01904 637000
www.redhouseyork.co.uk

Visit

NATIONAL RAILWAY MUSEUM

A national treasure, stuffed to the rafters with engineering marvels; some, such as Mallard (world speed record for steam engines), still occasionally venture out, but most simply bask silently in the adulation of visitors. It's not only for transport buffs; the history of the railways is an integral part of the social history of Britain, and this is explored in the showrooms of the outer galleries.

Leeman Road, York, North Yorkshire YO26 4XJ
0870 4214001
www.nrm.org.uk

SCAMPSTON GARDENS

An inspirational garden at elegant Scampston Hall; the mix of contemporary design with highly traditional flower borders and perennial meadows is the work of Chelsea Gold Medal winner Piet Oudolf. There's an award-winning restaurant here, too; the Hall itself is open to visitors only during July.

Malton, North Yorkshire YO17 8NG
01944 758224
www.scampston.co.uk

SUTTON PARK

Elegant furniture by Chippendale and Sheraton, an extensive collection of paintings and some fine textiles and needlework are set in rooms richly decorated with plasterwork by one of the masters of the craft, the Italian artist Cortese. Formal gardens and parkland designed by Capability Brown enhance the mansion.

Sutton on the Forest, North Yorkshire YO6 1DP
01347 810249
www.statelyhome.co.uk

Activity

BALLOONING

Undoubtedly the most relaxing way to fly, drifting with the wind with the silence only punctuated by occasional recharges of hot air. Flights are necessarily in the early morning or mid-evening when the air is at its most still; sometimes heading towards Nidderdale and the Dales, on other occasions over the rivers Ouse and Swale.

Moor Lane, Arkendale, Knaresborough, North Yorkshire HG5 0RQ
01423 340140
www.blueskyballoons.co.uk

FLIGHT SIMULATOR

Top Gun meets *Airport* in the chance to live out fantasies as gung-ho fighter pilot or airliner captain while firmly anchored to the ground. The state-of-the-art simulators reproduce either a Phantom fighter jet or a Boeing 737, giving plenty of scope to prove your mettle through turbulence, take-off and landing. This is training as used by professional pilots.

Moor Lane, Arkendale, Knaresborough, North Yorkshire HG5 0RQ
01423 340664
www.yorkshireflightcentre.co.uk

PONY TREKKING

With the North Yorkshire Moors on the doorstep, full-day treks can reach areas far-removed from traffic or the well-beaten tourist trail. Outright beginners can try a half-hour experience ride; options then depend on the confidence and competence of the rider.

Boltby Pony Trekking & Trail Riding Centre, Boltby, Thirsk, North Yorkshire YO7 2DY
01845 537392
www.boltbytrekking.co.uk

The Walk - Treasures of a Hidden City

A stroll through the streets of the historic walled city of York.

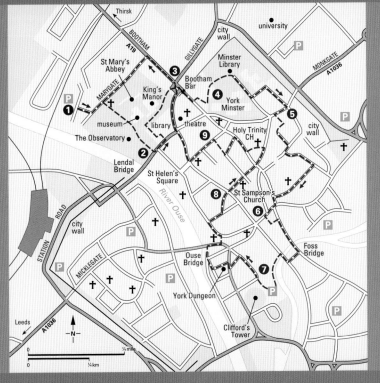

Walk Details

LENGTH: 3.25 miles (5.3km)

TIME: 1hr 30min

ASCENT: 82ft (25m)

PATHS: City pavements

SUGGESTED MAP: AA York streetplan

GRID REFERENCE: SE 598523

PARKING: Marygate Car Park, off Bootham

❶ Walk to Marygate, turn left, cross road; enter Museum Gardens through arch. Follow path ahead, passing Observatory; leave by lodge.

❷ Turn left, then left again. Go left through gate, and alongside library. Ascend steps; go through gate. At bottom of slope, turn right. Follow Abbey Wall into Exhibition Square.

❸ Cross at traffic lights; through Bootham Bar. Shortly on the left, take the passageway by the Hole in the Wall pub; turn right down Precentor's Court. By the Minster go left through the gate ('York Minster Library and Archives').

❹ Follow path left to library. Bend right through gate on to cobbled road. Turn left by post-box down Chapter House Street, bending right

into Ogleforth. At crossroads turn right, then left through archway.

❺ Bear right into Bartle Garth. At T-junction go right, then left on Spen Lane. Opposite Hilary House go right on St Saviourgate. At the T-junction turn left to crossroads, then right. Next to Jones's take passage, Lady Peckitt's Yard.

❻ Go under the building; turn left to Fossgate. Turn right, cross bridge. Turn right on Merchantgate. At T-junction, cross the road; take the passageway beside the bridge ('Jorvik Viking Centre') into the car park by Clifford's Tower.

❼ Bend right and go to right of the Hilton Hotel. Just before Job Centre, go left down Friargate, right along Clifford Street, then left by York

Dungeon. At the riverside turn right, ascend steps by Ouse Bridge; turn right. At the traffic lights turn left by the church. By the NatWest, go right, forking left by The Link shop.

❽ Cross Parliament Street and pass church. Keep ahead at crossroads into Goodramgate. Opposite Bon Marche, go through gateway into Holy Trinity churchyard; leave by passage to left, to reach Low Petergate. Turn right; turn left into Grape Lane. At bend left, turn right down Coffee Yard into Stonegate.

❾ Go left to St Helen's Square; turn right by TSB. Keep ahead at crossroads to Exhibition Square. At the traffic lights turn left up Bootham. Turn left down Marygate by the circular tower to the start.

The Blue Lion

North Yorkshire

The Inn

The location of this 18th-century coaching inn is idyllic, overlooking the green in a timeless estate village near the tumbledown ruins of Jervaulx Abbey. Since arriving here in 1990, Paul and Helen Klein have created one of the finest inns in North Yorkshire, popular with the country set and local shooting parties. Expect a good pubby atmosphere, with locals at the bar quaffing Black Sheep and Theakston ales, and a relaxed ambience in the two candle-lit bar rooms. Add tasteful prints and paintings, gilt mirrors, newspapers on poles, rustic high-backed settles, old Windsor chairs, rug-strewn flagstones and roaring log fires and you have one of the most evocative pub interiors in which to drink and dine.

Individually decorated rooms await you. Most of those in the inn are spacious and simply furnished with wooden beds and antiques, while the beamed stable rooms are really contemporary by comparison, with under-floor heating, plasma screens, leather furnishings and smart bathrooms. One has a big leather sleigh bed, another a metal four-poster, with bath and walk-in shower.

The Food

You can choose between a short menu in the intimate, antique-furnished dining room or the ambitious bar menu of classy modern dishes chalked on boards above a striking stone fireplace. As you can't book a table in the bar, it's best to arrive early to bag a seat – by the fire in winter, of course. First-class fashionable ingredients appear in starters like grilled king scallops with lemon and spring onion risotto, and soft shell crab deep-fried with garlic and ginger with a fennel salad.

Equally appealing main course options make good use of Yorkshire produce and might take in beef and onion suet pudding with dark onion sauce, slow-braised masala mutton with cumin sweet potato, roast cod served with pesto and Mediterranean vegetables, and chargrilled beef fillet with Shiraz sauce. A winter visit will reveal local game dishes, perhaps roast pheasant breast wrapped in bacon with butternut squash and red wine risotto. If you've room, indulge in a pud such as dark chocolate tart. Impressive global list of wines.

The Essentials

Time at the Bar!
11am–11pm
Food: 12–2.30pm; 6.30–8.30pm

What's the Damage?
Main courses from £13.50

Bitter Experience:
Black Sheep, Theakston

Sticky Fingers:
Children welcome

Muddy Paws:
Dogs welcome in bar and bedrooms

Zzzzz:
15 rooms £79–£120

Anything Else?
Garden, car park

What To Do

Shop

WENSLEYDALE CREAMERY

Based in the beautiful, tranquil village of Hawes, the Wensleydale Creamery is the only maker of real Yorkshire Wensleydale Cheese, created using an ancient recipe handed down from the French Cistercian monks who used to occupy Jervaulx Abbey. In the visitor centre is a museum, a specialist cheese shop, a gift shop with inevitable Wallace and Gromit items, and a restaurant where you can enjoy a range of cheesy dishes!

Hawes, North Yorkshire DL8 3RN

01969 667664

www.wensleydale.co.uk

DAVILL'S PATISSERIE

Kenneth Davill is an independent master baker making traditional bread and cakes, and one of TV chef Rick Stein's Food Heroes. His specialities, made on the premises, are chocolate products, especially Easter eggs – but you should buy the curd tart to take home with you for a genuine taste of Yorkshire.

Davill's, 24 Westgate, Ripon,

North Yorkshire HG4 2BQ

01765 603544

THE CRAFT YARD

Watch craftspeople at work and buy personalised gifts at this collection of local and individual craft businesses at Bedale Station. Products on sale range from contemporary and bespoke jewellery and model railways to gourmet Yorkshire food and gift hampers from Country Crossing.

Bedale Sation, The Bridge, Aiskew, Bedale,

North Yorkshire DL8 1BZ

Country Crossing, Unit 6; 01677 427772

www.countrycrossing.co.uk

Visit

JERVAULX ABBEY

Just walking amidst the crumbling ruins of this ancient Cistercian Abbey, with hundreds of wild flowers and fauna clinging to its walls, is a magical experience. Built in 1145, the Abbey was home to the French white monks.

Park House, Jervaulx, Ripon,

North Yorkshire HG4 4PH

01677 460226

www.jervaulxabbey.com

THORPE PERROW ARBORETUM

Here in the heart of the Yorkshire Dales are 1,750 species of the largest and rarest trees and shrubs collected from all over world – the most impressive collection in Europe. Enjoy delightful woodland walks, the beautiful lake with the manor house as a backdrop, and drop into the plant centre to buy one or two specimens to take home.

Thorpe Perrow, Bedale,

North Yorkshire DL8 2PR

01677 425323

www.thorpeperrow.com

FOUNTAINS ABBEY & STUDLEY ROYAL WATER GARDENS

There's a full day's worth of pleasure to be had here, starting with the dramatic remains of the Cistercian Abbey. There are 822 acres of parkland, with a medieval deer park, elegant ornamental lakes, temples, follies, statues, and the sumptuous Fountains Hall. You can get an excellent lunch in the Victorian tearooms at Studley Royal, overlooking the ornamental lake.

Fountains Abbey, Ripon,

North Yorkshire HG4 3DY

01765 608888

www.fountainsabbey.org.uk

Activity

THIRSK RACES

One of the county's prettiest venues, set between the North Yorkshire Moors and the Dales, Thirsk is a friendly, compact course with a track just a mile round. The action is never far from where you are.

Thirsk Racecourse, Station Road, Thirsk,

North Yorkshire YO7 1QL

01845 522276

www.thirskracecourse.net

WENSLEYDALE RAILWAY

Go as far or near as you like on the 22 miles (35 km) of scenic track from Northallerton to Redmire, deep in the heart of Wensleydale. Trundle through the Vale of York to the upland splendour of the Yorkshire Dales, passing through market towns, woodland and picturesque villages. Alight in historic Bedale and do a bit of shopping, visit Bedale Hall and break for lunch in one of the town's many cafes.

Leeming Bar Station, Leases Road,

Leeming Bar, Northallerton,

North Yorkshire DL7 9AR

08454 505474

www.wensleydalerailway.com

FALCONRY

Learn the art of falconry and handle many species of raptors, including owls, kites and eagles, on a full-day falconry course at Sion Hill Hall.

Falconry UK Ltd, Sion Hill Hall, Kirby Wiske,

Thirsk, North Yorkshire YO7 4EU

01845 587522

www.falconrycentre.co.uk

The Walk - A Kingdom for a Horse

From a castle and back via the gallops at Middleham.

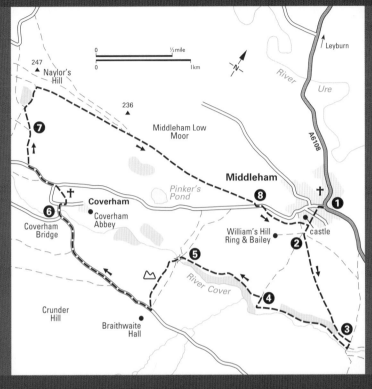

Walk Details

LENGTH: 7 miles (11.3km)

TIME: 2hrs 30min

ASCENT: 475ft (145m)

PATHS: Field paths and tracks, with some road walking, 18 stiles

SUGGESTED MAP: aqua3 OS Outdoor Leisure 30 Yorkshire Dales – Northern & Central

GRID REFERENCE: SE 127877

PARKING: In the square in centre of Middleham

❶ From the cross in the Square, walk uphill past the Black Swan Hotel. Just beyond, turn left up the passage beside tea rooms. Continue over road and left of castle to gate.

❷ Go half-left across field, following sign towards stepping stones. Cross next 3 fields, over waymarked stiles. After 3rd field, turn along side of field, ignoring track to right. Turn right at waymarked crossing wall to bank of River Cover by stones.

❸ Turn right (don't cross the stepping stones); follow riverside path, going through the gate and up steps. After returning to river bank, go right where path forks. Cross 2 more stiles, turning immediately right after 2nd stile. Follow the waymark uphill to the marker post.

❹ Turn left; follow line of wood. At end of field go left through waymarked stile, through trees to 2nd stile, then straight down field back to river bank. Cross waymarked stile and on to bridge.

❺ Go through gate over bridge. Follow track as it winds right and uphill through 2 gates on to road, opposite Braithwaite Hall. Turn right and follow road for 1 mile (1.6km) to Coverham Bridge. Turn right over bridge, then right again.

❻ Before gates, turn left through gate, walk beside waterfall and into churchyard. Leave by lychgate; turn left along the road. After 0.25 mile (400m) go through the gate on the right, opposite disused factory, bearing slightly left. Cross 3 stiles.

Go through the gate, pass between buildings, then cross 3 stiles through woodland.

❼ Cross the field to the gateway to the right of the wood. After passing a house, bend left to the gate on to the track. Turn right; go through the gate; turn right again. Don't follow the track, but go half-left to meet the bridleway across moor. Follow it for 1.5 miles (2.4km) to road.

❽ Turn left. Just before the sign ('Middleham') take the signposted path on the right. Turn left over the stile. Follow path parallel to road. Go through 2 more stiles, then take another towards Middleham Castle (favourite home of King Richard III), passing through the gate on to the lane. Turn left. Return to the square.

The Drunken Duck

Cumbria

The Inn

Take the Tarn Hows turning at Outgate off the B5286 to find this famous
17th-century inn, standing in splendid isolation high in the hills and
offering spectacular views across distant Lake Windermere to a backdrop
of craggy fells. It's worth the drive: the Duck is the perfect country pub
for the modern age – a classy inn with its own fishing tarn, microbrewery,
a relaxed country-style interior, innovative pub food and suitably stylish
accommodation. Whether you're supping pints of Cracker Ale in the oak-
floored bar, relaxing on the verandah after an invigorating fell walk and
soaking up that view, or lingering over a meal in one of the dining rooms
(which feature original beams, log fires, antiques and a wealth of landscape
and sporting prints), it's guaranteed you won't want to leave.

After all the fresh air and exercise, why not savour the creature comforts
of your individually designed bedroom? Rooms have charm and taste in
equal quantities, blending antique furnishings with designer fabrics, restful
Farrow & Ball colours, flat-screen TVs and impeccable bathrooms with
power showers and quality toiletries. Book the Garden Room for the best
views across the beautiful Langdale Valley.

The Essentials

Time at the Bar!
11am-11pm
Food: 12-2.15pm, 6-9pm

What's the Damage?
Main courses from £13

Bitter Experience:
Barngates Cracker, Tag Lag,
Cat Nap, Westmorland Gold and
Red Bull Terrier

Sticky Fingers:
Children welcome; smaller portions
available

Muddy Paws:
Dogs welcome in the bar

Zzzzz:
16 rooms, £120-£225

Anything Else?
Garden, car park, views

The Drunken Duck, Barngates, Ambleside, Cumbria LA22 0NG

The Food

The justifiably popular food makes good use of fresh local produce. Individual suppliers are listed on the daily menus, including venison from Holker Hall Estate and farm meats from named, traditionally reared herds. The simpler lunchtime bar menu offers interesting sandwiches – say, roast salmon with chive mayonnaise – which arrive wrapped in greaseproof paper, to eat in, outside or take away. Alternatives include Lancashire cheese ploughman's or beef casserole with pickled red cabbage.

More elaborate restaurant dishes may start with duck and spring onion confit with chilli jam or ham and pearl barley soup, while rump of Kendal rough-fell lamb with minted pea purée and rosemary jus or sea bass with mussel chowder are among main course options. Round off with bitter chocolate tart with warm chocolate sauce or a plate of local cheeses that may include Keldthwaite Gold, a pasteurised brie-style cheese made at Ivegill near Carlisle. As well as some cracking real ales brewed in the microbrewery behind the inn, you will find 20 wines by the glass from a carefully chosen list supplied by Staintons in Kendal.

01539 436347, www.drunkenduckinn.co.uk

What To Do

Shop

CARTMEL VILLAGE SHOP

This little shop in the picturesque square at Cartmel has a huge following for its famous sticky toffee pudding, lauded by TV food and travel programmes alike. But there are more strings to the bow here, with a delicatessen stocking umpteen cheeses, Lake District preserves, Lyth Valley damson and sloe gins and liqueurs and basketfuls of other delicacies.

Parkgate House, The Square, Cartmel, Cumbria LA1 6QB
01539 536280
www.stickytoffeepudding.co.uk

HEATON COOPER STUDIO

Alfred and William Heaton Cooper remain among England's favourite landscape painters of the past century. Originals by these masters, fine art prints and works by the current generation of this dynasty (painting, sculpture, ceramics) are displayed in this Grasmere gallery – some of the works are for sale.

Grasmere, Cumbria LA22 9SX
01539 435280
www.heatoncooper.co.uk

STAVELEY

This interesting village outside Kendal is well worth a visit. You'll find furniture makers and craft designers at Peter Hall, while Hawkshead Brewery is based in the nearby mill. Both welcome visitors. Lucy Cooks cookery school offers day-long courses to all levels.

01539 821633
www.peter-hall.co.uk
01539 822644
www.hawksheadbrewery.co.uk
01539 432288
www.lucycooks.co.uk

Visit

FURNESS ABBEY

Once one of the wealthiest abbeys in England. The substantial sandstone ruins slumber in the Vale of Nightshade near the southern tip of the Furness Peninsula. Discover the history of the foundation and the Cistercian monks whose order grew rich on wool. Easy walks meander up to the limestone plateau with views across Morecambe Bay.

Barrow-in-Furness, Cumbria LA13 0PJ
01229 823420
www.english-heritage.org.uk

HILL TOP

This cottage was home to Beatrix Potter for many years; it's been preserved in aspic since she died in 1943. Aficionados of her work will recognise many of the scenes from her books in the cottage garden and along the lanes of picturesque Near Sawrey. Head for the Beatrix Potter Gallery in nearby Hawkshead to view her original drawings.

Near Sawrey, Hawkshead, Ambleside, Cumbria LA22 0LF
01539 436269
www.nationaltrust.org.uk

RAVENGLASS & ESKDALE RAILWAY

England's steepest, most enjoyable mountain roads pass the lonely Roman fort at Hard Knott before plummeting into remote Eskdale and the hamlet of Boot. From here, a narrow-gauge steam railway slips down the beautiful valley to the ancient tidal port of Ravenglass, with further Roman remains and nearby Muncaster Castle.

Ravenglass, Cumbria CA18 1SW
01229 717171
www.ravenglass-railway.co.uk

Activity

GRIZEDALE FOREST CYCLING

Slinking across the Furness Fells above Coniston, Grizedale Forest's mix of old woodland and pines is laced by forest roads and tracks rising to sublime viewpoints. Ideal cycling territory, enhanced by the famous Sculpture Trail of around 80 works created over the years by a range of artists.

Grizedale Visitor Centre, Hawkshead, Cumbria LA22 0OJ
01229 860369
www.grizedalemountainbikes.co.uk

HAWKSHEAD TROUT FARM FLY FISHING

You can buy trout here, but it tastes much better if you've caught it yourself. Hire the tackle and book tuition in bank fishing and boat fishing techniques – you could land yourself a monster.

Boat House, Ridding Wood, Hawkshead, Cumbria LA22 0QF
01539 436541
www.hawksheadtrout.co.uk

SWINSIDE STONE CIRCLE WALK

One of the largest stone circles in Britain, this Neolithic monument is in an amazing setting below Black Combe. The walk up from the hamlet of The Green will find you in the company of few other people; this really is undiscovered Lakeland at its best. Beckstones microbrewery is based at The Green – try a pint at The Punchbowl Inn. Broughton-in-Furness, Cumbria.

www.visitcumbria.com

The Walk - *Lilies and Lakes at Ambleside*

A pretty walk above little Ambleside.

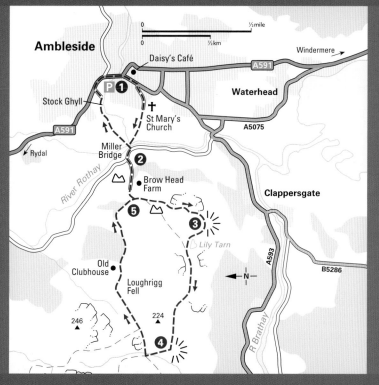

Walk Details

LENGTH: 3.25 miles (5.3km)

TIME: 1hr 45min

ASCENT: 575ft (175m)

PATHS: Road, paths and tracks, can be muddy in places, 3 stiles

SUGGESTED MAP: aqua3 OS Explorer OL7 The English Lakes (SE)

GRID REFERENCE: NY 375047

PARKING: Ambleside central car park

❶ Take the wooden footbridge from the car park; go right along Rydal road to pass the waterwheel and Bridge House. At the junction bear right along Compston Road. Continue to the next junction (cinema on corner); bear right to cross a side road and enter Vicarage Road alongside the chip shop. Pass the school; enter Rothay Park. Follow main path through park to emerge by flat bridge over Stock Ghyll Beck. Cross the beck, then go left to cross over stone arched Miller Bridge spanning River Rothay.
❷ Bear right along the road over the cattle grid until, in a few paces, a steep surfaced road rises to left. Climb the road, which becomes unsurfaced, by buildings of Brow Head. At S-bend, beyond buildings, stone stile leads up and off left. Pass through trees to find, in a few dozen paces, a stone squeeze stile. Pass through; climb open hillside above. The paths are well worn and there are various possible routes. For the best views keep diagonally left. Rising steeply at first, the path levels before rising again to ascend 1st rocky knoll. A higher, larger knoll follows and offers good views.
❸ Beyond this, the way descends to the right, dropping to a well-defined path. Follow the path to pass a little pond before cresting a rise and falling to little pocket-handkerchief Lily Tarn (flowers bloom late June to September). The path skirts the right edge of the tarn, roughly following the crest of Loughrigg Fell. A gate/stile leads to the base of a further knoll and this is ascended to another viewpoint.
❹ Take the path descending right to the track below. Bear right to the gate, which leads through the stone wall boundary of open fell and into field. Continue to descend track, passing the old golf clubhouse on left. Intercept the original route just above the buildings of Brow Head.
❺ Continue to cross Miller Bridge then, before the flat bridge, bear left to follow the track by the side of Stock Ghyll Beck. Beyond the meadows, a lane through houses leads to the main Rydal road. Bear right along the road to the car park beyond the fire station.

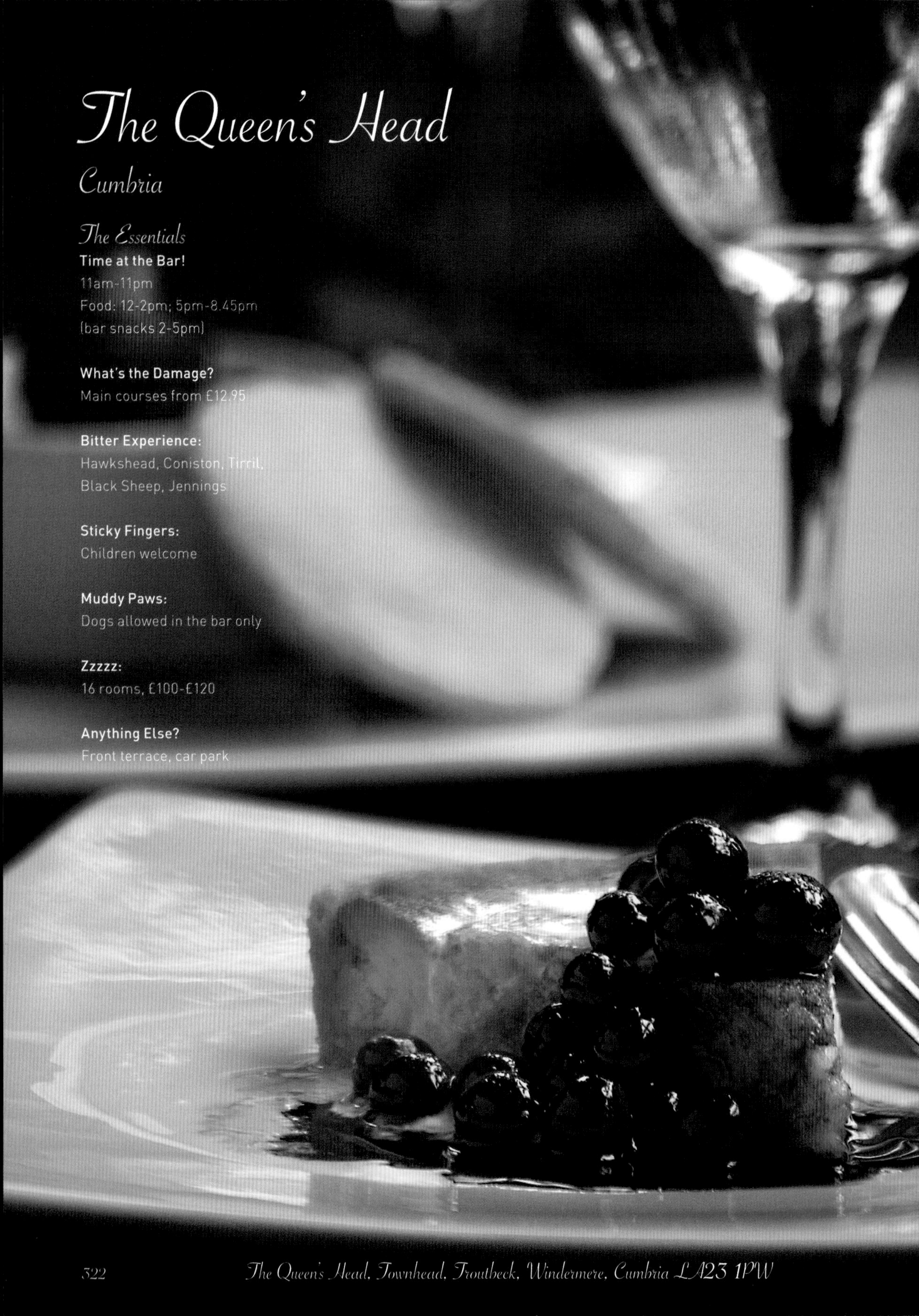

The Queen's Head

Cumbria

The Essentials

Time at the Bar!
11am-11pm
Food: 12-2pm; 5pm-8.45pm
(bar snacks 2-5pm)

What's the Damage?
Main courses from £12.95

Bitter Experience:
Hawkshead, Coniston, Tirril,
Black Sheep, Jennings

Sticky Fingers:
Children welcome

Muddy Paws:
Dogs allowed in the bar only

Zzzzz:
16 rooms, £100-£120

Anything Else?
Front terrace, car park

The Queen's Head, Townhead, Troutbeck, Windermere, Cumbria LA23 1PW

The Inn

For over 400 years this classic Lakeland hostelry has given shelter and sustenance to travellers journeying across the Kirkstone Pass between Penrith and Windermere – you'll find it in the shelter of the Troutbeck Valley with stunning views across the Garburn Pass to Applethwaite Moors. Little has changed in the solidly traditional interior since the inn's heyday as a thriving coaching inn, so you can expect oak beams, ancient carved settles, flagstone floors, sturdy old tables, crackling log fires and cosy alcoves for supping pints of local Hawkshead and Coniston ales. You can't miss the bar counter – it's fashioned from an Elizabethan four-poster bed that was once housed in Appleby Castle.

Classy rooms are split between the inn and the beautifully transformed ancient barn opposite. All sport contemporary bold striped or checked fabrics and wall coverings, colourful rugs and big beds, including some grand carved four-posters, all adorned with huge scatter cushions. Expect a host of modern-day comforts, smart bathrooms with power showers and top toiletries, and breathtaking Lakeland views.

The Food

Surroundings may be typical of many traditional Lakeland pubs but the food emanating from the busy kitchen is up-to-the-minute in both style and presentation. Dishes yield the promised full flavours due to the use of quality raw ingredients, some flair in the kitchen and general attention to detail on the plate – everything is made on the premises.

At lunchtimes, tuck into posh filled rolls, perhaps Cumbrian beef with Dijon mustard and watercress, and some cracking main courses – Lakeland lamb hotpot with pickled red cabbage or pan-fried ox liver with smoked bacon, onion gravy and creamed potatoes. Cooking moves up a gear or two in the evening to produce a varied range of modern-style dishes. Why not kick off with seared scallops with celeriac, crab and chive remoulade and shellfish oil, move on to roast Holker Hall venison served with roast potatoes cooked in duck fat, confit field mushrooms and plum jus, and finish with vanilla cheesecake with mixed berry compote or a plate of local cheeses? The set menu is excellent value.

What To Do

Shop

LOW SIZERGH BARN

Stock up on wonderful organic goodies and speciality Cumbrian foods at the farm shop then browse the craft galleries for hand-made knitwear or a locally made pot. Stop off for tea and cake in the tea room and watch the cows being milked, before following the 2-mile (3-km) trail around the farm at this award-winning farm complex close to the National Trust's Sizergh Castle.

Low Sizergh Farm, Sizergh, Kendal, Cumbria LA8 8AE

01539 560426

www.lowsizerghbarn.co.uk

OSHY GALLERY

Run by a talented artistic, design- and crafts-oriented family, OSHY specialises in unique designer/maker pieces and home accessories including sculptural furniture and lighting. As a souvenir of your stay you can also buy one of Marilyn Tordoff's evocative landscape paintings of the Lake District.

Old Stamp House Yard, Lake Road, Ambleside, Cumbria LA22 0AD

01539 432641

www.oshy-gallery.co.uk

HAWKSHEAD BREWERY

You've probably supped a pint of Lakeland Gold in the bar at the Queen's Head, so why not visit the brewery's state-of-the-art Beer Hall and taste the full range of Hawkshead beers and then buy some bottles to take home. You can tour the brewery on Saturdays between 12 and 3pm.

Staveley Mill Yard, Staveley, Cumbria LA8 9LR

01539 822644

www.hawksheadbrewery.co.uk

Visit

HILL TOP & BEATRIX POTTER GALLERY

If you enjoyed Beatrix Potter's enchanting tales, then you should visit this small 17th-century farmhouse tucked away in the fells above Lake Windermere. The house and area were her inspiration and it was here that she wrote many of the famous stories. Kept exactly as it was then, it is filled with her furniture, china and favourite possessions. The Hawkshead gallery exhibits her watercolours.

Hill Top, Near Sawrey, Hawkshead, Ambleside, Cumbria LA22 0LF

01539 436269

TOWNEND

This 17th-century stone and slate house is one of the finest examples of a 'statesman' farmer's house in Cumbria. Perfectly preserved, it was home to the Browne family for 300 years and you can see the original home-made carved furniture, books, paperwork and fascinating domestic utensils.

Troutbeck, Windermere, Cumbria LA23 1LB

01539 432628

www.nationaltrust.org.uk

RYDAL MOUNT

Overlooking mountains and Rydal Water, the family home of William Wordsworth from 1813 until his death in 1850 contains important family portraits, furniture and many of the poet's personal possessions, together with first editions of his work. Stroll through the beautiful gardens - see the spring daffodils or take an exclusive evening tour.

Rydal, Ambleside, Cumbria LA22 9LU

01539 433002

www.rydalmount.co.uk

Activity

SAILING

Why not learn to sail a Beneteau performance yacht on Lake Windermere with Outrun Sailing? Join one of the courses or just relax and soak up mountain views as you cruise the lake. See the sun set over the Langdale Pikes on the Sundowner Cruise.

Outrun Sailing, Outrun Nook, Crook, Cumbria LA8 9HS

01539 488981

www.outrunsailing.co.uk

COOKERY COURSES

Prepare to be inspired, educated and entertained, whatever your cooking experience and ability, on one of Lucy Nicholson's hands-on and interactive one-day cookery courses. Don your pinnie and cook your own lunch.

LucyCooks, Mill Yard, Staveley, Kendal, Cumbria LA8 9LR

01539 432288

www.lucycooks.co.uk

GRIZEDALE FOREST PARK

Explore a few of Cumbria's various waymarked woodland trails, from the 1-mile (1.6-km) Millwood Habitat Trail to the 9-mile (14-km) Silurian Way. You can do it on foot, or maybe hire a bike at the visitor centre, and explore the forest tracks on two wheels. There are routes to suit all biking abilities but, for something rather challenging, you should try the North Face Trail.

Hawkshead, Ambleside, Cumbria LA22 0QJ

01229 860373

www.forestry.gov.uk

www.grizedalemountainbikes.co.uk

The Walk - A Remote Valley at Kentmere

Once ravaged by Scottish rivers, this lovely remote valley now basks in tranquillity.

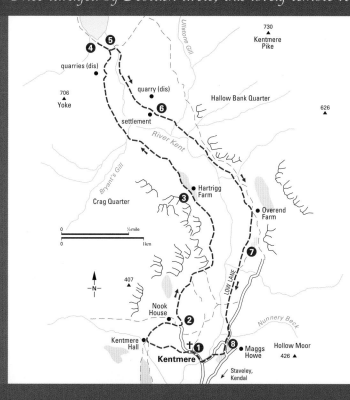

Walk Details

LENGTH: 6.75 miles (10.9km)

TIME: 2hrs 15min

ASCENT: 689ft (210m)

PATHS: Generally good tracks and paths, some open fields, 7 stiles

SUGGESTED MAP: aqua3 OS Explorer OL7 The English Lakes (SE)

GRID REFERENCE: SD 456040

PARKING: Very limited in Kentmere, but small field by Low Bridge is occasionally available

❶ Begin the walk on the bridleway ('Kentmere Hall') opposite to St Cuthbert's Church. Approach a farmyard and bear right behind the cattle pens, then right again through the side gate. A signpost ('Kentmere Reservoir') directs you up the field. Leave at the top and continue to the gate. Pass the barn and go through the gap to another gate, where the track leads past Nook House.

❷ Ignore the turn-off to Garburn, and immediately after the next house, Greenhead, go left. Still following signs to the reservoir, turn right through the gate, then right again at the 2nd fork to join the metalled track up the valley.

❸ The valley bottom here is wide and flat. Turn left past the entrance to Hartrigg Farm and continue on the track through the valley, now progressively squeezed between the craggy breasts of Yoke and Kentmere Pike. Eventually the dam appears, rising above spoil heaps of abandoned slate quarries.

❹ Continue walking on the track as far as the dam.

❺ The bridges below the dam take the return route across the outflows to the path just above, which then follows the River Kent downstream. Beyond the quarries, cross over the ladder stile into the enclosure by the barn and then leave this area by the gate on the left.

❻ The track continues through successive valley bottom fields, eventually leading to Overend

Farm. Ignore the tarmac lane and bear right through the gate on to the grass track. Where the track later drops from Hallow Bank, keep ahead along Low Lane.

❼ This old track ultimately emerges on to the lane. Carry on, at the next junction, to the waymarked stile on the right a little further on. The route now lies across the field but, for a break, continue to the 2nd junction and turn left to Maggs Howe, above the lane on right.

❽ Retrace your steps to the stile and walk down to the far bottom corner of the field. The steep path drops beside the stream through larch to emerge on to the lane. Turn left and, at the end, go right, back to St Cuthbert's Church.

The Weary

Cumbria

The Inn

Life is full of surprises. Set in a walkers' paradise with Hadrian's Wall, the Lakes and the Scottish Borders on the doorstep, Castle Carrock is not really the sort of place you'd expect to find an urbane inn. The Weary may retain its rustic 18th-century country inn charms outside, but within it gives way to a modern, good-looking interior. Ian and Gill Boyd took a gamble in 2001, taking the view that the inn should be refurbished with every attention paid to style and design, and it has paid off. Suede-style tub chairs or sofas mean that comfort is a prime consideration, while cask ales (available from the granite-topped bar) maintain pubby credentials.

Bedrooms may vary in size, but all have clean fresh colour schemes and feature superior beds with rich Egyptian cotton bedding. Statement headboards link to the room colour and make discreet homes for quality speakers. There are DVD and flat-screen options in both bed- and bathroom, with the latter also offering roomy power showers. Finishing touches include handsome Welsh glass hand-basins and tasteful lighting.

—

The Weary, Castle Carrock, Carlisle, Cumbria CA8 9LU

The Essentials

Time at the Bar!
11am-11pm; closed Mon;
Food: 12-2pm, 5.30-9pm (guests Mon)

What's the Damage?
Main courses from £11.50

Bitter Experience:
Derwent Parsons Pledge, Worthington

Sticky Fingers:
Children welcome, children's menu

Muddy Paws:
No dogs

Zzzzz:
5 rooms, £95-£145

Anything Else?
Walled garden, car park

The Food

The conservatory dining room continues the contemporary theme, and on fine evenings you can eat outside in the sheltered courtyard. Dedication goes into sourcing ingredients: a local farmer-cum-butcher supplies beef and lamb, for example, and there are four Cumbrian farmhouse cheeses on the cheeseboard.

Similarly, the kitchen focuses on allowing the principal ingredient to speak for itself. Everything is delicious and the best it can possibly be, from the selection of freshly baked bread to the popular crème brûlée made with free-range eggs supplied by a village boy who keeps a dozen hens (the eggs are also on the menu at breakfast).

Starters range from an imaginative carrot and spring onion mousse served with a chilled vegetable coulis to game sausage with bubble and squeak, given a tweak with a few streaks of date and chocolate sauce. Mains can take in baked salmon fillet, fresh asparagus and a light herb and lemon sauce, or Barbary duck breast on a pan-fried mushroom risotto cake with an orange Grand Marnier sauce. A simpler bar menu is available on Tuesday to Friday evenings.

What To Do

Shop

BROUGHAM HALL SMOKEHOUSE

Cumbrian cheeses, local estate-reared venison, rare-breed and organic meats, salmon, trout and hare are among the raw materials hand-prepared on site before hot or cold smoking over oak logs or shavings. The products are stocked by Harvey Nichols, Harrods and other top London stores known to be purveyors of good food. The Smokehouse is one of a range of craft food businesses here; Tirril Microbrewery is another.

Broughham, Penrith, Cumbria CA10 2DE
01768 867772
www.the-old-smokehouse.co.uk

CUMBRIAN ANTIQUES CENTRE

The centre houses around 40 dealers, with specialisms ranging from furniture to porcelain and paintings. All co-exist happily together in this Antiques Centre in the heart of Brampton. The town is acquiring a growing reputation for arts and crafts as well, including craftspeople specialising in glass.

St Martin's Hall, Brampton,
Cumbria LA8 1NT
01697 742515
www.cumbrianantiquescentre.co.uk

HIGH HEAD SCULPTURE VALLEY

Brass, wood, stone and iron sculptures are displayed beside the natural beauty of water, pasture and woodland in this secluded valley. The home gallery stages exhibitions of exciting new works by artists, ceramicists and sculptors, many of which are for sale.

High Head Farm, Ivegill, Carlisle,
Cumbria CA4 0PJ
01697 473552
www.highheadsculpturevalley.co.uk

Visit

ACORN BANK GARDEN

A National Trust garden recognised as the most comprehensive herbalist's garden in the north; a riot of colours and aromas. The collection of rare fruit and orchard trees is equally impressive. There's a watermill in the grounds. In the same village is Winderwath Gardens, with specimen trees, Himalayan and alpine rock gardens.

Temple Sowerby, Penrith,
Cumbria CA10 1SP
01768 361893
www.nationaltrust.org.uk

BIRDOSWALD

A lonely outpost on the Roman Empire's northern border, the five-acre fort at Birdoswald is one of the major sites on Hadrian's Wall; a well-preserved stretch leads to one of the milecastles, at Harrow Scar. Nearby is Lanercost Priory, parish church and medieval ruined Augustinian foundation.

Greenhead, Brampton, Cumbria CA8 7DD
01697 747602
www.english-heritage.co.uk

HUTTON-IN-THE-FOREST

At the heart of Inglewood Forest, this imposing baronial mansion, part redesigned by Arts and Crafts guru William Morris, enjoys a parkland setting in a landscape dappled with specimen trees, terraces, topiary and walled gardens. Centuries' worth of fine furniture, ceramics, tapestries and paintings complement this memorable location, with views to the high Pennines.

Penrith, Cumbria CA11 9TH
01768 484449
www.hutton-in-the-forest.co.uk

Activity

COUNTRY PURSUITS

The immense estate surrounding Greystoke Hall, near Penrith, offers tuition in country sports and pursuits. The art of fly casting, the skill of falconry, the practice of archery and the sheer challenge of clay-pigeon shooting are all taught here. More vigorous pursuits include off-road driving.

Greystoke Castle, Greystoke, Penrith,
Cumbria CA11 0TG
01768 483722
www.greystoke.com

SUNSOAR PARAGLIDING

A taster day of this exhilarating sport in the hills above the Eden Valley, one of the best places in the north of England to learn. Professional instruction ensures you'll soar to around 50ft (15m) by the end of the day.

Mallerstang, Kirkby Stephen,
Cumbria CA17 4JT
0870 199 7343
www.sunsoar-paragliding.com

WALKING THE SOLWAY COAST

Explore the haunting lowlands and seamarshes opposite the mountains of Galloway in Scotland. Villages are thick with history: at tiny Burgh-by-Sands King Edward I died; Port Carlisle is that city's failed, ghostly harbour; and Silloth a charming Edwardian seaside resort. The Solway Firth is one of Europe's foremost wetland reserves.

www.solwaycoastaonb.org.uk

The Walk - *Lime Kilns of Castle Carrock*

Discovering a wealth of fine industrial remains.

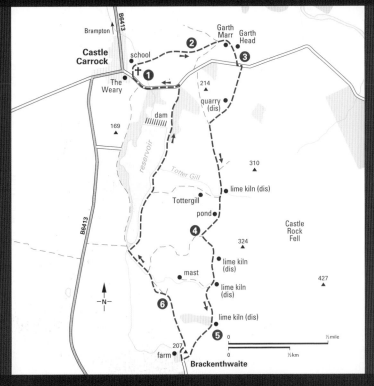

Walk Details

LENGTH: 4.5 miles (7.2km)

TIME: 2 hours

ASCENT: 476ft (145m)

PATHS: Field paths, farm tracks, metalled lanes, 7 stiles

SUGGESTED MAP: aqua3 OS Explorer 315 Carlisle

GRID REFERENCE: NY 543553

PARKING: On street between parish church and Watson Institute

❶ Facing the church turn left, then right past the school ('Garth Head'). Cross the bridge into field by stile. Ascend left of hedge and maintain direction through trees up to the gate on left. Keep hedge right and continue up hill, cutting corner of field. Continue with hedge right, up to stile in corner behind the bush.

❷ Bear slightly left up the bank and across the field, then go through the gate in top right corner. Follow lane through Garth Marr farmyard, then through 2 gates by Garth Head farmyard. Walk up track into field, turn right, up to gate on to the road.

❸ Go left for 20yds (18m), then right ('Brackenthwaite'). Walk along field edge to stile. Join track with wall on left. Follow until wall comes in right.

Go through gap. Follow track with wall now right. After 350yds (320m) cross stile. Eventually, go through gap in wall and join track from left. Descend to bridge with lime kiln up to left. Continue to left of wall, ahead. Track leads through reeds then left of the pond. Cross stile on far side. Bear right to fingerpost.

❹ Turn left up right edge of field to gate. Turn right alongside fence. Past lime kiln on left, path opens out and continues through gap in wall into boggy area. Keep left and continue along the base of hillside. Cross beck and pass the lime kiln. Continue along the track following wall on right. Go through stile right and follow the path with wall now left for 100yds (91m) to lime kiln.

❺ Turn right through the gap in the wall. Follow the track down to the left of the tin-roofed shed. Cross stile and bear right down track. Go through gate on to road. Turn right, round back of farmyard, signposted to reservoir. At the corner of yard, carry on through gateway, turning right in front of barn to gate on right. Walk up the field for 10yds (9m), turn left and cross 4 fields to the gate on to the road, just past green shed.

❻ Turn left. Follow the road for 0.5 mile (800m) to the junction. Turn right and follow the track by the reservoir, ignoring the turn to Tottergill. Pass the dam and go through the woods to the gate on to the road. Turn left and walk back into Castle Carrock and your car.

The Punch Bowl
Cumbria

The Inn

This handsomely renovated, rambling stone building sits back from the road between Kendal and nowhere, overlooking the stunningly lush Lyth Valley, alongside pretty St Mary's church. Owners Steph Barton and Paul Spencer couldn't have found a better-located inn to complement their other hugely successful pub – the famous Drunken Duck Inn not far away in Ambleside. This part of the Lake District is gentle and rolling, and the tranquil vibe is continued inside, where it's bliss to lounge in leather sofas with the newspaper and a pint or two of Westmorland Gold from the Duck's Barngates microbrewery. The impressive long bar is slate-topped, an appropriate complement to the stone floors, richly patinated oak furniture, open fires and flawlessly chalked boards listing delicious food and a raft of wines by the glass.

The nine bedrooms are individually designed, but all are equipped with retro Roberts radios, rich fabrics and furnishings, soothing Farrow & Ball colours, plasma TVs, roll-top baths standing on underfloor-heated limestone and separate power showers. Noble is an impressive suite occupying the whole third floor, its twin baths (for couples who are truly inseparable) enjoying wonderful views down the valley.

The Punch Bowl, Crosthwaite, Kendal, Cumbria LA8 8HR

The Essentials

Time at the Bar!
12-11pm
Food: 12-3pm, 6-9pm (light snacks
served 12-6pm)

What's the Damage?
Main courses from £9.50

Bitter Experience:
Barngates, Taglag, Westmorland Gold

Sticky Fingers:
Children welcome (no high chairs);
children's menu

Muddy Paws:
Dogs welcome in the bar

Zzzzz:
9 rooms, £110-£280

Anything Else?
Terrace, garden, car park